5/95

# FUNDAMENTALS
## OF
# RUSSIAN

# FUNDAMENTALS

## OF

# RUSSIAN

## FIRST RUSSIAN COURSE

*Revised Edition*

Reprint 1982

# HORACE G. LUNT

## Harvard University

## Slavica

Slavica publishes a wide variety of textbooks for the study of Russian at all levels, as well as books on the peoples, literatures, languages, linguistics, history, and folklore of the USSR and Eastern Europe. For a complete catalog, with prices and ordering information, write to:

Slavica Publishers, Inc.
PO Box 14388
Columbus, Ohio 43214

ISBN: 0-89357-097-4.

Printed in the United States of America.

# CONTENTS

# PREFACE

This book is designed to enable a beginner to master the fundamental structure of Russian as quickly as possible. Stress is laid on the indispensable forms and their uses. Vocabulary has been kept to a minimum so that the student will be encouraged to concentrate on all the possible combinations of the words he does know. The course provides, so to speak, samples of all the sizes, shapes, and textures of building materials and many examples of the most important ways in which they can be combined, but it does not give many specimens of each size and shape. Learning vocabulary is an endless process, for every language constantly creates new words and no one ever knows the total lexicon. But the patterns into which the words must fit if they are to be meaningful are relatively few, and it is the task of mastering these patterns that must be the primary concern of the student.

An English-speaking person will find Russian to be a difficult language for two obvious reasons: it is complex and it is foreign. By complex, I mean that there are many formal details which must be memorized. For example, one does not simply learn a Russian word that is equivalent to an English word; one cannot put such a word to work without first learning precisely which of a number of possible changes— regular or irregular—it may undergo in different contexts and with varying shades of meaning. By foreign, I mean that there are very few elements which are more or less immediately recognizable. This is in sharp contrast to German or the Romance languages, where an English-speaker finds from the outset essential words which he can guess at once or which he can easily memorize because of their similarity to things he already knows. Obviously, then, the complexity and foreignness of Russian put a greater load on one's powers of memorization, and progress will be slower for the beginning student than if he were attacking French or German.

None of the difficulties of Russian is insurmountable, however, and a growing number of Russian experts who are native speakers of English attest the fact that Russian can be mastered. Mastery is to be most quickly achieved by facing the difficulties squarely and working at them constantly. These lessons are intended to take the student over the direct but rocky road to Russian, giving him only the real necessities, without sugared pills or fun and games. We have found that this system brings results astonishingly quickly, but only if the student is willing to work, steadily and conscientiously.

The book was originally designed for an intensive course, to be completed in fifteen to twenty weeks with eight classroom hours per week. To furnish more variety for non-intensive use, several supplementary lessons were added, in which larger vocabulary and more exercises are supplied, but no new structural principles. This series of lessons has proved to be an excellent device for reviewing at the end of the intensive courses.

In the Harvard courses where this book was shaped, tested, re-shaped and re-tested for more than fifteen years, special emphasis has been laid on oral drill under the tutelage of a native speaker of Russian. The primary purpose of the drill is not so much to give the student a glib set of phrases for small-talk or for the practical exigencies of travel as to accustom him to automatic production of and reaction to typical Russian utterances. It is our belief that this kind of oral drill is fundamental to the acquisition of those basic patterns which constitute the structure of the language, and that it is just as valuable for the student whose aim is only a passive reading knowledge as for the student with more ambitious goals. A secure command of the patterns, built up through constant repetition, makes any use of the language thereafter far more efficient.

Yet audio-lingual drill is a time-consuming and, for many students, often frustrating way to acquire linguistic structures. An understanding of how the language works is much more rapidly achieved by direct discussion of the grammar and by trans-lation exercises from and into English. Experience has shown that students who have mastered the material in this book, even those who have had regrettably little opportunity for audio-lingual drills, are able very quickly to attain high levels in the active use of Russian when exposed to the spoken language. Students who wish to proceed directly to reading in their chosen fields do not feel that they have lost time in acquiring an oral fluency for which they had no use and which all too often has proved to be ephemeral. The materials offered here are indeed fundamental to any sort of use of Russian, passive or active. For those who desire more oral materials, a set of pattern drills has been devised by Robert D. Sholiton and Joseph A. Van Campen,* both now at Stanford University.

The statements of Russian grammar in this book often are not quite the familiar rules which have traveled from textbook to textbook for decades. The criteria for the innovations in order of presentation and in formulations of grammatical rules have been efficiency and effectiveness as proved in a long series of practical classroom trials. We have found over the years that students who have been through these lessons experience no difficulty in making use of advanced reference works cast in the traditional mold—and contemporary Soviet grammars and handbooks are, with a few encouraging exceptions, rigidly traditional.

This second edition differs from the first in many details and in certain major divisions. The old lessons which introduced the verb system, the noun plurals, and the comparison of adjectives (IV, VII, and XXI) were much too comprehensive and proved hard to handle in the classroom. Each has split into two, making the total number of lessons twenty-five. In the process the vocabulary from two of the early

* *Pattern Drills for Introductory Russian, especially designed to accompany "Fundamentals of Russian" by Horace G. Lunt*, Norton, 1968.

supplementary lessons (IIIa, Va) was incorporated into the regular series, largely to furnish regular nouns to illustrate plural formations. In many places new exercises have been provided, with special attention to review materials at points where our schedules at Harvard usually required examinations, particularly X, XIII, XVI, XIX and, for courses using the supplementary lessons, XIIIa. The final lessons contain a great deal of review material, and XXIa is essentially a summing-up of information about negation and a review incorporating some useful new words. The total increase in vocabulary amounts to about forty-five items, and there has been no attempt to treat grammatical structures that were not already in the first edition. One useful innovation is the distinction between stressed é and unstressed ё, which Professor Morris Halle of M.I.T. strongly urged me to adopt when the first edition was being prepared. In 1957 it struck me as too great a break with tradition, but in 1967 it seems a necessary, and even rather conservative, device.

The introduction to the first edition included a comprehensive account of pronunciation, but too many teachers ignored my prefatory advice to skip these details and use the account as a reference section. Therefore a new introduction has been provided to give the most important information, and the details have been relegated to Appendix I. Here too has gone the detailed treatment of patronymics, formerly in Lesson V. It is to be hoped that these pages will not be neglected: they contain vital information.

Since this book contains no connected Russian texts, we strongly recommend that a reader, preferably one with a small, controlled vocabulary, be used concomitantly starting with Lesson XII or XIII. It has been our practice to start to read unsimplified Russian with Lesson XXII. The student then knows nearly all of the structure of the language, and his major problem is to amass vocabulary pertinent to his special needs. We have found that Pushkin's tale *The Queen of Spades*, despite its large vocabulary, is read enthusiastically and without special difficulty at this point. A quite different but equally successful selection has been Chekhov's *Mal'chiki*. Both stories are included in the *Accented Russian Reader* (Книга для чтения) published by Mouton and Co., The Hague, and available through the Harvard Cooperative Society Bookstore, Cambridge, Mass. An introduction to scholarly prose, edited for students who have finished this course, is *A Lecture on Russian History*, by Professor Michael Karpovich, also published by Mouton.

The course owes a great deal to suggestions from teachers and students who have used it from the earliest versions in 1952 down to mimeographed copies of revised lessons in 1967, and it is my pleasurable duty to thank them at this time. The contributions of Professor Halle, Professor Irina Borisova-Morozova Lynch, now of Wellesley College, Professor Hugh McLean, now of the University of Chicago, and Tatiana Kosinski, now of the University of Massachusetts, were particularly valuable. Dr. Bayara Aroutunova of Harvard has assisted in the preparation of many of the exercises for both editions and made many valuable suggestions. Professor Van Campen and Robert Sholiton, in addition to their work on the pattern drills, took active part in rewriting the lessons on the comparison of adjectives; Mr. Sholiton also compiled the index. In spite of the efforts of these friends, some errors surely have gone unnoticed, and I should be grateful to have them called to my attention. I should also be glad to receive comments and suggestions for improving the book.

H. G. Lunt

Boylston Hall 301
Harvard University
Cambridge, Massachusetts 02138

May, 1967

# ABBREVIATIONS

A, Acc. – accusative case
aj. – adjective
av. – adverb
D – determined aspect
D, Dat. – dative case
*E* – see p. 351 § 4
*Epl* – see p. 350 § 2
*E pl obl* – see p. 351 § 3
f., fem. – feminine
G, Gen. – genitive case
I – imperfective aspect
I, Inst. – instrumental case
imv. – imperative
indecl. – indeclinable
Intro. – Introduction
m., masc. – masculine
n., neut. – neuter

N, Nom. – nominative
ND – non-determined aspect
neg. – negative, negated
P – perfective aspect
pl. – plural
Pr., Prep. – prepositional case
prep. – preposition
pron. – pronounced
*s* – see p. 351 § 9
sg., sing. – singular
*SNpl* – see p. 351 § 7
*S Npl Asg* – see p. 351 § 6
*Spl* – see p. 351 § 5
*Spl Asg* – see p. 351 § 8
trans. – transitive
/ = or; and/or
~ = versus
$\cong$ = approx. the same as

Cross-references are given by lesson (Roman numerals) and paragraph. Numeration of the paragraphs is decimal: every number to the right of the decimal point is to be read as a separate unit. Thus 6.123 = 6.1.2.3; i.e. the third subdivision of 6.12, which is the second subdivision of 6.1.

# INTRODUCTION

Russian is a Slavic language belonging to the East Slavic group, together with Ukrainian and Byelorussian.

They are closely related to the West Slavic (Polish, Czech, Slovak, and the Upper and Lower Sorbian languages of eastern Germany) and the South Slavic (Slovene, Serbo-Croatian, Macedonian, and Bulgarian) languages. The Slavic languages as a whole are related to the Baltic languages (Lithuanian and Latvian) and, less closely, to the other members which make up the Indo-European language family: Indic (Sanscrit and many modern Indian languages), Iranian (including modern Persian), Greek, Albanian, Italic (including Latin and the modern Romance languages), Germanic (including English), and Celtic. Russian and English are thus related, but both have undergone far-reaching changes from the hypothetical common prototype, and the relationship is not readily apparent except for a very few words (e.g. *brát* – brother, *sᵇistrá* – sister).

Russian is the mother tongue of over a hundred million Russians (often called Great Russians to distinguish them from Byelo-Russians or White Russians and from Ukrainians or Little-Russians). Moreover it is the administrative language of the Soviet Union and must be learned by the hundred million non-Russian inhabitants of that country. As a required subject in the schools of Eastern Europe and an important part of the curriculum in many schools in China, Russian is gaining ever more importance in the daily lives of more millions of non-Russians.

The Russians, when they accepted Christianity late in the tenth century, received the liturgical and other books which had been translated into the South Slavic language which is called Church Slavonic. They continued to write in this slightly foreign dialect into the eighteenth century, although the Church Slavonic became more and more Russianized. By the beginning of the nineteenth century the Russian of Moscow was accepted as the standard for literary use, but the Church Slavonic elements remain as vital and essential components of modern Russian as are the Latin elements in English.

Like any language, Russian is not entirely homogeneous: a peasant from the far north does not speak like a peasant from the south or far east, and none of them speaks like an intellectual from Leningrad or Tomsk. There is, however, a standard literary language whose written form is precisely codified and whose spoken form varies surprisingly little in usage over the whole enormous area. The recognized norm which actors and public speakers try to follow is based on the pronunciation of Moscow, but "Leningrad standard" is also entirely acceptable. The beginning student should endeavor to imitate as closely as possible the pronunciation of his teacher or of records made by an educated native.

## I. THE RUSSIAN SOUND SYSTEM

The sounds of Russian are represented by the writing system with much less ambiguity than is the case with English. Nevertheless, Russian spelling does not completely conform to the phonetic principle of one symbol for one sound: combinations of letters and their positions within the word play a great role in determining the phonetic value of the symbols. If one hears a Russian word, it is often difficult to know how to spell it, but it is nearly always possible to pronounce correctly a word whose written form is known. Normal Russian writing unfortunately does not mark the stress, but the information is usually given in dictionaries and texts for foreigners. Stress will be written throughout this book.

In order to illustrate as fully as possible the relationship between sound and spelling, we will use a transcription, beside the regular spelling, in the first four lessons. The transcription employs, with three exceptions, only the functional sound units which are significant in Russian, ignoring minor phonetic differences. We will first examine the meaning of the symbols in the transcription, and then see the relationship of the Russian spelling to the transcription.[1]

### 1. THE VOWELS

*a* – pronounced approximately as in English f*a*ther.

*ə* – as in sof*a*, *a*bout.[2]

*e* – about like b*e*t.

*ẹ* – close to English b*a*te.[2]

*i* – about like b*ee*t.

*ɨ* – a back vowel, pronounced with the tongue in position for the vowel of b*oo*t and the lips in position for the vowel of b*ee*t, i.e. not rounded; this vowel does not occur in English.

---

[1] Transcription represents the *sounds* of Russian by means of Roman letters and diacritics. Do not confuse it with transliteration, which uses Roman letters as a substitute for Russian *letters*. See Appendix II, pp. 344–345.

[2] *e*, *i*, and *ə* do not represent independent units, but variants of *e*, *i*, and *a*, respectively. Although the occurrence of these variants is predictable in terms of the sounds preceding and following, the three symbols are used here (contrary to the principles of strictly phonemic transcription) as a practical means to point up important and easily recognizable phonetic differences which the student should learn.

*o* – *o*r, in middle-western American pronunciation.
*u* – approximately as in b*oo*t.

The sounds *e*, *ę*, and *o* occur only under stress. The sound *ə* is found only in unstressed syllables.

*Stress* is marked by the acute accent ('): *á é ę́ í ɨ́ ó ú* (but unstressed *a i ɨ u ə*). NB: It is essential to learn the stress with every word!

## 2. THE CONSONANTS

**2.1**   Here are fifteen consonants defined as *non-palatalized*:

*p* – pronounced approximately as in "s*p*ot"; note that it lacks the puff of air (aspiration) which follows the *p* in "*p*ot".

*b*
*f*
*v*    pronounced approximately as in English.
*m*

*t* – pronounced with the tip of the tongue against the front teeth (not against the upper gum as in English) and without aspiration.

*d*
*n*    pronounced with the tip of the tongue against the front teeth.

*s* – approximately as in "*s*o".
*z* – approximately as in "*z*one".
*l* – pronounced with a *w*-colored quality like that in "ha*ll*". In English, this sound does not occur before a vowel.
*r* – trilled with the tip of the tongue, as in Spanish or Italian.
*k* – pronounced without aspiration, as in "s*k*ate".
*g* – approximately as in "*g*o".
*x* – does not occur in English. It is produced by placing the tongue in the position for *k* and lowering it slightly so that a stream of air passes between the back of the tongue and the roof of the mouth. (It is a sound that can be prolonged, like *s*, *f*, and *v*).

**2.2**   There is a series of Russian consonants for which no equivalents exist in English. These consonants are *palatalized*; that is, they have both the articulation of the non-palatalized consonant plus a second, palatal articulation. The tongue arches toward the middle of the roof of the mouth. The acoustic effect is one of higher pitch, and an English speaker often has the impression that the palatalized consonant is simply a hard consonant plus *y*. Actually this "y-quality" is simultaneous with and inseparable from the other quality.

**2.21** In transcription we use the superscript letter ь (ᵇ) to represent palatalization; it is to be regarded as *part of the preceding letter*. Thus *brát* differs from *brátᵇ* in that the last consonant of the former is *t* and the last consonant of the latter is *tᵇ*.

**2.3** The distinction of palatalized ∼ non-palatalized is fundamental for the Russian linguistic system. You must learn to recognize the differences when you hear them and to make them when you speak Russian.

**2.4** All the consonants listed in § 2.1 are paired with corresponding palatalized consonants:

*pᵇ* – very approximately as in "s*p*ew"
*bᵇ* – " " " " "im*b*ue"
*fᵇ* – " " " " "*f*ew"
*vᵇ* – " " " " "*v*iew"
*mᵇ* – " " " " "*m*use"
*tᵇ* – " " " " "s*t*ew" (British pronunciation)
*dᵇ* – " " " " "*d*ew" " "
*nᵇ* – " " " " "*n*ews" " "
*sᵇ* – " " " " "*s*uit" " "
*zᵇ* – " " " " "pre*s*ume" " "
*lᵇ* – " " " " "mi*ll*ion"
*rᵇ* – palatalized trilled *r*
*kᵇ* – very approximately as in "as*k*ew"
*gᵇ* – " " " " "ar*g*ue"
*xᵇ* – palatalized *x*

**2.5** Palatalized consonants are commonly referred to as "soft" and non-palatalized consonants as "hard". Those which occur in both "hard" and "soft" varieties are called *paired consonants*.

**2.51** In addition to the consonants listed in § 2.1, the following are grouped as "hard" (but without "soft" equivalents):
*c* – like the *ts* in "ha*ts*"; it functions as a single unit, not a combination of two units.
*š* – approximately as in "*sh*eep".
*ž* – approximately as in "a*z*ure, plea*s*ure".

**2.6**   In addition to the consonants listed in § 2.4, the following are grouped as "soft" (but without "hard" equivalents):

*j* – like the *y* in "*y*es" or "bo*y*ish".
*č* – approximately as in "*ch*eap".
*šč* – either a combination as written ("ra*sh ch*ild", "Dani*sh ch*eese") or a long, that is to say doubled, *š* ("ra*sh* sheik", "Dani*sh* sheep").

## 3.   STRESS

The vast majority of Russian words have one single stressed syllable which is in strong contrast to the other syllables, all of which are unstressed, however many there may be. The syllable immediately before the stress is slightly stronger than the other unstressed syllables, and syllables after the stress are much weaker. It is important for an English-speaking person to avoid the secondary stresses which are present in long English words like "incómprehènsibílity".

Some Russian words are stressless. Most of them are pronounced as an integral part of the stressed word which follows, but a few are pronounced as part of the stressed word that precedes. More specific information is to be found in Appendix I, § 13.

Here are some Russian sentences written in transcription. Listen carefully to your teacher or a recording as you hear them pronounced. Say them aloud, imitating your native model as closely as possible. Memorize the sentences and their meanings. Do not try to write them; the transcription is meant only to guide you when listening to the pronunciation. Learn these sentences as meaningful sequences of *sound*.

| | |
|---|---|
| *zdrástvujt*ᵇ*i.* | Hello. |
| *kák ví pəživájit*ᵇ*i?* | How are you? |
| *xərašó, spas*ᵇ*ibə.* | Fine, thanks. Well, thanks. |
| *n*ᵇ*ičivó, spas*ᵇ*ibə.* | OK, thanks. All right, thanks. |
| *ták s*ᵇ*ib*ᵇ*é.* | Fair. So-so. Not bad. |
| *a ví?* | And you? (i. e. And how are you?) |
| *óčin*ᵇ *xərašó.* | Very well. |
| *dóbrəjə útrə.* | Good morning. |
| *dóbrij d*ᵇ*ę́n*ᵇ*.* | Good afternoon. |
| *dóbrij v*ᵇ*ę́čir.* | Good evening. |
| *də sv*ᵇ*idán*ᵇ*jə.* | Goodbye. Au revoir. |

| | |
|---|---|
| *fsʲivó lúčšivə.* | All the best. Good luck. |
| *spakójnəj nóči.* | Good night. |
| *izvʲinʲítʲi.* | Excuse me. |
| *pəftarʲítʲi za mnój.* | Repeat after me. |
| *jiščó rás, pažálstə.* | Again please. Once more, please. |
| *skažɨ́tʲi jiščó rás.* | Say (it) again. |
| *étə nʲi ták.* | That's not right. |
| *nʲi ták.* | Not that way. |
| *ták. étə ták.* | That way. That's right. |
| *vɨ́ pənʲimájitʲi?* | Do you understand? |
| *dá, já pənʲimáju.* | Yes, I understand. |
| *nʲét, já nʲi pənʲimáju.* | No, I do not understand. |
| *štó vɨ́ skazálʲi?* | What did you say? |
| *étə lúčšɨ.* | That's better. |
| *gəvarʲítʲi grómči!* | Speak louder! |
| *nʲi ták bɨ́strə.* | Not so fast. |
| *nʲi ták mʲédlʲinnə.* | Not so slowly. |
| *nʲi gəvarʲítʲi paanglʲíjskʲi!* | Don't speak English! |
| *gəvarʲítʲi parúskʲi!* | Speak Russian! |
| *fsʲé vmʲę́stʲi.* | All together. |

## II. THE WRITING SYSTEM

Let us now examine the Russian alphabet[3] to see how the sounds of Russian are represented. The first column is the name of the letter written in transcription.

[3] The Russian alphabet is an adaptation of the old Slavonic alphabet called Cyrillic.

Tradition attributed its invention to St. Cyril (known also as Constantine the Philosopher), who with his brother St. Methodius made the first translations into Slavonic, in the 860's. As a matter of fact the alphabet elaborated by these "Slavic Apostles" was a totally different one, called glagolitic, but the Cyrillic letters were in use by the early tenth century and it was in this form that the Slavonic writings were imported by the Russians. Cyrillic is essentially the Greek alphabet, with additional letters for specifically Slavic sounds. The shapes of the letters were modified under Peter the Great (1708) in imitation of the style of Roman letters used in the West. Various adaptations of this "civil" Cyrillic (as opposed to the older "ecclesiastical" letters) are used by the Serbs, Macedonians, Bulgarians, Ukrainians and Byelorussians, and in recent decades alphabets based on Russian have been devised for the use of a large number of non-Slavic languages in the Soviet Union.

| á | **Аа** | ká | **Кк** | xá | **Хх** |
|---|---|---|---|---|---|
| bé | **Бб** | él<sup>ь</sup> | **Лл** | cé | **Цц** |
| vé | **Вв** | ém | **Мм** | čá | **Чч** |
| gé | **Гг** | én | **Нн** | šá | **Шш** |
| dé | **Дд** | ó | **Оо** | ščá | **Щщ** |
| jé | **Ее** | pé | **Пп** | *2 | **Ъ** |
| jó | **Ёё** | ér | **Рр** | jirɨ | **Ы** |
| žé | **Жж** | és | **Сс** | *3 | **Ь** |
| zé | **Зз** | té | **Тт** | *4 | **Ээ** |
| i | **Ии** | ú | **Уу** | jú | **Юю** |
| *1 | **Й** | éf | **Фф** | já | **Яя** |

*1 *i krátkəjə*, "short *i*".   *2 *tv<sup>ь</sup>órdɨj znák*, "hard sign".   *3 *m<sup>ь</sup>áxkəj znák*, "soft sign".   *4 *é*, or *é abarótnəjə*, "reversed *e*".

Note in particular the letters **в, н, р, с, у**, and **х**. They look like familiar Roman letters, but in Russian they represent quite different sounds.

Here are the same sentences you learned in transcription. This time they are given both in transcription and in the Russian spelling.

Здра́вствуйте.
*zdrástvujt<sup>ь</sup>i.*

Hello.

Ка́к вы поживáёте?
*kák vɨ pəživájit<sup>ь</sup>i?*

How are you?

Хорошо́, спаси́бо.
*xərašó, spas<sup>ь</sup>ibə.*

Fine, thanks. Well, thanks.

Ничёго, спаси́бо.
*n<sup>ь</sup>ičivó, spas<sup>ь</sup>ibə.*

OK, thanks. All right, thanks.

Та́к себе́.
*ták s<sup>b</sup>ib<sup>b</sup>é.*

Fair. So-so. Not bad.

А вы́?
*a ví?*

And you? (i. e. And how are you?)

О́чень хорошо́.
*óčin<sup>b</sup> xərašó.*

Very well.

До́брое у́тро.
*dóbrəjə útrə.*

Good morning.

До́брый де́нь.
*dóbrɨj d<sup>b</sup>én<sup>b</sup>.*

Good afternoon.

До́брый ве́чер.
*dóbrɨj v<sup>b</sup>éčir.*

Good evening.

До свида́ния.
*də sv<sup>b</sup>idán<sup>b</sup>jə.*

Goodbye. Au revoir.

Всего́ лу́чшего.
*fs<sup>b</sup>ivó lúčšɨvə.*

All the best. Good luck.

Споко́йной но́чи.
*spakójnəj nóči.*

Good night.

Извини́те.
*izv<sup>b</sup>in<sup>b</sup>ít<sup>b</sup>i.*

Excuse me.

Повтори́те за мно́й.
*pəftar<sup>b</sup>ít<sup>b</sup>i za mnój.*

Repeat after me.

Еще́ ра́з, пожа́луйста.
*jiščó rás, pažálstə.*

Again please. Once more, please.

Скажи́те еще́ ра́з.
*skažɨ́t<sup>b</sup>i jiščó rás.*

Say (it) again.

Э́то не та́к.
*étə n<sup>b</sup>i ták.*

That's not right.

Не та́к.
*n<sup>b</sup>i ták.*

Not that way.

Та́к. Э́то та́к.
*ták. étə ták.*

That way. That's right.

| | |
|---|---|
| Вы́ понима́ете?<br>*ví pən<sup>b</sup>imájit<sup>b</sup>i?* | Do you understand? |
| Да́, я понима́ю.<br>*dá, já pən<sup>b</sup>imáju.* | Yes, I understand. |
| Не́т, я не понима́ю.<br>*n<sup>b</sup>ét, já n<sup>b</sup>i pən<sup>b</sup>imáju.* | No, I do not understand. |
| Что́ вы́ сказа́ли?<br>*štó ví skazál<sup>b</sup>i?* | What did you say? |
| Это лу́чше.<br>*étə lúčš<sup>b</sup>i.* | That's better. |
| Говори́те гро́мче!<br>*gəvar<sup>b</sup>ít<sup>b</sup>i grómči!* | Speak louder! |
| Не та́к бы́стро.<br>*n<sup>b</sup>i ták bístrə.* | Not so fast. |
| Не та́к ме́дленно.<br>*n<sup>b</sup>i ták m<sup>b</sup>édl<sup>b</sup>innə.* | Not so slowly. |
| Не говори́те по-англи́йски!<br>*n<sup>b</sup>i gəvar<sup>b</sup>ít<sup>b</sup>i paangl<sup>b</sup>íjsk<sup>b</sup>i!* | Don't speak English! |
| Говори́те по-ру́сски!<br>*gəvar<sup>b</sup>ít<sup>b</sup>i parúsk<sup>b</sup>i!* | Speak Russian! |
| Всé вме́сте.<br>*fs<sup>b</sup>é vm<sup>b</sup>ést<sup>b</sup>i.* | All together. |

Study this text for relations between Russian letters and sounds.

**4. CONSONANT LETTERS**

Twenty-one letters are used to represent the Russian consonant sounds. Fifteen of them are *paired-consonant letters*, which represent, depending on the letter that follows them, either a hard or a soft paired-consonant sound. The other six are *non-paired consonant letters*, which regularly represent only a hard or a soft consonant sound regardless of the following letter. The three which represent only soft consonant sounds will be called *soft-consonant letters*. The remaining three regularly stand only for hard sounds, and will be called *hard-consonant letters*. The following table shows the consonant letters and their basic sound correspondences.

**4.1** Paired-consonant letters:

| | | |
|---|---|---|
| п – *p, pᵇ* | т – *t, tᵇ* | л – *l, lᵇ* |
| б – *b, bᵇ* | д – *d, dᵇ* | р – *r, rᵇ* |
| ф – *f, fᵇ* | с – *s, sᵇ* | к – *k, kᵇ* |
| в – *v, vᵇ* | з – *z, zᵇ* | г – *g, gᵇ* |
| м – *m, mᵇ* | н – *n, nᵇ* | х – *x, xᵇ* |

**4.2** Non-paired-consonant letters:

Soft-consonant letters:

| | | |
|---|---|---|
| ч – *č* | щ – *šč* | й – *j* |

Hard-consonant letters:

| | | |
|---|---|---|
| ш – *š* | ж – *ž* | ц – *c* |

**4.3** The "soft-sign" ь after a paired-consonant letter indicates that the consonant is soft.[4]

## 5. VOWEL LETTERS

There are ten vowel letters for representing the eight Russian vowel sounds. They are:

| | | | | |
|---|---|---|---|---|
| а | о | у | ы | э |
| я | ё | ю | и | е |

**5.11** After paired-consonant letters, the letters а, о, у, ы, э indicate that the preceding consonant is hard. For example, тáк — **ták**, дóбрый — **dóbrij**, лýчше — **lúčši**, вы́ — **ví**.

**5.12** The letters я, ё, ю, и, and е indicate that it is soft: говоря́т — **gəvarᵇát**, живéте — **živᵇótᵇi**, говорю́ — **gəvarᵇú**, говори́те — **gəvarᵇítᵇi**, нéт — **nᵇét**.

**5.2** After other vowel letters or ь, the letters я, ё, ю, и, е indicate that a *j* precedes the vowels they represent: моя́ — **majá**, моё — **majó**, мою́ — **majú**, мой — **maji**, моéй — **majéj**, статья́ — **statᵇjá**, статьéй — **statᵇjój**, статью́ — **statᵇjú**, статьи́ — **statᵇjí**, статьé — **statᵇjé**. In initial position, only я, ё, ю, е (not и[5]) have this significance: я́ — **já**, ещё — **jiščó**, ёгó — **jivó**, but извини́те — **izvᵇinᵇítᵇi**.

**5.3** All ten of these letters can occur with or without an accompanying

---

[4] The ь after a non-paired-consonant letter has no phonetic value. Cf. Appendix I, § 8.3, p. 326. The "hard-sign" ъ is very rare. For its use see Appendix I, § 9.1, p. 326.

[5] Exception: **jíx** 'theirs' и́х.

stress mark: **а а́, о о́, у у́, э э́, ы ы́, я я́, ё ё́, ю ю́, е е́, и и́**. Some of the vowel letters have significantly different values if they are not stressed.

**5.31** Letters whose pronunciation is not significantly affected by the presence or absence of the stress mark:

The letters **у (у́)\* ю (ю́)†‡** all represent the vowel *u* (or stressed *ú*). Examples: по-ру́сски — parúskᵇi, лу́чше — lúčṣ̌i, здра́вствуйте — zdrástvujtᵇi,⁶ понима́ю — pənᵇimáju, лю́бит — lᵇúbᵇit.

The letter **ы (ы́)\*** represents only the vowel sound *i* (stressed *í*). Example: бы́стро — bístrə.

The letter **и (и́)†‡** represents either the vowel *i* (*í*) or the vowel *i* (*í*). It stands for *i* (*í*) after the hard-consonant letters **ш, ж, ц**. Examples: скажи́те — skažị́tᵇi, поживáете — pəži̱vájitᵇi.

In all other cases, **и (и́)** represents *i* (*í*). Examples: извини́те — izvᵇinᵇítᵇi, сказáли — skazálᵇi, говори́те — gəvarᵇítᵇi, и — i, мой — mají.

**5.32** Letters whose pronunciation is significantly affected by the presence or absence of a stress mark.

**1. á : a\***

**á** always represents the vowel sound *á*. Examples: тáк — ták, кáк — kák, понимáете — pənᵇimájitᵇi.

**a** (unstressed) represents either *a* or *ə*.

It stands for *a* in initial position or immediately before a stressed syllable. Examples: сказáли — skazálᵇi, адвокáт — advakát, спаси́бо — spasᵇíbə.

It stands for *ə* in all other cases.⁷ Examples: пожáлуйста — pažálstə,⁸ карандáш — kərandáš.

---

\* For use of this letter indicating that a preceding paired-consonant letter represents the hard member of the pair, see § 5.11 above.

† For use of this letter indicating that a preceding paired-consonant letter represents the soft member of the pair, see § 5.12 above.

‡ For use of this letter to indicate that *j* precedes the vowel, see § 5.2 above.

⁶ In this greeting, used dozens of times daily, the first **в** is omitted in the pronunciation.

⁷ For more details, see Appendix I, § 12.

⁸ This extremely common word reduces the next-to-last syllable either completely: *pažálstə*, or partially, *pažálэstə*. The full pronunciation with *uj* as spelled is artificial.

**2. я́ : я†‡**

я́ always represents the vowel sound *á*. Examples: я́ — **já**, моя́ — **majá**, поня́ть — **panᵇátᵇ**.

я (unstressed) stands for either the sound *ə* or the sound *i*.

It represents *ə* in certain grammatical endings. Example: свида́ния — svᵇidánᵇjə.[9]

It represents *i* elsewhere. Examples: язы́к — **jizík**, по́нял — **pónᵇil**, поняла́ — **pənᵇilá**.

**3. о́ : о***

о́ always represents the sound *ó*. Examples: до́брый — **dóbrij**, о́чень — **óčinᵇ**.

о (unstressed) stands for *a* or *ə*.

It represents *a* in initial position or immediately before a stressed syllable. Examples: оте́ц — **atᵇéc**, споко́йный — **spakójnij**.

It represents *ə* in all other cases. Examples: спаси́бо — **spasᵇíbə**, понима́ю — **pənᵇimáju**, хорошо́ — **xərašó**, говорю́ — **gəvarᵇú**.

**4. ё́ : ё́†‡**

ё́ always represents the sound *ó*. Examples: моё́ — **majó**, Пётр — **pᵇótr**, ещё́ — **jiščó**.

ё (unstressed) stands for *ə*, *i*, or *i*.

It represents *ə* in certain grammatical endings. Examples: до́брое — **dóbrəjə**, ва́ше — **vášə**.

Otherwise, unstressed ё represents (a) *i* after the hard-consonant letters ш, ж, ц, and (b) *i* in all other cases. Examples: жёна́ — **žiná**, понима́ете — **pənᵇimájitᵇi**, сёстра́ — **sᵇistrá**, ничёго́ — **nᵇičivó**.

**5. э́ : э***

э́ represents *é* or *ę́*.

It stands for *ę́* before a soft-consonant sound (paired or unpaired). Example: э́ти — **ę́tᵇi**.

It represents *é* in all other cases. Example: э́то — **étə**.

э (unstressed) represents *i*. Example: экза́мен — **igzámᵇin**.

---

\* For use of this letter indicating that a preceding paired-consonant letter represents the hard member of the pair, see § 5.11 above.

† For use of this letter indicating that a preceding paired-consonant letter represents the soft member of the pair, see § 5.12 above.

‡ For use of this letter to indicate that *j* precedes the vowel, see § 5.2 above.

[9] The full pronunciation as spelled, -ánᵇijə, is possible, but it is not usual in the common phrase до свида́ния.

**6. é : e†‡**

**é** represents *é* or *ę̂*.

It stands for *ę̂* before a soft-consonant sound (paired or unpaired). Examples: день — dᵇę̂nᵇ, вечер — vᵇę̂čir.

It represents *é* in all other cases. Examples: себе — sᵇibᵇé, нет — nᵇét, медленно — mᵇédlᵇinnə, всё — fsᵇé.

**e** (unstressed) represents *i* or *i̇*.

It stands for *i̇* after the hard-consonant letters **ш, ж, ц**. Example: лучше — lúč*š*i̇.

It represents *i* in all other cases. Examples: себе — sᵇibᵇé, не — nᵇi.

**5.4**  The occurrence of the vowel letters after non-paired consonants (§ 4.2 above) and also **к, г, х** is arbitrary. For more details see §§ 5 and 6 of Appendix I, page 325.

These spelling rules are indispensable:

> *After* **к, г, х, ш, ж, ч, щ**     : *only* **и**.     [NEVER ы!]
> *After the same letters and also* **ц** : *only* **а, у**.     [NEVER я, ю!]

**6.**   The consonant sounds of Russian include two major groups: *voiced* and *voiceless* consonants. (More details are given in § 14 of Appendix I.)

| Voiced:    | b bᵇ | v vᵇ | d dᵇ | z zᵇ | ž | g | gᵇ |
|------------|------|------|------|------|---|---|----|
| Voiceless: | p pᵇ | f fᵇ | t tᵇ | s sᵇ | š | k | kᵇ |

The consonant letters **б, в, д, з, ж, г** normally, as we have seen, represent voiced consonants: **б** — *b* and *bᵇ*, **в** — *v* and *vᵇ*, **д** — *d/dᵇ*, **з** — *z/zᵇ*, **ж** — *ž*, **г** — *g/gᵇ*.

However, at the end of a word or else before a letter which represents a voiceless consonant these letters stand for the corresponding voiceless consonants: **б** — *p* and *pᵇ*, **в** — *f* and *fᵇ*, **д** — *t/tᵇ*, **з** — *s/sᵇ*, **ж** — *š*, **г** — *k/kᵇ*. Examples: раз — rás, повторите — pəftarᵇítᵇi, все — fsᵇé, всего — vsᵇivó, тетрадка — tᵇitrátkə.

The letters **п, ф, т, с, ш**, and **к** and also **ц, ч**, and **щ**, represent voiceless consonants. If they stand directly before letters that represent voiced consonants, they are pronounced voiced: также — tágži̇. See Appendix I, § 14.1, rule IIb, for more examples.

---

† For use of this letter indicating that a preceding paired-consonant letter represents the soft member of the pair, see § 5.12 above.

‡ For use of this letter to indicate that *j* precedes the vowel, see § 5.2 above.

## III. RUSSIAN HANDWRITING

Here is the Russian alphabet in italics and in script. Note that Russian italics are designed on the model of the script.

| | | | | | |
|---|---|---|---|---|---|
| **Аа** *Аа* | **Кк** *Кк* | **Хх** *Хх* |
| **Бб** *Бб* | **Лл** *Лл* | **Цц** *Цц* |
| **Вв** *Ввв* | **Мм** *Мм* | **Чч** *Чч* |
| **Гг** *Гг* | **Нн** *Нн* | **Шш** *Шш* |
| **Дд** *Дg* | **Оо** *Ооо* | **Щщ** *Щщ* |
| **Ее** *Ёе* | **Пп** *Пп* | **Ъ** *ъ* |
| **Ёё** *Ёё* | **Рр** *Рр* | **Ыы** *ы* |
| **Жж** *Жж* | **Сс** *Сс* | **Ьь** *ьь* |
| **Зз** *Зз* | **Тт** *Тт* | **Ээ** *Ээ* |
| **Ии** *Ии* | **Уу** *Уу* | **Юю** *Ююю* |
| **Йй** *й* | **Фф** *Фф* | **Яя** *Яя* |

Three letters have alternative written shapes: д has *д* beside *g* ; з has *з* beside *з* ; and т is written *т* as well as *т*. Further, it is common to add a cross-piece above the т and under ш: *т т*, *ш щ*. This helps very much in reading normal handwriting: e. g. **пишите** *пишите, пищите*, кот, кош *кот , кош*. Note that *ш* is *not* like English w.

It is very important to make the initial little hooks on л, м, я: e. g. **там, имя, взяла, воля, земля, Крым, стулья, дом** *там, имя, взяла, воля, земля, Крым, стулья, дом.*

The tails on ц *ц* and щ *щ* must be small, not long like у *у*: улицу *улицу*, щука *щука*.

The soft-sign ь and ы do not rise above the mid-line; в does: e. g. кровь *кровь*, вы *вы*, дверь *дверь*, объяснять *объяснить*.

Do not confuse л, г, and ч (or ч and ъ): гам, лам *гам, лам*, очаги, флаги, фланг *очаги, флаги, фланг*, дала, дача *дала, дача*, счёт, съехал *счёт, съехал*, долги, желчи *долги, желчи*.

Note that у *у* does not go below the line.

Note in particular the letters *В в, Г д, И и, Н, п, Р р, т, у, Х х* and *ч*. They look familiar to you, but represent other sounds in Russian than in English.

Here are the sentences from pages 7–9 in Russian script:

Здравствуйте!

Как вы поживаете?

Хорошо, спасибо.   Ничего, спасибо.

Так себе. А вы?   Очень хорошо.

Доброе утро.

Добрый день.

Добрый вечер.

До свидания.   Всего лучшего.

Спокойной ночи.

Извините.

Повторите за мной.

Ещё раз, пожалуйста.

Скажите ещё раз.

Это не так.

Не так.

Так. Это так.

Вы понимаете?

Да, я понимаю.

Нет, я не понимаю.

Что вы сказали?

Это лучше.

Говорите громче!

Не так быстро.

Не так медленно.

Не говорите по-английски!

Говорите по-русски!

Всё вместе!

Очень хорошо!

# LESSON I

Чтó э́то такóё?
*štó étǝ takójǝ?*

What's this?

Э́то кни́га.
*étǝ knᵇígǝ.*

That's a book.

Э́то каранда́ш.
*étǝ kǝrandáš.*

That's a pencil.

Э́то перó.
*étǝ pᵇiró.*

That's a pen.

Э́то стóл.
*étǝ stól.*

That's a table.

Э́то письмó.
*étǝ pᵇisᵇmó.*

That's a letter.

Э́то окнó. Гдé окнó? Вóт онó.
*étǝ aknó. gdᵇé aknó? vót anó.*

That's a window. Where is the window? There it is.

Э́то двéрь. Гдé двéрь? Вóт она́.
*étǝ dvᵇę́rᵇ. gdᵇé dvᵇę́rᵇ? vót aná.*

That's a door. Where is the door? There it is.

Э́то стýл. Гдé стýл? Вóт óн.
*étǝ stúl. gdᵇé stúl? vót ón.*

That's a chair. Where is the chair? There it is.

Э́то моя́ кни́га (тетра́дка).
*étǝ majá knᵇígǝ (tᵇitrátkǝ).*

That's my book (notebook).

Э́то мóй каранда́ш (стóл, стýл).
*étǝ mój kǝrandáš (stól, stúl).*

That's my pencil (table, chair).

Э́то моё перó (окнó, письмó).
*étǝ majó pᵇiró (aknó, pᵇisᵇmó).*

That's my pen (window, letter).

Э́то на́ша кóмната (двéрь).
*étǝ nášǝ kómnǝtǝ (dvᵇę́rᵇ).*

That's our room (door).

Э́то ва́шё окнó (перó).
*étǝ vášǝ aknó (pᵇiró).*

That's your window (pen).

Это егó кни́га (каранда́ш, перó).
*étə jivó knʲígə (kərandáš, pʲiró).*

That's his book (pencil, pen).

Это её кни́га.
*étə jijó knʲígə.*

That's her book.

Это и́х перó.
*étə jíx pʲiró.*

That's their pen.

Чéй э́то каранда́ш?
*čéj étə kərandáš?*

Whose pencil is this?

Чья́ э́то кни́га?
*čjá étə knʲígə?*

Whose book is this?

Чьё э́то письмó?
*čjó étə pʲisʲmó?*

Whose letter is this?

Это мóй каранда́ш.
*étə mój kərandáš.*

It's my pencil.

Это моя́ кни́га.
*étə majá knʲígə.*

It's my book.

Это моё письмó.
*étə majó pʲisʲmó.*

It's my letter.

Чéй э́тот каранда́ш?
*čéj étət kərandáš?*

Whose is this pencil?

Чья́ э́та кни́га?
*čjá étə knʲígə?*

Whose is this book?

Чьё э́то письмó?
*čjó étə pʲisʲmó?*

Whose is this letter?

Этот каранда́ш мóй.
*étət kərandáš mój.*

This pencil is mine.

Эта кни́га моя́.
*étə knʲígə majá.*

This book is mine.

Это перó моё.
*étə pʲiró majó.*

This pen is mine.

Этот стóл и́х (ёгó, её).
*étət stól jíx (jivó, jijó).*

This table is theirs (his, hers).

Гдé ва́ша кни́га? Вóт она́.
*gdʲé vášə knʲígə? vót aná.*

Where is your book? There it is.

Вóт моя́ кни́га.
*vót majá knʲígə.*

There is my book.

Гдé вáшё перó? Вóт онó.
*gdᵇé vášə pᵇiró?   vót anó.*
  Вóт моё́ перó.
  *vót majó pᵇiró.*

Where is your pen? There it is.

There is my pen.

Гдé вáш карандáш? Вóт óн.
*gdᵇé váš kərandáš?   vót ón.*
  Вóт мóй карандáш.
  *vót mój kərandáš.*

Where is your pencil? There it is.

There is my pencil.

Это стýл? Нéт, это стóл.
*étə stúl? nᵇét, étə stól.*

Is this a chair? No, it's a table.

Это егó тетрáдка йли вáша?
*étə jivó tᵇitrátkə ilᵇi vášə?*

Is this his notebook or yours?

Это перó йли карандáш?
*étə pᵇiró ilᵇi kərandáš?*

Is this a pen or a pencil?

---

**1.0**  Nouns in Russian belong arbitrarily to one of three classes called *genders* — masculine, feminine and neuter. (Abbreviated m, f, n.)

**1.1**  *Masculine nouns* normally end in a consonant: in spelling they end in a consonant-letter or the soft-sign ь (indicating a soft consonant). For example: стóл *stól* 'table', карандáш *kərandáš* 'pencil', (cf. дéнь *dᵇénᵇ* 'day').

**1.2**  *Neuter nouns* normally end in -*o* (which becomes -*ə* if unstressed), spelled -**о** if preceded by a hard consonant, and -**ё** otherwise: окнó *aknó* 'window', перó *pᵇiró* 'pen' (cf. здáниё *zdánᵇijə* 'building', пóлё *pólᵇə* 'field', ружьё́ *ružjó* 'gun').

**1.31**  *Most feminine nouns* end in -*a* (-*ə* if unstressed), spelled -**a** after hard consonants and **ч** and **щ**, and -**я** otherwise: доскá *daská* 'board', кнíга *knᵇígə* 'book' (cf. земля́ *zᵇimlᵇá* 'land', дерéвня *dᵇirᵇévnᵇə* 'village', Россíя *rasᵇíjə* 'Russia').

**1.32**  *Some feminine nouns* end in a soft consonant or *š* or *ž*; in spelling, the last letter is always -**ь**: двéрь *dvᵇérᵇ* 'door' (cf. нóчь *nóč* 'night').

**1.4**  In the vocabularies, nouns ending in a consonant-letter or **-ь** are masculine; nouns in **-o** or **-ё** are neuter; nouns in **-a** or **-я** are feminine. Feminines in **-ь** and exceptional cases will be specifically labelled: e.g. двéрь (f).

**2.0**  Most *pronouns* which accompany or refer to nouns change their forms in accordance with the gender of the noun:

|            | 'that'       | 'this'        | 'it, he, she' |
|------------|--------------|---------------|---------------|
| masculine: | **тóт** tót  | **э́тот** étət | **óн** ón     |
| neuter:    | **тó** tó    | **э́то** étə   | **онó** anó   |
| feminine:  | **тá** tá    | **э́та** étə   | **онá** aná   |

|            | 'my'          | 'our'          | 'your'         | 'whose'       |
|------------|---------------|----------------|----------------|---------------|
| masculine: | **мóй** mój   | **нáш** náš    | **вáш** váš    | **чéй** čéj   |
| neuter:    | **моё** majó  | **нáшё** nášə  | **вáшё** vášə  | **чьё** čjó   |
| feminine:  | **моя** majá  | **нáша** nášə  | **вáша** vášə  | **чья** čjá   |

**2.01**  This adaptation of certain features of one word to *agree with* another word which is presented as linguistically of more importance is called *agreement*. The word which dictates is a *head-word*, and the word which agrees is a *modifier*. Thus these *demonstrative pronouns* ('this, that') and *possessive pronouns* ('my, your, our') are said to agree in gender with the noun they modify.

**2.1**  The three possessive pronouns 'his' **егó** *jivó* (NB pronunciation, cf. App. I, § 17.3), 'her' **её** *jijó*, and 'their' **úx** *jíx*[1] NEVER change their forms to agree: e.g.

| | | |
|---|---|---|
| **егó кни́га** jivó knʰígə | **её кни́га** jijó knʰígə | **úx кни́га** jíx knʰígə |
| **егó стóл** jivó stól | **её стóл** jijó stól | **úx стóл** jíx stól |
| **егó перó** jivó pʰiró | **её перó** jijó pʰiró | **úx перó** jíx pʰiró |

**2.2**  Note that while in English the pronoun *it* is used unless speaking of male or female creatures (= *he, she*), in Russian the masculine and feminine forms óн, онá refer to *nouns of masculine or feminine gender*. Thus вóт *óн* means "there is someone or something normally referred to by means of a masculine noun": if the context tells us that this is a person, the translation is "There *he* is", but if the context indicates an object (e.g. стóл, карандáш), the translation is "There *it* is." Similarly, for "there *it* is", meaning a book or a door (кни́га, двéрь), the Russian says вóт *онá*.

---

[1] The *j* of *jíx* is weak; some Russians omit it entirely.

**2.3** The Russian pronoun э́тот (*étət*) indicates something relatively close to the speaker, while то́т (*tót*) points to something more distant. The two terms are roughly equivalent to *this* and *that* in English, but the student will frequently find э́тот where he would say *that*. The reason is that the boundary between э́тот and то́т is conceived of as being farther from the speaker than is the boundary between *this* and *that*, and there is an area of overlap between э́тот and *that*, thus:

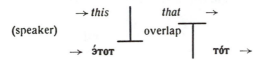

То́т is thus closer in meaning to "that over there", or dialect "that yonder, yon."

**2.31** For the English-Russian exercises in this book, "this" will be considered equivalent to э́тот and "that" to то́т, but the student should observe carefully how Russians use the terms in concrete situations.

**3.** *The verb 'to be'* is normally not expressed in the present tense in Russian. Я здесь, а вы та́м. já zdʰésʰ a ví tám. 'I *am* here and you *are* over there'. In writing, a dash is sometimes used to represent this "zero verb",[1] and in speaking, the intonation clearly delimits the two parts of the statement:

О́н — на́ш профе́ссор. ón náš prafʰésər. He is our professor.

**4.** The invariable pronoun э́то *étə* is used to refer to anything which has not yet been defined: э́то стол *étə stól* — 'this (undefined thing) is a table'; э́то на́ш профе́ссор *étə náš prafʰésər* — 'this (undefined object) is our professor'.

**5.** Two ways of indicating a question in Russian are: (a) rising tone of voice, e.g. *э́то кни́га?* *étə knʰígə?* 'is this a book?' ~ *э́то кни́га.* *étə knʰígə.* '*this is a book.*' (b) interrogative word: что́ *э́то тако́е?* *štó étə takójə?* 'what is this?'; че́й *э́то каранда́ш?* *čéj étə kərandáš?* 'whose pencil is this?'

### EXERCISES

**A.** Complete the sentence below by substituting the proper forms of мо́й *mój*, ва́ш *váš*, его́ *jivó*, на́ш *náš*, и́х *jíx* with each of the nouns given:

Э́то — кни́га (сто́л, ко́мната, перо́, две́рь, сту́л, тетра́дка).
étə — knʰígə (stól, kómnətə, pʰiró, dvʰérʰ, stúl, tʰitrátkə).

[1] Contrasting with the lack of "to be" in a present-tense statement there are explicit forms for "to be" in both past and future (as we shall see in Lesson VI). Thus it is convenient to say that the "zero verb-form" of the present is a unit in the normal three-way past-present-future system.

**B.**   On the patterns (1) **Чей** э́т**от** сту́л? čéj étət stúl? and (2) **Эта** дверь **мо**я́, étə dvʰḗrʰ majá, make all the possible sentences by substituting the other forms indicated:

1. Ч— эт—      (письмо́, кни́га, перо́, тетра́дка, дверь)?

2. Эт— [т—]      (окно́, тетра́дка, каранда́ш, ко́мната, сто́л, доска́, письмо́, сту́л, перо́) мо́ — (ва́ш, его́, её, на́ш, йх).

1. č— ét—      (pʰisʰmó, knʰígə, pʰiró, tʲitrátkə, dvʰḗrʰ)?

2. ét— (t—)      (aknó, tʲitrátkə, kərandáš, kómnətə, stól, daská, pʰisʰmó, stúl, pʰiró) moj— (váš, jivó, jijó, náš, jíx).

**C.**   Read and translate:

1. До́брый ве́чер. Ка́к вы́ пожива́ете? 2. О́чень хорошо́, спаси́бо, а вы́? —Та́к себе́. 3. Это ва́ше перо́? 4. Извини́те, я не понима́ю. Пожа́луйста, не говори́те та́к бы́стро. 5. Это перо́ ва́ше? 6. Не́т, э́то не мое́ перо́, э́то её перо́. 7. Во́т моя́ тетра́дка и его́ каранда́ш. 8. Где́ ва́ш каранда́ш? Во́т о́н. 9. Что́ э́то тако́е? Это доска́. 10. Повтори́те еще́ ра́з, все́ вме́сте, гро́мче. 11. Это письмо́ и́ли тетра́дка? Это тетра́дка. 12. Чья́ э́та ко́мната? Эта ко́мната на́ша. 13. Говори́те по-ру́сски, пожа́луйста. 14. Где́ на́ша дверь? Во́т она́. 15. Это мое́ письмо́ и́ли ва́ше? Это не мое́ письмо́. 16. *Во́т ва́ш профе́ссор.* 17. *Говори́те ме́дленно, пожа́луйста.* 18. *Это перо́ и́ли каранда́ш? Это каранда́ш.* 19. *Че́й э́тот сто́л? Этот сто́л мо́й.* 20. До свида́ния.

## VOCABULARY

| | | | |
|---|---|---|---|
| бы́стро | rapidly, fast | гро́мче | louder, more loudly |
| bístrə | | grómči | |
| ва́ш, ва́ше, ва́ша | your, yours | да́ | yes |
| váš, vášə, vášə | | dá | |
| вме́сте | together | дверь f. | door |
| vmʰéstʰi | | dvʰḗrʰ | |
| во́т | there, there is [pointing] | доска́ | board |
| vót | | daská | |
| вы́ | you | его́ | his |
| ví | | jivó (NB!) | |
| где́ | where | её | her |
| gdʰé | | jijó | |
| говори́те | speak! | | |
| gəvarʰítʰi | | | |

| | | | |
|---|---|---|---|
| ещё ра́з<br>jiščó rás | again, once more | по-англи́йски<br>paanglʰíjskʰi | in English |
| за мно́й<br>zamnój | after me | повтори́те<br>pəftarʰítʰi | repeat! |
| и<br>i | and | пожа́луйста<br>pəžálstə (NB) | please |
| и́ли<br>ílʰi | or | понима́ёте<br>pənʰimájitʰi | you understand |
| и́х<br>jíx | their | понима́ю<br>pənʰimáju | I understand |
| ка́к<br>kák | how, as | по-ру́сски<br>parúskʰi | in Russian |
| каранда́ш<br>kərandáš | pencil | профе́ссор<br>prafʰésər | professor |
| кни́га<br>knʰígə | book | скажи́те<br>skaží̇tʰi | say! |
| ко́мната<br>kómnətə | room | сказа́ли<br>skazálʰi | said (plural) |
| лу́чше<br>lúčṧi | better | спаси́бо<br>spasʰíbə | thanks |
| ме́дленно<br>mʰédlʰinnə | slowly | сто́л<br>stól | table |
| мо́й, мое́, моя́<br>mój, majó, majá | my, mine | сту́л<br>stúl | chair |
| на́ш, на́шё, на́ша<br>náš, nášə, nášə | our, ours | та́к<br>ták | so, thus |
| не (normally *un*stressed)<br>nʰi : if stressed, nʰé | not | тетра́дка<br>tʰitrátkə | notebook |
| не́т<br>nʰét | no | то́т, то́, та́<br>tót, tó, tá | that |
| окно́<br>aknó | window | хорошо́<br>xərašó | good, well |
| о́н, оно́, она́<br>ón, anó, .aná | he, it, she | че́й, чье́, чья́<br>čéj, čjó, čjá | whose? |
| о́чень<br>óčinʰ | very | что́<br>štó (NB!) | what? |
| перо́<br>pʰiró | pen | э́тот, э́то, э́та<br>étət, étə, étə | this |
| письмо́<br>pʰisʰmó | letter | я (NB: not capitalized)<br>já | I |

# LESSON II

Ваш до́м в го́роде йли
*váš dóm vgórədʰi ilʰi*
в дере́вне?
*vdʰirʰέvnʰi?*

Is your house in the city or

in the country?

Я живу́ зде́сь в э́том до́ме.
*já živú zdʰέsʰ vétəm dómʰi.*

I live here in this house.

Это зда́ниё музе́й.
*étə zdánʰijə muzʰέj.*

This building is a museum.

Музе́й та́м в то́м зда́нии.
*muzʰέj tám ʃtóm zdánʰiji.*

The museum is there in **that** building.

Она́ живёт в э́той ко́мнате, а
*aná živʰót vétəj kómnətʰi, a*
рабо́таёт в музе́е.
*rabótəjit vmuzʰέji.*

She lives in this room and

works in the museum.

Её ко́мната где́-то в э́том зда́нии.
*jijó kómnətə gdʰétə vétəm zdánʰiji.*

Her room is somewhere in **this** building.

Мы́ живём в дере́вне.
*mí živʰóm vdʰirʰέvnʰi.*

We live in the village (in the country).

Где́ вы живёте?
*gdʰé ví živʰótʰi?*

Where do you live?

Они́ живу́т в Босто́не, но́ йх
*anʰí živút vbostónʰi, nó jíx*
оте́ц живёт в Росси́и.
*atʰéc živʰót vrasʰíji.*

They live in Boston, but **their**

father lives in Russia.

О́н нигде́ не рабо́таёт.
*ón nʰigdʰé nʰirabótəjit.*

He doesn't work anywhere.

Я рабо́таю зде́сь, а мо́й оте́ц
*já rabótəju zdʰέsʰ a mój atʰéc*
рабо́таёт на фа́брике в го́роде.
*rabótəjit naʃábrʰikʰi vgórədʰi.*

I work here and my father **works**

in a factory in the city.

Мы́ рабо́таем вме́сте, когда́
*mí rabótəjim vmᵇə́stᵇi kagdá*
  мы́ до́ма.
  *mí dómə.*

We work together when

  we are at home.

Кто́ рабо́таёт здесь?
*któ rabótəjit zdᵇə́sᵇ?*

Who works here?

Кто́-то рабо́таёт та́м.
*któtə rabótəjit tám.*

Someone works there.

Зна́ёте ли вы́, где́ они́ рабо́тают?
*znájitᵇilᵇi ví gdᵇé anᵇi rabótəjut?*

Do you know where they work?

Я́ не зна́ю, где́ вы́ рабо́таёте.
*já nᵇiznáju gdᵇé ví rabótəjitᵇi.*

I don't know where you work.

Ва́шё перо́ та́м на сту́ле.
*vášə pᵇiró tám nastúlᵇi.*

Your pen is there on the chair.

Во́т моя́ кни́га на столе́.
*vót majá knᵇígə nəstalᵇé.*

There is my book on the table.

Они́ в саду́.
*anᵇi fsadú.*

They are in the garden.

О́н рабо́таёт в го́роде в Крыму́.
*ón rabótəjit vgórədᵇi fkrímú.*

He works in a city in the Crimea.

Они́ живу́т в лесу́ на Дону́.
*anᵇi živút vlᵇisú nədanú.*

They live in a forest on the Don.

О чём вы́ говори́те?
*ačóm ví gəvarᵇitᵇi?*

What are you talking about?

Я́ говорю́ о ва́шей дере́вне.
*já gəvarᵇú avášij dᵇirᵇę́vnᵇi.*

I'm talking about your village.

Они́ говоря́т о моём карандаше́.
*anᵇi gəvarᵇát amajóm kərəndašé.*

They are talking about my pencil.

Они́ говоря́т о ко́м-то.
*anᵇi gəvarᵇát akómtə.*

They are talking about someone.

Я́ не зна́ю, о ко́м они́ говоря́т.
*já nᵇiznáju akóm anᵇi gəvarᵇát.*

I don't know who they're talking about.

Они́ ни о ко́м не говоря́т.
*anᵇi nᵇiakóm nᵇigəvarᵇát.*

They aren't talking about anybody.

Они́ ни о чём не говоря́т.
*anᵇi nᵇiačóm nᵇigəvarᵇát.*

They aren't talking about anything.

Она́ говори́т о чём-то.
*aná gəvarʲit ačómtə.*

She is speaking about something.

Что́ говоря́т об отце́?
*štó gəvarʲát abatcé?*

What are they saying about father?

Почему́ вы́ не говори́те
*pəčimú vʲí nʲigəvarʲitʲi*
о ва́шей фа́брике?
*avášij fábrʲikʲi?*

Why don't you talk

about your factory?

Вы́ понима́ете, когда́ о́н
*vʲí pənʲimájitʲi kagdá ón*
говори́т по-ру́сски?
*gəvarʲit parúskʲi?*

Do you understand when he

speaks Russian?

———

Most Russian words can be analyzed as *stem + ending*. The ending is defined, and the remaining part of the word is then the stem. The stem itself may be further analyzable. It contains a *root* which may be accompanied by one or more *affixes*. Affixes are of two types: *prefixes*, which precede the root, and *suffixes*, which follow the root. We use the term *ending* specifically for those suffixes which always occur at the very end of the word. The study of these endings is *morphology*, and is one of the chief concerns of this course. The study of other word-elements is *derivation* or *word-formation*: it is of less importance for beginners and will not be dealt with systematically here.

Russian nouns, pronouns, and adjectives change their forms to indicate the different relationships within a sentence. The forms which signify one category of relationships are said to belong to the same *case*.

**1.0** *The prepositional case* is *always* accompanied by one of five prepositions, the most important of which are **в** 'in', **на** 'on', and **о** 'about'.

**1.10** The prepositional case-ending for nearly all nouns is -*e* (or rather -*e* if stressed but -*i* when unstressed, cf. page 13, § 5.32: 6).

For most nouns, this suffix is spelled -**e**. Note that the consonant preceding the ending is "softened" if possible: сто́л stol — на столе́ nə stalʲé, письмо́ pʲisʲmó — в письме́ f pʲisʲmʲé, доска́ daská — на доске́ nə daskʲé, сту́л stúl — на сту́ле na stúlʲi; but (cf. page 4, § 2.51) каранда́ш kərandáš — на карандаше́ nə kərəndašé, оте́ц atʲéc — об отце́ ab atcé.

**1.11** This suffix is spelled -**и**, however, (1) if the stem of the noun ends in -**и**- (that is, if the nominative ends in -**ий**, -**иё**, -**ия**), or (2) if the noun is a feminine ending in a soft-sign:

(1), ге́ний gᵇéⁿᵇij ('genius') — о ге́нии а gᵇéⁿᵇiji

зда́ниё zdánᵇijə — о зда́нии а zdánᵇiji

Росси́я rasᵇijə — в Росси́и v rasᵇiji

(2) дверь dvᵇérᵇ — о две́ри а dvᵇérᵇi

**2.0**  In masculine nouns whose nominative ends in a consonant, there are sometimes differences between the nominative and the stems used for the prepositional (and other cases):

(1) an -e-, -ё-, or -o- preceding the last consonant may be lost:[1]

оте́ц atᵇéc — об отце́ ab atcé

(2) an important change not indicated in the spelling is that a final voiceless consonant of the nominative is replaced by the corresponding voiced consonant elsewhere (cf. page 13, § 6): górət ∼ górədᵇi (cf. genitive górədə), spelled го́род, в го́роде (го́рода).

**2.1**  Note that often the accent in the masculine nouns may shift onto the suffix: стол stól — столе́ stalᵇé; каранда́ш kərandáš — карандаше́ kərəndašé. It is extremely important to learn such changes as they occur. They will be noted in the vocabularies.

**3.**  Certain masculine nouns have besides the normal prepositional suffix -e a special stressed suffix -ú (spelled -y, -ю) which specifically indicates *location*, and occurs only with the prepositions в v and на *na*:

| Она́ в саду́. | aná f sadú. | She is *in* the garden. |
| Он живёт в лесу́. | ón živᵇót v lᵇisú. | He lives *in* the forest. |
| Дере́вня на Дону́. | dᵇirᵇévnᵇə nə danú. | A village *on* the Don. |

BUT: Он говори́т о са́де. ón gəvarᵇít a sádᵇi.  } He is    { the garden.
         о ле́се.        a lᵇésᵇi.  } speaking  { the forest.
         о До́не.        a dónᵇi.  } about     { the Don.
         о Кры́ме.       a krímᵇi.  }          { the Crimea.

[There are about 80 nouns which have this special locative ending, but nearly half of them are rare in literature. This form (which some authorities term a separate case, the locative) will always be indicated in the vocabularies.]

---

[1] Strictly speaking, this vowel is added in the nominative rather than lost in the other forms. Such "inserted vowels" are found elsewhere; in the genitive plural of neuter and feminine nouns (VIII 1.2312), in the "short" masculine form of adjectives (XII 2.11), in some irregular past verb forms, and in a few isolated forms like the pronoun 'whose' — n. čjó, f. čjá: m. čéj. In all of these cases the forms with such vowels can be said to have a zero suffix — the absence of a suffix is just as much a signal as the presence of a suffix in the other forms. The masc. nom. sing. suffix is, then, zero. The "inserted vowels" do, however, appear in some instances where there is a suffix other than zero.

**4.** Pronouns and adjectives have different endings than nouns. In the prepositional case, masculine and neuter pronouns have identical forms.

|       | I | you | we | you | he | it | she | they | who? | what? |
|-------|---|-----|----|----|----|----|-----|------|------|-------|
| Nom. | я<br>*já* | ты<br>*tí* | мы́<br>*mí* | вы́<br>*ví* | он<br>*ón* | оно́<br>*anó* | она́<br>*aná* | они́<br>*an<sup>b</sup>í* | кто́<br>*któ* | что́<br>*štó* |
| Prep. | мне́<br>*mn<sup>b</sup>é* | тебе́<br>*t<sup>b</sup>ib<sup>b</sup>é* | нас<br>*nás* | вас<br>*vás* | нём<br>*n<sup>b</sup>óm* | | ней<br>*n<sup>b</sup>éj* | них<br>*n<sup>b</sup>íx* | ко́м<br>*kóm* | чём<br>*čóm* |

|       | masculine and neuter | | | | | |
|-------|----------------------|--|--|--|--|--|
| Nom. | то́т то́<br>*tót tó* | э́тот э́то<br>*étət étə* | мо́й мое́<br>*mój majó* | на́ш на́шё<br>*náš nášə* | ва́ш ва́шё<br>*váš vášə* | че́й чьё́<br>*č<u>é</u>j čjó* |
| Prep. | то́м<br>*tóm* | э́том<br>*étəm* | мое́м<br>*majóm* | на́шем<br>*nášəm* | ва́шем<br>*vášəm* | чьё́м<br>*čjóm* |
|       | feminine | | | | | |
| Nom. | та́<br>*tá* | э́та<br>*étə* | моя́<br>*majá* | на́ша<br>*nášə* | ва́ша<br>*vášə* | чья́<br>*čjá* |
| Prep. | то́й<br>*tój* | э́той<br>*étəj* | мое́й<br>*maj<u>é</u>j* | на́шей<br>*náš<u>ɨ</u>j* | ва́шей<br>*váš<u>ɨ</u>j* | чье́й<br>*čj<u>é</u>j* |

**5.1** The interrogative pronouns кто́ *któ* and что́ *štó* become negative if preceded by the particle ни *n<sup>b</sup>i*: никто́ *n<sup>b</sup>iktó* 'no one', ничто́ *n<sup>b</sup>ištó* 'nothing'. The nominative ничто́ is rare, but the other forms are common.

When used with a preposition, the ни *n<sup>b</sup>i precedes* the preposition, and the three units are written separately: ни о ко́м *n<sup>b</sup>iakóm* 'concerning no one', ни о чём *n<sup>b</sup>iačóm* 'concerning nothing'.

**5.2** The interrogative adverb где́ *gd<sup>b</sup>é* 'where?' also is made negative by the prefix ни *n<sup>b</sup>i* — нигде́ *n<sup>b</sup>igd<sup>b</sup>é* 'nowhere'.

**5.3** NOTE that any verb used with никто́, ничто́, нигде́ must be *negated*:

Óн нигде́ *не* рабо́таёт,          Никто́ та́м *не* живёт.
*ón n<sup>b</sup>igd<sup>b</sup>é* n<sup>b</sup>i *rabótəjit.*          *n<sup>b</sup>iktó tám* n<sup>b</sup>i *žɨv<sup>b</sup>ót.*
            Они́ ни о чём *не* говоря́т.
            *an<sup>b</sup>i n<sup>b</sup>iačóm* n<sup>b</sup>i *gəvar<sup>b</sup>át.*

**5.4** -то *tə* suffixed to кто́, что́, and где́ makes them less definite: кто́-то *któtə* 'someone', что́-то *štótə* 'something', где́-то *gd<sup>b</sup>étə* 'somewhere'.

**6.0**  The present tense of the Russian verb has six forms, each of which expresses both person and tense. Like all Russian verb-forms, these present tense forms consist of a *stem* and an *ending*. We define the ending, and the remaining part is, by definition, the stem.

**6.01**  The verb is a modifier (cf. page 20, § 2.01) which agrees in *person* and *number* (singular or plural) with the subject, which is normally a noun or pronoun.

**6.1**  The *endings* are:

|  | singular | | plural | |
|---|---|---|---|---|
| 1st person (speaker) | 'I' | -*u*   -у/-ю | 'we'   -*m* | -м |
| 2nd person (addressee) | 'you'   -*š* | -шь | 'you'   -*t<sup>ь</sup>i* | -те |
| 3rd person (spoken of) | 'he, she, it' } -*t* | -т | 'they'   -*t* | -т |

Do not forget that both **y** and **ю** represent the vowel *u*, but that the letter **ю** after a vowel-letter indicates the consonant *j* + the vowel *u* (работаю = rabótə*ju*), while after a consonant-letter it indicates the palatalized or "soft" variety of the consonant concerned (говор**ю** = gəvar<sup>ь</sup>*ú*).

**6.2**  Except in the 1st person singular, the endings are preceded by a *stem-vowel*. For the 3rd person plural it is -*u*- or -*a*-, spelled **y** or **ю**, **a** or **я**.

The 3rd plural is the key form, from which we can predict the other forms, and it must be memorized.[1] When it ends in -**ут** or -**ют**, the other persons have the stem-vowel -**e**-: when the 3rd person plural is in -**aт** or -**ят**, the other persons have the stem-vowel -**и**-.

If the ending of the 3rd plural is stressed, then the stem-vowel in the other persons will be stressed.

For example:

| | | | | | |
|---|---|---|---|---|---|
| 1 sg | (я) | жив-ý | žɨv-ú | рабóта[й]-ю | rabótəj-u |
| 2 sg | (ты) | жив-ё-шь | žɨv<sup>ь</sup>-ó-š | рабóта[й]-е-шь | rabótəj-i-š |
| 3 sg | (óн) | жив-ё-т | žɨv<sup>ь</sup>-ó-t | рабóта[й]-е-т | rabótəj-i-t |
| 1 pl | (мы́) | жив-ё-м | žɨv<sup>ь</sup>-ó-m | рабóта[й]-е-м | rabótəj-i-m |
| 2 pl | (вы́) | жив-ё-те | žɨv<sup>ь</sup>-ó-t<sup>ь</sup>i | рабóта[й]-е-те | rabótəj-i-t<sup>ь</sup>i |
| 3 pl | (они́) | жив-ý-т | žɨv-ú-t | рабóта[й]-ю-т | rabótəj-u-t |

[1] To predict the whole conjugation of a verb, not only the 3rd plural must be memorized, but also the infinitive. Both forms will be given in the vocabularies.

| 1 sg | (я)   | виж-у[1]    | vᵇíž-u         | говор-ю      | gəvarᵇ-ú         |
|------|-------|-------------|----------------|--------------|------------------|
| 2 sg | (ты)  | вид-и-шь    | vᵇídᵇ-i-š      | говор-и-шь   | gəvarᵇ-í-š       |
| 3 sg | (он)  | вид-и-т     | vᵇídᵇ-i-t      | говор-и-т    | gəvarᵇ-í-t       |
| 1 pl | (мы)  | вид-и-м     | vᵇídᵇ-i-m      | говор-и-м    | gəvarᵇ-í-m       |
| 2 pl | (вы)  | вид-и-те    | vᵇídᵇ-i-tᵇi    | говор-и-те   | gəvarᵇ-í-tᵇi     |
| 3 pl | (они) | вид-я-т     | vᵇídᵇ-ə-t (-u-t) | говор-я-т  | gəvarᵇ-á-t       |

The normal Russian spellings in the paradigm of **работают** are deceptive: it is important to understand that the stem really ends in the *consonant j*, which is spelled ю (*j* + *u*) in two forms and ё (*j* + *o*)[2] in the other four: работаю, работаешь, работает, etc.

Note that the 3rd plural ending spelled **-ат, -ят** is pronounced with the vowel *ə* when unstressed. It may also be pronounced *u* in accordance with the older Moscow norm: vᵇídᵇ-*u-t*.

**7.**   The second person singular, with the pronoun **ты** *tí*, is used by Russians when addressing relatives and intimate friends, or, on the other hand, persons considered as socially inferior. The second person plural, with the pronoun **вы** *ví*, is the normal polite way of addressing a single person, and is the only way of addressing more than one person. In the exercises in this book, "you" is to be translated by **вы** *ví* unless otherwise indicated.

The possessive "your" corresponding to **вы** *ví* is **ваш, ваше, ваша** *váš, vášə, vášə*, while for **ты** *tí* the forms are **твой, твоё, твоя** *tvój, tvajó, tvajá*.

**8.**   Beside the types of question-sentences mentioned in I 5 (= Lesson I, § 5), there is a third. For a neutral yes-or-no question, the verb is put in first place, followed by the interrogative particle **ли** *lᵇi* (stressless):

Работает ли он в музее?
*rabótəjit lᵇi ón v muzᵇéji?*          Does he work in the museum?

If the question stresses some word other than the verb, that word may stand in first place, followed by the **ли**:

В городе ли работает ваш отец?     Is it in the city that your father
*v górədᵇi lᵇi rabótəjit váš atᵇéc?*     works?

Ваш ли отец работает там?
*váš lᵇi atᵇéc rabótəjit tám?*          Does *your* father work there?

----

[1] The change of stem in the verb 'see' (вижу but видишь) will be explained in the more detailed discussion of the verb system in Lesson V.

[2] Being unstressed and after a soft consonant, the *o* is automatically pronounced *i*; cf. Introduction § 5.32, 4 (and Appendix I, § 11.01).

**9.** Prepositions are pronounced as an integral part of the following word, even though in normal writing they are separated from that word by a space. Prepositions are thus subject to the same automatic changes of pronunciation, depending on the neighboring sounds and the place of stress, that take place within words.

1. The preposition **в** is normally pronounced *v*, but it automatically becomes *f* if the following word begins with the consonants *p t k c č f s š x*. These are *voiceless* consonants, and the voiced *v* must become voiceless to match (see § 6 of the Introduction). For example:

| | (voiced) | | but | | (voiceless) | |
|---|---|---|---|---|---|---|
| in this | vétəm | в э́том | в то́м | | ftóm | in that |
| in your | vvášəm | в ва́шём | в че́м | | fčóm | in what |
| in my | vmajóm | в мое́м | в чьём | | fčjóm | in whose |
| in his | vjivó | в ёго́ | в твоём | | ftvajóm | in your |
| in their | vjíx | в и́х | в письме́ | | fpᵇisᵇmᵇé | in a letter |
| in Boston | vbastónᵇi | в Босто́не | в ко́мнате | | fkómnatᵇi | in the room |
| in the house | vdómᵇi | в до́ме | в столе́ | | fstalᵇé | in the desk |
| in a building | vzdánᵇiji | в зда́нии | | | | |

We have not yet had suitable words beginning with *f c š x*, but compare в феврале́ 'in February', в це́ркви 'in church', в шко́ле 'in school', в Харби́не 'in Harbin': *ffᵇivralᵇé, fcérkvᵇi, fškólᵇi, fxarbᵇínᵇi*.

The preposition sometimes adds a vowel and is spelled **во**, thus preserving the voiced consonant. This usually happens before words pronounced with initial *f* + *consonant*: во Фра́нции 'in France', во вто́рник 'on Tuesday' — *vafráncɨji, vaftórnᵇik*.

2. The preposition **на** is normally pronounced *nə* if the accented syllable does not immediately follow it (cf. Introduction § 5.31, 1). Thus:

| на сту́ле | nastúlᵇi | but | nəstalᵇé | на столе́ |
|---|---|---|---|---|
| на э́том сту́ле | naétəm stúlᵇi | | nəpᵇisᵇmᵇé | на письме́ |
| на ва́шём до́ме | navášəm dómᵇi | | nəmajóm dómᵇi | на моём до́ме |
| | | | nəkərəndašé | на карандаше́ |

**10.** The conjunction **и** *i* 'and' joins words which are on the same level. It represents equality or addition. **a** has no exact equivalent in English, and sometimes is to be translated as 'and' and sometimes as 'but'. Я́ зде́сь, **a** о́н та́м *já zdᵇésᵇ, a ón tám* 'I am here and/but he is there'. **a** denotes a contrast of two items: here **я́** and **о́н** are contrasted, and **зде́сь** is opposed to **та́м**. If there is a negation, this counts as one of the items contrasted, for it is compared to the positive: я́ не та́м, а зде́сь *já nᵇi tám, a zdᵇésᵇ* 'I am *not* (1) there (2), but [I am (1)] here (2)'.

The conjunction **нó** *nó* 'but' always specifies a contradiction, something contrary to expectation. The attitude of the speaker is clearly revealed in such a sentence as: Oнá живёт здéсь, **нó** её отéц живёт тáм *aná živᵇót zdᵇęsᵇ, nó jijó atᵇéc živᵇót tám* 'She lives here, but her father lives there'. The speaker presents this as a contradiction, showing that he expects the two to live in the same place. The same sentence with **a** instead of **нó** tells us nothing about the attitude of the speaker; he is merely presenting a twofold contrast.

Note: in the transcription of the sentences on pp. 24–6, the prepositions and the verbal negation have been written just as pronounced, as a part of the word that follows. Elsewhere the transcription leaves a space between these units just as Russian spelling does. Do not forget, however, that the unstressed prepositions and the negative particle behave differently from stressed monosyllables. Cf. App. I, § 13.4.

## EXERCISES

**A.** 1. Be prepared to say and write in Russian all possible combinations of:
a. in this (that) city (room, house, garden, village, book, door, forest).
b. on my (your, his, her, our, their) table (book, house, chair, notebook).
c. about my (your, his, her, our, their, this, that, whose) father (professor, museum, city, pencil, forest, letter, room, building, notebook, book, garden, door, village).

Give all present-tense forms of the verbs: work, live, speak, understand, know.

**B.** Read and translate:

1. Eгó кни́га и её письмó тáм на столé, а моя́ кни́га на сту́ле. 2. Óн говори́т бы́стро. Мы́ не понимáем. 3. Когдá мы́ вмéсте в дерéвне, мы́ не рабóтаем. 4. Дóма ли вáш отéц? Дá, óн в саду́. 5. До свидáния, всегó лу́чшего! 6. Профéссор живёт в э́той кóмнате, а рабóтает в тóм здáнии. 7. Они́ говоря́т о вáс и о вáшем дóме. 8. Чтó э́то такóё? Э́то мóй карандáш. 9. Нáша фáбрика в э́той дерéвне. 10. Э́то не тáк. Скажи́те ещё рáз. 11. Понимáете ли вы́, когдá онá говори́т бы́стро? 12. Знáет ли и́х отéц, гдé я́ живу́? 13. Э́то вáш карандáш? Нéт, э́то егó карандáш. 14. Гдé фáбрика, гдé вы́ рабóтаете? 15. О чём онá говори́т? О нём ли? 16. Они́ ни о кóм не говоря́т. 17. Óн рабóтает в саду́ и в лесу́. 18. Eгó отéц живёт в Росси́и, на Дону́. 19. Они́ рабóтают гдé-то в Крыму́. 20. Вы́ понимáете, о чём мы́ говори́м? Дá, я́ хорошó понимáю.

21. Вы живёте там в этом доме? Нет, я живу в деревне. 22. О ком говорят отец и профессор? Мы не знаем, о ком они говорят. 23. Это наша фабрика. 24. Вы знаете, где мой отец? 25. Это не ваша Дверь. 26. Почему вы говорите об отце? 27. Скажите ещё раз, пожалуйста. 28. Я не понимаю. 29. Их дом в лесу. 30. До свидания.

**C.** Supplemental sentences:

1. Ва́ша кни́га на столе́.
   vášə knᵇígə nəstalᵇé.

2. О чём вы говори́те?
   ačóm vɨ gəvarᵇítᵇi?

3. Я́ говорю́ о мое́й кни́ге.
   já gəvarᵇú amajéj knᵇígᵇi.

4. Она́ на э́том столе́.
   aná naétəm stalᵇé.

5. Что́ э́то в кни́ге? Это письмо́.
   štó étə fknᵇígᵇi? étə pᵇisᵇmó.

6. В э́той кни́ге письмо́.
   vétəj knᵇígᵇi pᵇisᵇmó.

7. А что́ э́то на кни́ге?
   a štó étə naknᵇígᵇi?

8. На чём? На ва́шей кни́ге.
   načóm? naváš ̣ij knᵇígᵇi.

9. На кни́ге каранда́ш.
   naknᵇígᵇi kərandáš.

10. Каранда́ш на кни́ге а письмо́ в кни́ге.
    kərandáš naknᵇígᵇi a pᵇisᵇmó fknᵇígᵇi.

11. Мы́ говори́м о карандаше́ и о письме́.
    mɨ́ gəvarᵇim akərəndašé i apᵇisᵇmᵇé.

12. О чьём письме́ они́ говоря́т?
    ačjóm pᵇisᵇmᵇé anᵇi gəvarᵇát?

13. Они́ говоря́т о моём письме́.
    anᵇi gəvarᵇát amajóm pᵇisᵇmᵇé.

14. Моё письмо́ в ва́шем столе́.
    majó pᵇisᵇmó vvášəm stalᵇé.

15. Я́ говорю́ и понима́ю по-
    ру́сски.
    já gəvarʰú i panʰimáju parúskʰi.

16. Она́ не говори́т, но́ понима́ет.
    aná nʰigəvarʰít, nó pənʰimájit.

17. Мы́ хорошо́ говори́м и
    mɨ́ xərašó gəvarʰím i
        понима́ем.
        pənʰimájim.

18. Вы́ не понима́ете по-ру́сски?
    vɨ́ nʰipənʰimájitʰi parúskʰi?

19. Они́ понима́ют по-англи́йски.
    anʰí pənʰimájut paanglʰíjskʰi.

20. На́ш го́род — Босто́н.
    naš górət — bastón.

21. Вы́ здесь живе́те?
    vɨ́ zdʰésʰ žɨvʰótʰi?

22. Да́, мо́й до́м в го́роде.
    dá, mój dóm vgórədʰi.

23. Я́ живу́ в Босто́не.
    já žɨvú vbastónʰi.

24. Мы́ живе́м в дере́вне.
    mɨ́ žɨvʰóm vdʰirʰévnʰi.

25. Та́м са́д и ле́с.
    tám sát i lʰés.

26. Во́т мо́й сту́л в саду́.
    vót mój stúl fsadú.

27. Кто́ живе́т та́м в лесу́?
    któ žɨvʰót tám vlʰisú?

28. Никто́ та́м не живе́т.
    nʰiktó tám nʰižɨvʰót.

29. О ко́м вы́ говори́те?
    akóm vɨ́ gəvarʰítʰi?

30. Мы́ ни о ко́м не говори́м.
    mɨ́ nʰiakóm nʰigəvarʰím.

31. Кто́-то говори́т о мое́м са́де.
    któtə gəvarʰít amajóm sádʰi.

32. О́н живе́т где́-то в дере́вне.
    ón žɨvʰót gdʰétə vdʰirʰévnʰi.

33. В чье́й ко́мнате о́н живе́т?
    fčjéj kómnətʰi ón žɨvʰót?

## VOCABULARY

| а | a | and, but (§ 10) |
| в | v, f | in, on  (§ 9) |
| (preposition with prepositional case) | | |
| ви́дят (3 pl.) | vʰídʰət (-ut) | see |
| ви́деть (inf.) | vʰídʰitʰ | |
| где́-то | gdʰétə | somewhere |
| ге́ний | gʰénʰij | genius |
| говоря́т (3 pl.) | gəvarʰát | speak, say, talk, tell |
| говори́ть (inf.) | gəvarʰítʰ | |
| го́род | górət | city |
| дере́вня | dʰirʰévnʰə | village          [country |
| в дере́вне | vdʰirʰévnʰi | in the village, in the |
| До́н | dón | Don (river) |
| на Дону́ | nə dar.ú | on the Don |
| до́м | dóm | house |
| до́ма (adv.) | dómə | at home |

| | | |
|---|---|---|
| живу́т (3 pl.) | živút | live |
| жи́ть (inf.) | žítʲ | |
| зда́ниё | zdánʲijə | building |
| здесь | zdʲésʲ | here |
| зна́ют (3 pl.) | znájut | know |
| зна́ть (inf.) | znátʲ | |
| когда́ | kagdá | when |
| Кры́м | krɨ́m | Crimea |
| в Крыму́ | f krɨmú | in the Crimea |
| кто́ | któ | who |
| кто́-то | któtə | someone |
| лес | lʲés | forest |
| в лесу́ | v lʲisú | in the forest |
| музе́й | muzʲéj | museum |
| на | na, nə | on, in (§ 9) |
| (preposition with prepositional case) | | |
| нигде́ | nʲigdʲé | nowhere (§ 5.3) |
| никто́ | nʲiktó | no one (§ 5.1–3) |
| ничто́ | nʲištó | nothing (§ 5.1–3) |
| но́ | nó | but (§ 10) |
| о (об before vowels) | a/ab | about, concerning |
| (preposition with prepositional case) | | |
| они́ | anʲí | they |
| отец (stem отц-) | atʲéc, atc- | father (§ 2.0,1) |
| понима́ют (3 pl.) | pənʲimájut | understand |
| понима́ть (inf.) | pənʲimátʲ | |
| почёму́ | pəčimú | why? |
| рабо́тают (3 pl.) | rabótəjut | work |
| рабо́тать (inf.) | rabótətʲ | |
| Росси́я | rasʲíjə | Russia |
| са́д | sát | garden |
| в саду́ | f sadú | in the garden |
| та́м | tám | there |
| тво́й | tvój | your (§ 7) |
| ты́ | tɨ́ | you (§ 7) |
| фа́брика | fábrʲikə | factory |
| на фа́брике | na fábrʲikʲi | at/in the factory |
| что́-то | štótə | something |
| Ялта | jáltə | Jalta (Yalta) |

# LESSON III

| | | |
|---|---|---|
| Кого́ вы́ зна́ёте? | kavó ví znájitʰi? | Whom do you know? |
| Вы́ зна́ёте мою́ сёстру́? | ví znájitʰi majú sʰistrú? | Do you know my sister? |
| Да́, я хорошо́ зна́ю ва́шу сёстру́. | dá, já xərašó znáju vášu sʰistrú. | Yes, I know your sister well. |
| Не́т, я не зна́ю ва́шей сёстры́. | nʰét, já nʰi znáju vášij sʰistrɨ́. | No, I don't know your sister. |
| Вы́ зна́ёте кого́-нибудь здесь? | ví znájitʰi kavónʰibutʰ zdʰésʰ? | Do you know anyone here? |
| Не́т, я никого́ не зна́ю. | nʰét, já nʰikavó nʰi znáju. | No, I don't know anyone. |
| Что́ вы́ ви́дите? | štó ví vʰídʰitʰi? | What do you see? |
| Вы́ ви́дите кни́гу? | ví vʰídʰitʰi knʰígu? | Do you see the book? |
| Не́т, я не ви́жу кни́ги. | nʰét, já nʰi vʰížu knʰígʰi. | No, I don't see a book. |
| Я ничёго́ не ви́жу. | já nʰičivó nʰi vʰížu. | I don't see anything. |
| Да́, я ви́жу что́-то, но́ не зна́ю, что́ э́то тако́ё. | dá, já vʰížu štótə, nó nʰi znáju štó étə takójə. | Yes, I see something, but I don't know what it is. |
| Зна́ёте ли вы́ на́шёго учи́теля? | znájitʰi lʰi ví nášivə učítʰilʰə? | Do you know our teacher? |
| Да́, мы́ ёго́ зна́ём. | dá, mɨ́ jivó znájim. | Yes, we know him. |
| Не́т, мы́ ёго́ не зна́ём. | nʰét, mɨ́ jivó nʰi znájim. | No, we don't know him. |
| Да́, мы́ зна́ём ва́шёго профе́ссора. | dá, mɨ́ znájim vášivə prafʰésərə. | Yes, we know your professor. |
| Где́ моё перо́? Я ёго́ нигде́ не ви́жу. | gdʰé majó pʰiró? já jivó nʰigdʰé nʰi vʰížu. | Where is my pen? I don't see it anywhere. |

| | | |
|---|---|---|
| Áх, вóт онó, тáм на столé. | áx, vót anó tám nə stalʲé. | Oh, there it is over there on the table. |
| Тепéрь я ёгó вѝжу. | tʲipʲérʲ já jivó vʲížu. | Now I see it. |
| Ктó тепéрь читáет? | któ tʲipʲérʲ čitájit? | Who is reading now? |
| Мы̀ тепéрь читáем э́ту кнѝгу. | mí tʲipʲérʲ čitájim étu knʲígu. | We are now reading this book. |
| Вы̀ её не читáете? | ví jijó nʲi čitájitʲi? | Aren't you reading it? |
| Ктó понимáет э́тот урóк? | któ pənʲimájit étət urók? | Who understands this lesson? |
| Понимáет ли ктó-нибудь э́тот урóк? | pənʲimájit lʲi któnʲi-butʲ étət urók? | Does anyone understand this lesson? |
| Нéт, я не понимáю э́того урóка. | nʲét, já nʲi pənʲimáju étəvə urókə. | No, I don't understand this lesson. |
| Нéт, никтó не понимáет урóка. | nʲét, nʲiktó nʲi pənʲimájit urókə. | No, no one understands the lesson. |
| Дá, конéчно, я понимáю э́тот урóк. | dá, kanʲéšnə, já pənʲimáju étət urók. | Yes, of course, I understand this lesson. |
| Рабóтает ли óн гдé-нибудь? | rabótəjit lʲi ón gdʲénʲibutʲ? | Does he work anywhere? |
| Учѝтель меня́ не знáет. | učítʲilʲ mʲinʲá nʲi znájit. | The teacher does not know me. |
| Я вáс не понимáю; не говорѝте тáк бы́стро, пожáлуйста. | já vás nʲi pənʲimáju; nʲi gəvarʲítʲi ták bístrə, pažálstə. | I don't understand you; please don't talk so fast. |
| Вы̀ вѝдите окнó? | ví vʲídʲitʲi aknó? | Do you see the window? |
| дóску? | dósku? | board? |
| двéрь? | dvʲérʲ? | door? |
| Óн не вѝдит окнá. | ón nʲi vʲídʲit akná. | He doesn't see the window. |
| доскѝ. | daskʲí. | board. |
| двéри. | dvʲérʲi. | door. |

| Я не ви́жу | já nʲi vʲižu kərəndašá. | I don't see the pencil. |
| карандашá. | | |
| столá. | stalá. | table. |
| дóма. | dómə. | house. |
| Я ничегó не ви́жу. | já nʲičivó nʲi vʲižu. | I don't see anything. |
| Я никогó не ви́жу. | já nʲikavó nʲi vʲižu. | I don't see anyone. |
| Я не ви́жу жёны́. | já nʲi vʲižu žɨnɨ́. | I don't see (my/the) wife. |
| му́жа. | múžə. | husband. |
| Я егó не ви́жу. | já jivó nʲi vʲižu. | I don't see him [it]. |
| её́ | jijó | her [it]. |
| и́х | jíx | them. |
| вáс | vás | you. |

---

**1.1**   All Russian nouns belong to form-groups called declensions. There are three regular declensions. To the first belong masculine and neuter nouns (e.g. сту́л, отéц, учи́тель, музéй, письмó, здáниё); to the second belong feminine (and a few masculine) nouns ending in -a, spelled -**a** or -**я** (e.g. кни́г**а**, дерéв**ня**, Росси́**я**); to the third declension belong feminine nouns ending in a soft consonant or š or ž — their last letter is always -**ь**.

**1.2**   A Russian declension has six cases. The *nominative* is the "name-form", the form used in dictionaries. It indicates that the thing or person is directly concerned in the utterance, and its most frequent use is as subject of the sentence. The *accusative* presents the person or thing as entirely enveloped by the action of the verb; it functions most frequently as the direct object. The *genitive* presents the thing or person as somehow limited or even completely eliminated. The *dative* is somewhat like the accusative in that it denotes that the person or thing in question is presented as the receiver or goal of some action, but it is the *in*direct object. The *instrumental* expresses a variety of meanings which may be described as attendant circumstance. The *prepositional* denotes an extreme limitation, always specifically defined by the governing preposition.

These are general definitions of the total meanings of each case: each case has a number of more specific meanings which are determined by the context of the utterance in which a given form occurs.

**2.**   The *forms* of the ACCUSATIVE are:

(1) the suffix -*u* (**-y, -ю**) replaces the nominative -*a* (**-а, -я**) of 2nd-declension nouns: кни́г*а* — кни́г**у**, дере́вн*я* — дере́вн**ю**, Росси́*я* — Росси́**ю**.

(2) The suffix -*a* (which automatically becomes -*ə* if unstressed) is added to masculine nouns denoting living creatures (persons, animals): such masculine nouns are called *animate*. The suffix is spelled **-а** if the stem ends in a hard consonant; otherwise it is spelled with the letter **-я**, which replaces the **-ь** or **-й** of the Nom. sg.   E.g.:

профе́ссор — профе́ссор**а**, учи́тель — учи́тел**я**, ге́ний — ге́ни**я**.

(3) with all neuter nouns, all non-animate masculines of the 1st declension, and all 3rd-declension feminines, the accusative form is identical with the nominative.

**3.**   The *forms* of the GENITIVE case are as follows:

(1) all nouns of the 1st declension (i.e. masculines and neuters) have the genitive suffix -*a*, (which automatically becomes -*ə* if unstressed), spelled **-а, -я**. **а** is added to masculines whose last letter is a consonant, and it replaces the **-о** of neuters; **-я** replaces the **-ь** or **-й** of masculines and the **ё** of neuters:   до́м — до́м**а**, учи́тель — учи́тел**я**; пер*о́* — пер**а́**, зда́ни*ё* — зда́ни**я**. The "inserted vowel" of Nom. sing. disappears (cf. II 2): оте́ц — отц**а́**.

(2) all feminine nouns (i.e. nouns of the 2nd and 3rd declensions) take the ending **-ы/-и**. **-ы** replaces the nominative **-а**, and **-и** replaces the nominative **-я** or **-ь**. HOWEVER, if the nominative ends in **-ка, -га, -ха, -ша, -жа, -ча, -ща**, the genitive is **-ки, -ги, -хи, -ши, -жи, -чи, -щи**. (See page 13, § 5.4.)

**4.**   In tabular form, then, all endings so far discussed are:

|  | first declension | | | 2nd declens. | 3rd decl. |
|---|---|---|---|---|---|
|  | masculine | | neuter | | |
|  | animate | non-animate | | | |
| Nom. | (–) -,   **-ь** | (–) -,   **-ь** | (-*o*) **о, ё** | (-*a*) **-а, -я** | (–) **-ь** |
| Acc. | (-*a*) **-а, -я** | (–) -,   **-ь** | (-*o*) **о, ё** | (-*u*) **-у, -ю** | (–) **-ь** |
| Gen. | (-*a*) **-а, -я** | | | (-*i*) **-ы, -и** | (-*i*) **-и** |
| Prep. | (-*e*) **-е** or, after **и, -и** | | | | (-*i*) **-и** |

For example:

| N | дóм | стóл | музéй | профéссор | отéц | учи́тель | гéний |
|---|---|---|---|---|---|---|---|
| A. | дóм | стóл | музéй | профéссора | отцá | учи́теля | гéния |
| G. | дóма | столá | музéя | профéссора | отцá | учи́теля | гéния |
| P. | дóме | столé | музéе | профéссоре | отцé | учи́теле | гéнии |

| N. | dóm | stól | muzʰéj | prafʰésər | atʰéc | učítʰilʰ | gʰéɲʰij |
|---|---|---|---|---|---|---|---|
| A. | dóm | stól | muzʰéj | prafʰésərə | atcá | učítʰilʰə | gʰéɲʰijə |
| G. | dómə | stalá | muzʰéjə | prafʰésərə | atcá | učítʰilʰə | gʰéɲʰijə |
| P. | dómʰi | stalʰé | muzʰéji | prafʰésərʰi | atcé | učítʰilʰi | gʰéɲʰiji |

| N. | перó | здáниѥ | кóмната | кни́га | доскá | дерéвня | Росси́я | двéрь |
|---|---|---|---|---|---|---|---|
| A. | перó | здáниѥ | кóмнату | кни́гу | дóску | дерéвню | Росси́ю | двéрь |
| G. | перá | здáния | кóмнаты | кни́ги | доски́ | дерéвни | Росси́и | двéри |
| P. | перé | здáнии | кóмнате | кни́ге | доскé | дерéвне | Росси́и | двéри |

| N. | pʰiró | zdánʰijə | kómnətə | knʰígə | daská | dʰirʰévnʰə | rasʰíjə | dvʰérʰ |
|---|---|---|---|---|---|---|---|
| A. | pʰiró | zdánʰijə | kómnətu | knʰígu | dósku | dʰirʰévnʰu | rasʰíju | dvʰérʰ |
| G. | pʰirá | zdánʰijə | kómnətɨ | knʰígʰi | daskʰí | dʰirʰévnʰi | rasʰíji | dvʰérʰi |
| P. | pʰirʰé | zdánʰiji | kómnətʰi | knʰígʰi | daskʰé | dʰirʰévnʰi | rasʰíji | dvʰérʰi |

**5.** Note that sometimes the *accent shifts* from one syllable of the stem or suffix to another syllable. These shifts must be learned with every noun, since there are no adequate rules to cover them.

**5.1** Many masculine nouns always stress the suffix (стóл, столá, столé; карандáш, карандашá, карандашé, etc.).

**5.2** In the 2nd declension, a few nouns which in other cases have the stress on the ending shift it to the first syllable of the stem in the accusative: доскá, доски́ and доскé; but дóску.

**6.1** Personal pronouns have identical genitive and accusative forms.

(Notice: the masculine-neuter suffix spelled **-го** is pronounced *-vó/və*.)

| N. | я́ | ты́ | мы́ | вы́ | óн | онó | онá | они́ | ктó | чтó |
|---|---|---|---|---|---|---|---|---|---|---|
| A. | меня́ | тебя́ | нác | вác | ѐгó | её | и́х | когó | чтó |
| G. | меня́ | тебя́ | нác | вác | ѐгó | её | и́х | когó | чегó |
| P. | мнé | тебé | нác | вác | нём | нéй | ни́х | кóм | чём |

| N. | já | tɨ́ | mɨ́ | vɨ́ | ón | anó | aná | anʰí | któ | štó |
|---|---|---|---|---|---|---|---|---|---|---|
| A. | mʰinʰá | tʰibʰá | nás | vás | jivó | jijó | jíx | kavó | štó |
| G. | mʰinʰá | tʰibʰá | nás | vás | jivó | jijó | jíx | kavó | čivó |
| P. | mɲé | tʰibʰé | nás | vás | nʰóm | nʰéj | nʰíx | kóm | čóm |

**6.2** Demonstrative and possessive pronouns have separate forms for animate and inanimate accusative. Here are the forms for all cases so far:

| | тот то́т тó | э́тот э́то | мóй моё́ | нáш нáшё | вáш вáшё | чéй чьё́ |
|---|---|---|---|---|---|---|
| N. | тóт тó | э́тот э́то | мóй моё́ | нáш нáшё | вáш вáшё | чéй чьё́ |
| Non-an. A. | тóт тó | э́тот э́то | мóй моё́ | нáш нáшё | вáш вáшё | чéй чьё́ |
| Animate A. | тогó — | э́того — | моегó — | нáшёго — | вáшёго — | чьёгó — |
| G. | тогó | э́того | моегó | нáшёго | вáшёго | чьёгó |
| P. | тóм | э́том | моё́м | нáшё́м | вáшё́м | чьё́м |
| N. | tót tó | étət étə | mój majó | náš nášə | váš vášə | čéj čjó |
| Non-an. A. | tót tó | étət étə | mój majó | náš nášə | váš vášə | čéj čjó |
| Animate A. | tavó — | étəvə — | məjivó — | nášivə — | vášivə — | čjivó — |
| G. | tavó | étəvə | məjivó | nášivə | vášivə | čjivó |
| P. | tóm | étəm | məjóm | nášəm | vášəm | čjóm |
| N. | тá | э́та | моя́ | нáша | вáша | чья́ |
| A. | тý | э́ту | мою́ | нáшу | вáшу | чью́ |
| G. | тóй | э́той | моéй | нáшей | вáшей | чьéй |
| P. | тóй | э́той | моéй | нáшей | вáшей | чьéй |
| N. | tá | étə | majá | nášə | vášə | čjá |
| A. | tú | étu | majú | nášu | vášu | čjú |
| G. | tój | étəj | majéj | nášɨj | vášɨj | čjéj |
| P. | tój | étəj | majéj | nášɨj | vášɨj | čjéj |

**7.** From these tables it is clear that with *masculine* nouns and pronouns the *animate accusative form is identical with the genitive* form, while the non-animate form is the same as the nominative.

**8.** The principal *use* of the ACCUSATIVE is as the *direct object* of positive verbs:

| | | |
|---|---|---|
| Я ви́жу **сестру́**. | já vʲížu sʲistrú. | I see (my) *sister*. |
| Сестра́ ви́дит **отца́**. | sʲistrá vʲídʲit atcá. | Sister sees *father*. |

**9.** However the GENITIVE case is regularly required for the direct object of *negated* verbs. This construction is particularly foreign to western languages and therefore should be noted especially. For example:

| | | |
|---|---|---|
| Я **не** ви́жу **сестры́**. | já nʲi vʲížu sʲistrí. | I don't see (my) sister. |
| Я **не** ви́жу **стола́**. | já nʲi vʲížu stalá. | I don't see a/the table. |

**10.** The GENITIVE is also used to express *possession*. For example:

| | | |
|---|---|---|
| Это кни́га **моего́ отца́**. | étə knʲígə majivó atcá. | This is *my father's* book. |
| Óн брáт **учи́тельницы**. | ón brát učítʲilʲnʲicɨ. | He is the *teacher's* brother. |
| Онá в саду́ **брáта**. | aná f sadú brátə. | She is in *brother's* garden. |

Notice that the genitive normally *follows* the word representing the thing possessed. This word-order is obligatory if the thing possessed is also expressed by a genitive: e.g.

| | | |
|---|---|---|
| Это дóм **сестры́ учи́теля**. | étə dóm sʲistrí učítʲilʲə. | This is the house of the teacher's sister. |

Это до́м **учи́теля сёстры́**. étə dóm *učit'il'ə s'istrí*.     This is the house of
sister's teacher.

**10.1** The genitives of the 1st and 2nd personal pronouns (**меня́, тебя́, на́с, ва́с**) are never used with the sense of possession, for the special possessive pronouns **мо́й, тво́й, на́ш, ва́ш** fulfil this function. On the other hand, the genitives of the 3rd personal pronoun, ёго́, её, и́х, do serve to signify possession. Since they are genitives, they do not change form to agree with the word they modify.

**11.1** -**нибудь** added to **кто́, что́, где́,** and **когда́** (and a number of other interrogatives) gives the completely general meaning of "any at all":

> Вы́ зна́ете **кого́-нибудь** зде́сь?  Do you know *anyone at all* here?
> Рабо́тает ли о́н **где́-нибудь**?  Does he work *anywhere at all*?
> Говори́т ли о́н **когда́-нибудь**?  Does he *ever* speak *at all*?

It indicates that there is a choice among a range of possibilities which may include negation: "Do you know one or more of the persons who are present, or no one at all?" The answer can be either "Yes, I know *x* (or *x* and others)" or else "No, I don't know anyone here."

**11.2** -**то** added to the same interrogatives does not imply any alternative or choice, although the meaning is non-specified: the person, thing, place or time is definite, but the speaker does not choose to give the exact description (either because he doesn't want to or because he doesn't know). For example:

> О́н зна́ет **кого́-то** зде́сь.   He knows *someone* here. (I'm not saying who it is, but there is a person here whom he knows.)
>
> О́н рабо́тает **где́-то**.   He works *somewhere*. (I'm not saying where, but he does work in a certain spot.)

**11.3** Note that in English the meaning of "any" is dependent on the presence or absence of negation: "not anyone" is equivalent to "no one", "not anywhere" = "nowhere", etc. Russian has no choice. For example:

> Are you reading *anything*?   Вы́ чита́ете что́-**нибудь**?
> No, I'm *not* reading *anything*. ⎫
> No, I'm reading *nothing*.     ⎬  Не́т, я́ **ничего́ не** чита́ю.
>                                 ⎭

Notice that -**нибудь** cannot be used in a negative sentence.

**12.**   The possessive pronoun **свой** *svój* has the same forms as **мой** *mój* 'my'. Observe the usage:

| | | |
|---|---|---|
| Я читаю **свою** книгу. | *já čitáju svajú knʲígu.* | *I* am reading *my* (own) book. |
| Он читает **свою** книгу. | *ón čitájit svajú knʲígu.* | *He* is reading *his own* book. |
| Она читает **свою** книгу. | *aná čitájit svajú knʲígu.* | *She* is reading *her* own book. |
| Мы читаем **свою** книгу. | *mí čitájim svajú knʲígu.* | *We* are reading *our* (own) book. |
| Вы читаете **свою** книгу. | *ví čitájitʲi svajú knʲígu.* | *You* are reading *your* (own) book. |
| Они читают **свою** книгу. | *anʲí čitájut svajú knʲígu.* | *They* are reading *their own* book. |

In the 1st and 2nd persons it is possible to substitute the suitable form of **мой**, **твой**, **наш** or **ваш**, for special emphasis on the person (*my*, *your*), but in the 3rd person the use of **свой** is obligatory, for **свой** regularly refers back to the *subject* of the sentence. Compare:

| | | |
|---|---|---|
| Он читает **его** книгу. | *ón čitájit jivó knʲígu.* | He is reading *his* (NOT his own, but somebody else's) book. |

Note that with nouns signifying relatives, Russian normally omits the possessive, although it may be used for emphasis or contrast:

| | | |
|---|---|---|
| Он понимает отца. | *ón panʲimájit atcá.* | He understands *his* father. |
| Он не понимает своего отца. | *ón nʲi panʲimájit svajivó atcá.* | He doesn't understand his own father. |

**13.**   Notice that where English nouns may refer to either male or female persons (or other animates), Russian usually has two nouns specifying sex: e.g.

| masculine | | feminine | | |
|---|---|---|---|---|
| студент | *studʲént* | студентка | *studʲéntkə* | student |
| учитель | *učítʲilʲ* | учительница | *učítʲilʲnʲicə* | teacher |

In relatively rare instances, the masc. noun may be used for women, e.g.:

| | | |
|---|---|---|
| Она профессор. | *aná prafʲésər.* | She is a professor. |

## EXERCISES

**A.** For oral drill. Complete the sentences by using the proper form of the words in parentheses:

1. a. Я ви́жу —.      (кни́га, перо́, каранда́ш, бра́т, письмо́, доска́,
                               сёстра́, са́д, зда́ниё, фа́брика, го́род, дере́вня,
   б. Я не ви́жу —.   отец́, окно́, тетра́дка, учи́тель, учи́тельница, ле́с,
                               ко́мната, студе́нтка, студе́нт, сту́л, ге́ний, до́м,
   в. Говоря́т о —.    профе́ссор, уро́к)

2. Repeat, using *this* (*that, my, your, our, his, her, their*) before each of the nouns.

**B.** Read aloud and translate:

1. Эта студе́нтка здесь никого́ не зна́ёт. 2. Она́ живёт в Крыму́. 3. Учи́тельница чита́ёт кни́гу о на́шём го́роде. 4. Вы́ когда́-нибудь чита́ёте по-ру́сски? 5. Они́ тепе́рь живу́т в своём до́ме. 6. Они́ живу́т в и́х до́ме. 7. Где́ письмо́ му́жа? 8. Сёстра́ ёго́ жёны́ рабо́тает на фа́брике профе́ссора. 9. Чей э́то каранда́ш? 10. Кто́-то та́м в лесу́. 11. Да́, я ёго́ ви́жу, но ёго́ не зна́ю. 12. А я ёго́ зна́ю. Это отец наше́го учи́теля. 13. В чье́й ко́мнате они́ рабо́тают? 14. Почёму́ вы́ не говори́те по-ру́сски? 15. Эта тетра́дка ва́ша и́ли ва́шего бра́та? 16. Говори́те ме́дленно и гро́мче. Хорошо́, э́то та́к. 17. Студе́нтка тепе́рь на уро́ке. 18. В э́том зда́нии фа́брика. 19. Они́ говоря́т о профе́ссоре и ёго́ учи́тельнице. 20. Они́ где́-нибудь рабо́тают? 21. Они́ э́то чита́ют до́ма. 22. Почёму́ вы́ не понима́ёте уро́ка? 23. Мы́ чита́ём о́чень ме́дленно по-ру́сски. 24. В Росси́и говоря́т не по-англи́йски, а по-ру́сски. 25. Её бра́т ге́ний. 26. Чью́ кни́гу о́н чита́ёт? 27. Мы́ её зна́ём. 28. Чей му́ж говори́т тепе́рь? 29. Почёму́ вы́ чита́ёте моё письмо́? 30. Спаси́бо, до свида́ния. Споко́йной но́чи.

1. Что́ де́лает жёна́ э́того студе́нта?
2. Чью́ кни́гу вы́ чита́ёте, Ве́ра?
3. Профе́ссор не живёт в э́том зда́нии. 4. Они́ рабо́тают в саду́ отца́.
5. Он говори́т ме́дленно. 6. Я не ви́жу свое́й тетра́дки. 7. Ва́ша сёстра́ говори́т по-англи́йски?
8. Извини́те, я не понима́ю, о чём

вы говорите. 9. Он не видит своей женой. 10. Ты пишешь книгу? 11. Они говорят о тебе. 12. Она не читает своей книги. 13. Он хорошо пишет и читает по-русски, но ничего не понимает, когда учитель говорит. 14. Наташа теперь где-то в деревне. 15. Ты не читаешь по-русски? 16. Она не понимает своего брата. 17. Пишет ли кто-нибудь на доске? 18 Иван учитель брата. 19. Что вы сказали о них? 20. Мы пишем книгу о лесе.

C. For oral and/or written translation into Russian.

1. Whom do you see? 2. I see the teacher (m) and a student (f). 3. I see the teacher (f) and a student (m). 4. I see the student (m) but I don't see the girl student. 5. He sees his (own) wife. 6. He sees his (not his own) wife. 7. We do not know your brother's wife. 8. Do you know my wife's brother? 9. That teacher is the husband of a student. 10. That student is the husband of a teacher. 11. Does she see anyone? I don't know. 12. They understand the lesson very well. 13. Someone is in the garden. 14. Where is my brother's notebook? There it is, on the chair. 15. Whose book are you reading? I am reading my own book. 16. The teacher is not reading my book. 17. We are talking about the genius and his wife. 18. The genius is talking about his wife. 19. They live somewhere in Russia. 20. Do you see that village? Where? I don't see a village. 21. What are you doing? I am reading John's book. 22. The teacher asks Vera, but Vera does not answer. 23. Ivan doesn't understand Vera. 24. Vera and (her) father are writing a book about Russia. 25. My sister is writing a letter in class.

**D.** 1. Complete the questions and corresponding answers by supplying the proper verbal ending to go with each pronoun:

Чтó *вы́* (*óн, онá, они́*) дéла . . . ? *Я́* (*мы́, óн, онá, они́*) рабóта . . . .

2. By changing pronouns and verbal endings, make all possible meaningful combinations:

*Я́* (*óн, онá, мы́, вы́, они́*) спрáшива . . . по-англи́йски и *óн* (*я, онá, мы́, вы́*) отвечá . . . по-рýсски.

3. On the model "I ask Ivan", make sentences with all the possible meaningful combinations:

$$Я́ \begin{cases} \text{мы́, онá,} \\ \text{брáт и сёстрá,} \\ \text{вы́, её мýж,} \\ \text{Вéра, они́} \end{cases} \text{спрáшива} \ldots \text{Ивáн} \ldots \begin{cases} \text{Вéра, отéц, я́, мы́,} \\ \text{онá, они́, студéнт,} \\ \text{студéнтка, мýж,} \\ \text{жёнá, брáт и сёстрá,} \\ \text{профéссор и учи́тель-} \\ \text{ница} \end{cases}$$

**E.** Read aloud and translate:

Мы́ в клáссе. Мы́ рабóтаем. Вóт доскá. Ктó-то пи́шёт на доскé. — Ктó пи́шёт? спрáшиваёт Вéра. — Чтó óн пи́шёт? Я́ не ви́жу доски́. Её брáт отвечáёт, — Это Ивáн. Óн пи́шёт чтó-то по-рýсски, нó я́ не понимáю. Óн нехорошó пи́шёт. Учи́тель говори́т, — Нéт, Ивáн, э́то не тáк. Вы́ нехорошó пи́шёте. Мы́ не понимáем.

Вóт, э́то тáк. Тепéрь э́то хорошó. Спаси́бо.

## VOCABULARY

| | | |
|---|---|---|
| áх | áx | oh! |
| брáт | brát | brother |
| Вéра | vᵇérə | Vera |
| дéлают | dᵇéləjut | (3 pl.) do, |
| (дéлать | dᵇélətᵇ | inf.) make |
| жёнá | žiná | wife |
| Ивáн | ivá | Ivan (·John) |
| клáсс | klás | class, class-room |
| конéчно | kanᵇéšnə NB š! | of course |
| мýж | múš | husband |
| -нибудь | nᵇibutᵇ | see § 11.1 |
| обо | (form of the preposition o, об used with the pronoun мнé) | |
| обо мнé | abamnᵇé | about me |
| отвечáют | atvᵇičájut | (3pl.) answer |
| (отвечáть | atvᵇičátᵇ | inf.) |

| | | |
|---|---|---|
| пи́шут | pᵇíšut | (3pl.) write |
| (писáть | pᵇisátᵇ | inf.) |
| свóй | svój | see § 12 |
| сёстрá | sᵇistrá | sister |
| спрáши-вают | sprášivəjut | (3pl.) ask |
| (спрáши-вать | sprášivətᵇ | inf.) |
| студéнт | studᵇént | student |
| студéнтка | studᵇéntkə | student (f) |
| тепéрь | tᵇipᵇérᵇ | now |
| урóк | urók | lesson |
| на урóке | nə urókᵇi | at the l. |
| учи́тель | učítᵇilᵇ | teacher |
| учи́тель-ница | učítᵇilᵇ-nᵇicə | teacher (f) |
| читáют | čitájut | (3pl.) read |
| (читáть | čitátᵇ | inf.) |

# LESSON IV

1. Óн ча́сто спра́шивал жёну́ об э́том.

He often asked his wife about that.

2. Она́ до́лго спра́шивала му́жа.

She questioned her husband for a long time.

3. Писа́тельница всегда́ хорошо́ отвеча́ла.

The writer always answered well.

4. Ни о́н ни она́ ещё не отвеча́ли.

Neither he nor she has yet answered.

5. Я никогда́ не чита́л расска́за э́того писа́теля.

I never read a story by that author.

6. Та́ня что́-то говори́ла, но́ мы́ не понима́ли.

Tanja was saying something, but we didn't understand.

7. Я хочу́ писа́ть расска́з.

I want to write a story.

8. Па́вёл и Наде́жда хотя́т чита́ть э́ту статью́.

Pavel and Nadežda want to read that article.

9. Они́ почёму́-то хоте́ли отвеча́ть.

They wanted to answer for some reason.

10. Серге́й не зна́л что де́лать.

Sergej didn't know what to do.

11. Со́ня хо́чёт жи́ть в Евро́пе.

Sonja wants to live in Europe.

12. Её сёстра́ до́лго жила́ в Пари́же, и она́ всегда́ хоте́ла жи́ть та́м.

Her sister lived in Paris for a long time, and she always wanted to live there.

1. ón částə spráši̯vəl ži̯nú ab étəm.
2. aná dólgə spráši̯vələ múžə.
3. pʰisátʰilʰnʰicə fsʰigdá xərašó atvʰičálə.
4. nʰi ón nʰi aná jiščó nʰi atvʰičálʰi.
5. já nʰikagdá nʰi čitál raskázə étəvə pʰisátʰilʰə.
6. tánjə štótə gəvarʰílə, nó mí nʰi pənʰimálʰi.
7. já xačú pʰisátʰ raskás.
8. pávʰil i nadʰéždə xatʰát čitátʰ étu statʰjú.
9. anʰí pəčimútə xatʰél̦ʰi atvʰičátʰ.
10. sʰirgʰéj nʰi znál stó dʰélətʰ.
11. sónʰə xóčit žíțʰ v jivrópʰi.
12. jijó sʰistrá dólgə žilá f parʰíži̱, i aná.fsʰigdá xatʰélə žíțʰ tám.

13. Алексе́й до́лго хоте́л рабо́тать в на́шей лаборато́рии. — Aleksej long wanted to work in our laboratory.

14. Никола́й уже́ ча́сто рабо́тал та́м. — Nikolaj has worked there often already.

15. Му́ж Со́ни не́ жил в Пари́же. — Sonja's husband didn't live in Paris.

16. Кто́ бы́л та́м? — Who was there?

17. О́льга была́ та́м. — Ol'ga was there.

18. Мы́ бы́ли та́м. — We were there.

19. Писа́тельница и её адвока́т бы́ли на фа́брике. — The writer and her lawyer were at the factory.

20. Что́ бы́ло в углу́? — What was in the corner?

21. Ла́мпа стоя́ла в углу́. — A lamp stood in the corner.

22. Карти́на моего́ бра́та стои́т на её столе́. — A picture of my brother stands on her desk.

23. Мо́й кошелёк лёжа́л на столе́. — My purse was lying on the table.

24. Моё перо́ лёжа́ло на э́той по́лке. — My pen was lying on this shelf.

25. Вы́ ви́дели мою́ шля́пу и мо́й кошелёк, Пётр? — Have you seen my hat and my purse, Peter?

26. Не́т, я́ и́х не ви́дел. — No, I haven't seen them.

27. Мо́жёт бы́ть Наде́жда и́х ви́дела. — Perhaps Nadežda has seen them.

28. Во́т кре́сло. — There is the armchair.

29. Моя́ су́мка была́ на э́том кре́сле, и в су́мке бы́л кошелёк. — My bag was on this armchair, and in the bag was my purse.

---

13. alᵇiksᵇéj dólgə xatᵇél rabótətᵇ v nášɨj ləbəratórᵇiji.

14. nᵇikaláj užé částə rabótəl tám.

15. múš sónᵇi nᵇé žɨl f parᵇížɨ.

16. któ bɨ́l tám?

17. ólᵇgə bɨlá tám.

18. mɨ́ bɨ́lᵇi tám.

19. pᵇisátᵇilᵇnᵇicə i jijó advakát bɨ́lᵇi na fábrᵇikᵇi.

20. štó bɨ́lə v uglú?

21. lámpə stajálə v uglú.

22. kartᵇínə məjivó brátə stajít nə jijó stalᵇé.

23. mój kəšɨlᵇók lᵇižál nə stalᵇé.

24. majó pᵇiró lᵇižálə na étəj pólkᵇi.

25. vɨ́ vᵇídᵇilᵇi majú šlᵇápu i mój kəšɨlᵇók, pᵇótr?

26. nᵇét, já jíx nᵇi vᵇídᵇil.

27. móžɨt bɨ́tᵇ nadᵇéždə jíx vᵇídᵇilə.

28. vót krᵇéslə.

29. majá súmkə bɨlá na étəm krᵇéslᵇi, i f súmkᵇi bɨ́l kəšɨlᵇók.

| | |
|---|---|
| 30. Ты́ ви́дела мою́ су́мку, Та́ня? | Have you seen my bag, Tanja? |
| 31. Не́т, я́ не ви́дела ни су́мки ни кошелька́. | No, I haven't seen either the bag or the purse. |
| 32. О чьём кошельке́ она́ говори́ла? | Whose purse was she talking about? |
| 33. И О́льга и Пётр сиде́ли на дива́не. Они́ ещё та́м сидя́т. | Both Ol'ga and Peter were sitting on the sofa. They're still sitting there. |
| 34. Ва́ша ша́пка лёжа́ла на полу́. | Your cap was lying on the floor. |
| 35. Почему́ она́ ча́сто лёжи́т на полу́? | Why does it lie on the floor often? |
| 36. Мы́ хорошо́ по́мнили э́ту ка́рту Евро́пы. | We remembered this map of Europe well. |
| 37. Она́ всегда́ висе́ла в ко́мнате Ве́ры, вы́ не по́мните? | It always hung in Vera's room, don't you remember? |
| 38. Что́ висе́ло здесь на э́той стене́? | What used to hang on this wall? |
| 39. Что́ э́то за кни́га? | What sort of book is that? |
| 40. Это а́тлас. | It's an atlas. |
| 41. Что́ э́то за ка́рта? | What sort of map is that? |
| 42. Это ка́рта Берли́на. | It's a map of Berlin. |
| 43. Она́ виси́т на стене́. | It is hanging on the wall. |

30. tɨ vʲídʲilə majú súmku, tánjə?

31. nʲét, já nʲi vʲídʲilə nʲi súmkʲi nʲi kəšɨlʲká.

32. a čjóm kəšɨlʲkʲé aná gəvarʲílə?

33. i ólʲgə i pʲótr sʲidʲélʲi nə dʲivánʲi. anʲɨ́ jiščó tám sʲidʲát.

34. vášə šápkə lʲižálə nə palú.

35. pəčimú aná částə lʲižɨ́t na palú?

36. mɨ́ xərašó pómnʲilʲi étu kártu jivrópɨ.

37. aná fsʲigdá vʲisʲélə f kómnətʲi vʲérɨ, vɨ́ nʲi pómnʲitʲi?

38. štó vʲisʲéləzdʲésʲ na étəj stʲinʲé?

39. štó étə za knʲígə?

40. étə átləs.

41. štó étə za kártə?

42. étə kártə bʲirlʲínə.

43. aná vʲisʲít nə stʲinʲé.

---

**1.** The key forms of the Russian verb are the third person plural present and the infinitive. (Further particulars are given in Lesson V.)

**2.0** There are three possible **infinitive** endings: **-ть, -ти** and **-чь. -ти** and **-чь** are relatively rare, and will be discussed later.

**2.1**   The *infinitive stem* is the form minus -ть:

чита́-ть, рабо́та-ть, говори́-ть, ви́де-ть, стоя́-ть, взя́-ть, жи́-ть

**3.**   One of the chief uses of the infinitive (which is ordinarily translated into English "to —") is as complement of such verbs as "want, be able, like". For example:

Я хочу́ де́лать э́то.             I want *to do* that.

**4.**   **The past tense** in Russian differs from the present (and future) in that the endings do not express person, but only gender (m, n, f) *or* plural (Russian *never* makes gender distinctions in the plural). For example:

| | | |
|---|---|---|
| я отвеча́ла | I was answering. | (female speaking) |
| ты́ по́мнила | You remembered. | (female being addressed) |
| она́ чита́ла | She was reading. | |
| говори́ли | They said. | (plural, person unspecified) |

**4.1**   To the *infinitive stem* (cf. 2.1 above) are added the past-tense suffixes:

-л for masculine singular        -ла for feminine singular
-ло for neuter singular           -ли for plural

e. g.   писа́-ть    — писа́л, писа́ло, писа́ла, писа́ли
       стоя́-ть    — стоя́л, стоя́ло, стоя́ла, стоя́ли
       говори́-ть   — говори́л, говори́ло, говори́ла, говори́ли

**4.2**   Note that the past tense of the verbs given so far may be translated into English in several ways:

я писа́л — I wrote, I have written, I was writing, I used to write.

**5.**   The past of **бы́ть** 'to be' has stress on the suffix in the feminine: была́ as opposed to бы́л, бы́ло, бы́ли. With negation, the stress falls on the negative particle in the non-feminine forms: не́ был, не́ было, не́ были : не была́. Similarly **жи́ть** 'to live'; жи́л, не́ жил; жи́ло, не́ жило; жи́ли, не́ жили : жила́, не жила́.

**6.**   The verb **хоте́ть хотя́т** 'to want' is irregular in the second and third persons of the present singular:

я хочу́,[1] ты́ хо́чешь, о́н хо́чет; мы́ хоти́м, вы́ хоти́те, они́ хотя́т.

---

[1] The change of *t* to *č* in **хочу́** parallels the change of *d* to *ž* in **ви́жу** 'I see' and is regular. The rule is given in Lesson V.

The past is normal: хотéл, хотéло, хотéла, хотéли.

**7.** With **никогдá** 'never', the verb must also be negated (cf. II 5.3):

| | |
|---|---|
| Óн никогдá *не* читáёт. | He never (doesn't ever) reads. |
| Óн никогдá нигдé *не* рабóтал. | He never worked anywhere. |
| Онá никогдá ничёгó *не* читáла. | She never read anything. |

## EXERCISES

**A.** Вы́ читáёте эту кни́гу? Дá, я её читáю. Я́ читáю эту кни́гу.

1. For "book", in the above question, substitute "story, article, letter, document", making the appropriate changes in the answers.
2. Repeat, putting the verbs in the past tense.

Вы́ ви́дите эту кáрту? Дá, я её ви́жу. Я́ ви́жу эту кáрту.

3. For "map" in the above question, substitute "purse, armchair, shelf, sofa, wall", making the appropriate changes in the answers.
4. Repeat, putting the verbs in the past tense.

**B.** Read aloud and translate:

1. Чья́ это шáпка на полу́? Это не моя́ шáпка, моя́ шáпка здéсь, на столé.

Чтó это такóе? Это карти́на. Чтó мы́ ви́дим на карти́не? Мы́ ви́дим кóмнату. Вóт стенá, вóт двéрь, вóт потолóк. На полу́ лёжи́т кошелёк. Чéй это кошелёк? Это кошелёк Вéры. Чтó вы́ ви́дите в углу́? Я́ ви́жу лáмпу на столé. Лáмпа стои́т на столé. Тáм тáкже кни́га, карандáш, перó и сýмка. Кни́га, карандáш, перó и сýмка лёжáт на столé.

Вы́ ви́дите эту стéну? Дá, мы́ её ви́дим. Чтó на стенé? На этой стенé кáрта и карти́на. Кáрта и карти́на вися́т на стенé. А на тóй стенé тóже виси́т кáрта. Это кáрта Росси́и, а вóт тáм кáрта Амéрики.

Чтó это такóё? Это пóлка. Гдé онá? Я́ не ви́жу. Вóт онá, вы́ не ви́дите? Пóлка виси́т на стенé. Áх, тепéрь я́ ви́жу пóлку. На пóлке сýмка нáшей учи́тельницы.

2. Чья́ шáпка былá на полу́? Это не былá шáпка Пётрá; ёгó шáпка висéла на стенé.

3. Что́ вы́ ви́дели на карти́не? Мы́ ви́дели ко́мнату. Мы́ ви́дели сте́ну и две́рь и потоло́к. На полу́ лежа́л кошелёк. Че́й э́то бы́л кошелёк? Э́то бы́л кошелёк Та́ни. Что́ вы́ ви́дели в углу́? Я́ ви́дел ла́мпу на столе́. Ла́мпа стоя́ла на столе́. Та́м та́кже бы́ли кни́га, каранда́ш, перо́ и су́мка. Кни́га, каранда́ш, перо́ и су́мка лежа́ли на столе́. Мы́ и́х хорошо́ ви́дели на карти́не. На стене́ мы́ ви́дели ка́рту и карти́ну. Ка́рта и карти́на висе́ли на э́той стене́. А на то́й стене́ то́же висе́ла ка́рта. Э́то была́ ка́рта Аме́рики, а во́т та́м была́ ка́рта Пари́жа.

**C.** Read aloud and translate:

1. Мы́ ча́сто де́лали э́то. 2. Э́та писа́тельница здесь никого́ не зна́ла. 3. Студе́нтка чита́ла кни́гу о на́шем го́роде. 4. Почему́ вы́ не говори́ли по-ру́сски? 5. Она́ говори́ла ме́дленно и Серге́й хорошо́ её понима́л. 6. Когда́ адвока́т бы́стро говори́л, я́ его́ не понима́ла. 7. Му́ж бы́л до́ма вчера́. 8. Со́ня жила́ в Крыму́. 9. Они́ до́лго жи́ли в своём до́ме. 10. Когда́ они́ бы́ли в Росси́и, Серге́й и Па́вел жи́ли в и́х до́ме. 11. Они́ где́-нибудь рабо́тали вчера́? 12. Жена́ писа́теля рабо́тала на фа́брике адвока́та. 13. В э́том зда́нии была́ фа́брика. 14. Почему́ о́н чита́л моё письмо́? 15. Наде́жда была́ где́-то в дере́вне.

16. О́льга ча́сто не хоте́ла рабо́тать. Вы́ э́то понима́ете? 17. Они́ до́лго говори́ли о его́ расска́зе. О чьём расска́зе? 18. Писа́тельница не хо́чет отвеча́ть. Она́ почему́-то никогда́ не хоте́ла отвеча́ть. 19. Вы́ чита́ли статью́ Серге́я? Не́т, я́ её ещё не ви́дел. 20. Ива́н меня́ ча́сто спра́шивал об э́том. Я́ никогда́ не отвеча́л. 21. Она́ стоя́ла на сту́ле. Она́ ча́сто стои́т та́м? 22. Вы́ бы́ли когда́-нибудь в Москве́? Да́, я́ бы́л та́м. 23. Мо́жет бы́ть они́ хотя́т рабо́тать здесь. 24. Я́ ещё не чита́л докуме́нта. Где́ о́н? Вы́ его́ не ви́дели? 25. Никола́й писа́л расска́з о до́ме в Пари́же.

26. Писа́тельница и учи́тель почему́-то его́ не понима́ли. 27. Па́вел стоя́л в углу́ и ничего́ не де́лал. 28. Вы́ когда́-нибудь писа́ли по-ру́сски? Не́т, никогда́. 29. Вы́ по́мните э́ту карти́ну? Да́, мы́ её хорошо́ по́мним. Мы́ её ви́дели, когда́ бы́ли в Пари́же. 30. Кого́ вы́ ви́дели на э́той карти́не? Я́ ви́дела писа́теля, Никола́я Го́голя. О́н лежа́л на дива́не и писа́л что́-то.

**D.** Re-read exercise C, changing the verb forms from present to past or from past to present, wherever the sense allows.

**E.**   For oral and/or written translation:

1. Where is your house? Our house is there on the corner. Do you see it? 2. On the wall hangs a picture of my (his, her) sister. Do you see it? 3. Her hat is lying on the shelf. Her purse is there too. Her hat and purse are on the shelf. Do you see them? 4. What are you doing? I am reading a book about Leningrad. 5. What were you doing yesterday? I was working. I was reading this document. 6. The lamp stands on the table in the corner. Don't you see it? 7. That armchair stood in the corner in Peter's room. Didn't you see it? 8. A map of Moscow was lying on a chair in the laboratory. Did you see it? 9. He didn't live in Moscow, he lived in Leningrad. I remember his house very well. 10. Her handbag is on the table in the corner. Don't you see it? 11. The writer's (f) pen and pencil were in her handbag. 12. In his classroom a map of our city hangs on the wall. 13. When we lived in the village we worked together in the forest. 14. There is a picture of your museum. 15. The lawyer's hat was lying on the floor. 16. I don't see [= I see neither] a picture [n]or a pen on that shelf. Do you see the picture? 17. What is hanging there on the wall? Is it a picture or a map? 18. That teacher always spoke very rapidly and my brother and my sister never understood anything. 19. Nikolaj's sister did not understand Russian, don't you remember? 20. At home Ol'ga, Nadezhda and Aleksej used to speak Russian, but now they speak English. 21. That lady didn't remember my brother. 22. Do you want to read this document? No, thank you. 23. Excuse me, I want to sit here in this armchair, please. 24. The writer wants to read your father's article. 25. Sonja and Pavel wanted to work in Paris.

## VOCABULARY

| | | | |
|---|---|---|---|
| адвока́т | lawyer | докуме́нт | document |
| а́тлас | atlas | до́лго | for a long time |
| Берли́н | Berlin | Евро́па | Europe |
| всёгда́ | always | ещё | still |
| вчера́ | yesterday | ещё не | not yet |
| да́ма | lady | и...и | both ... and |
| дива́н | sofa | ка́рта | map |

| | | | |
|---|---|---|---|
| карти́на | picture | статья́ | article |
| кошелёк | purse | стена́ | wall |
| кошелька́, о кошельке́ | | Acc. сте́ну; cf. III 5.2 | |
| кре́сло | armchair | су́мка | handbag |
| лаборато́рия | laboratory | та́юже tágži (Intro. § 6) | likewise |
| ла́мпа | lamp | то́же | also |
| Ленингра́д | Leningrad | у́гол | corner |
| мо́жёт бы́ть | perhaps | угла́, в углу́ | |
| Москва́ | Moscow | уже́ | already |
| ни…ни | neither … nor | уже́ не | no longer |
| никогда́ (§ 7) | never | ча́сто | often |
| Пари́ж | Paris | что́ за (+ Nom.) | what a, |
| писа́тель | writer | | what sort of |
| писа́тельница | writer (f) | ша́пка | cap |
| пол | floor | шля́па | hat |
| на полу́ | on the floor | висе́ть вися́т | hang, be hanging |
| по́лка | shelf | лёжа́ть лёжа́т | lie, be lying |
| потоло́к | ceiling | по́мнить по́мнят | remember |
| потолка́, о потолке́ | | сиде́ть сидя́т | sit, be sitting |
| почёму́-то | for some reason | стоя́ть стоя́т | stand, be standing |
| расска́з | story | хоте́ть хотя́т (§ 6) | want |

## Some Personal Names

| | | | |
|---|---|---|---|
| Алексе́й | Aleksej, Alexis | Наде́жда | Nadezhda |
| Никола́й | Nikolaj, Nicolas | О́льга | Ol'ga, Olga |
| Па́вёл, Па́вла | Pavel, Paul | Со́ня | Sonja, Sonia |
| Пётр, Пётра́ | Peter | Та́ня | Tanja, Tania |
| Серге́й | Sergej, Sergius | | |

# LESSON V

| | |
|---|---|
| Я тепéрь пишý письмó. | I am now writing a letter. |
| Зáвтра я бýду писáть пи́сьма. | Tomorrow I will write letters. |
| Зáвтра я напишý э́то письмó. | Tomorrow I'll write that letter. |
| Чтó вы дéлаете? Я закрывáю двéрь. | What are you doing? I'm closing the door. |
| Зáвтра я егó не встрéчу. | I won't run into him tomorrow. |
| Конéчно они́ отвéтят зáвтра. | Of course they will answer tomorrow. |
| Они́ бýдут на фáбрике зáвтра. | They will be at the factory tomorrow. |
| Я сегóдня получи́л письмó, и сейчáс же отвéчу. | I received a letter today, and I'll answer it at once. |
| Брáт всегдá отвечáет, когдá óн получáет пи́сьма. | My brother always answers when he receives letters. |
| Éсли óн спрóсит, я отвéчу. | If he asks, I shall answer. |
| Профéссор диктýет. | The professor is dictating. |
| Они́ всегдá молчáт в клáссе. | They are always silent in class. |
| Пётр бýдет лёжáть на дивáне. | Peter will be lying on the sofa. |
| Не открывáйте окнá, пожáлуйста! | Please don't open the window! |
| Закрóйте двéрь! | Shut the door! |
| Не забывáйте закрывáть двéрь! <br> Не забýдьте закры́ть двéрь! } | Don't forget to shut the door. |
| Пиши́те диктóвку! | Write dictation. |
| Отвéтьте, пожáлуйста. | Answer, please! |
| Повторя́йте э́то чáсто! | Repeat this often. |
| Не диктýйте тáк бы́стро, пожáлуйста. | Don't dictate so fast, please. |
| Молчи́те! | Be quiet! |
| Спроси́ когó-нибудь. | Ask someone. |
| Не спрáшивайте никогó! | Don't ask anyone! |

| | |
|---|---|
| Пожа́луйста, возьми́те мою́ кни́гу. | Please take my book. |
| Вчера́ я писа́л пи́сьма, когда́ оте́ц откры́л окно́. | Yesterday I was writing letters when father opened the window. |
| Вчера́ я написа́л письмо́. | Yesterday I wrote a letter. |
| Студе́нтка реша́ла э́ту зада́чу, но не реши́ла. | The student was working at this problem, but she didn't solve it. |
| На́ш учи́тель закры́л окно́. | Our teacher closed the window. |
| Она́ почему́-то всегда́ закрыва́ла э́то окно́. | For some reason she always used to close this window. |
| Сего́дня я встре́тил бра́та в лаборато́рии. | Today I met (my) brother at the laboratory. |
| Мы́ его́ ча́сто встреча́ли в музе́е. | We often met him at the museum. |
| Что́ она́ отве́тила? Я́ не по́нял. | What did she answer? I didn't understand. |
| Она́ всегда́ хорошо́ отвеча́ла, но я не всегда́ понима́л. | She always answered well, but I didn't always understand. |
| Вы́ получи́ли его́ статью́? | Have you received his article? |
| Я получа́л э́тот журна́л. | I used to receive this magazine. |
| Я доста́л э́тот рома́н в Пари́же. | I obtained this novel in Paris. |
| Что́ вы́ де́лали? | What were you doing? |
| Что́ вы́ сде́лали? | What did you do? |
| Мы́ повторя́ли уро́к. | We were reviewing the lesson. |
| Она́ повтори́ла фра́зу. | She repeated the sentence. |
| Он смотре́л на сте́ну и молча́л. | He was looking at the wall and not saying anything. |
| Он посмотре́л на Та́ню и замолча́л. | He looked at Tanja and fell silent. |
| Учи́тельница продиктова́ла упражне́ние. | The teacher dictated an exercise. |
| Кто́-то взя́л ва́ш каранда́ш. | Someone took your pencil. |

---

**1.1** Every Russian verb necessarily belongs to one of two classes called *aspects*: perfective or imperfective. The *perfective aspect* denotes that the action of the verb has *one single end or termination*, and attention is focused on that end. The *imperfective* aspect does not say anything about the end of the action: it can thus mean that the action is conceived of as having several ends (repeated or habitual action) or no end at all (incomplete action or action in progress).

**1.2**   It is obvious that for every verbal idea there must usually be a pair of Russian verbs, one perfective and one imperfective. The verbs of such aspect-pairs are normally very closely related in form. The usual types of relationship are:

(A)   The imperfective has *no prefix* ~ the perfective has a *prefix*:[1] e.g.

| 'write' | писа́ть пи́шут | ( I ) | написа́ть напи́шут | (P) |
| 'read' | чита́ть чита́ют | | прочита́ть прочита́ют | |
| 'do' | де́лать де́лают | | сде́лать сде́лают | |
| 'see' | ви́деть ви́дят | | уви́деть уви́дят | |

(B)   The imperfective has a different *suffix* than the perfective:

| 'receive' | получа́ть получа́ют | ( I ) | получи́ть полу́чат | (P) |
| 'meet' | встреча́ть встреча́ют | | встре́тить встре́тят | |
| 'answer' | отвеча́ть отвеча́ют | | отве́тить отве́тят | |
| 'obtain' | достава́ть достаю́т | | доста́ть доста́нут | |

(C)   The imperfective and perfective stems are entirely different:

| 'speak' | говори́ть говоря́т | (I) | сказа́ть ска́жут | (P) |
| 'take' | бра́ть беру́т | | взя́ть возьму́т | |

In the vocabularies, verbs will be given in both imperfective (I) and perfective (P) forms. Both must be memorized.

**1.3**   Only imperfective verbs can have a true present tense. The "present" forms of perfective verbs normally refer to future events; the action is envisioned as completed in the future. Thus:

*Imperfective*:  Я **закрыва́ю** окно́.    I am (now in the process of) closing the window.

OR,   I (regularly, habitually) close the window.

*Perfective*:  Я **закро́ю** окно́.    I shall close the window (once, definitely).

**2.**   To be able to predict all the forms of any Russian verb, one must memorize the *3rd person plural present* (including "perfective present") and *the infinitive*. From the point of view of *form*, verbs of both aspects follow the same rules. It is in *use* and *meaning* that they differ.

---

[1] The most common prefixes in this function are **вы-, за-, на-, по-, при-, про-, с-,** and **у-**.

**3.** The infinitive endings and stem were discussed in IV 2.

**4.0** All remarks about the present tense made in Lesson II apply to "perfective present" as well as to the imperfective verbs discussed there. Here are some more particulars.

**4.1** In some stems there is an alternation of consonants (called *substitutive softening*) whereby the **first singular** differs from other forms:

If the 3rd plural ends in **-ят**, the final consonant in the present stem (i.e. 3 pl. minus **-ят**) is replaced according to the following table:

|      | п  | б  | м  | в  | т | д | з | с | ст | зд | *replaced* |
|------|----|----|----|----|---|---|---|---|----|----|------------|
| *by* | пл | бл | мл | вл | ч | ж | ж | ш | щ  | зж |            |

Examples: люби́ть лю́бят — люблю́; шуме́ть шумя́т — шумлю́; отве́тить отве́тят — отве́чу; ви́деть ви́дят — ви́жу; проси́ть про́сят — прошу́; чи́стить чи́стят — чи́щу; е́здить, е́здят, е́зжу.

**4.11** The ending of the 1st sing. is normally spelled **-у** if the 3 pl. is **-ут** or **-ат**, and **-ю** if the 3 pl. is **-ют** or **-ят**. However, when the *stem* of the 1st sing. ends in **ш, ж, ч,** or **щ** as a result of substitutive softening, then **-у** must be written. Look at the spelling rules on p. 13, § 5.4!

**4.2 Accentuation** of the present tense follows one of three patterns. The stress
   (I)  is constant, remaining
            (a) on the *stem* throughout, or
            (b) on the *endings* throughout; or else it is mobile and
  (II) falls on the ending (-ú) in the 1st person singular but on the stem in all other persons:

| (Ia) ви́жу | (Ib) говорю́ | (II) пишу́ | получу́ |
|-----------|-------------|-----------|---------|
| ви́дишь | говори́шь | пи́шешь | полу́чишь |
| ви́дит | говори́т | пи́шет | полу́чит |
| ви́дим | говори́м | пи́шем | полу́чим |
| ви́дите | говори́те | пи́шете | полу́чите |
| ви́дят | говоря́т | пи́шут | полу́чат |

All forms of the present tense follow the accent of the 3rd person plural (type I, either *a* or *b*) *unless the stress in the 3rd plural is one syllable closer to the beginning of the word than in the infinitive*, in which case we have type II:

| | | | | | |
|---|---|---|---|---|---|
| ви́де-ть | | | *but* получи́-ть | | |
| ви́д-ят | — | ви́жу | полу́ч-ат | *so* | получу́ |
| чита́-ть | | | писа́-ть | | |
| чита́-ют | — | чита́ю | *but* пи́ш-ут | *so* | пишу́ |

**4.21**  Verbs with infinitive in -ова́ть always have 3rd pl. in -ую́т and fixed stress throughout the present, including 1st sg.: диктова́ть дикту́ют; я дикту́ю. This group of verbs constitutes an important exception to the stress rule above.

**5.  The imperfective future** tense is formed by the future of the verb 'to be' (3 pl. бу́дут, cf. § 8 below) plus the imperfective infinitive: я бу́ду писа́ть — I will be writing, I will write (repeatedly); вы бу́дете получа́ть you will receive, be receiving.

**6.1**  The past-tense *accent* is normally that of the infinitive. But if the infinitive is monosyllabic, the feminine suffix is usually stressed. E.g.:

бра́ть   —   бра́л, бра́ло, бра́ли : брала́
взя́ть   —   взя́л, взя́ло, взя́ли : взяла́

Exception: зна́ть has зна́ла, like зна́ло and зна́ли.

**6.2**  The perfective **поня́ть пойму́т** 'understand' has the past forms по́нял, по́няло, по́няли : поняла́ (pónʰil, pónʰilə, pónʰilʰi : pənʰilá).

**7.0**  The **imperative** has two forms, one for giving a command to a person addressed as **ты**, and a plural and polite form for a person or persons addressed as **вы**.

**7.1**  The *imperative stem* is the same as the present stem (3 pl. minus *-ut*, *-at*). *The singular imperative suffix is either zero* (i.e. no ending at all: the bare stem remains) *or* -**и**. For the *plural*, -**те** is added to the singular imperative. To form the imperative, apply these rules in order:

1. If the last stem *letter* is a vowel, add -**й**:[1]
2. Otherwise —
   a. If the ending of the *first* person singular present is stressed (cf. 4.2 above), add stressed -**й**.
   b. If first singular present has an *un*stressed ending, and
      i. the stem ends in two consonants, add -**и** (unstressed).
      ii. the stem ends in one consonant, add -**ь**.[2]

[1] The rules are stated in terms of spelling; here the suffix is actually zero, for the stem ends in the consonant *j* (cf. II 6.2).

[2] This spelling rule tacitly includes the requirement that the final hard consonant of a stem is palatalized before the zero suffix if possible. The **ь** thus denotes the soft consonant; **ь** is arbitrarily used after non-paired consonants too (p. 326, § 8.32).

|      | infinitive-3rd plural | 1st singular | imperative sing. – plural | |
|------|----------------------|--------------|---------------------------|----------|
| 1.   | чита́ть чита́-ют      | чита́ю       | **чита́й**[1]              | **чита́йте** |
|      | стоя́ть сто-я́т       | стою́        | **сто́й**[1]               | **сто́йте** |
|      | диктова́ть дикту́-ют  | дикту́ю      | **дикту́й**[1]             | **дикту́йте** |
| 2a.  | говори́ть говор-я́т   | говорю́      | **говори́**                | **говори́те** |
|      | писа́ть пи́ш-ут       | пишу́        | **пиши́**                  | **пиши́те** |
|      | бра́ть бер-у́т        | беру́        | **бери́**                  | **бери́те** |
|      | взя́ть возьм-у́т      | возьму́      | **возьми́**                | **возьми́те** |
| 2bi. | по́мнить по́мн-ят     | по́мню       | **по́мни**                 | **по́мните** |
| 2bii.| отве́тить отве́т-ят   | отве́чу      | **отве́ть**[2]             | **отве́тьте** |
|      | доста́ть доста́н-ут   | доста́ну     | **доста́нь**[2]            | **доста́ньте** |

Note 1. The imperative of the verb 'to be' is **бу́дь бу́дьте.**

Note 2. The verb *ви́деть* 'see' has no imperative: it is replaced by **смотри́ смотри́те**; cf. смотре́ть смо́трят 'to look'.

Note 3. *Достава́ть* has **достава́й достава́йте.**

**7.2**   As a useful general rule, it may be said that the perfective imperative is ordinarily used in commands, while the imperfective imperative is used in prohibitions, i.e. negative commands: *Закро́йте две́рь!* 'Shut the door'; but *Не закрыва́йте две́ри!* 'Don't shut the door!' However, the speaker is free to choose the aspectual form — the perfective focuses attention on the completion of the action (often implying the result of the completion); the imperfective focuses on the action or process itself.

When the perfective is used in a negated imperative, it usually signifies a warning against an action the person might inadvertently or unintentionally complete (e. g. 'don't fall.''). Thus 'don't forget!' is normally perfective, *не забу́дьте.*

It is normal to use such imperfective imperatives as *пиши́те* 'write' and *чита́йте* 'read' — i. e. "do some writing/reading". The perfective imperatives *напиши́те* and *прочита́йте* are to be translated "write/read *it*". The perfective specifies the completion of a single act, and with these particular actions, some object must be supplied. English demands an expressed object; Russian does not.

---

[1] Here the suffix is zero, for the stem ends in the consonant *j* (cf. II 6.2): *čitáj*-ut *čitáju* — *čitáj*; *staj*-át *staj*-ú — *stój.*

[2] Here the suffix is also zero; the ь denotes the palatalized consonant of the stem: *atvʲét*ᵇ-ət — *atvʲét*ᵇ; *dastán*-ut — *dastán*ᵇ (see footnote 2 on previous page).

**8.** The verb 'to be' lacks a present tense (cf. I 3), but has all other forms: infinitive **быть**; (3 pl.) future **бу́дут**; past **был** (IV 5), imperative **бу́дь**.

**9.** Sometimes the English rendering of the two members of a pair of Russian verbs belonging to opposite aspects will differ. Thus *решáть* means 'try to solve, work at, try to decide' as well as to 'solve repeatedly, make several decisions', as opposed to the perfective *решúть* 'solve, reach a solution; decide, make a decision'. The verb *вúдеть* means 'see; have the power of sight', while the perfective *увúдеть* is 'catch sight of, perform an individual act of seeing':

Compare:  **Я ви́дел** её в саду́.        I *saw* her in the garden.
          **Я уви́дел** её в саду́.        I *caught sight of* her in the garden.

The imperfective *говорúть* means 'speak or talk (in general), say or tell (repeatedly)'', whereas the perfective (*сказáть*), being restricted to a single act of speaking, i.e. a single utterance, means only 'say, tell':

e.g.:    Óн э́то сказáл.              He said that.
         Óн э́то всегдá говори́л.      He always said that.
         Óн всегдá говори́л.          He always spoke.

**10.** Verbs like *сидéть, стоя́ть, лежáть, висéть, пóмнить*, and *рабóтать* have meanings which stress the continuing nature of the action or state they express: 'be sitting, standing, lying, hanging, remembering, working'. They do not have corresponding perfectives, although there are related verb pairs that express somewhat similar notions; they will be discussed later.

**11.1** *Смотрéть/посмотрéть на* + Acc. means 'look at':

Óн смóтрит на кáрту.              He's looking at the map.

**11.21** *Смотрéть в* + Acc. usually means 'look into'.

Óн смóтрит { в учéбник.          He's looking into { the textbook.
            в áтлас.                                { the atlas.

**11.22** *Смотрéть в окнó* (Acc.) = 'look *out of* the window'.

**12.** The object of an infinitive that is governed by a negated verb may be either in the genitive (III 9) or the accusative. For example:

Я **не** хочу́ прочитáть { статьи́.        I don't want to read the article.
                        { статью́.

Examples of complete conjugations.

| | | IMPERFECTIVE | | | PERFECTIVE | | |
|---|---|---|---|---|---|---|---|
| | | писа́ть | получа́ть | брать | написа́ть | получи́ть | взять |
| **INFINITIVE** | | писа́ть | получа́ть | брать | написа́ть | получи́ть | взять |
| **FUTURE** sg 1 | бу́ду | писа́ть, | получа́ть, | брать | напишу́ | получу́ | возьму́ |
| sg 2 | бу́дешь | писа́ть, | получа́ть, | брать | напи́шешь | полу́чишь | возьмёшь |
| sg 3 | бу́дет | писа́ть, | получа́ть, | брать | напи́шет | полу́чит | возьмёт |
| pl 1 | бу́дем | писа́ть, | получа́ть, | брать | напи́шем | полу́чим | возьмём |
| pl 2 | бу́дете | писа́ть, | получа́ть, | брать | напи́шете | полу́чите | возьмёте |
| pl 3 | бу́дут | писа́ть, | получа́ть, | брать | напи́шут | полу́чат | возьму́т |
| **PRESENT** sg 1 | | пишу́ | получа́ю | беру́ | | | |
| sg 2 | | пи́шешь | получа́ешь | берёшь | N O N E | | |
| sg 3 | | пи́шет | получа́ет | берёт | | | |
| pl 1 | | пи́шем | получа́ем | берём | | | |
| pl 2 | | пи́шете | получа́ете | берёте | | | |
| pl 3 | | пи́шут | получа́ют | беру́т | | | |
| **PAST** m | я, он | писа́л, | получа́л, | брал | написа́л | получи́л | взял |
| n | оно́ | писа́ло, | получа́ло, | бра́ло | написа́ло | получи́ло | взя́ло |
| f | я, она́, ты | писа́ла, | получа́ла, | брала́ | написа́ла | получи́ла | взяла́ |
| pl | мы, вы, они́ | писа́ли, | получа́ли, | бра́ли | написа́ли | получи́ли | взя́ли |
| **IMPERATIVE** sg | | пиши́ | получа́й | бери́ | напиши́ | получи́ | возьми́ |
| pl | | пиши́те | получа́йте | бери́те | напиши́те | получи́те | возьми́те |

**13.** As examples of complete conjugations, the table on page 62 gives all the forms of the verbs 'write' (писа́ть пи́шут [I] — написа́ть напи́шут [P]), 'receive' (получа́ть получа́ют [I] — получи́ть полу́чат [P]), and 'take' (бра́ть беру́т [I] — взя́ть возьму́т [P]).

## EXERCISES

**A.** I. The following exchange is based on the command "Open the door":

— *Откро́йте две́рь!* говори́т учи́тельница. Ива́н *открыва́ет две́рь.* — Что́ вы́ де́лаете? спра́шиваёт учи́тельница. — *Я́ открыва́ю две́рь,* отвеча́ёт Ива́н. — Да́, говори́т учи́тельница, вы́ *открыва́ёте две́рь.*

Use the following commands to make similar exchanges:
1. Write a sentence! 2. Answer! 3. Speak Russian! 3a. Say it in Russian! 4. Do it again! 5. Take my notebook! 6. Read the book! 7. Solve this problem! 8. Ask Anna! 9. Close the window! 10. Work! (Imperfective only.)

IIa. Ива́н *откры́л (открыва́л) две́рь.* — Что́ вы́ де́лали (сде́лали)? — *Я́ откры́л (открыва́л) две́рь.*

Repeat, using the past (both perfective and imperfective) of each verbal expression from exercise I above.

IIb. Repeat IIa, substituting А́нна and then мы́ for Ива́н and making the necessary changes in the verb-forms.

**B.** Read and translate:

1. Где́ вы́ бу́дёте рабо́тать? Я́ бу́ду рабо́тать до́ма, бу́ду писа́ть. 2. Я́ не закро́ю о́кна.˙ 3. Вы́ бу́дёте жи́ть в лесу́? 4. Они́ спро́сят о ва́с. 5. Моя́ учи́тельница напи́шёт кни́гу о на́шей дере́вне. 6. Я́ э́то забу́ду, е́сли не напишу́. 7. Вы́ бу́дёте чита́ть э́тот журна́л? 8. Я́ прочита́ю его́ письмо́, и сейча́с же отве́чу. 9. Вы́ бу́дёте за́втра на фа́брике? 10. Она́ возьмёт мою́ тетра́дку и прочита́ёт уро́к. 11. Мы́ уви́дим ге́ния за́втра. 12. Что́ мы́ бу́дём ви́деть? 13. Что́ ты́ бу́дёшь де́лать та́м? 14. Никола́й и О́льга бу́дут сиде́ть та́м в углу́ и писа́ть сочине́ниё. 15. Вы́ писа́ли на доске́ вчера́? Да́, мы́ всегда́ пи́шём на доске́. 16. Вы́ написа́ли пи́сьма? Не́т, я́ ничего́ не писа́ла. 17. Э́та студе́нтка никогда́ не открыва́ла уче́бника. 18. Вы́ получа-

ли газéту, когдá вы́ жи́ли на Донý?    19. Когдá я её встрéтил сегóдня, онá спроси́ла меня́ ещё рáз об э́том.    20. Óн дóлго смотрéл
в окнó, а ничегó не говори́л.    21. Писáтельница взялá мою́ статью́.
Онá хотéла прочитáть её.    22. Чтó вы пóняли? Я́ ничегó не понялá.
23. Чтó вы сказáли вчерá, и чтó вы скáжете сегóдня?    24. В чьéй
кóмнате вы откры́ли окнó?    25. Óн нé был вчерá на урóке, óн не
читáл задáчи, и тепéрь óн ничегó ни о чём не знáет.    26. Учи́тель
нé жил в дерéвне, óн жил и живёт в гóроде.    27. Извини́те, я за-
бы́ла свою́ кни́гу дóма.    28. Чтó óн написáл в тетрáдке?    29. Гово-
ри́те грóмче, и óн вáс поймёт.    30. Открóйте кни́гу и читáйте
урóк!

31. Пиши́те на доскé, пожáлуйста! Напиши́те э́то!    32. Скажи́те
чтó-нибудь по-рýсски!    33. Закрóйте кни́гу, и мы́ бýдем говори́ть
об урóке.    34. Решáй э́ту задáчу!    35. Реши́ э́ту задáчу!    36. Пов-
тори́те за мнóй!    37. Отвéть сейчáс же!    38. Не забывáйте нáшего
гóрода!    39. Не забýдьте достáть газéту.    40. Почемý онá не отвé-
тила? Спроси́те учи́тельницу.    41. Скажи́те э́то и её адвокáт сейчáс
же замолчи́т.    42. Óн решáет задáчу.    43. Онá реши́т задáчу.
44. Возьми́те егó тетрáдку!    45. Вы возьмёте егó тетрáдку?    46. Óн
берёт вáшу газéту и вáш журнáл.    47. Мóй мýж получáет э́ту газéту,
нó никогдá её не читáет.    48. Вы пóмните мою́ сестрý? Дá, óчень
хорошó пóмню. Дóбрый вéчер!    49. Онá открывáет тетрáдку и
пи́шет.    50. Онá всегдá говори́ла о Я́лте и Пари́же.

51. *Ты́ пи́шешь по-рýсски?* 52. *Почемý стýл бы́л на столé?* 53. *Конéчно, мы́
э́то реши́м.* 54. *Сестрá былá на урóке.* 55. *Я́ её тáм встрéтила.* 56. *Онá
не понялá.* 57. *Мы́ хорошó пóняли.* 58. *Её мýж бýдет тáм.* 59. *Женá забы́ла
закры́ть окнó.* 60. *Я́ откры́л тетрáдку.* 61. *Когó онá встрéтила?* 62. *Вы́
бýдете здéсь?* 63. *Возьми́те свою́ кни́гу.* 64. *Ктó егó спроси́л?* 65. *Мы́ нé
жи́ли тáм.* 66. *Óн бы́л в Росси́и.* 67. *Вы́ сегóдня писáли на доскé?* 68. *Ивáн
чáсто э́то говори́т.* 69. *Вы́ не получи́ли газéты сегóдня?* 70. *Вóт э́то нáш
дóм, смотри́те.*

**C.**  For oral and/or written translation:

1. What shall we do tomorrow? We'll be in the country and we won't
do anything.    2. Have you read this story in this magazine? No, I'll
read it today.    3. What were they doing? They were closing the window. They weren't doing anything.    4. Whom did he ask? He asked
the genius. He didn't ask anyone.    5. Did they close the window? I
don't remember.    6. When I saw Aleksej, he was writing letters.    7.
Nikolaj wrote a letter yesterday. Sonja received it today.    8. Whom

did they use to meet in the garden? They met the teacher, his sister and her husband. Did they meet them yesterday? They met the teacher, but they did not meet the sister or her husband. Today they met no one.   9. His father didn't read Russian well, but he spoke well.

10. I asked him and he answered, but I didn't understand. Why don't you ask [P future] again?   11. We'll meet that writer in Moscow tomorrow.   12. Today you will receive his book. We received it yesterday.   13. Why didn't your wife close the window? Perhaps she forgot. 14. The teacher (f) dictated the sentence in English and we wrote it in Russian.   15. He will take Nadezhda's pencil.   16. Whose pen did Tanja take?   17. Why didn't you read the article? I wanted to talk about it.   18. Nikolaj's father said something about the village. He's always talking about it.   19. The lady opened the door and looked into the garden. She didn't see anyone.

20. Excuse me, I forgot to get the newspaper and the magazine.   21. Do it at once! (omit 'it').   22. Answer! What did you ask?   23. Look at Ivan! What is he doing? He's looking out the window.   24. Write a letter! I'll write it at once.   25. No, do not open the door! Close it! 26. Take this! Don't take that!   27. Please dictate slowly. When you speak fast I don't understand.   28. Do you want to read my composition? It's in this notebook. Please take it.   29. Read this article, and tomorrow we shall talk about it.   30. What did she say? I (f) did not understand. Please repeat.

## VOCABULARY

| | | | |
|---|---|---|---|
| газе́та | newspaper | сейча́с же | at once, right away |
| дикто́вка | dictation | сочине́ние | written work, composition, paper |
| е́сли | if | | |
| журна́л | magazine | уче́бник | textbook |
| за́втра | tomorrow | упражне́ние | exercise |
| зада́ча | task, assignment, problem | фра́за | sentence |
| пи́сьма Nom.-Acc.plural of письмо́ | | что (always unstressed *štə*) | that (a connective) |
| рома́н | novel | | |
| сего́дня (NB sʲivódnʲə) | today | | |

| | | | | |
|---|---|---|---|---|
| бы́ть бу́дут | to be: see § 8 | открыва́ть открыва́ют I | | open |
| бра́ть беру́т I | } take | откры́ть откро́ют P | | |
| взя́ть возьму́т P | | отвеча́ть отвеча́ют I | | answer |
| ви́деть ви́дят I | } see § 9 | отве́тить отве́тят P | | |
| уви́деть уви́дят P | | писа́ть пи́шут I | | write |
| встреча́ть встреча́ют I | } meet (by chance) | написа́ть напи́шут P | | |
| встре́тить встре́тят P | | повторя́т повторя́ют I | | repeat, review |
| говори́ть говоря́т I | } speak, say, talk, tell | повтори́ть повторя́т P | | |
| сказа́ть ска́жут P | | получа́ть получа́ют I | | receive, get |
| де́лать де́лают I | } do, make | получи́ть полу́чат P | | |
| сде́лать сде́лают P | | понима́ть понима́ют I | | under-stand |
| диктова́ть -у́ют I § 4.21 | } dictate | поня́ть пойму́т P (§ 6.3) | | |
| продиктова́ть -у́ют P | | реша́ть реша́ют I | | decide, solve (§ 9) |
| достава́ть достаю́т I | } obtain | реши́ть реша́т P | | |
| доста́ть доста́нут P | | смотре́ть смо́трят I | | look (§ 11) |
| забыва́ть забыва́ют I | } forget | посмотре́ть посмо́трят P | | |
| забы́ть забу́дут P | | спра́шивать спра́шивают I | | ask a question |
| закрыва́ть закрыва́ют I | } close, shut | спроси́ть спро́сят P | | |
| закры́ть закро́ют P | | чита́ть чита́ют I | | read |
| молча́ть молча́т I | } be silent, not speak | прочита́ть прочита́ют P | | |
| замолча́ть замолча́т P | } fall silent | | | |

## For review

**A.** Read aloud and translate:

1. Где висела шапка Николая? Я ее не видел в его комнате, может быть она была в комнате его сестры.  2. Извините, я забыл свой учебник дома. Не знаю что мы будем делать сегодня в классе.  3. Вы не помните Алексея и его брата Павла? Они работали где-то в городе, может быть в лаборатории. —Нет, я их не помню.  4. Посмотрите! Что вы там видите? —Я вижу что-то, но не знаю что это такое.  5. Она сидит в своей комнате и пишет сочинение.  6. Может быть вы хотите прочитать этот рассказ? —Спасибо, я его уже прочитал.  7. Она тоже хорошо говорит по-русски. Она долго жила в Ленинграде, вы не знали?  8. Сумка этой писательницы была на этом кресле, а в сумке был кошелек. Где они теперь?  9. Ольга и Петр

еще не достали этого документа. Может быть достанут завтра. 10. Надежда меня часто спрашивала об этом адвокате, но я молчал. Я не хотел и не хочу говорить о нем.

**B.** For oral and/or written translation into Russian:

1. Look at the sentence and repeat it slowly once more. 2. What will your wife be doing tomorrow? She will be in town. She will be talking about the picture and the map in the magazine. 3. When you meet the genius, don't forget to ask him about the letter. 4. Does anyone live in that building? No, that is a museum and of course no one lives in it. 5. Please close the door in our room. Never open that window. 6. Was the lamp standing on the table or lying on the floor? Whose lamp are you talking about? The professor's lamp, of course. 7. My brother thinks that no one will ever write the assignment. 8. Excuse me, what did the teacher (f) say about our lesson? I did not understand. 9. I see neither the purse nor the hat in the corner. 10. Solve the problem now and tomorrow we shall talk about it. 11. What are you always thinking about, Nicholas? I won't say. I don't want to say. 12. Take your pencil and your notebook and write the dictation in Russian. 13. Why doesn't Vera look at her own map of Russia? She doesn't know where it is. 14. Don't ask the genius about the lesson; ask your teacher in class. 15. Neither the lamp nor the picture is hanging on the wall; they are lying in the corner of the room on the floor.

16. Did you used to get a newspaper when you lived in the forest? 17. Nadezhda and her sister are sitting in their father's garden, where they are writing a story about the Crimea. 18. I don't understand you. Repeat it once more, please. Remember, I understand very well when you speak slowly. 19. Ivan's wife forgot to close the door. For some reason she always forgets to close it. 20. Please don't dictate the sentence so quickly! 21. I'm not going to write an exercise tonight. Goodnight. 22. I know that you don't understand the lesson now, but read it once again and you will understand it tomorrow. 23. If my sister asks you about it, say that you have read her story. 24. Of course you remember her. She is the wife of that writer. 25. They say that they will meet us at the factory tomorrow. 26. Nikolaj and Nadezhda are no longer silent in class, they talk often. 27. I worked for a long time in her father's laboratory. Where is it? There it is. 28. Whose purse is this? Where did you get it? 29. Our lawyer wants to read your article about the wall in Berlin. His wife has already read it. 30. Don't forget us when you are [= will be] in Paris!

# LESSON Va

| | |
|---|---|
| Мы слу́шаем учи́тельницу. | We are listening to the teacher. |
| Она́ чита́ет анекдо́т. | She is reading a funny story. |
| Когда́ она́ ко́нчит чита́ть, мы напи́шем анекдо́т. | When she finishes reading, we will write the joke down. |
| Я сде́лал оши́бку, и профе́ссор меня́ попра́вил. | I made a mistake and the professor corrected me. |
| Переведи́те э́то на англи́йский! | Translate this into English. |
| Она́ пра́вильно перевела́ отве́т на ру́сский. | She translated the answer into Russian correctly. |
| Она́ начала́ переводи́ть с ру́сского. | She began to translate from Russian. |
| Э́то пра́вильно! | That's correct! |
| Я не переводи́л э́того упражне́ния. | I didn't translate this exercise. |
| Он спра́шивал уро́к и пото́м на́чал диктова́ть. | He asked questions about the lesson and then began to dictate. |
| Что́ он сказа́л? Я не слу́шал. | What did he say? I wasn't listening. |
| Вы не понима́ете вопро́са? | Don't you understand the question? |

---

**1.** A few verbs have infinitives ending in **-ти́**. The past forms are slightly irregular and should be memorized. Other forms are derived by the regular rules (II 6; V 7).

An example is the perfective *перевести́ переведу́т* 'translate':

present: **переведу́т, переведу́ переведёшь переведёт**, etc.
past: **перевёл, перевела́, перевело́, перевели́.**

**2.** The past of the perfective нача́ть начну́т 'begin' has mobile stress like that of поня́ть (V 6.2): на́чал, на́чало, на́чали : начала́.

**3.** Note the forms[1] used in rendering 'translate *from* Russian/English *to* English/Russian':

с рýсск**ого**      **на** англ**и**́йск**ий**

с англ**и**́йск**ого на** рýсск**ий**

The **г** in the **-ого** suffix is pronounced *v*: *srúskəvə, sangl*ᵇ*íjskəvə*.

*NB*: **на** рýсск**ий**, англ**и**́йск**ий**, but **по**-рýсск**и**, **по**-англ**и**́йск**и**.

**4.** Note that any infinitive after verbs meaning "begin, start" or "end, finish" must be *im*perfective.

**5.** Notice the difference between two types of «that»:

| | |
|---|---|
| Я дýмаю, что | I think *that*₁ |
| {  э́тот студéнт здéсь. | {  *that*₂ student is here. |
| э́та студéнтка здéсь. | |
| э́то письмó тáм на пóлке. | *that*₂ letter is there on the shelf. |

"*That*₂" is a demonstrative pronoun, an identifier; in Russian it is *э́тот, э́та, э́то*, etc. "*That*₁" is a connective whose only function is to join two parts of a compound sentence. Both in Russian and English the connective is unstressed.

Do not confuse the unstressed connective **что** *štə* 'that₁' with the stressed interrogative **чтó** *štó* 'what'.

**6.** Notice that the English word *paper* is used not only for the material (Russian **бумáга**) but also as a term for a written composition (**сочинé-ниё**) and as a short way of saying 'newspaper' (**газéта**). When translating, keep the ambiguity of the English word in mind.

**7.** *Дáльше* 'further' is used to mean "go on", or "next", i.e. as a command for the next person to take his turn, e.g. at recitation.

**EXERCISES**

**A.** Use the following imperative phrases to make exchanges on the model of Exercise V A 1.

1. Translate this sentence!    2. Begin to read!    3. Take paper and write!

---

[1] These forms will be explained in detail in Lesson XIV. At present, just learn ther.ɪ as fixed phrases.

4. Think about the exercise!   5. Finish the story!   6. Look at the board!
7. Dictate!

**B.** Read aloud and translate:

1. Мы́ в кла́ссе. Кто́-то пи́шет зада́чу на доске́. Звоно́к. Пора́ начина́ть уро́к. Учи́тельница закрыва́ет две́рь и говори́т: «До́брое у́тро». «До́брое у́тро, А́нна Па́вловна,» — отвеча́ем мы́. «Смотри́те на до́ску, —говори́т она́. Ве́ра, начина́йте вы́, пожа́луйста. Прочита́йте э́ту фра́зу.  Не́т, э́то не та́к. Повтори́те! Та́к, тепе́рь лу́чше; повтори́те ещё ра́з. Да́льше. Ива́н, чита́йте, пожа́луйста.»

Учи́тельница начина́ет спра́шивать уро́к. Она́ спра́шивает Наде́жду. Наде́жда хорошо́ зна́ет уро́к и отвеча́ет пра́вильно. «О́чень хорошо́,» —говори́т А́нна Па́вловна. Она́ ви́дит, что Пётр смо́трит в окно́. Она́ его́ спра́шивает, но он не зна́ет отве́та. Пото́м она́ спра́шивает Никола́я. Никола́й ду́мает, что зна́ет отве́т на вопро́с, но когда́ он начина́ет говори́ть по-ру́сски, он де́лает оши́бку. Учи́тельница его́ поправля́ет, и он повторя́ет фра́зу.

«Тепе́рь напи́шем дикто́вку, —говори́т учи́тельница. Возьми́те бума́гу и пиши́те.» Она́ чита́ет ме́дленно по-ру́сски и мы́ пи́шем. Мы́ конча́ем писа́ть дикто́вку. Пото́м мы́ начина́ем чита́ть по-ру́сски и переводи́ть с ру́сского на англи́йский. Звоно́к: пора́ конча́ть! Учи́тельница открыва́ет две́рь и говори́т: «До свида́ния.»

2.  Вчера́ в кла́ссе никто́ не писа́л на доске́. Учи́тель спра́шивал уро́к, но никто́ его́ не зна́л. Он спроси́л меня́, но я́ не по́нял вопро́са. «Повтори́те, пожа́луйста, вопро́с,» —сказа́л я́. Он повтори́л и я́ по́нял, но не зна́л отве́та. «Э́то о́чень нехорошо́,» —сказа́л учи́тель. Пото́м он на́чал чита́ть дикто́вку по-ру́сски, а мы́ писа́ли. Он прочита́л дикто́вку ещё ра́з. Пото́м мы́ чита́ли расска́з, а он на́с поправля́л.

3.  Repeat No. 2 in Russian, making both the teacher and the narrator feminine.

**C.**  Read aloud and translate:

1. Мы́ спра́шиваем учи́теля, но он не отвеча́ет.   2. Она́ берёт ва́ш рома́н.   3. Учи́тельница ме́дленно чита́ет сочине́ние Никола́я.   4. Вы́ не перево́дите э́того упражне́ния с ру́сского на англи́йский? 5. О́льга слу́шает писа́тельницу. 6. Я́ получа́ю э́ту газе́ту. 7. Алексе́й открыва́ет две́рь. 8. Па́вел пи́шет сочине́ние об э́той статье́. 9. Пётр и Со́ня понима́ют э́тот анекдо́т, а Наде́жда не понима́ет. 10. Та́ня встреча́ет своего́ учи́теля в э́том кла́ссе.

**D.** Read exercise C again, putting all verbs first into imperfective past, and then into perfective past.

**E.** For oral and/or written translation into Russian:

1. Sit here in the armchair; we'll sit on the sofa.   2. Excuse me, I didn't understand your question; repeat it please.   3. Where did you get that hat, Nadezhda? I got it in Paris.   4. Ask Tanja, she will answer at once. She always knows the answer.   5. Look at the map of Russia on that wall. Do you see Moscow?   6. We will translate this story into Russian tomorrow in class.   7. Anna took her (own) handbag. Vera took her (someone else's) handbag.   8. We will always translate from Russian into English and also from English into Russian.   9. Be quiet and listen to me. I want to say something. You don't know anything. You never want to listen to anyone.   10. Don't you know the answer? Didn't you repeat the exercise?   11. Your textbook will always be standing on this shelf.   12. I will read a sentence in Russian; you write it (down).   13. Now translate it into English.   14. When I make a mistake the teacher corrects me.   15. Look, you've made a mistake; correct it!

## VOCABULARY

| | | | |
|---|---|---|---|
| анекдо́т | joke, funny story | ду́мать ду́мают I<br>поду́мать -ают Р | think |
| бума́га | paper | | |
| вопро́с | question | конча́ть конча́ют I<br>ко́нчить ко́нчат Р | end, finish |
| да́льше | see § 7 | | |
| звоно́к | bell | начина́ть начина́ют I<br>нача́ть начну́т Р § 2 | begin |
| [Gen. звонка́, Pr. звонке́] | | | |
| непра́вильно | incorrect(ly) | слу́шать слу́шают I<br>послу́шать -ают Р | listen |
| отве́т | answer | | |
| отве́т на + Acc. | (the) answer to | переводи́ть перево́дят I<br>перевести́ переведу́т Р § 1 | translate |
| оши́бка | mistake | | |
| пора́ (+ inf.) | it's time to | поправля́ть поправля́ют I<br>попра́вить попра́вят Р | correct |
| пото́м | then, afterwards | | |
| пра́вильно | correct(ly) | | |

# LESSON VI

| | |
|---|---|
| У вáс éсть кни́га? | Do you have a book? |
| Дá, у меня́ éсть кни́га. | Yes, I have a book. |
| Нéт, у меня́ нéт кни́ги. | No, I have no book. I don't have a book. |
| Éсть ли у когó-нибудь кни́га? | Does anyone have a book? |
| Нéт, ни у когó нéт кни́ги. | No, no one has a book. |
| У вáс éсть и́ли каранда́ш и́ли перó? | Do you have either a pencil or a pen? |
| У вáс бы́л каранда́ш? | Did you have a pencil? |
| Нéт, у меня́ нé было карандаша́. | No, I had no pencil. |
| Нéт, нó у меня́ бы́ло перó. | No, but I had a pen. |
| Нéт, у меня́ нé было ни пера́ ни карандаша́. | No, I had neither a pen nor a pencil. |
| Вы́ знáете э́то слóво? | Do you know this word? |
| Посмотри́те в словáрь. | Look in the dictionary. |
| Э́того слóва нéт в словарé. | This word isn't in the dictionary. |
| Платóк тáм на шкафý. | The handkerchief is there on the wardrobe. |
| У неё в рукé клю́ч. | In her hand is a key. |
| У негó в карма́не нéт ни платка́, ни ключа́. | He has neither a handerchief nor a key in his pocket. |
| У вáс éсть сы́н и́ли дóчь? | Do you have a son or daughter? |
| У нáс éсть сы́н, нó дóчери нéт. | We have a son but no daughter. |
| Сы́н тепéрь студéнт в Бостóне. | (Our) son is now a student in Boston. |
| Дóчь нáшей соседки госпожи́ Петрóвой тóже студéнтка. | The daughter of our neighbor Mrs. Petrov is also a student. |
| Ктó э́тот человéк? | Who is that man? |
| Это Пётр Ивáнович. | That's Pëtr Ivanovich. |
| Кáк его́ фами́лия? | What's his surname? |
| Семёнов. Óн меха́ник. | Semënov. He's a mechanic. |

| Тá дáма егó мáть, Нúна Алексéёвна. | That woman is his mother, Nina Alekseevna. |
|---|---|
| У Петрá Ивáновича éсть сестрá, Нúна Ивáновна. | Pëtr Ivanovich has a sister, Nina Ivanovna. |
| Марúя Юрьевна сидúт у окнá. | Marija Jur'evna is sitting at the window. |
| У неё éсть сосéд, дóктор Поливáнов. Вы ёгó знáете? | She has a neighbor, Dr. Polivanov. Do you know him? |
| Кáк ёгó úмя óтчество? | What is his first name and patronymic? |
| Алексáндр Николáёвич. | Aleksandr Nikolaevich. |
| Нéт, я не знáю этого дóктора Поливáнова. | No, I don't know *that* Dr. Polivanov. |
| Я встрéтил господúна Семёнова у мáтери моёгó сосéда. | I met Mr. Semënov at my neighbor's mother's. |
| Дóктор дóма? | Is the doctor at home? |
| Дóктора нéт дóма. | The doctor is not at home. |
| Дóктор не дóма, óн в гóроде. | The doctor isn't home; he's in town. |
| Дóктора не бýдёт дóма сегóдня. | The doctor will not be home today. |
| Дóктор не бýдёт дóма сегóдня, óн бýдёт в гóроде. | The doctor won't be home today; he'll be in town. |
| Я никогдá нé был в Россúи, нó был в Лóндоне. | I never was in Russia, but I've been in London. |

---

**1.0** Éсть is a general statement of existence, 'there is'. (NB: in English, the word *there* in this phrase does not *point* to anything, nor does it define *position* by itself; it merely denotes the general validity of the statement which it introduces. Compare French *il y a*, German *es gibt*.)

| В этом гóроде **éсть** дóктор. | *There is* a doctor in that town. |
|---|---|
| **Éсть** кнúга об этом. | *There is* a book about that. |
| Тáм в гóроде **éсть** дóктор. | In the town there, *there is* a doctor. |

**1.1** The negative (i.e. *general denial of existence*) is **нéт** 'there is not' (*il n'y a pas, es gibt nicht*). It ALWAYS requires the GENITIVE. For example:

| Тáм **нéт** дóктор*а*. | *There is no* doctor there. |
|---|---|
| Об этом **нéт** кнú*ги*. | *There is no* book on that. |

**1.2** In the past tense, **éсть** is represented by the forms **бы́л, бы́ло, была́, бы́ли:**

| | |
|---|---|
| В э́том го́роде **бы́л** до́ктор. | *There was* a doctor in that town. |
| **Была́** кни́га об э́том. | *There was* a book about that. |

Here there may be ambiguity:

| | |
|---|---|
| Та́м бы́л до́ктор. | { The/A doctor was there. <br> { There there was a doctor. |

In such cases the context makes it clear which is meant.

**1.3** The past of **нéт** is the invariable impersonal (neuter) form **нé бы́ло**, which likewise of course demands the genitive:

| | |
|---|---|
| Та́м **нé бы́ло** до́ктор*а*. | *There wasn't* a doctor there. |
| Никогда́ **нé бы́ло** кни́г*и* об э́том. | *There never was* a book about that. |

**1.41** The future of **éсть** is **бу́дёт** for the singular and **бу́дут** for the plural.

| | |
|---|---|
| В э́том го́роде **бу́дёт** до́ктор. | *There will be* a doctor in that town. <br> (or: The/A doctor will be...) |
| [В э́том го́роде **бу́дут** док-тора́ (Nom. pl.)] | [ *There will be* doctors in that town.] <br> (or: [the] doctors will be...) |

**1.42** The future of **нéт** is **не бу́дёт**.

| | |
|---|---|
| Та́м **не бу́дёт** до́ктор*а*. | *There will not be* a doctor there. |
| [Та́м **не бу́дёт** доктор*о́в*.] <br> (Gen. pl.) | [*There won't be* doctors there.] |

**2.** Notice that in stating the absence of someone or something from a given place, there are two possibilities. If only the absence is to be mentioned, then *нéт + genitive*: до́ктор*а* нéт до́ма; кни́г*и* на столе́ нéт. The doctor and the book are absent, and the subject is closed. If, however, the whereabouts of the person or thing is to be defined, then *nominative + не*: До́ктор *не* до́ма, а в го́роде; кни́г*а* *не* на столе́, а на сту́ле.

**3.0** The preposition **у** takes the *genitive* case. Its general meaning is 'close by, at', but in different contexts it must be rendered in English by a number of expressions. With nouns denoting place, **у** normally can be translated 'at, by': она́ стоя́ла *у доски́* — 'She was standing *by* the blackboard.' With nouns or pronouns denoting persons, **у** can be translated 'at the home of, at the office of, in the country of' and the like, depending on the context:

| | |
|---|---|
| Моя́ сосе́дка рабо́таёт **у до́ктора.** | My neighbor works *at the doctor's.* |

Она́ тепе́рь **у ни́х**.                 She is now *at their place.*
**У на́с** в го́роде не́т музе́я.          In *our* town there is no museum.
Ива́н живёт **у до́чери**.              Ivan lives *at his daughter's.*

**3.1**   Like most prepositions, **у** also has purely idiomatic uses which are best learned as separate vocabulary items. For example, it is more usual to use *у* + *Gen.* than the simple Acc. with **спра́шивать/спроси́ть**; e.g. 'I asked the teacher': я спроси́л **у учи́тельницы** or я спроси́л учи́тельницу. To 'take *from*' a person is бра́ть/взя́ть **у кого́-нибудь**:

Я взял э́ту кни́гу **у учи́тель-**      I took this book *from* the teacher.
  ницы.

But NB:

Я взял кни́гу **в** библиоте́ке.   I took a book *from* the library.

**4.**   NOTE that the pronominal forms for 'he, she, it, they' add an initial **н-** when they are used as objects of prepositions: **у него́, у неё, у них**. Normal genitive — **его́, её, их**: with prepositions — **него́, неё, них**.

**5.0**   **У** plus a noun or pronoun and the general expression of existence **есть** is the normal Russian equivalent of the English verb 'to have':

**У** его́ **ма́тери есть** до́м (ко́мната,        His *mother has* a house (room,
                               перо́).                              pen).

The negative of course employs **не́т** and the genitive:

**У** неё **не́т** до́м*а* (ко́мнат*ы*, пер*а́*).     *She has no* house (room, pen).

In the past tense, the positive has the gender forms **был, бы́ло, была́, бы́ли**:

**У госпожи́ Семёновой был** до́м.        Mrs. Semënov *had* a house.
                        **была́** ко́мната.                              a room.
                        **бы́ло** перо́.                                 a pen.
                        **бы́ли** пи́сьма.                             letters.

The negative past uses the invariable impersonal **не́ было** + genitive:

**У Петра́ Серге́евича не́ было** до́м*а*.    Pëtr Sergeevich *had no* house.
                        **не́ было** ко́мнат*ы*.                        *no* room.
                        **не́ было** пер*а́*.                            *no* pen.
                        **не́ было** *пи́сём* (Gen pl).               *no* letters.

**5.1**   In this construction the nominative (or genitive) forms of **свой** are used to refer to the *logical subject*, i.e. the grammatical object of **у**:

У меня́ есть **своя́** кни́га.             I have *my own* book.
У неё не́т **свое́й** ко́мнаты.          She does not have a room of *her own.*

  As a practical rule, the nominative case forms of **свой** occur *only* in this construction.

**5.2**   In the "have"-construction with **у**, the expected **éсть** may be omitted if the emphasis is on the thing possessed (particularly its description or location) rather than on the fact of possession. For example:

| | |
|---|---|
| У меня́ éсть учéбник. | I have a textbook. |
| У меня́ нóвый[1] учéбник. | I have a new textbook. |
| У неё в рукé словáрь. | She has a dictionary in her hand. |
| Чтó у нёгó в кармáне? | What has he in his pocket? |
| Чтó э́то у меня́ в рукé? | What is it I have in my hand? |
| Чья́ э́то у неё шля́па? | Whose hat is it that she has? |

**6.**   Both **здесь** and **тýт** render English "here". **Здéсь** is more general, while **тýт** specifies an immediate connection with the speaker and the moment of speech; it is very likely to be accompanied by pointing. For example:

| | |
|---|---|
| Кни́га гдé-то *здéсь;* | The book is somewhere *here* [e.g., in this room]; |
| áх, *тýт* онá! | oh, *here* it is [right here, where I'm pointing]. |

**7.0**   A Russian name consists of three parts: the Christian name **и́мя**, the patronymic **óтчество**, and the surname **фами́лия**. The normal polite form of address is to use the first two (*и́мя óтчество* is the usual pronunciation, with *и* 'and' omitted).

**7.1**   The patronymic means "son of…" or "daughter of…". It consists of the stem of the father's Christian name plus either the masculine suffix **-ович** or the feminine **-овна**. If the underlying name is a soft-stem, the suffixes are **-ёвич**, **-ёвна**; for names ending in **-ий** the patronymics are spelled **-ьёвич**, **-ьёвна**. For example:

| Father's name (+Gen. sg.): | patronymic | Father | patronymic |
|---|---|---|---|
| **Ивáн** | Ивáн**ович** | **Леони́д** | Леони́д**ович** |
| Ivan (John) | Ивáн**овна** | Leonid | Леони́д**овна** |
| **Пётр (Петрá)** | Петр**óвич** | **И́горь** | И́горь**евич** |
| Pëtr (Peter) | Петр**óвна** | Igor' | И́горь**евна** |
| **Пáвел (Пáвла)** | Пáвл**ович** | **Сергéй** | Сергéй**евич** |
| Pavel (Paul) | Пáвл**овна** | Sergej (Serge) | Сергéй**евна** |
| **Лéв (Львá)** | Льв**óвич** | **Юрий** | Ю́рь**евич** |
| Lev (Leo) | Льв**óвна** | Jurij (George) | Ю́рь**евна** |

[1] This adjective is given here only as a typical illustration of this usage: adjectives will not be used until Lesson XII.

## Sample Declensions of Full Names

| | Masculine | | | | Feminine | | |
|---|---|---|---|---|---|---|---|
| | Name | Patronymic | Surname | | Name | Patronymic | Surname |
| N | Ива́н | Ива́нович | Ива́нов | N | Ве́ра | Ива́новна | Ива́нова |
| A | Ива́на | Ива́новича | Ива́нова | A | Ве́ру | Ива́новну | Ива́нову |
| G | Ива́на | Ива́новича | Ива́нова | G | Ве́ры | Ива́новны | Ива́новой |
| P | Ива́не | Ива́новиче | Ива́нове | P | Ве́ре | Ива́новне | Ива́новой |
| N | Андре́й | Семёнович | Луки́н | N | Любо́вь | Семёновна | Лукина́ |
| A | Андре́я | Семёновича | Лукина́ | A | Любо́вь | Семёновну | Лукину́ |
| G | Андре́я | Семёновича | Лукина́ | G | Любви́ | Семёновны | Лукино́й |
| P | Андре́е | Семёновиче | Лукине́ | P | Любви́ | Семёновне | Лукино́й |
| N | Лёв | Льво́вич | Шми́т | N | О́льга | Льво́вна | Шми́т |
| A | Льва́ | Льво́вича | Шми́та | A | О́льгу | Льво́вну | Шми́т |
| G | Льва́ | Льво́вича | Шми́та | G | О́льги | Льво́вны | Шми́т |
| P | Льве́ | Льво́виче | Шми́те | P | О́льге | Льво́вне | Шми́т |
| N | Юрий | Андре́ёвич | Жива́го | N | Ната́лия | Андре́ёвна | Жива́го |
| A | Юрия | Андре́ёвича | Жива́го | A | Ната́лию | Андре́ёвну | Жива́го |
| G | Юрия | Андре́ёвича | Жива́го | G | Ната́лии | Андре́ёвны | Жива́го |
| P | Юрии | Андре́ёвиче | Жива́го | P | Ната́лии | Андре́ёвне | Жива́го |

When the patronymics are used alone (which is rare), they are pronounced as spelled, but when used in conjunction with the *и́мя* they normally are shortened by one syllable. The full pronunciation occurs only in a formal, almost artificial style of speaking, but many Russians are scarcely aware of the fact that they omit a syllable or make further reductions in pronouncing a patronymic, and the short forms are rarely written. Soviet authorities on pronunciation for radio and stage agree that the shortening is good usage. The foreign student is best advised to use the full spelling forms until he has had a great deal of experience in hearing conversational Russian. Details on the shortened forms are given in Appendix I, § 17.9.

**7.11**  Patronymics, like Christian names, are ordinary nouns and have the same regular noun endings.

**7.2**  *Russian surnames* frequently have the suffix **-ов (-ёв)** in the masculine and **-ова (-ёва)** in the feminine: Петро́в, Петро́ва; Соловьёв, Соловьёва; Турге́нёв, Турге́нёва; Семёнов, Семёнова.
  Another common suffix is **-ин** (m), **-ина** (f): Пу́шкин, Пу́шкина.

*Masculine surnames* in **-ов** and **-ин** follow the normal masculine animate noun declension for all cases so far discussed. If the suffix **-ин** is stressed, the case-ending will be stressed throughout: Бороди́н, Бороди́на́, о Бороди́не́.

*Feminine surnames* in **-ина** and **-ова** have the *pronominal* declension, like *э́та*. If the masculine ends in stressed **-и́н**, the feminine is **-ина́** and the stress remains on the ending throughout. For example:

| Nom. | Пётро́ва | Пу́шкина | Бороди́на́ |
| Acc. | Пётро́ву | Пу́шкину | Бороди́ну́ |
| Gen./Prep. | Пётро́вой | Пу́шкиной | Бороди́но́й |

Other surnames (excepting those in **-ий** or **-ой**, which will be treated later) have no feminine forms. Names ending in a consonant are declined like other masculine animate nouns if they refer to men, but do not change form at all when referring to women. Surnames ending in a vowel are normally indeclinable:

| господи́н Бра́ун, госпожа́ Бра́ун | Mr. Brown, Mrs. Brown |
| Вы зна́ете господи́на Бра́уна? | Do you know Mr. Brown? |
| госпожу́ Бра́уна? | Mrs. Brown? |
| у господи́на Бра́уна | at Mr. Brown's |
| у госпожи́ Бра́ун | at Mrs. Brown's |
| у профе́ссора Дурново́ | at Prof. Durnovo's |

**8.** The nouns **господи́н** 'gentleman, master' and **госпожа́** 'lady, mistress' may be used with the surname: *господи́н Пётро́в* Mr. Petrov, *госпожа́ Пётро́ва* Mrs. or Miss Petrov. In the USSR these terms are mostly employed for referring to foreigners, but they are regularly used by Russian-speakers elsewhere.

In the USSR the term **граждани́н** 'citizen' and the feminine **гражда́нка** are used instead. In place of either may stand **това́рищ** 'comrade': *това́рищ Пётро́в* Comrade Petrov; *това́рищ Пётро́ва* Comrade Petrov (female). **Това́рищ** may occur with a title: *това́рищ до́ктор, това́рищ учи́тельница.*

**9.** The feminine nouns **мать** 'mother' and **дочь** 'daughter' are irregular: in cases other than the nominative and accusative they add **-ер-** before the suffixes of the *third* declension:

| Nom. | мать | дочь | (дверь) |
| Acc. | мать | дочь | (дверь) |
| Gen. | ма́тери | до́чери | (две́ри) |
| Prep. | ма́тери | до́чери | (две́ри) |

**10.**   **Имя** *ím<sup>ь</sup>a* 'Christian name' is an irregular noun:

N-A и́мя, Gen.-Prep. и́мёни.

**11.**   In speech, **не́ту** sometimes replaces **не́т** ('there is not') as a slightly more emphatic form. This colloquial form is rarely written.

**12.**   *A note on word-order.* Because of the distinctive grammatical forms of most Russian words, the order in which they occur in a sentence may frequently be varied.

For example, the three words сестра́, ви́дит, and учи́теля may be combined in all of the six mathematically possible arrangements and still the fundamental meaning remains "Sister sees the teacher." To an English-speaking person, accustomed to the relatively rigid order of his native language, the variations in Russian word-order may seem always to be thus utterly free, limited only by mathematical possibility. As a matter of fact, however, every type of sentence has one pattern which is semantically neutral. Any departure from the basic order is necessarily accompanied by a greater or lesser change in the emphasis, in the relative importance of the semantic units. Thus, сестра́ учи́теля ви́дит stresses the verb, implying that there might be some question about it; she *sees*, not hears or asks or strikes. Учи́теля сестра́ ви́дит stresses the direct object, emphasizing that it is the teacher and not someone else whom sister sees.

For this type of sentence the neutral statement has the order subject-verb-object: сестра́ ви́дит учи́теля. This order becomes obligatory when the words have forms which may be ambiguous: До́чь ви́дит ма́ть means only "The daughter sees the mother", and Ма́ть ви́дит до́чь "The mother sees the daughter."

If the object is a pronoun, the neutral order is subject-object-verb: сестра́ ёго́ ви́дит; я э́то зна́л.

Modifiers that have gender-case agreement (i.e. pronouns like мо́й and э́тот, and adjectives, which will be treated in Lesson XII and after) normally precede the word they modify: моя́ кни́га. Modifiers which do not agree usually follow (e.g. the genitive of possession, cf. III 10; ёго́, её and и́х are exceptions to this rule).

The neutral positions of adverbs within a sentence are too varied to treat at this point. Adverbs of manner usually go between subject and verb, e.g. Óн хорошо́ говори́т.

The position of the negative particle **не** should be noticed. For example, the neutral *Я́ не говори́л об э́том* "I didn't speak of that" is opposed to *Не я́ говори́л об э́том* "It was not I [but someone else] who spoke of it", and *Я́ говори́л не об э́том* "It was not that [but something else] I was talking about". You will find that the Russian distinguishes between Óн не рабо́таёт хорошо́ "He doesn't work well", where the whole complex "works-well" is negated, and Óн рабо́таёт нехорошо́, negating only the adverb "well": "He works [—yes, but] not well." There are sentences where this type of distinction can be of great importance.

The beginner should stick to the neutral, unemphatic patterns of word-order when speaking or writing Russian. But he must be alert to the fact that Russians will use far more variety and he should try to observe just what shades of emphasis are conveyed by the variations. While it is only after a great deal of experience that he will be able to handle these subtleties actively, he should not find it difficult to learn to recognize them.

13.   In a printed text, Russian may use *italics* or **boldface** to show special emphasis, very much as in English books. A far more common device, however, and one which the English reader is likely to overlook, is s p a c i n g, where the individual letters of a word are separated by small spaces. E.g.

| | |
|---|---|
| Э́то м о я́ кни́га. | This is *my* book. |
| Э́то Ива́н Пётро́вич, не Ива́н Льво́вич. | It's Ivan *Petrovich*, not Ivan *L'vovich*. |

## EXERCISES

**A.**   Be prepared to say in Russian all possible combinations of:

1. я, ты, вы, он, она́, мы́, они́, кто́ } { live(s)/lived / work(s)/worked } у { ма́ть, отéц, до́ктор, Вéра Ива́новна, бра́т, Пётр Петро́вич, сестра́, меха́ник, госпожа́ Семёнова, Бороди́н, Бородина́, э́та да́ма, сосéд[ка] }

2. I, you, he, she, they, who, mother, daughter, the professor, Marija } { has/have / had } a { сестра́, отéц, ма́ть, бра́т, до́чь, сы́н, газéта, каранда́ш, библиотéка, письмо́, са́д, ко́мната, до́м, перо́, учи́тель[ница], ба́нк, сосéд[ка]. }

3. Repeat no. 2 in the negative.

4. учи́тель[ница], еë отéц, я, и́х ма́ть, госпожа́ Ту́мина, мы́, они́ } { is/are / were } speaking about { э́то, музéй, они́, кто́-то, моя́ жёна́; са́д мое́й жёны́; его́ бра́т; Росси́я, на́ша зада́ча, о́н; то́ окно́; ты́, э́та доска́, и́х профéссор, она́, това́рищ Бороди́н, Любо́вь, мы́. }

5. I (you, he, she, we, they) see(s)/saw — (substitute items at end of 2 and 5).

6. Repeat no. 5 in the negative.

7. Это сочине́ниё Пу́шкина.

Мы́ чита́ём Пу́шкина.

Он писа́л о Пу́шкине.

This is a work by Pushkin [of Pushkin's].

We are reading Pushkin.

He has written about Pushkin.

7a. Repeat the three sentences in 7, using the full name Алекса́ндр Серге́ёвич Пу́шкин.

7b. Repeat, substituting the names Анто́н Па́влович Че́хов, Бори́с Леони́дович Пастерна́к, Никола́й Васи́льёвич Го́голь, Михаи́л Алекса́ндрович Шо́лохов, А́нна Андре́ёвна Ахма́това, Мари́на Ива́новна Цвета́ёва, Зинаи́да Никола́ёвна Ги́ппиус.

**B.** Read and translate:

1. У ва́с е́сть перо́? Да́, у меня́ е́сть перо́. Во́т оно́.  2. У сёстры́ И́горя е́сть до́м? Не́т, у ёго́ сёстры́ не́т до́ма, но́ у нёго́ е́сть до́м. 3. У неё е́сть и ба́нк и фа́брика.  4. У её ма́тери живёт профе́ссор Ива́нов.  5. Этот меха́ник рабо́тал у и́х отца́.  6. У ни́х не́ было са́да.  7. Когда́ вы́ доста́ли э́ту ка́рту университе́та?  8. У тебя́ ли была́ моя́ кни́га?  9. И́х не́ было до́ма вчера́.  10. Почёму́ вы́ не чита́ли э́той кни́ги? Я́ забы́л, но́ она́ стои́т у меня́ на столе́.  11. Она́ не напи́шёт письма́ сего́дня. У неё не́т ни пера́ ни карандаша́.  12. Я́ хорошо́ зна́ла Татья́ну Миха́йловну Пётро́ву в Крыму́. Она́ жила́ у на́шей сосе́дки, Татья́ны Ива́новны Ива́новой.  13. Я́ никогда́ не встреча́л граждани́на Воробьёва. Он не́ жил в на́шём го́роде.

14. Вы́ бу́дёте у до́ктора Моро́зова сего́дня? Не́т, я́ бу́ду и́ли на фа́брике и́ли у ма́тери.  15. Ма́ть зна́ёт Алексе́я Алекса́ндровича. Он рабо́тал у её отца́.  16. У э́той да́мы е́сть ко́мната у госпожи́ Фёдоровой.  17. Кто́ взя́л моё сочине́ниё? Я́ не бра́л.  18. В на́шём кла́ссе сего́дня не́ было учи́тельницы.  19. Любо́вь Льво́вна бу́дёт жи́ть в дере́вне, и мы́ бу́дём её встреча́ть у госпожи́ Джо́нз.  20. У ва́с в университе́те е́сть библиоте́ка?  21. Ни у меня́ ни у Людми́лы Серге́ёвны не́ было платка́.  22. Я́ не зна́ю э́того сло́ва, и у меня́ ту́т не́т словаря́. —Спроси́те у А́нны Пётро́вны.  23. У Дми́трия Юрье́вича в ко́мнате виси́т календа́рь на стене́ у шка́фа.  24. На календаре́ карти́на. Что́ на карти́не? На карти́не мы́ ви́дим ле́с.  25. Кто́ написа́л э́то сло́во на доске́?

**C.** For written and/or oral translation into Russian:

1. This lady's husband has a forest on the Don, a bank in the city, and a house in the village. 2. Comrade Ptáshin has a room at the university. 3. Anna Borísovna is not at home. 4. Comrade (f) Petrov has

the magazine. She took it from Vera Pavlovna. 5. Ivan Ivanovich will not be home tomorrow, he will be sitting in the library, in Prof. Ivanov's room. 6. We have both a university and a museum in our town, but you have neither a university nor a museum. 7. He has a daughter and she has a son. 8. Their son lives with (= at) our neighbor, Sergej Solov'ëv. 9. My wife, Nadezhda, works with Mr. Brown in the museum. 10. Is that the building where Citizen Jones and Citizeness Morozov used to work? Yes, they worked in that building. 11. Andrej is standing by the window and writing the assignment on the board. 12. I don't remember; ask comrade Tamara Borodiná, she knows. 13. Boris Nikolaevich, please read her article once more. 14. Did you see anything in the forest yesterday, Ol'ga? No, I didn't see anything. 15. Do not take the letter, Oleg, mother hasn't read it.

16. Do you receive letters in the country, Mr. Petrov? 17. Leonid, did you meet anyone at the factory today? Yes, I met Alekséj Sergéevich Borodín and Ekaterína Borísovna Ivánov. 18. I don't see my newspaper, did someone [III 11.1] take it? Igor', why don't you (sg) read your own newspaper? 19. Nina Aleksandrovna and her husband will live in the Crimea, in Jalta. 20. Mikhail, don't close that window, close this one [omit 'one' in R.]! 21. What will you be doing tomorrow? I'll be solving a problem either at home or at my comrade's. 22. Excuse me, comrade, I have forgotten your name. 23. Does the teacher always open that window? 24. Has your mother ever been in Russia? No, neither she nor father have been there. 25. Fine! I'll do it right away. 26. That man has lived both at the doctor's and the mechanic's. 27. Why weren't you in class today? 28. Who has my notebook? 29. Say something in Russian. Why are you speaking English? 30. Tat'jana wasn't home yesterday or [ни] today, but she will be home tomorrow.

**D.** For oral and/or written translation into Russian:

1. This word isn't in my dictionary, is it in yours? 2. The key wasn't in my pocket. It was on the floor by the wardrobe. 3. Igor' has my key. He will open the door. 4. His father, Pëtr Ivanovich, has his dictionary. 5. There's a textbook there on the wardrobe. My textbook is here on the shelf. 6. I'll write that word down; I have a notebook and pencil in my bag. 7. Her handkerchief is on a shelf in that wardrobe in the corner, and her sister's pocketbook is there on the table. 8. Have you a lamp in your room, Aleksej Petrovich? There was no lamp there yesterday, but I obtained a lamp today. 9. The key is there on the dictionary, don't you see it? 10. Repeat this exercise once more.

## СЛОВАРЬ

| | |
|---|---|
| ба́нк | bank |
| библиоте́ка | library |
| господи́н | Mr., master, gentleman |
| госпожа́ | Mrs., Miss, mistress |
| до́ктор | doctor |
| до́чь (§ 9) | daughter |
| е́сть (§ 1) | there is |
| и́ли … и́ли | either…or |
| и́мя (neuter, § 10) | Christian name |
| календа́рь (m, *E*) | calendar |
| карма́н | pocket |
| клю́ч (*E*, p. 351 § 4) | key |
| ма́ть (§ 9) | mother |
| меха́ник | mechanic |
| не́т (+ Gen.; § 1.1) | there is not |
| о́тчество | patronymic |
| плато́к (G платка́) | handkerchief |

| | |
|---|---|
| рука́ | hand, arm |
| (Acc. ру́ку, cf. III 5.2) | |
| слова́рь (m, *E*) | dictionary, vocabulary |
| сло́во | word |
| сосе́д | neighbor (m) |
| сосе́дка | neighbor (f) |
| сы́н | son |
| това́рищ | comrade |
| ту́т | there (§ 6) |
| у (prep. + Gen.) | at, by (§§ 3, 5) |
| университе́т | university |
| фами́лия | surname |
| челове́к | man, human being |
| шка́ф | wardrobe, standing cupboard |
| [в, на шкафу́] | |

Some common Russian feminine names (NB, read Appendix II carefully):

| | | | | | | |
|---|---|---|---|---|---|---|
| А́нна | Еле́на | Зинаи́да | Анаста́сия | Людми́ла | Ду́ня | А́ся |
| Ли́за | Ири́на | Катери́на | Валенти́на | Ната́лия | Зо́я | Ра́я |
| Ни́на | Мари́я | Ксе́ния | Екатери́на | Тама́ра | Ма́ша | Же́ня |
| | Софи́я | Любо́вь [3rd decl.] | Елизаве́та | Татья́на | Ва́ря | Ка́тя |

Some common Russian masculine names:

| | | |
|---|---|---|
| Алекса́ндр | Васи́лий | И́горь |
| Андре́й | Влади́мир | Макси́м |
| Анто́н | Вячесла́в | Михаи́л |
| Арсе́ний | Дми́трий | Сёмён |
| Бори́с | Евге́ний | Фёдор |

| | |
|---|---|
| Куда́ вы́ идёте? | Where are you going? |
| Мы́ идём на фа́брику, где́ рабо́таем. | We are going to the factory where we work. |
| Вы́ зна́ете, куда́ о́н идёт? | Do you know where he is going? |
| Обыкнове́нно мы́ туда́ е́здим на автомоби́ле. | Usually we go there by automobile. |
| Куда́ вы́ е́дете? | Where are you going? |
| Я́ тепе́рь е́ду в ба́нк, а пото́м пря́мо на конце́рт. | I am going to the bank now, and then straight to the concert. |
| Серге́й Алексе́ёвич бу́дет говори́ть на собра́нии. | Sergej Alekseevich will speak at the meeting. |
| Идёмте в теа́тр! | Let's go to the theater. |
| Она́ ре́дко ходи́ла в то́т магази́н, но́ сего́дня она́ туда́ пошла́. | She seldom went to that store, but today she went there. |
| Мы́ реши́ли пойти́ в теа́тр сего́дня. | We have decided to go to the theater today. |
| Я́ ча́сто е́зжу в дере́вню. | I often go to the country. |
| Вы́ е́здите ча́сто в дере́вню? | Do you go to the country often? |
| Зна́ете ли вы́, е́здит ли о́н туда́? | Do you know whether he goes there often? |
| Сего́дня сестра́ е́дет то́же. | Today sister is going too. |
| Они́ уже́ пое́хали домо́й. | They've already gone home. |
| Вчера́, когда́ мы́ шли́ в рестора́н, мы́ уви́дели Ве́ру Ива́новну Семёнову. | Yesterday when we were on our way to the restaurant we saw Vera Ivanovna Semënov. |
| Неси́те мою́ кни́гу! | Carry my book! |
| Пу́сть кто́-нибудь несёт её кни́гу! | Let someone carry her book! |
| Начнём. Дава́йте чита́ть. | Let's begin. Let's read. |
| О́н шёл куда́-то, когда́ мы́ его́ встре́тили. | He was on his way somewhere when we met him. |
| Пойдёмте куда́-нибудь! | Let's go somewhere! |

| | |
|---|---|
| Óн никуда́ не ходи́л. | He didn't go anywhere. |
| Óн не отвеча́л на мóй вопрóс. | He didn't answer my question. |

---

**1.** *The "going-verbs".* In certain Russian verbs indicating locomotion, the imperfective aspect is represented by two sets of forms: one is called the *determined* aspect, the other the *non-determined.* Besides this there is the normal perfective, which is *not* subdivided. The *determined aspect* (D) denotes that the action is viewed as a whole, as an undivided unit, usually an action carried out at one time and in one direction. The *non-determined aspect* (ND) does not imply any such quality of the action. For example:

**ходи́ть хо́дят (ND) — идти́ иду́т (D) :: пойти́ пойду́т (P)**

| | |
|---|---|
| *a.* Я иду́ в шко́лу. | I am on the way to school. |
| *b.* Она́ шла́ в шко́лу, когда́ мы её встре́тили. | She was on the way to school when we met her. |
| *c.* Я хожу́ в шко́лу. | I go to school. |
| Я хожу́ в э́ту шко́лу. | I attend this school. |
| *d.* Она́ ходи́ла в шко́лу. | She went to school. |
| Она́ ходи́ла в шко́лу в Росси́и. | She attended school in Russia. |
| *e.* Óн пошёл в шко́лу. | He went to school. He set out for school. |

In examples *a* and *b*, the use of the determined verb **идти́** (see below for forms) shows that the action is specific: one single trip in one direction is envisaged. Examples *c* and *d* illustrate the ND **ходи́ть**: the action is not one, but more than one, and hence normally repeated or habitual.

(On *e*, the perfective, see sections 3.2 and 4, below.)

**1.1** The past tense of **идти́** is irregular: **шёл** (m), **шло́** (n), **шла́** (f), **шли́** (pl). Similarly **пойти́**: **пошёл, пошло́, пошла́, пошли́.**

The infinitive is often spelled *итти́.*

**1.2** The verb-complex **éздить éздят (ND) — éхать éдут (D) :: поéхать поéдут (P)** specifies 'to ride, be conveyed', and must be carefully distinguished from the **ходи́ть** verb-complex, whose meaning is 'to go on foot or under one's own power'. When translating such a sentence as "He went to town" into Russian, one must decide whether the locomotion was accomplished by vehicle or not — Russian simply does not have a general verb 'go'. Therefore either Óн **поéхал** *or* Óн **пошёл** в го́род.

A sentence like *Он пошёл в Париж* 'He went to Paris' automatically includes the information that the person set out from someplace in France or Europe from which a journey to Paris on foot is possible.

**1.201**  The imperative of both **éхать** and **поéхать** is **поезжáй|те|**.

**1.21**  If a clear specification of walking is desired, the adverb **пешкóм** 'afoot' may be used with ходи́ть-идти́-пойти́.

**1.3**  Note further that the directional distinction of English *come* vs. *go* is not insisted on by the Russian. While *come* can be expressed by a separate verb (as will be explained in XVI), this emphasis is not necessary:

| | |
|---|---|
| Вóт идёт Ивáн Пётрóвич. | Here comes Ivan Petrovich. |
| Вóт Пётр идёт в шкóлу. | { There's Peter going to school.<br>{ There goes Peter to school. |

**2.**  The verb 'to carry' also has determined/non-determined forms:

**носи́ть нóсят (ND) — нести́ несу́т (D) :: понести́ понесу́т (P)**
**Нести́** and **понести́** have the past forms **(по)нёс, (по)неслá, (по)несли́**. See § 5, below.

**3.1**  The present determined (**иду́т, éдут, несу́т**) is the normal way to express the future of such verbs, being in this something like the "present perfective" of other verbs. It is only the context which shows that a future action is referred to: e.g. Мы́ éдем *зáвтра* 'We're going tomorrow.'

**3.2**  The prefixed perfective forms (**пойду́т, поéдут, понесу́т**) have a somewhat different meaning: they focus on the future *start* of the action:

Мы́ поéдём зáвтра.                  We'll set out tomorrow.

This meaning of inceptiveness is in the prefix: the inherent perfectiveness of the verb shows that the "act of starting to go (carry, etc.)" is viewed as certain of completion.

As a practical rule, you can translate with D when English uses a present with an adverb that explicitly denotes future (e. g. 'tomorrow') and with P when English has a clear future using 'will/shall'.

**3.3**  Both ND and D infinitives may be used with the forms of **бу́дут** to indicate futures which have the same fundamental aspectual meaning as the present and past usages:

| | |
|---|---|
| Я́ бу́ду идти́ мéдленно. | I will be walking slowly (on this specific occasion). |
| Я́ бу́ду éздить на фáбрику на автомоби́ле. | I will go (repeatedly) to the factory by car. |

**4.**  Note that the past *non*-determined is normally used for a round-trip:

Онá éздила в гóрод.                  She went to town (and came back).

The determined form (**éxaла**) is impossible in this meaning, for it *specifies* one trip *in one direction*. The perfective **поéхала** *specifies* the departure, without saying what happens next. The ND **éздила** does not *specify* a round-trip, and, since it is imperfective, it does not specify any completion of activity, but unless the context adds some specification, such a sentence as the example here will regularly *be interpreted as* denoting a complete round trip.

**5.** Verbs whose infinitives end in **-ти** or in **-сть**, **-зть** or **-чь** usually form their past tenses from the *present* stem, which ends in a consonant. A stem-final **т** or **д** is lost before the **-л** of the past-tense suffix: клад-ýт, клá-л, клá-ла. Any other stem-final consonant is retained, but the **-л** of the suffix is lost in the masculine form: нёс-ýт, нёс, нёс-лá.

**6.1** The first person plural of a perfective verb (or of a *determined* "going-verb"), if pronounced with the intonation of a command, expresses an exhortation in which the speaker includes himself:

| | |
|---|---|
| Éдём! Пойдём! | Let's go. |
| Закрóем окнó! | Let's close the window. |

This form is the only one which can be used for a person addressed as **ты**, that is, when the implied "we" means **я + ты**.

To *specify* more than one person, or a single person addressed as **вы**, the suffix **-те** may be added: éдёмте, пойдёмте, закрóемте. Решúмте эту задáчу. — Let's solve this problem.

The addition of **давáй**, **давáйте** (literally, 'give') softens the command somewhat: давáй закрóем (я + ты), давáйте поéдём (я + вы).

**6.2** With imperfective verbs, exhortations are expressed only by means of **давáй**, **давáйте** *plus* **infinitive:**

| | | |
|---|---|---|
| Давáй читáть! | Let's[1] read. | (ты + я) |
| Давáйте рабóтать! | Let's work. | (вы + я) |

**7.** Third person imperatives are expressed by **пýсть** (or its exact equivalent **пускáй**) plus the regular 3rd person form of imperfective present (D or ND) or perfective future.

| | |
|---|---|
| Я не пойдý, пýсть идýт они! | I won't go; let[1] them go. |
| Пýсть ктó-нибудь открóет окнó! | Somebody open the window! Let someone[2] open the window! |

---

[1] Note that this 'let' in English does not mean 'permit', but only expresses an exhortation that someone do something.

[2] **-нибудь** here because there is *choice* (cf. III 11.1) among all the people who can possibly perform the action.

**8.** Certain Russian prepositions may be used with more than one case and consequent differences of meaning. Thus **в** and **на** with the prepositional mean 'in, on', but with the accusative they mean 'in*to*, on*to*': see the table below.

| | *prepositional* case = **location** | *accusative* case = **motion** |
|---|---|---|
| **в** | в го́роде        '*in* the city'<br>Она́ жила́ в го́роде.<br>       She lived in town.<br>в шко́ле        '*in* school'<br>Мы́ бы́ли в шко́ле.<br>       We were in (the) school. | в го́род        '*into* the city'<br>Она́ пое́хала в го́род.<br>       She went to town (riding).<br>в шко́лу        '(*in*)*to* school'<br>Мы́ его́ понесли́ в шко́лу.<br>       We carried him to the school. |
| **на** | **на** столе́        '*on* the table'<br>Ва́ша кни́га на столе́.<br>       Your book is on the table.<br>**на** фа́брике    '*at* the factory'<br>Он рабо́таёт на фа́брике.<br>       He works at a factory. | **на** сто́л        '*onto* the table'<br>Я́ положи́л кни́гу на сто́л.<br>       I put the book on the table.<br>**на** фа́брику    '*to* the factory'<br>Он пошёл на фа́брику.<br>       He's gone to the factory. |

**8.1** This distinction of rest ("place where") versus motion ("place to which") exists also in adverbs:

| where? in what place? | где́ | — | куда́ | whither? to what place? |
|---|---|---|---|---|
| there, in that place | та́м | — | туда́ | thither, to that place |
| here, in this place | здесь | — | сюда́ | hither, to this place |
| at home | до́ма | — | домо́й | home, to home |

Also: где́-нибудь — куда́-нибудь; где́-то — куда́-то; нигде́ — никуда́.

**9.0** Note that both the prepositions **в** and **на** may be translated in English by *in, into, to, at*. The general meaning of **в** is *at* (or, with Acc., *to*) *a position within, inside*; while **на** means *on* (or, with Acc., *to*) *a position on the top, surface of* — e.g. в ко́мнате, but **на** столе́. However with a number of nouns denoting gathering-place or working-place or gathering, Russian regularly uses **на**: **на** фа́брике, ста́нции, конце́рте, собра́нии, et al. Since this general statement does not consititute a clear rule, such cases will be noted in the vocabularies.

**9.1** Do not confuse **в** and **на** with **у** just because the English equivalents overlap. Reread VI 3 (defining **у**) and study the following phrases:

| в магази́не | at/in the store | у магази́на | by/near the store |
|---|---|---|---|
| в университе́те | at/in the university | у университе́та | by/near the university |

| в шко́ле | at/in (the) school | у шко́лы | by/near the school |
|---|---|---|---|
| у доски́ | at/by the board | у окна́ | at/by the window |
| у стола́ | by/near the table | у отца́ | at father's |
| в столе́ | in the table | в отце́ | inside father |
| на столе́ | on the table | на отце́ | on father |

**10.** Уже́ 'already' (уже́ не 'no longer') implies change, a different state of affairs, while ещё 'still' (ещё не 'not yet') *specifies* a lack of change:

Он уже́ рабо́таёт.                He's already working (≈ he started).
Он уже́ не рабо́таёт.            He's no longer working (≈ he stopped).
Он ещё рабо́таёт.                He's still working.
Он ещё не рабо́таёт.            He's not yet (= still not) working.  } (no change)

## EXERCISES

**A.**   Be prepared to read aloud in Russian and to translate:

Вчера́, когда́ я шёл в го́род, меня́ уви́дел профе́ссор Лео́нов. — Здра́вствуйте, Ива́н Пётро́вич! сказа́л он. — Где́ вы? Я ва́с никогда́ нигде́ не встреча́ю. — Здра́вствуйте, Никола́й Алекса́ндрыч, сказа́л я. — Вы́ не зна́ете? Мы́ тепе́рь не живём здесь в го́роде. — Не́т, я не зна́л. Я ду́мал, что вы́ ещё у Ни́ны Алексе́евны. — Я на́чал рабо́тать на на́шей фа́брике в дере́вне. Мы́ живём у ма́тери в лесу́. У неё та́м есть до́м. Бра́т ча́сто е́здит сюда́. Он пи́шет кни́гу. Обыкнове́нно он рабо́таёт в музе́е. Он чита́ёт та́м в библиоте́ке. Я тепе́рь туда́ иду́, а пото́м мы́ пойдём вме́сте в клу́б. В клу́бе бу́дёт собра́ние. Пожа́луйста, пойди́те и вы́! — Спаси́бо, отве́тил профе́ссор, но́ я иду́ в ба́нк, а пото́м е́ду пря́мо домо́й. — Ну́, до свида́ния, сказа́л я. — До свида́ния, отве́тил Никола́й Алекса́ндрович, всего́ лу́чшего!

**B.**   Using all possible personal pronouns as subject, and both "riding" and "afoot" verbs for *go*, translate the various possible combinations below:

1. Now I am going (D)
2. I usually go (ND)
3. Tomorrow I shall go (P)
4. Tomorrow I shall go (ND) often
5. Yesterday I was going (D)
6. Yesterday I went (P)
7. I used to go (ND)

to school, to that bank, to the garden, to our club, to the meeting, to Jalta, to that factory, to the station, to the Crimea, to town, to the store, there, to the library, to the country, to the theater, somewhere, home, to his restaurant, to the forest, to the concert, to your class.

**C.** 1. Мо́й сосе́д идёт в ба́нк. 2. У нёго́ е́сть автомоби́ль, но́ я́ ду́маю, что о́н всегда́ хо́дит пешко́м. 3. Его́ до́чь ча́сто е́здит в дере́вню. 4. Вчера́ я́ её ви́дел, когда́ она́ е́хала на ста́нцию. 5. Вы́ реши́ли ва́шу зада́чу? 6. Мы́ ходи́ли в го́род на собра́ниё. 7. Я́ не рабо́тал сего́дня, но пошёл в дере́вню. 8. Моя́ ма́ть пое́хала в дере́вню. Я́ её встре́тил та́м, у бра́та в саду́. 9. Почёму́ о́н всёгда́ но́сит кни́гу? 10. Иди́те сюда́, пожа́луйста! 11. Она́ начала́ чита́ть э́ту кни́гу. 12. Она́ начина́ла чита́ть по-ру́сски. 13. Моя́ сёстра́ уже́ хо́дит в шко́лу и начина́ёт чита́ть и писа́ть. 14. Я́ на́чал писа́ть письмо́. 15. О́н за́втра начнёт рабо́тать у до́чери сосе́дки. 16. На че́й вопро́с вы́ отве́тите? 17. Куда́ о́н шёл? Пу́сть о́н ска́жёт. 18. Она́ е́хала домо́й. 19. Пу́сть кто́-нибудь закро́ёт две́рь. 20. Я́ не поняла́ ва́шёго отве́та; где́ сиди́т ма́ть?

**D.** For written and/or oral translation into Russian:

1. Our neighbor works at that store. She usually goes to the store by auto, but today she walked to the store. 2. Today I will be reading in the library at the university. I will walk to the library. 3. The doctor has a car. He usually rides to town. There he goes (riding). 4a. Where've you been? Where were you going (walking) when I saw you at the station? 4b. I have been at a meeting in the museum and I was going to the club. 5. Let's work at home today. 6. At the club I met Dmitrij Ivanovich and we drove home. 7. I put your newspaper on the table. Do you see it there? 8. I put your magazine there. Do you see it there on the table? 9. We rarely go to that restaurant. We are all going there together now. 10. Let's walk to town at once. 11. I often go to the country. 12. He's gone somewhere (afoot), I don't know where. 13. She has started in her car to someplace in town, I don't know where. 14. Let her answer my question! 15. Someone answer his question, I don't know the answer. 16a. He usually goes to the bank, then to the club, then to a restaurant, and then straight home. 16b. I often meet Sergej Ivanovich in the bank or in the club or in the restaurant, but today I didn't see him. He usually sits by the window. 17. Go straight home! (a. riding, b. on foot). 18. Let's carry this table and this chair into that room. 19. What is he carrying? I don't know, I can't see (transl. 'don't see'). 20. Please put the book and the magazine on that chair. 21. Are you going to the theater? Let's go together! 22. He said it[1] at the meeting yesterday and he will say it again at the meeting today. 23. She was speaking there yesterday and she will be speaking here at your school tomorrow. 24. Do you go to the university? No, I don't go anywhere. 25. Let's do it at once.

---

[1] When "it" has no clear antecedent, use *э́то*.

## СЛОВАРЬ

| | | | |
|---|---|---|---|
| автомоби́ль | automobile | отве́т | answer |
|   на автомоби́ле | by auto | пешко́м | on foot, afoot |
| вопро́с | question | пото́м | then, afterwards |
| дава́й[те] | see § 6 | пря́мо | directly, straight |
| домо́й | home(wards) | пу́сть (пуска́й) | let (§ 7) |
| клу́б | club | ре́дко | rarely, seldom |
| конце́рт | concert | рестора́н | restaurant |
|   на конце́рте | at (the) concert | собра́ниё | meeting |
| куда́ | where, to where, whither |   на собра́нии | at (the) meeting |
|   куда́-нибудь, куда́-то | (cf. III 11) | ста́нция | station |
| магази́н | store |   на ста́нции | at (the) station |
| никуда́ (+ не, cf. II 5.3) | to nowhere | сюда́ | here, to here, hither |
| | | теа́тр | theater |
| ну́ | well | туда́ | there, to there, thither |
| обыкнове́нно | usually | шко́ла | school |

---

| | | | |
|---|---|---|---|
| ду́мать ду́мают I <br> поду́мать поду́мают P | } think | начина́ть начина́ют I <br> нача́ть начну́т P <br>   past на́чал, на́чало, <br>   на́чали; начала́ | } begin |
| кла́сть кладу́т I <br>   past кла́л, кла́ло, <br>   кла́ла, кла́ли <br> положи́ть поло́жат P | } put | отвеча́ть/отве́тить на вопро́с <br> answer a question | |

| NON-DETERMINED | DETERMINED | PERFECTIVE | |
|---|---|---|---|
| ходи́ть хо́дят | идти́ иду́т | пойти́ пойду́т | go afoot § 1.1 |
| е́здить е́здят | е́хать е́дут | пое́хать пое́дут | ride, go § 1.201 |
| носи́ть но́сят | нёсти́ нёсу́т | понёсти́ понёсу́т | carry |
| IMPERFECTIVE | | PERFECTIVE | |

# LESSON VIII

У вас есть романы?  
      газеты?  
      книги?  

Do you have any novels?  
      newspapers?  
      books?  

Нет, у меня нет романов.  
      газет.  
      книг.  

No, I have no novels.  
      newspapers.  
      books.  

Я читаю эти романы.  
      газеты.  
      книги.  

I'm reading these novels.  
      newspapers.  
      books.  

Мы читали о ваших романах во всех газетах.  

We read about your novels in all the papers.  

У вас есть товарищи?  
      автомобили?  
      карандаши?  

Do you have any comrades?  
      automobiles?  
      pencils?  

Нет, у меня нет товарищей.  
      автомобилей.  
      карандашей.  

No, I have no comrades.  
      automobiles.  
      pencils.  

Петровы поехали в автомобилях ваших товарищей.  

The Petrovs went off in the automobiles of your comrades.  

У окна стояла моя кровать.  

My bed stood by the window.  

Здесь наши кресла, столы и кровати.  

Here are our arm-chairs, tables, and beds.  

Там не было ни кресёл, ни столов, ни кроватей.  

There were neither arm-chairs nor tables nor beds there.  

У Петровых было много комнат.  
      фабрик.  
      идей.  
      фотографий.  

The Petrovs had a lot of rooms.  
      factories.  
      ideas.  
      photographs.  
      [textbook.  

В учебнике мало фраз.  
      упражнений.  
      рассказов.  

There are (too) few sentences in the exercises stories  

Иван герой и его сестра геройня.  

Ivan is a hero and his sister is a heroine.

| | |
|---|---|
| В его расска́зах мно́го геро́ев и геройнь. | In his stories there are many heroes and heroines. |
| Все они́ геро́и и геройни. | All of them are heroes and heroines. |
| Все они́ адвока́ты. | All of them are lawyers. |
| журнали́сты. | journalists. |
| геро́и. | heroes. |
| писа́тели. | writers. |
| Он спроси́л всех адвока́тов. | He asked all the lawyers. |
| журнали́стов. | journalists. |
| геро́ев. | heroes. |
| писа́телей. | writers. |
| Здесь нет адвока́тов. | Here there are no lawyers. |
| журнали́стов. | journalists. |
| геро́ев. | heroes. |
| писа́телей. | writers. |
| Они́ спра́шивают о всех адвока́тах. | They ask about all the lawyers. |
| журнали́стах. | journalists. |
| геро́ях. | heroes. |
| писа́телях. | writers. |
| Они́ все да́мы. | They are all ladies. |
| журнали́стки. | journalists. |
| де́вочки. | little girls. |
| писа́тельницы. | writers. |
| геройни. | heroines. |
| Здесь нет дам. | Here there are no ladies. |
| журнали́сток. | journalists. |
| де́вочёк. | little girls. |
| писа́тельниц. | writers. |
| геройнь. | heroines. |
| Говоря́т о да́мах. | They are talking about ladies. |
| журнали́стках. | journalists |
| де́вочках. | little girls. |
| писа́тельницах | writers. |
| геройнях. | heroines. |
| Куда́ вы несёте | Where are you taking |
| все э́ти кни́ги? | all these books? |
| газе́ты? | papers? |
| карандаши́? | pencils? |

| | |
|---|---|
| В на́шем го́роде не́т музе́ев. | In our town there are no museums. |
|       библиоте́к. | libraries. |
|       лаборато́рий. | laboratories. |
| Вы́ понима́ете все́ упражне́ния? | Do you understand all the exercises? |
| Я не понима́ю все́х упражне́ний. | I do not understand all the exercises. |
| Во́т зда́ния, где́ живу́т студе́нты и студе́нтки. | There are the buildings where the students live. |
| Мно́го студе́нтов и студе́нток рабо́тают в рестора́нах. | Many students work in restaurants. |
| О чьи́х де́вочках говори́ли э́ти студе́нтки? | About whose little girls were these (female) students speaking? |
| За́втра бу́дет собра́ние все́х учите́лей, учи́тельниц и профессоро́в. | Tomorrow will be a meeting of all teachers and professors. |
| Учителя́, учи́тельницы и профессора́ иду́т на собра́ния. | The teachers and professors are on their way to the meetings. |
| Писа́тели и учителя́ пошли́ домо́й. | The writers and teachers went home. |
| Я не встре́тил ни писа́телей ни учителе́й. | I didn't meet any writers or teachers. |
| У на́с у все́х е́сть уче́бники.[1] | We all have textbooks. |
| У на́с е́сть все́ уче́бники. | We have all the textbooks. |

---

## 1. THE PLURAL OF NOUNS

**1.10**  The NOMINATIVE PLURAL has the suffixes *-i* and *-a*.

On the whole, the nominative plural will be in *-i* (spelled и/ы, see below), except that neuters in *-o*/-ё regularly have plurals in *-a*/-я.

NOTE that a number of the very common nouns in Russian have irregularities in their declensional forms, especially in the formation of the plural (compare English *child*, *man*, *wife* ~ child*ren*, m*en*, wi*ves*). This lesson purposely omits discussion of the relatively large number of such words whose singular forms you already know; they will be treated in the next lesson.

[1] Repetition of the preposition is exceptional here.

**1.11** The suffix *-i* is used with all feminine and most masculine nouns: it is spelled **-ы** or **-и**:

(a) Masculines ending in a consonant-letter add **-ы** and feminines in **-a** replace it with **-ы**, *unless the stem ends in* **к, г, х, ш, ж, ч, щ**, in which case the letter **ы** is excluded and **и** must be written (see page 325, §§ 5–7).

(b) A noun ending in the letter **-я, -ь**, or **-й** replaces it with **-и**.

Examples:

(a) диван — дива́ны      ко́мната — ко́мнаты
    па́рк — па́рки       това́рищ — това́рищи

(b) ста́нция — ста́нции     музе́й — музе́и
    автомоби́ль — автомоби́ли    крова́ть — крова́ти

**1.12** *-a* (spelled **-а/-я**) is the regular suffix for neuter nouns; it also occurs in an important group of some 150 masculine nouns.

**-a** is written if the Nom. sg. ends in **-o** or a consonant-letter:

кре́сло — кре́сла       до́м — дома́

**-я** is written if the Nom. sg. ends in **-ё** or **-ь**:

зда́ниё — зда́ния       учи́тель — учителя́

When used with masculines, the suffix *-a* is always stressed. Since there is no way to recognize which masculines take this ending, you must memorize the plural with each of these words. So far we have had only:

до́м — дома́        до́ктор — доктора́
го́род — города́      профе́ссор — профессора́
ле́с — леса́         учи́тель — учителя́

NOTE that while учи́тель belongs to this group, писа́тель does not; учи́тель is exceptional, писа́тель is regular.

**1.20** The GENITIVE PLURAL has the suffixes *-ov*, *-ej*, and zero (i. e. no suffix at all — the bare stem remains).

The most generally valid rule is that the form must be different from the nominative singular. On the whole, if Nom. sg. has an ending, Gen. pl. will have zero-suffix; if Nom. sg. has zero-ending, Gen. pl. will have a suffix: *-ej* is the suffix for feminines and for masculines whose stems end in *š, ž*, or any soft consonant except *j*; *-ov* goes for all other masculines.

These are the regularities (see table p. 97), BUT there are many exceptions, the most important of which will be taken up in Lesson IX.

**1.21**   *-ov* (spelled **-ов** or **-ёв**) is used with masculine nouns ending in *j* or any hard consonant except *š* or *ž*.²

If the Nom. sg. ends in **-й**, the gen. pl. is spelled **-ёв**:

музе́й — музе́ёв [= -ейов]      ге́ний — ге́ниёв [= -ийов]

(ча́й 'tea' — чае́в [= чайо́в] 'kinds of tea')³

(Also, *un*stressed suffix after **ц**: не́мец 'German' Gen. pl. не́мцёв; but stressed отцо́в, cf. p. 326, § 7.1.)

If the Nom. sg. ends in any consonant-letter except **ш, ж, ч, щ, й** (cf. 1.22 below), the Gen. pl. is spelled **-ов**:

дива́н — дива́нов      студе́нт — студе́нтов      до́м — домо́в

**1.22**   *-ej* (spelled **-ей**) is used (1) with third-declension nouns, and (2) with masculines whose stem ends in *š*, *ž*, or any soft consonant except *-j*.

In practice this means all nouns whose nominative singular ends in **-ь** or in **ш, ж, ч,** or **щ**.

крова́ть — крова́тей          каранда́ш — карандаше́й
автомоби́ль — автомоби́лей    клю́ч — ключе́й
писа́тель — писа́телей        това́рищ — това́рищей

**1.23**   The zero-suffix is used (1) with second-declension feminines, and (2) with neuters. That is,

(a) with nouns in **-а/-я**: e. g.  кни́га — кни́г
(b) with nouns in **-о/-ё**: e. g.  о́тчество — о́тчеств

If the **-я** of the Nom. sg. is preceded by a consonant-letter, then the Gen. pl. is spelled with **-ь**:

геро́йня [= и́нья] — геро́йнь

If the **-я** or **-ё** of the Nom. sg. is preceded by a vowel-letter, then the Gen. pl. is spelled with **-й**:

ста́нция [= -цийа] — ста́нций    зда́ниё [= -ийо] — зда́ний
иде́я [= иде́йа] — иде́й

---

² The formula *-ov* denotes the suffix with the stressed vowel: when the suffix is unstressed it becomes *-əf* or *-if* (*-ĭf*) automatically, in accordance with the ordinary rules given in § 11.01, p. 327. Examples: damóf (čijóf), studᵇéntəf, muzᵇéjif, (nᵇémcĭf): домо́в (чае́в), студе́нтов, музе́ёв, (не́мцёв).

³ Words given in parentheses here and in similar instances are included as examples for the sake of completeness in illustrating the rule in question: they are not to be learned at present.

## The Normal Relationship Between Nominative Singular and Genitive Plural

*plus* means a real ending: *minus* means a zero-suffix

| Nom. sg. *plus* | therefore | Gen. pl. *minus* | Nom. sg. *minus* | therefore | Gen. pl. *plus* |
|---|---|---|---|---|---|
| газе́та | | газе́т | дива́н | | дива́нов |
| о́тчество | | о́тчеств | сто́л | | столо́в |
| геро́йня | | геро́йнь | геро́й | | геро́ев |
| gʰirajínʰə | | gʰirajínʰ | gʰirój | | gʰirójif |
| фами́лия | | фами́лий | писа́тель | | писа́телей |
| famʰílʰijə | | famʰílʰij | pʰisátʰilʰ | | pʰisátʰilʰij |
| зда́ниё | | зда́ний | крова́ть | | крова́тей |
| zdánʰijə | | zdánʰij | kravátʰ | | kravátʰij |

### With inserted vowel before zero-suffix

| | | | | | |
|---|---|---|---|---|---|
| су́мка | | су́мок | потоло́к | | потолко́в |
| де́вочка | | де́вочёк | кошелёк | | кошелько́в |
| кре́сло | | кре́сёл | у́гол | | угло́в |
| статья́ | | стате́й | | | |
| statʰjá | | statʰéj | отце́ц | | отцо́в |
| (овца́ 'sheep' | | овёц) | | | |
| (afcá | | avʰéc) | | | |

**1.231**   If the stem ends in a group of two or more consonants, a vowel is usually inserted before the final consonant. The consonant-groups **ств**, **ст**, and **зд**, however, do not admit an inserted vowel.[4]

**1.2311**   If the final consonant is *hard* (except **ц**), the vowel *o* is inserted.
(a) It is nearly always spelled **ё**:

    сёстра́ — сёстёр    кре́сло — кре́сёл    де́вочка — де́вочёк

Note that a **ь** which precedes the final consonant will be replaced by the **ё**:

    письмо́ — пи́сём    (де́ньги [Nom. pl. 'money'] — де́нёг)

---

[4] No vowel is inserted in *ка́рта, ла́мпа* — Gen. pl. *ка́рт, ла́мп*. Stems that take an inserted vowel will be indicated in the vocabularies.

(b) With feminines whose nominative singular ends in **-ка** preceded by a consonant other than **ш, ж, ч, щ,** or **й,** the inserted vowel is spelled **o**:

шáпка — шáпок                    студéнтка — студéнток
*but* дéвочка — девочёк

[Note that **й** is not needed before **ё**: копéйка 'kopeck' копéёк — kapᵇéjkə kapᵇéjik.]

**1.2312**   If the final consonant is *soft* or **ц,** the inserted vowel is *ę* or *e,* spelled **e**:

дерéвня — деревéнь; (овцá 'sheep' овéц; сéрдцё 'heart' сердéц).

Note that stems ending in **-ья** and **-ьё** contain the soft consonant *j* and therefore a consonant cluster, so that they too require an inserted vowel: e. g.

статья́ — статéй                   statᵇj-á statᵇę̇j
(питьё́ 'beverage' питéй            pitᵇj-ó pitᵇę̇j)

**1.3**   The ACCUSATIVE PLURAL form of **all** *nouns denoting living creatures* (*feminine* and *neuter* as well as masculine!) is the same as the genitive form. The accusative plural form of all other nouns is the same as the nominative.

**1.4**   The PREPOSITIONAL PLURAL for *all* nouns is *-ax* (spelled **-ах, -ях**) added to the *plural* stem. (If unstressed, always pronounced *-əx*).

**-ях** is used if the nominative singular ends in **-я, -ё, -й,** or **-ь** (except **-шь, -жь, -чь, -щь**: see App. I, § 8.3).

**-ах** is used in all other instances.

For example:
идéя — идéях                      здáниё — здáниях
музéй — музéях                    кровáть — кровáтях
писáтель — писáтелях              дивáн — дивáнах
дóм — домáх                       кнúга — кнúгах

## 1.5   ACCENTUATION

**1.51**   For the overwhelming majority of nouns, the stress is either on the stem in all forms (plural as well as singular) or on the ending in all forms. Since the stress cannot, of course, fall on a zero-suffix, the ending-stress of masculine nouns cannot be recognized in the nominative singular. You must memorize the genitive singular; this kind of stress-pattern will be indicated in the vocabularies by the letter *E*. For nouns with a real suffix in the nominative singular, the stress in all other forms corresponds to that of Nom. sg.

A. кни́га — кни́ги кни́гах                    кре́сло — кре́сла кре́слах
   дива́н — дива́ны дива́нах                   крова́ть — крова́ти крова́тях

B. госпожа́ — госпожи́ госпожа́х              слова́рь — словари́ словаря́х
   сто́л — столы́ столо́в стола́х               платóк — платки́ платкóв
   кошелёк — кошельки́                        платка́х
   кошелькóв кошелька́х

**1.52**  Masculines that have stressed *á* in the nominative plural (1.12 above) stress the endings throughout the plural: e. g. дóм, G sg. дóма — N pl. дома́, домóв, дома́х; учи́тель учи́теля — учителя́, учителéй, учителя́х.

**2.**  The PLURAL FORMS of **PRONOUNS**. The plural personal pronouns were given in Lesson III. The forms for the demonstratives **тóт** and **э́тот** and the possessives **мóй, твóй, на́ш, ва́ш, чéй** [**свóй** goes like **мóй, твóй**] are:

| N   | тé  | э́ти  | мои́  | твои́  | на́ши  | ва́ши  | чьи́  |
|-----|-----|------|------|-------|-------|-------|------|
| A   |     | (same as genitive or nominative) | | | | | |
| G   | тéх | э́тих | мои́х | твои́х | на́ших | ва́ших | чьи́х |
| Pr. | тéх | э́тих | мои́х | твои́х | на́ших | ва́ших | чьи́х |

The accusative plural form of words modifying or standing for plural animate nouns (1.3 above) is identical with the genitive plural form: the non-animate plural accusative form is like the nominative. (NB: in the plural there is never a grammatical gender distinction in Russian.)

**3.**  The PLURAL FORM of SURNAMES in **-ин** and **-ов (-ёв)** has the suffix **-ых** in the Acc.-Gen. and the Prep.:

'the Pëtrovs', N Пётрóвы, G-A-P Пётрóвых.

**3.1**  The plural of the surname must be used when more than one individual is involved: e.g.

бра́т и сестра́ Луки́ны                    the Lukín brother and sister
Пётр и Любóвь Сóболёвы                 Pëtr and Ljubov' Sóbolev

Here are some sample plural declensions of cases treated so far:

| | | | | | |
|---|---|---|---|---|---|
| Nsg | дива́н | адвока́т | па́рк | това́рищ | кре́сло |
| Npl | дива́ны | адвока́ты | па́рки | това́рищи | кре́сла |
| A | дива́ны | адвока́тов | па́рки | това́рищей | кре́сла |
| G | дива́нов | адвока́тов | па́рков | това́рищей | кре́сёл |
| P | дива́нах | адвока́тах | па́рках | това́рищах | кре́слах |

| | | | | | |
|---|---|---|---|---|---|
| Nsg | портфе́ль | писа́тель | сто́л | слова́рь | зда́ниё |
| Npl | портфе́ли | писа́тели | столы́ | словари́ | зда́ния |
| A | портфе́ли | писа́телей | столы́ | словари́ | зда́ния |
| G | портфе́лей | писа́телей | столо́в | словаре́й | зда́ний |
| P | портфе́лях | писа́телях | стола́х | словаря́х | зда́ниях |

| | | | | | |
|---|---|---|---|---|---|
| Nsg | музе́й | ге́ний | до́м | до́ктор | крова́ть |
| Npl | музе́и | ге́нии | дома́ | доктора́ | крова́ти |
| A | музе́и | ге́ниев | дома́ | докторо́в | крова́ти |
| G | музе́ев | ге́ниев | домо́в | докторо́в | крова́тей |
| P | музе́ях | ге́ниях | дома́х | доктора́х | крова́тях |

| | | | | | |
|---|---|---|---|---|---|
| Nsg | шля́па | да́ма | ша́пка | студе́нтка | де́вочка |
| Npl | шля́пы | да́мы | ша́пки | студе́нтки | де́вочки |
| A | шля́пы | да́м | ша́пки | студе́нток | де́вочёк |
| G | шля́п | да́м | ша́пок | студе́нток | де́вочёк |
| P | шля́пах | да́мах | ша́пках | студе́нтках | де́вочках |

| | | | | | |
|---|---|---|---|---|---|
| Nsg | иде́я | геройня | оте́ц | Пу́шкин | Пу́шкина |
| Npl | иде́и | геройни | отцы́ | Пу́шкины | |
| A | иде́и | геройнь | отцо́в | Пу́шкиных | |
| G | иде́й | геройнь | отцо́в | Пу́шкиных | |
| P | иде́ях | геройнях | отца́х | Пу́шкиных | |

**4.** The words **мно́го** and **ма́ло** have two separate functions:

  a. as adverb. О́н мно́го (ма́ло) чита́ет. He reads a lot (little).

  b. as indefinite, neuter expressions of number, followed by the *genitive plural.*

| | |
|---|---|
| О́н написа́л мно́го кни́г. | He has written many books. |
| В э́той кни́ге ма́ло расска́зов. | There are few stories in this book. |
| Мно́го кни́г бы́ло на столе́. | Many books were on the table. |

**4.1** Two other common expressions of indefinite quantity are **немно́го** 'a little' and **не́сколько** 'several'. They also take the genitive plural and are grammatically singular.

While in some contexts there is little difference between **ма́ло** and **немно́го**, **немно́го** usually means '*a* little, *a* few, *a* little bit', and **ма́ло** means 'few, little', very frequently with the idea of '*too* little, not enough'.

**5.** The pronominal adjective **ве́сь** 'all, the whole' has the stem **вс-**:

|      | m         | n      | f     | pl        |
|------|-----------|--------|-------|-----------|
| Nom  | ве́сь     | всё́   | вся́  | все́      |
| Acc  | (= N, G)  | всё́   | всю́  | (= N, G)  |
| Gen  | всего́    |        | все́й | все́х     |
| Prep | всё́м     |        | все́й | все́х     |

**5.1** The neuter **всё́** frequently means 'everything'. The plural **все́** may mean 'everyone'.

| Óн всё́ зна́ет. | He knows everything. |
| Óн все́х зна́ет. | He knows everyone. |

**6.** Note that the preposition **в** has the form **во** before this root: **во всё́м** до́ме 'in the whole house', **во все́х** клу́бах 'in all clubs', etc.

## EXERCISES

**A.**  i. Read and translate the following sentences.
  ii. In each sentence, put into the plural all forms that the sense allows, e. g.

У студе́нт**а** е́сть кни́г**а**. — У студе́нт**ов** е́сть кни́г**и**.
Мо́**й** това́рищ чита́**ет** кни́гу. — Мо**и́** това́рищ**и** чита́**ют** кни́г**и**.

Also change **ты́ (тво́й)** to **вы́ (ва́ш)**. e. g. **Ты́** ви́дишь кни́гу? — **Вы́** ви́дите кни́ги?

1. Че́й э́то каранда́ш?  2. Во́т моё сочине́ние.  3. Студе́нт повторя́л фра́зу.  4. У студе́нта не́т автомоби́ля.  5. Ты́ не по́мнишь отве́та?
6. Закро́й тетра́дку!  7. Вы́ не ви́дите мое́й кни́ги?  8. На́ш магази́н в то́м зда́нии.  9. Собра́ния не́ было.  10. Чьё э́то кре́сло?
11. Ты́ не брала́ моего́ карандаша́?  12. Э́то слова́рь учи́теля или

писа́теля? 13. Вот твоя́ зада́ча: чита́й э́ту кни́гу. 14. Что́ он говори́т об отце́? 15. Там нет ни рестора́на ни ба́нка. 16. Он доста́нет ключ у писа́тельницы. 17. У адвока́та нет ключа́. 18. Эта да́ма не хо́чет чита́ть ва́шей статьи́? 19. В э́том а́тласе нет ка́рты Евро́пы. 20. Учи́тель и писа́тель до́лго говори́ли об э́том рома́не.

21. Профе́ссор писа́л дикто́вку. 22. Меха́ник смо́трит на фотогра́фию и молчи́т. 23. Учи́тельница не дикту́ет упражне́ния. 24. У э́той госпожи́ есть дом в го́роде. 25. Профе́ссор отвеча́ет на вопро́с студе́нтки. 26. Студе́нтка отвеча́ла на вопро́с профе́ссора. 27. Карти́на де́вочки лежи́т на по́лке. 28. Ла́мпа стои́т в углу́ в лаборато́рии. 29. У э́той да́мы на столе́ есть фотогра́фия Петро́ва. 30. Почему́ твой това́рищ сиди́т на словаре́?

31. Студе́нтка поняла́ учи́тельницу. 32. Адвока́т до́лго чита́л рома́н о Карама́зове. 33. Оте́ц э́того студе́нта ге́ний. 34. Кошелёк был в су́мке на э́том кре́сле. 35. У меня́ нет ни шля́пы ни ша́пки. 36. В ко́мнате нет ни кре́сла ни дива́на. 37. Оте́ц рабо́тает у адвока́та. 38. Пусть э́та студе́нтка продикту́ет фра́зу. 39. Куда́ де́вочка положи́ла уче́бник? Туда́ на стол. 40. Чья э́то крова́ть?

41. Това́рищ забы́л взять слова́рь. 42. Я не понима́ю его́ иде́и. 43. Журнали́ст встреча́л журнали́стку в па́рке. 44. Я всегда́ чита́ю э́ту газе́ту и э́тот журна́л. 45. В том го́роде есть фа́брика? Нет, фа́брики там нет. 46. Куда́ ты несёшь мой портфе́ль? 47. Учи́тельница жила́ у Петро́вой. 48. Герои́ня э́того расска́за де́вочка. 49. Геро́й моего́ рома́на ма́льчик. 50. Па́влов там встре́тил Лукина́.

iii.

a. Он студе́нт. (Она́ студе́нтка.)　б. Они́ студе́нты (студе́нтки).

в. Он спроси́л студе́нта
　　　　(студе́нтку).

г. Он спроси́л студе́нтов
　　　　(студе́нток).

д. Здесь нет студе́нта
　　　　(студе́нтки).

е. Здесь нет студе́нтов
　　　　(студе́нток).

ж. Говоря́т о студе́нте
　　　　(студе́нтке).

з. Говоря́т о студе́нтах
　　　　(студе́нтках).

For студе́нт (студе́нтка) in the above 8 sentences, substitute the following nouns: адвока́т, журнали́ст, меха́ник, ма́льчик, това́рищ, ге́ний, геро́й, писа́тель, до́ктор, профе́ссор, учи́тель; да́ма, журнали́стка, де́вочка, писа́тельница, учи́тельница.

iv. Repeat, adding the proper form of the pronoun "this" before the nouns.

v.   On the model of the 6 sentences below, substitute for "(our) store" the nouns given after the models; make each sentence first without the pronoun "our", then with it.

а. Это (наш) магазин.                        б. Это (наши) магазины.
в. Здесь нет (нашего) магазина.       г. Нет (наших) магазинов.
д. Говорят о (нашем) магазине.        е. Говорят о (наших) магазинах.

диван, театр, университет, парк, музей, стол, дом, портфель, автомобиль, календарь, словарь, ключ; школа, библиотека, фабрика, идея, лаборатория, полка, статья, здание, кресло, кровать.

**B.**   Read and translate:

1. Посмотрите на эти книги и журналы.  2. Что это за учебники? Где вы их достаёте?  3. В этих атласах есть карты всех городов России.  4. В наших уроках было много задач. Я не всё решил. 5. Я не всё решал.  6. Товарищи, пойдёмте в ресторан!  7. Если ты не понимаешь, спроси учительницу.  8. На всех концертах было много журналистов и журналисток.  9. Что за радость! Мать Петровых достала все документы!  10. Эти писательницы почему-то хотят писать несколько статей обо всех этих документах.  11. На собраниях не было студенток.  12. Вы не видели фотографий в её комнатах? Нет, я их не видел, потому что я никогда не был у неё. 13. В школе будет много концертов.  14. Этот гений прочитал все книги во всех библиотеках в городе.  15. Кто-то взял все карандаши.  16. Я ничего об этом не знаю, потому что все обо всём молчали.  17. Я не понял ваших ответов, потому что вы говорили очень быстро.  18. У Ивановых в магазине много журналов, газет и книг.  19. В деревне было несколько собраний.  20. Павел и Ольга Новиковы тогда долго ездили в Европе.  21. Девочки лежали на всех кроватях.  22. Пусть кто-нибудь встретит студенток на станции. 23. Петровы не достали ни романов ни словарей.  24. Ивановы встретили почти всех этих адвокатов, когда мы ездили в Париж. 25. Извините, я забыл ваши фамилии.  26. У Петровых тогда было много фабрик и лабораторий во всех этих городах.

**C.**   For written and/or oral translation into Russian:

1. These ladies are all teachers, journalists, or writers.  2. Almost all these professors, teachers and lawyers have houses in that village.

3. There are several libraries in our university.    4. There are (too) few libraries and laboratories in those cities.    5. We always walk to the meetings at the restaurant.    6. Where did you put my newspapers and magazines?  7. Someone carry these beds and armchairs into those rooms, please.  8. Let the students (m, f) answer the teachers' (f) questions!  9. There will be many concerts at the museum, and several at the library. We will go to all the concerts.    10. There are no sofas or armchairs in these rooms.    11. We met all the teachers (m, f) and writers (m, f) at the meetings in the lawyers' club.    12. When we met the students (f) at the station, they at once began to talk about the theater and the concerts.    13. When we go to the theater, we usually meet the Petrovs, Pëtr Ivanovich and Vera Dmitr'evna, there.    14. In our classes there are no geniuses.    15. Have you read the lessons? Yes, I read them, but I did not solve all the problems.

## СЛОВАРЬ

| | | | |
|---|---|---|---|
| ве́сь всё вся (§ 5) | all, the whole | мно́го (§ 4) | much, a lot |
| геройня | heroine | немно́го (§ 4) | a few, a little |
| геро́й | hero | не́сколько (§ 4) | several |
| де́вочка (Gpl -чёк) | little girl | па́рк | park |
| журнали́ст | journalist | портфе́ль (m) | briefcase |
| журнали́стка | journalist (f) | потому́ что | because |
| (Gpl -ток) | | почти́ | almost |
| иде́я | idea | ра́дость (f) | joy |
| крова́ть (f) | bed | тогда́ | then, at that time; |
| ма́ло (§ 4) | little, too little | | afterward |
| ма́льчик | little boy | фотогра́фия | photograph |

# LESSON IX

Вы́ зна́ете все́ слова́ в э́той фра́зе?

Do you know all the words in this sentence?

Я зна́ю э́то сло́во, но́ не зна́ю все́х слов.

I know this word, but I don't know all the words.

У ва́с е́сть де́ньги?
        часы́?
        пи́сьма?

Do you have any money?
        a watch?
        any letters?

Не́т, у меня́ не́т де́нег.
        часо́в.
        пи́сем.

No, I have no money.
        watch.
        letters.

О́н нашёл ва́ши часы́ и де́ньги.

He found your watch and money.

Почему́ вы́ не закрыва́ете о́кон и двере́й?

Why don't you close the windows and doors?

Пу́сть кто́-нибудь закро́ет о́кна и две́ри.

Someone close the windows and doors.

Кто́ э́ти господа́? Ва́ши сосе́ди?

Who are these gentlemen? Your neighbors?

О́н потеря́л мои́ пе́рья.

He lost my pens.

Вы́ не ви́дели мои́х пе́рьев?

Haven't you seen my pens?

Сыновья́, мужья́ и бра́тья несли́ сту́лья.

The sons, husbands, and brothers were carrying chairs.

Да́мы слу́шали сынове́й, муже́й и бра́тьев.

The ladies were listening to their sons, husbands, and brothers.

Жёны и сёстры слу́шали Петро́вых.

The wives and sisters were listening to the Petrovs.

Ма́тери и до́чери бы́ли в сада́х.

The mothers and daughters were in the garden.

Во́т карти́ны на́ших матере́й и дочере́й.

There are pictures of our mothers and daughters.

О чьи́х дочеря́х говори́ли э́ти лю́ди?

Whose daughters were these people talking about?

| | |
|---|---|
| Всё её сёстры и бра́тья живу́т здесь. | All her sisters and brothers live here. |
| Вчера́ я встре́тил её сестёр и бра́тьев. | Yesterday I met her sisters and brothers. |
| Óн ча́сто говори́т о свои́х сёстрах и бра́тьях. | He often speaks of his sisters and brothers. |
| Профе́ссор зна́ет имёна́ все́х. | The professor knows everyone's names. |
| Я не по́мню ни имён ни о́тчеств. | I don't remember names or patronymics. |
| Óн рабо́таёт в поля́х. | He works in the fields. |
| Они́ сиде́ли в угла́х и молча́ли; вы́ и́х не заме́тили? | They sat in the corners and kept quiet; didn't you notice them? |

---

**1.0** There is a tendency in Russian to contrast the plural stem to the singular, either by stress (see 8 below) or by other changes in the make-up of the stem.

**1.1** The plural stem of a small number of masculine and neuter nouns differs from the singular stem by the addition of the consonant $j$ before the plural suffixes. They take the suffix -$a$ in the nominative, and the resulting compound suffix is spelled -ья (cf. App. I, §9.1). These plurals must be memorized with the individual nouns. So far we have had:

| | | | |
|---|---|---|---|
| бра́т — бра́тья | | brát | brátᵇjə |
| му́ж — мужья́ | | múš | mužjá |
| сту́л — сту́лья | | stúl | stúlᵇjə |
| перо́ — пе́рья | | pᵇiró | pᵇέrᵇjə |

**1.2** The selection of genitive plural suffix depends on the stress of the plural stem.

(a) Nearly all are stem-stressed and take -$ov$:

| | |
|---|---|
| бра́тьёв | brátᵇjif/brátᵇjəf[1] |
| сту́льёв | stúlᵇjif/stúlᵇjəf |
| пе́рьёв | pᵇέrᵇjif/pᵇέrᵇjəf |

---

[1] For the pronunciation of the final vowel here, see App. I, § 11.011.

(b) A few exceptional nouns are suffix-stressed and take the zero-suffix; an inserted vowel must therefore appear before the stem-final consonant *j* :

| Nom. pl. | мужья́ | mužjá |
| Gen. pl. | муже́й | mužéj |

**1.3** The addition of the regular prepositional suffix -*ax* to the stem-final *j* is spelled -**ьях**: бра́тьях, сту́льях, мужья́х, пе́рьях.

**2.0** The noun **сы́н** 'son' suffixes -*ovᵇj*- to form the plural stem, which has suffix stress: сыновья́ (sɨnavᵇjá). The genitive therefore (1.2 above) has zero-suffix and an inserted vowel: сынове́й (sɨnavᵇéj).

**3.1** The plural of **граждани́н** 'citizen' is **гра́ждане** (shift of accent, loss of -**ин**, special suffix -**e**). The genitive plural has zero suffix: **гра́ждан**.
   This is one of an important class of words where the plural (in -**e**) signifies a social group, and the singular (in -**ин**) is an individual belonging to the group.

**3.2** The plural of **господи́н** 'gentleman' is господа́, госпо́д, господа́х. It may be used to mean 'ladies and gentleman'.

**4.** The noun **сосе́д** 'neighbor' has a softened consonant in the plural stem: hence, N pl. сосе́ди, G-A сосе́дей, Prep. сосе́дях.

**5.** The plural of **челове́к** is **лю́ди** 'people', G-A люде́й, Prep. лю́дях.

**6.** **И́мя** 'name' has the plural N-A имена́, G имён, Prep. имёна́х.

**7.** The plural of **ма́ть** and **до́чь** retains the -**ер**- but the accent shifts to the suffix in all plural endings except nominative:

**ма́ть** — ма́тери матере́й матеря́х; **до́чь** — до́чери дочере́й дочеря́х.

## 8. ACCENTUATION

Many nouns contrast the stress of the singular to that of the plural, and there are instances where the stress of individual cases is opposed to other forms in the same number. A full survey is given in Appendix III, pp. 350–352.

**8.1** You have seen that nouns with stressed -*á* in the plural nominative stress the endings throughout the plural: дома́, домо́в, дома́х.

**8.2** About fifty other masculines (some very common) stress the stem in the singular (excepting, perhaps, a "second locative") and the suffix in the plural. We have had only: са́д, са́да о са́де [в саду́, II 3]; сады́ садо́в сада́х; шка́ф [в шкафу́]; шкафы́ шкафо́в шкафа́х.

**8.3** A limited but important group of feminines, whose Nom. sing. stress is on the ending, shift it to the stem in certain forms. We've had:

| N sg | Acc sg | Nom pl | Gen pl | Prep pl |
|------|--------|--------|--------|---------|
| рука́ | ру́ку | ру́ки | ру́к | рука́х |
| стена́ | сте́ну | сте́ны | сте́н | стена́х |
| доска́ | до́ску | до́ски | досо́к | доска́х |
| сёстра́ | сёстру́ | сёстры | сёстёр | сёстрах |
| жёна́ | жёну́ | жёны | жён | жёнах |

**8.31** There are some exceptional cases. Дере́вня has the plural forms N-A дере́вни, G дереве́нь, Prep. деревня́х.

**8.4** *Feminines of the 3rd declension* have either:
  a. stress on the stem throughout the paradigm: ра́дость — ра́дости, ра́достях; крова́ть — крова́ти, крова́тях.
  b. stress on the stem in the singular and the Nom-Acc plural, but on the suffix in the other plural cases: N-A две́рь, G-Pr sg две́ри, N-A pl две́ри — Gen pl двере́й, Prep дверя́х.
There are about 70 nouns of this pattern, many of them extremely common ones.

**8.5** *Neuters.* Neuters in **-иё** and **-ство** (зда́ниё, о́тчество) keep the stress of the Nom. sg. Otherwise the stress is on the stem in the singular and on the ending in the plural or vice versa:

| N sg | G sg | N-A pl | G pl | Prep pl |
|------|------|--------|------|---------|
| письмо́ | письма́ | пи́сьма | пи́сём | пи́сьмах |
| окно́ | окна́ | о́кна | о́кон | о́кнах |
| сло́во | сло́ва | слова́ | сло́в | слова́х |
| по́лё[1] | по́ля | поля́ | полей | поля́х |

But кре́сло has fixed stress: кре́сла, кре́сёл, кре́слах.

[1] Note that **по́лё** 'field' and **мо́рё** 'sea' are the only two neuters ending in consonant-letter + **ё**: they both take **-ей** in the genitive plural: полей, морей.

The plurals of some words treated in this lesson:

| N sg | сту́л | бра́т | сы́н | сосе́д | граждани́н |
|------|-------|-------|------|--------|------------|
| Nom | сту́лья | бра́тья | сыновья́ | сосе́ди | гра́ждане |
| Acc | сту́лья | бра́тьев | сынове́й | сосе́дей | гра́ждан |
| Gen | сту́льев | бра́тьев | сынове́й | сосе́дей | гра́ждан |
| Prep | сту́льях | бра́тьях | сыновя́х | сосе́дях | гра́жданах |

| N sg | письмо́ | окно́ | перо́ | по́лё | и́мя | челове́к |
|------|---------|-------|-------|-------|------|----------|
| Nom | пи́сьма | о́кна | пе́рья | поля́ | имена́ | лю́ди |
| Acc | пи́сьма | о́кна | пе́рья | поля́ | имена́ | люде́й |
| Gen | пи́сём | око́н* | пе́рьев | поле́й | имён | люде́й |
| Prep | пи́сьмах | о́кнах | пе́рьях | поля́х | имена́х | лю́дях |

| N sg | дере́вня | доска́ | жёна́ | сёстра́ | две́рь | до́чь |
|------|----------|--------|-------|---------|--------|-------|
| Nom | дере́вни | до́ски | жёны | сёстры | две́ри | до́чери |
| Acc | дере́вни | до́ски | жён | сёстёр | две́ри | дочере́й |
| Gen | дереве́нь | досо́к | жён | сёстёр | двере́й | дочере́й |
| Prep | деревня́х | доска́х | жёнах | сёстрах | дверя́х | дочеря́х |

* Two accents written on a word means that either stress is permissible.

**9.1** Де́ньги 'money' is found only in the plural. Gen. де́нёг, Prep. деньга́х.

**9.2** Часы́ 'watch, clock, timepiece' is found only in the plural. Gen. часо́в, Prep. часа́х.

**10.** Corresponding to the (intransitive) verbs *стоя́ть, лежа́ть, сиде́ть* and *висе́ть* are (transitive) verbs meaning "cause to stand (lie, sit, hang)":

ста́вить ста́вят I ⎫
поста́вить поста́вят P ⎭  
*cause to stand, put in a standing position, stand, put*

О́н поста́вил кни́гу на сто́л.  
He stood the book on the table.

Кни́га стои́т на столе́.  
The book is standing on the table.

О́н почти́ всёгда́ ста́вит свои́ кни́ги туда́ на э́ту по́лку.  
He almost always puts his books there on that shelf.

| | |
|---|---|
| **кла́сть/положи́ть** | *put, lay, cause to lie* |
| Он положи́л кни́гу на сто́л. | He laid the book on the table. |
| Кни́га лёжи́т на столе́. | The book is lying on the table. |
| **сажа́ть сажа́ют** I <br> **посади́ть поса́дят** P | *cause to sit, seat, sit* |
| Он посади́л до́чь на сту́л. | He sat his daughter on the chair. |
| Она́ сиди́т на сту́ле. | She is sitting on the chair. |
| **ве́шать ве́шают** I <br> **пове́сить пове́сят** P | *cause to hang, put in a hanging position, hang* |
| Он пове́сил ша́пку в шка́ф. | He hung his cap in the cupboard. The cap is still hanging there. |
| Ша́пка ещё та́м виси́т. | |
| Пове́сь ла́мпу та́м в углу́. | Hang the lamp there in the corner. |

Notice that *ста́вить/поста́вить* is often translated "put", like *кла́сть/положи́ть*, but the Russian distinguishes carefully objects which normally stand (e.g. a lamp) from those which normally lie (e.g. a newspaper), and he selects the appropriate verb for those which may do either (e.g. a book).

*Кла́сть/положи́ть*, besides specifying a lying position, has a broader sense: e.g. *кла́сть де́ньги в карма́н, кни́ги в портфе́ль.*

## УПРАЖНЕНИЯ

**A.**  i. Read and translate the following sentences.

ii. In each sentence, put into the plural all forms that the sense allows, e.g.

У студе́нт**а** е́сть кни́г**а**. — У студе́нт**ов** е́сть кни́г**и**.
Мо́**й** бра́т чита́**ет** кни́г**у**. — Мо́**й** бра́т**ья** чита́**ют** кни́г**и**.

Also change **ты́ (тво́й)** to **вы́ (ва́ш)**. e.g. **Ты́** ви́дишь кни́г**у**?
— **Вы́** ви́дите кни́г**и**?

1. Че́й э́то слова́рь? 2. Во́т моё окно́! 3. Ма́льчик повторя́л э́то сло́во. 4. У ма́льчика е́сть портфе́ль. 5. Ты́ не спра́шивал о бра́те? 6. Откро́й две́рь! 7. Ты́ не ви́дишь мое́й руки́? 8. Её плато́к в э́том шкафу́. 9. В углу́ не́ было крова́ти. 10. Чьё э́то письмо́?

11. Ты́ не брала́ моего́ портфе́ля? 12. Э́тот господи́н студе́нт и́ли профе́ссор? 13. Во́т твоя́ зада́ча: пиши́ статью́ о лаборато́рии. 14. Что́ де́вочка говори́т о ма́тери? 15. На стене́ не́т ни календаря́

ни карти́ны.  16. У отца́ éсть са́д.  17. У сы́на нéт са́да.  18. Это
ва́шё перо́?  19. Куда́ ты́ нёсёшь сту́л?  20. Учи́тель ча́сто говори́л
о своём до́ме в дерéвне.

21. Механик писа́л сло́во на стенé.  22. Му́ж и жёна́ иду́т в го́род
пешко́м.  23. Отéц и сы́н бы́ли на собра́нии в клу́бе.  24. У сёстры́
éсть до́м в лесу́.  25. Куда́ этот человéк несёт этот сту́л?  26. Твоя́
шля́па та́м на сту́ле.  27. Ма́ть говори́ла о до́чери и её учи́теле.
28. Пу́сть сы́н и́ли до́чь откро́ёт двéрь.  29. Что́ у того́ граждани́на
в рукé?  30. Куда́ этот человéк положи́л моё письмо́? Туда́ на сту́л.

31. Посмотри́ на эту стéну!  32. Гражда́нка Ивано́ва говори́ла об
этом человéке.  33. Ты́ хо́чёшь написа́ть письмо́?  34. Сосéд ча́сто
встреча́ёт на́шёго до́ктора на концéрте.  35. До́чь не зна́ла этого
сло́ва.  36. Жёна́ зна́ёт и́мя ва́шёго това́рища?  37. Му́ж моéй
сосéдки ча́сто хо́дит в библиотéку.  38. Сосéдка моёго́ му́жа ча́сто
говори́ла в библиотéке.  39. Това́рищ и́х сы́на хо́дит в эту шко́лу.
40. Этот граждани́н всёгда́ сиди́т у окна́ в этой ко́мнате.

41. Ма́ть не получа́ла письма́.  42. Учи́тельница забы́ла газéту
сёстры́ в кла́ссе.  43. Сы́н сосéда рабо́та́ёт в саду́.  44. Мо́й сы́н
забы́л твоё и́мя.  45. Моя́ сёстра́ то́же не по́мнит и́мёни.  46. Почёму́
эта да́ма стои́т на сту́ле?  47. Что́ он сказа́л об этом человéке?
48. Учи́тель рабо́та́ёт и у бра́та и у отца́.  49. Бра́т спро́сит о Пётро́ве.
50. Пётро́в спра́шивал о бра́те.

iii.   For "brother" in the 6 sentences below, substitute the nouns that
follow, saying each sentence first without "our" and then with it.

a. Это (на́ш) бра́т.               б. Это (на́ши) бра́тья.
в. Он спроси́л (на́шёго) бра́та.   г. Он спроси́л (на́ших) бра́тьёв.
д. Спра́шивают о (на́шём) бра́те.  е. Спра́шивают о (на́ших)
                                                      бра́тьях.

му́ж, отéц, сы́н, студéнт, бра́т, сосéд, человéк, до́ктор, граждани́н;
сёстра́, ма́ть, учи́тельница, до́чь, студéнтка, жёна́.

iv.   a. Он тепéрь пи́шёт  фра́зу.        статья́, кни́га, сочинéниё,
      б. Он пи́шёт фра́зы.                расска́з, учéбник, письмо́,
      в. Он написа́л мно́го  фра́з.       слова́рь, сло́во, дикто́вка,
      г. Он говори́т о свои́х  фра́зах.    упражнéниё

In the patterns of the four sentences above on the left, substitute
each of the nouns listed above on the right.

**B.** Чтó э́то вы́ тудá положи́ли, Ве́ра? Э́то вáша сýмка. А чтó э́то лёжит тýт у меня́ на столе́? Э́то моя́ сýмка. Э́то нáши сýмки.

Пётр Ивáнович, чтó в нáших сýмках? — Я́ не знáю: мóжет быть тáм и платки́, и карандаши́, и фотогрáфии, и пéрья, и календари́, и ключи́, и бумáги, и кáрты и дáже дéньги.

Мóжет быть. А чтó у вáс в кармáнах?

У меня́ в кармáнах почти́ ничегó нéт, тóлько платки́, ключи́ и перó, а нéт ни кошелькá, ни дéнег.

**C.**  Read and translate:

1. У вáс éсть брáтья и́ли сёстры? 2. У меня́ éсть и брáтья и сёстры. 3. У меня́ нéт ни брáтьев ни сестёр. 4. Я́ где́-то потеря́л часы́, вы́ и́х не ви́дели? 5. Мáльчики не знáют всé словá в э́тих пи́сьмах. 6. Господá, поéдемте! 7. Жёны нáших сосéдей дóлго слýшали э́тих журнали́сток. 8. Сосéди мои́х дочерéй жи́ли и рабóтали в Росси́и, в деревня́х и городáх. 9. Они́ рабóтали и в поля́х и в магази́нах. 10. У негó в кóмнате на стенáх éсть фотогрáфии отцá, мáтери, сыновéй, дóчери, домóв, полéй и лéса. 11. У дéвочек нé было пéрьев. 12. Мы́ бýдем писáть в тетрáдках, потомý что в э́тих клáссах нéт досóк. 13. Сёстры Луки́ны достáли óчень мнóго шáпок и шля́п в э́тих магази́нах. 14. Пожáлуйста, закрóйте всé óкна. 15. Мы́ нашли́ э́ти платки́ у сестёр Ивáновых. 16. Э́ти грáждане и граждáнки нé жили в Крымý. 17. Не открывáйте дверéй. 18. Всé э́ти лю́ди бы́ли вчерá на концéрте у нáших сосéдей. 19. Я́ не знáю, когдá óн пошёл домóй; у меня́ нé было часóв. 20. Мáтери и мужья́ студéнток хóдят в шкóлу на концéрты.

**D.**  For written and/or oral translation into Russian:

1. Our neighbors, Ivan and Marija Morózov, work in those stores. 2. Those doctors have automobiles, but their wives have no automobiles. 3. The daughter of those writers have no hats. 4. There are (too) few schools in those villages in the forest. 5. The husband of those writers didn't obtain briefcases. 6a. Vera Ivanovna Petrov's sisters lost their purses in the park yesterday. 6b. No one has found them yet. 6c. There was a lot of money in them. 7a. Have you (any) magazines? 7b. No, we have no magazines now because our neighbors took them all yesterday. 8. I have several pens and pencils. 9. We listened to those people yesterday at the Petrovs'. 10. In the professors' house there is a room where there are neither doors nor windows. 11. I don't know

where the museums are. Ask those people. 12. Let's write all the sentences on the blackboard, gentlemen. 13. If you repeat all the words, you will remember them. 14. Why did the Petrovs forget to open the windows? 15. I don't want to see the Petrovs today, they will talk about their brothers and sisters and about their brothers' wives and their sisters' husbands, and I don't want to listen. 16. The mechanic hasn't received the money yet. 17. Why didn't the citizens close the doors and windows in their rooms? Because they forgot. 18. Excuse me, I am going home now. I forgot my watch somewhere. I almost always forget it. 19. I found Anna Semënova's watch in the laboratory. 20. In all his books and articles, Petrov writes about his neighbors. 21. I'll get many pictures of all those buildings. 22. Pavel and Vera Lukín want to write letters home tonight. 23. Please put all your textbooks and dictionaries on those shelves. 24. The teacher will seat the mothers and fathers near the blackboard. 25. Did you notice the picture of the Ivanovs' sons on the wall?

## СЛОВАРЬ

де́ньги (pl. only, § 9.1) money
лю́ди (§ 5) people
по́ле (pl. поля́, поле́й) field
часы́ (pl. only; § 9.2) watch, clock

ве́шать/пове́сить ⎫
сажа́ть/посади́ть ⎬ see § 10
ста́вить/поста́вить ⎭

замеча́ть замеча́ют I ⎫
заме́тить заме́тят P ⎬ notice

находи́ть нахо́дят I ⎫
найти́ найду́т P ⎬ find
   past нашёл, нашла́, нашли́

слу́шать слу́шают I ⎫
послу́шать -ают P ⎬ listen to

теря́ть теря́ют I ⎫
потеря́ть -яют P ⎬ lose

# LESSON IXa

| | |
|---|---|
| Сегóдня какóй дéнь? | What day is it today? |
| Сегóдня воскресéньё. | Today is Sunday. |
| Вчерá былá средá. | Yesterday was Wednesday. |
| По суббóтам мы́ éздили в дерéвню. | On Saturdays we used to go to the country. |
| В суббóту журналúст пошёл в óперу. | On Saturday the journalist went to the opera. |
| Я́ ни рáзу нé был в óпере. | I haven't been to the opera once. |
| Онá не рáз былá в э́том универмáге. | She's been in that department store more than once. |
| Óн иногдá нóсит портфéль, нó во втóрник у нёгó нé было портфéля. | He sometimes carries a briefcase, but on Tuesday he had no briefcase. |
| Двá рáза в недéлю, по средáм и по пя́тницам, онú тудá хóдят. | Twice a week, Wednesdays and Fridays, they go there. |
| Онá всегдá ходúла в цéрковь трú рáза в дéнь. | She always went to church three times a day. |
| На бýдущей недéле я́ кáждый дéнь бýду ходúть в пáрк. | Next week I shall go to the park every day. |
| На прóшлой недéле я́ иногдá встречáл журналúстку в пáрке. | Last week I sometimes met the newspaper woman in the park. |
| У нáс нé было диктóвок на слéдующей недéле. | The next week we had no dictations. |
| Óн поéдёт домóй на канúкулы. | He will go home for vacation. |
| Я́ бýду здéсь на канúкулах. | I'll be here during vacation. |

---

**1.** To render English "in" and "on" with time expressions, Russian uses a variety of prepositions and cases. We will treat only selected examples in this course.

**1.1**  **В** plus the *accusative* of the name of a week-day means "on (this specific day)":

| | |
|---|---|
| **Во вто́рник** о́н получи́л письмо́. | He received the letter on Tuesday. |
| **В сре́ду** о́н написа́л отве́т. | On Wednesday he wrote an answer. |
| **В э́ту пя́тницу** о́н начнёт. | He will begin this Friday. |

| Similarly: | **в э́тот (то́т) де́нь** | on this/that day |
|---|---|---|
| | **в како́й де́нь**? | on what day? |

**1.2**  **По** plus the *dative plural*[1] means "on (this day as a rule)":

| | |
|---|---|
| **По воскресе́ньям** о́н хо́дит в це́рковь. | He goes to church on Sunday (Sundays). |
| **По понеде́льникам** о́н рабо́тает до́ма. | He works at home Mondays. |
| **По вто́рникам** о́н получа́ет пи́сьма. | He receives letters Tuesdays. |
| **По среда́м** о́н отвеча́ет. | He answers on Wednesdays. |
| **По четверга́м** они́ сидя́т в рестора́не. | They sit in the restaurant on Thursdays. |
| Что́ вы́ де́лаете **по пя́тницам**? | What do you usually do on Friday? |

**2.**  Other expressions of time given in this lesson are to be learned simply as set phrases:

| | | | |
|---|---|---|---|
| **на э́той неде́ле** | this week | **ра́з** | once |
| **на про́шлой неде́ле** | last week | **ра́з в де́нь** | once a day |
| **на бу́дущей неде́ле** | next week | **ра́з в неде́лю** | once a week |
| **на сле́дующей неде́ле** | the next week | **не ра́з** | more than once |
| **ка́ждый де́нь** | every day | **два́ ра́за** | twice |
| **ка́ждую неде́лю** | every week | **два́ ра́за в де́нь** | twice a day |
| **ни ра́зу** [+ **не**] | not once | **три́ ра́за** | three times |

Note that with *ни ра́зу* (as with *никогда́*, *нигде́*; cf. II 5.3), the verb *must* be negated.

**3.**  *На кани́кулы* (Acc.) = 'for (the) vacation' in the sense of "to spend the (whole period of) vacation"; *на кани́кулах* (Prep.) = 'in (during) vacation'.

**4.**  The particle **же** serves to emphasize the *preceding* word. **И**, when it is not the connective 'and', underlines the *following* word.

**5.**  *Расска́зывать/рассказа́ть* means 'tell, narrate', implying a speech of some length, not just a simple statement.

---

[1] The forms will be explained in Lesson XIII; learn them now as set phrases.

## УПРАЖНЕНИЯ

**A.**  For oral drill.

1. On Monday          – I – was on the way/went/will go – to the theater.
   В понеде́льник      – я́ – шёл/пошёл/пойду́            – в теа́тр.

   On Mondays          – I – used to go /go/will go        – to the theater.
   По понеде́льникам – я́ – ходи́л/хожу́/бу́ду ходи́ть  – в теа́тр.

On the above models, make sentences using all the days of the week, all the possible personal pronoun subjects (*I, you, he, she, we, you, they*), both "riding" and "walking" verbs, and the following destinations: *opera, church, park, village, there, class, nowhere, the museum, somewhere.*

2.  Repeat the above, substituting for "go" the phrase "carry a textbook".

**B.**  Be prepared to say in Russian all possible combinations, first in the singular, then in the plural:

1. Сестра́, о́н, учи́тель[ница],       календа́рь, ла́мпа, вопро́с,
   я́, оте́ц, сосе́д[ка], госпожа́  } has/have { ка́рта, шка́ф, ша́пка,
   Лукина́, она́, её ма́ть, бра́т,      had       звоно́к, до́чь, словарь,
   они́, ты́, кто́-то                                упражне́ние, его́ уче́бник,
                                                        шля́па, плато́к

2.  Repeat the above in the negative.

3.  I (you, he, she, we, they) see(s)/saw ____ (substitute items from the end of 1, above).

4.  Repeat no. 3 in the negative.

5. Я́, мы́,              { (*a*) is/are asking }              (substitute the
   бра́т и сестра́,            were asking      } about ____  same list as
   э́та госпожа́         { (*b*) will ask (P)   }              above).
                               asked (P)       }

**C.**  Read aloud and translate:

1. На про́шлой неде́ле мы́ два́ ра́за пошли́ в о́перу, в понеде́льник и в четве́рг. На э́той неде́ле мы́ никуда́ не бу́дем ходи́ть, но́ на бу́дущей неде́ле мы́ пое́дем куда́-нибудь на автомоби́ле.  Поезжа́йте с на́ми!  2. В како́й де́нь И́горь пойдёт на собра́ние?  3. У на́с бу́дет дикто́вка в четве́рг и́ли в пя́тницу.  4. Почему́ вы́ не несёте и́х портфе́лей?  5. Ле́в Льво́вич ка́ждый де́нь ходи́л в це́рковь, а его́ жена́ ходи́ла то́лько по воскресе́ньям.  6. Её не́ было в це́ркви в воскресе́нье.  7. Пу́сть они́ хо́дят туда́ три́ ра́за в де́нь. 8. На

будущей неделе — каникулы. Я поеду в город, пойду в универмаг и куплю портфель. На следующей неделе, когда буду ходить в университет, я буду носить учебники и словарь в портфеле. 9. Когда будут каникулы? 10. Мы начали читать этот рассказ на прошлой неделе, не знаю, когда кончим.

**D.** —Какой сегодня день? —спросила учительница. —Посмотрите, пожалуйста, в календарь, Игорь.

—Сегодня вторник, —ответил Игорь. —Когда у нас будет диктовка, Наталья Сергеевна?

—Диктовка у нас будет в четверг. А в субботу —начало каникул. Расскажите, что вы будете делать на каникулах, Игорь.

—На этой неделе я буду читать и переводить рассказы с английского на русский и с русского на английский. В четверг мы будем писать в школе диктовку. Но потом, на будущей неделе, мы пойдём во вторник и в пятницу в оперу. В среду мы идём на концерт. Моя мама работает в универмаге только по четвергам. Каждую неделю, по субботам, мы ездим в деревню.

—Спасибо, Игорь. Очень хорошо! Ольга, теперь вы расскажите нам о клубе. В какой день недели вы ходите в клуб?

—В пятницу. У нас каждую неделю по пятницам в клубе собрания, а иногда и концерты. Поезжайте с нами, Наталья Сергеевна!

—Ходите ли вы в церковь, Оля? —спросила учительница.

—Я хожу в церковь только раз в неделю, по воскресеньям. Но мой отец, Лев Львович, ходит в церковь каждый день. Мама говорит: «Пусть он ходит туда два раза в день!» Она же ходит в церковь только раз в неделю, по воскресеньям.

**E.** Read aloud and translate:

Иван, закройте дверь, пожалуйста. Пора начинать урок.

Вера, скажите, пожалуйста, что это у меня в руке? Это моя сумка. У вас тоже есть сумка? Что у вас в сумке? Это ваше перо, ваш карандаш и ваш кошелёк, а это — что такое? Вы не знаете слова? Посмотрите в словарь. Правильно, это платок, это ваш платок.

Пётр, скажите, пожалуйста, у вас есть платок? Где он? Он у вас в кармане? У вас там также кошелёк?

Надежда, откройте учебник и прочитайте рассказ. Что, у вас нет учебника? Возьмите у Ивана, а завтра не забудьте своего учебника дома. Вы, Алексей, пишите, пожалуйста, на доске.

Спасибо, Надежда, вы читали очень хорошо.

Смотри́те на до́ску. Алексе́й, у ва́с оши́бка в э́той фра́зе, вы́ её не ви́дите? Ви́дит ли кто́-нибудь оши́бку? Вы́ непра́вильно написа́ли во́т э́то сло́во. Попра́вьте его́. Та́к, тепе́рь пра́вильно.

Да́льше! Ива́н, чита́йте э́ту фра́зу на доске́ по-ру́сски и переведи́те на англи́йский. Не́т, э́то не та́к, та́м «у шка́фа», а не «на шкафу́». Пра́вильно; не забыва́йте э́того.

А́, во́т звоно́к! Уже́ пора́ конча́ть.

**F.** For written and/or oral translation into Russian:

1. Last week he carried my dictionary home on Tuesday, and on Wednesday he forgot it at home. 2. On Thursday and Friday we will not have class this week. 3a. Let's go to the opera this Saturday. 3b. Let's go to the opera every week. 4. I sometimes meet the journalist's wife in the department store on Thursdays. 5. They used to go to the park every day, but now they go only twice a week. 6. Next week we'll translate this article from English into Russian. 7. Let Boris carry your book and briefcase to class. 8. What were you carrying when I saw you in the park on Sunday? I was carrying my wife's pocketbook. 9. You haven't once answered a question correctly. Why didn't you read the lesson two or three times? 10. He goes to the restaurant only once a day.

## СЛОВАРЬ

Learn the forms and expressions given in §§ 1.2 and 2.

| | | | |
|---|---|---|---|
| воскресе́ньё | Sunday | с на́ми | with us |
| вто́рник | Tuesday | среда́ [A sg. сре́ду] | Wednesday |
| де́нь [G дня́, Pr. дне́] | day | суббо́та | Saturday |
| же | see § 4 | то́лько | only |
| иногда́ | sometimes | универма́г | department store |
| кани́кулы [pl. only, G кани́кул] | vacation | це́рковь (f.) [G-Pr. це́ркви; pl. N-A це́ркви, G церкве́й, Pr. церква́х] | church |
| ма́ма | mama | четве́рг (*E*) | Thursday |
| нача́ло | beginning | покупа́ть -а́ют I ⎫ купи́ть ку́пят P ⎭ | buy |
| неде́ля | week | | |
| о́пера | opera | | |
| понеде́льник | Monday | расска́зывать -ают I ⎫ рассказа́ть расска́жут P ⎭ | tell (§ 5) |
| пя́тница | Friday | | |

# LESSON X

Эта америка́нка ча́сто смеётся.

This American woman often laughs.

Они́ мно́го бу́дут смея́ться.

They will laugh a lot.

Почему́ англича́нка смея́лась?

Why was the Englishwoman laughing?

Англича́нин засмея́лся.

The Englishman burst out laughing.

Мы́ зна́ли, что она́ ча́сто смеётся.

We knew that she laughed often.

Я́ наде́ялся, что они́ бу́дут смея́ться мно́го.

I hoped that they would laugh a lot.

О́н спро́сит, почему́ она́ смея́лась.

He will ask why she was laughing.

Э́ти гра́ждане, мо́жет быть, англича́не.

Those citizens are perhaps Englishmen.

Она́ ду́мала, что они́ англича́не.

She thought that they were Englishmen.

Е́сли о́н меня́ спро́сит, я́ отве́чу.

If he asks me, I shall answer.

Е́сли бы о́н меня́ спроси́л, я́ отве́тил бы.

{ If he'd asked me, I'd've answered.
{ If he should ask me, I'd answer.

Е́сли бы у меня́ бы́ли де́ньги, я́ бы купи́л автомоби́ль у э́тих англича́н.

{ If I had money, I would buy
{ If I'd had money, I'd have bought
{    a car from those Englishmen.

Я́ хочу́, что́бы ты́ купи́ла э́ти ве́щи.

I want you to buy those things.

Я́ не смо́г купи́ть э́тих веще́й, потому́ что у меня́ бы́ло ма́ло де́нег.

I couldn't buy those things because I didn't have enough money.

Вы́ покупа́ете э́тот журна́л?

Do you buy this magazine?

О́н спроси́л, покупа́ю ли я́ э́тот журна́л.

He asked whether I bought this magazine.

| | |
|---|---|
| Óн не мóжет поéхать ýтром. | He can't go in the morning. |
| Онú боя́тся учúтельницы. | They're afraid of the teacher. |
| Онú надéялись, что онá кýпит их домá. | They hoped that she would buy their houses. |
| Óн спросúл, кудá я несý пúсьма. | He asked where I was taking the letters. |
| Óн хотéл, чтоб я понёс егó вéщи в метрó. | He wanted me to carry his things to the subway. |
| Онá хóчет, чтобы мы́ всé пошлú в кинó сегóдня вéчером. | She wants us all to go to the movies tonight. |

---

**1.** Russian verbs often occur with a suffixed particle which has the form **-ся** after a consonant-letter or the "soft-sign" **-ь**, and **-сь** after a vowel:

> e.g. смея́ться "to laugh"
>
> | | |
> |---|---|
> | ты́ смеёшься | я́ смею́сь |
> | óн смеётся | вы́ смеётесь |
> | мы́ смеёмся | |
> | онú смею́тся | онá смея́лась |
> | óн смея́лся | мы́ смея́лись |
> | смéйся! | смéйтесь! |

The infinitive and 3rd person endings are *always* pronounced as though spelled **-тца** (*-tcə*, cf. App. I, § 17.1). In other cases the **с** is preferably pronounced hard (i. e. sm<sup>ь</sup>ijús, sm<sup>ь</sup>ijáləs, sm<sup>ь</sup>ijómsə, sm<sup>ь</sup>éjsə), but many Russians pronounce it soft, as spelled.

**2.** Most *ся*-verbs occur also without **-ся**, and there is a difference in meaning. Such verbs will be treated in Lesson XV; at present we will introduce only verbs which never occur without **-ся**.

**3.** Notice the difference between English and Russian usage when one speaker reports another's statements or questions: In Russian (1) a reported statement or question remains *in the same tense* as the original, only the person being changed; (2) a reported question, in the absence of a specific question-word, is indicated by the particle **ли**, translated 'whether'. For example (first direct quotation, then indirect):

| | |
|---|---|
| Óн говори́т: «Она́ рабо́таёт». | He says, "She works." |
| Óн говори́т, что она́ рабо́таёт. | He says that she works. |
| | |
| Óн сказа́л: «Она́ рабо́таёт». | He said, "She works." |
| Óн сказа́л, что она́ рабо́таёт. | He said that she work*ed*. |
| | |
| Óн говори́т: «Она́ рабо́тала». | He says, "She worked." |
| Óн говори́т, что она́ рабо́тала. | He says that she worked. |

<br>

Óн сказа́л, что она́ рабо́тала.

He said that she
$\begin{cases} \text{worked.} \\ \text{used to work.} \\ \text{had worked.} \end{cases}$

| | |
|---|---|
| Óн сказа́л: «Она́ бу́дёт рабо́тать». | He said, "She will work." |
| Óн сказа́л, что она́ бу́дёт рабо́тать. | He said that she *would* work. |
| | |
| Óн спра́шиваёт: «Вы́ ёго́ ви́дите?» | He asks, "Do you see him?" |
| Óн спра́шиваёт, ви́дит ли она́ ёго́. | He asks *whether* she sees him. |
| | |
| Óн спроси́л: «Вы́ ёго́ ви́дите?» | He asked, "Do you see him?" |
| Óн спроси́л, ви́дит ли она́ ёго́. | He asked *whether* she *saw* him. |
| | |
| Óн спроси́л: «Что́ вы́ де́лаёте?» | He asked, "What are you doing?" |
| Óн спроси́л, что́ она́ де́лаёт. | He asked what she *was* doing. |
| | |
| Óн спроси́л: «Что́ вы́ де́лали?» | He asked, "What were you doing?" |
| Óн спроси́л, что́ она́ де́лала. | He asked what she *had been* doing. |
| | |
| Óн спро́сит: «Что́ вы́ бу́дете де́лать?» | He will ask, "What will you do?" |
| Óн спро́сит, что́ она́ бу́дёт де́лать. | He will ask what she will do. |
| | |
| Óн спроси́л, что́ она́ бу́дёт де́лать. | He asked what she *would* do. |

Note that the **что́** in the last examples is stressed *štó*: it is the interrogative used as a relative and means 'what' or sometimes 'that which'. The **что** in the other examples is *un*stressed *štə* and is merely a connective, the English 'that'. The visual identity of these two can be confusing, and sometimes the relative *štó* is marked with an accent (**что̀, что́**) in Russian books which write no other accents.

In translating indirect quotations from English to Russian, try first to reconstruct the direct statement. In isolated sentences there may be ambiguity in English (cf. the 4th and 6th and perhaps the 7th of the examples above).

The same sort of indirectly reported speech may be introduced by other verbs also, like "answer, know, hope."

| | |
|---|---|
| Óн отвéтил, что онá бýдет рабóтать. | He answered that she would work. |
| Я знáл, что вы́ э́то замéтите. | I knew that you would notice that. |
| Мы́ всегдá надéялись, что óн кýпит нáшё пóлё. | We always hoped that he would buy our field. |

**4.** A reported command is changed from the imperative into the past tense, and introduced by the conjunction **чтобы** (**чтоб**), a word which is normally stressless, *štəbi* or *štəp*.

| | |
|---|---|
| Возьми́те мою́ тетрáдку! | Take my notebook! |
| Óн говори́т, чтобы я́ взя́л ёгó тетрáдку. | He says for me to take his notebook. |
| Óн сказáл, чтобы я́ взя́л ёгó тетрáдку. | He told me to take his notebook. |
| Пýсть онá возьмёт мою́ тетрáдку. | Let her take my notebook. |
| Óн говори́т, чтобы онá взялá ёгó тетрáдку. | He says for her to take his notebook. |
| Óн сказáл, чтобы онá взялá ёгó тетрáдку. | He said she should ⎱ take his <br> He told her to ⎰ notebook. |

**5.1** A condition which is believed possible of fulfilment is expressed by **éсли** 'if':

| | |
|---|---|
| Éсли óн рабóтаёт тáм, мóй отéц ёгó знáет. | If he works there, my father knows him. |
| Éсли óн бы́л в теáтре, (тó) óн ви́дел «Гáмлета». | If he was at the theater, he saw "Hamlet". |
| Éсли óн бýдет тáм, тó спроси́те ёгó об э́том. | If he's there, ask him about it. |

When the consequence-clause follows the if-clause, the particle **тó** may be used to mark its beginning. **Тó** may be omitted in translation or rendered by "then".

Notice that in English we use the present tense with *if* to express a *future* condition viewed as probable: "If I *meet* him *tomorrow*, I'll ask him about it." Russian must have the future: Éсли я́ ёгó *встрéчу* зáвтра, тó спрошý ёгó об э́том.

**5.2** If, however, the fulfilment is viewed as doubtful or impossible, because the condition is improbable or contrary to fact, then "if" is éсли бы (éсли б) and the unreal consequence is expressed by the past tense plus the unstressed particle бы or б:

Éсли бы óн **рабóтал** тáм, мой          If he $\begin{Bmatrix} \text{worked (were working)} \\ \text{had been working} \end{Bmatrix}$ there

отéц **бы** ёгó **знáл.**          my father $\begin{Bmatrix} \text{would know} \\ \text{would have known} \end{Bmatrix}$ him.

Éсли бы óн **бы́л** в теáтре,          If he $\begin{Bmatrix} \text{were} \\ \text{had been} \end{Bmatrix}$ at the theater

мы́ **бы** ёгó **ви́дели.**          we $\begin{Bmatrix} \text{would see} \\ \text{would have seen} \end{Bmatrix}$ him.

The particle **бы** excludes the possibility of using any present (including the perfective future) tense form in a clause, so that *only the past tense forms can be used* here. Thus there is no distinction between present and past contrary-to-fact or unreal conditions, and one must be guided by the context in translating into English.

**5.21**   Either half of such a condition may occur alone: (1) with **éсли бы,** to express a wish: Éсли бы óн бы́л здéсь! 'if he were only here!' (2) with **бы,** to indicate a willingness or inclination to act (granting the fulfilment of some unnamed and unlikely condition): я́ бы спáл 'I'd like to sleep (if only circumstances were right).'

   Note: In some books éсли бы is written with a hyphen or as a single word: éсли-бы éсли-б éслибы éслиб.

**5.3**   Note that although "whether" may occasionally be replaced by "if" in English, Russian makes a clear distinction between **éсли** "if, if it is so that, in case that" and **ли,** which specifies a question, direct or indirect. Thus "whether" is to be translated as **ли,** *following* the word questioned:

   Do you know whether (if) he          Вы́ знáете, отвéтит **ли** óн?
   will answer?
   Ask her if (whether) she under-          Спроси́те её, понимáет **ли** онá.
   stands.

**6.0**   Like **хотéть** (IV 6), the perfective **захотéть захотя́т** has irregular forms in the 2nd and 3rd persons of the present singular: ты́ захóчёшь, óн захóчёт. It means "take a liking, start to want," and sometimes is used as a perfective for **хотéть:**

   Éсли я́ захочу́, пойду́.          If I (shall) want to, I'll go.

**6.1**   Notice the translation of "want to do":

(a) Я хочу́ написа́ть э́то.          I want to write that down.

Она́ бы хоте́ла написа́ть э́то.  She would like to write that down.

(b) Я хочу́,          ⎫
    Она́ бы хоте́ла, ⎬ что́бы вы          I want          ⎫ you to write it
                              ⎭          She would like ⎬ down.
    э́то написа́ли.

In (a) the same person "wants" and "writes", and the infinitive is used, but in (b) the person who "wants" is different from the person who "writes" and **что́бы** plus past tense must be used. Compare § 4 above.

**6.2**   Observe that "would like" is rendered by **хоте́л бы**.

**7.**   The verb **мочь мо́гут** (I) "to be physically able" has an irregular accent in the 1st person singular present, **могу́**, and replaces the stem-consonant *g* (**г**) with *ž* (**ж**) in all other persons of the present: **мо́жешь, мо́жет, мо́жем, мо́жете**. The imperative is not used. The past forms are **мог, могло́, могла́, могли́**.

The perfective **смочь смо́гут** has similar forms. It is used for the future of **мочь** (which is not found with **бу́дут**), and in the past it normally occurs with negation, signifying "tried and failed":

Я не смогу́ сде́лать э́того.        I won't be able to do that.

Я не смог реши́ть э́ту зада́чу.   I couldn't manage to solve the problem.

**8.**   **Мочь** is illustrative of verbs with infinitives in **-чь**. Such verbs have stems either in *-g-* or *-k-* (**г, к**) which are replaced by *-ž-* or *-č-* (**ж, ч**) respectively, in all present forms except 1st singular and 3rd plural.

For past, cf. VII 5.

**9.**   The verb **боя́ться** 'fear, be afraid of' takes a genitive (never an accusative):

Он бои́тся (свое́й) сестры́.      He is afraid of his sister.

**10.**   The third person plural verb-forms, without the pronoun **они́**, express an action with no specified actor or actors.

Говоря́т, что он ма́ло смеётся.   *They say* he doesn't laugh much.

Frequently such a Russian construction is best rendered by an English passive:

Ле́том его́ ви́дели в Москве́.    *He was seen* in Moscow in the summer.

Здесь говоря́т по-ру́сски.        Russian *is spoken* here.

**11.** A tiny number of Russian neuter nouns have no declensional forms: e.g.

| | |
|---|---|
| **кино́** 'cinema, movie-theater, film' | Óн *в то́м кино́*. |
| | Та́м *кино́* не́ было. |
| **метро́** 'subway(-train)' | В э́том го́роде не́т *метро́*. |
| | Она́ е́здит *на метро́*. |

Here belong place-names whose endings do not fit any Russian declension, such as **Баку́** 'Baku': о́н живёт в *Баку́*, е́дет в *Баку́*.

**12.** Note that the adverb **ве́чером** 'in the evening' refers to the time approximately from sundown until bed-time. In English we often say 'night' for this time, so NB 'tonight' = **сего́дня ве́чером**; 'last night' = **вчера́ ве́чером**, 'tomorrow night' = **за́втра ве́чером**.

**13.** *A note on punctuation.* In English, the effort is usually made to write a comma only where one makes a pause in speaking. Russian uses the comma with less regard for actual speech, and Russian school-children learn such rules as to "write a comma before *а, но, что, чтобы, если, когда, где, кто,*" and some similar words. The general rule is that *any* subordinate clause (and most independent clauses) must be set off by commas. In this book little attention will be devoted to explaining Russian punctuation, but all Russian examples are punctuated according to the current rules.


## УПРАЖНЕНИЯ


**A.** For oral drill:

1. Make each of the model sentences in IX into indirect statements by prefacing them with as many of the following as the sense will allow:

(а) *О́н говори́т,* (б) *о́н сказа́л,* (в) *о́н спра́шивает,* (г) *о́н спроси́л.*

2. Give all persons of this sentence in present, past, and future:
*Они́ хотя́т идти́, но́ не мо́гут.*

**B.** Read and translate:

1a. Они́ чита́ют кни́гу мое́й до́чери.    1b. Пётр Петро́вич сказа́л, что они́ чита́ют кни́гу его́ до́чери.    2a. Они́ покупа́ют фа́брику свои́х сынове́й.    2b. Ива́н Ива́нович сказа́л, что они́ покупа́ют поля́ свои́х сынове́й.    3. Éсли б я зна́л э́то, я бы не спроси́л у докторо́в.    4. Я не могу́ е́хать на метро́, потому́ что у меня́ не́т де́нег.    5. Ма́ть сказа́ла, что она́ ча́сто встреча́ет Алексе́я Алекса́ндровича в рестора́нах.    6. Мы́ надééмся, что ле́том уже́ бу́дет у на́с автомоби́ль.    7. Éсли бы у ни́х не́ было автомоби́лей, они́ бы не́ жили в дере́вне.    8a. У на́с в

шко́ле нет англича́нок. 8b. Сосе́ди говори́ли, что у них в университе́те
нет америка́нцев. 9. Е́сли бы това́рищи жи́ли в Росси́и, то они́ хорошо́
говори́ли бы по-ру́сски. 10a. Пусть кто́-нибудь ку́пит газе́ту сего́дня
ве́чером! 10b. Зо́я Петро́вна хоте́ла, чтобы А́ся купи́ла журна́лы.
11. Е́сли уви́дишь э́ту кни́гу, купи́ её, пожа́луйста. 12. Э́ти англича́не
и англича́нки говоря́т о́чень хорошо́ по-ру́сски. Говоря́т, что они́
бы́ли в Росси́и ле́том. 13. Да, коне́чно я э́то сде́лаю — е́сли не забу́ду.
14. Е́сли вы напи́шете кни́гу, то я её прочита́ю. 15. Е́сли бы ты
написа́л кни́гу, я её прочита́л бы. 16. Пётр говори́т, что е́сли Ива́н
напи́шет кни́гу, Пётр её прочита́ет. 17. Пётр сказа́л, что е́сли бы
Ива́н написа́л кни́гу, он бы её прочита́л. 18a. Вы америка́нка? Нет,
я англича́нка, но оте́ц был америка́нец и муж и сын то́же америка́нцы.
18b. До́ктор спроси́л, англича́нка ли э́та да́ма. Она́ отве́тила, что
она́ америка́нка, а что муж англича́нин. 19. Америка́нцы хоте́ли,
чтобы все э́ти англича́не то́же пое́хали в Баку́. 20. Е́сли бы вы пошли́
в теа́тр вчера́ ве́чером, вы бы встре́тили англича́н. 21. Говоря́т, что
Петро́вы мо́жет быть ку́пят кино́. 22. За́втра у́тром я хочу́ взять у
америка́нок все э́ти сту́лья. 23. Е́сли бы вы бы́ли в кла́ссе сего́дня
у́тром, вы бы зна́ли, о чём студе́нтки говоря́т. 24. Е́сли Арка́дий
Серге́евич не до́ма, то он или в библиоте́ке или в рестора́не. 25. Е́сли
бы вы жи́ли в го́роде, ваш сын и моя́ дочь могли́ бы ходи́ть в шко́лу
вме́сте. 26. Мы наде́ялись встре́тить вас всех у сосе́дей вчера́ ве́чером,
но вас не́ было. 27. Е́сли у Зо́и бы́ло своё перо́, то почему́ она́ взяла́
перо́ Ду́ни? 28. Е́сли б А́нна Петро́вна спроси́ла, она́ получи́ла бы
отве́т сейча́с же. 29. Е́сли ты всё понима́ешь, почему́ спра́шиваешь?
30. Е́сли бы вы повторя́ли все фра́зы, вы бы хорошо́ зна́ли все слова́
на уро́ке. 31. Дми́трий сказа́л, что ле́том учи́тельница мо́жет быть
напи́шет кни́гу об имена́х. 32. Вы ви́дели фотогра́фии го́рода Баку́
у него́ на стене́? 33. Е́сли вы получа́ете э́ти газе́ты, то почему́ вы
их никогда́ не чита́ете? 34. Дава́йте ку́пим её автомоби́ль! Я хоте́л
бы, но у меня́ нет де́нег. 35. Зинаи́да Алексе́евна хо́чет, чтобы мы
все пошли́ за́втра ве́чером в теа́тр на «Макбе́та».

**C.** For written and/or oral translation into Russian:

1. These ladies can't often go to the movie, to the theater, or to
concerts, because they live in the country and have no car. If they lived
in the city they could go by subway or (walk) on foot. 2a. What do you
want, sir? 2b. The Englishwoman asked the American what he wanted.
3. If the teacher would speak slowly, we'd all understand better.
4. The teacher laughed and said that she couldn't speak slowly in

Russian.   5. I hope that you and your wife will be at the meeting to-morrow morning.   6. What are you going to do in the summer? Perhaps we will go somewhere in our car.   7. Why were they afraid of their wives and daughters?   8. If you didn't understand the Englishman, why are you laughing?   9a. Those Englishmen are talking about the Petrovs' factories.   9b. I knew that the Americans were talking about the English-men's houses.   10a. Do you understand this article, comrade?   10b. The mechanic asked his comrade whether he understood the article.   11. Haven't you seen the Americans' gardens?   12. Don't forget that we're all going to the movies together tonight.   13. If I had an automobile, I'd never walk to the factory, I'd always ride.   14. Ask, and you will receive an answer at once, because we want you to know all the answers.   15. They say that he works in the movie(-theater) now.   16a. I want to go to the movies tomorrow night.   16b. I want you to go to the movies.   17a. Stand by the door!   17b. I want you to stand by the door.   17c. Ivan Petrovich wanted all the students to stand at the blackboard.   18. I was sitting at home and reading a magazine.   19a. What are you afraid of?   19b. He is asking you what you are afraid of.   19c. He asked what she was afraid of.   20. If he had been sitting there, I would have seen him.   21a. Please carry these things to the station.   21b. The Americans (f) wanted me to carry all their things to the station.   22. The doctor said he had forgotten his watch at home.   23a. No, the Petrovs have no tables.   23b. The Ivanovs said that there were no tables at the Petrovs.   24. She said that this citizen was an Englishman and that his wife was an American.   25. If their husbands lived in that village, my brothers would know them.

## СЛОВАРЬ

америка́нец          American (m)
  [-нца] (App. I, § 7.1.2)
америка́нка          American (f)
  [Gen. pl. -нок]
англича́нин          Englishman
  [pl. англича́не, G англича́н]
англича́нка          Englishwoman
  [Gen. pl. -нок]
бы (§ 5.2)     conditional particle
ве́чером (§ 12)      in the evening
ве́щь (f: cf. IX 8.4b)          thing

кино́ (neut. indecl. § 11)      movie
ле́том                in the summer
метро́ (neut. indecl. § 11)   subway

у́тром            in the morning
  вчера́ у́тром          yesterday
                 morning
  за́втра у́тром         tomorrow
                 morning
  сего́дня у́тром     this morning

чтобы § 4, 6.1b             that

| | | | | |
|---|---|---|---|---|
| боя́ться боя́тся I (+ Gen.) fear (§9) | | надея́ться наде́ются I | | hope |
| покупа́ть покупа́ют I<br>купи́ть ку́пят P } | buy | смея́ться смею́тся I<br>засмея́ться P } | | laugh |
| мо́чь мо́гут I<br>смо́чь смо́гут P } (§ 7) | be able | хоте́ть хотя́т<br>захоте́ть P (§ 6) } | | want |

## For review

**A.**  Когда Михаил ехал домой на метро, он встретил своих соседей, Бориса и Ирину Ивановых.

—Здравствуйте, Михаил Петрович, —сказал Борис. Почему вы несете все эти книги? Вы их взяли в библиотеке?

—Нет, —ответил Михаил. Я их купил в магазине нашего университета. Обыкновенно там мало книг, но вчера они получили много книг, журналов, газет из России, и я купил всё, что мог. У меня никогда нет денег, потому что я всегда покупаю книги. В магазине я встретил нашего профессора истории. Он спросил, почему я покупаю так много рома́нов. Я думаю, он боится, что я не читаю учебников. Когда я его об этом спросил, он засмеялся и сказал: «Если бы вы бо́льше[1] работали, то вы были бы очень хороший студент.»

—Не думаете ли вы, что кто-нибудь сказал, что вы пишете рассказы? —спросила Ирина. Может быть он их прочитал в журнале «Наша литература»?

—Никто не понимает людей, которые пишут! Мои отец тоже надо мной смеется и часто повторяет: «Если ты не будешь писать своих рассказов, то ты, конечно, начнешь лучше писать экзамены.[2]»

Михаил спросил у Бориса и Ирины, что́ они будут делать сегодня вечером. Он спросил, не хотят ли они пойти на концерт.

—Мы бы очень хотели пойти, но не можем, —сказал Борис. Нас ждут[3] сёстры Ирины в ресторане, а потом мы все идем в театр.

Ирина засмеялась.

—Когда мы жили в деревне, мы никогда никуда не ходили, потому что там не было ни театра, ни кино, ни библиотеки, ни ресторанов. Я сидела дома и читала, а летом работала в саду. Здесь же в городе я редко сижу дома. Мы никогда не можем решить, куда идти вечером: так много здесь всего.

---

[1] more.   [2] экза́мен exam.   [3] are awaiting.

**B.** For oral or written translation:

1. Ivan met his friend Sergej Borodin near the library. 2. "Where are you going and what are you carrying?" Ivan asked him. 3. "I am going to the library and I am taking some books there; I'd like you to go with me. Let's go together," said Sergej. 4. "No," answered Ivan, "I'd like to go, but I can't. 5. I'm going to a meeting now at Professor Ivanov's; several Americans and Englishmen will be there. 6. All the students and professors will also be there. 7. Professor Nikoláev will speak about Russia and America. 8. Tomorrow morning I will see you at the laboratory and we can talk about it all."

9. Ivan went to the meeting, and Sergej went to the library. 10. Usually Sergej read at the library for many hours, but today he could not read. 11. He decided to go to a movie. 12. He saw "The Brothers Karamazov". 13. Then he went to a store and bought several books and magazines. 14. He went home by subway.

15. At home his mother said that if he had not gone to the library in the morning, he would have seen her brother, Andrej Andreevich, the writer. 16. "You know," said Sergej's mother, "Andrej lives in the country and rarely goes to town. 17. Today there is a concert at the Petrovs'. 18. He's gone to the concert. 19. He wanted to see you, and I said that you would be home in the evening, but he said that he wants to go straight to the country." 20. "I think that he will be here again and then I will see him," said Sergej. 21. "Good night, mother," he said and went to his room.

**C.** 1. If you had only said that you wanted me to buy the books! 2. My brothers didn't go to school yesterday because they were afraid of their teachers. 3. When I repeated that there were no people in the garden, they burst out laughing for some reason. 4. These students don't know their husbands' first names! 5. I often go to the meetings in town by automobile. 6. Always read the lessons and write the sentences at home.—But yesterday you told us not to write the sentences. 7a. The professor's wife asked, "Why don't we ever go anywhere?" 7b. Mrs. Ivanov wanted to know why they never went anywhere. 8. Mrs. Petrov and Mrs. Brown had a lot of money, but their neighbors the Borodins didn't have anything. 9. Let's talk about the villages and fields of Russia. 10. Where did you put my things? I carried them into your room. 11. Somebody answer my question. Who say Ivan Borisovich Lukin today? 12. Those people want everyone to know everything about them. 13. Do you see the books there on the chairs?

Please put them here in this room. 14a. Yesterday evening comrade Petrov set off on foot for the theater because she had no automobile. 14b. Her friends had forgotten that she wanted to go with them.   15. If you see Mikhail, ask him what he is doing tonight and whether he wants to go to a concert.

# LESSON Xa

| | |
|---|---|
| После лекций мы будем играть в футбол. | After the lectures we will play soccer. |
| Этот писатель теперь ходит на все лекции нашего профессора. | This writer now attends all the lectures of our professor. |
| Он читает лекции по средам, не правда ли? | He gives lectures on Wednesdays, doesn't he? |
| Вы заметили, что она теперь делает успехи, не правда ли? | You noticed that she is now making progress, didn't you? |

'To play (a game)' is expressed by the verb **играть** followed by **в** + Acc.: *Вы играете в шахматы, не правда ли?* 'You play chess, don't you?'

Many Russian sport terms are borrowed. Can you guess the following: баскетбол, бейсбол, воллейбол, гольф, теннис, хоккей?

## УПРАЖНЕНИЯ

**A.** Complete the sentences, giving both singular and plural forms for each of the nouns:

1. **Я вижу** _____
2. **Я не вижу** _____
3. **Я говорил о** _____

рука, парк, календарь, церковь, ошибка, карман, упражнение, учебник, шапка, платок, лампа, кошелёк, ключ, полка, портфель, сумка, словарь, шляпа, шкаф, карта

**В.** 1. Закройте двери, пожалуйста, и начнёмте читать упражнения. 2. Теперь переведём рассказ с английского на русский. 3. Если ты повесил шляпу в шкаф, почему её там нет теперь? 4. Мы все будем ходить на лекции писательницы. Вы будете тоже ходить? 5. Куда вы идёте после уроков? Я иду в парк играть в бейсбол. 6. Он посадит журналистку в автомобиль. Она будет ездить на автомобиле. 7. Писатель поставил лампу на полку. Лампа теперь стоит на полке. 8. Вы заметили, что она боится звонков? 9. Если вы ходите на все лекции и уроки, вы будете делать успехи. 10. Я заметил, что он положил мои карты в свой карман. 11. Сергей

Па́влович пове́сил ла́мпу на сте́ну. Ла́мпа тепе́рь виси́т на стене́. 12. Она́ всё замеча́ет. 13. У Петро́вых говори́ли, что сыновья́ журнали́стки Ива́новой в пя́тницу бу́дут игра́ть в футбо́л у нас в дере́вне. 14. Па́вел Серге́евич сказа́л, чтобы я вас посади́л на э́тот сту́л у окна́. Посмотри́те в сад. 15. Вы де́лаете оши́бки, когда́ вы говори́те по-ру́сски, но вы та́кже де́лаете и успе́хи.

**C.** Сего́дня по́сле ле́кций Па́вел Петро́в спроси́л меня́:

—Куда́ вы тепе́рь идёте?

—Я иду́ в па́рк игра́ть в те́ннис, —отве́тила я. —Вы иногда́ хо́дите туда́ то́же, не пра́вда ли?

—Да, почти́ ка́ждый день. Я и сего́дня пойду́. У меня́ тут автомоби́ль, пое́демте вме́сте!

Па́вел посади́л меня́ в автомоби́ль и вдру́г уви́дел, что нигде́ нет ключе́й.

—Мы не мо́жем е́хать, —сказа́л он.

—Мо́жет быть ключи́ у вас в карма́не? —спроси́ла я. —Посмотри́те!

—У меня́ в карма́не почти́ ничего́ нет, то́лько плато́к, кошелёк и каранда́ш, а ключе́й нет нигде́. Пойдёмте в конто́ру.

Мы пошли́. Па́вел всегда́ но́сит портфе́ль, когда́ хо́дит в университе́т. Тепе́рь же я заме́тила, что сего́дня он забы́л свой портфе́ль.

—Где ваш портфе́ль, Па́вел?

—У́тром я его́ взял.

—Е́сли вы взя́ли портфе́ль у́тром, то почему́ его́ нет тепе́рь?

В конто́ре закры́ты[1] все о́кна. В углу́ стои́т ла́мпа. Я поста́вила ла́мпу на стол.

—Что э́то лежи́т у меня́ на столе́? Да э́то мой портфе́ль!

Па́вел откры́л портфе́ль. Там бы́ли и бума́ги, и карандаши́, и фотогра́фии, и ка́рты и да́же де́ньги, но ключе́й не́ было.

—Ключе́й нигде́ нет, —повтори́л Па́вел.

—Смотри́те, смотри́те вот там, на полу́ у шка́фа... вы их не ви́дите?

На полу́, в углу́ у шка́фа, лежа́ли ключи́ Петро́ва.

—Тепе́рь е́дем. Пора́! —сказа́л Па́вел.

Он закрыва́ет дверь. Я замеча́ю, что он положи́л ключи́ в свой карма́н.

Мы — в автомоби́ле. Говори́м о том, что[2] писа́тельница Ивано́ва бу́дет чита́ть в клу́бе ле́кции два ра́за в неде́лю, а её сыновья́ бу́дут игра́ть в суббо́ту у нас в университе́те в хокке́й.

---

[1] закры́ты = are closed.   [2] о том, что = about the fact that.

Потóм Пáвёл сказáл мнé:

—Вы́, Вéра, не хóдите на всé лéкции. Я дýмаю, что éсли вы́ не хóдите в университéт, а рабóтаёте тóлько дóма, тó вы́ не сдéлаёте успéхов. Потóм... тогдá я не бýду ви́деть вáс кáждый дéнь.

**D.**   For written and/or oral translation.

1. The teacher said last night after the lecture that all the students in our class were making progress. 2. They asked Peter Ivanovich what he had in his pockets. 3a. Hang the picture on that wall! 3b. The writer wanted the journalist to hang the picture on the wall, didn't he? 4. If our husbands want to go to the opera tonight, you and I can play chess here at home. 5. Put the chair in the corner by the bed. 6. Are there many pictures in your churches in Russia? 7. Does anyone want to play tennis? We're driving to the park. 8. Let's go to the department store. My wife and I are going to buy a bed, a wardrobe, and perhaps chairs. 9. The students played basketball every day last week, didn't they? 10. I noticed that she was carrying his briefcase to the office. 11. My wife wants me to go to the department store on Friday. 12. Our teachers want us all to make progress. 13. I want you to play chess Saturday after the concert. 14. I suddenly noticed that he had put all the letters into his briefcase. 15. The laywers want me to give a lecture at their club about these documents. 16. Why didn't she want you to go to the country with us last week? 17. My father wanted us to go to church, but we rarely went. 18. The journalists asked whether I had lost my watch. 19a. Will Vladimir go to the lectures on Thursdays? 19b. I asked Nadezhda whether she knew if Vladimir would go to the lectures on Tuesdays. 20. Tomorrow after the lessons they will want us all to play soccer.

## СЛОВАРЬ

| | | | |
|---|---|---|---|
| вдрýг | suddenly | успéх | success |
| да (unstressed) | why! | дéлать успéхи | make progress |
| кáрта | playing-card | футбóл | soccer |
| контóра | office | шáхматы | chess |
| лéкция | lecture | [pl. only,  G шáхмат] | |
| читáть лéкцию | give (a) lecture | | |
| пóсле + Gen. | after | игрáть -áют I | play |
| прáвда | truth | сыгрáть -áют P | |
| не прáвда ли? | isn't it so? | | |

# LESSON XI

Чём вы пи́шёте?

What are you writing with?

Я всегда́ пишу́ карандашо́м.

I always write with a pencil.

Его́ дру́г бы́л до́ктором.

His friend was a doctor.

Её бра́тья ре́дко е́здят по́ездом в Москву́.

Her brothers rarely go by train to Moscow.

Пое́хали сёстры трамва́ём и́ли на метро́?

Did the sisters go by street-car or on the subway?

Он говори́л об автомоби́лях с меха́никами перед рестора́ном.

He was talking about automobiles with the mechanics in front of the restaurant.

Де́вочка стоя́ла за ма́льчиком.

The little girl was standing behind the little boy.

Она́ игра́ла с детьми́ в саду́ за шко́лой.

She was playing with the children in the garden behind the school.

Он попроси́л меня́ пое́хать с ни́ми.

He asked me to go with them.

С ке́м они́ е́здили? С друзья́ми.

With whom did they go? With friends.

Я ни с ке́м не говори́л о ребёнке.

I didn't talk with anyone about the child.

Пое́ду ли я́ с ва́ми, и́ли вы́ пое́дете со мно́й?

Shall I go with you, or will you go with me?

Мы́ с тобо́й реши́ли все́ зада́чи.

You and I have solved all the problems.

Мы́ с Пётро́вым уже́ бы́ли у те́х люде́й.

Petrov and I have already been to see those people.

Он сиде́л за столо́м с гра́жданами Ива́новым и Бороди́ным.

He was sitting at a table with citizens Ivanov and Borodín.

Мы́ пое́дем те́ми же поезда́ми.

We will travel by the same trains.

Они́ жи́ли в то́й же дере́вне между Москво́й и Смоле́нском.

They lived in the same village between Moscow and Smolensk.

| | |
|---|---|
| Óн чáсто éздил в Москвý пóездом, нó в Смолéнск обыкновéнно éздил автóбусом. | He often went to Moscow by train, but he usually went to Smolensk by bus. |
| Тóмск гóрод за Óмском. | Tomsk is a city beyond Omsk. |

---

**1.** The INSTRUMENTAL CASE is expressed by the following *noun* suffixes:

**1.1** *Singular* — (*-om* 1.11; *-oj* 1.12; *-ju* 1.13).

**1.11** *-om* (spelled **-ом, -ём**) for 1st declension nouns. **-ём** is written if the Nom. ends in **-ь, -й,** or **-ё,** or if the stem ends in **ш, ж, ч, щ,** or **ц** and the suffix is *not* stressed (App. I, § 7.1). In all other cases **-ом** is written.

For example:

| | |
|---|---|
| учи́тель — учи́тел**ём** | музéй — музéй**ём** |
| словáр ь — словарём | пóлё — пóл**ём** |
| здáниё — здáни**ём** | (питьé — пить**ём**) |
| товáрищ — товáрищ**ём** | америкáнец — америкáнц**ём** |
| дóм — дóм**ом** | стóл — стол**óм** |
| слóв*о* — слóв**ом** | перó — пер**óм** |
| карандáш — карандаш**óм** | отéц — отц**óм** |

**1.111** The irregular neuter *и́мя* (VI 10) has **и́мёнём.**

**1.12** *-oj* (spelled **-ой, -ей**) for 2nd declension nouns. **-ей** is written if the Nom. ends in **-я** or *u*nstressed **-ша, -жа, -ча, -ща,** or **-ца** (App. I, §7.1); **-ой** is written in all other cases. For example:

| | |
|---|---|
| дерéвн*я* — дерéвн**ей** | Росси́*я* — Росси́**ей** |
| задáч*а* — задáч**ей** | учи́тельниц*а* — учи́тельниц**ей** |
| кóмнат*а* — кóмнат**ой** | госпожá — госпож**óй** |

See also paragraph 3, below.

**1.13** *-ju* (spelled **-ью**) for 3rd declension nouns: двéр ь — двéр**ью,** рáдость — рáдост**ью.**

Note: here also мáт ь — мá**терью,** дóч ь — дó**черью.**

**1.2** *Plural* — (*-amᵇi* 1.21; *-mᵇi* 1.22).

**1.21** *-amᵇi* (spelled **-ами, -ями**) for nearly all nouns. **-ями** corresponds to **-ях** in the prepositional pl.; **-ами** to **-ах:** see VIII 1.4. For example:

| | |
|---|---|
| брáть*я* — брáть**ями** | пéрь*я* — пéрь**ями** |
| (недéл*я* — недéл**ями**) | фотогрáфи*я* — фотогрáфи**ями** |
| пóл*ё* — пол**я́ми** | здáни*ё* — здáни**ями** |
| музéй — музé**ями** | учи́тель — учител**я́ми** |

| дверь — дверя́ми | мать — матеря́ми (NB) |
|---|---|
| стол — стола́ми | го́род — города́ми |
| оте́ц — отца́ми | каранда́ш — карандаша́ми |
| граждани́н — гра́жданами | и́мя — имена́ми |

**1.22** -*mʰi* (spelled -**ьми**) for four exceptional cases: *челове́к* — **людьми́**, *до́чь* — до**че́рьми́**, (*ло́шадь* 'horse' [3rd decl. f] — лошадьми́), N pl. де́ти 'children' — детьми́.

**2.** *Pronouns* have the following forms in the instrumental:

| Sg. N | кто́ | что́ | я́ | ты́ | о́н оно́ она́ |
|---|---|---|---|---|---|
| I | ке́м | че́м | мно́й | тобо́й | и́м   е́й |
| Pl. N | | | мы́ | вы́ | они́ |
| I | | | на́ми | ва́ми | и́ми |

| Sg. N | мо́й моё́ моя́ | на́ш на́шё на́ша | че́й чьё́ чья́ |
|---|---|---|---|
| I | мои́м мое́й | на́шим на́шей | чьи́м чье́й |
| Pl. N | мои́ | на́ши | чьи́ |
| I | мои́ми | на́шими | чьи́ми |

| Sg. N | э́тот э́то э́та | то́т то́ та́ | ве́сь всё́ вся́ |
|---|---|---|---|
| I | э́тим э́той | те́м то́й | всём всей |
| Pl. N | э́ти | те́ | всё́ |
| I | э́тими | те́ми | все́ми |

The forms of **тво́й** and **сво́й** are like those of **мо́й**, and **ва́ш** goes like **на́ш**. The forms of the third person pronoun prefix an **н-** when used with a preposition (cf. VI 4): e.g. с ни́м 'with him', за не́й 'after her', перед ни́ми 'in front of them'.

**3.** All nominal and pronominal forms with the endings -**ой** or -**ей** may replace the -**й** by -**ю** (i.e. add *u* to -*ój*/-*əj*/-*ệj*/-*ij*): ко́мнато**ю**, госпожо́**ю** статье́**ю**, дере́вне**ю**, учи́тельнице**ю**, мно́**ю**, е́**ю**, на́ше**ю**, and the like. These longer forms are rarely used in speaking, but occur frequently in print.

**4.** *Surnames* in -**ин** and -**ов** (-**ёв**) (VI 7.2, VIII 3) have in the instrumental singular the pronominal endings in both *masculine* and *feminine*: Пётро́вым, Пу́шкиным — Пётро́вой, Пу́шкиной. (This is the only case where the *masculine* singular deviates from the normal animate masculine noun declension. In the feminine, the pronominal declension is regular throughout.)

The plural has the suffix -**ыми**: Пётро́выми, Пу́шкиными, Бороди́ными.

**5.**  Frequent USES of the *instrumental* are —

**5.1**  To express instrument or agent:

Я пишу́ ёго перо́м.  I'm writing with (by means of) his

Мы́ пое́дем трамва́ем.  We'll go by street-car.        [pen.

**5.2**  To express a temporary or impermanent state:

Её оте́ц бы́л до́ктором.  Her father was a doctor.

О́н бу́дет меха́ником.  He will be a mechanic.

Она́ хо́чет бы́ть учи́тель-  She wants to be a teacher.
ницей.

This is the normal construction for this type of sentence, with the past, future, or infinitive of the verb 'to be' and a noun (or adjective) which does not express an inherent, unchanging state. Thus one says о́н бы́л америка́нец 'he was an American', since nationality is regarded as being unchanging, at least as far as grammar is concerned.

[The use of the instrumental here appears to be spreading at the expense of the nominative, and not uncommonly it is found simply as the second member of a definition (in past or future), regardless of permanency.]

**5.3**  With a limited number of nouns, to express the medium or sur-roundings *through which*: Мы́ шли́ по́лем и ле́сом. 'We went by field and forest.'

**5.4**  With certain prepositions:

| | | | |
|---|---|---|---|
| с | with,[1] accompanying | между | between, among |
| над | above, over | перед | in front of, before |
| под | under, below | за | behind, beyond |

For example:

Я́ пойду́ **с** ни́ми.  I'll go with them.

Ёго кварти́ра **над** музе́ём.  His flat is above the museum.

Музе́й **под** ёго кварти́рой.  The museum is below his flat.

Сто́л **между** окно́м и две́рью.  The table is between the window and the door.

Автомоби́ль уже́ **перед** до́мом.  The car is already in front of the house.

**За** две́рью.  Behind the door.

**За** поля́ми.  Beyond the fields.

**6.**  Certain of these prepositions have variant phonetic forms: **с** becomes **со** before the root **вс-** 'all, whole' (**со** все́ми людьми́ 'with all

[1] Do not forget the fact that the English preposition *with* means at least two separate things. In the sense of *accompanying*, it is translated by the Russian **с** + Instrumental case. But in the sense of *by means of, through the agency of*, it is translated by the instrumental case alone.

men', **со** всём го́родом 'with the whole town'), before **мно́й** 'me', and before most words beginning with a **с, ш** or **з** which is followed by another consonant: e.g. **со столо́м**.

**Над, под,** and **перед** become надо, подо, передо before the pronoun **мно́й**: **передо** мно́й 'in front of me'.

Перед and между, although normally without stress, accent the first syllable if they are pronounced with special emphasis.

**7.** The prepositions **под** and **за** are used with the *accusative* case to denote motion:

| | |
|---|---|
| Она́ положи́ла перо́ **под** те́ кни́ги. | She put the pen under those books. |
| Он пошёл **за** шко́лу. | He's gone behind the school. |

**8.** *Special cases*: за столо́м means '*at* (the) table'. За́ го́родом (note the accent) 'beyond the city' usually means 'in the country'. When motion is expressed, the accusative is used: Пое́демте за́ город. 'Let's go to the country'.

**8.1** Notice that 'laugh at' is смея́ться **над** + Instr.

**9.** The plural of **друг** 'close friend' is **друзья́**. The Gen. pl. has zero suffix and inserted vowel: **друзе́й** (cf. сынове́й, муже́й), Instr. **друзья́ми**.

**10.** The plural of the noun **ребёнок** 'child' is **де́ти**, Acc.-Gen. **дете́й**, Prep. **де́тях**, Instr. **детьми́** (cf. 1.22 above).

**11.** The particle **же** (*ži* or *žə*, always unstressed), sometimes shortened to **ж** (*š*), has a number of different meanings. One of the most important is to serve as emphasis for the *preceding* word.

| | |
|---|---|
| Я э́то сде́лаю сего́дня же. | I'll do it *today* (no later!). |
| Он рабо́тает здесь же. | { He works right here. / It's here that he works. |

Note the following special meanings:

| | |
|---|---|
| Э́то за то́й стено́й. | It's beyond that wall. |
| Э́то за то́й же стено́й. | It's beyond *the same* wall. |
| Он рабо́тает та́м же. | He works *in the same place* (*right there*). |
| Он то́же пойдёт. | He's going *too, as well*. |
| Вы его́ зна́ете? Я то́же. | Do you know him? I do *too*. |
| Он то́же не зна́ет. | He doesn't know *either*. |
| У меня́ то́же нет де́нег. | I don't have any money *either*. |

**12.** **Тóт** sometimes means "the right one", that is, the one which has been discussed. Even more common is the negation **не тóт** meaning 'the wrong one.'

Это тóт каранда́ш?    Is this the (right) pencil?

Это не тó перó.    { That's not the right pen.
{ That's the wrong pen.

**13.** The verb **проси́ть прóсят** I / **попроси́ть** P means 'request (someone to do something)'. Do not confuse it with **спра́шивать / спроси́ть** 'ask (a question)':

Я **по**проси́л ёгó сде́лать э́то.    I asked him to do it.

Я **с**проси́л ёгó, сде́лал ли óн    I asked him whether he had
э́то.    done it.

## УПРАЖНЕНИЯ

**A.** Translate: 1. *with* this man, that lady, our teacher (m, f), their neighbor (m, f), your doctor, him, her, my mother, her son, that mechanic, your comrade, his friend, citizen Ivanov, Mrs. Petrov, father, the American (m, f), the Englishman, the Englishwoman, the little boy, the little girl.

2. *under* that table, her chair, this window, their house, the letter, my notebook.

3. *behind* that apartment, the museum, that building, the bank, my door.

4. *in front of* this factory, that station, our house, their club, that movie, this theater, your restaurant, the library.

5–8. Repeat the above, putting all nouns into the plural, if possible. Translate all possible combinations of:

9. I, you, he, she, we, they, my brother(s), your sister(s), the doctor(s) { work(s) / worked / will work } with { me, you, her, him, them, us, those men, that man, all the teachers (m, f), their neighbors (m, f), these mechanics, our friends, the children

10. between { him, her, them, the students (m, f), the villages, that house, Lev, your school, her garden, us, Sergej, Pëtr, Dmitrij } and { those buildings, our houses, the museum, these factories, that field, those fields, the wall, the station, that forest, those forests, Zoja, Marija, Tanja, Irina

**B.** Read and translate:

1. Эта дере́вня ме́жду Ки́евом и Оде́ссой. 2. Наде́жда сиди́т в кла́ссе ме́жду Ива́ном и Со́ней. 3. Ле́том мы е́здили с госпожо́й Бу́ниной и господи́ном Ма́ловым. 4. Бра́тья мои́х това́рищей рабо́тали в деревня́х за Ки́евом. 5. Ма́льчик стоя́л перед кла́ссом и говори́л о поезда́х. 6. Мы пое́хали в дере́вню, куда́ ча́сто ходи́л мой оте́ц. 7. Пойдёмте туда́ с мои́м отцо́м и с америка́нцем. 8. У меня́ нет ни пера́ ни карандаша́. Чем я бу́ду писа́ть? 9. Что э́то там под сту́льями де́вочек? 10. Не́сколько друзе́й сиде́ло за столо́м с Любо́вью Андре́евной перед рестора́ном. 11. Не хоти́те ли игра́ть с ма́льчиками, де́вочки? Нет, они́ всегда́ смею́тся над на́ми! 12. Англича́нка ча́сто хо́дит за́ город в лес с детьми́. 13. Она́ хоте́ла, что́бы все мы, студе́нты, жи́ли на той же кварти́ре над её магази́ном. 14. Когда́ он был ребёнком, он о́чень боя́лся поездо́в и авто́бусов. 15. Они́ спроси́ли, куда́ он кладёт свои́ де́ньги. 16. Вы зна́ете, кто живёт за э́той стено́й? Да, там живёт на́ша учи́тельница с му́жем и сыновья́ми. 17. Кто положи́л мои́ фотогра́фии за дверь? Мо́жет быть, де́ти положи́ли. 18. У них в го́роде не́ было метро́. Она́ е́здила в го́род трамва́ем. 19. Пойдёмте со мно́й в кино́! 20. Любо́вь Никола́евна шла в теа́тр с дочерьми́ и сы́ном, когда́ мы её встре́тили перед ба́нком.

21. Дава́йте рабо́тать с э́тими гра́жданами и гражда́нками. 22. Э́того он не ска́жет перед свои́ми това́рищами. 23. Я ду́мал, что э́ти америка́нцы бы́ли со студе́нтками у сосе́дей. 24. Она́ не хоте́ла, что́бы де́ти говори́ли с меха́никами. 25. Е́сли вы не хоти́те пое́хать с Петро́вым на автомоби́ле, мо́жете пое́хать с на́шей до́черью авто́бусом. 26. Ду́ня хоте́ла бы игра́ть с ке́м-нибудь, но здесь в дере́вне нет ни де́вочек ни ма́льчиков. 27. На доске́ мы пи́шем ме́лом, а в тетра́дках мы пи́шем карандашо́м и́ли перо́м. 28. Мы встре́тили дру́га перед ста́нцией. Он е́хал в А́страхань. Я бы пое́хал с ним! 29. Я наде́юсь, что вы мо́жете пойти́ с на́ми в лес за́втра у́тром. 30. У неё в столе́ не́сколько пе́рьев и карандаше́й, но она́ спра́шивает, чем она́ бу́дет писа́ть! Я не понима́ю э́той де́вочки. 31. Е́сли в кла́ссе нет ме́ла, то не бу́дем писа́ть на доске́ сего́дня. Откро́йте кни́ги, пожа́луйста. Госпожа́ Смит, чита́йте по-ру́сски! Так, э́то хорошо́. 32. Повтори́те э́то сло́во за учи́тельницей. Так, э́то лу́чше. Тепе́рь напиши́те э́ту фра́зу. 33. Она́ нас попроси́ла написа́ть фра́зу. 34а. Спро́сим Ива́на Серге́евича, хо́чет ли он е́здить с на́ми в дере́вню ле́том. 34б. Това́рищ до́ктор, вы не хоте́ли бы е́здить за́ город со все́ми на́ми? 35а. Сосе́ди попроси́ли Серге́я Ива́новича пое́хать с ни́ми. 35б. Пожа́луйста, поезжа́йте (VII 1.201) с на́ми! 36а. Пусть ма́льчики

играют с э́тими детьми́. 36б. Ма́ть сказа́ла, чтобы они́ игра́ли с сосе́дями. 37а. Дава́йте начина́ть уро́к. Вы́ чита́ли все́ фра́зы? 37б. Профе́ссор хоте́л, чтобы мы́ начина́ли уро́к. О́н спроси́л, чита́ли ли мы́ все́ фра́зы. 38а. Де́ти, ке́м вы́ хоти́те бы́ть? 38б. Учи́тельница спроси́ла у дете́й, ке́м они́ хотя́т бы́ть. 39. Почёму́ вы́ откры́ли моё письмо́? Потому́ что я́ ду́мал, что оно́ моё, извини́те. 40. А́х, вы́ чита́ли не ту́ кни́гу. Вы́ мо́жете сего́дня не отвеча́ть.

**C.** For written and/or oral translation into Russian:

1. What are you doing? I'm writing. 2. What are you writing with? I'm writing with a pencil. 3. With whose pen are you writing? I'm writing with my brother's pen. 4. What will you write with your mother's pencil? Perhaps I shall write a book about children in cities. 5. You are reading the wrong lesson. You won't be able to answer in class, because you won't understand the professor's questions. 6. The doctors live with their mother, their sisters, and a brother in the house in the garden behind the museum. 7. With whom were those people talking? They were talking with the doctor. 8. We worked with the same people in the factory and in the theater. 9. The children all worked on (cf. V 9) the same problem this morning, and they all solved it. 10. Tomorrow morning you can play with the same little girls and boys. 11. When I was walking to the university last night with my sister and her teachers (f), I met Ivan Petrovich in front of the theater. 12. He was a mechanic at that time (vocab. VIII), he is now a teacher, and he wants to be a doctor. 13. Do you speak Russian with your father? Rarely; he speaks very rapidly and I do not understand everything. 14. Mrs. Leonov often opens the windows in the doctor's apartment, but his daughter closes them right away. 15. When they were students, they always spoke English at home. 16. Her father was an American, but he had lived in Russia and spoke Russian very well. 17. Perhaps you want to come to the meeting with us? An Englishwoman is speaking at the museum about gardens. 18. If I had a pen, I'd write a letter. If you don't have a pen, (then) write with a pencil. 19. She wanted me to write about the same things. 20. Your book is there under the magazines on the table by the window. 21. Ask him to write with my pen. 22. Ask him with whose pen he is writing. 23. The boy asked me to go to the movies with him. 24. The little girl asked whether I wanted to go to the concert. 25. That's all, goodbye!

## СЛОВАРЬ

| | |
|---|---|
| автобус | bus |
| дети (pl. of ребёнок, § 10) | children |
| друг [pl. друзья, § 9] | friend |
| же | see § 11 |
| за + Instr. (§ 6) | behind, beyond |
| за + Acc. (§ 7) | (to) behind, beyond |
| квартира | apartment, flat |
| на квартире<br>в квартире | in the apt. |
| между + Instr. (§ 5.4) | between |
| мёл | chalk |
| над + Instr. (§ 6) | above, over |
| перед + Instr. (§ 6) | before, in front of |
| под + Instr. (§ 6) | under, below |
| + Acc. (§ 7) | (to) under |
| поезд [pl. поезда] | train |
| ребёнок | child |
| [Gen. sing. ребёнка, pl. дети] | |
| с + Instr. (§ 6) | with, accompanying |
| там же (§ 11) | in the same place |
| тоже (§ 11) | also, too |
| тот же (§ 11) | the same |
| не тот (§ 12) | wrong |
| трамвай | street-car |

---

| | | |
|---|---|---|
| играть играют I<br>сыграть сыграют Р | play | |
| просить просят I<br>попросить Р | request (§ 13) | |

Some cities in the Soviet Union:

Москва, Одесса, Ленинград, Киёв, Смоленск, Харьков, Новгород, Архангельск, Владивосток, Ташкент, Тифлис, Астрахань, Казань.

Этот худо́жник знако́м с ни́ми со все́ми.

This artist is acquainted with them all.

Éсли я́ не ошиба́юсь, она́ уже́ знако́ма с э́тими офице́рами.

She is already acquainted with these officers, if I'm not mistaken.

Музыка́нты знако́мы с худо́жницами.

The musicians are acquainted with the artists (f.).

Адвока́т за́втра познако́мится с купцо́м.

The lawyer will make the acquaintance of the merchant tomorrow.

Ра́зве вы́ не знако́мы?

Why, aren't you acquainted?

Познако́мьтесь: И́горь Бори́сович Ма́льцёв — Ка́рл И́горёвич Леско́в.

Let me introduce: Igor' Borisovich Mal'cev — Karl Igorevich Leskov.

—О́чень прия́тно [познако́миться с ва́ми]!

I'm glad to meet you.

Ра́зве они́ не зна́ли, что мо́й бра́т актёр?

Didn't they know that my brother is an actor?

Эта актри́са ста́ла секрета́ршей коммерса́нта Воро́нина.
—Неуже́ли!

That actress has become the secretary of Voronin, the businessman.
You don't mean to say so!

Поэ́ты ре́дко стано́вятся генера́лами.

Poets rarely become generals.

Майо́р взя́л музыка́нтшу за́ руку и они́ пошли́ куда́-то.

The major took the musician (f.) by the hand and they went somewhere.

Секрета́рь на́шёго клу́ба собира́лся пое́хать в Евро́пу.

The secretary of our club was about to go to Europe.

Ра́зве ты́ оши́блась?

Were you really mistaken?

Извини́те, я́ оши́бся.

Excuse me, I was mistaken.

**1.** 'To be acquainted (with)' is expressed by the gender forms *знако́м* (m.), *знако́ма* (f.), *знако́мы* (pl.), plus *с* + instrumental. [*Знако́м* is an example of the short-form adjectives, discussed in XII 2.3.]

**2.** *Станови́ться/стать* 'become' is accompanied by the instrumental case of a noun: e.g., *Он ста́нет секретаре́м.* 'He will become secretary.'

**3.** Поэ́т 'poet' may refer to women (cf. III 13).

**4.** The past of ошиби́ться ошибу́тся is formed from the present stem (cf. VII 5): о́н **оши́бся**, она́ **оши́блась**, они́ **оши́блись**.

**5.1** *Неуже́ли* introduces (or implies) a question expecting a strong positive answer:

| | |
|---|---|
| Неуже́ли вы́ не познако́мились та́м с капита́ном Льво́вым? | Is it possible that you didn't meet Captain L'vov there? |
| Лейтена́нт Ро́зов собира́ется ста́ть актёром. — Неуже́ли! | Lt. Rozov is about to become an actor. You don't mean to say so! |

**5.2** *Ра́зве* adds a note of surprise to a question or implied question:

| | |
|---|---|
| О́н та́м бы́л. — Ра́зве? | He was there. Was he really? |
| Ра́зве о́н и́х не ви́дел? | *Didn't* he see them? |

**6.** *Быва́ть* 'to be' connotes a frequent or habitual, intermittent, non-continuous state.

| | |
|---|---|
| О́н быва́ет у адвока́та по среда́м. | He is usually at the lawyer's on Wednesdays. |

**7.** Note that *(по)знако́миться* can be translated "meet", but it specifically means "make the acquaintance of." *Встреча́ть/встре́тить* means "meet" rather in the sense of "run into, happen upon" or "meet by appointment".

## УПРАЖНЕНИЯ

**A.** Translate into Russian all the possible combinations of the following:

1. He/She wants to / They want to become (a) musician, officer, lawyer, merchant, soldier, artist, actor, poet, writer, journalist, student, teacher.

2a. under the calendar, hat, handkerchief, shelf, church, briefcase, bed, map, purse, pocketbook, key, cap, dictionary, floor

2b. Repeat 2a in the plural.

**B.** 1. Надёжда хотёла стáть писáтельницёй, нó у неё нёт талáнта. 2. Неужёли вы́ не замётили, с кём э́та музыкáнтша былá в цéркви? 3. Я́ не знакóма с Вéрой, нó познакóмилась с её мýжём у худóжницы на прóшлой недéле. 4. Бумáга тáм на столé. Вы́ мóжёте писáть э́тим перóм. 5. Фотогрáфия генерáла висéла над доскóй между кáртой Еврóпы и окнóм. 6. Онá иногдá диктовáла óчень бы́стро. 7. Нéсколько солдáт игрáли в футбóл на пóле за цéрковью. 8. Вáша секретáрша меня́ не рáз поправля́ла. 9. Адвокáт бы́л тогдá капитáном, нó потóм óн стáл майóром. 10. Чтó э́то тáм на полý между шкáфом и кровáтью?

**C.** Мы́ сиди́м в пáрке. Со мнóй мóй брáт Алексéй, музыкáнт, и ёгó друзья́. Я́ ужé знакóма с ни́ми со всéми. Здéсь худóжники, актёры, адвокáт и офицéр. Éсли я́ не ошибáюсь, актёры знакóмы с худóжниками, нó адвокáт и майóр ещё не знакóмы.

—Познакóмьтесь: майóр Бори́с Николáёвич Фóкин и Николáй Кáрлович Мáйков.

—Óчень прия́тно, —говори́т адвокáт Мáйков.

—Рáзве вы́ не знáли, что майóр Фóкин пи́шёт? Óн собирáётся стáть писáтелём, —сказáла я́.

—Неужéли? Генерáлы станóвятся поэ́тами! Я́ дýмал, что э́то бывáёт рéдко. Тепéрь я́ ви́жу, что оши́бся. Я́ чáсто ошибáюсь. Вóт вчерá я́ познакóмился с купцóм Морóзовым и óн сказáл, что ёгó дóчь, моя́ секретáрша, тепéрь стáла актри́сой и собирáётся éхать в Москвý. Конéчно, не я́ откры́л её талáнт!

**D.** For oral and/or written translation.

1. Are you acquainted with the secretary of our class? 2. Yes, I made his acquaintance last week, when we played tennis with the artists and musicians. 3. Excuse me, I think you're mistaken. 4. We are going to the country with the officers and soldiers. 5. The writer (f.) always went to church on Sunday with her brothers, the merchant and the actor. I met them in front of the church yesterday. 6. Many soldiers were at the opera Saturday evening. 7. I hope that I will make the acquaintance of that actress at your office next week. 8a. Have you translated this story from Russian? 8b. The lieutenant asked the major whether he had translated the exercises into English. 9. If I'm not mistaken, she has carried your briefcase to the office. 10. Do you want to go with us to Moscow for the vacation?

## СЛОВАРЬ

| | | | |
|---|---|---|---|
| актёр | actor | солда́т [G pl. солда́т] | soldier |
| актри́са | actress | тала́нт | talent |
| генера́л | general | | |
| знако́м | see § 1 | худо́жник ⎫<br>худо́жница ⎬ | artist |
| капита́н | captain | | |
| коммерса́нт | businessman | быва́ть быва́ют I | be (§ 6) |
| купе́ц [G купца́] | merchant | | |
| лейтена́нт | lieutenant | знако́миться ⎫ | make |
| майо́р | major | знако́мятся I ⎬ | acquain- |
| музыка́нт ⎫<br>музыка́нтша ⎬ | musician | познако́миться P ⎭ | tance |
| неуже́ли | see § 5.1 | ошиба́ться -а́ются I ⎫<br>ошиби́ться P see § 4 ⎬ | be<br>mistaken |
| офице́р | officer | | |
| поэ́т | poet | собира́ться -а́ются I ⎫<br>собра́ться соберу́тся P ⎬ | be about<br>to (+inf.) |
| прия́тно | pleasant(ly) | | |
| ра́зве | see § 5.2 | станови́ться ⎫ | |
| секрета́рь (m.) E ⎫<br>секрета́рша ⎬ | secretary | стано́вятся I ⎬<br>ста́ть ста́нут P ⎭ | become |

# LESSON XII

Вóт тá нóвая кни́га, котóрую мы́ тепéрь читáем.

That's the new book which we're reading now.

Óн читáет тý нóвую кни́гу, котóрая тáм на столé.

He is reading the new book which is there on the table.

Мы́ не получи́ли тóй нóвой кни́ги, о котóрой вы́ говори́ли.

We didn't receive the new book of which you were speaking.

Говоря́т о тóй нóвой кни́ге, котóрой я́ не хочý читáть.

They are talking about the new book I don't want to read.

Газéта под тóй нóвой кни́гой, котóрую вы́ ви́дите тáм.

The paper is under that new book which you see there.

Óн тóт стáрый дóктор, с котóрым вы́ говори́ли вчерá.

He is the old doctor with whom you were speaking yesterday.

Вы́ не знáете тогó стáрого дóктора, котóрый бы́л тогдá у нáс?

Don't you know that old doctor who was at our house at that time?

Мы́ ви́дели тогó стáрого дóктора, у котóрого вы́ жи́ли.

We saw the old doctor at whose place you used to live.

Óн поéхал с тéм стáрым дóктором, о котóром мы́ говори́ли.

He went with the old doctor of whom we were speaking.

Чтó вы́ знáете о тóм стáром дóкторе, котóрого мы́ тáм встрéтили?

What do you know about the old doctor whom we met there?

Э́то тó (сáмое) пóлё, на котóром дéти всегдá игрáют.

This is the (very) field in which the children always play.

Вы́ знáете тó (сáмое) пóлё, котóроё за университéтом?

You know that (very) field, which is behind the university?

Мы́ говори́м о тóм (сáмом) пóле, котóроё мы́ ви́дели вчерá.

We are speaking about that (very) field which we saw yesterday.

Э́то тó (сáмое) перó, котóрым писáл Пýшкин.

This is the (very) pen with which Pushkin wrote.

| | |
|---|---|
| Они говоря́т о то́м (са́мом) де́ле, кото́рого о́н боя́лся. | They are speaking of the (very) matter which he feared. |
| Говоря́т о те́х (са́мых) лю́дях, кото́рые живу́т та́м. | They are speaking of the (very) people who live there. |
| Мы́ встре́тили те́х (са́мых) люде́й, с кото́рыми мы́ тогда́ е́здили. | We met the (very) people with whom we had travelled at that time. |
| Э́то те́ (са́мые) лю́ди, о кото́рых все́ говори́ли. | They are the (very) people of whom everyone was speaking. |
| Во́т до́м те́х (са́мых) люде́й, у кото́рых вы́ рабо́таете. | There is the house of the (very) people for whom you work. |
| Му́ж рабо́тает с те́ми (са́мыми) людьми́, кото́рых я́ встреча́ла в Москве́. | My husband works with the (very) people whom I used to meet in Moscow. |
| Они́ чита́ют э́ту ста́рую, но́ интере́сную кни́гу, а мы́ чита́ем но́вую, но́ ску́чную кни́гу. | They are reading this old but interesting book, and we are reading a new but boring book. |
| Его́ жена́ молода́я, у́мная и краси́вая англича́нка. | His wife is a young, intelligent, and pretty Englishwoman. |
| Бе́дный Ива́н не мо́жет реши́ть э́того тру́дного вопро́са. | Poor Ivan can't decide this difficult question. |
| На́ш сосе́д ста́рый, дово́льно бога́тый, и весёлый челове́к. | Our neighbor is an old, rather rich, and jolly person. |
| Во́т интере́сная ве́щь, кото́рую я́ сего́дня купи́л. | Here's an interesting thing that I bought today. |
| Во́т то́т ва́жный журна́л, о кото́ром госпожа́ Толста́я говори́ла. | Here's that important magazine that Mrs. Tolstoj was talking about. |

---

**ADJECTIVES.** Russian adjectives are words which present their semantic content as qualities and have, like pronouns, different forms to agree in *gender*, *number*, and *case* with the nouns they modify.

**1.0** Except for the nominative and accusative, the adjective endings are nearly identical with the pronominal suffixes. (But note that in

adjectives the stress cannot fall on the last syllable of the suffix: молодóго — тогó).

There is a single adjectival declension, but spelling rules cause some
difficulty to the beginner, and therefore this lesson presents only adjectives whose stems end in a hard consonant (excluding š, ž). The other
variants will appear in Lessons XIII and XV. If you learn the first
20 model sentences in this lesson thoroughly, you should have no trouble
with adjective-forms thereafter.

**1.01**   Here is a sample declension, with the pronominal forms added for
comparison:

|      | masculine | neuter | feminine | plural |   |
|------|-----------|--------|----------|--------|---|
| Nom. | [э́тот] нóв-**ый** | э́т-**о** нóв-**оё** | э́т-**а** нóв-**ая** | э́т-**и** нóв-**ые** | N |
| Acc. | (like N or G) | э́т-**о** нóв-**оё** | э́т-**у** нóв-**ую** | (= N, G) | A |
| Gen. | э́т-**ого** нóв-**ого** | | э́т-**ой** нóв-**ой** | э́т-**их** нóв-**ых** | G |
| Prep. | э́т-**ом** нóв-**ом** | | э́т-**ой** нóв-**ой** | э́т-**их** нóв-**ых**. | P |
| Inst. | э́т-**им** нóв-**ым** | | э́т-**ой** нóв-**ой** | э́т-**ими** нóв-**ыми** | I |
|      |           |        | (э́т-**ою** нóв-**ою**) | | |

Note: the **-г-** in the masculine-neuter genitive singular is pronounced *v*.

**1.02**   The masculine and neuter forms are identical except in nominative
and accusative. The accusative forms of adjectives modifying animate
masculine singular or any animate plural nouns are like the genitive
forms.

**1.03**   When the suffix is stressed, the masc. Nom. sg. is **-ой**: молодóй.

**1.04**   Some surnames are formally adjectives with this type of declension; e.g. 'Belyj' Бéл**ый**, Бéл**ая**; 'Tolstoj' Толстóй, Толстáя.

**2.0**   Beside the normal forms, many Russian adjectives have "short-
forms" of the *nominative* (but *not of other cases*). They are used only as
the predicate; never attributively.[1]

**2.1**   The *masculine* short forms have a zero suffix in place of the masculine long ending **-ый (-ой)**:

| нóв**ый** — **нóв** | Э́то нóвый дóм. | Дóм нóв. |
|-----|-----|-----|
| 'new' | This is a new house. | The house is new. |
| стáр**ый** — **стáр** | Э́то стáрый профéссор. | Профéссор стáр. |
| 'old' | That's the old professor. | The professor is old. |

[1] In English, *mine* and *ours* are predicate forms, *my* and *our* attributive.

**2.11** Before the zero suffix, most consonant clusters take an inserted vowel, usually -ё- (but sometimes -o- ).

интере́сный журна́л          Э́тот журна́л интере́сен.

   an interesting magazine          This magazine is interesting.

Similarly обыкнове́нный — обыкнове́нен, печа́льный — печа́лен.

**2.2** The *feminine, neuter,* and *plural* short forms add respectively -a, -o, and -ы to the stems:

интере́сн**ая** газе́та     Газе́та интере́сн**а**.     The paper is interesting.

интере́сн**оё** письмо́     Письмо́ интере́сн**о**.     The letter is interesting.

интере́сн**ые** музе́и     Музе́и интере́сн**ы**.     The museums are interesting.

**2.3** Normally (always if the stem has three or more syllables), the stress of the short forms is like that of the long ones, but in a number of the most common adjectives there is a shift of stress. The most usual type (**A**) has stress on the feminine suffix, opposed to stress on the first syllable of the stem elsewhere (cf. past-tense stress, V 6.1–2). A less common type (**B**) stresses the suffix in all forms, or the last stem-syllable for masculine. NB: *for both types,* the "inserted vowel" is ignored in counting syllables.

| A: | | m. | n. | pl. | ~ | f. |
|---|---|---|---|---|---|---|
| но́вый | new | но́в | но́во | но́вы | | нова́ |
| бы́стрый | quick | бы́стр | бы́стро | бы́стры | | быстра́ |
| молодо́й | young | мо́лод | мо́лодо | мо́лоды | | молода́ |
| весё́лый | gay | весё́л | весё́ло | весё́лы | | весела́ |
| бе́дный | poor | бе́ден | бе́дно | бе́дны | | бедна́ |
| ва́жный | important | ва́жен | ва́жно | ва́жны | | важна́ |
| ску́чный | dull | ску́чен | ску́чно | ску́чны | | скучна́ |
| тру́дный | hard | тру́ден | тру́дно | тру́дны | | трудна́ |

(There are no examples of type B in this lesson.)

**2.31** Some adjectives do not fit either type, usually because they admit variant accents. There are forms which can equally correctly be stressed on different syllables, and other forms where good usage prefers the stress on a certain syllable but accepts an alternative possibility. The neuter and the plural are particularly likely to have variants. Two accents written on a word means equally valid variants, but the mark ` signifies the less desirable variant: у́мны́ = у́мны, умны́; у́мно̀ = у́мно preferred, умно́ acceptable.

It may be noted here that with individual adjectives the authoritative Soviet dictionaries and grammars often flatly contradict each other, and the usage of individual Russians will vary widely. Occasionally a difference in accent will be accompanied by a difference in shade of meaning.

The only variants and mixed types in this lesson are:

|          |             | m.    | n.    | pl.   | f.    |
|----------|-------------|-------|-------|-------|-------|
| бе́лый    | white       | бе́л   | бело́  | бе́лы́  | бела́  |
| ста́рый   | old         | ста́р  | старо́ | ста́ры́ | стара́ |
| у́мный    | intelligent | умён  | у́мно̀  | у́мны̀  | умна́  |

**3.**  The short form is restricted to the predicate, but the long form may be used here too. Usage is quite idiomatic, and a rule of thumb can be "when in doubt, use the long form." But there is a difference in meaning. Óн умён means simply "He is intelligent" — a statement noting a characteristic of the particular individual under discussion. Óн у́мный also is to be translated "He is intelligent", but the use of the long form in Russian implies the omission of a noun, i.e. approximately "a bright one, an intelligent person" and thus signals a comparison with other individuals who are intelligent.

**4.**  The short neuter forms serve as adverbs. We have already met бы́стро, ме́дленно, обыкнове́нно. Compare the adjectives from which they are derived:

| бы́стрый автомоби́ль | a fast car |
| ме́дленный по́езд | a slow train |
| обыкнове́нный челове́к | an ordinary man |

Examples of adverbs from adjectives new in this lesson:

| Они́ живу́т бе́дно, но ве́сёло. | They live poorly but gaily. |
| Óн говори́т интере́сно, но пи́шет ску́чно. | He speaks interestingly but writes boringly. |

NB: This sort of adjectival adverb will not be given in the vocabularies unless there is an additional meaning peculiar to the adverbial form.

**5.**  An adjective in Russian may be used without a noun, but the noun to be understood is usually clear from the context. English demands either the use of the noun or the substitute "one, ones".

| Áх, ты́ бе́дная! | Oh you poor *thing*! |
| Вы́ купи́ли кни́гу? Не́т, не́ было но́вых. | Did you buy a book? No, there were no new *ones*. |

**6.**  The relative pronoun meaning 'who, which, that' has purely adjectival forms: **кото́рый**, **кото́рая**, etc. (Cf. the model sentences.) Notice that the case of **кото́рый** is determined by its use in the clause in which it occurs, *not* by the word to which it refers:

| Это доктора́, | They are doctors ( = N.) |
| кото́р**ых** она́ зна́ла. | whom ( = Acc.) she knew. |
| с кото́р**ыми** мы́ говори́ли. | with whom ( = Inst.) we talked. |
| о кото́р**ых** мы́ говори́ли. | about whom ( = Pr.) we talked. |

**6.1**  When the *который*-clause is very closely associated with the noun which it defines, that noun may be preceded by the proper form of **тот** (cf. model sentences). In English, this **тот** is best translated simply "the": **тá** кнńга, **котóрая** (о **котóрой**)... '*the* book *which* (about *which*)'. Conversely, when translating from English, one must remember to render the English definite article as *тот* in such cases.

**6.2**  Note that the relative ('who, which, that') is sometimes omitted in English: котóрый *cannot* be omitted in Russian. E.g. 'That's a (the) book I bought yesterday' — Это (тá) кнńга, **котóрую** я купńл вчерá.

**6.3**  The relative "whose" is translated by the genitive of **котóрый**, which then *follows* the noun it modifies (cf. III 10):

| | |
|---|---|
| Дóктор, дóчь котóрого вы́ знáете ... | The doctor whose daughter you know ... |
| Дáма, о кнńгах котóрой мы́ говорńли ... | The woman of whose books we spoke ... |
| Нáши сосéди, с детьмń котóрых вы́ игрáли ... | Our neighbors, with whose children you played ... |

In poetic style, the forms of **чéй** may be found as relatives (e.g. чью́ дóчь, о чьńх кнńгах, с чьńми детьмń), but the foreigner should avoid the construction.

**6.4**  A comma is always written before a clause containing котóрый (cf. X 13).

**7.**  Another pronoun with purely adjectival forms is **сáмый**, which serves to identify accompanying words more closely. Its specific meaning depends on the context. Compare:

| | |
|---|---|
| (a) в сáмой Москвé | in Moscow itself; right in Moscow |
| в сáмый лéс | into the very wood, right into the wood |
| сáмый фáкт | the very fact |
| на сáмом дéле | in actual fact, really |
| э́та сáмая кнńга | this very book |
| тá же сáмая дáма (XI 11) | the very same woman, that very same woman |
| тó сáмоё перó, котóроё... | the very pen which ... |
| (b) в сáмом нóвом дóме | in the newest house |
| о сáмой интерéсной кнńге | about the most interesting book. |

The examples under (a) illustrate **сáмый** directly modifying a *noun*, with the meaning "precisely this one, no other". Frequently a demonstrative pronoun (э́тот, тóт, тóт же) is used in such constructions to make the definition even more precise. Under (b) are examples showing **са́мый** directly preceding an *adjective*. The quality presented by the adjective is emphasized as being present in the highest degree: it is the *superlative*.

**8.** The adverb **бо́лее** 'more' plus adjective makes up a construction corresponding to the English comparative (cf. handsom*er* = more handsome):

в бо́лее но́вом до́ме         in a newer house

о бо́лее интере́сной кни́ге    about a more interesting book

NB: the superlative **са́мый интере́сный** and the comparative **бо́лее интере́сный** correspond to the non-compared *long* adjective. There are special forms for the nominative predicate comparative which correspond to the short-form adjectives. They will be treated in Lessons **XXII** and **XXIII**.

## УПРАЖНЕНИЯ

**A.** For oral drill:

1a. У ва́с есть но́в—— кни́га?    Да́, у меня́ есть но́в—— кни́га.

                                     Не́т, у меня́ не́т но́в—— кни́ги.

 б. У ва́с есть но́в—— кни́ги?    Да́, у меня́ есть но́в—— кни́ги.

                                     Не́т, у меня́ не́т но́в—— кни́г.

 в. Я ви́жу но́в—— кни́гу; но́в—— кни́ги.

 г. Говоря́т о но́в—— кни́г——; но́в—— кни́гах.

 д. с но́в—— кни́гой; с но́в—— кни́гами.

2. Repeat, substituting all possible combinations of the following adjectives and nouns:

ста́рый, интере́сный \
скучный, ва́жный    } + { газе́та, журна́л, вопро́с, де́ло, кварти́ра, автомоби́ль, до́м

бога́тый, бе́дный, умный, \
молодо́й, ста́рый, весёлый } + { му́ж, жена́, до́чь, учи́тель[ница] \
студе́нт[ка], сосе́д[ка], до́ктор, \
печа́льный, краси́вый              ребёнок, бра́т

**B.** Here are some pairs of related sentences. Make each pair into a single sentence joined by the appropriate form of *который*. For example:

Вóт нóвый учéбник.    Я *егó* купúл вчерá.

→ Вóт нóвый учéбник, **котóрый** я́ вчерá купúл.

1. Вóт бéлая шáпка.    Я её купúл вчерá.
2. Я потеря́л нóвые часы́.    Я и́х достáл в Еврóпе.
3. Приéхали егó богáтые друзья́.    Ивáн жúл у нúх в Еврóпе.
4. Я замéтил стáрую дáму.    Онá сидéла на дивáне в углý.
5. Это трýдный вопрóс.    Я не могý на негó отвéтить.
6. Я достáл вáжный докумéнт.    Вы́ егó хотéли вúдеть.
7 а. Я купúла бéлую шля́пу.    Мы́ говорúли о нéй вчерá.
  б. Я купúла бéлую шля́пу.    Мы́ её вúдели в магазúне.
8. Ктó написáл эту скýчную статью́?    Всё говоря́т о нéй.
9 а. Вы́ пóмните úмя óтчество молодóго журналúста?    Óн сидéл перед нáми на концéрте.
  б. Вы́ пóмните úмя óтчество молодóго журналúста?    Мы́ сидéли перед нúм на концéрте.
10 а. Вы́ знáете эту весёлую дéвочку?    Мы́ смея́лись над нéй перед шкóлой.
  б. Вы́ знáете эту весёлую дéвочку?    Онá смея́лась над нáми.
11. Вóт эта красúвая дéвочка.    Её мáть и отéц купúли нáш дóм.
12. Вóт стóл.    Я хочý сидéть за нúм.
13. Вы́ не встречáли этих весёлых молоды́х людéй?    Мы́ с нúми éздили в Россúю.
14. Это моё письмó.    Вы́ егó откры́ли.
15 а. Онú спросúли о стáром адвокáте.    Вы́ егó знáете.
  б. Онú спросúли о стáром адвокáте.    Вы́ о нём чáсто спрáшиваёте.
  в. Онú спросúли о стáром адвокáте.    Ивáн рабóтал у негó.

**C.** Read and translate:

1. У нáс в библиотéке нéт нóвых журнáлов, éсть тóлько стáрые.
2. Кудá вы́ положúли мою́ нóвую кнúгу? Я не вúдел нóвой кнúги.
3. Éсли ты́ хóчешь нóвый бéлый автомобúль, тó почемý не кýпишь?
4. Егó женá былá молодá, красúва и весёла, но óн бы́л стáр и печáлен.
5. Кудá вы́ éздили с весёлой америкáнкой на этом стáром автомобúле?    6. Моя́ сестрá обыкновéнно пúшет интерéсные пúсьма о всéх нóвых делáх.    7. Егó отéц встрéтил молодóго Толстóго в тóм сáмом садý.    8. Стáрая учúтельница печáльно смея́лась, но ничегó не

ответила на его вопрос. 9. Если вы покупаете все новые книги, у вас не будет денег. 10. Знает ли кто-нибудь, кто эта очень красивая дама, с которой профессор Бородин шёл вчера? Да, все знают; это умная и довольно богатая студентка. 11. Толстые были на новой квартире у матери наших новых соседей. 12. Вера Павловна Толстая, дочь доктора Леонова, работала с тем самым американцем, о котором писали в газетах. 13. Он красиво говорит, но молодые студенты не понимают его. 14. Иван Львович самый умный человек в университете. Вера Алексеевна тоже умна. 15. Бородины жили в самом бедном доме во всём городе; но потом они получили деньги, и теперь у них красивая квартира. 16. Он очень много говорил о неинтересных людях и их скучных делах, но когда его спросили о более важных вопросах, он замолчал. 17. В саду Набоковых Игорь встретил интересную и весёлую, но очень молодую студентку, Лолиту Владимировну Сирину. 18. Пожалуйста, не вешайте этой старой шляпы там на двери, положите её на полку над моей кроватью. 19. Ирина Белая-Ларина поехала в Москву со своим старым отцом, Игорём Игорёвичём Корсаковым. 20. Завтра я наконец достану этот старый журнал, который я так долго не мог найти. В нём есть несколько важных статей с очень интересными картами.

**D.** For oral and/or written translation. Before you start this exercise, read paragraph 6.2 above and think about the English of the sentences.

1. I have the stories you bought yesterday. 2. Do you remember the village in which mother lived? 3. He's the boy we usually play with. 4. I couldn't find the handbag mother wanted me to get. 5. Did you notice the keys he put in his pocket? 6. Ask a student who has a car to do it. 7. Ask the man who is standing in front of the door where the professor is. 8. Our neighbors want to buy the lamp which used to stand there by the table. 9. Those are the chairs on which we will be sitting. 10. She asked about the little girl the children were laughing at. 11. In her hand was the dictionary that I had lost at school. 12. We met the professor in whose laboratory Pavel works. 13. The museum is the building behind that laboratory in which Nadezhda used to work. 14. Where's the atlas in which are all the maps of Europe? 15. Who are the people with whom you were speaking Russian?

**E.** For written and/or oral translation:

1. That's the sad lady who always wants to talk only about handsome Englishmen. 2. Mrs. Tolstoj has an old white house in an interesting village where she lives in the summer. 3. There are several new tables in the old restaurant. 4. The new teachers were talking boringly about very important and interesting letters which Churchill wrote. 5. She met there the same dull young man who had taken her new pen in class in the morning. 6. The little boy doesn't want to answer the boring question. 7. She's writing a new book about rich young men and gay young ladies. 8. That sad young man who is sitting at the old table by the window is a rather intelligent student. 9. I think that it's the oldest newspaper (which) they have, and I know that it's the dullest. 10. Haven't you read the sad but interesting letter of my old friend, which I received yesterday? 11. I hope that the young students have taken all the new chairs from the old Englishmen (VI 3.1). 12. Do you remember the surname of the old professor behind whom we were sitting at the theater? 13. Perhaps we will meet the young American and his intelligent old mother at Dr. Tolstoj's. 14. At the meeting she met the very same handsome American about whom her sister had been talking. 15. They are the mothers of those pretty little girls and jolly little boys who play with your children. 16. That's the very same dull affair they were talking about yesterday with the very same people at the very same table in the very same room of the very same restaurant. 17. That poor teacher (f) lives in a pretty apartment with a rich young student (f) whom she knew at home in Moscow. 18. Did you see the pretty photographs of the newest houses which were on the walls in our club last night? 19. They're talking about the very same American woman whom we met at the old Englishwomen's yesterday morning. 20. The pretty ladies gaily laughed at the poor students who were slowly solving the rather difficult problems. 21. She lives with her jolly children, her old mother, and her handsome husband in the old building between the old bank and the new movie. 22. If the poor student had money, he'd buy the newest magazine. 23. I never received an interesting or important letter. 24. She asked me to buy Shóloxov's new book. 25. The pretty student asked me whether I had read Leonov's new books.

## СЛОВАРЬ

| | | | |
|---|---|---|---|
| бе́дный | poor | ме́нее (av.) | less |
| бе́лый | white | молодо́й | young |
| бога́тый | rich | наконе́ц | at last, finally |
| бо́лее | see § 8 | но́вый | new |
| бы́стрый | fast | обыкнове́нный | ordinary |
| ва́жный | important | печа́льный | sad |
| весёлый | gay, jolly | са́мый | see § 7 |
| де́ло [pl. дела́] | matter, affair | ску́чный [pron. -шн-] | boring, dull |
| дово́льно | rather | ста́рый | old |
| интере́сный | interesting | то́лько | only |
| кото́рый (§ 6) | who, which, that | тру́дный | difficult, hard |
| краси́вый | pretty, handsome | у́мный | intelligent |
| ме́дленный | slow | фа́кт | fact |

# LESSON XIII

| | |
|---|---|
| Кому́ вы́ да́ли письмо́? | To whom did you give the letter? |
| Кому́ вы́ помогли́ реша́ть зада́чи? | Whom did you help solve problems? |
| Таки́м лю́дям всё равно́. | It's all the same to such people. |
| Мне́ жа́ль госпожу́ Толсту́ю. | I'm sorry for Mrs. Tolstoj. |
| Ива́н Ива́нович, ва́м письмо́! | Ivan Ivanovich, a letter for you. |
| Сде́лаю ва́м э́то сейча́с же. | I'll do it for you at once. |
| О́н пи́шет друзья́м. | He is writing to his friends. |
| На письме́ о́н написа́л «До́ктору Пётру́ Ива́новичу Толсто́му». | On the letter he wrote, "To Doctor Pëtr Ivanovich Tolstoj". |
| Скажи́те ему́, чтобы о́н помо́г на́м. | Tell him to help us. |
| Что́ вы́ сказа́ли э́той молодо́й же́нщине? | What did you say to that young woman? |
| О́н е́й сказа́л, что о́н да́ст ва́м отве́т за́втра ве́чером. | He told her that he will give you an answer tomorrow evening. |
| Е́сли ты́ мне́ не да́шь кни́ги, я скажу́ ма́тери! | If you don't give me the book, I'll tell mother! |
| Я́ ему́ отве́тил, что не могу́ пое́хать с ни́м. | I answered him that I couldn't go with him. |
| Я́ не могу́ обеща́ть ва́м. | I can't promise you. |
| Покажи́те мне́ но́вые фотогра́фии. | Show me the new photographs. |
| Я́ не ве́рю тому́ молодо́му челове́ку. | I don't believe that young man. |
| Профе́ссор на́м объясня́л уро́к, но́ я́ не по́нял. | The professor explained the lesson to us, but I didn't understand. |
| Я́ ва́м объясню́ пото́м. | I'll explain it to you afterwards. |
| Сестре́ бы́ло уже́ пора́ идти́. | It was already time for sister to go. |
| Ва́м ску́чно в шко́ле? Не́т, мне́ о́чень интере́сно. | Are you bored in school? No, it's very interesting for me. |

| | |
|---|---|
| Ива́ну Пётро́вичу бы́ло всё равно́. | It was all the same to Ivan Petrovich. |
| Мы́ поéхали к ёго́ ма́тери в деревню. | We went to visit his mother in the country. |
| Мы́ мо́жёт быть пойдём к нёму́ зимо́й. | We will go to his place in the winter perhaps. |
| Идéмте к Пётру́ на кварти́ру. | Let's go to Peter's apartment. |
| Иди́те к доскé! Пиши́те на доскé! | Go to the board. Write on the board. |
| Ты́ ни к кому́ не пойдёшь! | You aren't going to see anyone! |
| Óн ча́сто хо́дит по го́роду. | He often walks about the city. |
| Óн ходи́л по рестора́нам. | He went from restaurant to restaurant. |
| Ка́к по-ва́шёму, интерéсна ли э́та кни́га? Нéт, по-мо́ёму о́чень скучна́. | What do you think, is the book interesting? No, in my opinion it's very dull. |

---

**1. The DATIVE CASE. The forms —**

**1.1** NOUNS: **1.11** *First declension nouns* (masc. and neut.) have the suffix -*u*, spelled -**y** or -**ю**. **Ю** is written if the nominative ends in -**й**, -**ь**, -**е**, or -**ё**; -**y** in all other cases: музéю, гéнию, учи́телю, по́лю, зда́нию, (питью́); столу́, отцу́, карандашу́, окну́, дéлу.

**1.12** For *all feminine nouns* the dative form is identical with the prepositional: сёстрé, доскé, ко́мнате, фотогра́фии, двéри, до́чери, ма́тери.

**1.13** The *plural* suffix for *all* nouns is -*am*, spelled -**ам** or -**ям**, added to the *plural* stem. Practically speaking, it is the prepositional plural with -**м** instead of -**х** (see VIII and IX): теа́трам, това́рищам, стола́м, отца́м, дома́м, учителя́м, сту́льям, бра́тьям, ко́мнатам, фотогра́фиям, жéнщинам, сосéдкам, доска́м, сёстрам, жёнам, имёна́м, пи́сьмам, о́кнам, пéрьям, поля́м, дверя́м, дочеря́м, матеря́м, лю́дям.

**1.14** The *accent* of the dative singular is always like that of the genitive; that of the dative plural is like the prepositional plural. See VIII and IX.

**1.2** PRONOUNS and ADJECTIVES have similar dative suffixes:

**1.21** The masculine-neuter singular is *-omu*, spelled **-ому** or **-ёму**. If the stress falls on the pronominal suffix, it is on *-мú*, but in the adjective suffix on *-ó-*: тому́, э́тому, моёму́, всёму́, на́шёму; молодо́му, но́вому.

**1.22** The feminine dative and prepositional forms are identical: то́й, э́той, мое́й, все́й, на́шей; молодо́й, но́вой.

**1.23** The dative plural adjectival suffix is *-im*, spelled **-ым/-им**. Pronouns have either **-им** or **-ем**. As a practical rule, the dative suffix is the prepositional suffix with **-м** instead of **-х**: те́м, э́тим, мои́м, все́м, на́шим; молоды́м, но́вым.

**1.3** The dative forms of the personal and interrogative pronouns are:

| N | я́ | ты́ | о́н | оно́ | она́ | мы́ | вы́ | они́ | кто́ | что́ |
|---|----|-----|-----|------|------|-----|-----|------|------|------|
| D | мне́ | тебе́ | ёму́ | е́й | на́м | ва́м | и́м | кому́ | чёму́ | |

**1.31** With prepositions, the forms **ёму́, е́й, и́м** prefix an **н-** (cf. VI 4): к нёму́, по нёму́, к не́й, по не́й, к ни́м, по ни́м.

**1.4** *Surnames* in **-ов (-ёв)** and **-ин** have masculine dative singular in **-у**, feminine singular in **-ой**, and plural in **-ым**:

Пётро́ву, Пу́шкину; Пётро́вой, Пу́шкиной : Пётро́вым, Пу́шкиным.

**2.** Uses of the dative case:

**2.1** To express a weakly specified "intended for", "directed to", "having reference to": письмо́ Пу́шкину 'a letter *to/for* Pushkin.'

**2.21** As the indirect object with a number of verbs: e.g.

| "answer" | О́н мне́ отве́тил. | He answered me. |
|---|---|---|
| "aid, help" | Она́ на́м помога́ла. | She used to help us. |
| "promise" | О́н ёму́ обеща́л. | He promised him. |
| "believe" | Коне́чно, я ва́м ве́рю. | Of course I believe you. |

**2.22** As indirect object with verbs which also have a direct object: e.g.

| "give" | О́н мне́ да́л кни́гу. | He gave me a book. |
|---|---|---|
| "explain" | Объясни́те ёму́ э́то. | Explain it to him. |

This type often corresponds exactly to the English construction.

Note that negation of the verb has no effect on the dative *in*direct object; it affects only the accusative *direct* object (III 9). For example: Она́ *на́м* **не** помога́ла. О́н *мне́* **не** да́л кни́ги.

**2.3**   With certain subjectless expressions: e.g.

| | |
|---|---|
| Ему́ пора́ идти́. | It's time for him to go. |
| Ему́ всё равно́. | It's indifferent to him. |
| Мне́ жа́ль сёстру́. | I'm sorry for sister. |
| Ива́ну ску́чно. | Ivan is bored. |
| Ива́ну здесь интере́сно. | It's interesting for Ivan here. |
| Ему́ тру́дно. | It's hard for him. |
| Пётру́ печа́льно. | Peter feels sad. |
| Йгорю бы́ло лёгко́. | It was easy for Igor'. |
| Ва́м не бу́дёт ску́чно. | You won't be bored. |

Note that in this type of construction there is no grammatical subject in Russian, just as in some of the English equivalents the "it" is merely an introductory word ("it's boring here, it's time to go"). This introductory English "it", if it refers to anything at all, includes the general situation and not any one specific thing. Many short-form adjectives (like ску́чно and интере́сно) can be used in this kind of Russian construction.

**2.4**   With a few prepositions, mainly к 'toward, in the direction of' and по 'on, along, by, according to'.

**3.1**   К implies motion: к доске́ 'to the board'.

It is regularly used with nouns and pronouns denoting persons, and often renders "to the side of, to the home (office, place, country) of": e.g.

| | |
|---|---|
| Óн е́дёт к бра́ту в го́род. | He's on his way to his brother's in town. |
| Она́ поéхала к ма́тери в дере́вню. | She's left for her mother's in the country. |
| Мы́ ча́сто хо́дим к ни́м. | We often go to their place. |

This is a common construction with going-verbs, and may be translated "go to see" or "visit": e.g. "He's going to see his brother in town"; "She's gone to visit her mother in the country"; "We often visit (go to see) them."

Note that к + dative is used to denote motion with the same expressions with which у + genitive denotes rest. Compare:

| | |
|---|---|
| Óн живёт у бра́та в го́роде. | He lives at his brother's in town. |
| Она́ живёт у ма́тери в де-ре́вне. | She lives at her mother's in the country. |
| Мы́ бы́ли у ни́х. | We were at their place. |

**3.11**   This preposition has the form **ко** in **ко мне́, ко всему́, ко всем,** and a small number of other cases.

**3.2**   **По** has a variety of meanings when used with the dative. (It is also found with the accusative and with the prepositional: these cases will be treated later.)

(a) It is used for motion all about a surface or for things located at various scattered points on a surface:

| | |
|---|---|
| Он хо́дит **по** у́лице. | He walks along the street. |
| Он хо́дит **по** го́роду. | He walks all over the city. |
| В города́х **по** все́й Росси́и. | In towns all over Russia. |
| У него́ в ко́мнате всю́ду кни́ги — и **по** стола́м и **по** сту́льям. | Everywhere in his room there are books — even on the tables and chairs. |

(b) From one place to another:

| | |
|---|---|
| Он хо́дит **по** рестора́нам. | He goes from restaurant to restaurant. |

(c) "According to": at present we need consider only the idioms **по-ва́шему (по-тво́ему)** and **по-мо́ему** 'in your opinion, in my opinion'. Note the exceptional stress: по-мо́ему, по-тво́ему.

(d) "Concerned with, on":

| | |
|---|---|
| Он специали́ст **по** исто́рии Москвы́. | He's a specialist on the history of Moscow. |

(e) Certain idiomatic uses, e.g.: по телефо́ну 'by telephone'

| | |
|---|---|
| Я говори́л с И́горем по телефо́ну. | I spoke with Igor' by telephone. |

**4.1**   The perfective verb **да́ть даду́т** has irregular forms:
(present) я **да́м,** ты **да́шь,** он **да́ст;** мы **дади́м,** вы **дади́те,** они **даду́т:** (imperative) **да́й, да́йте:** (past) **да́л, да́ло, да́ли — дала́** [не́ дал, не́ дало, не́ дали — не дала́].

**4.2**   The imperfective **дава́ть даю́т** has the irregular imperative **дава́й, дава́йте.**

*NB: all verbs in* **-ава́ть -аю́т** *have imperatives in* **-ава́й -ава́йте.**

**5.**   The perfective **помо́чь помо́гут** 'help' follows the same pattern as **мо́чь** (cf. X 7), except that it has an imperative: **помоги́, помоги́те.**
Its imperfective mate *помога́ть помога́ют* is regular.

**6.** The short adjective **до́лжён, должно́, должна́, должны́** is used to mean "must, have to, ought":

| | |
|---|---|
| Я до́лжён идти́. | I must go. |
| Она́ должна́ рабо́тать. | She has to work. |
| Мы́ должны́ бы́ли отвеча́ть. | We had to answer. |
| Он до́лжён бы́ть здесь. | He ought to be here. |

Note the idiomatic usage of **должно́ бы́ть**:

| | |
|---|---|
| Он, должно́ бы́ть, та́м. | He is probably there. |
| Вы́, должно́ бы́ть, зна́ете. | You probably know. |
| Она́, должно́ бы́ть, пое́хала. | She must have set out. |

**7.** **Звони́ть/позвони́ть** means 'ring'. For example:

| | |
|---|---|
| Кто́-то звони́т у две́ри. | Someone is ringing at the door. ( ≅ is ringing the doorbell). |

**Звони́ть по телефо́ну** means 'to telephone'; it takes the dative of person and is directional as to place:

| | |
|---|---|
| Позвони́те ему́ *сюда́*. | Call him up here. |
| Он вчера́ позвони́л в Москву́ по телефо́ну. | Yesterday he made a telephone call to Moscow. |
| Вы́ не туда́ звони́ли. | You've got the wrong number. (XI 12) |

Note that the qualifying по телефо́ну is often omitted.

**8.** Notice that the verb-pair **говори́ть/сказа́ть** usually means 'say' when there is only a direct object, but 'tell' if there is also an indirect object:

| | |
|---|---|
| Он э́то сказа́л вчера́. | He said that yesterday. |
| Он ча́сто говори́л э́то. | He often said that. |
| Он мне́ уже́ сказа́л. | He already told me. |
| Он всё́ говори́т жене́. | He tells his wife everything. |

The perfective сказа́ть is somewhat more restricted in meaning than говори́ть, for it focuses on the completion of the action and implies a result (cf. V 9), "say, tell *something*". Говори́ть too may have this meaning of saying *something* (without specifying one single completion), but it may also mean "have the power of speech, use the power of speech", i.e. 'speak, talk':

| | |
|---|---|
| Ве́рочка уже́ хо́дит, но́ она́ ещё́ не говори́т. | Verochka already walks, but she doesn't talk yet. |
| Васи́лий хорошо́ говори́т. | Vasilij speaks well. |
| Я ча́сто говори́л с ни́ми. | I often talked with them. |

**9.** **Же́нщина** is the generic word for 'woman', differing from **да́ма** 'lady' in approximately the same way the two English words differ: да́ма is slightly more polite.

**10.** A limited number of verbs can be modified directly by **о́чень**, which denotes intensity of the action. So far we have had only two of these verbs, *проси́ть/попроси́ть* and *помога́ть/помо́чь*.

О́чень прошу́!

Он о́чень нам помо́г.

I beg you!

He helped us very much.
He was a great help to us.

## УПРАЖНЕНИЯ

**A.** 1. Да́йте *мне* э́то. Repeat, substituting for "me" the following: him, her, them, us, that old friend, that beautiful woman, her father and mother, Semën and Nikolaj, those people, Dr. Tolstoj, Prof. Borodín, Mrs. Petrov, our teachers (m, f), his sisters, those mothers, the doctors, husbands and wives.

2. *Нам* пора́ идти́. Repeat, substituting for "us" the following: you, me, her, her sister(s), him, his brother(s), them, their friend(s), those gentlemen, the Petrovs, the Tolstojs, all of us, all those students.

**B.** Read and translate:

1. Вам уже́ пора́ рабо́тать в саду́. 2. Мне всё равно́, обеща́ет ли Семён и́ли нет. 3. Когда́ молода́я жена́ чита́ла весёлую кни́гу, я писа́л письмо́ ста́рому дру́гу. 4. Извини́те, я не могу́ тепе́рь показа́ть господа́м Семёновым ко́мнату. 5. Зимо́й наш сосе́д даёт уро́ки мое́й сестре́. Он бе́дный студе́нт. 6. Моя́ мать хо́чет, чтобы мы лу́чше говори́ли и чита́ли по-ру́сски. 7. Я мо́жет быть напишу́ об э́том ва́шему отцу́. 8. Я сего́дня иду́ к тому́ до́ктору, у кото́рого есть кварти́ра над ба́нком. 9. Обыкнове́нно мы хо́дим к Ива́ну Никола́евичу. 10. Почему́ вы ей не помогли́? Дава́йте ей помо́жем! 11. Э́то краси́вые слова́, но я им не ве́рю! Я ве́рю то́лько дела́м! 12. Почему́ вы ему́ не да́ли отве́та?

13. Óн хóчет, чтобы я писáл этим карандашóм. 14. Нáм говорят, что Петрý жáль молодýю сосéдку. 15. Повéрьте мнé, мóй дрýг, у меня нéт дéнег. Я не могý вáм дáть ничегó. 16. Онá егó спросúла, нó óн не мóг отвéтить. 17. Вы никогдá не помогáете друзьям. 18. Учúтельница емý объясняла, объясняла, нó óн ничегó не понимáет. 19. По-мóему, это сáмый трýдный урóк в кнúге! 20. Борúс Яковлёвич обещáет нáм, что óн зáвтра вéчером покáжет всéм у Бéлых свои интерéсные кнúги. 21. Молодым людям скýчно жúть в дерéвне. Им тáм ничегó не интерéсно. 22. К комý вы идéте? К Бéлым. 23. Кáк ты дýмаешь, что Лéв Юрьевич тебé дáст? Я надéюсь, что óн мнé дáст тý вéщь, котóрую óн покáзывал дáмам вчерá. 24. Игорь обещáл написáть éй сегóдня же вéчером. 25. Скажúте мнé, где вы были вчерá? — Я покáзывал музéй молодым друзьям сёстры нáших сосéдей. 26. Не давáйте этого никомý! 27. Гдé Юрий обыкновéнно сидúт? За тéм столóм у окнá. 28. Яков Борúсович дóлжен был быть на собрáнии, нó егó нé было. Óн никомý ничегó не сказáл, и когдá я тудá позвонúл, нé было отвéта. 29. Я не понимáю задáчи; покажú отцý, мóжет быть óн помóжет тебé. 30. Было тáм óчень вéсело у нúх; я рéдко говорúл с бóлее интерéсными людьмú.

**C.** For oral and/or written translation into Russian:

1. Tell me why you don't believe me. 2. Help my old mother: she is going to (see) Dr. Leónov at his apartment. 3. It's all the same to that young man. 4. I want to show Pëtr Petrovich Petrov several interesting letters which my father received. 5. Perhaps I will explain these photographs to all the students (m, f) tomorrow. 6. Why don't you telephone your young friends? 7. I wanted to tell him yesterday. 8. She promised my daughter to give her my new book. 9. It's a pity that I did not read the new lesson. I won't be able to answer the professor tomorrow in class. 10. Here's a more interesting book for Vera Aleksandrovna Petrov. 11. I'm sorry for that poor old woman. She lives here in town, but doesn't understand anything in English. 12. He helped me close the windows. 13. Help your friend; he can't solve all those difficult problems. 14. He told me that Igor' wants us to go to the country tomorrow. Will you be able to go with him? 15. He says he wants to help us, but I don't believe him. 16. She asked the teacher (f) to explain the sentence to her again. 17. Give Zoja the book and show her the difficult sentence which we're talking about. 18. I think she is beginning to understand now. 19. If he calls you (ты) tonight, explain to him that I couldn't help anyone. 20. Ol'ga had to work yesterday; she couldn't go to see Vera

Pavlovna Ivanov. 21. Let's all go to the board. 22. You ought to buy a new watch. 23. Someone help Sergej and Ol'ga. 24. No one explained the problem to the children. 25. It's time for the girls to call their mother. 26. He's on his way to see (§ 3.1) young Boris Ivanovich Borodín. 27. Promise me that you will explain everything to everyone! 28. We often go to see the Tolstojs at their new home in the country. 29. If you want to help us, call me this evening. 30. There's a difficult problem for you!

## СЛОВАРЬ

| | |
|---|---|
| всю́ду | everywhere |
| до́лжён | see § 6 |
| жа́ль + Dat. (+ Acc.) | be sorry (for) |
| [о́чень] жа́ль, что ... | it's a (great) pity that |
| же́нщина | woman (§ 9) |
| зимо́й | in winter |
| к (ко) + Dat. (§ 3.1) | to, toward |
| по (prep. with Dative) | see § 3.2 |
| пора́ + Dat. | it's time (for) |
| (равно́) | (evenly, equally) |
| всё равно́ + Dat. | it's all the same to |
| специали́ст | specialist |
| телефо́н | telephone |
| по телефо́ну | by phone |
| у́лица | street |
| фи́льм | film |

ве́рить ве́рят I / пове́рить P } + Dat. believe

дава́ть даю́т I (§ 4.2) / да́ть даду́т P (§ 4.1) } give

звони́ть звоня́т I / позвони́ть P } (§ 7) ring, call

обеща́ть IP / обеща́ют } + Dat. promise

объясня́ть объясня́ют I / объясни́ть объясня́т P } explain

пока́зывать пока́зывают I / показа́ть пока́жут P } show

помога́ть помога́ют I / помо́чь помо́гут P (§ 5) } + Dat. help

**For review**

**A.** 1. Добрый день. Пожалуйста начните писать. Я буду диктовать медленно. Слушайте! 2. Извините, как ваше имя отчество? Я почти всегда забываю имена. 3. Пусть Петр напишет свое сочинение! 4. Здравствуйте, как вы поживаете? Говорят, вы уже не работаете в лесу? 5. Над полкой висела необыкновенная карта. Она, должно быть, очень старая. 6. Наконец кто-то решил попросить учителя повторить и говорить менее быстро. 7. Трудно понять, почему у Тани в сумке был словарь моего мужа. 8. Чей это кошелек тут перед шкафом? —Не мой. 9. Когда у нас будут деньги, мы тоже будем ходить по ресторанам. Давайте пойдем в этот новый ресторан сегодня вечером! 10. Он еще стоял тут же. 11. Он был на собрании с англичанкой, которую он встретил в парке. Она молодая журналистка, которая поедет в Африку. Ах, если бы только я могла поехать с ней! Жаль, что отец не хочет дать мне денег. 12. Под лампой висело что-то. Что это могло быть такое? 13. Ребенок хотел написать на доске «доброе утро», но мела не было. 14. Посмотрите и в карманах, может быть там лежат ключи. 15. Пусть она несет ее тетрадку. Чью тетрадку? 16. Пойдите прямо и вы увидите за стеной белое здание. Это — новая лаборатория, где работают ваши друзья. 17. Он очень редко об этом говорит, но он, должно быть, специалист по этому вопросу. 18. Куда ваш товарищ кладет свои вещи вечером? 19. Поезжай со мной купить часы в универмаге. Хорошо, поедем сейчас же. 20. Она несла шляпу, платки, учебник англичанина и бумагу. 21. По-моему, письмо журналистки госпоже Семеновой начало все это. 22. Бородин всегда спрашивает у девочек, кем они хотят быть. 23. Вчера утром тут на полу не было портфеля. 24. Автобусы уже не шли. Мы не знали, что делать, и поехали не тем трамваем. 25. Пора вам идти домой. До свидания! Всего лучшего!

**B.** 1a. Igor' wanted Nadezhda to help him find something. b. He said, "I've lost my keys, please help me find them. c. I thought I put them here on the desk. d. They must be here somewhere. e. "There they are, under those documents." f. "Thank you, I probably wouldn't have found them if you hadn't noticed them there."

2a. Gentlemen, they always told me that Englishmen were dull, but did you notice that young Englishwoman who was standing near the door with old doctor Kórsakov? b. She's beautiful and I believe she must be very interesting. c. In actual fact I know she's interesting; she wants me to meet her in front of the new restaurant in the park this evening.

3a. I asked my mother about everything, but she didn't explain very well and I didn't understand. b. Let the doctor explain these matters to you; he's intelligent and he knows the answers to all your questions.

4a. I cannot understand how he could have bought a new house if he had no money. b. He must have gotten money.

5. It's very difficult for me to tell you this, but in actual fact I'm afraid those mechanics probably can't help you; they're very poor.

6a. It's a great pity that Irína Mikhajlovna Kórsakov's brother no longer lives with us. b. He's a jolly person, and when he laughs, everybody laughs with him. c. We all used to have a good time at table when he was home.

7a. I know that my friends the Borodín's have not forgotten me and that somewhere they are thinking about me. b. I'd like to write them a letter, but I don't know where they are. c. They must be somewhere in Europe.

8a. Why are we standing here on the corner? b. Let's go somewhere. c. — It's interesting for me to watch the people. d. I have no money and can't go anywhere. e. If you're bored, why don't you go home? f. Don't you remember you have to write a composition? g. — I can't forget it, but I don't want to talk about it, and I don't want you to talk about it. h. — You'll have to write several sentences on the board tomorrow morning. i. The teacher said she wanted you to review all the new exercises. j. — Be quiet!

9a. We usually go to town by bus, but today we had Igor' Smirnóv's car. b. In town we went to the movies with my wife's friends and their husbands and saw a rather interesting new film, "Who's afraid of Virginia?"

10. She gave her father's oldest notebook to Elizavéta Pávlovna Goncharóv, because there is an important article in it which Elizaveta Pavlovna wants to read.

11a. I asked your brothers where they were going. b. They answered me that they were going from apartment to apartment (XIII 3.2b) and buying old magazines. c. They want to give them to the poor children who live in our sister's village.

12a. Sit here at the table and don't look out the window! b. It's time for you to work. c. You have to finish your article this evening! d. Ivanov wants you to give it to him at the meeting tomorrow.

13a. Were you there when Vera carried her things into our room? b. I was sorry for her, it was so sad to look at her.   c. It all must be very hard for her.   d. When Peter was a child, he used to play with our neighbors' children, Tanja and Igor'.   e. Now he still goes to their place often.

14a. American women don't like to sit at home when their husbands are not there. b. They don't have to work very much and they like to go from store to store and look at hats and handbags.

15a. Someone telephone Sergej Tolstoj and tell him to meet us at the concert.   b. He must be at his sister's place.   c. Call there.   d. — There's no answer at the Tolstojs'.   e. Perhaps he's at the Borodíns'.

16a. Promise us never to dictate so fast.   b. The students asked the teacher (f) to promise to dictate slowly.

# LESSON XIIIa

## REVIEW

**A.** 1. Я хочу вам рассказать что-нибудь о доме, в котором мы живем, о наших соседях и друзьях.

2. Наш дом — довольно красивое здание перед старым университетом. 3. В квартирах много комнат. 4. В моей комнате стоит стол, стулья и шкаф с полками. 5. На стенах висят картины и карта России. 6. На столе стоят книги, — учебники и словари, и лежит несколько журналов. 7. За столом я делаю уроки, читаю и пишу письма.

8. Со мной живет мой друг Иван. 9. Он очень умный и веселый молодой человек. 10. Говорят, что его отец гений. 11. Они бедные, и Иван поэтому не ходит в университет, а работает на фабрике. 12. У него мало книг, он их обыкновенно не покупает, а читает в библиотеке.

13. У нашего соседа Петра есть жена, Вера, и мальчик и девочка. 14. Иногда мы играем с их детьми. 15. Вера помогает нам писать упражнения и переводить трудные фразы. 16. Она жила в Москве и хорошо пишет и читает по-русски, но дети говорят дома только по-английски. 17. Петру трудно понимать их.

18. Надежда, сестра Веры, работает в музее на углу нашей улицы. 19. По субботам она дома. 20. Она смеется надо мной, потому что я боюсь ездить в метро. 21. У меня нет автомобиля, и мы часто ходим пешком, в кино или в театр.

22. Профессор Браун, который живет в том же доме, очень интересный человек. 23. Его отец — американец, а мать — англичанка. 24. Он никогда не был в России. 25. Я с ним хожу по средам на собрания в клуб, где мы встречаем наших друзей. 26. На следующей неделе он едет в Париж, и я надеюсь, что буду получать письма, в которых он мне расскажет обо всем, что он видел и что он будет делать. 27. Жаль, что его не будет здесь.

28. У моей сестры, детей которой вы знаете, есть дом в лесу у самой деревни. 29. Она — учительница, а ее муж — специалист по садам. 30. Они очень богатые люди. 31. Я к ним езжу часто на каникулы. 32. Когда я у них, мы или ходим по полям, или сидим перед домом и говорим с соседями.

33. Еслы бы вы хорошо понимали по-русски, я бы вам рассказал еще что-нибудь.   34. Надеюсь, что вам не будет скучно.   35. Думаю, что вы сможете перевести все это на английский язык.

**B.**   1. Here's a story about a jolly little boy.   2. My teachers don't think that I'm very intelligent, but my mother wants me to go the university in order to be an engineer and get a lot of money.   3. Last week she finally went to my school to explain me to my teachers.   4. "Don't tell me about the mistakes my son makes when he answers your questions!   5. Excuse me, that's nothing.   6. I want you to know that he's a very bright child.   7. Remember, no one knew that the young Einstein was a genius.   8. Believe me, my Ivan will be a genius too!   9. You will all see!   10. How can he understand anything in your classes?   11. He'd answer better if you'd explain the problems and exercises to the poor students better.   12. It's a pity that you don't understand geniuses!   13. I don't believe you understand ordinary students (m. + f.)!   14. Why don't you help the more intelligent children?"

15. No one understands me, but let them talk, it's all the same to me.   16. I'll be silent.   17. Let them think that I don't understand them.   18. How can I go to school where it's boring, when all the joys of the city lie before me, in my very hands?   19. Interesting films are running in the movie-theaters, there are concerts and operas almost every day.   20. And at concerts and in museums in which they are showing new pictures you meet people who talk about everything more interestingly than [чём + nom.] professors.   21. Of course it's rather difficult when I don't get any money from either father or mother, because then I sit at home in the corner by the window and read the dull magazines which my father receives.   22. Or I lie on my bed and look at the ceiling, and I think about the maps in my atlas of Europe and all the interesting cities I want to see.   23. Our neighbors have no children with whom I could play, and I have few friends.   24. Sometimes I go to town by foot, but usually someone gives me money and I can ride the subway.   25. Perhaps it'd be fun [jolly] to go to the Crimea by slow train and live at my brothers'.   26. My brothers have been living there in the Crimea for a long time.   27. Vasilij works in the new laboratory with professor Kórsakov.   28. Dmitrij was a mechanic in a factory which they closed in the winter.   29. Now he hopes to work in a new store which his friends the Tolstojs opened in the town in which he and Vasilij live.   30. In the sad letter mother got from Dmitrij on Wednes-

day, he wrote that they had promised him work [рабо́та], but they
still hadn't called him.    31. When he was still a student he used to tell
me about the girls [де́вушка] he met at the library.    32. Somehow he
knew only rich girls, not poor ones.    33. I remember a girl who had a
beautiful fast automobile in which she used to drive to the country on
Saturdays.    34. She told jokes very well. 35. She used to laugh at
me because I wanted to ride with her and my brother.    36. I could
tell you a lot about them if only I knew the Russian words.

37. It's time to go home.    38. All the best!

# LESSON XIV

Какоё это у вас перо?
Это новоё немецкоё перо —
такое хорошёё! Но очень
дорогоё!

Дайте мне какую-нибудь
хорошую русскую книгу.

Вы читали какие-нибудь русские
романы? Нет, не читал.

Это недорогие часы.

Какой-то француз вас там
спрашиваёт.

Никто не покупал никаких
романов.

У неё была когда-то такая же
книга.

Мы ни с какими японцами не
говорили.

Можно мне идти?

Конечно, можно.

Большоё вам спасибо. Не за что.
                                    [nьézəštə]
Нет, дорогой, нельзя.

Нельзя здесь говорить
по-английски!

Эта китаянка умеёт говорить и
по-польски и по-немецки. Она
такая умная!

Маленькая Вера умеёт писать.

Я не могу писать, потому что у
меня теперь нет ни пера ни
карандаша.

What sort of a pen is it you have?
It's a new German pen — such a
good one! But very expensive.

Give me a good Russian book.

Have you read any Russian
novels? No, I haven't read any.

This is an inexpensive watch.

A Frenchman is asking for you
there.

No one bought any novels.

She once had the same sort of book.

We didn't speak with any Japanese.

May I go?

Of course you may.

Thank you very much. Not at all.

No, my dear, you may not.

It is forbidden to speak English
here.

This Chinese woman knows how to
speak both Polish and German.
She's so intelligent!

Little Vera knows how to write.

I can't write, because I don't have
either a pen or a pencil now.

XIV 174

| | |
|---|---|
| Он это делаёт, как умеёт. | He does it as best he knows how. |
| Он не умеёт делать этого. | He can't do that. |
| Это можно делать. | This can be done. |
| Можно мне говорить с Анной? | May I speak with Anna? |
| Об этом нельзя и подумать. | One can't even think about that. |
| Она берёт уроки немецкого языка у французского профессора. | She takes German lessons from a French professor. |
| Кого он учит? | Whom does he teach? |
| Он учит французских студенток. | He teaches French students. |
| Чему он их учит? | What does he teach them? |
| Он их учит русскому языку. | He teaches them Russian. |
| Игорь учит Веру музыке. | Igor' is teaching music to Vera. |
| На каком языке он пишет? | In what language does he write? |
| Он пишет и по-французски и по-испански. | He writes both in French and Spanish. |
| Он переводит книги с японского языка на итальянский. | He translates books from Japanese into Italian. |

---

**1.** Adjectives with stems in **к**, **г** or **х** differ from the adjectives you have already learned only in the operation of the "indispensable spelling rules" given in Appendix I, § 7: since the **ы** *cannot* stand after these letters, it is automatically replaced by **и**. This happens in all the plural forms and in the singular masc. Nom.[1] and the masc.-neut. Inst.: нов-*ый* русск-**ий**; (с) нов-*ым* русск-**им**; нов-*ые* русск-**ие**, нов-*ых* русск-**их**, нов-*ым* русск-**им**, нов-*ыми* русск-**ими**.

**1.01·** If the suffix is stressed, the Nom. sg. masc. is **-ой**: плохой 'bad'. There are a few surnames in **-ской** or **-цкой**, e.g. *Ланской*, *Трубецкой*.

**1.11** In the short forms, the plural suffix is of course **-и** (cf. XII 2.3 for stress):

| | | | | |
|---|---|---|---|---|
| **A.** дорогой | dear | дорог | дорого | дороги | дорога |
| плохой | bad | плох | плохо | плохи | плоха |

**1.12** Adjectives in **-ский** and **-ской** do not have short forms.

---

[1] In the N sg. masc. the unstressed **-кий -гий -хий** is *-kəj -gəj -xəj* in standard Muscovite pronunciation, although *-kʰij -gʰij -xʰij* is also now recognized as "correct". All other forms are pronounced according to the normal rules, pp. 327–330.

**1.13**   Adjectives whose stems end in consonant (except **c**) plus **к** usually have the inserted vowel **o** in the masculine short form:

**A.** ре́дкий      rare          ре́док   ре́дко   ре́дки   редка́
**B.** лёгкий      light, easy   лёгок   лёгко́   лёгки́   лёгка́

*NB*: the -гк- is pronounced as though spelled -хк- (App. I, § 17.7).

**1.141**   **Большо́й** 'big, large' has no short form from the same stem. In its place is found **вели́к, -о, -и, -а**. With suffix-stress (**велико́, -и́, -а́**), it usually connotes 'too big, bigger than necessary':

Ко́мната велика́.                    The room is (too) big.

**1.142**   Similarly, the short forms corresponding to **ма́ленький** 'small, little' are **мал, -о, -ы; мала́**. The feminine form always has suffix-stress, but when the neuter and plural have suffix-stress (**мало́, малы́**), they ordinarily connote '*too* little':

Э́ти ко́мнаты на́м малы́.            These rooms are (too) small for us.

**1.2**   The many Russian surnames in -**ский** are declined like adjectives: Достое́вский, Достое́вского, к Достое́вскому, с Достое́вским.

**2.1**   Adjectives whose stems end in **ш, ж, ч,** or **щ** are likewise spelled in accordance with the "indispensable spelling rules", but the place of the stress also affects the spelling (Intro. 5.4). If the stress is on the *suffix*, the forms are identical with suffix-stressed stems in **к, г, х**: но́в-*ый* плох-**о́й** больш-**о́й**; Inst. sg. masc.-neut. но́в-*ым* плох-**и́м** больш-**и́м**; но́в-*ые* плох-**и́е** больш-**и́е**, etc.

Short forms:

**B.** хоро́ший good   хоро́ш   хорошо́   хороши́   хороша́

**2.2**   If, however, the *stem* is stressed, then (beside the replacement of **ы** by **и**) the suffixes beginning in -o- are spelled with -ё-:

но́в-*оё*   ру́сск-*оё*   хоро́ш-**ёё**   но́в-*ого*   ру́сск-*ого*   хоро́ш-**ёго**
о но́в-*ом*   ру́сск-*ом*   хоро́ш-**ём**   к но́в-*ому*   ру́сск-*ому*   хоро́ш-**ёму**
                 fem. G-D-P-I sg.   но́в-*ой*   ру́сск-*ой*   хоро́ш-**ёй**

**3.**   The normal adjectival declension can thus be divided into types by these spelling rules. The stem may be stressed (type B) or unstressed (type A). The stem may end in **ш, ж, ч, щ,** (3A *большо́й*; 3B *хоро́ший*), in **к, г, х** (2A *плохо́й*; 2B *ру́сский*), or in some other consonant (1A *молодо́й*, 1B *но́вый*). Types 2A and 3A are identical and we separate them only because of the contrast between 2B and 3B. Sample declensions are given in Appendix III, p. 353.

**4.** Certain adjectives regularly serve as nouns. Thus **ру́сский**, without any noun, means 'a Russian', **ру́сская** 'a Russian woman', **ру́сские** 'Russians'.

*NB*: This use of the adjective of nationality as a noun is quite rare; normally there is a separate noun. See the next paragraph for typical examples.

**5.** Here are the names of some countries, the words for male and female inhabitants of the countries, and the adjectives referring to them. Note that only the name of the country is written with a capital letter.

|  |  | m. (+ Gen. sg.) | f. | aj. |
|---|---|---|---|---|
| America | Аме́рика | америка́нец -нца | америка́нка | америка́нский |
| England | А́нглия | англича́нин (pl. англича́не) | англича́нка | англи́йский |
| Germany | Герма́ния | не́мец, не́мца | не́мка | неме́цкий |
| Europe | Евро́па | европе́ец, -пе́йца | европе́йка | европе́йский |
| Spain | Испа́ния | испа́нец, испа́нца | испа́нка | испа́нский |
| Italy | Ита́лия | италья́нец, италья́нца | италья́нка | италья́нский |
| China | Кита́й | кита́ец, кита́йца | китая́нка | кита́йский |
| Poland | По́льша | поля́к | по́лька | по́льский |
| France | Фра́нция | францу́з | францу́женка | францу́зский |
| Japan | Япо́ния | япо́нец, япо́нца | япо́нка | япо́нский |

**5.1** Note the plural of "Englishman"; cf. IX 3.1.

**5.2** The genitive plural of the feminines in **-нка** is in **-нок**: *не́мок, испа́нок*. The genitive plurals of **по́лька** and **европе́йка** are, respectively, *по́лёк, европе́ек*. (Cf. VIII 1.2311.)

**5.3** The language name is the adjective plus the noun **язы́к** 'language, tongue': **кита́йский язы́к** 'Chinese, the Chinese language'. The noun must not be omitted.

To say 'in (the language)', an adverb is formed by means of the particle **по-** with the adjective minus the final **-й**: **по-кита́йски** 'in Chinese'.

Read § 3 of Lesson Va, p. 69.

**5.4** Note: The English phrase "Russian professor" is ambiguous, for it can refer to the nationality of the professor or to the subject he teaches. But ру́сский профе́ссор means only the nationality; to express the other meaning of the English phrase, one says профе́ссор ру́сского языка́. "Russian lesson" is normally уро́к ру́сского языка́.

**6.1**   Ordinarily a noun (with its modifiers) which is in *apposition* with another noun (i.e. which identifies it by giving it a different name) is in the same case:

| | |
|---|---|
| Óн говори́л с францу́женкой, ма́терью своего́ дру́га. | He was speaking with a Frenchwoman, the mother of his friend. |
| Я встре́тил дру́га, профе́ссора Воло́цкого. | I met my friend, Professor Volockij. |

**6.2**   However, the title of a book, play, newspaper, or the like, when used in apposition, normally remains in the nominative. Thus:

| | |
|---|---|
| Мы́ чита́ем «Идио́та». | We are reading *The Idiot.* |
| but Мы́ чита́ем рома́н «Идио́т». | We are reading the novel *The Idiot.* (apposition) |
| Я э́то чита́л в «Но́вом ру́сском сло́ве». | I read it in *The New Russian Word.* |
| but Я э́то чита́л в газе́те «Но́вое ру́сское сло́во». | I read it in the newspaper *The New Russian Word.* (apposition) |
| Кто́ геро́й «Анны Каре́ниной» Толсто́го? | Who is the hero of Tolstoj's *Anna Karenin?* |
| but Кто́ геро́й рома́на Толсто́го «Анна Каре́нина»? | Who is the hero of Tolstoj's novel *Anna Karenin?* (apposition) |

**7.**   The verb уме́ть means 'know how to, have the skill to', as opposed to мо́чь 'have the physical power or opportunity to'.

**8.1**   The impersonal form мо́жно (мо́жно бы́ло, мо́жно бу́дет) means 'it is possible', or with the dative 'one may, one can, one is permitted to'.

**8.2**   Its negative is нельзя́ (нельзя́ бы́ло, нельзя́ бу́дет), meaning 'it is impossible, one cannot, it is not allowed, one must not'.

**9.**   The verb учи́ть 'teach' (with the P научи́ть) takes the accusative of the person taught and the dative of the thing taught.[1]

**9.1**   Colloquially, учи́ть also means 'learn'. *Я учу́ уро́к.* 'I'm learning the lesson.' The perfective in this sense is вы́учить. (Note the accent!)

[1] Historically speaking, this verb meant "make accustomed to". Thus the construction is "make someone (Acc.) used to something (Dat.)."

**10.** The verb with the adjective **никако́й** 'no, none' must be negated (cf. II 5.3, p. 28). Notice that the first syllable *precedes* any preposition (cf. II 5.1), and the form is then written as three words: e.g. **ни у како́го, ни о како́й, ни к како́му, ни перед како́ю, ни с каки́ми.**

**11.** Hyphenated surnames decline both parts in accordance with the appropriate rules (cf. VI 7.2). For example:

| | | |
|---|---|---|
| N | Ри́мск**ий**-Ко́рсаков | Серге́ев-Це́нск**ий** |
| A-G | Ри́мск**ого**-Ко́рсаков**а** | Серге́ев**а**-Це́нск**ого** |
| P | о Ри́мск**ом**-Ко́рсаков**е** | о Серге́ев**е**-Це́нск**ом** |
| D | Ри́мск**ому**-Ко́рсаков**у** | Серге́ев**у**-Це́нск**ому** |
| I | с Ри́мск**им**-Ко́рсаков**ым** | с Серге́ев**ым**-Це́нск**им** |
| N | Ве́ра Ри́мск**ая**-Ко́рсаков**а** | О́льга Серге́ев**а**-Це́нск**ая** |
| A | Ве́ру Ри́мск**ую**-Ко́рсаков**у** | О́льгу Серге́ев**у**-Це́нск**ую** |
| G | Ве́ры Ри́мск**ой**-Ко́рсаков**ой** | О́льги Серге́ев**ой**-Це́нск**ой** |
| P-D $\left. {o \atop к} \right\}$ | Ве́ре Ри́мск**ой**-Ко́рсаков**ой** | $\left. {o \atop к} \right\}$ О́льге Серге́ев**ой**-Це́нск**ой** |
| I | с Ве́рой Ри́мск**ой**-Ко́рсаков**ой** | с О́льгой Серге́ев**ой**-Це́нск**ой** |

## УПРАЖНЕНИЯ

**A.** Supply in place of the blanks first the singular and then the plural forms for all the nouns and their modifiers:

1. Я ви́жу —. у́мн— не́мец, ма́леньк— не́мка, так'— же лёгк— зада́ча, хоро́ш— испа́нск— рома́н, доро́г'— бе́л— ша́пка, то́ бо́льш'— зда́ниё, молод'— ру́сск— му́ж, бе́д— кита́йск—

2. Я не ви́жу —. дере́вня, э́та плох'— у́лица, А́нна Арка́дьёвна Каре́нина, Ле́в Никола́ёвич Толсто́й, Фёдор Достое́вский, ста́р— и ме́дленн— автомоби́ль, э́тот неме́цк— фи́льм, небольш'— англи́йск—

3. О[б] —.

4. К —. са́д, са́мый весёл— ма́льчик, ре́дк— ста́р— кни́га, Пу́шкин и Достое́вский, Пу́шкина и

5. С —. Достое́вская, Бесту́жёв-Ма́рлинский.

**B.** Read and translate:

1. Мо́жно на́м пойти́ в теа́тр сего́дня ве́чером? Не́т, дороги́е друзья́, нельзя́. Вы́ все́ должны́ рабо́тать. 2. Вы́ бы́ли во Фра́нции и́ли в

Италии? 3. У каки́х профессоро́в вы́ чита́ли таки́е ве́щи? 4. Но́вая студе́нтка, францу́женка, дала́ учи́телю дово́льно хоро́ший отве́т. Поля́к ему́ то́же хорошо́ отве́тил. 5. Кто́ дава́л са́мые плохи́е отве́ты? 6. Нельзя́ писа́ть таки́м плохи́м перо́м! Пу́сть мне́ даду́т бо́лее но́воё. 7. Вы́ смотре́ли то́т ста́рый ру́сский фи́льм, кото́рый пока́зывали та́м вчера́? Не́т, но наде́юсь, что мы́ посмо́трим э́тот о́чень интере́сный и краси́вый япо́нский фи́льм, о кото́ром все́ тепе́рь говоря́т. 8. Э́тот рома́н меня́ не интересу́ёт, да́йте мне́ друго́й, пожа́луйста. 9. У него́ е́сть мно́го кни́г на все́х языка́х по эконо́мике и есте́ственным нау́кам. 10. Вчера́ на собра́нии в америка́нском клу́бе говори́ли не́сколько кита́йцёв и япо́нцёв. На́м все́м бы́ло о́чень интере́сно. 11. Она́ перевёла́ его́ исто́рию неме́цкой литерату́ры с францу́зского на англи́й-ский язы́к. 12. Мы́ е́здили ещё ра́з к те́м печа́льным ста́рым европе́й-цам, кото́рых ва́м бы́ло та́к жа́ль, когда́ вы́ и́х ви́дели на конце́рте. 13. Мо́жно та́к сказа́ть по-ру́сски? Не́т, нельзя́. 14. Бори́с Пётро́вич у́чит меха́ника, францу́за, хи́мии. 15. Тебе́ нельзя́ чита́ть э́ту кни́гу. Да́й её мне́ сейча́с же! 16. Не лёгко́ отвеча́ть на тако́й вопро́с. 17. Ва́м не ску́чно жи́ть на тако́й кварти́ре в тако́м го́роде? 18. Она́ получи́ла письмо́ на кита́йском языке́ и коне́чно не могла́ его́ про-чита́ть. Но зде́сь е́сть ста́рый не́мец, кото́рый жи́л когда́-то в Кита́е, и о́н е́й помо́г. 19. Перед таки́ми людьми́ нельзя́ та́к говори́ть! 20. Она́ бу́дёт бра́ть уро́ки неме́цкого языка́ у не́мки, госпожи́ Мюллер, жёны́ на́шёго до́ктора. 21. Суме́л ли Васи́лий перевести́ э́ту францу́зскую фра́зу? Да́, о́н хорошо́ перевёл её́. 22. Вы́ должны́ вы́учить все́ но́вые ру́сские слова́. 23. Ва́м лёгко́ переводи́ть с ру́сского языка́? 24. Е́сли ты́ реши́шь все́ зада́чи сего́дня ве́чером, ты́ мо́жёшь не рабо́тать за́втра. 25. Когда́ мы́ ва́с нау́чим ру́сскому языку́?

**C.** For written and/or oral translation into Russian:

1. They asked whether we lived in a little apartment or a big house. 2. We had a nice big apartment in Moscow. 3. One can't talk with such people. 4. That's an easy question! Such questions don't interest intelligent people. 5. The Russian lady asked me to buy a (some) good Russian novel. She wants to give a Russian book to her neighbor, a German, to whom she is teaching Russian. 6. Tell Anna Bródskij to show you the pretty but inexpensive things which she bought in Spain and Italy. 7. Do you know whether they (X 10) have translated Leónov's novel *The Russian Forest*? 8. Sergej was teaching Marija Bélskij mathe-matics and natural sciences, and Marija was teaching him history and literature. 9. Please help me to translate this letter into French. It's rather difficult. 10. I believe that I read about that in Tolstoj's novel,

*Anna Karenin.* 11. Several Chinese live in the little house behind the French school. 12. To whose daughter did he say that? 13. You may go with Sergej Petrovich Ivanov to the country. 14. Our Russian professor used to live in Germany, and he speaks German very well and has many German books. 15. He is working very hard [= much]; he must translate many sentences into English. 16. Medicine and natural sciences interest my friend. 17. Lev was sitting at a large table by the little window and reading a Russian newspaper. 18. One can't buy French or German newspapers here in town, but one can buy Spanish newspapers in the little store which is in our street beyond the big factory. 19. I hope that you won't forget to tell your wife to call me tomorrow morning. 20. I met an old friend, Igor' Vasil'evich Trónskij, at the English club last night.

## СЛОВАРЬ

| | | | |
|---|---|---|---|
| большо́й | big, large | мо́жно | one may; see § 8.1 |
| вели́к | see § 1.141 | му́зыка | music |
| дорого́й (§ 1.11) | dear, expensive | нау́ка | science |
| друго́й | other, another | небольшо́й | small, not large |
| есте́ственный | natural | недорого́й | inexpensive |
| есте́ственные нау́ки | natural sciences | нельзя́ | one may not; see § 8.2 |
| идио́т | idiot | никако́й (§10) | no, of no kind |
| исто́рия | history | плохо́й | bad |
| како́й | what, of what kind | ре́дкий | rare |
| како́й-нибудь | some, a, of some kind | ру́сский | Russian |
| | | ру́сский ⎫ § 4 | a Russian (m) |
| како́й-то | some, of a certain kind (III 11.2) | ру́сская ⎭ | a Russian (f) |
| | | с [со] + Gen. | from |
| лёгкий (App. I, § 17.7) | light, easy | тако́й | such, of such kind |
| литерату́ра | literature | тако́й же | of the same kind |
| ма́л | see § 1.142 | хи́мия | chemistry |
| ма́ленький | small, little | хоро́ший | good |
| матема́тика | mathematics | эконо́мика | economics |
| медици́на | medicine | язы́к *E* (see p. 351) | language, tongue |

SEE ALSO PARAGRAPH 5, page 176

интересова́ть  
    интересу́ют I ⎱ interest  
заинтересова́ть P ⎰  
переводи́ть перево́дят I ⎱ translate  
перевести́ переведу́т P ⎰  
    past перевёл, -вела́, -вели́

уме́ть уме́ют I ⎱ know how to (§ 7)  
суме́ть P ⎰  
учи́ть у́чат I ⎱ (see § 9) teach  
научи́ть P ⎰  
учи́ть у́чат I ⎱ (§9.1) learn  
вы́учить вы́учат P ⎰

# LESSON XIVa

Вы́ ему́ меша́ете.

You're bothering him.

Из газе́т я ви́жу, что же́нщинам меша́ют рабо́тать на э́той фа́брике.

From the papers I see that they are preventing women from working at that factory.

Э́то помеша́ет ему́ пое́хать в Москву́.

This will hinder him from going to Moscow.

Незнако́мая да́ма ему́ меша́ла чита́ть.

An unknown lady was hindering him from reading.

Он нам мно́го рассказа́л о роди́телях и знако́мых.

He told us a lot about his parents and acquaintances.

Ваш знако́мый получи́л откры́тку от роди́телей.

Your acquaintance received a postcard from his parents.

Они́ про́сят переда́ть вам приве́т от друзе́й.

They asked (me) to pass on to you greetings from your friends.

[Переда́йте] приве́т му́жу!

[Give] my best to your husband!

Она́ ему́ передала́ уче́бник.

She handed the textbook to him.

По како́му а́дресу мо́жно вам посыла́ть телегра́ммы?

To what address can one send you telegrams?

Телеграфи́руйте сейча́с же роди́телям.

Telegraph your parents at once.

Что́ вам сове́товали роди́тели?

What did your parents advise?

Они́ посове́товали посла́ть телегра́мму знако́мому адвока́ту в Оде́ссу.

They advised to send a telegram to my lawyer acquaintance in Odessa.

Ва́ша знако́мая дово́льна но́вой су́мкой.

Your acquaintance is pleased with her new handbag.

Мне́ ну́жен ваш слова́рь.

I need your dictionary.

---

**1.** Read § 5 of Lesson XXI, on *ну́жный* and *ну́жно*.

**2.** *Передава́ть* and *переда́ть* have the same forms as *дава́ть/да́ть* (cf. XII 4). Note the shift of stress in the perfective past: пе́редал -о -и;

передала́. The meaning is literally 'give over, transfer'. It may be used of concrete objects or of messages. With *по ра́дио* (expressed or understood) it is the usual term for 'broadcast'.

| | |
|---|---|
| О́н мне́ пе́редал откры́тку. | He passed me the postcard. |
| Ему́ пе́редали ва́ш приве́т. | Your greeting was passed on to him. |

**3.** Compound adjectives like "Polish-German" or "Russo-Japanese" in Russian have the first element ending in -o, and the second with the normal declensional endings: по́льско-неме́цкий, ру́сско-япо́нский. The stress on the first stem is weaker than that on the second.

## УПРАЖНЕНИЯ

**A.** For oral drill:

| | |
|---|---|
| 1. О́н быва́л у [адвока́та]. | He used to visit the [lawyer]. |
| 2. О́н ходи́л к [адвока́ту]. | He used to go to see the [lawyer]. |

On these two models, make sentences using the following, in both singular and plural: *писа́тель[ница], купе́ц, солда́т, знако́мый, знако́мая, журнали́ст[ка], музыка́нт[ша], секрета́рь, секрета́рша, худо́жник, худо́жница.*

Repeat, adding the proper forms of the adjectives *бога́тый ру́сский* as modifiers for the nouns.

**B.** Read aloud and translate:

1. Роди́тели хотя́т, чтобы я́ и́м посыла́л краси́вые откры́тки. 2. Извини́те, не мо́жете ли вы́ мне́ сказа́ть, где́ э́тот а́дрес? —Не́т, э́та у́лица мне́ незнако́ма.  3. Я́ о́чень недово́лен ва́шими упражне́ниями. Вы́ все́ сде́лали мно́го оши́бок. Напиши́те то́ же само́е еще́ ра́з и попра́вьте все́ оши́бки.  4. Почему́ она́ дикту́ет бы́стро? Студе́нтам тру́дно понима́ть и коне́чно они́ пи́шут непра́вильно. 5. У него́ конто́ра в универма́ге. Во́т а́дрес, по кото́рому ну́жно писа́ть. 6. По календарю́ я́ ви́жу, что не бу́дет ле́кций в э́ту пя́тницу.  7. Ра́зве о́н ва́м не пе́редал моего́ приве́та?  8. Лейтена́нт ему́ не посове́товал переда́ть телегра́мму жене́.  9. Неуже́ли вы́ ничего́ не получи́ли от ни́х? Ну́жно бы телеграфи́ровать, чтобы они́ сейча́с же ва́м посла́ли отве́т. 10. А́х, э́то то́лько ру́сско-англи́йский слова́рь, о́н мне́ не помо́жет. Мне́ ну́жен англи́йско-ру́сский слова́рь.

11. Кака́я оши́бка! Е́сли бы то́лько я́ не познако́мился с не́й! 12а. Он хоте́л бы посове́товаться с каки́м-то худо́жником об э́том. 12б. Он хоте́л бы посове́товаться с каки́м-нибудь худо́жником об э́том. 13. Неуже́ли вы́ ещё не доста́ли никаки́х докуме́нтов? Тру́дно пове́рить э́тому. 14. Вы́, должно́ быть, оши́блись. Тама́ра на́м говори́ла, что она́ о́чень дово́льна все́ми на́шими сочине́ниями. 15. Е́сли бы то́лько о́н получи́л мою́ телегра́мму!

**C.** На бу́дущей неде́ле кани́кулы. Куда́ е́хать? Сего́дня я́ хочу́ реши́ть э́то.

—До́брое у́тро, Серге́й! Я́ получи́ла откры́тку от бра́та. Он про́сит переда́ть ва́м приве́т от все́х знако́мых.

—Спаси́бо, напиши́те ему́, чтобы и о́н все́м и́м пе́редал от меня́ приве́т. Скажи́те, Ири́на, куда́ вы́ реши́ли е́хать?

—Я́ ещё не реши́ла.

—Что́ же ва́м посове́товал ва́ш знако́мый?

—Он не сове́тует е́хать туда́ зимо́й.

—Я́ не меша́ю ва́м, наде́юсь?

—Не́т, мне́ то́лько ну́жно телеграфи́ровать роди́телям сво́й но́вый а́дрес. Я́ не получа́ю пи́сем, кото́рые они́ посыла́ют по ста́рому а́дресу. Бра́т обеща́л посыла́ть телегра́ммы ка́ждую неде́лю, но́ не де́лает э́того. Да́, на про́шлой неде́ле у меня́ бы́л незнако́мый молодо́й челове́к с приве́том от роди́телей. Он на́м мно́го расска́зывал о ни́х. Мне́ пе́редал неме́цко-англи́йский слова́рь от бра́та.

—А ка́к ва́ши успе́хи в францу́зском языке́?

—Учи́тельница о́чень дово́льна мои́ми успе́хами. Я́ мно́го рабо́таю. Тепе́рь мне́ ну́жен но́вый уче́бник. Не́т ли его́ у ва́с?

—Е́сть, но я́ его́ да́л това́рищу. Тепе́рь мне́ ну́жно идти́. Я́ наде́юсь, что ничто́ не помеша́ет ва́шим кани́кулам, Ири́на.

—До свида́ния, Серге́й! Приве́т жене́!

**D.** *Переведи́те на ру́сский язы́к:*

1. Send me a telegram every day. 2. Don't bother the artists. 3. Tell your acquaintances about the opera we heard on the radio last night. 4. Is the merchant satisfied with his new office? 5. Did he advise you to hand over the keys to the lawyers? I think he is mistaken. 6. If you had told your parents your new address, they wouldn't be sending telegrams to the old address. 7. The writer has a pretty new hat, but the actress has a newer and prettier [one]. 8. This was an easier dictation than the story which she dictated to us on Wednesday, wasn't it? 9. The artist was playing chess with the journalist. 10. The

students gave the old professor a new briefcase. He's very pleased [= satisfied] with it.   11. The actress has many pretty postcards which she has received from friends and acquaintances.   12. If you write to your parents tonight, give them my best [= greeting].   13. I'd advise you to hinder him from doing that.   14. Igor' sent his new story to a writer who works in Moscow. He hopes the writer will hand it on to someone who can help.   15. You ought to advise the soldiers what to do.

## СЛОВАРЬ

а́дрес [*Epl.* адреса́]        address

дово́льный ( + Inst.)        satisfied (with)

знако́мый (aj.)        familiar, known
  (aj. as noun)        acquaintance

недово́льный ( + Inst.) dissatis- fied (with)

незнако́мый (aj.)        unfamiliar
  (aj. as noun)        unknown person

ну́жно  }
ну́жный  }        *see* XXI 5

от + Gen.        from

откры́тка [G pl. -ток]        postcard

приве́т        greeting

роди́тели        parents
  [pl. only, G роди́телей]

телегра́мма        telegram

меша́ть
  -а́ют I        } + Dat.        bother, disturb, hinder (from)
помеша́ть
  -а́ют P

передава́ть -даю́т I }        hand over,
переда́ть -да́м *etc.* P }        pass on (§2)

посыла́ть -а́ют I }        send
посла́ть пошлю́т P }

сове́товать
  -туют I        } + Dat.        advise, counsel
посове́товать
  -туют P

телеграфи́ровать IP }        telegraph
телеграфи́руют }

# LESSON XV

| | |
|---|---|
| Нра́вится ли ва́м э́тот дива́н? | Do you like this sofa? |
| Они́ о́чень понра́вились дру́г дру́гу. | They took a great liking to each other. |
| Э́то ему́ мо́жет понра́виться. | He might like this. |
| Ему́ понра́вилось ходи́ть туда́. | He took a liking to going there. |
| Че́м вы́ бо́льше интересу́етесь, исто́рией и́ли эконо́микой? | What are you more interested in, history or economics? |
| Эконо́мика мне́ ме́ньше нра́вится че́м исто́рия. | I like economics less than history. |
| Фома́ всегда́ хорошо́ гото́вил уро́ки. | Foma (Tom) always prepared his lessons well. |
| Илья́ гото́вился к экза́мену. | Il'ja (Elija) was getting ready for an examination. |
| Ба́бушка приготови́ла у́жин. | Grandmother prepared supper. |
| Они́ интересу́ются дру́г дру́гом. | They are interested in each other. |
| Ве́ра Ники́тична хорошо́ одева́ется. | Vera Nikitichna dresses well. |
| Ма́ленький Ва́ня уже́ са́м одева́ется. | Little Vanja (Jack) already dresses himself. |
| О́н ра́но встаёт и по́здно ложи́тся спа́ть. | He gets up early and goes to bed late. |
| На́ш кла́сс начина́ется ра́ньше и конча́ется по́зже, че́м ва́ш. | Our class begins earlier and ends later than yours. |
| Вста́ньте, оде́ньтесь сейча́с же и иди́те со мно́й. | Get up, get dressed at once, and come with me. |
| За́втра Ники́та вста́нет ра́ньше на́с. | Tomorrow Nikita will get up before us. |
| Ва́ш дя́дя слу́шал ра́дио, а ва́ша тётя гото́вила у́жин. | Your uncle was listening to the radio, and your aunt was preparing supper. |

| | |
|---|---|
| Са́ша и Ко́стя никого́ не слу́шаются. | Sasha (Alec) and Kostja don't obey anybody. |
| Пожа́луйста, сади́тесь за сто́л. | Please sit down at the table. |
| Вчера́ ве́чером судья́ лёг спа́ть по́зже ва́с. | The judge went to bed later than you last night. |
| Како́й-то мужчи́на стоя́л та́м же и жда́л трамва́я. | Some man was standing in the same place and waiting for a streetcar. |
| Ко́ля жда́л своего́ дя́дю и мою́ тётю. | Kolja (Nick) was waiting for his uncle and my aunt. |
| Мне́ не спи́тся. | I'm not sleepy. |
| Кто́ э́тот мужчи́на? | Who is that man? |
| Кото́рый? То́т мо́й дя́дя, а э́тот мо́й де́душка. | Which one? That one is my uncle and this one is my grandfather. |
| Вы́ зна́ете моего́ дя́дю Ива́на Ильича́ и́ли моего́ бра́та Илью́? | Do you know my uncle Ivan Il'jíč or my brother Il'já? |
| Ники́та взя́л ва́шу тетра́дку с собо́й. | Nikita took your notebook with him. |
| Уже́ пора́ конча́ть. | It's already time to finish. |

---

**1.1** Verb-forms with the particle -ся/-сь (cf. Lesson X) are traditionally (but somewhat misleadingly) called *reflexive*. Their meaning is simply *intransitive*: they may never take an accusative, a direct object. The goal of the action, if mentioned, is inseparable from the grammatical subject. Four categories may be distinguished:

(A) *Simply intransitive* (there is no goal). For example:

| | | |
|---|---|---|
| laugh | Она́ мно́го смеётся. | She laughs a lot. |
| fear | Я бою́сь. | I'm afraid. |
| be pleasing | Э́то мне нра́вится. | This pleases me. ($\cong$ I like it.) |

(B) *Passive*. The grammatical subject is the goal (or receiver) of the action. The actor may be expressed by the instrumental case, but only if the verb is *im*perfective. For example:

| | |
|---|---|
| Ка́к пи́шется его́ фами́лия? | How is his surname spelled? |
| Зада́ча реша́ется студе́нтами. | The problem is being solved by the students. |

(C) *True reflexive*. The grammatical subject is both the actor and the goal of the action, the performer and the receiver. For example:

Бра́т одева́ется о́чень бы́стро.    Brother dresses very quickly.
(Бра́т одева́ет ребёнка.)    (Brother dresses the child.)

(D) *Reciprocal*. The grammatical subject is again both actor and goal, but there is another performer (or performers), and the action is mutual or reciprocal. For example:

Мы́ ви́делись вчера́.    We saw *each other* yesterday.
О́н ви́делся со свои́м дру́гом.    He met his friend [and his friend met, saw, him].

**1.2** There are verbs which never occur without the -ся, as we saw in Lesson X, but the majority of verbs may occur either with or without it, and with a difference in meaning. For example:

Мы́ на́чали уро́к ра́но.    We began the lesson early.
  (ко́нчили)    (finished)
Уро́к ра́но начался́.    The lesson began early.
  (ко́нчился).    (ended)

О́н обеща́л на́м помо́чь.    He promised to help us.
О́н всегда́ обеща́ется.    He is always making promises.

Слу́шайте ма́ть.    Listen to your mother.
Слу́шайтесь ма́тери.    Obey your mother.

Она́ встре́тила Ива́на.    She met Ivan.
Она́ встре́тилась с Ива́ном    She met Ivan [and he met her].
Они́ встре́тились.    They met [each other].

**2.** While -ся/-сь is a *positive* indication of intransitivity, there are many intransitive verbs without the particle. Some verbs may be either intransitive or transitive without change in form (like most English verbs): e.g.,

Мы́ ви́дим.    We see.    (intransitive)
Мы́ ви́дим поля́.    We see the fields.    (transitive)
О́н понима́ет.    He understands.    (intransitive)
О́н ва́с понима́ет.    He understands you. (transitive)

And some verbs are exclusively intransitive: e.g.,

О́н се́л за сто́л.    He sat down at the table.
О́н стоя́л у окна́.    He was standing by the window.

**3.** Verbs with the particle -ся/-сь cannot take an object in the accusative case, but they are often accompanied by some other case or by a preposition with the appropriate case. For example:

| | | |
|---|---|---|
| *gen.* | Он бои́тся сёстры́. | He fears (is afraid of) his sister. |
| *dat.* | Автомоби́ль нра́вится ёму́. | The automobile pleases him. |
| *inst.* | Она́ интересу́ётся автомоби́лями. | She's interested in automobiles. |
| *над* + *inst.* | Он смеётся надо мно́й. | He's laughing at me, making fun of me. |

**3.1**  Note: **Нра́виться** is usually turned around in English translation, so that the Russian dative becomes the English subject, and the Russian nominative becomes the English object:

| | |
|---|---|
| Я **ей** нра́влюсь. | I please **her**. ≅ **She** likes me. |
| Это **ёму́** понра́вилось. | This pleased **him**. ≅ **He** took a liking to it. |

**3.2**  Учи́ть**ся** means 'learn, study':

| | |
|---|---|
| Я учу́сь ру́сскому языку́. | I'm learning Russian. |
| cf. Ива́н меня́ у́чит ру́сскому языку́. | Ivan is teaching me Russian. |

**4.**  The third person (neuter) of certain verbs may be used with -**ся** in a subjectless construction where the logical actor (if presented at all) is in the dative case. E.g. *хоте́ться*:

| | |
|---|---|
| Ёму́ хоте́лось пое́хать куда́-нибудь. | He felt like going somewhere. |
| Ёму́ не спи́тся. | He doesn't feel like sleeping = He's not sleepy. |
| Ёму́ не спа́лось. | He didn't feel like sleeping = He wasn't sleepy. |

With the negation, many verbs can be so used:

Он до́лжен { рабо́тать, чита́ть, переводи́ть,     но́ *ёму́* **не** { рабо́таётся. чита́ётся. перево́дится.

He ought to { work, read, translate,     but he doesn't feel like it (or, working.) reading.) translating.)

The English "feel like" is not an accurate equivalent of the Russian, for it specifies a real actor. In Russian the verbal action is presented as quite autonomous, impinging on the logical actor only indirectly — the actor is not responsible for the action, but is somehow affected by it.

This construction occurs often enough so that you need to recognize it. In speaking, however, it is well to use it very sparingly.

**5.** The verbs **сиде́ть сидя́т** 'sit', **стоя́ть стоя́т** 'stand', **лёжа́ть лёжа́т** 'lie' have no perfective equivalents (but cf. XXIV 7). They denote a state rather than an action, and mean "to be in a [sitting/standing/lying] position". To them correspond verbs denoting action and meaning "to assume a ... position":

| | | | |
|---|---|---|---|
| сади́ться садя́тся | (I) | се́сть ся́дут (P) | to sit down |
| встава́ть встаю́т | | вста́ть вста́нут | to stand up, get up |
| ложи́ться ложа́тся | | ле́чь ля́гут | to lie down, go to bed |

For example:

Óн се́л на сту́л, сиде́л на сту́ле две́ мину́ты и вста́л со сту́ла.

He sat down in the chair, sat in the chair two minutes, and got up from the chair.

Óн ча́сто сади́лся на э́тот сту́л.

He often used to sit down in that chair.

**5.1** The past tense forms of **се́сть** are **се́л, се́ло, се́ли, се́ла.** (Cf. VII 5.)

**5.2** The present (= future) of **ле́чь** has ž instead of g in all forms but 1st sg. and 3rd pl. (cf. X 8): **ля́гу, ля́жешь, ля́жёт; ля́жём, ля́жёте, ля́гут.** The imperative is **ля́г, ля́гте.** Past: **лёг, легло́, легли́, легла́.**

**5.3** The imperfective imperatives **сади́тесь** and **ложи́тесь** are normally used in preference to the perfectives **ся́дь[те], ля́г[те]**, which are considered somewhat abrupt and therefore tend to be rude. (Review V, 7.2, p. 60.)

**5.4** Note that the verbs **сади́ться/се́сть** and **ложи́ться/ле́чь** are treated as verbs of motion and therefore take prepositions with the accusative (cf. VII 8):

Куда́ óн ля́жёт? На э́тот дива́н.

Where is he going to lie down? On that sofa.

Óн се́л в э́то кре́сло.

He sat down in this armchair.

**5.5** For the imperative of **встава́ть**, look at XII 4.2.

**6.** The personal pronoun to which **свой** corresponds has no nominative case. The other forms are: Acc.-Gen. **себя́**, Prep.-Dat. **себе́**, Inst. **собо́й (собо́ю).**

Возьми́те э́ту кни́гу с собо́й.

Take this book with *you*.

Я́ не хочу́ говори́ть о себе́.

I don't want to talk about *myself*.

Óн ушёл к себе́.

He went off to *his own place*.
[for the verb, see next lesson]

**7.** The emphatic personal pronoun "self" has the following forms:

|        | m.       | n.     | f.           | plural     |
|--------|----------|--------|--------------|------------|
| Nom.   | са́м     | само́  | сама́        | са́ми      |
| Acc.   | (= N, G) | само́  | самоё, саму́ | (= N, G)   |
| Gen.   | самого́  |        | само́й       | сами́х     |
| Prep.  | само́м   |        | само́й       | сами́х     |
| Dat.   | самому́  |        | само́й       | сами́м     |
| Inst.  | сами́м   |        | само́й (-о́ю) | сами́ми   |

**7.1** Some uses and appropriate translations can be seen from the following:

| | |
|---|---|
| Я са́м э́то сде́лаю. | I'll do it myself. |
| Са́м сде́лай! | Do it yourself! |
| Окно́ само́ закры́лось. | The window closed by itself. |
| О́н ча́сто са́м с собо́й говори́т. | He often talks to himself. |
| О́н са́м смеётся над собо́ю. | He himself laughs at himself. |
| Она́ сама́ себя́ спра́шивает и сама́ себе́ отвеча́ет. | She asks herself questions and answers herself. |
| Она́ не ве́рит самому́ ге́нию! | She doesn't believe the genius himself! |
| Мы ви́дели самого́ геро́я. | We saw the hero himself. |

**8.** Note the following cases where the reciprocal character of the action (cf. 1.1 D, above) is specifically underlined by means of a special pronoun:

| | |
|---|---|
| Вы понима́ете дру́г дру́га. | You understand each other. |
| Они́ боя́тся дру́г дру́га. | They are afraid of each other. |
| Студе́нтки говори́ли дру́г о дру́ге. | The students were talking about each other. |
| Мы помога́ли дру́г дру́гу. | We helped each other. |
| Де́ти смея́лись дру́г над дру́гом. | The children laughed at each other. |

The first element (**дру́г**) remains unchanged, and the second (**дру́га, дру́ге,** etc.) expresses the cases.

**9. Жда́ть/подожда́ть** 'wait for' normally takes the accusative of person but genitive of thing:

| | |
|---|---|
| Я жду́ ма́ть. | I'm waiting for mother. |
| Я жду́ трамва́я. | I'm waiting for a streetcar. |

## 10.  *Masculine nouns in* -**а**/-**я**.

There is a small number of nouns which belong to the second declension, but which are of *masculine* gender. They all signify male persons. Their forms are exactly like the feminine 2nd-declension nouns, but the masculine gender is expressed in the agreement of pronouns, adjectives and verbs:

| | |
|---|---|
| Э́тот молодо́й мужчи́на не зна́ет своего́ дя́ди. | That young man does not know his own uncle. |
| Мо́й дя́дя Илья́ говори́л со ста́рым судьёй. | My uncle Il'ja was speaking with the old judge. |
| Фома́ зна́л того́ молодо́го мужчи́ну. | Foma (Thomas) knew that young man. |

**10.01**  Patronymics from names in -*a*:

| | | | |
|---|---|---|---|
| Илья́: | Ильи́ч, Илья́нична | Фома́: | Фоми́ч, Фоми́нична |
| Лука́: | Луки́ч, Луки́нична | Ники́та: | Ники́тич, Ники́тична |

-*чн*- is pronounced -шн- here.

Note that Ильи́ч, Луки́ч, and Фоми́ч are suffix-stressed: Ильича́, Лукичо́м, Фомичу́, etc.

**10.1**  This group is widely represented by familiar forms of common personal names (like Jack, Jacky, Bill): e.g. **Алёша** (Алексе́й), **Бо́ря** (Бори́с), **Ва́ня** (Ива́н), **Ва́ся** (Васи́лий), **Воло́дя** (Влади́мир), **Гри́ша** (Григо́рий), **Ко́ля** (Никола́й), **Ко́стя** (Константи́н), **Ми́тя**, **Ди́ма** (Дми́трий), **Ми́ша** (Михаи́л), **Пе́тя** (Пётр), **Са́ша** (Алекса́ндр), **Серёжа** (Серге́й), **Фе́дя** (Фёдор), **Я́ша** (Я́ков).

Such nicknames are normally used to refer only to children or to relatives and friends. The list given here is merely a sampling. Not only are there many more similar names, but many of the names here have still other forms which express varying degrees of endearment or annoyance.

**11.**  It has been pointed out that some masculine nouns may be used when referring to women (cf. p. 43). Note that these words take masculine modifiers:

| | |
|---|---|
| Она́ хоро́ший до́ктор. | She is a good doctor. |

Such words are *до́ктор, профе́ссор, меха́ник, това́рищ, судья́, дру́г.*

*Note.* The word **подру́га** 'girl-friend' is used chiefly to refer to the friend of a woman. A man says of a woman 'She is my (close) friend' — Она́ *мой дру́г.*

**12.** The adverbs **бо́лее** and **ме́нее** (XII) are rarely used except to modify adjectives, e.g. в *бо́лее* (*ме́нее*) *но́вом* до́ме 'in a *newer* (*less new*) house'. To modify verbs, the forms **бо́льше** 'more' and **ме́ньше** 'less' are used:

| | |
|---|---|
| Лу́чше слу́шать бо́льше, а говори́ть ме́ньше. | It's better to listen more and talk less. |

**13.** The adverb **ра́ньше** means 'earlier, earlier than, before' and also 'formerly'; similarly, **по́зже** 'later, later than; later on'.

| | |
|---|---|
| Они́ ко́нчили ра́ньше нас. | They finished before us, earlier than we did. |
| Они́ ра́ньше жи́ли в Евро́пе. | Formerly they lived in Europe. |
| Он вста́л по́зже вас. | He got up later than you, later than you did, after you. |
| Он вста́нет по́зже. | He'll get up later on. |

**14.** Note in the examples in the preceding paragraph that "than" in the comparisons is expressed by the genitive case: compare

| | |
|---|---|
| Он пи́шет лу́чше сёстры́. | He writes better than his sister. |

The use of the genitive in such a construction is limited (and will be defined in Lesson XXII). "Than" may be rendered by **чём**: e.g.,

| | |
|---|---|
| Лу́чше по́здно, чём никогда́. | Better late than never. |
| Он лу́чше говори́т по-англи́йски, чём по-ру́сски. | He speaks English better than [he speaks] Russian. |
| Она́ бо́льше говори́т, чём слу́шает. | She talks more than she listens. |
| Он живёт на бо́лее краси́вой кварти́ре, чём вы. | He lives in a nicer apartment than you. |

## УПРАЖНЕНИЯ

**A-1.** On the pattern Он мне́ нра́вится (нра́вился), "I like (liked) him", translate all the possible combinations of:

You, he, she, we, they, the children, the wives, those uncles, our friends, those citizens, that German, the teachers (m, f) everyone, no one } { like/s/ liked } { her, us, them, these children, their wives, the same judges, those people, Mrs. Petrov, the beautiful streets, Chinese literature, forests and fields.

A-2.  Complete each of the following six sentences with each of the
      phrases in parentheses, first in singular, then (if possible) in plural:

a. Where is/are ___ ?
b. I see ___.
c. I do not see ___.
d. They were talking about ___.
e. They were talking to ___.
f. They were talking with ___.

the old judge, the old doctor, my
father, my dear uncle, my dear
aunt, our grandfather, our grandmother, that child, her son and
daughter, his sister and brother;
Il'ja Fomič, uncle Ivan, uncle
Vanja, my uncle and your aunt;
your aunt Ljubov' and my uncle
Aleksej, Petr Il'ič Čajkovskij, all
the children, they.

B.  Read and translate:

1. Скажи́те, пожа́луйста, почему́ вы́ не слу́шаёте, когда́ учи́тельница
говори́т? 2. Э́ти де́вочки никогда́ не слу́шались ма́тери. 3. Фома́
приго́товил не то́т уро́к, и все́ студе́нтки смея́лись над ни́м. 4. Ся́дьте
туда́ на дива́н. Я́ не хочу́ сиде́ть, спаси́бо. 5. В то́й же дере́вне бы́ло
мно́го больши́х но́вых зда́ний, кото́рых мы́ ра́ньше не ви́дели. 6. Са́-
ша жда́л его́ ба́бушку. Чью́ ба́бушку? 7. Е́сли в библиоте́ке э́той
са́мой но́вой кни́ги не́т, ка́к могу́ я́ гото́виться к экза́мену? 8. Его́
кни́га хорошо́ чита́ется. 9. У на́с не́ было ни геро́ев ни геро́инь.
10. У мое́й подру́ги е́сть краси́воё но́воё кре́сло. 11. Мне́ всё́ равно́,
когда́ я́ ложу́сь спа́ть. 12. Тётя Та́ня заинтересова́лась ру́сским
теа́тром. 13. Вы́ у́читесь како́й-нибудь есте́ственной нау́ке? Не́т, я́
студе́нт языко́в и литерату́ры. 14. Я́ не понима́ю, ка́к о́н мо́жёт та́к
бы́стро одева́ться. 15. Что́ э́ти мужчи́ны пока́зывали дру́г дру́гу?
Я́ не зна́ю, я́ ничего́ не ви́дел. 16. Уже́ по́здно, пора́ спа́ть. Ва́м не
спи́тся? 17. Илья́ Луки́ч спроси́л самого́ судью́, но́ отве́та не получи́л.
18. Кто́ мо́г бы да́ть Ва́не э́тот рома́н? Де́тям нельзя́ чита́ть таку́ю
кни́гу. 19. Кого́ вы́ ждёте? Я́ жду́ Фому́ Ча́цкого, кото́рый сейча́с
е́дёт на своём но́вом автомоби́ле. 20. Я́ то́же жду́ автомоби́ля. 21. У
кого́ вы́ у́читесь ру́сскому языку́? Я́ учу́сь у Тама́ры Ники́тичны
Бороди́но́й и то́же у её му́жа, Ильи́ Фомича́. 22. Я́ та́м не́ был,
когда́ собра́ниё начало́сь. Что́ говори́л судья́? 23. Ста́рый дива́н
тёте бо́льше нра́вится чём то́т но́вый, кото́рый де́душка вчера́ купи́л.
24. Мы́ сиде́ли за у́жином, когда́ вы́ позвони́ли. 25. Сего́дня я́ вста́л
ра́ньше чём обыкнове́нно, потому́ что я́ до́лжён мно́го рабо́тать, но́
мне́ не рабо́таётся.

**C.** For written and/or oral translation into Russian:

1. I hope that my girl-friend will not forget to call uncle Ivan. 2. We all liked his idea and we started to work at once. 3. Foma took the wrong Russian book. He's an idiot — why didn't he take his own? 4. Did you like the heroine in that dull novel which grandfather gave you yesterday? 5. The judges went to the meeting with all their uncles and aunts and sisters and brothers and wives and children. 6. To whose grandfather did uncle say that? 7. Our Vanja is very much interested in schools and books and lessons and problems. 8. Formerly we worked with the genius himself, but now we may not work in the new building. 9. There will be an examination tomorrow. Get ready for the examination. 10. My uncles usually get up late in winter, but today they got up very early — earlier than grandfather. 11. The professors used to get up early and go to bed late — later than the neighbors. 12. Tomorrow we will get up very late and perhaps go to bed very early. 13. How do you do? Did you sleep well? 14. I don't want to get up, I want to sleep. 15. My uncle does not like your aunt. Your aunt does not like my uncle. They do not like each other. 16. Natasha got supper herself last night; neither her mother nor her aunt were at home. 17. Please sit down and wait here for the doctor. 18. The mechanics were waiting for their wives in the street in front of the French restaurant. 19. What were the children doing? Anna was writing her French sentences and Nikita was listening to the radio. 20a. Obey your mother and father! 20b. Grandfather always told us to obey our mother and father. 21. Vasilij told her to get up, get dressed at once, and go with him. 22. He told them to sit down at the table. 23. I'm not sleepy. Give me a good novel and you (= yourself) go to bed. 24. Someone close the door! Close it yourself! 25. Aren't you sorry for little Vanja? He is afraid of autos and busses and streetcars and everything!

## СЛОВАРЬ

| | | | |
|---|---|---|---|
| бабушка | grandmother | друг дру́га § 8 | each other |
| [Gen. pl. -шёк] | | дя́дя masc. [G pl. дя́дей] | uncle |
| бо́льше | more; see § 12 | ме́ньше | less; § 12 |
| де́душка masc. | grandfather | мужчи́на masc. | man, male |
| [G pl. -шёк] | | подру́га § 11 | girl-friend |

по́здно (ро*z*пэ, App. I, § 17.5) late
по́зже § 13 later
ра́дио neut. indecl. radio
ра́но early
ра́ньше § 13 earlier
са́м § 7 self
себя́ себе́ собо́й see § 6; self

судья́ masc. judge
[N pl. су́дьи; суде́й, су́дьях]
тётя [G pl. тётей] aunt
у́жин supper
за у́жином at supper
чём § 14 than
экза́мен examination
(по + Dat.) (on)

---

вставать встаю́т I ⎫
imv. вставай[те] ⎬ stand up, get up (§ 5)
встать вста́нут P ⎭

гото́вить гото́вят I ⎫
приготовить P ⎬ prepare

гото́виться I ⎫
пригото́- ⎬ к + Dat. get ready for
виться P ⎭

жда́ть жду́т I ⎫
подожда́ть ⎬ § 9 wait for
подожду́т P ⎭
past подожда́л -о -и; подождала́

интересо- ⎫
ва́ться I ⎬ + Inst. be interested in
заинтересо- ⎪
ва́ться P ⎭

конча́ть конча́ют I ⎫ finish, end
ко́нчить ко́нчат P ⎭ (trans.)

конча́ться/ко́нчиться end (intrans.)

ложи́ться ложа́тся I ⎫ lie down
ле́чь ля́гут P (§ 5.2) ⎭ (§ 5)

начина́ться ⎫
-а́ются I ⎪ start, begin
нача́ться ⎬ (intrans.)
начну́тся P ⎭
past начался́ -ло́сь -ли́сь -ла́сь

нра́виться ⎫
нра́вятся I ⎬ + D. please (§ 3.1)
понра́виться P ⎭

одева́ть одева́ют I ⎫ dress (trans.)
оде́ть оде́нут P ⎭

одева́ться/оде́ться get dressed

сади́ться садя́тся I ⎫ sit down
се́сть ся́дут P (§ 5.1) ⎭ (§ 5)

слу́шаться ⎫
послу́шаться ⎬ + Gen. obey

спа́ть спя́т I sleep

учи́ться ⎫ learn
у́чатся I ⎬ + Dat. (something)
научи́ться P ⎭

# LESSON XVI

Дéдушка приходи́л домо́й с фа́брики о́чень по́здно.

Grandfather used to come home from the factory very late.

Говоря́т, что но́вый судья́ приезжа́ет ско́рым по́ездом за́втра, ра́но у́тром.

They say that the new judge is arriving by fast train tomorrow, early in the morning.

Извини́те, за́втра я́ не смогу́ прийти́ на уро́к.

Excuse me, I won't be able to come to the lesson tomorrow.

Я́ до́лжен уе́хать сего́дня же ве́чером.

I must leave this evening.

Когда́ уезжа́ют друзья́ ва́шего дя́ди?

When are the friends of your uncle leaving?

Су́дьи ско́ро прие́дут на собра́ние.

The judges will arrive soon for a meeting.

Лука́ унёс э́ти ру́сские кни́ги, я́ не зна́ю почёму.

Luke took those Russian books away, I don't know why.

Кто́ прино́сит дя́де Ива́ну газе́ту?

Who brings Uncle Ivan the paper?

Молодо́й мужчи́на то́лько что вы́шел из ко́мнаты моего́ де́душки.

A young man has just left my grandfather's room.

Мы́ прошли́ че́рез поля́ ми́мо ма́ленького ле́са в дере́вню.

We went through the fields past a little wood into the village.

Отку́да вы́ тепе́рь?

Where are you coming from now?

Я́ от ба́бушки, а Ива́н из шко́лы; мы́ встре́тились на у́лице.

I'm coming from grandmother's and Ivan is from school; we met in the street.

Возьми́те газе́ту из-под сту́ла!

Take the newspaper out from under the chair!

Ба́бушка должна́ была́ вы́йти отту́да.

Grandmother had to leave there.

Они́ подъе́хали к до́му.

They approached the house.

О́н ни ра́зу не приезжа́л к на́м.

He didn't come to see us once.

О́н не ра́з приезжа́л к на́м.

He came to see us more than once.

| | |
|---|---|
| Óн ра́з прие́хал к на́м на неде́лю. | Once he came to visit us for a week. |
| Э́тот судья́ здесь (уже́) почти́ го́д. | This judge has been here for almost a year. |
| Игорь прие́дет сюда́ на ме́сяц. | Igor's coming here for a month. |
| Тогда́ óн уже́ рабо́тал та́м то́лько одну́ неде́лю. | At that time he had been working there for only a week. |
| Она́ еще́ живёт в то́м же до́ме. | She still lives in the same house. |
| Моя́ тётя всё еще́ живёт та́м. | My aunt still lives there. |
| Тогда́ óн еще́ не рабо́тал та́м. | At that time he hadn't yet worked there. |
| Тогда́ дя́дя уже́ не рабо́тал та́м. | At that time my uncle was no longer working there. |
| Илья́ Ильи́ч то́лько что прие́хал. | Il'ja Il'ich just arrived. |
| Ники́та уже́ вы́шел с собра́ния. | Nikita has already left the meeting. |
| Фома́ еще́ не пришёл туда́. | Foma hasn't arrived there yet. |
| Óн всё еще́ прихо́дит сюда́. | He still keeps coming here. |
| Óн уже́ не прихо́дит к на́м. | He doesn't come to see us any more. |
| Óн уже́ го́д сюда́ хо́дит. | He has been coming here for a year. |
| Она́ давно́ живёт здесь. | She has been living here for a long time. |
| Она́ до́лго жила́ та́м. | She lived there for a long time. |
| Я давно́ не ви́дел Ильи́ Ники́тича. | I haven't seen Il'ja Nikitich for a long time. |
| Ка́к до́лго вы́ здесь бу́дете? | How long will you be here? |
| Ка́к до́лго вы́ здесь? | How long have you been here? |
| Вы́ здесь давно́? | Have you been here long? |

---

**1.01** The imperfective verb **приходи́ть прихо́дят** means 'come, arrive (*under own power*)' and **приезжа́ть приезжа́ют** correspondingly means 'come, arrive (*being conveyed*)'.

Они́ ча́сто приходи́ли к на́м.⎫
Они́ ча́сто приезжа́ли к на́м.⎬ They often came to our place.

The perfective equivalents are **прийти́ приду́т** and **прие́хать прие́дут**, respectively. Similarly there are verbs with other directional prefixes: e.g.

| | | |
|---|---|---|
| входи́ть вхо́дят     I | войти́ войду́т   Р | to enter, go in |
| въезжа́ть въезжа́ют | въе́хать въе́дут | (+ в + Acc.) |
| уходи́ть ухо́дят | уйти́ уйду́т | to go away from |
| уезжа́ть уезжа́ют | уе́хать уе́дут | (leave a point) |
| выходи́ть выхо́дят | вы́йти вы́йдут | to exit, go out of |
| выезжа́ть выезжа́ют | вы́ехать вы́едут | (leave from within) |
| подходи́ть подхо́дят | подойти́ подойду́т | to approach |
| подъезжа́ть подъезжа́ют | подъе́хать подъе́дут | (+ к + Dat.) |
| проходи́ть прохо́дят | пройти́ пройду́т | to go past; |
| проезжа́ть проезжа́ют | прое́хать прое́дут | to go through |

**1.02**   These verbs are simple imperfective-perfective pairs, like any other such pair. There is no further distinction of determined/non-determined within the imperfective. It is important to note that the non-determined verb **ходи́ть** *remains imperfective* upon the addition of a prefix, but the determined verbs **идти́** and **е́хать** *become perfective* with the addition of the prefix.

**1.1**   The past tenses of the compounds of **идти́** [**-йти́**] are:

| | | | | |
|---|---|---|---|---|
| прийти́ : | пришёл | пришло́ | пришла́ | пришли́ |
| войти́ | вошёл | вошло́ | вошла́ | вошли́ |
| уйти́ | ушёл | ушло́ | ушла́ | ушли́ |
| вы́йти | вы́шел | вы́шло | вы́шла | вы́шли (← accent!) |
| подойти́ | подошёл | подошло́ | подошла́ | подошли́ |
| пройти́ | прошёл | прошло́ | прошла́ | прошли́ |

**1.11**   The infinitive **прийти́** is pronounced *prʲitʲtʲi* and sometimes spelled придти or притти. Present (= future) forms from **прийду́т** are now archaic, but they are not infrequent in older books.

**1.2**   The compounds of **е́хать** do not have imperative forms, but use the corresponding forms of **-езжа́ть.** Thus the imperative for both *прие́хать* and *приезжа́ть* is **приезжа́й[те].**

Note that **-зж-** in this root represents *-žʲžʲ-* (*-jižʲžʲáj-*): cf. App. I, § 15.

**1.3**   The prefixes added to the verb "to carry" [**носи́ть** (ND)/**нёсти́** (D)] give imperfective/perfective verb-pairs:

| | | |
|---|---|---|
| приноси́ть прино́сят   I | принёсти́ принёсу́т   Р | bring (carrying) |
| уноси́ть уно́сят | унёсти́ унёсу́т | carry away |
| вноси́ть вно́сят | внёсти́ внёсу́т | carry into |

| выноси́ть выно́сят | вы́нести вы́несут | carry out of |
| подноси́ть подно́сят | поднести́ поднесу́т | carry up to, offer |
| проноси́ть проно́сят | пронести́ пронесу́т | carry thru/past |

The past forms of the perfective verbs are like those of нести́ (VII 2): *принёс, унёс, внёс, поднёс, пронёс; принесла́, унесла́, внесла́, поднесла́, пронесла́.* Note that the forms of **вы́нести** always have the stress on the first syllable: *вы́нёс, вы́нёсло, вы́нёсла, вы́нёсли.* The imperative is irregular (cf. 1.61 below): *вы́неси[те].*

**1.4**   The verbs with the prefix в- [въ-, во-] meaning 'enter', *must* be accompanied by the preposition **в** + accusative:

Он **вошёл в** ко́мнату.                    He entered the room.

О́н **внёс** стул { в мою́ ко́мнату.        He carried the chair
                   { ко мне́ **в** ко́мнату.        into my room.

**1.5**   The meaning of the verbs with the prefix у- is 'go away from', and the point of departure (if mentioned) is regarded simply as a point:

О́н **ушёл** на фа́брику.                He's left for the factory; gone
                                                     away, headed for the factory.

О́н **уе́хал** от на́с.                    He's left us.

О́н **ушёл** от ни́х.                     He went away from them.

**1.6**   The verbs with the prefix вы- have the meaning 'go out of', where the point of departure is regarded as a container:

Она́ **вы́шла из** ко́мнаты.            She left the room, went out of
                                                     the room.

Мы́ уже́ **вы́ехали из** го́рода.       We've already gotten out of the
                                                     city.

**1.61**   Note that *all* **perfective** verbs with this prefix stress the вы- in all forms. The imperative forms retain the и which is found in the same verb without prefix or with other prefixes, e.g. иди́ иди́те, приди́ приди́те — *вы́йди, вы́йдите;* неси́[те] — *вы́неси*[те]; cf. учи́, учи́те, научи́[те] — *вы́учи, вы́учите.*

**1.7**   The verbs with the prefix про- mean 'go past, by, through'. Used with an accusative direct object, or with **ми́мо** + Gen., they mean 'past':

Мы́ **прое́хали** го́род.                We went past the town [the
                                                     road did not take us through
                                                     the town].

Мы́ **прое́хали ми́мо** ва́шего        We drove past your house.
до́ма.

With **че́рез** + Acc., these verbs mean 'go through':

Мы́ **прошли́ че́рез** са́д.            We went through the garden.

**1.71 Проходи́ть/пройти́** is used in a number of cases where actual locomotion is not involved,[1] e.g.: Мы́ уже́ прошли́ то́т уро́к. 'We've already gone through that lesson.'

**1.8** The verbs with the prefix **под- (подо- подъ-)** mean 'come up close to, draw near, approach' and the goal being approached is expressed by **к** + dative.

По́езд **подходи́л к** ста́нции.     The train came up to the station.
Она́ **поднесла́** кни́гу **к ни́м**.     She brought the book to them.

**2.** Notice the following adverbs of place:

| whither?<br>to what place?<br>**куда́** | where?<br>in what place?<br>**где́** | whence?<br>from what place?<br>**отку́да** |
|---|---|---|
| thither<br>to that place<br>**туда́** | there<br>in that place<br>**та́м** | thence<br>from that place<br>**отту́да** |
| hither<br>to this place<br>**сюда́** | here<br>in this place<br>**зде́сь** | hence<br>from this place<br>**отсю́да** |

**3.** The same threefold division is expressed by groups of prepositions:

The question **куда́?**    is answered by **в** + Accusative: *в го́род.* →

The question **где́?**    is answered by **в** + Prepositional: *в го́роде.* ×

The question **отку́да?** is answered by **из** + Genitive: *из го́рода.* ×→

Other correspondences:

| **куда́?** | **где́?** | **отку́да?** | |
|---|---|---|---|
| **на** + accusative | **на** + prepositional | **с (со)** + *genitive* | |
| **к** + dative | **у** + genitive | **от** + genitive | |
| **под** + accusative | **под** + instrumental | **из-под** + genitive | |
| **за** + accusative | **за** + instrumental | **из-за** + genitive | |

---

[1] The other verbs in this lesson also may have transferred, non-concrete meanings, but they will not be discussed here.

For example:

*Куда́ вы иде́те?*   *в го́род;*   *на фа́брику;*   *к до́ктору;*   *за ба́нк.*
*Где́ вы бы́ли?*   *в го́роде;*   *на фа́брике;*   *у до́ктора;*   *за ба́нком.*
*Отку́да вы иде́те?*  *из го́рода;*  *с фа́брики;*   *от до́ктора;*   *из-за ба́нка.*

**3.1**  The preposition **до** (+ genitive) means *up to, as far as, attaining* (but not entering):

> Э́тот трамва́й идёт до фа́брики.    This streetcar goes as far as the factory.

*From a certain point* is expressed by **от**: от ба́нка до теа́тра.

**3.2**  The preposition **о́коло** (+ genitive) means (1) *near, in the vicinity of*: *о́коло стола́* 'near the table' (2) *around, surrounding*: *О́коло на́шего до́ма* е́сть больши́е поля́. 'Around our house there are big fields.' (3) with numbers or quantitative expressions, *about, approximately*: Я рабо́тал *о́коло ча́са*. 'I worked for about an hour.'

**3.21**  **О́коло** with persons specifies 'near' or 'around', while **у** has the less concrete meaning discussed in VI 3. **У** with non-animate nouns is practically equivalent to **о́коло** in the meaning 'at, near' (though о́коло may also mean 'around'). **О́коло** thus would figure in the examples in § 3 in the same place as **у**: *к до́ктору — о́коло до́ктора — от до́ктора*: *к окну́ — у/о́коло окна́ — от окна́*.

**3.3**  The preposition **че́рез** + *accusative* (on accent, see App. I, § 13.4) means (1) *through, via, across*:

> Мы́ проезжа́ли че́рез ле́с.          We were going through the woods.

> Э́тот по́езд идёт из Ленин-          This train goes from Leningrad
> гра́да че́рез Москву́ до              via Moscow to Stalingrad.
> Сталингра́да.

> Автомоби́ль шёл че́рез мо́ст.      The automobile was going across
>                                                        the bridge.

(2) With a time expression, **че́рез** means *in, after the passage of*:

> Я приду́ че́рез ча́с.               I'll come in an hour.
> Он прие́хал че́рез ча́с.          He arrived after an hour.

**3.4**  **Для** + genitive translates English "for" in various senses:

> Он э́то сде́лает для неё.         He'll do it for her.

**3.5** The preposition **за** + instrumental or accusative means *behind* or *beyond*, but it also has other meanings. With the instrumental it may mean *for* or *after* in the sense of *to fetch*:

Са́ша пошёл за до́ктором.          Sasha has gone for a doctor.

Notice these cases:

Оте́ц рабо́таёт за больши́м          Father works at a big table.
  столо́м.
О́н мно́го говори́л за у́жином.          He talked a lot at supper.
Она́ писа́ла кни́гу за кни́гой.          She wrote book after book.
Спаси́бо за письмо́ и кни́гу.          Thanks for the letter and book.

**3.6** **На** + the accusative of many time expressions usually means *for*, with the connotation "to spend this length of time":

О́н прие́хал на неде́лю.          He came for a week.
Они́ прие́дут на не́сколько          They will come for several days.
дне́й.

Note that there is a notion of purpose here, and that the period of time does not begin until after the completion of the act expressed by the verb; in the two examples above, the subjects have to arrive before the count of days starts. Contrast this to the use of the accusative discussed in § 4 below, and observe that there too English may use the preposition "for".

**3.7** When defining a part of a group, "of" is expressed by **из** + Gen.:

        оди́н из студе́нтов          one of the students
  *NB* не́сколько из кни́г          several of the books
  but  не́сколько кни́г          several books

**4.** Note that the accusative of the time expression used without preposition means *during*, *for*, connoting that the whole period is occupied by the action:

О́н ве́сь де́нь та́м сиде́л.          He sat there all day.
О́н та́м жи́л ме́сяц.          He lived there for a month.
О́н зде́сь бу́дет рабо́тать одну́          He will work here for a week.
неде́лю.

**5.** The regular genitive plural **годо́в** from **го́д** 'year' is not used with numerical expressions, but is replaced by **ле́т**: не́сколько, мно́го **ле́т** 'several, many years'.

Годо́в is used in other constructions, however; e.g. лю́ди *тех годо́в* 'men of those years'.

**6.  Ско́ро** means both 'soon' and 'quickly'. **Бы́стро** denotes a greater degree of speed than **ско́ро**: e.g. Он бы́стро/ско́ро говори́т. 'He speaks rapidly.'

The normal term for 'fast train' is ско́рый по́езд.

**7.**  The adverb **всё** stresses the continuousness or frequent repetition of an action: *Она́ всё спра́шивает.* 'She keeps asking, is continually asking.' The combination **всё ещё** indicates that this type of action has gone on in the past and is still continuing: *Она́ всё ещё спра́шивает.* 'She is still always asking questions, she still keeps on asking.' (Review VII 10.)

**8.  Оди́н одно́ одна́** 'one' has the pronominal declension:

|       | m.      | n.       | f.            | pl.          |   |
|-------|---------|----------|---------------|--------------|---|
| Nom.  | оди́н   | одно́    | одна́         | одни́        | N |
| Acc.  | (N, G)  | одно́    | одну́         | (N, G)       | A |
| Gen.  | одного́ |          | одно́й        | одни́х       | G |
| Prep. | одно́м  |          | одно́й        | одни́х       | P |
| Dat.  | одному́ |          | одно́й        | одни́м       | D |
| Inst. | одни́м  |          | одно́й (-о́ю)  | одни́ми      | I |

Beside meaning *one*, it may mean *only, alone*: *Она́ там одна́.* 'She's there alone.' It may sometimes be translated simply "a (an)"; e.g., *Я там встре́тил одну́ да́му, кото́рая вас зна́ет.* 'I met a lady there who knows you.'

The plural forms are used (1) with nouns which are plural in form but singular in meaning, or (2) to signify 'some', or 'only, alone'.

| | |
|---|---|
| одни́ часы́ | one clock, watch, timepiece |
| Одни́ хоте́ли, други́е не хоте́ли. | Some wanted to, others didn't want to. |
| Там живу́т одни́ студе́нты. | Only students live there. |

**8.1  Ни оди́н**, with **не** before the verb, or with **нет**, means "not a single, no":

| | |
|---|---|
| Ни оди́н студе́нт не мог реши́ть зада́чу. | No student was able to solve the problem. |
| Я не по́нял ни одного́ сло́ва. | I didn't understand a single word. |
| Во всём до́ме не́ было ни одно́й кни́ги. | There wasn't a book in the whole house. |

But note well that the omission of **ни** changes the meaning drastically:

| | |
|---|---|
| Один студе́нт не мо́г реши́ть зада́чу. | One student was unable to solve the problem. |
| Я не по́нял одного́ сло́ва. | There was one word I didn't understand. |
| Одно́й кни́ги не́ было. | One book was missing. |

**9.** Notice the difference between **то́лько что** (+ *verb*) 'just' and **то́лько** 'only, merely':

| | |
|---|---|
| То́лько вчера́ я с ни́м встре́тился. | I met him only yesterday. |
| Я то́лько что встре́тился с ни́м. | I just met him. |
| (Я встре́тился с ни́м одни́м.) | (I met only him, him alone.) |

**10.** The adverb **до́лго** means "covering a long period". **Давно́** refers primarily to a moment that was a long time ago, and it may include the whole period from that distant moment up to the time of action or of speaking.

| | |
|---|---|
| Он уе́хал в Пари́ж **давно́** и **до́лго** не писа́л. | He went off to Paris a long time ago and didn't write for a long time. |
| Она́ **давно́** молчи́т о сы́не. **До́лго** не хоте́ла, что́бы мы́ о нём говори́ли. | She has not talked about her son for a long time. For a long time she didn't want us to talk about him. |

The last example means that she ceased talking about her son at a definite time in the past and has been maintaining silence since then; in the meantime there was a long period, now finished, when she objected to other people speaking about him.

## УПРАЖНЕНИЯ

**A.** Read and translate:

1. Пожа́луйста, принеси́ мне́ свои́ часы́.   2. Моему́ ста́рому де́душке интере́сно сиде́ть здесь у окна́. Отсю́да он мо́жет ви́деть, как лю́ди прихо́дят и ухо́дят.   3. Приди́те ра́ньше други́х, и мы мо́жем спроси́ть судью́ об э́том.   4. У меня́ де́нег не́т, но ещё ра́но, я не могу́ войти́ в ба́нк.   5. Илья́ Ильи́ч на́м не ра́з говори́л: «Когда́ гото́витесь к экза́мену, повторя́йте всё ру́сские слова́ и фра́зы.»   6. Дя́дя господи́на Чайко́вского мно́го е́здит. Он то́лько что прие́хал из Ленингра́да, а уже́ за́втра он уе́дет в То́мск (через О́мск) и отту́да в Краснoя́рск.

7. Ва́ня говори́т, что не зна́ет, что́ де́лать. Пу́сть де́лает ка́к уме́ет!
8. Я ду́маю, что они́ из Ми́нска и́ли из Смоле́нска, но́ они́ уже́ давно́ живу́т зде́сь в Москве́. Должно́ быть, они́ давно́ прие́хали сюда́.
9. Пройдёмте ми́мо до́ма ва́шего де́душки; говоря́т, что его́ са́д тепе́рь о́чень краси́вый. 10. Переведи́те мне́ э́то, пожа́луйста. 11. Бе́дная тётя Лю́ба ещё не мо́жет выходи́ть. 12. Краси́вая да́ма подошла́ к Алёше на у́лице и попроси́ла его́ показа́ть ей, ка́к пройти́ на ста́нцию метро́. 13. Я уже́ мно́го чита́л обо все́х э́тих дела́х, но у меня́ е́сть ещё мно́го вопро́сов. 14. Вы́несите все́ э́ти ста́рые сту́лья. Сейча́с принесу́т но́вые, кото́рые на́м купи́л на́ш дру́г, судья́ Бороди́н. 15. От него́ я ничего́ не получу́. Он никогда́ не даёт ничего́ никому́. 16. Э́ти студе́нтки неда́вно перевели́ кни́гу по эконо́мике с англи́йского языка́. 17. Мари́я Ильи́нична наде́ется получи́ть через неде́лю письмо́ с деньга́ми от своего́ ста́рого дру́га Илья́ Ильича́. 18. Я с ва́ми пое́ду до магази́на, а пото́м пойду́ са́м в шко́лу. 19. Ба́бушка давно́ уе́хала к сёстре́. 20. Мы́ встре́тили на мосту́ Серге́я Лукича́ с Луко́й Серге́евичем. 21. Како́й-то мужчи́на ва́с спра́шивал та́м в друго́й ко́мнате. 22. Я в э́том году́ ни ра́зу не выезжа́л из го́рода; я то́лько сижу́ до́ма и рабо́таю. Моя́ жена́ не ра́з была́ за́ городом с друзья́ми.

23. Ниотку́да не́т пи́сем. 24. Они́ встава́ли из-за стола́, когда́ мы́ вошли́ к ни́м в кварти́ру. 25. У его́ ста́рого дя́ди е́сть не́сколько дороги́х часо́в. 26. Мо́й дя́дя прие́хал то́лько на оди́н ме́сяц, но́ о́н у на́с уже́ бо́льше го́да. 27. Тётя Тама́ра то́лько что уе́хала в Кита́й с Алёшей Соловьёвым. 28. Ва́ня, подойди́ к ба́бушке и скажи́ до́брый ве́чер! 29. Они́ сиде́ли на дива́не и слу́шали по ра́дио ту́ са́мую симфо́нию Чайко́вского, о кото́рой мы́ то́лько что говори́ли. 30. По́езд пройдёт через ча́с. 31. Ско́лько неде́ль вы́ бы́ли у дя́ди зимо́й в Крыму́? То́лько одну́ неде́лю. 32. Когда́ мы́ вошли́ к Ники́те в ко́мнату, я сейча́с же уви́дел, что на стене́ одно́й фотогра́фии не́т. 33. Бы́ло ещё ра́но, когда́ Фома́ вы́шел со ста́нции. На у́лице не́ было ни одного́ челове́ка. 34. Ско́лько интере́сных кни́г у ва́с! —Возьми́те, пожа́луйста, не́сколько из ни́х с собо́й на не́сколько дне́й, е́сли хоти́те. 35. Когда́ учи́тельница начала́ чита́ть зада́чу, одно́й студе́нтки ещё не́ было.

**B.** For written and/or oral translation into Russian:

1. I'm sorry, your uncle has just left the meeting. 2. Where will you go [riding] when you leave this city? 3. Old Foma Petrov has been here for almost a year. 4. My grandfather and your aunt are coming tomorrow

by train.   5. He is coming here for a week.   6. He has been working here for a month.   7. These Russian women had been working there for a week. 8. Please come in and sit down.   9. We arrived from Moscow today in the judge's beautiful expensive new automobile.   10. They entered the city [(a) riding, (b) afoot].   11. From here we go by train to Odessa, and from there via Kiev to Moscow.   12. Did grandmother bring any letters today? Yes, there were letters for your uncle.   13. Where did she put the letters? On the table in your room.   14. This is very interesting: Nikita has not written for a long time, and now I receive several letters.   15. I will read the letters and then answer him at once.   16. How many times have you seen that film?   17. I have seen it only once.   18. I just saw it yesterday [§ 9].   19. She had no watch. We did not know that it was late.   20. Please go with me as far as [до] the factory.   21. Take [= carry] that chair into the other room.   22. Last night I met Il'ja with a very pretty young lady, and this morning I saw him coming out of the bank [as he came out of] with another lady. Which one is he interested in? 23. I (f) went with the children from their mother's house to [but not into] the school.   24. The children keep opening the doors and their mothers keep closing them.   25. Vasilij Igorevich will give you an old German book and several new French magazines.

## СЛОВАРЬ

всё .       }
всё ещё }                          see § 7

год                                year
   [в году́ II 3; *Epl obl*]
давно́ (§10)    a long time ago; for
                            a long time
для + Gen.                         for
до + Gen.    up to, until, before
до́лгий (aj.)         long (in time)
до́лго (av.)    long, for a long time
из + Gen. (§ 3.7)                 from
из-за + Gen.          from behind;
                         because of
из-под + Gen.         from under
лет (G pl.)                 see § 5
ме́сяц                           month

ми́мо + Gen.                      past
мост                           bridge
   [на мосту́ II 3; pl. мосты́]
на + Acc. of time expression:  for
            (a time in relative future)
неда́вно    not long ago, recently
неде́ля                          week
ниотку́да               from nowhere
   (with neg. verb; cf. II 5.3, XIV 10)
оди́н одно́ одна́          one (§ 8)
о́коло + Gen.        (§ 3.2) about,
                            around
от + Gen.                        from
отку́да                  from where
отсю́да                   from here
отту́да                  from there

| | | | |
|---|---|---|---|
| ра́з [Gen. pl. ра́з] | time, occasion | ско́ро (§ 6) | soon: quickly |
| ра́з (av.) | once | ско́рый (§ 6) | fast |
| не ра́з | more than once | то́лько | only (§ 9) |
| ни ра́зу (+ neg. verb) | not once | то́лько что | just (§ 9) |
| с [со] + genitive | from, down from | ча́с | hour, time |
| симфо́ния | symphony | [в часу́ II 3; pl. часы́] | |
| ско́лько (+ G pl.) | how many | че́рез + Acc. (§ 1.9, 3.3) | through, in |

входи́ть въезжа́ть вноси́ть
выходи́ть выезжа́ть выноси́ть
подходи́ть подъезжа́ть подноси́ть
приходи́ть приезжа́ть приноси́ть     } See paragraphs 1.1—1.9.
проходи́ть проезжа́ть проноси́ть
уходи́ть уезжа́ть уноси́ть

### For review

1a. Promise me that you won't say a single word about this to anyone! 1b. Why do you want me to promise? You know I'm always silent about matters of this kind. 2. Marija Il'ichna Smirnóv-Bélyj is one of the Russian students who recently came to America for a year. 3. I hope that you have prepared for the exam because there will be many difficult questions. 4. When I called Foma Fomich Petrov this morning, he told me to meet him at the library tomorrow. 5. The Rímskij-Kórsakovs just arrived here by train from Leningrad. 6. That boring student who just got up from the table only wants to talk about himself. 7a. The teacher herself could not translate the letter which Sasha received from his friend in China. 7b. A long time ago she lived in China for a long time, and she says she used to read Chinese well. 8. My grandfather is coming to Moscow tomorrow for a week. 9. Our professor promised to explain all the difficult sentences to us today, but it's already time to begin the lesson and he hasn't come to class yet. 10. It's all the same to me whether you like my new hat or not.

11. If we read Russian better, we would be able to understand these interesting but difficult books which your uncle bought in Moscow and Leningrad. 12a. Please sit down at that table over there in front of

the little French restaurant and wait for my sister.    12b. She should
be here soon.    13. Just yesterday that handsome Italian asked me
whether I wanted him to teach me Italian.    14. The lawyer entered
the room, went up to the judge who had just walked away from the
window, said a few words to him, and went out.    15a. Vanja's mother
is a good doctor.    15b. His father is an old judge who rarely listens to
his wife and never obeys her.    16. Sergej is teaching his sons natural
sciences and music.    17. Il'ja must prepare for an exam today; he got
up earlier than the others, dressed quickly, sat down at his desk, and
began to work.    18a. Nikita was studying French but was more interested in medicine.    18b. Now he has decided he wants to be a doctor.
19. Nadezhda was the most intelligent student in the class and more
than once she helped me translate sentences from English to German.
20. I had been waiting for the streetcar for a long time when some man
walked up to me and said that I was standing on the wrong corner.

21a. How many times have you read the new lesson?    21b. I haven't
even read it once.    21c. Explain it to me.    22. Nikita's friend came
for a week, but she has already been at our place for a month.    23a.
Those pretty Spaniards (f) who are standing on the bridge are talking
about *The Idiot, The Brothers Karamazov,* and *Poor People.*    23b. They
told me they love Dostoevskij and want to read everything that he
wrote.    24. She said that she was very interested in Russian literature,
but I didn't believe her because she thought that Anna Karenina was
our new neighbor.    25a. We were told that the new armchair would
arrive here in a week.    25b. It was very expensive and I didn't want
my wife to buy it.    26a. Someone find the chalk for Il'ja Nikitič.    26b.
He wants to write something on the blackboard.    27a. Let Nikita sleep.
27b. I can finish this myself.    28a. I've lost my Russian dictionary, do
you know where it might be?    28b. I'm sorry, I haven't seen it for a
long time.    28c. I don't know what I'll do if I don't find it right away.
29. Get ready to answer some difficult questions.    30a. If you won't
help me, I'll have to go to the Rimskij-Korsakovs'.    30b. Someone
there will help me write my composition.

| | |
|---|---|
| Ва́ши бра́тья жена́ты? | Are your brothers married? |
| Ва́ши сёстры за́мужём? | Are your sisters married? |
| Когда́ о́н жени́лся? | When did he get married? |
| Когда́ она́ вы́шла за́муж? | When did she get married? |
| На ко́м о́н жена́т? | Who's he married to? |
| О́н неда́вно жени́лся на актри́се. | He married an actress recently. |
| За ке́м она́ за́мужём? | Who's she married to? |
| Она́ вы́йдёт за́муж за ва́шего знако́мого Щу́кина. —Что́ вы говори́те! Во́т но́вость! | She will marry your acquaintance Shchukin. You don't mean to say so! That's news! |
| У её жениха́ све́тлые и́ли тёмные во́лосы? | Does her fiancé have light or dark hair? |
| На столе́ у него́ стоя́л портре́т краси́вой де́вушки с голубы́ми глаза́ми и све́тлыми волоса́ми. | On his desk stood the portrait of a pretty girl with blue eyes and light hair. |
| У неё чёрные глаза́. | She has black eyes. |
| Предста́вьте меня́ ва́шей неве́сте! | Present me to your fiancée! |
| Что́ случи́лось? | What happened? |
| Что́ э́то сло́во зна́чит? | What does this word mean? |

---

**1.** Russian terms for "marry" depend on the sex of the subject. For a man: *жени́ться на* + *Prep.* For a woman: *выходи́ть/вы́йти за́муж за* + *Acc.*

На ко́м о́н жени́лся?
За кого́ она́ вы́шла за́муж?

Whom did {he / she} marry?

"Married" is rendered by the adjective *жена́тый* for a man, and by the indeclinable form *за́мужём* for a woman:

О́н жена́т.
Она́ за́мужём.

He / She is married.

*Жениться* may refer to a couple:

Когда они женились?                    When did they get married?

*Жениться* is both perfective and imperfective. Occasionally the perfective *пожениться* is used to avoid ambiguity.

Когда мы поженимся, мы        After we get married, we're
поедём в Европу на шесть      going to Europe for six weeks.
недель.

**2.** Notice that *волос* 'hair' refers to *one* hair; the plural is by far more usual. Note the stress-shift in plural (*E pl obl,* cf. p. 351, § 3): N-A *волосы,* G *волос,* Pr. *волосах.*

**3.** The segment of the color spectrum identified as "blue" in English is divided into two parts by Russian. The lighter shade, typical of the bright sky, is *голубой.* [The darker shade, more toward purple, is *синий,* given in XVII.]

**4.** Случаться/случиться 'happen' is impersonal: it has only 3rd singular (neuter) forms.

## УПРАЖНЕНИЯ

**A.**  **1.** Read and translate these sentences as they stand.
      **2.** Change the direct to indirect discourse. For example:

Он ей сказал: «Я поиду!»   →   Он ей сказал, что он пойдет.
Он ей сказал: «Иди!»        →   Он ей сказал, чтобы она шла.

 1. Игорь меня спросил: «Когда вы наконец женитесь?»
 2. Она всёгда спрашиваёт: «Вы слышали, что случилось?»
 3. Анна нам сказала: «Мне очень не нравится этот портрет.»
 4. Он ей посоветовал: «Пошли телеграмму сейчас же!»
 5. Невеста его спросила: «Вы знакомы с моим другом?»
 6. Сестра сказала Ване: «Молчи! Не мешай моим знакомым!»
 7. Он сказал Анне: «Нет, дорогая, вы ошибаётесь.»
 8. Вера мне сказала: «Я не собираюсь стать его женой!»
 9. Дети меня попросили: «Расскажите нам о своих успехах!»
10. Саша мне сказал: «Передай привет невесте!»

**B.**  **1.** Разве вы не знакомы с Ниной? Вчера она была на собрании. У неё светлые волосы и голубые глаза. **2.** На будущей неделе Алексей Петров уезжаёт в Москву. **3.** В прошлом году мы ездили в Крым поездом, но в этом году решили ехать автомобилём. **4.** Мой сы́н Вади́м конча́ет шко́лу. Посове́туйте, куда́ его́ посла́ть учи́ться да́льше. Мно́гие ду́мают, что у него́ тала́нт к теа́тру, но мо́жет быть они́ ошиба́ются. 5. У на́с в шко́ле все́ игра́ют в баскетбо́л. 6. Неуже́ли вы́ не зна́ете, что А́ся Воробьёва наконе́ц вы́шла за́муж за Ивано́ва? Поэ́тому она́ и уезжа́ет в Ки́ев. 7. Мо́й дру́г Васи́льев тепе́рь солда́т в а́рмии, но о́н ещё хо́чет учи́ться в университе́те и ста́ть до́ктором. 8. Почти́ все́ де́вушки, кото́рые бы́ли в на́шем кла́ссе, тепе́рь за́мужем. То́лько Ва́ля Лугова́я ещё не вы́шла за́муж. Она́ адвока́т. 9. Ску́чно всегда́ сиде́ть в тёмной ко́мнате и чита́ть, пойдёмте куда́-нибудь де́лать что́-нибудь. 10. Вы́йти за́муж за кого́-нибудь зна́чит ста́ть жёною кого́-нибудь, не пра́вда ли?

C. —У на́с но́вость: же́нится мо́й дя́дя, Ива́н Петро́вич Стра́хов.

—Ка́к, ра́зве о́н ещё не жена́т?

—Не́т, но на бу́дущей неде́ле же́нится. Кста́ти, же́нится о́н на знако́мой ва́м да́ме, секрета́рше адвока́та Петро́ва. Вы́ зна́ете, э́та краси́вая, с о́чень све́тлыми волоса́ми и чёрными глаза́ми.

—Неуже́ли? А я́ ду́мал, что и она́ уже́ давно́ за́мужем!

—Не́т. Она́ когда́-то собира́лась вы́йти за́муж за како́го-то писа́теля, но что́-то между ни́ми случи́лось.

—Что́ вы́ говори́те? Слу́шайте, На́дя, тепе́рь должны́ вы́йти за́муж вы́.

—О, я́ э́то сде́лаю, когда́ ко́нчу университе́т. Кста́ти мо́й жени́х тепе́рь в а́рмии, о́н сейча́с в Герма́нии.

—А я́ ду́мал, что о́н студе́нт.

—О́н студе́нт, но тепе́рь в а́рмии. Во́т о́н, я́ ва́с с ни́м познако́млю, смотри́те.

На стене́ висе́л портре́т незнако́мого мне́ молодо́го лейтена́нта с тёмными волоса́ми и голубы́ми глаза́ми.

—Это мо́й жени́х, —сказа́ла На́дя. —На сле́дующей неде́ле о́н прие́дет, и я́ ва́м предста́влю его́.

D.    For oral and/or written translation into Russian.

1. Good morning, Ivan, how are you? Are you acquainted with my sister's husband, Sergej Petrovich Volóshin?

Why yes, we met last week, after the opera, in that little French restaurant where we always go. Isn't that so, Sergej Petrovich?

Of course, I remember. You were with several artists and musicians, weren't you, Ivan Igorevich?

That's right. We always go to the opera together. But I didn't know that you were married to Boris's sister.

Yes, I got married a long time ago.

2. Who's that pretty woman? —Which one? — The one [= that] with the officer there at the little table? The little woman with the dark hair? —No, no, with light hair and blue eyes; she's sitting in the corner by the window with a major. —Oh yes, now I see her. I don't think I am acquainted with her. But the officer is Ivan Tróickij. We were good friends at the university. I haven't seen him for a long time. That's probably his wife. Not long ago people (omit) were saying that he had met a beautiful German musician in Berlin and was about to get married. Do you want me to introduce you to him? —No, it's not necessary...if she's married. — If you don't meet them, you won't know (P) whether she's married or not. —Good. Let's go. — Hello, Vanja, how long have you [ты] been in Moscow? I thought you were still in Germany. —Vasja! How are you! We just arrived this morning. This is my bride, Ol'ga Petrovna. Olja, this is my old friend Vasilij Zhúkov from Leningrad; we studied together at the university. — I'm pleased to meet you. May I present my comrade Nikíta Fílin. I see your wife speaks Russian. —Why of course, why shouldn't she?— They (omit) told me you married a German. —Who said that? Ol'ga is a Russian, and has always lived in Moscow. —But I thought you said that you just arrived from Berlin. —Just arrived...but from the Crimea. I left Berlin long ago. —Excuse me, Nikíta and I [trans. we with N.] must go now. Goodbye.

## СЛОВАРЬ

| | |
|---|---|
| а́рмия | army |
| во́лос | hair (§ 2) |
| гла́з | eye |
| [Epl глаза́, G глаз] | |
| голубо́й | (light) blue (§ 3) |
| жена́тый | married (§ 1) |
| жени́х | fiancé; bridegroom; newlywed |
| за́муж[ём] | see § 1 |
| кста́ти | by the way |
| неве́ста | fiancée; bride; newlywed |
| но́вость (f.) | news, novelty |
| портре́т | portrait |
| све́тлый | light |
| [све́тёл све́тло -ы: светла́] | |

| | |
|---|---|
| тёмный | dark |
| [тёмен, тёмно́ -ы: тёмна́] | |
| чёрный | black |
| [чёрен, черно́ -ы́ -а́] | |
| знако́мить -мят I | acquaint |
| познако́мить P | |
| жени́ться же́нятся IP | marry (§ 1) |
| зна́чить зна́чат I | mean |
| представля́ть -я́ют I | present, introduce |
| предста́вить -вят P | |
| случа́ться -а́ется I | happen (§ 4) |
| случи́ться -чи́тся P | |

# LESSON XVII

| | |
|---|---|
| Эта си́няя кни́га — его́ тре́тья. | That blue book is his third. |
| Вы́ чита́ли его́ после́днюю кни́гу? | Have you read his last book? |
| Мне́ бо́льше нра́вится вече́рняя газе́та чем у́тренняя. | I like the evening paper better than the morning one. |
| Они́ живу́т в тре́тьем до́ме за библиоте́кой на э́той же у́лице. | They live in the third house beyond the library in this same street. |
| Вы́ мо́жете пое́хать после́дним по́ездом, в три́ часа́. | You can go by the last train, at three o'clock. |
| Она́ хо́чет писа́ть си́ним карандашо́м. | She wants to write with a blue pencil. |
| Я́ его́ ви́дел в после́дний ра́з четы́ре дня́ тому́ наза́д. | I saw him for the last time four days ago. |
| На столе́ лёжа́ло пя́ть си́них кни́г и две́ кра́сных тетра́дки. | On the table lay five blue books and two red notebooks. |
| У меня́ в ко́мнате два́ но́вых сту́ла, оди́н но́вый сто́л, одна́ две́рь и то́лько одно́ ма́ленькое окно́. | In my room I have two new chairs, a new table, a door, and only one little window. |
| У ни́х три́ краси́вых кре́сла, два́ стола́, две́ две́ри и четы́ре больши́х окна́. | They have three nice armchairs, two tables, two doors, and four big windows. |
| Они́ приезжа́ют ка́ждую зи́му на́ три дня́. | They come for three days every winter. |
| Тре́тьего дня́ они́ прие́хали на́ две неде́ли. | Day before yesterday they arrived for two weeks. |
| У на́с собра́ния два́ ра́за в неде́лю. | We have meetings twice a week. |
| Челове́к двена́дцать бы́ло на собра́нии в сре́ду. | About a dozen people were at the meeting on Wednesday. |

| | |
|---|---|
| Óн приéхал в пéрвый рáз в октябрé, а в слéдующий рáз óн приéдёт в ноябрé. | He came the first time in October, but next time he's coming in November. |
| Скóлько часóв в дéнь вы́ рабóтаёте? | How many hours a day do you work? |
| Я́ обыкновéнно рабóтаю вóсемь и́ли дéвять часóв, нó иногдá я́ дóлжён рабóтать ещё часá двá вéчером. | I usually work for eight or nine hours, but sometimes I have to work another couple of hours in the evening. |
| В суббóту и в воскресéньё я́ рéдко рабóтаю. | On Saturday and Sunday I rarely work. |
| Бу́дущей вёснóй óн уéдёт в Москву́ нá пять недéль. | Next spring he's going off to Moscow for five weeks. |
| Нáм остаю́тся тóлько сéмь днéй. | We have only seven days left. |
| Кáк дóлго вы́ тáм остáлись? | How long did you stay there? |

----

1.    A relatively small number of adjectives have a stem ending in a soft consonant. As a practical rule, the Nom. sg. masc. ends in **-ний**. The softness of the stem-final consonant must be indicated throughout the declension by the first letter of the suffix. Therefore the suffixes all must begin with **ё, и, я, ю**. The full declension of **послéдний** 'last' is on p. 352.

2.    A few adjectives, mostly formed from names of animals, have a variant declension. The suffix in nominative and accusative neuter, feminine, and plural has only one syllable. The rest of the declension has the regular suffixes spelled with the "soft vowel-letters", added to a stem ending in **-ь**: e.g. **трéтий** 'third', neut. N-A **трéтьё**; fem N **трéтья**, A **трéтью**; pl. N **трéтьи**. The full declension is given in App. III, p. 357.

3.    The use of Russian numerals is complex. In this lesson only certain preliminary notions will be presented.

3.1    The numeral 'one' was given in XVI 8.

3.2    The numeral 'two' has one form when it refers to masculine or neuter nouns and another when it refers to feminine nouns. The nouns themselves must be in the *genitive singular* form:

    **двá** столá, **двá** сту́ла, **двá** карандашá: **двá** окнá, **двá** письмá
    **двé** кни́ги, **двé** доски́, **двé** стены́, **двé** кóмнаты, **двé** дóчери

The accusative form of **двá/двé** is like the nominative only for non-animate; we will not use the animate accusative for the time being.

**3.31** The numerals 'three' **три** and 'four' **четы́ре** also take the *genitive singular*: **три** сту́ла, **четы́ре** до́ма, **три** окна́, **четы́ре** доски́.

**3.32** An adjective modifying a noun after *2, 3, 4* may be in the *genitive* PLURAL or, less commonly, the *nominative plural*:

**две́** ру́сских кни́ги   or   **две́** ру́сские кни́ги   two Russian books
**два́** но́вых сту́ла     or   **два́** но́вые сту́ла     two new chairs

**3.41** The numbers *5* to *12* are as follows:

| | | |
|---|---|---|
| 5 пя́ть | 8 во́семь | 11 оди́ннадцать |
| 6 ше́сть | 9 де́вять | 12 двена́дцать |
| 7 се́мь | 10 де́сять | |

**3.42** They are followed by the *genitive plural* of the noun and any modifiers:

**пя́ть** столо́в [кни́г, ле́т]       five tables (books, years)
**ше́сть** кра́сных карандаше́й     six red pencils
**се́мь** краси́вых де́вушёк         seven beautiful girls

**4.** When a number *follows* a noun, its meaning is weakened: кни́ги две́ 'a couple of books', го́да три 'about 3 years', ра́за четы́ре 'approximately four times', ле́т де́сять 'about 10 years', челове́к двена́дцать 'about a dozen men'.

   In such inversions, a preposition remains **before** the numeral: дней **на́** пять 'for about 5 days', часо́в **через** ше́сть 'in about 6 hours'.

**5.** When a number other than 'one' is the subject of a sentence, the verb may be either in the 3rd singular neuter (grammatical agreement) or the 3rd plural (logical agreement). The plural is, however, only rarely used for inanimates.

Три́ студе́нтки та́м сиде́л**о**. }     Three students were sitting
Три́ студе́нтки та́м сиде́л**и**. }      there.

**6.** Indefinite numerals (i.e. expressions of quantity) take the genitive *plural*:

ско́лько но́в**ых** кни́г           How many new books?
не́сколько пе́рьёв             Several pens.
ма́ло карандаше́й              Not enough pencils.
мно́го студе́нтов              A lot of students.

**6.1** Instead of **мно́го** and **немно́го** + genitive plural, the regular adjectives **мно́гие** and **немно́гие** may be used. These adjectives *must* be used for cases other than Nom. and Acc.: **о мно́гих студе́нтах, с немно́гими студе́нтками**.

**6.11**   In the Nom. and Acc. мно́го/немно́го indicate "a group of many (few)", while the adjectives show "a (small) number of individuals [e.g. students]".

**6.2**   Similarly, не́сколько 'several' is replaced by regular plural adjectival forms in cases other than the nominative and accusative: де́ти *не́скольких* учи́тельниц, в *не́скольких* города́х, к *не́скольким* де́вушкам, с *не́сколькими* людьми́.

**7.**   Note that *челове́к* has a special genitive plural, identical with the Nom. sing., used with numerals: *пять челове́к* '5 men'.

**8.**   With numerals and expressions of quantity, еще́ means "more, in addition":

| | |
|---|---|
| еще́ оди́н уро́к | one more lesson |
| еще́ пять зада́ч | five more problems |
| еще́ ра́з | one more time, again |
| еще́ не́сколько дне́й | a few more days |

**9.**   Note the following time expressions:

| | | | |
|---|---|---|---|
| ча́с | one o'clock | в ча́с | at one o'clock |
| два́ часа́ | two o'clock | в два́ часа́ | at two o'clock |
| три́ часа́ | three o'clock | к три́ часа́ | at three o'clock |
| четы́ре часа́ | four o'clock | в четы́ре часа́ | at four o'clock |
| пять часо́в | five o'clock | в пять часо́в | at five o'clock |

*Six* to *twelve* of course have the same pattern as 'five o'clock'.

**10.**   Ча́с 'hour, time' has two possible accents in the genitive singular. With the numerals *2, 3, 4*, the suffix is stressed: два́ часа́ '2 hours, two o'clock'. In any other usage the stem is stressed: *до э́того* ча́са 'until that hour', *о́коло* ча́са 'about an hour, about 1 o'clock'.

In the plural, the endings are always stressed (cf. VIII 1.51 B).

**11.**   The accent of у́тро 'morning' is variable also. The genitive sing. утра́ is used with time expressions, with до and с; otherwise у́тра. Dative sing. к утру́ 'toward morning'; otherwise у́тру. Dative pl. по утра́м 'mornings (regularly)'; otherwise у́трам. In all other cases stress remains on the first syllable.

**12.**   Feminine nouns with stressed suffix in Nom. sg. may have some other syllable stressed in other forms (cf. IX 8.3). The only possible change in the singular is that the accusative may have a stressed initial syllable. In the plural, the Nom.-Acc. form may be opposed to the other forms (the so-called oblique cases). Some stress the first syllable in N-A pl. only, others have stem-stress throughout the plural, and still others admit either accentuation, although one is usually preferred.

| N | G | A sg. | | N-A pl. | G | P | D | I |
|---|---|---|---|---|---|---|---|---|
| среда́ | среды́ | сре́ду | Wednesday | сре́ды | сред | среда́х | (-а́м, -а́ми) | |
| зима́ | зимы́ | зи́му | winter | зи́мы | зим | зи́мах | (-ам, -ами) | |
| весна́ | весны́ | весну́ | spring | вёсны | вёсен | вёснах | (-ам, -ами) | |

**13.** There are some instances when a preposition will take the stress of the group "preposition + noun". So far we have had: **на́** зиму, **за́** город, **за́** городом, **на́** год, **на́** ночь. The stressed preposition may be found in combinations of **на** (or **за**) plus the numerals два́ [две́], три́, пя́ть, ше́сть, се́мь, во́семь, де́вять, де́сять.

This sort of stress-shift is slowly disappearing from the language, and at present there are very few cases where it is obligatory. Some people will, for example, say **на́** ночь very frequently, others rarely or not at all. As a general rule, the foreigner can safely put the stress on the noun. Occasionally the phrase with shifted accent is taken as a fixed idiom; thus for some speakers **за́** городом means 'in the country', and is not the same as за го́родом 'beyond the city'.

**14.** *Time expressions.*

**14.1** "At, on, in", meaning 'time when' is translated variously (and not always consistently) in Russian:

**14.11** With a *month*, *year*, or *century*, **в** + *prepositional* case:

| | |
|---|---|
| **в** ию́не э́того го́да | (in) this June |
| **в** ма́е про́шлого го́да | last May |
| **в** ию́ле бу́дущего го́да | next July |
| **В** то́м ме́сяце о́н бы́л в Москве́. | That month he was in Moscow. |
| Она́ прие́хала **в** про́шлом году́. | She arrived last year. |
| (**в** тре́тьем ве́ке) | (in the third century) |

Also:

| | |
|---|---|
| **в** про́шлом, **в** бу́дущем | in the past, in the future |

**14.12** With *day*, *part of day*, *week-day*, or *time*, **в** + *accusative*:

| | |
|---|---|
| О́н прие́хал **в** то́т де́нь, когда́ вы́ здесь бы́ли. | He arrived the day you were here. |
| О́н уе́хал **в** то́т же ве́чер. | He left the same evening. |
| **в** ту́ же ночь. | the same night. |
| Всё начало́сь **в** э́то у́тро. | Everything began (on) that morning. |
| **в** (э́ту) сре́ду, **в** пя́тницу | on (this) Wednesday, on Friday |
| **в** пе́рвый (после́дний) ра́з | for the first (last) time |

But note these special expressions:

| | |
|---|---|
| **на** сле́дующий де́нь (ве́чер) | on the following day (evening) |
| **на** друго́й де́нь | on the next day |
| **на** сле́дующее у́тро | (on) the following morning |

**14.13**  With *week*, **на** + *prepositional* case:

| | |
|---|---|
| **на** про́шлой неде́ле | last week |
| **на** э́той неде́ле | this week |
| **на** бу́дущей неде́ле | next week |

**14.14**  With an *hour* there may be a distinction:

| | |
|---|---|
| в ча́с | at one o'clock |
| во второ́м часу́ | in the second hour = after one o'clock |

**14.15**  With the name of a *season*, the *instrumental* is used without preposition:

| | |
|---|---|
| Э́тим ле́том мы́ жи́ли в дере́вне. | This summer we lived in the village. |
| Бу́дущей о́сенью он прие́дет в Босто́н. | Next fall he's coming to Boston. |
| Зимо́й он мно́го рабо́тает. | He works a lot in winter. |
| О́н уе́хал про́шлой весно́й. | He left last spring. |

**14.2**  With the adjective **ка́ждый** 'every', only the accusative is used:

| | |
|---|---|
| Они́ приезжа́ют ка́ждую зи́му. | They come every winter. |
| ка́ждый го́д | every year. |
| ка́ждый де́нь. | every day. |

**14.3**  To express "per", **в** + accusative is used:

| | |
|---|---|
| Она́ рабо́тает четы́ре часа́ *в де́нь.* | She works four hours a day. |
| Трамва́и прохо́дят пя́ть ра́з *в ча́с.* | Streetcars go by five times an hour. |

**14.4**  Do not forget the use of **через, на**, and the prepositionless accusative in time expressions. Cf. XVI 3.3 (2), 3.6, 4.

**15.**  The names of the months and days are not capitalized in Russian.
The months are all masculine. The six from September through February are stressed on the endings: e.g. в сентябре́, до сентября́.

**16.**  Де́вочка is a 'little girl', up to the age of adolescence. Де́вушка is past adolescence, but unmarried. The word sometimes means 'servant girl', also 'virgin'. It may be used, colloquially, to call or refer to a waitress or salesgirl.

**17.** Notice:

| | |
|---|---|
| Я его видел на прошлой не-деле в пе́рвый и, наде́юсь, после́дний ра́з. | I saw him for the first and I hope for the last time last week. |
| Про́шлый уро́к бы́л после́дним в э́том году́. | The last lesson was the final one this year. |
| После́дний уро́к бу́дет в бу́ду-щую сре́ду. | The last lesson will be next Wednesday. |
| После́дний уро́к до́лжен бы́л бы́ть в сле́дующую сре́ду. | The last lesson was to have been on the next Wednesday. |

**Про́шлый** means 'past, belonging in the past'; in phrases with words denoting time-units (e.g. *неде́ля, ме́сяц, год, ра́з*) it is usually translated into English as "last". Its opposite is **бу́дущий** 'future'. **После́дний** refers to the end of a series (not necessarily a time-series); its opposite is **пе́рвый** 'first'.

**Бу́дущий** specifies 'future': it means 'next' only from the point of view of the moment of speaking. '*The* next', with relation to any other time, is **сле́дующий**, literally 'the following'.

## УПРАЖНЕНИЯ

**A.** For oral drill:

1. Count the following objects from 1–12 (i.e. "1 day, 2 days", etc.): day, year, month, week, field, chair, woman, child, girl, language, city, pen, pencil, notebook, automobile, building, thing, photograph, word, door.

2. Count from 1–12 the following: blue pencil, red pen, expensive handbag, big window, little door, difficult problem, morning paper, evening train, last bus, intelligent Englishwoman, new word, Russian name, Chinese novel, jolly child, dull meeting, rich girl.

3. Recite the days of the week; repeat with "on" ("on Monday, on Tuesday", etc.).

4. Recite the months; repeat with "in" ("in Jan., in Feb.", etc.).

5а. У ва́с е́сть после́дн__ журна́л?

         Да́, у меня́ е́сть после́дн__ журна́л.

         Не́т, у меня́ не́т после́дн__ журна́ла.

б. У ва́с е́сть после́дн__ журна́лы?

         Да́, у меня́ е́сть после́дн__ журна́лы.

         Не́т, у меня́ не́т после́дн__ журна́лов.

в. Я ви́жу после́дн__ журна́л; после́дн__ журна́лы.

г. Что́ вы́ ду́маете о после́дн__ журна́ле; о после́дн__ журна́лах?

д.  к послѐдн___ журнѐлу; к послѐдн___ журнѐлам.

е.  с послѐдн___ журнѐлом; с послѐдн___ журнѐлами.

6. Repeat, substituting the following adjectives and nouns: ѝтренн___ газѐта; слѐдующ___ урѐк; трѐт___ фотографѝя; послѐдн___ фрѐза; вечѐрн___ собрѐниё; нѐв___ больш'___ сѝн___ автомобѝль; трѐт___слѐво.

**B.**  Read and translate:

1. Онѝ поѐхали в Еврѐпу на шесть недѐль, нѐ остѐлись трѝ мѐсяца. 2. Наш пѐрвый урѐк рѝсского языкѐ был в трѐтью срѐду в сентябрѐ прѐшлого гѐда.  3. Я это читѐл в однѐм из тех немѐцких журнѐлов, котѐрые Фомѐ мне недѐвно купѝл у нѐмки в гѐроде.  4. Дѐвушки рѐньше жѝли в ѐтом крѐсном дѐме за послѐдней фѐбрикой, а прѐшлой вёснѐй онѝ себѐ купѝли красѝвый сѝний дѐм зѐ городом.  5. В бѝдущую пѝтницу бѝдёт экзѐмен по послѐднему урѐку. Не забѝдьте! 6. Ваш дрѝг Вѝня позвонѝл час томѝ назѐд и попросѝл менѝ сказѐть тебѐ, что ты дѐлжён быть у Ивѐновых с дѐвушками в вѐсемь часѐв. 7. На прѐшлой недѐле судьѝ нѐ был на вечѐрнём собрѐнии.  8. Скѐль- ко у вѐс рѝсских книг?  9. Я ужѐ не получѐю пѝсём от дѝди Алѐши; в послѐдний рѐз я получѝл в прѐшлом годѝ, недѐль дѐсять томѝ назѐд.  10. Через двѐ недѐли мы поѐдём во Флорѝду нѐ зиму. Не хотѝте ли вы поѐхать с нѐми? —Хотѐл бы, но не могѝ.  11. Вѝня говорѝт, что сѐмый послѐдний пѐезд ужѐ ушёл, и он хѐчёт остѐться у нѐс нѐ ночь.  12. Он нам принѐсит журнѐлы кѐждую недѐлю. 13. В четвѐрг приѐхали Петрѐвы, и в слѐдующеё воскресѐньё мы всѐ пошлѝ с мѐтерью в лес.  14. На послѐднём концѐрте игрѐли трѐтью симфѐнию Шостакѐвича. Онѐ мне не ѐчень понрѐвилась.  15. Онѐ былѐ дрѝгом моегѐ дѐдушки мнѐго лет томѝ назѐд в Еврѐпе, когдѐ онѝ были детьмѝ.  16. Скѐлько тѐтей у ѐтих дѐвушёк?  У них тѐлько трѝ тѐти.  17. На прѐшлой недѐле онѐ переводѝла всѐ урѐки ѐчень хорошѐ, но на ѐтой недѐле, должнѐ быть, онѐ не готѐвилась, и ничегѐ не мѐжёт перевѐсти.  18. Какѝю ѝтреннюю газѐту вы получѐ- ёте? Мы не получѐём никакѐй ѝтренней газѐты, а читѐем «Вечѐрнюю Москвѝ».  19. Он иногдѐ приезжѐл к нѐм с женѐй и дѐдушкой, нѐ ѐтим лѐтом онѝ ни рѐзу не приезжѐли.  20. У Алѐши сѐмый стѐрый автомобѝль в гѐроде. Егѐ мѐть не хѐчёт дѐже ѐздить на нём.  21.Через недѐлю Бородѝны уѐдут в Крым. Онѝ там остѐнутся до октябрѝ. 22. Дѐвушка звонѝла емѝ шесть рѐз, нѐ егѐ всѐ нѐ было.  23. Никѝта ужѐ трѐтью недѐлю на Донѝ.  24. Мѝтя пѝшёт, что он однѐго письмѐ не получѝл. Мы написѐли пѝть пѝсём, из котѐрых он получѝл тѐлько четѝре.  25. Остѐньтесь у нѐс до четвергѐ! Тогдѐ бѝдёт послѐднеё собрѐниё у Бѐлых. Вѐм бѝдёт интерѐсно и мѐжёт быть дѐже вѐсёло.

C. For written and/or oral translation into Russian:

1. We receive the evening paper every day at six o'clock.    2. Father buys the morning paper from (VI 3.1) the little boy at the station when he is on his way [use D] to the factory.    3. In a week we will get two new blue automobiles.    4. Did you read about Vanja's grandfather, the judge, in the evening paper?    5. In their new apartment are five big rooms and two small ones.    6. Boris Dmitr'evich has one Chinese book on music, two Japanese magazines with many photographs, and seven old Russian newspapers which, he says, are rather interesting. 7. Every April the Tolstojs and Petrovs go to the Crimea for two or three weeks.    8. I saw a Russian film for the first time last week. 9. Next time you can go with us.    10. Dmitrij gives mathematics lessons (cf. XIV 5.4, last sentence) to Vanja five times a week from September to May.    11. How did you like the two Russian books which we read last year?    12. Last autumn Mark usually didn't come to class, and now it's very hard for him to understand.    13. Please write the last two sentences on the board.    14. What are you going to do (= will you do) next summer?    15. If I have any money in the spring, I shall buy a dozen Russian novels.    16. They say he writes two books every month.    17. In the winter Igor' goes to school in Italy and in the summer he works for several weeks in his grandfather's factory.    18. The Ivanovs will stay here for the first three days of June and then go to Odessa for about ten days and from there to Yalta for two weeks or a month.    19. We will be home all day on Saturday and perhaps Sunday; please phone in the morning.    20. You can come by the morning train at ten o'clock, or by the evening bus at seven o'clock.

## СЛОВАРЬ

| | | | |
|---|---|---|---|
| See § 3 for numerals 1–12. | | осень f. | autumn |
| бу́дущий | future | осенью | in autumn |
| бу́дущёё (n. aj. as noun) | the future | пе́рвый | first |
| | | после́дний | last |
| вёсна́ (§ 12) | spring | про́шлый | past |
| вёсно́й | in spring | про́шлоё (n. aj. as noun) | the past |
| ве́чер [pl. вечера́] | evening | | |
| вече́рний (aj.) | evening | си́ний | (darkish) blue |
| второ́й | second | сле́дующий | following, next |
| да́же | even | тому́ наза́д | ago |
| де́вушка [G pl. -шёк] | girl (§ 16) | тре́тий (§ 2) | third |
| де́нь [G дня́] | day | тре́тьего дня | day before yesterday |
| зима́ (§ 12) | winter | | |
| иногда́ | sometimes | у́тренний (aj.) | morning |
| ка́ждый (§ 14.2) | every | у́тро (§ 11) | morning |
| кра́сный | red | остава́ться | |
| ле́то | summer | остаю́тся I | remain, stay, |
| наза́д | back; ago | оста́ться | be left |
| но́чь (f. IX 8.4b) § 13 | night | оста́нутся P | |

| | |
|---|---|
| понеде́льник | Monday |
| вто́рник | Tuesday |
| среда́ (§ 12) | Wednesday |
| четве́рг *E* | Thursday |
| пя́тница | Friday |
| суббо́та | Saturday |
| воскресе́ньё | Sunday |

| | | | |
|---|---|---|---|
| сентя́брь [-бря́] | September | ма́рт | March |
| октя́брь [-бря́] | October | апре́ль | April |
| ноя́брь [-бря́] | November | ма́й | May |
| дека́брь [-бря́] | December | ию́нь | June |
| янва́рь [-ря́] | January | ию́ль | July |
| февра́ль [-ля́] | February | а́вгуст | August |

# LESSON XVIII

| | |
|---|---|
| Ско́лько ва́м ле́т? | How old are you? |
| Мне́ два́дцать ле́т. | I'm twenty years old. |
| Моему́ дя́де Алёше три́дцать оди́н го́д. | My uncle Alec is thirty-one. |
| Ему́ бы́ло два́дцать два́ го́да, когда́ о́н в пе́рвый ра́з встре́тил свою́ жену́. | He was twenty-two when he met his wife for the first time. |
| Ей бы́ло то́лько семна́дцать ле́т. | She was only seventeen. |
| Ско́лько ва́м бы́ло ле́т три́ го́да тому́ наза́д? | How old were you three years ago? |
| Ско́лько ва́м бу́дет ле́т через пя́ть ле́т? | How old will you be in five years? |
| Кото́рый ча́с? | What time is it? |
| Уже́ во́семь. Я до́лжен идти́. | It's already eight. I must go. |
| Уже́ восьмо́й ча́с! Пора́ у́жинать. | It's already after seven! Time to have supper! |
| Тепе́рь полови́на седьмо́го; я приду́ через полчаса́, ро́вно в се́мь. | It's now six thirty; I'll come in half an hour, at seven sharp. |
| В кото́ром часу́ отхо́дит после́дний по́езд? В ча́с два́дцать оди́н. | At what time does the last train leave? At 1:21 AM. |
| Ива́н пришёл домо́й но́чью, в два́дцать одну́ мину́ту второ́го. | Ivan came home at 1:21 in the morning. |
| Обыкнове́нно мы́ у́жинаем в полови́не восьмо́го. | Usually we have supper at seven-thirty. |
| Ве́ра прие́дет в восьмо́м часу́. | Vera is coming between seven and 7:30. |
| Я до́лжен бы́ть та́м ро́вно в се́мь. | I must be there at seven sharp. |

| | |
|---|---|
| Приди послезавтра часов в семь. | Come day after tomorrow at about seven. |
| Она ложится спать около десяти. | She goes to bed at about ten. |
| Какая сегодня погода? | What is the weather like today? |
| В среду было очень приятно, но вчера рано утром пошёл снег. | On Wednesday it was very pleasant, but yesterday morning early it started to snow. |
| Снег шёл с утра до вечера, а ночью пошёл дождь. | It snowed from morning till evening, but in the night it began to rain. |
| В субботу было уже не так холодно, а сегодня тепло. | Saturday it wasn't so cold any more, and today it's warm. |
| В пятницу было солнце. | On Friday there was sunshine. |
| Вчера не было солнца. | Yesterday there was no sun. |
| Он работал с девяти утра до шести вечера. | He used to work from nine in the morning to six in the evening. |
| Я встал без десяти восемь. | I got up at ten minutes to eight. |
| Она встала в десять минут восьмого. | She got up at ten minutes after seven. |
| Я буду работать до ужина. | I will work till supper. |
| Я зайду к вам после ужина. | I'll drop in at your place after supper. |
| Он сказал, что будет работать до ужина, а зайдёт сюда после ужина. | He said that he would work until supper and would drop in here after supper. |
| Он им дал деньги, чтобы купить дом за городом. | He gave them the money to buy a house in the country. |
| Он им дал деньги, чтобы они могли купить новый дом. | He gave them money so that they could buy a new house. |
| Письма отсюда туда идут теперь очень быстро. | Letters go from here to there very quickly now. |

---

1. In the subdivisions of this paragraph we are dealing with numerals in the **nominative** case, except where the accusative is specifically mentioned.

**1.1** All numerals in the nominative case whose last element is **один**, **одна**, **одно** take the *nominative SINGULAR*, as do any accompanying adjectives:

| | |
|---|---|
| двадцать один большой стол | 21 big tables |
| тридцать одна новая книга | 31 new books |
| сорок одно маленькое окно | 41 small windows |

**1.11** In the accusative, the noun remains singular, while modifiers including the numeral **один**, take the appropriate singular gender form:

| | |
|---|---|
| двадцать один большой стол. | 21 big tables. |
| Мы купили | We bought |
| тридцать одну новую книгу. | 31 new books. |

**1.12** In short, the grammatical number remains singular, and *21, 31, 321, 58741* behave just like **один**. In this book only the nominative and accusative forms will be used, because of the complications in the declension of other numerals.

**1.2** All numerals whose last element is **два/две**, **три**, or **четыре** take the *genitive SINGULAR*, like *два, три, четыре:*

| | |
|---|---|
| двадцать две книги | 22 books |
| тридцать три стола | 33 tables |
| девяносто четыре окна | 94 windows |

Adjectives may be genitive plural or nominative plural. (Review XVII 3.32!)

Note that the numerals *11* through *14*, since their last element is **-надцать**, belong in § 1.3, and not with the basic numerals treated in §§ 1.1 and 1.2.

**1.3** All numerals not covered in the paragraphs above have a single form for nominative and accusative[1] and take the genitive plural:

| | |
|---|---|
| одиннадцать книг | 11 books |
| двенадцать вещей | 12 things |
| шестнадцать стульев | 16 chairs |
| сорок девять старых газет | 49 old newspapers |

**2.** Observe the use of the dative in expressing **age**:

| | |
|---|---|
| Мне двадцать один год. | I am twenty-one years old. |

---

[1] NB: This does *not* include the *animate* accusative forms, which will not be used in this book.

| | |
|---|---|
| Ему́ со́рок четы́ре го́да. | He is forty-four years old. |
| Ей одиннадцать лет. | She is eleven. |

The past has **бы́ло**, the future **бу́дет**:

| | |
|---|---|
| Ему́ бы́ло четы́рнадцать лет. | He was fourteen years old. |
| Ему́ бу́дет девяно́сто лет. | He will be ninety. |

**3.** When a person's age is presented as an attribute, the genitive of the numeral (see § 5 below) is used:

| | |
|---|---|
| У неё есть сын пятна́дцати лет. | She has a son 15 years old. |
| Челове́к лет пяти́десяти вошёл. | A man of about 50 entered. |

**4.1** In **telling time** for official usage (railroads, radio, the army, etc.), the twenty-four hour clock is used: the word "hour" is normally omitted, "minute" is always omitted (and the masculine numerals are used):

| | |
|---|---|
| 6:23 | шесть (часо́в) два́дцать три |
| 14:37 | четы́рнадцать (часо́в) три́дцать семь |
| 23:41 | два́дцать три (часа́) со́рок оди́н |
| 23:52 | два́дцать три (часа́) пятьдеся́т два́ |

**4.2** Normal every-day usage is far more complex.

**4.21** **Пе́рвый час** is the time from 12 to 1. **В пе́рвом часу́** thus means any time during this hour, but it normally is interpreted as meaning from 12 to 12:30. **Второ́й час** = 1 to 2 (chiefly 1–1:30), and so on.

**4.220** "It is x o'clock" is expressed in two different ways: one for the first half of the hour and the other for the second half —

**4.221** Between the hour and half-past (the word "minute" must not be omitted):

| | | |
|---|---|---|
| 12:02 | (*1:02*) | две мину́ты пе́рвого (*второ́го*) |
| 12:05 | (*2:05*) | пять мину́т пе́рвого (*тре́тьего*) |
| → 12:15 | (*3:15*) | че́тверть пе́рвого (*четве́ртого*) |
| 12:29 | (*4:29*) | два́дцать де́вять мину́т пе́рвого (*пя́того*) |
| 12:30 | (*5:30*) | полови́на пе́рвого (*шесто́го*) |

"At" is here translated by **в** + accusative: **в пять мину́т пе́рвого**, except with the half-hour, which takes the prepositional: **в полови́не пя́того.**[1]

---

[1] Colloquially, "at half-past" is often simply the nominative without preposition (полови́на пя́того), but this is considered incorrect. Do NOT write it!

**4.222** The second half hour entails the use of the preposition **без** ('without, minus') with the genitive of the numeral (forms below). The word "minute" may be omitted (and the часá or часóв 'o'clock' usually is).

| | | |
|---|---|---|
| 12:31 | *(6:31)* | без двадцати́ девяти́ [мину́т] ча́с (*се́мь [часо́в]*) |
| 12:35 | *(7:35)* | без двадцати́ пяти́ [мину́т] ча́с (*во́семь [часо́в]*) |
| 12:39 | *(4:39)* | без двадцати́ одно́й [мину́ты] ча́с (*пя́ть [часо́в]*) |
| → 12:45 | *(8:45)* | без че́тверти ча́с (*де́вять [часо́в]*) |
| 12:57 | *(9:57)* | без трёх [мину́т] ча́с (*де́сять [часо́в]*) |

"At" may not be translated at all, or **в** may be used with the hour preceding the minutes: без трёх [мину́т] ча́с — в ча́с без трёх [мину́т].

**4.3** In contemporary conversational language, the questions *What time is it?* and *At what time?* are frequently **Ско́лько вре́мени?** (not Кото́рый ча́с?) and **Во ско́лько?** or **Во ско́лько часо́в?** (not В кото́ром часу́?). Soviet teachers and lexicographers do not approve of this usage, and it is therefore not recommended for the foreigner.

**5.0** The numerals have full declensions, but their use is extremely complicated and not important for an elementary course. The forms and an outline of uses can be found in the Appendix. For now, only the genitives are to be learned, since they are frequent in telling time. They occur, for example, with **без** 'without', **до** 'before, up to', and **о́коло** 'about, at approximately'.

**5.1** *2, 3, 4, 40, 90, 100* have genitives which do not fit into any regular declension: **дву́х, трёх, четырёх; сорокá, девяно́ста, стá.**

**5.2** Most other numerals have the 3rd declension suffix **-и**:

пяти́, шести́, семи́, восьми́, девяти́, десяти́, оди́ннадцати, двена́д-цати, трина́дцати, четы́рнадцати, пятна́дцати, шестна́дцати, семна́дцати, восемна́дцати, девятна́дцати; двадцати́, тридцати́.

**5.3** *50, 60, 70, 80* inflect both component members of the numeral:

пяти́десяти, шести́десяти, семи́десяти, восьми́десяти.

**6.** Note that there are no specific terms for AM and PM. The calendar day consists rather of: the time when people are usually asleep — *но́чь*; the time from dawn to dinner — *у́тро* (roughly 6–12); from dinner to dark — *де́нь* (in its narrow sense); and the period from sunset to bedtime — *ве́чер* (roughly 6 to midnight). If the time is specified, the genitive forms of these nouns are used: ча́с но́чи 'one AM', се́мь часо́в утра́ '7 AM', ча́с дня́ 'one PM', се́мь часо́в ве́чера '7 PM'. Otherwise the instrumental forms are used as adverbs: **но́чью** 'at night', **у́тром** 'in the morning', **днём** 'in the afternoon', **ве́чером** 'in the evening'.

**7.1**   The verb **ехать éдут** specifies that something or someone capable of locomotion is being transported. **Идти идут** has no such specification, but simply means motion. As such it is used of the motion of most vehicles:

| | |
|---|---|
| Идёт трамвай. | The streetcar is coming. |
| Этот автобус идёт прямо в город. | This bus goes right into town. |

But it is also used of things which are not expected to go of themselves:

| | |
|---|---|
| Письмо идёт отсюда в Москву три-четыре дня. | A letter goes from here to Moscow in three or four days. |

**7.11**   Automobiles, contrary to the general rule, ordinarily **éдут**:

| | |
|---|---|
| Автомобиль éхал быстро. | The car was going fast. |

**7.2**   **Идти**, as a normal imperfective verb, is often used to mean "function, run, work":

| | |
|---|---|
| Сегодня поезда опять идут. | The trains are running again today. |
| Ваш новый автомобиль хорошо идёт. | Your new car runs well. (i.e. the motor) |
| Эти часы плохо идут. | This watch runs badly. |

**7.3**   It is used idiomatically in the expressions *дождь идёт* 'it rains' and *снег идёт* 'it snows'. In these expressions the perfective **пойти [пойдёт]** means '*start to* (rain, snow)': *Дождь пошёл.* 'It started to rain.' *Дождь (снег) прошёл* means 'it stopped raining (snowing)'.

**7.4**   It is used of a play, opera, or film, and certain regular activities:

| | |
|---|---|
| Что идёт сегодня в кино? | What's playing at the movies today? |
| Сегодня идёт «Гамлет». | "Hamlet" is on today. |
| Здесь идёт урок русского языка. | A Russian lesson is in progress here. |

**8.1**   The verb **отходить отходят** I / **отойти отойдут** P is regularly used for the departure of trains and the like. Used of a person, it means "move away from" and implies a movement within a relatively limited space. **Отъезжать** I / **отъехать** P is used of a person departing by means of a vehicle, and implies the point of departure. The past of *отойти* is *отошёл, отошла,* etc.

**8.2** The "going-verbs" with the prefix **за-** mean "drop in", i.e. stop in somewhere for a short time while on the way to another destination: **заходи́ть захо́дят** I/**зайти́ зайду́т** P (**зашёл, зашла́**); **заезжа́ть заезжа́ют** I/**зае́хать зае́дут** P.

| | |
|---|---|
| Я зашёл к нему́ на мину́ту. | I dropped in to see him for a minute. |
| Заезжа́йте ко мне́. | Drop in and see me. |

The verb **заноси́ть зано́сят** I/ **занести́ занесу́т** P (**занёс, занесла́**) occasionally has this meaning, but it usually has other meanings which will not be mentioned here:

| | |
|---|---|
| Она́ занесла́ его́ письмо́ к ним. | She dropped in at their place, bringing his letter. |

**9.** Purpose is expressed by the conjunction *чтобы* or *чтоб* 'in order to':

| | |
|---|---|
| Он рабо́таёт, чтобы жи́ть, а она́ живёт, чтобы рабо́тать. | He works (in order) to live, but she lives (in order) to work. |
| Он взя́л твоё перо́, чтобы написа́ть письмо́. | He took your pen (in order) to write a letter. |

Note that Russian *must* use *чтобы* although English often has simply the infinitive. Only with going-verbs may the *чтобы* be omitted:

| | |
|---|---|
| Он пошёл, (чтобы) получи́ть де́ньги. | He's gone to receive his money. |

Note that if there is a change of subject, the past tense is used instead of the infinitive (compare the "explanatory" use of *чтобы* in X 4, 5.1, page 122):

| | |
|---|---|
| Он рабо́таёт, чтоб она́ могла́ жи́ть. | He works so that she may live. |

**9.1** The compound conjunction **для того́ чтобы** has the same meaning, but is slightly more emphatic. This longer form is normally used if the purpose clause stands *before* the main clause:

| | |
|---|---|
| Для гого́ чтобы по́мнить все́ слова́, вы́ должны́ повторя́ть и́х мно́го ра́з. | In order to remember all the words, you ought to go over them many times. |
| Он написа́л кни́гу для того́, чтобы все́ хорошо́ понима́ли ёго иде́и. | He wrote the book so that everyone would understand his ideas well. |

**10.** Notice the use of the dative with expressions of heat and cold (cf. XIII 2.3):

| | |
|---|---|
| Мне́ бы́ло хо́лодно. | I was cold. |
| Ва́м зде́сь жа́рко? | Is it (too) hot here for you? |

**11.** The verb **люби́ть лю́бят** ranges in meaning from English "love" to "be fond of". When used with a noun object, it is almost exactly equivalent in meaning to **нра́виться**. Óн лю́бит кни́ги = кни́ги ему́ нра́вятся, although the latter may imply a new impression and the former familiarity.

To translate "like to (do something)", **люби́ть** is more usual:

Óн (о́чень) лю́бит чита́ть.          He likes to read (very much).

Remember that "would like" is **хоте́л бы** (cf. X 6.1):

Она́ (о́чень) бы хоте́ла чита́ть.     She would like (very much) to read.

**12.** **В** + accusative of time expression may be used to express "period during which" an action was accomplished. For example:

Óн написа́л э́ту статью в два́     He wrote that article in two дня́.                              days.

## УПРАЖНЕНИЯ

**A.** Be prepared to count in Russian from one to 100; to give your present age, your age ten (five, three, two) years ago and various years in the future; to elicit from your fellow-students this information and to ask and answer questions concerning the ages of various relatives; to give all possible answers to the questions "What time is it?" and "At what time...?"

**B.** Read and translate:

1. Же́нщины ча́сто не хотя́т отвеча́ть, когда́ и́х спра́шивают, ско́лько и́м ле́т.   2. Ско́рый по́езд прихо́дит дне́м, без че́тверти ча́с. 3. Ско́ро ли придёт по́езд?   4. После́дний по́езд отхо́дит но́чью в че́тверть второ́го.   5. Уже́ три́ дня́ мы́ не ви́дим со́лнца.   6. Что́ идёт сего́дня в кино́? Я́ ду́маю, что ещё пока́зывают то́т же ску́чный фи́льм, кото́рый мы́ уже́ ви́дели два́ ра́за.   7. Вчера́ бы́л холо́дный де́нь. Сне́г шёл до трёх, а пото́м пошёл до́ждь.   8. Я́ дала́ Ва́не

де́ньги, чтоб о́н мо́г на́м купи́ть вече́рнюю газе́ту, но́ о́н забы́л зайти́ в магази́н. 9. По́сле пе́рвого уро́ка ру́сского языка́, мы́ зна́ли ка́к сказа́ть и до́брый ве́чер и споко́йной но́чи. 10. Ка́к вы́ ду́маете, бу́дет наконе́ц до́ждь сего́дня? 11. Заéдемте к нему́ в дере́вню! Мы́ мо́жем поу́жинать и́ли у него́ и́ли, е́сли его́ не́т до́ма, в ма́леньком рестора́не та́м. 12. Говоря́т, что вчера́ но́чью учи́тельница уе́хала с краси́вым молоды́м челове́ком, ле́т двадцати́ четырёх. 13. Ва́ня, тво́й дру́г зашёл за тобо́й (XVI 3. 5). 14. Де́ти не хоте́ли пойти́ в шко́лу, потому́ что шёл до́ждь. 15. Ма́ть на́м всё повторя́ла: чего́ в друго́м не лю́бишь, того́ и са́м не де́лай! 16. Друзья́ мое́й жены́ е́здят в Калифо́рнию ка́ждую ве́сну и всегда́ заезжа́ют к на́м дня́ на́ три. 17. Мы́ ва́с подождём на у́лице перед кино́ и пото́м мы́ все́ пойдём вме́сте во францу́зский рестора́н. 18. До тре́тьего ма́я пого́да не была́ прия́тной. 19. Де́вушка отошла́ от окна́. 20. В э́ти до́лгие холо́дные вечера́ мы́ лю́бим сиде́ть в тёплой ко́мнате и чита́ть. 21. Е́сли до́ждь бу́дет идти́ ещё по́сле у́жина, то́ мы́ не пойдём на собра́ние. 22. Говоря́т, что О́льга прочита́ла два́дцать одну́ кни́гу в три́ дня́. 23. Зайди́те по́сле у́жина к мои́м бра́тьям и мы́ все́ пойдём в кино́ в полови́не восьмо́го. 24. Алексе́й Петро́вич позвони́л, чтобы сказа́ть, что о́н занесёт твою́ кни́гу в суббо́ту. 25. На́м бы́ло о́чень ве́село в Крыму́. Пого́да была́ хоро́шая и мы́ мно́го бы́ли на со́лнце.

**C.** For written and/or oral translation into Russian:

1. He said Andrej would be here at six o'clock sharp. 2. I waited until quarter past six, but he still had not come, and I had to leave. 3. They arrived about ten days ago, on Monday or Tuesday. 4. Today is the eleventh day without sunshine. 5. I'll call Igor' in a quarter of an hour and ask whether they can come to our house to have supper. 6. His mother is about fifty, but his father is nearly [almost] seventy-five. 7. His train will leave at 8:25 PM. 8. It's unpleasant to work in this building when it's hot. 9. Do you like to speak Russian? 10. When they arrived at the station the last train had already left. 11. On a cold, unpleasant day at seven thirty in the morning they set out (afoot) from Moscow. 12. I will go to bed in half an hour. 13. Did you like the film which we saw day before yesterday? 14. Ol'ga translated the lesson in twenty minutes. 15. She'll be here in twenty minutes. 16. It's very pleasant and warm to sit here in the sun. 17. Their son Vanja is two years old, and their daughter Nadja is five years old. 18. In the 12th class last year there were 41 female students and 44 male students, and this year there are 49 female students and 51 male students. 19. I'd like to stay and help the girls, but I have to be at uncle's in ten minutes.

20. Boris took some books with him to read on the train.　21. When you come tonight, drop in at the store to buy the newest magazines. 22. Mother called to ask you to bring these things.　23. If you had been here last winter, you could have helped us a great deal.　24. It's very hot here in July and August, and we always go away somewhere for a month or six weeks.　25. It sometimes snows there in September, and every year it snows often in October.　26. I'm cold; let's go into a warmer room.　27. They have two new red chairs and five old blue chairs. 28. You must get up at ten to seven.　29. If you stay there for a week, we will see you.　30. Excuse me, I must go home to write my Russian sentences.

## СЛОВАРЬ

Learn all the cardinal numerals through *100* and the ordinals through *12th*: See App. III, pp. 355–356.

| | |
|---|---|
| без + Gen. | without |
| днём (§ 6) | in the afternoon |
| до́ждь m. *E* | rain |
| (*dóšč, daž<sup>ь</sup>ž<sup>ь</sup>á*; cf. App. I, § 15) | |
| жа́ркий | hot |
| (жа́рок, жа́рко -и; жарка́) | |
| мину́та | minute |
| непого́да | poor weather |
| неприя́тный | unpleasant |
| но́чью (§ 6) | at night |
| пого́да | weather |
| полови́на | half |
| полчаса́ (not declined) | half hour |
| по́сле + Gen. | after |
| послеза́втра | day after tomorrow |
| прия́тный | pleasant |

| | |
|---|---|
| ро́вно | (with time expressions) sharp, exactly |
| с (+ Gen.) | from, since, beginning with |
| сне́г (pl. снега́) | snow |
| [в, на снегу́ II 3] | |
| со́лнцē | sun |
| (pronounced *sónɔ*: no *l*!) | |
| на со́лнце | in the sun |
| тёплый | warm |
| (тёпёл, тёпло́ -а́, тёплы́) | |
| холо́дный | cold |
| (хо́лоден, -дно, -дны; холодна́) | |
| че́тверть f. | quarter |
| чтобы (§ 9; App. I, 13.1) | in order to |
| для того́ чтобы | cf. § 9.1 |

―――――――

люби́ть лю́бят I ⎫
полюби́ть Р ⎭ love, like (§ 11)

у́жинать у́жинают I ⎫
поу́жинать Р ⎭ have supper

заходи́ть заезжа́ть заноси́ть ⎫
отходи́ть отъезжа́ть [относи́ть] ⎭ etc. see § 8

# ДЕВЯТНА́ДЦАТЫЙ УРО́К

| | |
|---|---|
| Ты́ хо́чёшь ча́ю? | Do you want some tea? |
| Ми́ша хо́чёт сы́ру. | Misha wants some cheese. |
| Фома́ вы́пил ча́й. | Foma drank the tea. |
| Фома́ вы́пил ча́ю. | Foma took a drink of the tea. |
| Вы́ купи́ли сы́ру и са́хару? | Did you buy some cheese and some sugar? |
| Де́душка иногда́ пьёт ко́фе без са́хара. | Grandfather sometimes drinks coffee without sugar. |
| Вы́пейте, пожа́луйста, ещё ча́шку ча́ю! | Please have another cup of tea! |
| Доктора́ пошли́ пи́ть ко́фе. | The doctors have gone to drink coffee. |
| Судья́ съе́л хле́б с ма́слом и вы́пил ча́шку ча́ю с са́харом. | The judge ate bread and butter and drank a cup of tea with sugar. |
| На обе́д о́н обыкнове́нно е́ст су́п, мя́со, хле́б, сы́р и пьёт ча́й и́ли ко́фе. | For dinner he usually eats soup, meat, bread, cheese, and drinks tea or coffee. |
| Сего́дня у на́с е́сть су́п, но́ я́ не е́м су́па. | Today we are having soup, but I don't eat soup. |
| Почёму́ ты́ е́шь та́к ма́ло? | Why are you eating so little? |
| Я́ уже́ съе́л мно́го су́пу. | I have already had a lot of soup. |
| Како́е сего́дня число́? | What's the date today? |
| Сего́дня второ́е декабря́. | Today is December second. |
| Сего́дня среда́ седьмо́го апре́ля. | Today is Wednesday, April seventh. |
| Вчера́ бы́ло тре́тье ма́рта. | Yesterday was March third. |
| За́втра бу́дёт два́дцать шесто́е октября́. | Tomorrow will be October twenty-sixth. |
| Э́то бы́ло деся́того января́. | That was on the tenth of January. |

| Царь у́мёр в сре́ду, три́дцать пе́р-вого ию́ля. | The tsar died on Wednesday, July thirty-first. |
| У ни́х роди́лся сы́н двена́дцатого февраля́. | Their son was born on February twelfth. |
| Она́ родила́сь два́дцать тре́тьего а́вгуста, а умёрла́ два́дцать четвёртого, когда́ е́й бы́ло во́семьдесят ле́т. | She was born on August 23rd, and died on the 24th, when she was eighty years old. |
| Мы́ оста́немся та́м с четвёртого по восемна́дцатоё а́вгуста. | We will stay there from the 4th through the 18th of August. |
| Они́ гуля́ли от ча́са до трёх. | They walked from one to three. |

---

**1.**   *Partitive expressions*

**1.0**   The genitive form of nouns denoting divisible substances may be used with the meaning "some of":

| Ба́бушка купи́ла хле́б**а**, мя́с**а** и во́дк**и**. | Grandmother bought *some* bread, *some* meat, and *some* vodka. |

**1.1**   Certain masculine nouns have a special "second genitive" form, with the suffix -*u* (spelled -**у**/-**ю**), which is used in such cases: e.g.,

| Я́ вы́пил ча́**ю**. | I drank *some of the tea*. |

Nouns which have this special form will be noted in the vocabularies.

**1.2**   The *partitive genitive* (as this usage of the genitive case is called) is most frequently used after expressions of quantity, definite or indefinite.

| ча́шка ча́ю | *a cup* of tea |
| мно́го хле́ба | *a lot* of bread |
| ма́ло су́пу | *little* soup |

The genitive *plural* gives a different meaning:

| мно́го чаёв | many kinds of tea |
| мно́го сахаро́в | many sugars (technical chemical term) |
| ма́ло сыро́в | few cheeses |

**1.3**   Nouns with the special genitive in -*u* (-**у**/-**ю**) have the normal suffix -*a* (-**а**/-**я**) in nearly all other uses: e.g. *без* су́п**а**, ча́**я**, са́хар**а** 'without soup, tea, sugar'.

**2.** Certain other masculine nouns have a genitive in *-u* which is used in fixed expressions only: Óн сегóдня не вы́шел *из дому* — 'He did not leave the house today.' Here it is also possible to say *из дóма*, however, and if there is anything between the preposition and noun, the latter must have the regular genitive form: *из э́того дóма*. Similarly *дó часу* or *до чáса* 'up to one o'clock'; *из лесу* or *из лéса* 'out of the forest'.

**3.** The verb **éсть едя́т** I 'to eat' and its perfective mate **съéсть съедя́т** 'eat up, consume' are irregular in the present singular, the imperative, and the past: я **éм (съéм)**, ты́ **éшь, (съéшь)**, óн **éст (съéст)**; **[съ]éшь!** **[съ]éшьте!**; óн **[съ]éл**, онá **[съ]éла**, они́ **[съ]éли**.

**4.** The verbs **пи́ть пью́т** I 'drink' and **вы́пить вы́пьют** P 'drink up, finish drinking' have irregular imperative forms:[1] **пéй, пéйте; вы́пей, вы́пейте**.

The accent of the past tense forms of **пи́ть** is like that of **бы́ть, жи́ть** (IV 5, V 6.2).

The stress of *all* forms of **вы́пить** is on the first syllable: cf. XVI 1.61.

**5.** The masculine noun **кóфе** (pronounced *kófʰi* or *kófʰə*) is indeclinable.

**6.** *Time expressions*

**6.1** The day of the month is expressed by means of the *ordinal* numeral, in the neuter nominative, with or without the noun **числó** 'number, date':

пéрвоё [числó] ноября́           November 1st.

**6.2** To express "on" a certain date, the expression is put in the genitive:

пéрв**ого** октября́           *On* October 1st.

Note the genitive in: Сегóдня пя́тница пя́т**ого** мáя. 'Today is Friday, May 5th.'

**6.3** **По** + *accusative* means "up to (and including)":

Мы́ тáм бу́дём с пéрвого **по**           We will be there from the first
пя́т**оё** июля.           to (= through) the fifth of
                         July.

In the past three decades this specific sense has rapidly been dissipated, and **по** in current language is essentially a bookish form, equivalent in sense to **до**. For clear specification with either preposition, the adverb **включи́тельно** 'inclusively' is added: *по пя́тоё июля включи́тельно* or *до пя́того июля включи́тельно*.

---

[1] The stem here consists only of two consonants: **пью́т** = *pʰj-út*. The imperative form is the bare stem with an inserted vowel (II 2.0 fn.): *pʰéj* (and, with the stressed prefix, *vípʰij*).

**6.4** "From... to" may be rendered in various ways. **С** + Gen. means "starting with", and is often correlated with **по** to give inclusive dates: *с сентября по январь* 'from September to January'. It is used with **до** in more or less fixed phrases like *с утра до вечера* 'from morning to evening'.

With hours, **от...до** is usual: *от двух до пяти* 'from 2 to 5', but **с** also occurs.

## УПРАЖНЕНИЯ

**A.** Be prepared to give today's date, yesterday's date, tomorrow's date, and to say "on" all those dates. Include the day of the week.

**B.** Read and translate:

1. В семнадцатом веке в России было много войн. 2. Помните ли вы тот день, когда кончилась война в Европе? 3. Мы завтракаем в семь часов. 4. Вы хотите ещё чаю? 5. Они читают нашу газету каждое утро, никогда не покупают своей. 6. Отец получает второй завтрак на фабрике, а дети в школе, часов в девять. 7. Сколько было революций в восемнадцатом веке? 8. Мы в городе обыкновенно обедаем в два часа дня, но в деревне у дедушки обедают около двенадцати. 9. Погода была очень неприятная той зимой. Я не помню более холодной зимы. 10. Иногда мы обедаем часа в четыре или в пять, когда отец уже приходит домой с фабрики. 11. Ужин может быть в восемь или в девять часов вечера. 12. Я не хочу идти в кино сегодня вечером. Этот фильм будет идти две недели. 13. Марья Ильинична была подругой её тёти. 14. Вы видели, сколько чашек чаю выпил Фома? 15. Этот мужчина очень любит сады. Он работает и в своём саду, и в саду судьи, и в садах соседей моих дядей. Он всё говорит только о саде. 16. Первым царём всей России был Иван Четвёртый. 17. Весной Аким Игоревич только лежит на солнце в саду, читает романы и пьёт холодный чай. 18. Борис Годунов хотел, чтобы его сын был царём. 19. Сколько часов в день работал Осип? Двенадцать или тринадцать. 20. Яша сел за стол и съел всё, что было на нём.

**C.** For written and/or oral translation into Russian:

1. They arrived last autumn on September 12th. 2. Write 50 sentences! 3. Drink up your tea and let's go. 4. Do you like vodka more than wine

( XV 14)?  5. Give me money to buy sugar and tea.  6. Vanja took a drink of milk.  7. Give Sasha bread and butter, cheese and coffee for breakfast in the morning.  8. Did you sleep well? Here's a cup of tea for you. 9. Russians came to America for the first time in the eighteenth century. 10. Who started the second war between France and Germany?  11. He called from Europe day before yesterday at 4:30 AM.  12. We dined at grandfather's at 12:30 and then walked about the city.  13. We often walk in the afternoon.  14. Uncle Ivan likes to walk very early in the morning when everyone else is (= all others are) asleep.  15. Grand-mother usually walks from 10 to 11 in the morning.  16. Next time I'll explain this same lesson once more.  17. They lived in Russia for several years before the revolution.  18. Sofija Igorevna is interested in French and German literature of the nineteenth century.  19. She did not leave the house today.  20. They will come to spend the summer, and will stay from June 8th to August 24th, inclusive.  21. Igor's grandfather has been dying for three days.  22. Old judge Petrushévskij died several days ago, on May 4th or 5th.  23. I was born on February 29th, and my sister would have been born on February 29th, but there wasn't such a date that year. Do you understand that?  24. They say that her child will be born in December.  25. Their son Vanja was born two years ago, on September 10th, and their daughter Nadezhda was born five years ago, on October 9th.

## СЛОВАРЬ

Learn the ordinal numerals through *100th*:  App. III, p. 356.

| | |
|---|---|
| вéк (pl. векá) | century; age |
| винó (pl. вúна) | wine |
| водá | water |
| (A sg. вóду; pl. вóды) | |
| вóдка | vodka |
| войнá (pl. вóйны, вóйн) | war |
| зáвтрак | breakfast; lunch |
| кóфе masc. indecl. | coffee |
| мáсло | butter |
| молокó | milk |
| мя́со | meat |
| обéд | dinner |
| пúво | beer |
| по + Acc. § 6.3 | to (and including) |
| револю́ция | revolution |
| сáхар | sugar |
| (2nd Gen. сáхару; pl. сахарá) | |
| сýп | soup |
| (2nd Gen. сýпу; pl. супы́) | |
| сы́р | cheese |
| (2nd Gen. сы́ру; pl. сыры́) | |
| хлéб | bread |
| цáрь E | tsar, emperor |
| чáй (2nd Gen. чáю; pl. чай) | tea |
| чáшка (G. pl. чáшёк) | cup |
| числó (pl. чúсла, чúсёл) | number; date |

| | | |
|---|---|---|
| гуля́ть гуля́ют I<br>погуля́ть Р | } | walk, stroll |

| | | |
|---|---|---|
| е́сть едя́т I<br>съе́сть Р | } §3 | eat |

| | | |
|---|---|---|
| за́втракать -кают I<br>поза́втракать Р | } | breakfast,<br>lunch |

| | | |
|---|---|---|
| обе́дать обе́дают I<br>пообе́дать Р | } | dine, have<br>dinner |

| | | |
|---|---|---|
| пи́ть пью́т I<br>вы́пить вы́пьют Р | } §4 | drink |

роди́ться родя́тся I/P    be born
   past  роди́лся  роди́ли́сь
   родила́сь

| | | |
|---|---|---|
| умира́ть умира́ют I<br>умёре́ть умру́т Р | } | die |

   past у́мёр, у́мёрли; умёрла́

## For review

**A.**    Прочита́йте и переведи́те:

| | |
|---|---|
| 1. Она сказала, что Иван ушел. | Она сказала, чтобы Иван ушел. |
| 2. Я раз там играл. | Я не раз там играл. |
| 3. Я сегодня не получил<br>   письма. | Я не сегодня получил письмо. |
| 4. Мы были там. | Мы были там же. |
| 5. Олег обещал дать Ольге<br>   какую-то книгу. | Олег обещал дать Ольге<br>   какую-нибудь книгу. |
| 6. Он сидел за столом. | Он сидел у стола. |
| 7. Самое трудное время зима. | Самое трудное время зимой. |
| 8. Когда я пришел домой, все<br>   уже обедали. | Когда я пришел домой, все<br>   уже пообедали. |
| 9. Он долго говорил с Петровым. | Он давно говорил с Петровым. |
| 10. Пришло пять человек. | Пришло человек пять. |
| 11. Он приехал на два дня. | Он приехал через два дня. |
| 12. Когда начался дождь,<br>   мы пришли домой. | Когда начался дождь,<br>   мы шли домой. |
| 13. Они ехали в снегу. | Они ехали в снег. |
| 14. Она читала рассказ. | Она читала час. |
| 15. Никита выпил чай. | Никита выпил чаю. |
| 16. Там не было одного мальчика. | Там не было ни одного мальчика. |
| 17. Судья пришла. | Судья пришел. |
| 18. Я не раз обедал там. | Я ни разу не обедал там. |
| 19. Он едет в город. | Он ездит в город. |

**B.** 1. There is no library in our village, and one can't get books in any language at any of our stores. 2. In my notebook I am writing the names and patronymics of my friends, so that I'll remember them all in the future. 3a. Irina is poor and never comes to school by automobile. 3b. Ivan Petrovich always carries her books and opens doors for her. 4. When I was a boy in Russia, there were neither busses nor automobiles, and all the children in our village beyond Omsk had to go on foot to a little school in another village. 5. Let's show our neighbors, the Bélkin-Petróvskijs, the interesting photographs of the old Polish woman we met in Poland last year. 6. Her brothers never thought that she would put those new French books with the interesting photographs on the tables in the library. 7. The professors asked whether Anna had ever read *Fomá Gordéev*, a rather dull novel by [= of] Maksím Gór'kij. 8. The little girl asked her friends to put all the magazines under the same table where they had put the old books for the poor children. 9. My watch is running badly, but I think the meeting must have already begun.

10a. Please be silent about that pretty Englishwoman you saw me talking to in the park yesterday afternoon. 10b. Mother doesn't want me to see her any more, and I don't want her to know that we are still meeting. 11a. Do you know that Japanese man who can speak Russian so well? 11b. He translated several important documents for our lawyers from Russian into Japanese last month. 12. Formerly the boys were afraid of each other, but now they like each other and like to play with each other. 13a. Do you know Vera Fëdorovna Panóva's *Serëzha*? 13b. It's a novel I liked very much, and I'd like my aunt to read it. 13c. But she doesn't like to read novels. 14. They will come to fetch Tanja Knipóvich's children in a week. 15. Some say there was not a single student in class yesterday; others say the professor told them not to come. 16. In order to get to bed earlier than Vera, you will have to finish all the exercises at eight-thirty. 17a. It's now a quarter to six. 17b. They are expecting me at the restaurant in thirteen minutes, but it is very pleasant here and I don't feel like leaving the house. 17c. Let them wait a few minutes.

18a. The Soviet writer we met at the club last night has lived in Paris for three years, with his wife and children. 18b. He is about forty, his wife is thirty-three, their son soon will be fourteen, and their daughter is twenty-one. 19a. Please drink up your wine and take some soup. 19b. But you know I never eat soup. 20a. All right, let's have breakfast together at the little restaurant by the bridge at seven thirty next Thursday.    20b. No, that's very early for me, let's say ten-fifteen.    20c. I have to be at the museum before that, I'll see you at nine-thirty-five.    21. At the last lesson Dmitrij Ivanovich said that today we would read through two more exercises, 21 more sentences, and that he would give us 55 important new words.    22. We dropped in to see the doctor for a minute so that he would understand that the meeting would be at 4:45 PM.    23. This year he is living in Moscow, but he goes to Kiev every month and last week he was at his neighbors' in the country.    24. Next week I will buy twelve big tables, twenty-seven new chairs, and two small blackboards for the English club.    25. He will be at the library in the laboratory on Mondays from two to three and on Tuesdays from four to five.

# ДВАДЦА́ТЫЙ УРО́К

Алекса́ндр Серге́евич Пу́шкин родился́ в Москве́ два́дцать шесто́го ма́я, ты́сяча семьсо́т девяно́сто девя́того го́да.

Aleksandr Sergeevich Pushkin was born in Moscow on May 26th, 1799.

Вели́кий поэ́т у́мер в Санкт-петербу́рге девя́того января́, ты́сяча восемьсо́т три́дцать седьмо́го го́да.

The great poet died in St. Petersburg on January 9, 1837.

Фёдор Миха́йлович Достое́вский родился́ тридца́того октября́, ты́сяча восемьсо́т два́дцать пе́рвого го́да и у́мер в ты́сяча восемьсо́т во́семьдесят пе́рвом году́, в январе́ ме́сяце.

Fëdor Mikhajlovich Dostoevskij was born on October 30, 1821, and died in 1881, in January.

Ле́в Никола́евич Толсто́й родился́ в а́вгусте ты́сяча восемьсо́т два́дцать восьмо́го го́да и у́мер седьмо́го ноября́ ты́сяча девятьсо́т деся́того го́да.

Lev Nikolaevich Tolstoj was born in August, 1828, and died on November 7, 1910.

Собра́ния быва́ют по четверга́м, но на э́той неде́ле собра́ние бу́дет в пя́тницу.

Meetings take place on Thursdays, but this week the meeting will be on Friday.

В сентябре́ быва́ет хо́лодно по вечера́м.

In September it is usually cold in the evenings.

В како́е вре́мя го́да вы быва́ете в Крыму́?

In what season do you visit the Crimea?

В то́ вре́мя война́ ещё не начала́сь.

At that time the war had not yet started.

Где́ вы бы́ли во вре́мя войны́?

Where were you during the war?

Я до́лжен бы́л встава́ть в ше́сть, чтобы прийти́ на фа́брику во́время.

I had to get up at six in order to get to the factory on time.

Зайдите к нам сегодня вечером, если у вас будет время.

Drop in to see us this evening, if you have time.

Извините, что я вам не позвонил вчера, у меня не было времени.

Excuse me for not calling you yesterday; I had no time.

Мы заезжаем к нему в деревню, время от времени.

We drop in on him in the country from time to time.

Он кончил работу в первых числах апреля.

He finished the work early in April.

Как быстро прошло время!

How quickly the time passed!

Главным городом СССР является Москва.     [эсэсэсэр]

Moscow is the chief city of the USSR.

После того он стал доктором.

After that he became a doctor.

Он должен явиться к судье тринадцатого числа этого месяца.

He must report to the judge on the thirteenth of this month.

Всё лето было жарко, а вчера вдруг стало очень холодно.

All summer it was hot, but yesterday it suddenly got very cold.

----

**1.** *Time expressions*

**1.1** The year in Russian is defined by means of the *ordinal* numeral:

тысяча девятьсот *сороковой* год     1940 (lit. 'the 1940th year')

**1.2** When the specific day is followed by the year, the year goes into the *genitive*; i.e. one says "the (first) date *of* (October) *of* the (1950th) year":

первое октября тысяча         October 1st, 1950
девятьсот пятидеся**того** го**да**

**1.31** "In" with the name of a month, but without a specific date, is **в** + *prepositional*, cf. XVII 14.11. The year remains in the genitive:

в декабре тысяча восемьсот      in December, 1893
девяносто третьего года

**1.32** "In" with the year alone is **в** + *prepositional*:

в тысяча девятисот**ом** году      in 1900

**1.4** To denote regular repetition on a certain day (or other unit of time), **по** + *dative plural* is used:

| | |
|---|---|
| Óн рабóтаёт дóма **по** средáм. | He works at home on Wednesdays. |
| **по** ночáм. | nights. |
| **по** вечерáм. | evenings. |

**1.5** Note the use of the ordinals to express decades:

| | |
|---|---|
| двадцáтые гóды | the '20's |
| в шестидесятых годáх девятнáдцатого вéка | in the 1860's |
| Óн интересýётся совéтской литератýрой сороковы́х годóв. | He's interested in Soviet literature of the 'forties. |

**2.** The verb **быва́ть быва́ют** means "to be, frequently or repeatedly":

| | |
|---|---|
| Зи́мы у нáс быва́ют холóдные. | Winters are usually cold in our country. |
| Óн чáсто бывáл в Москвé. | He was often in Moscow. |
| Óн у нáс рéдко быва́ёт. | He rarely visits us. |
| Собрáния быва́ют в клýбе рáз в мéсяц. | Meetings take place in the club once a month. |

**3.** The verb **явля́ться** I/**яви́ться** P means "appear, present oneself, report":

| | |
|---|---|
| Когдá ты́ я́вишься на рабóту? | When do you report for work? |
| Передо мнóй яви́лась ты́. | You appeared before me. |

The imperfective is commonly used in definitions, and takes the *instrumental* (cf. XI 5.2):

| | |
|---|---|
| Судьéй явля́ется товáрищ Пётрóв. | Comrade Petrov *is* the judge. |

This is a bookish construction, rare in conversation, but extremely common in journalistic, scholarly, and technical writings.

**4.** The verbs **станови́ться** I **стáть** P mean "become" when followed by a noun or adjective:

| | |
|---|---|
| Ивáн стáл дóктором. | Ivan became a doctor. |
| Тáня стáнёт учи́тельницей. | Tanja will become a teacher. |
| Всéм стáло скýчно. | Everyone got bored. |

When followed by an infinitive, the perfective **стáть** means "begin" or else has a meaning nearly identical with that of **бýду** (**бýдёшь**, etc.):

| Óн стáл говорúть. | He started to talk. |
| Я не стáну отвечáть. | I won't answer. |

Note that the instrumental is used for the noun or adjective *except* in the impersonal construction: i.e. всém бы́ло скýчно — всém стáло скýчно.

| В начáле кнúга былá интерéсной, а к концý стáла скýчн**ой**. | At the beginning the book was interesting, but toward the end it got dull. |

These verbs may also mean "take a standing position", although here the notion of 'standing' may not be important:

| Перед нúми стáла трýдная задáча. | Before them was (appeared, came to be) a difficult task. |
| Óн стáл на стýл. | He got up on the chair (standing). |

**5.** Notice the various possible equivalents for the present tense of the English verb "to be":

(1) *zero*; may be written with a dash to indicate the intonation:

| Товáрищ Пётрóв — судья́. | Comrade Petrov *is* a judge. |

This is the most common construction and the normal one in speech.

(2) In a definition, the zero may be replaced by **éсть**, representing any person or number:

| Времёнá гóда éсть: óсень, зимá, вёснá, лéто. | The seasons *are*: autumn, winter, spring, summer. |
| Я и éсть Пётрóв. | I *am* Petrov. |

(3) To specify the function of a person or thing in a definition, **являться**:

| Глáвными городáми СССР являются Москвá и Ленинрáд. | Moscow and Leningrad *are* the chief cities of the USSR. |

[Types (2) and (3) are essentially interchangeable: both are bookish.]

(4) To specify location, **нахóдиться нахóдятся**:

| Гдé нахóдится нóвый теáтр? | Where *is* the new theater? |

(5) To indicate frequent, habitual, but intermittent existence, **бывáть**:

| Здéсь бывáют холóдные нóчи в ию́не. | There *are* cold nights here in June. |
| Óн бывáёт у мáтери по воскресéньям. | He *is* usually at his mother's on Sundays. |

**6.** The preposition **при** takes the prepositional case. It has a general meaning of closeness and attachment, which has various more specific nuances and is rendered in a number of different ways in English: e.g.

| | |
|---|---|
| Óн живёт при стáнции. | His house is attached to the station. |
| Этого не говорúте при дéтях! | Don't say that in the presence of the children. |
| У меня́ перá при себé нéт. | I don't have my pen with (on, about) me. |
| При Пýшкине нóвая рýсская литератýра тóлько начинáлась. | In Pushkin's time modern Russian literature was just beginning. |
| При Пётрé Велúком бы́ло мнóго вóйн. | Under Peter the Great there were many wars. |
| При всём тóм я́ вáм не вéрю! | Moreover I don't believe you! |
| Нó при всём тóм óн мнé дáл дéньги. | But for all that, he gave me the money. |

**7.** Врéмя 'time' is a neuter declined like úмя:

| N-A sg. | G-P-D sg. | I sg. | N-A pl. | G pl. | P | D | I |
|---|---|---|---|---|---|---|---|
| врéмя | врéмени | врéмёнём | временá | времён | времёнáх | –áм | –áми |
| úмя | úмёни | úмёнём | именá | имён | имёнáх | –áм | –áми |

Note that *врéмя идёт*. Проходúть *пройтú* (cf. XVI 1.71) is more specific to mean "pass, go by" of time. It is used chiefly in the past and the future:

| | |
|---|---|
| Прошлó пя́ть лéт (векóв). | Five years (centuries) went by. |
| Прошлó мнóго врéмёни. | Much time passed. |

**8.** **Перед** with time expressions denotes a time immediately before, while **до** is without specification. Thus *перед* револю́циёй семнáдцатого гóда means late in 1916 or early in 1917, whereas *до* револю́ции could mean any time at all prior to the revolution.

**9.1** In writing dates with numerals, it is the Russian custom to put the day first, with an Arabic numeral, followed by the month, which is symbolized by a *Roman* numeral: 5/IV = April 5th.

**9.2** As an abbreviation for the ordinal which denotes a century, Roman numerals are used: в XX веке = в двадцáтом вéке; войны XVII в. = вóйны семнáдцатого вéка.

## УПРАЖНЕНИЯ

**A.** Here are some dates of Russian rulers (cf. § 9 above). The first is the birth, the second the date of accession to the throne, the last the death.

For each ruler make the following sentences:

1. ___ was born in ___.
2. He became tsar in ___, when he was ___ years old.
3. He died in ___, when he was ___ years old.
4. He was tsar for ___ years, from ___ to ___.

In the cases where a more specific date is given, state the dates first with day and month and year, then with month and year only, and finally with year alone.

| | | | | | |
|---|---|---|---|---|---|
| Ива́н IV Васи́льевич | | 1530 | | 1533 | 1584 |
| Фёдор Ива́нович | 11/V | 1557 | | 1584 | 6/I 1598 |
| Бори́с Годуно́в | о́коло | 1551 | | 1598 | 13/IV 1605 |
| Васи́лий Ива́нович Шу́йский | | 1552 | | 1606 | 1610 |
| Михаи́л Фёдорович Рома́нов | | 1596 | 21/II | 1613 | 1645 |
| Алексе́й Миха́йлович | | 1631 | | 1645 | 1676 |
| Фёдор Алексе́евич | | 1662 | | 1676 | IV 1682 |
| Пётр I (Вели́кий) | 30/V | 1672 | | 1682 | 28/I 1725 |
| Екатери́на I Алексе́евна | | 1684 | | 1725 | 1727 |
| Пётр II | | 1715 | | 1727 | 1730 |
| А́нна | | 1693 | | 1730 | 1740 |
| Иоа́нн (Ива́н) VI Анто́нович | 12/VIII | 1740 | 5/X | 1740 | 1741 |
| Елизаве́та Петро́вна | 18/XII | 1709 | | 1741 | 25/XII 1761 |
| Пётр III Фёдорович | | 1728 | | 1761 | 1762 |
| Екатери́на II (Вели́кая) | | 1729 | | 1762 | 1796 |
| Па́вел | | 1754 | | 1796 | 11/III 1801 |
| Алекса́ндр I | | 1777 | | 1801 | 1825 |
| Никола́й I | | 1796 | | 1825 | 1855 |
| Алекса́ндр II | | 1818 | | 1855 | 1/III 1881 |
| Алекса́ндр III | | 1845 | | 1881 | 20/X 1894 |
| Никола́й II | | 1868 | | 1894 | 1917 |

Note: from Peter I on, the official title was импера́тор (императри́ца) but царь (цари́ца) continued to be used.

**B.** Read and translate:[1]

1. Где вы́ бы́ли четы́рнадцатого ию́ля ты́сяча девятьсо́т три́дцать второ́го го́да в полови́не тре́тьего но́чи? 2. В Сою́зе Сове́тских Социалисти́ческих Респу́блик живёт две́сти миллио́нов челове́к. 3. Когда́ Ю́рий Аки́мович ста́л судьёй? 4. Мо́й оте́ц бы́л в Росси́и в ты́сяча девятьсо́т трина́дцатом году́ и опя́ть по́сле войны́, в два́дцатом и́ли два́дцать пе́рвом году́. 5. Госпожа́ Никола́евская уже́ забыва́ет францу́зский язы́к, хотя́ при жи́зни му́жа у ни́х до́ма почти́ всегда́ говори́ли по-францу́зски. 6. Хотя́ мо́й оте́ц роди́лся в Росси́и, о́н почти́ всю́ жи́знь жи́л в Аме́рике. То́лько оди́н ра́з, в ты́сяча восемьсо́т деся́том году́, о́н пое́хал туда́, чтоб уви́деть свою́ ба́бушку. 7. Сы́н Алексе́я Миха́йловича ста́л ру́сским царём в ты́сяча шестьсо́т во́семьдесят второ́м году́. 8. По́сле сме́рти свое́й жены́ до́ктор Васи́льев ста́л мно́го пи́ть. 9. В оди́ннадцатом ве́ке гла́вными ру́сскими города́ми явля́лись Ки́ев и Но́вгород. В то́ вре́мя ещё не́ было Москвы́. О Москве́ мы́ ничего́ не зна́ем до ты́сяча сто́ со́рок седьмо́го го́да. 10. В ты́сяча семисо́том году́ Росси́я начала́ войну́ с Ка́рлом Двена́дцатым. 11. Колу́мб откры́л Аме́рику оди́ннадцатого октября́ ты́сяча четы́реста девяно́сто второ́го го́да. 12. При жи́зни моего́ де́душки Герма́ния начина́ла войну́ два́ ра́за, в ты́сяча восемьсо́т семидеся́том году́ и опя́ть в ты́сяча девятьсо́т три́дцать девя́том году́. 13. Всю́ неде́лю, когда́ мы́ на рабо́те, вре́мя идёт ме́дленно, а суббо́та и воскресе́нье прохо́дят о́чень бы́стро. 14. Она́ мне́ позвони́ла то́лько для того́, чтобы спроси́ть како́е сего́дня число́. 15. При каки́х царя́х жи́л Пу́шкин? О́н жи́л в пе́рвой че́тверти девятна́дцатого ве́ка, то́-есть при Па́вле Петро́виче, Алекса́ндре Па́вловиче и Никола́е Па́вловиче.

16. При Никола́е Второ́м бы́ло три́ револю́ции: пе́рвая в ты́сяча девятьсо́т пя́том году́ и две́ в ты́сяча девятьсо́т семна́дцатом году́, одна́ в феврале́ ме́сяце, а друга́я в октябре́. 17. Девятна́дцатого апре́ля ты́сяча семьсо́т се́мьдесят четвёртого го́да По́ль Реви́р пое́хал из Босто́на в Лексингто́н. Та́к ли э́то? 18. В како́м шта́те вы́ живёте? 19. Éсли вы́ не слу́шаете во вре́мя уро́ка, вы́ не бу́дете по́мнить, что́ говори́ла учи́тельница. 20. Кто́ бы́л после́дним царём Кита́я?

---

[1] From this point the distinction between stressed é and unstressed e will no longer be made in exercises, though it will be retained in examples and vocabularies. Therefore ё occurs only in the stressed syllable, and the difference between unstressed e and ё is unmarked. This conforms to accepted usage for stressed texts; in ordinary Russian books neither the accent-mark nor the two dots are used, apart from exceptional cases. Cf. App. I, § 11.1322.

Когда́ о́н у́мер? 21. Она́ сказа́ла, что Вашингто́н ста́л президе́нтом но́вой америка́нской респу́блики в ты́сяча семьсо́т восьмидеся́том году́, но́ э́то не та́к. 22. По́сле револю́ции, в феврале́ ты́сяча девятьсо́т семна́дцатого го́да, Росси́я ста́ла респу́бликой. 23. Они́ вы́ехали из Росси́и во вре́мя пе́рвой войны́, но́ перед револю́цией. 24. Е́сли ты́ не придёшь во́время сего́дня ве́чером, мы́ уе́дем и без тебя́. 25. Ива́ну в дере́вне бы́ло ску́чно, но́ вдру́г о́н уви́дел краси́вую де́вушку, и сейча́с же ему́ ста́ло ве́село. 26. Когда́ вы́ бу́дете идти́ сюда́, пожа́луйста, зайди́те в магази́н за вече́рней газе́той. 27. К концу́ ма́я его́ бра́тья прие́дут из Ки́ева, и в пе́рвых чи́слах ию́ня они́ все́ пое́дут в Кры́м дне́й на четы́рнадцать. 28. Когда́ они́ прие́хали в Соединённые Шта́ты? В двадца́тых года́х, о́коло два́дцать пя́того и́ли два́дцать шесто́го го́да. Они́ здесь уже́ че́тверть ве́ка. 29. Ты́сяча восемьсо́т со́рок восьмо́й го́д явля́лся го́дом револю́ций. 30. Е́сли бы вы́ послу́шались моего́ сове́та , ва́с бы́ли бы де́ньги, чтобы купи́ть всё э́то.

**C.** Say in Russian (a) "It was —" and (b) "on —", supplying each of these dates:

**1**. 2/V 1893. **2**. 5/II 1839. **3**. 15/VII 1937. **4**. 25/XII 1476. **5**. 21/X 1840. **6**. 3/III 1952. **7**. 4/IV 1521. **8**. 6/VI 1900. **9**. 19/XI 1953. **10**. 18/VIII 1803. **11**. 24/V 1899. **12**. 2/I 1922. **13**. 7/IX 1930. **14**. 8/VI 1948. **15**. 29/IV 1918. **16**. 30/III 1333. **17**. 14/VIII 1414. **18**. 17/I 1717. **19** 11/XI 1907. **20**. 31/XII 1919.

**D.** Write in Russian:

1. Why don't you drop in to see us next Tuesday? She always visits us on Tuesdays. 2. They will arrive in three months. 3. We are going to the country for the summer. We will be there from June 8th through Aug. 21st. 4. He writes so that he can live. 5. Last May it got very hot, but this spring it has been very pleasant in town. 6. There are 423 male students and 541 female students here. 7. He received the money from his mother in time, and he was able to buy the automobile. 8. What time is it? Oh, it's already after eight! 9. If I had time, I'd help you, but I ought to be at work in five minutes. 10. Has your friend found an apartment yet, or is he still living with you? 11. The war started on Sunday, Sept. 1, 1939. 12. In 1938 my friends went to Florida for three weeks in the spring. 13. In September the mornings are cold but the days are pleasantly warm. 14. She almost never arrives on time. 15. Take this money and buy some tea, some sugar, some milk, and two new cups.

16. Who became emperor after the death of Peter I?    17. Let's ask Mrs. Semënov whether she wants to go to the movies with us tomorrow evening at seven thirty.    18. They say that Ol'ga wants to become a teacher.    19. I talked with him by phone on the 23rd, and he said to tell you that he arrives by train on Monday the 5th.    20. During (при) his father's life, Peter Slonskij remained in Odessa, but after his death he went to Kiev and became a mechanic.    21. She called at 4:30, and although I told her you would be in town until supper she called again at quarter past five.    22. Did you see in the paper that Dr. Ivanov died in China last week? What a life he must have had!    23. He understands Russian only very little, although he has been in the Soviet Union several times, both during the war and since [= after] the war.    24. Did Nikita arrive on Tuesday or on Wednesday?    25. The Borodin brothers are still at work now, but it's almost time for them to come home.

## СЛОВАРЬ

Learn the rest of the cardinals *and* ordinals through *million/millionth*.

| | |
|---|---|
| вдру́г | suddenly, all at once |
| вели́кий | great |
| во́время (av.) | on time |
| вре́мя (neuter, § 7) | time |
| гла́вный (aj.) | chief |
| жизнь f. | life |
| импера́тор | emperor |
| императри́ца | empress |
| конéц (G. концá) | end |
| нача́ло | beginning |
| опя́ть | again |
| поэ́т | poet |
| президéнт | president |
| при (prep. + Prep. case) | see § 6 |
| рабо́та | work |
| на рабо́те | at work |
| респу́блика | republic |
| смéрть f. (IX 8.4b) | death |
| совéт | advice, counsel; council; soviet |
| совéтский (aj.) | soviet |
| соединённый | united |
| (соединён, -инёна́, -о́ -ы́) | |
| социалисти́ческий | socialist[ic] |
| сою́з | union; alliance; league |
| СССР [эсэсэсэ́р] | USSR |
| = Сою́з Совéтских Социалисти́ческих Респу́блик | |
| США [эсшаа́] | USA |
| =Соединённые Шта́ты Амéрики | |
| то́-есть (т.е.) | that is (i.e.) |
| хотя́ (и) | although |
| цари́ца | empress; tsaritsa |
| штáт | state (in US, Australia) |

| | | | |
|---|---|---|---|
| быва́ть быва́ют I | be (§ 2) | становѝться становѝтся I ⎫<br>ста́ть ста́нут Р ⎬<br>past ста́л, ста́ла, -о, -и ⎭ | become, begin, see § 4 |
| находѝться I ⎫<br>найтѝсь Р ⎭ | find self, be found, be situated | явля́ться явля́ются I ⎫<br>явѝться я́вятся Р ⎭ | be (§ 3), appear |

# ДВА́ДЦАТЬ ПЕ́РВЫЙ УРО́К

Она́ всегда́ во́дит дете́й в шко́лу.⎫
Она́ всегда́ во́зит дете́й в шко́лу.⎭

She always takes the children to school.

Он вёзёт да́му в го́род.

He is driving the lady into town.

Куда́ вёдёт э́та доро́га?

Where does this road lead?

Он вёл за́ руку весёлого ма́льчика, а на рука́х он нёс печа́льную де́вочку.

He was leading a jolly little boy by the hand, and carrying a sad little girl in his arms.

Она́ провела́ почти́ всю жизнь за грани́цей.

She spent almost her whole life abroad.

Лёта́ли ли вы на самолёте?

Have you been up in an airplane?

Мне́ необходи́мо бы́ть та́м за́втра у́тром; на́до туда́ лёте́ть.

It is absolutely necessary for me to be there tomorrow morning; I must fly there.

Ока́зывается, что они́ уже́ прилёте́ли из-за грани́цы.

It turns out that they have already arrived from abroad.

На́м придётся перее́хать за грани́цу, в Ита́лию.

We will have to move abroad, to Italy.

Он меня́ попроси́л перевёзти́ де́вочёк с го́р домо́й в го́род.

He asked me to drive the little girls home from the mountains to the city.

Этот лётчик перелёта́ет океа́н два́ ра́за в неде́лю.

This aviator flies across the ocean twice a week.

На́до бежа́ть, чтобы не опозда́ть на по́езд.

You must run so as not to miss the train.

Ма́льчики вы́бежали из шко́лы и ве́сёло бе́гали по двору́.

The little boys ran out of the school and gaily ran about the yard.

Что́ ва́м ну́жно?

What do you need?

Мне́ ну́жён каранда́ш.

I need a pencil.

Кому́ ну́жны э́ти ве́щи?

Who needs these things?

Это ну́жно сде́лать сего́дня.

This must be done today.

| Всё вéщи, котóрые óн привёз с собóй, оказáлись ненýжными. | All the things he brought with him turned out to be unnecessary. |
|---|---|
| Вáм не кáжётся, что бýдёт дóждь? | Don't you think it'll rain? |
| Óн казáлся богáтым, нó оказáлся совсéм бéдным. | He seemed rich, but turned out to be quite poor. |
| Ктó занимáёт эту квартúру? | Who is occupying this apartment? |
| Чéм вы занимáётесь? | What's your business? / What are you studying? |
| Я занимáюсь эконóмикой. | I'm studying economics. |
| Онá тáк умнá, чтó éй не нáдо мнóго занимáться. | She is so bright that she doesn't have to study much. |

---

**1.** Here are four more "going-verbs" (cf. VII, XVI).

| Imperfective | | Perfective | |
|---|---|---|---|
| Non-Determined | Determined | | |
| возúть вóзят | вёзтú вёзýт | повёзтú повёзýт | convey |
| водúть вóдят | вёстú вёдýт | повёстú повёдýт | lead |
| лётáть лётáют | лётéть лётя́т | полётéть полётя́т | fly |
| бéгать бéгают | бёжáть бегýт | побёжáть побёгýт | run |
| ND | D | Perfective | |

**1.01** The present forms of **бёжáть** (and **побёжáть**), are irregular: бегý and бегýт, but бежúшь, бежúт, бежúм, бежúте: побёгý, побёжúшь, etc.

**1.02** Note the past tense forms (cf. VII 5):

> вёзтú (повёзтú) — вёз, вёзлó, вёзлú, вёзлá (повёз)
> вёстú (повёстú) — вёл, вёлó, вёлú, вёлá (повёл)

**1.1** When compounded with prefixes, the ND becomes a simple imperfective and the D a perfective verb. The directional prefixes have the same meanings as with other going-verbs (see XVI; XVIII 8):

| I | P | | I | P | |
|---|---|---|---|---|---|
| ввози́ть | ввёзти́ | convey in, import | вводи́ть | ввести́ | lead in |
| вывози́ть | вы́везти | convey out, export | выводи́ть | вы́вести | lead out |
| привози́ть | привёзти́ | bring | приводи́ть | привёсти́ | bring |
| провози́ть | провёзти́ | convey thru, by | проводи́ть | провёсти́ | lead thru, by |
| отвози́ть | отвёзти́ | take away | отводи́ть | отвёсти́ | take away |
| увози́ть | увёзти́ | take away | уводи́ть | увёсти́ | take away |
| влета́ть | влете́ть | fly in | вбега́ть | вбежа́ть | run in |
| вылета́ть | вы́лететь | fly out | выбега́ть | вы́бежать | run out |
| подлета́ть | подлете́ть | fly up to | подбега́ть | подбежа́ть | run up to |
| прилета́ть | прилете́ть | come flying | прибега́ть | прибежа́ть | come running |
| пролета́ть | пролете́ть | fly thru, by | пробега́ть | пробежа́ть | run thru, by |
| отлета́ть | отлете́ть | fly away | отбега́ть | отбежа́ть | run away |
| улета́ть | улете́ть | fly away | убега́ть | убежа́ть | run away |

(It may be noted that certain of these verbs have additional meanings, not directly concerned with locomotion, which will not be mentioned here.)

**1.11**  Notice that the ND verb бе́гать бе́гают stresses the root, but with prefixes the imperfective stresses the -**а**: -бега́ть -бега́ют.

**1.2**  You can see that the English words "carry, take, bring" may translate various of the going-verbs. Keep in mind the distinctions of Russian and translate accordingly: **носи́ть** means "carry in one's hands, on one's person"; **води́ть** is "lead (by the hand) while walking"; **вози́ть** is "convey, carry, haul by means of some vehicle." For example:

| | |
|---|---|
| Он принёс кни́ги. | He brought the books (in his hands, walking). |
| Он привёз кни́ги. | He brought the books (by vehicle). |
| Он привёл дете́й. | He brought the children (walking, leading them). |
| Он унёс студе́нта. | He carried the student off (bodily, on his back). |
| Он увёл студе́нта. | He took the student away (leading him, walking). |
| Он увёз студе́нта. | He took the student away (in a vehicle). |

Similarly, the English "he arrived (departed)" may translate он пришёл (ушёл), он приéхал (уéхал), он прилéтéл (улéтéл).

**2.**   We have already had the verb **переводи́ть перевёсти́** in the derived
sense of "translate". The concrete meaning of the prefix **пере-** is "from
one place to another; across". For example,

| | |
|---|---|
| Егó перевёли́ на другу́ю ра-  <br>бóту. | They transferred him to other <br>work. |

**2.1**   The same prefix is used also with the other going-verbs:

переходи́ть перейти́ (перешёл, перешла́)
переезжа́ть переéхать
переноси́ть перенéсти́ (перенёс, перенёсла́)
перевози́ть перевёзти́ (перевёз, перевёзла́)
перелёта́ть перелётéть
перебега́ть перебежа́ть

There are some cases where they take an accusative object, others
where they use **через** + accusative, and there are also some less concrete,
derived meanings. E.g.:

| | |
|---|---|
| Óн перевёз детéй из дерéвни <br>в гóрод. | He moved the children from the <br>village into the city. |
| Óн йх перевёз через рéку. | He ferried them across the river. |
| Мы́ переéхали через мóст. | We drove across the bridge. |
| Óн перенóсит кни́ги на нóвую <br>кварти́ру. | He is carrying the books over <br>to the new apartment. |
| Когда́ óн переходи́л через <br>у́лицу, егó переéхал авто- <br>мóби́ль. | When he was crossing the street, <br>an automobile ran over him. |
| Они́ перешли́ грани́цу. | They crossed the frontier. |
| Перейдём к слéдующёму во- <br>прóсу. | Let us pass on to the next <br>question. |

**3.**   **Проводи́ть провёсти́** is used to mean "spend", of time:

| | |
|---|---|
| Ка́к вы́ проводи́ли та́м <br>врéмя? | How did you spend your time <br>(pass the time) there? |

**4.**   Notice that the D вёсти́ is used of roads, paths, halls, and the like:

| | |
|---|---|
| Эта у́лица вёдёт к университ <br>тéту. | This street leads to the uni- <br>versity. |

**5.1**  The adjective **нужный**, most frequently found in its short forms **нужён**, **нужно**, **нужна́**, **нужны** (or **нужны́**), means 'necessary' and may take a dative:

| | |
|---|---|
| Это ну́жная кни́га. | That is a necessary book. |
| Это всем ну́жная кни́га. | That is a book necessary for everyone. |

This adjective is the normal means for rendering English "to need":

| | |
|---|---|
| Эта кни́га мне́ нужна́. | This book *is necessary to me* ≅ *I need* this book. |

The negative particle **не** is written together with this adjective:

| | |
|---|---|
| Это никому́ нену́жная кни́га. | This is a book nobody needs. |

**5.2**  The short neuter form **ну́жно** is used to mean "it is necessary", or, with a dative representing the logical subject, "must, should, ought":

| | |
|---|---|
| Это ну́жно сде́лать. | This must be done. |
| Мне́ ну́жно сде́лать это. | I need to do this. |
| Ему́ не ну́жно приходи́ть, е́сли он не хо́чет. | He needn't come if he doesn't want to. |
| Тебе́ не ну́жно боя́ться. | You needn't be afraid. |
| Не ну́жно бы́ло говори́ть ему́ это. | You didn't have to tell him that |

Here the negative particle **не** is written separately.

**5.21**  With infinitives, *ну́жно* may be replaced by **на́до**: это на́до сде́лать, мне́ на́до сде́лать это, ему́ не на́до приходи́ть, не на́до боя́ться.

**6.**  The impersonal **прихо́дится** (**придётся**, **приходи́лось**, **пришло́сь**) means "it is absolutely necessary, unavoidable", and takes a dative:

| | |
|---|---|
| Мне́ пришло́сь вы́йти ра́но. | I had to leave early. |
| Ва́м придётся рабо́тать всю ночь. | You will have to work all night. |

**7.1**  Notice that the verb **каза́ться** I **показа́ться** P 'appear' may be used (1) as a personal verb, with the subject in the nominative and with a predicate instrumental, (2) as an impersonal, in 3rd singular neuter, with a dative, or (3) as a parenthetical phrase with adverbial meaning. For example:

| | |
|---|---|
| 1) Он ка́жется у́мным. | He appears to be intelligent. |
| Он ка́жется ребёнком. | He looks like a child, seems a child. |

2) Мне́ ка́жется, что о́н уме́н.　　It seems ⎰　　⎱ ⎰he is intelligent.
　 Мне́ ка́жется, что о́н ребёнок.　 to me ⎱ that ⎰he's a child.
　 Мне́ ка́жется, что бу́дет до́ждь.　I think ⎰　　 ⎱it will rain.
　 Мне́ ка́жется, что э́то хоро́-　　　　　　　　　⎱this is a good
　 шая кни́га.　　　　　　　　　　　　　　　　　 book.

3) Ка́жется, о́н не понима́ет.　　Apparently he doesn't understand.
　 Он, ка́жется, зна́ет де́ло.　　He seems to know his business.
　 Ка́жется, бу́дет до́ждь.　　　It looks like rain.
　 Всё, каза́лось, шло хорошо́.　Everything was apparently going
　　　　　　　　　　　　　　　well.

**7.2**　The closely related verb **ока́зываться** I **оказа́ться** P is used to mean "prove to be, turn out"; for example:

　 Он оказа́лся у́мным.　　　　He turned out to be intelligent.
　 Оказа́лось, что о́н уме́н.　　It turned out that he was in-
　　　　　　　　　　　　　　　telligent.

**8.1**　Note these means for expressing the *result* of an action:

　 Он *та́к* бы́стро говори́т, *что* я́　He speaks *so* fast *that* I don't
　 не понима́ю.　　　　　　　　understand.
　 Он бы́стро говори́т, *та́к что* я́　He speaks rapidly, *so* (with the
　 не понима́ю.　　　　　　　　result) *that* I don't understand.
　 *Поэ́тому* я́ не понима́ю.　　　*Therefore* I don't understand.

**8.11**　Observe that English "so that" is sometimes ambiguous, for it may also express purpose, "in order to". The context usually makes the meaning clear. Compare:

　 Он объясня́л *та́к, что́бы* мы́ всё　He explained *so that* we all
　 понима́ли.　　　　　　　　　*might understand.*
　 Он объясня́л *та́к, что* мы́ всё　He explained *so that* we all
　 понима́ли.　　　　　　　　　*understood.*

The *та́к* in either sentence could also be rendered "in such a way that".

**8.2**　To express *cause:*

　 *Та́к как* о́н бы́стро говори́т, я́　*Since* he speaks rapidly, I don't
　 не понима́ю.　　　　　　　　understand.
　 Я́ не понима́ю, *потому́ что* о́н　I don't understand *because* he
　 бы́стро говори́т.　　　　　　speaks rapidly.

**9.** The nouns **река́** 'river', **рука́** 'hand, arm', **гора́** 'mountain' and **голова́** 'head' have shifting accents (cf. XVII 12 and App. III, p. 351).

| N | G | A sg. | N-A | Prep. |
|---|---|-------|-----|-------|
| река́ | реки́ | ре́ку | ре́ки | река́х |
|  |  | за́ реку |  |  |
| рука́ | руки́ | ру́ку | ру́ки | рука́х |
|  |  | за́ руку | на́ руки |  |
| гора́ | горы́ | го́ру | го́ры | гора́х |
|  |  | по́д гору |  |  |
| голова́ | головы́ | го́лову | го́ловы | голова́х |
|  |  | на́ голову |  |  |

За́ реку means '(to) beyond the river', за́ руку 'by the hand'; compare по́д руку 'by the arm'. На́ руки is 'into the arms', на рука́х 'in the arms'. В го́ру means 'uphill', по́д гору 'downhill'.

**10.** English "not until" is rendered by "only at", without negation. For example, О́н прилете́л то́лько в се́мь 'he arrived only at seven' ≅ He didn't arrive until seven.

**11.** You will have observed that while there is quite a number of possible formal relationships between the infinitive and the third person plural, some of the relationships occur in a larger number of verbs than others. Indeed, five patterns account for the overwhelming majority of Russian verbs, although the other types are represented by many of the most common and useful verbs.

For the commonest patterns (the so-called *productive* patterns, to which any newly-coined verb will belong), it is enough to know only one form in order to predict all the others. From now on, therefore, only the infinitive will be given for the 5 groups defined below: the 3rd plural and all other forms can be predicted from the infinitive alone.

(1) infinitive in **-овать** (**-евать**) implies 3rd pl. in **-уют** (**-юют**). End-stress in infinitive (**-ва́ть**) means **-у́ют** [see V 4.21]: stress on any other syllable is constant for all forms: интересова́ть интересу́ют; сове́товать сове́туют.

(2) other infinitives in **-ать** (or **-ять**) imply 3rd pl. in **-ают** (**-яют**), with the stress on the same syllable: чита́ть чита́ют, объясня́ть объясня́ют, де́лать де́лают.

(3) infinitive in **-е́ть** implies 3rd pl. in **-е́ют**: уме́ть уме́ют.

(4) infinitive in **-нуть** implies 3rd pl. in **-нут**, with the same stress: верну́ть верну́т, дви́нуть дви́нут.

(5) infinitive in **-ить** implies 3rd pl. in **-ят** (**-ат**) with no change of stress: говори́ть говоря́т, реши́ть реша́т; гото́вить гото́вят, ко́нчить ко́нчат.

We will of course continue to give the 3rd plural for all other cases: for the relatively common types like *писа́ть, лежа́ть, стоя́ть*, and *получи́ть*, and for rarer patterns like those of *умере́ть, пить, сесть, мочь,* and *войти́*.

In the vocabularies, the 3rd pl. is given only once if it is the same for perfective and imperfective: e.g. **каза́ться ка́жутся** I **показа́ться** P implies **пока́жутся**.

## УПРАЖНЕНИЯ

**A.** Using the proper forms of **ну́жный**, translate all the possible combinations:

| I, you, he, she, we, the judge, Uncle Peter, that pilot, those Englishmen, my mother, poor grandfather | need/s/ need needed | a new automobile, a big apartment, that French magazine, a cup of coffee, my pen, work; new autos, big apartments, those French magazines, my pens and pencils. |
|---|---|---|

**B.** Read and translate:

1. Счастли́вая Ли́за побежа́ла в свою́ ко́мнату.  2. В про́шлом году́ мо́й бра́т ста́л занима́ться медици́ной. Че́рез три́ го́да о́н бу́дет до́ктором.  3. За́втра я́ перее́ду на но́вую кварти́ру.  4. Пти́ца пролете́ла над мое́й голово́й.  5. Молода́я по́лька занима́лась амери́канской литерату́рой восемна́дцатого ве́ка.  6. Бори́с Ива́нович о́чень бога́тый.  У него́ е́сть да́же сво́й аэропла́н, та́к что о́н мо́жет лета́ть, куда́ хо́чет.  7. Де́ти бе́гали по поля́м.  8. Цари́ца та́к гро́мко звони́ла, что три́ де́вушки вбежа́ли в одну́ две́рь, а четвёртая в другу́ю.  9. Она́ на́с всю́ду вози́ла, всю́ду води́ла и пока́зывала всё, что бы́ло ну́жно ви́деть в го́роде.  10. Ники́та с бра́тьями Петро́выми уже́ всё сде́лали, та́к что тебе́ не придётся рабо́тать.  11. Ка́к ва́м нра́вится на́ш но́вый профе́ссор? Не ка́жется ли о́н у́мным и весёлым?  12. Кни́ги до́ктора Сми́та занима́ют мно́го ме́ста в э́той ко́мнате. Я́ хочу́, что́бы о́н и́х перенёс в до́м свое́й ма́тери.

13. Ко́стя опя́ть опозда́л, хотя́ я ему́ сто́ ра́з говори́л, что мы́ хоти́м улете́ть ро́вно в се́мь.   14. Хотя́ о́н и бои́тся лета́ть, бе́дный де́душка реши́л полете́ть сего́дня в По́льшу, где́ умира́ет его́ бра́т.   15. Оказа́лось, что э́та доро́га ле́сом ведёт в ту́ бе́дную дере́вню, где́ ба́бушка про́шлым ле́том покупа́ла сы́р и ма́сло.

16. На большо́м аэродро́ме самолёты прилета́ют ка́ждые два́дцать мину́т.   17. Доро́га оказа́лась плохо́й. На́м пришло́сь е́хать о́чень ме́дленно.   18. Мо́й дя́дя всегда́ говори́л, что америка́нцам языки́ не нужны́, но во вре́мя войны́ оказа́лось, что о́н са́м до́лжен бы́л учи́ться кита́йскому языку́.   19. Илья́ Ильи́ч опозда́л на собра́ние докторо́в в Ки́еве, хотя́ о́н и прилете́л на пе́рвом аэропла́не.   20. Вы́ уже́ лета́ли когда́-нибудь? Коне́чно я лета́л, я да́же перелете́л океа́н четы́рнадцать ра́з.   21. Попроси́те её купи́ть на́м ча́ю и вина́.   22. Спроси́те до́ктора, где́ его́ жена́ купи́ла э́ти ве́щи.   23. Её тётя всегда́ каза́лась счастли́вой, но оказа́лось, что она́ совсе́м несча́стлива.   24. Для э́той де́вочки то́лько лётчики мо́гут бы́ть геро́ями. Она́ говори́т, что сама́ бу́дет лётчицей и геро́йней.   25. Я́сно бы́ло, что о́н не отве́тит на вопро́с учи́теля.   26. Э́та де́вушка о́чень умна́, та́к что е́й не на́до мно́го занима́ться.   27. Хотя́ пого́да сего́дня плоха́я, самолёты, ка́жется, летя́т.   28. Каки́м о́бразом вы́ гото́витесь к экза́мену?   29. Она́ ка́жется совсе́м ребёнком, хотя́ е́й уже́ семна́дцатый го́д.   30. Я́ шёл домо́й не то́й доро́гой и таки́м о́бразом не встре́тил ва́с.

31. Каза́лось, о́н не понима́л, хотя́ вы́ и говори́ли по-ру́сски.   32. Я́ в сре́ду лечу́ в Кры́м.   33. Я́ слы́шал, ка́к о́н не́сколько ра́з выбега́л в коридо́р, когда́ звони́ли у две́ри.   34. В Москве́ судья́ вози́л на́с всю́ду и да́же води́л на́с по музе́ям.   35. Францу́зский студе́нт ка́ждый де́нь получа́ет пи́сьма и газе́ты из-за грани́цы.   36. Ма́ленькая пти́ца влете́ла в окно́ и до́лго лета́ла по ко́мнате. Наконе́ц она́ опя́ть нашла́ окно́ и вы́летела.   37. Э́та две́рь ведёт пря́мо на у́лицу.   38. Мы́ ви́дели, ка́к де́ти бежа́ли за ни́м.   39. Каки́м о́бразом вы́ е́дете в А́страхань? Вы́ пое́дете автомоби́лем и́ли по́ездом и́ли полети́те на самолёте?   40. У ни́х бы́ло о́чень ве́село, ме́сяц пролете́л как оди́н де́нь.   41. Ива́н бе́ден, зато́ умён, ве́сел и сча́стлив.   42. Мне́ не совсе́м я́сно, почему́ э́ти гра́ждане перее́дут отсю́да.   43. Обыкнове́нно мы́ е́здим в го́род у́тренним по́ездом, но сего́дня мы́ опозда́ли на него́ и на́м пришло́сь дово́льно до́лго жда́ть авто́буса.   44. Пти́цы прилета́ют весно́й, а улета́ют опя́ть о́сенью.   45. Где́ они́ прово́дят ле́то? Ка́жется в гора́х.   46. На́ш самолёт вы́летел ра́но у́тром.   47. О́н говори́л гро́мко и я́сно, та́к что все́ хорошо́ слы́шали и

понима́ли.   48. Э́ти лётчики лета́ют из Испа́нии в Герма́нию ра́з в ме́сяц.   49. Де́ньги мне́ нужны́ не послеза́втра, а сего́дня!   50. Во́т что́ Пу́шкин написа́л о саранче́ [locust] в ты́сяча восемьсо́т два́дцать четвёртом году́:

Саранча́
Летѐ́ла, летѐ́ла —
И сѐ́ла.
Сиде́ла, сиде́ла,
Всё съѐ́ла,
И вно́вь улетѐ́ла.          [вно́вь = опя́ть]

**C.**   For written and/or oral translation into Russian:

1. Yesterday Ivan Borisovich arrived by train from Nóvgorod and then he left at once for Moscow on a big new French airplane.   2. The plane on which he flew usually leaves the airport at 5:30 in the morning, but yesterday it was late and did not leave (§ 10) until ten to eight.   3. When we were waiting with him, we saw many planes arrive (trans. 'saw how ... arrived') from airdromes in America and (from) abroad.   4. The judge'll arrive (flying) in Moscow tomorrow, late in the evening. The plane usually arrives at 10:25.   5. He himself is a flier, you know, and flies almost every day.   6. Man flew for the first time only in the 20th century, in 1903.   7. It was a pleasant warm evening; the children were gaily running about the yard and birds were flying about over their heads.   8. One of the children, a pretty little girl, suddenly ran into the house and after a minute she came running out again; she was carrying something in her hand.   9. All the citizens (m + f) were running across the fields toward the river.   10. See the Chinese woman whom Ivan is taking into that restaurant!   11. Ivan is going to the movies tonight, but he won't take me with him!   12. If you will take these books and carry them to my car, which is in front of the Petrovs' house, I will take them over to the new apartment for you. Someone will have to take them out of the car; I cannot carry anything.   13. You don't have to talk so loudly; we all hear you well.   14. He seemed to be a flier, but it turned out that he had never been up in an airplane.   15. He brought me the wrong book. This is a book no one needs.   16. When she was little she was interested in medicine and wanted to become a doctor. Then in school she became interested in languages, and in the university she started to study languages. Now two days ago she met a flier and says she is going to learn to fly.   17. These useless books take up a lot of room. Can't you

take them away, or give them to somebody? 18. The poor old teacher (f)
asked me to buy these things, and although they seemed quite useless
to me, I felt very sorry for her, and so I bought them. Now I must ask
my wife whether there is room in the house for them. 19. When it is clear,
we can (= it is possible for us to) see the mountains, and the road which
leads across the river up (= uphill) and into the forest. 20. Ask Ivan
when he can bring the children to (see) us, and ask him to bring my
watch at the same time. It must be on the table in his mother's room.

## СЛОВАРЬ

| | | | |
|---|---|---|---|
| аэродро́м | airdrome | несчастли́вый | unhappy |
| голова́ (§ 9) | head | (несча́стлив) | |
| гора́ (§ 9) | mountain | ну́жно (§ 5.2) | one must |
| в го́ру | uphill | ну́жный | necessary |
| под го́ру | downhill | (ну́жён ну́жно ну́жны́ нужна́) | |
| грани́ца | frontier, border | [о́браз] | (shape, form, mode, image) |
| за грани́цей | abroad | | |
| за грани́цу | (to) abroad | каки́м о́бразом | how? in what way? |
| из-за грани́цы | from abroad | таки́м о́бразом | thus, in this way |
| гро́мкий | loud | океа́н | ocean |
| (гро́мок, -мко; громка́) | | поэ́тому | therefore |
| двор E | yard, court | пти́ца | bird |
| на дворе́ | outside, outdoors | река́ (§ 9) | river |
| при дворе́ | at court (royal) | самолёт | airplane |
| доро́га | road | совсе́м | entirely, quite |
| зато́ | instead; to make up for it | счастли́вый | happy |
| коридо́р | hall, corridor | (сча́стлив -а) | |
| лётчик | aviator ⎱ flier | так как | since, for |
| лётчица | aviatrix ⎰ | так что | with the result that |
| ме́сто (pl. места́) | place | так ... что | so ... that |
| на́до + Dat. + inf. (§ 5.21) | one must | я́сный | clear |
| нену́жный | unnecessary | (я́сён я́сно; ясна́) | |
| необходи́мый | indispensable | | |

занима́ть I
заня́ть займу́т Р } оссиру, take up

past за́нял, -о, -и; заняла́

занима́ться I
заня́ться Р } be occupied with (Instr.), be engaged in; study

past занялся́, -ло́сь -ла́сь -ли́сь

каза́ться ка́жутся I
показа́ться Р } seem (see § 7.1)

ока́зываться I
оказа́ться
ока́жутся Р } turn out (§ 7.2)

опа́здывать I
опозда́ть Р } [на + Acc.] be late (for)

пере- see § 2

прихо́дится
приходи́лось
придётся
пришло́сь } + Dat. + inf. must, have to

сади́ться I
се́сть Р } land (of planes), come to rest, perch (of birds, etc.)

слы́шать слы́шат I
imperative слу́шай[те]
услы́шать Р } hear

води́ть вёсти повести́;  в-, вы-, при-, про-, от- у-води́ть
вози́ть вёзти повезти́:  в-, вы-, при-, про-, от- у-вози́ть
бе́гать бежа́ть побежа́ть: в-, вы-, при-, про-, от- у-бега́ть
лёта́ть лёте́ть полёте́ть: в-, вы-, при-, про-, от- у-лёта́ть } see § 1

## For review

**A.**  1. Remember, don't write anything.  2. I will explain everything once more.

3. At exactly a quarter to eleven on Saturday  June fifth, the comrade will be walking slowly on 34th street toward the station.  4. When you catch sight of him you will approach him and say, "Hello, the weather is fine today; do you think it will rain?" 5. He will answer, "It rarely rains on Tuesdays, give me some sugar please." 6. You will give him the photographs and walk quickly away.  7. The next day, either at 8:30 AM or between three and four PM, a woman will phone you at the club.  8. She will say, "Let someone who speaks Russian come to the phone!"  9. You must answer, "Vanja cannot go out today, please ask Vera to come visit him here."  10. The woman will then tell you where you must go to receive the money which was promised to you.

11. Now repeat! Don't forget anything!

**B.** 1. Have you seen an old big blue book with photographs of people and towns and villages and fields and forests and many other things? 2. It's a Russian book which I took from the library yesterday afternoon for Marija Ivanovna Petrov. 3. Mrs. Petrov explained to me why she wanted to see it. 4. Friends at the meeting last Wednesday told her they had read about the book in the morning paper. 5. It is very rare and expensive, and the library just got it from a Russian general who died recently. 6. They say that in it there are several photographs of Nóvgorod, the city in which she was born, and perhaps even a photograph of the very factory in which her father worked for many years. 7. You remember that after the death of the father, when she was only four years old, she moved to her grandmother's. 8. With Anna Petrovna Tolstoj and Igor' Sergeevich Ivanov she used to go to the Crimea every winter for two months. 9. They stayed in the Crimea from January fifth to March second. 10. Marija Ivanovna had to study music and French there. 11. [It was] there [that] she first met Ivan Petrovich. 12. He was a poor but handsome and jolly student who gave lessons to rich young ladies. 13. Since he never had any money, he dressed very badly and ate only soup, bread, and tea— without sugar, of course. 14. Then he still wanted to be a poet and was studying literature. 15. Later he suddenly became interesting in natural sciences and decided to become a doctor. 16. During the revolution he and the Borodin brothers left [travelled away from] Russian for [= to] China. 17. From there he came to the United States with his comrades. 18. She had arrived here from Germany in 1931.

# УРО́К ДВА́ДЦАТЬ ПЕ́РВЫЙ а

| | |
|---|---|
| Я уве́рен, что здесь продаю́т ну́жные нам материа́лы. | I'm sure that they sell the materials we need here. |
| Как то́лько ко́нчится семе́стр, я улечу́ в Евро́пу. | As soon as the semester ends I'll fly to Europe. |
| Они́ пригласи́ли всех тала́нтливых арти́стов на ве́чер. | They invited all the talented performers to a party. |
| Должно́ быть, пригласят и вас. | Probably they'll invite you too. |
| Мы пое́дем к ним в го́сти. | We'll go visit them. |
| Я не знако́м ни с го́стем ни с го́стьей. | I'm not acquainted either with the male guest or the female guest. |
| Го́стью предста́вили арти́сту. | They presented the guest to the performer. |
| Го́стю предста́вили худо́жницу. | They presented the artist to the guest. |
| В про́шлом семе́стре у нас бы́ли заня́тия по ру́сскому языку́. | Last semester we had Russian lessons. |
| Заня́тия продолжа́ются и в э́том семе́стре. | The lessons continue this semester too. |
| Она́ продолжа́ла крича́ть на го́стя. | She continued to shout at the guest. |
| На́ша го́стья бу́дет игра́ть роль А́нны Каре́ниной. | Our guest will play the part of Anna Karenina. |
| Он там игра́ет большу́ю роль. | He's very important there. |
| К сча́стью, э́то не игра́ет ро́ли. | Fortunately it is of no importance. |
| Э́то как раз тот материа́л, кото́рый мне ну́жен. | This is precisely the material I need. |
| Предста́вьте себе́, как то́лько муж уе́хал, она́ продала́ дом. | Just imagine, as soon as her husband went away, she sold the house! |
| Я то́лько стара́юсь помо́чь вам. | I'm only trying to help you. |

**1.** Summary of negation in Russian.

**1.1** The most general negative is the particle **не** placed immediately before the word it negates (cf. VI 11, XI 12). Some examples:

| | | |
|---|---|---|
| *i* | Она́ **не** пи́шет хорошо́. | She doesn't write well. |
| *ii* | Она́ **нехорошо́** пи́шет. | " |
| *iii* | Она́ пи́шет **не** о́чень хорошо́. | She doesn't write very well. |
| *iv* | Она́ пи́шет о́чень **нехорошо́**. | She writes very poorly. |
| *v* | **Не** кричи́те на меня́! | Don't shout at me! |
| *vi* | Кричи́те **не** на меня́! | Don't shout at *me* (...)! |
| *vii* | Я **не** купи́ла шля́пу. | I didn't buy the[1] hat. |
| *viii* | **Не** я купи́ла шля́пу. | *I* didn't buy a/the hat. |
| *ix* | Я купи́ла **не** шля́пу ... | I bought not a hat ... |

*i* and *ii* differ in emphasis as in the examples on page 79. That it is the adverb which is negated is emphasized by omitting the space between the negation and the adverb (although this usage is not clear to many Russian writers). *iv* has a more strongly negated adverb, since the *о́чень* modifies the negation itself. *v* is a normal prohibition, but *vi* is rather "Go ahead and do some shouting, but don't shout at me, shout at someone else." Ordinarily the other person would be named (*а на Ва́ню* 'but at Vanja'). *vii* is a normally negated statement, but in *viii* it is the subject that is denied, not the statement: "*I* wasn't the person who bought a (or the) hat, although perhaps someone else did so." *ix* negates the object, but not the subject or the verb. It is unfinished, since it implies that the act was completed but with a different object (*а ша́пку* 'but rather a cap').

**1.2** **Нет** can be regarded as two separate words:

**1.21** It is the general impersonal negation 'there is/are not' and represents the present tense, with **не́ было** for past and **не бу́дет** for future (VI 1.1, 1.3, 1.42). It is often used in conjunction with **не** + genitive to mean "not have" (VI 5). It *always* requires the genitive of the object or objects whose absence is being specified.

| | |
|---|---|
| **Нет** ли у ва́с госте́й? | Don't you have guests? |
| **Не́ было** об э́том анекдо́та? | Wasn't there a joke about that? |

NB: Do not confuse the genitive *required* by the impersonal **нет** with the genitive that ordinarily replaces the accusative after a negated transitive verb: see § 5 below.

[1] See § 5 below.

**1.22**   It is the particle or sentence-substitute 'no'.

| | |
|---|---|
| Вы понима́ете? **Не́т**, не понима́ю. | Do you understand? No, I don't. |
| Óн про́дал до́м? **Не́т**, не про́дал. | Did he sell the house? No, he didn't. |

Note that the Russian is likely to omit the **не́т** and merely give the negated verb (Не понима́ю. Не про́дал.).

It is used as a sentence-substitute in asking about alternatives:

| | |
|---|---|
| Ты пойдёшь или **не́т**? | Are you going or not (or aren't you)? |
| Óн э́то сде́лал или **не́т**? | Did he do it or not (or didn't he)? |

**1.221**   Contrary to English usage, the Russian **да́** and **не́т** ordinarily confirm or deny the correctness of a question:

| | |
|---|---|
| Вы его́ не зна́ете? Да́, не зна́ю. | Don't you know him? No. |
| Ты не закры́ла две́ри? Не́т, закры́ла. | Didn't you close the door? Yes. |

Roughly, then, the first means, "Yes, the negative statement is true; I do not know him", and the second, "No, the negative statement is not true, for I did close it." However one can also answer the first question with a simple **не́т**.

**1.3**   **Ни** is an emphatic negative, always used in conjunction with **не** or **не́т** (present of не́ было). Doubled, it renders "neither...nor" or "not either...or":

| | |
|---|---|
| Я́ **не** чита́л **ни** статьи́ **ни** расска́за. | I didn't read either the article or the story. |

Remember the use of **ни** with forms of **оди́н** (XVI 8.1) and the phrase **ни ра́зу** (IXa 2). Contrast the sentences:

| | |
|---|---|
| **Ни** оди́н го́сть меня́ **не** зна́л. | Оди́н го́сть меня́ **не** зна́л. |
| Мы́ **ни** ра́зу **не** приглаша́ли его́. | Мы́ **не** ра́з его́ приглаша́ли. |

**Ни** combines with interrogative pronouns and adverbs to make them negative: **никто́, ниче́й, ничто́, никако́й, никогда́, нигде́, никуда́, ниотку́да** (II 5.1, 5.3). Remember that English has alternate forms: not *any*body/*no*body, *not any*thing/*no*thing, *not any*where/*no*where, etc. One single negative in a sentence is enough in English: *No*where did I see anyone or hear anything. Russian demands repeated specification of the negative: Я **нигде́ не** ви́дел **ни**кого́ и **не** слы́шал **ни**чего́.

Do not forget that when forms of **никто́, ниче́й, ничто́, никако́й** are used with prepositions, the preposition is inserted *after* the **ни** and the expression is written as three units (XIV 10).

| | |
|---|---|
| Я **ни** с **каки́ми** солда́тами **ни** о **чём** не говори́л. | I didn't talk about anything with any soldiers. |

**2.** Observe the force of the double negatives:

| | |
|---|---|
| Я **не** мо́г и́м **не** жела́ть сча́стья.[1] | I couldn't help wishing them luck. |
| Это **не** мо́жет **не** игра́ть та́м ро́ли. | This can't help but be of importance there. |

**3.** Notice that English "unless" is approximately equivalent to "if... not"; in Russian always **е́сли не**:

| | |
|---|---|
| I'll come *unless* it rains. ≅ I'll come *if* it doesn*'t* rain. | Я приду́, **е́сли не** пойдёт до́ждь. |

**4.** For English "not until", see XXI 10.

**5.** The genitive is regularly required as the direct object of a negated verb (III 9). Yet the accusative does occur, especially in colloquial language. No one has managed to delimit this usage, and many of the statements grammarians have made are demonstrably faulty. Here are some general considerations.

The accusative direct object of a negated verb ordinarily designates something quite concrete; it is very clearly specified and really the logical focal point of the sentence. Most commonly it will be a person (specified by name or status), but it may be a thing that is defined either by concretizing modifiers (like "this, my") in the same sentence or else by its general importance and previous specification in the larger context. For example:

| | |
|---|---|
| Вы́ не встреча́ли **Та́ню** и **Пе́тю**? | Didn't you run into *Tanja* and *Petja*? |
| Он не понима́ет **жену́**. | He doesn't understand *his wife*. |
| Я не чита́л **его́ статью́**. | I haven't read *his article*. |

[1] Read Lessson XXV, § 5.

This specific and emphatic accusative is very likely to be put at the beginning of the sentence as a further underlining of its logical importance:

| | |
|---|---|
| **Письмо́** я не получи́л. | I didn't get *the letter.* |
| **Рабо́ту** я ещё не ко́нчил. | I haven't finished *the work* yet. |

Note here the English use of "the"; translation omitting this definitizer would be inaccurate. Cf. *Письма́* я не получи́л — a more general denial 'I didn't get *a (any)* letter'.

The direct object of an infinitive that is governed by a negated verb may be genitive, but in today's language it is more likely to be accusative (V 12). Use of the genitive tends to strengthen the negation, but the nuance of meaning is insignificant.

| | |
|---|---|
| Я не могу́ посла́ть **телегра́мму**, нет де́нег. | I can't send a/the telegram, I have no money. |
| Я не хочу́ посыла́ть **откры́тки** всем знако́мым, э́то ску́чно. | I don't want to send postcards to all my acquaintances, it's boring. |

The use of the accusative is extremely rarely *required* after a negated transitive verb, but there are instances where it is preferred. The genitive then sounds somewhat stilted. On the other hand, there are a great many contexts that do require the genitive. The foreigner is safer to use the genitive always, running the risk of sounding stilted from time to time, but avoiding the greater risk of being downright wrong.

**6.** **Уро́к** is the most general word for "lesson" in all senses. It sometimes means "homework". **Заня́тие** 'occupation, work' is more commonly used, ordinarily in the plural, for "studies, classes" at the college level.

| | |
|---|---|
| Э́то бу́дет хоро́ший уро́к для него́! | That'll be a good lesson for him! |
| Все бы́ли { на уро́ке. { на заня́тиях. | Everyone was { at the lesson. { in class. |
| Каки́е у тебя́ уро́ки в шко́ле? | What sort of lessons do you have in school? |
| Каки́е у вас заня́тия в университе́те? | What sort of studies do you have at the university? |
| У нас мно́го уро́ков. | We have a lot of homework. |

## УПРАЖНЕНИЯ

**A.** **1.** Read and translate these sentences as they stand.

**2.** Change the direct to indirect discourse. For example:

Он ей сказал: «Я пойду!» → Он ей сказал, что он пойдет.

Он ей сказал: «Иди!» → Он ей сказал, чтобы она шла.

1. Он спросил: «Когда начнутся занятия?»
2. Он попросил её: «Продайте мне эту синюю птицу!»
3. Он сказал нам: «Я позвоню Римскому-Корсакову, как только приду домой.»
4. «Я уверена, что занятия продолжаются до июня,» — объясняла нам она.
5. «Уйди, ты мне мешаешь,» он крикнул на Илью.
6. Как только Анна вошла, она закричала: «Муж почему-то продал нашу кровать!»
7. Гости спрашивали: «Почему этот ребёнок всё кричит и кричит?»
8. Она вам скажет: «Продолжайте вашу работу, я подожду.»
9. Она крикнула: «Сядь и сиди!»
10. Они спросили меня: «Можно пригласить ещё несколько гостей?»

**B.** 1. Say in Russian all possible combinations of the following:

| He | $\left\{ \begin{array}{l} \text{came} \\ \text{will come} \end{array} \right\}$ | $\left\{ \begin{array}{l} \text{this} \\ \text{last} \\ \text{next} \end{array} \right\}$ | $\left\{ \begin{array}{l} \text{Wednesday, year, summer, Octo-} \\ \text{ber, week, Sunday, spring, month,} \\ \text{June, evening, Friday, fall, April,} \\ \text{Tuesday, winter} \end{array} \right.$ |
|---|---|---|---|

2. Say in Russian: "It happened on —", substituting each of the dates given:

**1.** 9/XII 1984. **2.** 4/II 1010. **3.** 6/VI 1919. **4.** 3/VII 1487. **5.** 12/X 323. **6.** 11/VIII 1902. **7.** 18/X 1260. **8.** 5/IX 909. **9.** 19/II 1975. **10.** 1/III 1504. **11.** 8/XI 1940. **12.** 24/VII 1899. **13.** 31/I 296. **14.** 10/IV 1865. **15.** 14/VIII 746. **16.** 13/XII 2001. **17.** 17/III 1230. **18.** 16/VI 1790. **19.** 2/V 1356. **20.** 15/V 1803. **21.** 7/I 1666. **22.** 20/XI 1748. **23.** 23/VI 1790. **24.** 21/IV 1111. **25.** 30/IX 1910.

**C.** 1. Он кричит, что мы не по той дороге поехали. 2. Что-то очень важное, кажется, случилось в Китае. Вы не слышали последние новости по радио? —Да, я не слышал. Ничего не знаю. 3. Гости приезжают, главным образом, на своих автомобилях. 4. Вы, должно́ бы́ть, почему́-нибудь не хоти́те мне́ э́того сказа́ть. —Не́т, я́ вам сейча́с скажу́. 5. Ничьи́ дела́ его́ не интересу́ют? —Да́, о́н интересу́ется то́лько сами́м собо́й. 6. Ва́ша го́стья говори́ла та́к гро́мко, что её нельзя́ бы́ло не слы́шать во всём до́ме. 7. Е́сли бы то́лько я́ посове́товался с ва́ми об э́том! Но́ к сожале́нию ва́с не́ было в лаборато́рии. 8. Оте́ц хоте́л, что́бы я́ пе́редал ва́м приве́т и пожела́л от него́ всего́ лу́чшего. 9. На его́ сча́стье, о́н мо́жет продолжа́ть рабо́ту у Па́влова в лаборато́рии. 10а. Мы́ как ра́з об э́том говори́ли. 10б. Мы́ то́лько об э́том говори́ли. 10в. Мы́ то́лько что говори́ли об э́том. 10г. Как то́лько мы́ об э́том на́чали говори́ть, И́горь ушёл.

11. Ни сло́ва да́льше! Молчи́! Не засме́йся! 12. Вы́ уве́рены, что о́н все́х пригласи́л к на́м пи́ть ча́й? Е́сли та́к, ну́жно сейча́с же нача́ть гото́виться. 13. Она́ не все́х пригласи́т. 14. Петро́в да́л Ири́не ва́жную ро́ль, но к сожале́нию она́ почему́-то оказа́лась для неё о́чень тру́дной. Жа́ль, потому́ что она́ та́к хо́чет бы́ть арти́сткой! 15. Во вре́мя заня́тий Людми́ла Ю́рьевна всё молча́ла, и как то́лько услы́шала звоно́к, она́ вы́бежала куда́-то. Должно́ быть, что́-то случи́лось у неё до́ма. 16. На́ш го́сть говори́т, что не хо́чет ни на ко́м жени́ться. 17. Неуже́ли они́ собира́ются перее́хать отсю́да? —Да́, они́ переезжа́ют в Оде́ссу. 18. Несча́стный И́горь! Но́, ка́к всегда́ повторя́ла ба́бушка, не в деньга́х сча́стье. 19. Вы́ пришли́ как ра́з во́время, фи́льм сейча́с начнётся. 20. Когда́ же́нимся, —продолжа́л о́н, —то́ пойдём вме́сте в дере́вню, дорога́я моя́, бу́дем та́м рабо́тать!

21. Предста́вьте себе́, Бе́лый ста́л игра́ть большу́ю ро́ль в уни-верситете! 22а. В це́ркви не́ было ни одного́ ребёнка. 22б. В це́ркви не́ было одного́ ребёнка. 23. Я́ постара́лся объясни́ть ему́ свои́ иде́и, но о́н ника́к не понима́л. 24. Мы́ телеграфи́ровали его́ роди́телям, чтоб они́ продолжа́ли посыла́ть де́ньги его́ адвока́ту. 25. Нельзя́ не ве́рить, что она́ живёт то́лько для того́, чтобы сде́лать все́х люде́й счастли́выми. 26. Я́ о́чень стара́лся найти́ и́х но́вый а́дрес, но к сожале́нию ока́зывается, что никто́ не зна́ет, куда́ они́ перее́хали. 27. Нельзя́ бы́ло не заме́тить, что И́горя не́ было на собра́нии. 28. Она́ о́чень стара́ется, но ну́жно сказа́ть, что она́ не уме́ет рабо́тать. Но ка́к она́ мо́жет рабо́тать без уче́бников и словаря́? 29. На по́лке стоя́ло три́ рома́на: «Весна́ начала́сь ра́но», «Начина́лась жи́знь» и «Ключи́ сча́стья». Ни одного́ из ни́х мне́ не хоте́лось чита́ть. 30. По-мо́ему, на́ши заня́тия интере́снее в э́том семе́стре, че́м в про́шлом.

**D.** 1. Прочитайте фразу два раза по-русски, потом переведите ее на английский язык. 2. Эта красивая молодая дама казалась студенткой, но оказалось, что она одна из новых учительниц. 3. Книги являются моими хорошими друзьями. 4. Мы часто гуляли по этому старому парку. 5. Принесите мне какую-нибудь интересную книгу. 6. Его дядя мог рассказывать о самых интересных вещах! 7. Только сегодня мне дали пять журналов, которые мне обещали две недели тому назад. 8. Вам тоже, должно быть, было очень приятно видеть успехи нашего Саши. 9. Петров почему-то должен был уехать за границу. 10. Тебе нужно будет перед экзаменом повторить еще раз все эти уроки.

**E.** 1. Try to read through this story and these articles before Wednesday.

2a. Did you notice that the actor took the keys from the shelf over Igor's desk? b. Yes, I couldn't help noticing.

3a. Are you going anywhere for the summer? b. No, we're not going anywhere. c. I have to work all summer.

4. I'm sure that he will continue to try to sell those old chairs for you.

5. Let's invite the Rimskij-Korsakovs and the Sergeev-Censkijs to the club on Friday; they've invited us to their places [to themselves] several times, but we're never invited them anywhere.

6a. As soon as someone buys this last newspaper I can go have dinner. b. Unless I sell it, I'll have to stay here until seven o'clock.

7a. I'm sorry my aunt shouted at you. b. It doesn't mean anything. c. Unfortunately she always shouts at people she's talking with. d. Poor thing, she thinks that because she herself hears poorly no one will understand her unless she shouts.

8a. Please continue to read, I don't want to bother you. b. I'll just sit here and listen to the radio.

9a. The Petrovs have finally opened their own little store on the corner of the street behind the bank and that other street that leads to the new bridge. b. What can one buy there? c. They sell newspapers and magazines, and also tea, sugar, cheese, butter, and milk, but they don't sell books or meat or wine or beer.

10a. Someone was shouting in the street in front of our house this morning. b. Do you know what happened? c. — No, I didn't hear anyone.

**F.**  1. We need to review some of the materials we have gone through.
2. Let's start with a few easy sentences.  3. Here in our classroom we
see the walls and the floor and the ceiling and the windows and the door.
4. What else do you see, Ivan?  5. I see the blackboard, chalk, my own
notebook, an atlas, a Russian dictionary, and other students.  6. What
did he talk about, Vera?  7. He talked about several things; about the
blackboard, the chalk, his own notebook, about some book, a Russian
dictionary, and the other students.  8. What else do you see, Vera?
9. I see a lot of books on a shelf which is hanging on the wall, a map in
the corner, chairs, and through the window I see a very pretty garden,
and beyond the river is the forest.  10. Let's not think about gardens
and other things outside, let's talk about the things and people in this
room.

**G.**  1. That pretty student was only 17 when she met the handsome
young judge two years ago.  2. He asked her to marry him the next
week, but she didn't give him an answer for several months.  3. It's
clear that he loves her very much and that they are very happy.  4.
Have you ever dined at their place?  5. I visit there often.  6. I went
there last Friday and it was great fun [very jolly].  7. There were many
guests, I have rarely spoken with more interesting people.  8. Did you
know that the judge was a flier in Europe during the war?  9. Before
the war he lived for almost five years in Germany, and he speaks
German, French and Russian very well.

## СЛОВАРЬ

артист ⎫ performing
артистка [-ток] ⎭ artist, actor
гость m. *Epl obl* guest
(идти) в гости (go) visiting
(быть) в гостях (be) visiting
гостья [f., Gpl гостий] guest
занятиё (§ 6) occupation, work, pastime, studies, class
как раз just, exactly, precisely
как только as soon as
материал material

несчастьё unhappiness, misfortune, ill luck, calamity
несчастный unhappy, unfortunate, miserable; (aj as noun) wretch
никак (+ не) in no way
ничей ничьё ничья (+ не) nobody's, no one's
роль f. *Epl obl* role, part (in play)
семестр semester

к сожалéнию unfortunately  
счáстьё happiness, luck, fortune  
к счáстью luckily, fortunately  
на (моё) счáстьё luckily for (me)

талáнтливый talented  
увéренный sure, confident  
(short) увéрен увéрена  
(adverb) увéренно

---

желáть I  
пожелáть P $\Big\}$ (+ Gen.) desire

кричáть кричáт I shout  
крúкнуть P (give one) shout  
закричáть -чáт P (start to) shout

представлять  
предстáвить $\Big\}$ себé imagine

приглашáть I  
пригласúть P $\Big\}$ invite

продавáть продаю́т I  
продавáй[те]  
продáть продаду́т P $\Bigg\}$ sell  
продáм (XIII 4.1)  
прóдал -о -и, продалá

продолжáть I  
продóлжить P $\Big\}$ continue (transitive)

продолжáться I  
продóлжиться P $\Big\}$ continue (intransitive)

# ДВА́ДЦАТЬ ВТОРО́Й УРО́К

Их дом нове́е на́шего.

Their house is newer than ours.

Этот уро́к для ва́с ле́гче и́ли трудне́е девятна́дцатого?

Is this lesson easier or harder for you than the nineteenth?

Этот уро́к трудне́е все́х.

This lesson is the hardest of all.

Э́та зада́ча гора́здо ле́гче че́м та́.

This problem is much easier than that one.

Моя́ зада́ча была́ гора́здо интере́снее ва́шей.

My problem was much more interesting than yours.

Она́ лу́чше все́х говори́т по-неме́цки.

She speaks German better than anyone else.

Он лу́чше всего́ говори́т по-по́льски.

He speaks Polish better than anything else.

Его́ бра́т моло́же его́, а зато́ умне́е.

His brother is younger than he, but to make up for it he's brighter.

Его́ сестра́ ста́рше и бога́че его́.

His sister is older and richer than he.

Че́м да́льше я чита́л, те́м бо́льше мне́ нра́вился расска́з.

The further I read, the more I liked the story.

Дни́ тепе́рь стано́вятся всё длинне́е и длинне́е.

The days are now getting longer and longer.

Звони́те ка́к мо́жно ча́ще.

Call up as often as possible.

Говори́те ещё гро́мче!

Speak still more loudly!

Его́ мла́дший бра́т уже́ ста́л ста́ршим лейтена́нтом.

His younger brother has already become a senior lieutenant.

## COMPARISON

Russian does not have the clearcut three-fold division of degrees of comparison which is normal in English (high, high*er*, high*est*). It has beside the *positive* (the non-compared form) two sets of suffixes which indicate a greater degree of the quality expressed by the adjective (or adverb), but only from the context is it clear whether the meaning is *comparative* (e.g. high*er*) or *superlative* (e.g. high*est*).

### 1.0 FORMS

**1.1** The **simple comparative** is an unchanging form which is restricted in use (see § 2 below). Many adjectives do not have such forms, particularly adjectives in **-ский (-ско́й)** or **-овый (-ово́й)**.

There are two suffixes: **-e** and **-ee**.

**1.11** **-e** (which is never stressed) is regularly used with stems ending in **-к**, **-г**, or **-х** (which change to **-ч**, **-ж**, **-ш**, respectively) and with monosyllabic stems in **-ст** (which changes to **-щ**). The accent falls on the syllable immediately before **-e**.

| | | | | | |
|---|---|---|---|---|---|
| hot | жа́ркий | жа́рче | clean | чи́стый | чи́ще |
| loud | гро́мкий | гро́мче | dear | дорого́й | доро́же |
| soft | мя́гкий | мя́гче | stern | стро́гий | стро́же |
| simple | просто́й | про́ще | quiet | ти́хий | ти́ше |
| frequent | ча́стый | ча́ще | | | |

**1.12** **-ee** (-*éjə* or -*ijə*) is regularly used with all other stems. It is added to the stem of the positive (i. e. the N sg. masc. minus -ый, -ой, -ий). If the positive has only two syllables, or if the feminine short-form suffix is stressed, then the comparative suffix is stressed **-е́е**; otherwise the stress remains on the same stem-syllable as in the positive. For example:

| | positive | comparative | (short fem.) |
|---|---|---|---|
| new | но́вый | нов**е́е** | нова́ |
| fast | бы́стрый | быстр**е́е** | быстра́ |
| warm | тёплый | тепл**е́е** | тёпла́ |
| gay | весёлый | весел**е́е** | весела́ |
| cold | холо́дный | холодн**е́е** | холодна́ |
| interesting | интере́сный | интере́сн**ее** | интере́сна |
| pretty | краси́вый | краси́в**ее** | краси́ва |
| ordinary | обыкнове́нный | обыкнове́нн**ее** | обыкнове́нна |

In conversation, this suffix (particularly when stressed) may lose its final vowel, becoming -*éj* (-*ij*), but these forms are not often written: нов**éй**, быстр**éй**.

## 1.2   IRREGULARITIES

**1.21**   **-e** occurs only with a few stems not ending in **к г х** or **ст**:

| young | молодóй | молóже | rich | богáтый | богáче |

**1.22**   A number of stems have more complex changes before **-e**. Here are the most important of them:

| easy | лёгкий | лéгче | cheap | дёшёвый | дёшéвле |
| high | высóкий | вы́ше | long | дóлгий | дóльше |
| broad | ширóкий | ши́ре | low | ни́зкий | ни́же |
| far | далёкий | дáльше | narrow | у́зкий | у́же |
|  |  | дáлее | near | бли́зкий | бли́же |
| deep | глубóкий | глу́бже | short | корóткий | корóче |
| thin | тóнкий | тóньше | rare | рéдкий | рéже |

**1.23**   Anomalous:

| good | хорóший | лу́чше | big | большóй | бóльше |
| bad | плохóй | ху́же | small | мáленький | мéньше |

**1.24**   **Бóльше** and **мéньше** (whose adverbial use was mentioned in XV 12) serve as comparatives both to *большóй* and *мáленький* and to *мнóго* and *мáло*, that is, they may refer to quantity as well as size. The forms **бóлее** and **мéнее** ('more; less') are specialized as part of the compound comparative (cf. XII 8, and § 3 below), but they also occur in some common fixed phrases, such as **бóлее и́ли мéнее** 'more or less', and **тéм бóлее** 'the more so'.

**2.0**   These indeclinable forms in -e/-ee do not have any specific marks of gender, number or case, and their functions are limited. They are used (1) as predicate adjectives or (2) as adverbs (see § 5 below) or (3), in conjunction with the prefix **по-**, as a sort of encapsulated relative clause (see § 7 below).

**2.1**   As predicate adjectives they occur after some form of the verb 'to be', including the zero present tense, or after a limited number of verbs denoting change of status, like **стáть, сдéлаться** 'become'. In the first type they represent nominative case; in the second they take the place of instrumentals. For example:

| | |
|---|---|
| Я стро́г и она́ строга́. | I am stern and she is stern. |
| Я стро́г, а она́ стро́же. | I am stern but she is sterner. |
| Я ста́л стро́гим. | I became stern. |
| Я ста́л стро́же. | I became sterner. |

**2.2** In their function as predicate adjectives, the simple comparative forms ordinarily have the meaning of comparative.

| | |
|---|---|
| Ю́рий вы́ше меня́. | Jurij is taller than I. |

**2.21** However, when one member of a class is compared to all the other members of the same class, the English translation is usually a superlative:

| | |
|---|---|
| Ива́н вы́ше всех. | Ivan is tallest of all. |
| Во́лга длинне́е всех рек Евро́пы. | The Volga is Europe's longest river. |

That is, Ivan is taller than all the other people who might be involved in the comparison, and the Volga is longer than all the other rivers of Europe.

**3.** The **compound comparative,** formed by combining the adverb **бо́лее** 'more' with any of the declensional forms of an adjective, expresses the comparative (cf. XII 8).

| | |
|---|---|
| бо́лее дли́нный расска́з | a longer story |
| бо́лее широ́кая у́лица | a wider street |
| бо́лее жа́ркое ле́то | a hotter summer |
| бо́лее гро́мкие голоса́ | louder voices |
| в бо́лее но́вом до́ме | in a newer house |
| о бо́лее тру́дных рабо́тах | about harder jobs |
| бо́лее ти́хим го́лосом | in a softer voice |

**3.11** This construction is not used with the four adjectives *big, little, good,* and *bad,* but there are special adjectives expressing the comparative:

| | | | |
|---|---|---|---|
| big | **большо́й** | bigger | **бо́льший** |
| small | **ма́ленький** | smaller | **ме́ньший** |
| good | **хоро́ший** | better | **лу́чший** |
| bad | **плохо́й** | worse | **ху́дший** |

**3.12**  NOTE carefully the accent of **бóльший**. In many of the declensional forms only the accent distinguishes the comparative from the positive: e.g. *бóльшая*.

**3.13**  **Лýчший** and **хýдший** function also as superlatives: see XXIII 2.2.

## 4.  *Special cases.*

**4.1**  The adjective **стáрый** 'old' has both **старéе** and **стáрше**. The meaning of the latter is specifically "senior in the family or society", i.e. it is used only of the age of persons or of seniority in rank.

| | |
|---|---|
| Он стáрше брáта. | He is older than his brother. |
| *but:* Это здáниё старéе тогó. | This building is older than that one. |

**4.2**  Corresponding is the adjective **стáрший** "senior, elder". Analogous is **млáдший** "junior, born later, of lesser status". Contrasting to the concrete meaning of the comparatives **бóлее высóкий**, 'taller, higher' and **бóлее нúзкий** 'lower' is the abstract meaning of **вы́сший** and **нúзший**, which are used of status, not of actual size:

| | |
|---|---|
| стáрший брáт | elder brother, oldest brother |
| стáрший лейтенáнт | senior lieutenant (ranks above лейтенáнт) |
| млáдшая сёстрá | younger sister, youngest sister |
| млáдший лейтенáнт | second lieutenant (ranks below лейтенáнт) |
| нúзшая шкóла | lower school, elementary school |
| вы́сшая шкóла | superior school (i.e. college level) |

**5.**  For adverbs, the comparative may be expressed by the forms in **-е/-ее**.

| | |
|---|---|
| Он ужé работáёт бы стрéе. | He is already working more rapidly. |
| Он пúшёт лýчше меня. | He writes better than I do. |

**5.1**  Note that when one member of a class is compared with all the other members, the English translation frequently uses a superlative, as was the case with the adjective (2.21 above).

When the comparison is between *persons*, the Russian form for 'all' is **всéх**.

| | |
|---|---|
| Он пúшёт лýчше всéх. | He writes best of all. |

That is, *he* writes better than *everyone else* writes.

When *actions* are compared, the Russian form is **всего́**.

| | |
|---|---|
| Он пи́шет лу́чше всего́. | He writes best of all. |

That is, he *writes* better than he *does* anything else.

**6.**   Many adverbs in -o, particularly if they contain more than two syllables, may make a comparative by using **бо́лее**; e. g. *бо́лее обыкнове́нно* 'more ordinarily, more usually'.

**7.**   The prefix **по-**, used with the comparative forms in -**e**, softens the comparative meaning: e.g., **поме́ньше** 'a little bit less', **похолодне́е** 'somewhat colder, a little colder'. Comparatives with **по-** may follow a noun to which they refer, the meaning being approximately that of a relative clause ('which is/are ...'): e.g.

| | |
|---|---|
| Да́йте воды́ похолодне́е. | Give me somewhat colder water (water that's a bit colder). |
| Я хочу́ ко́мнату почи́ще и подёше́вле. | I want a room [which will be] a bit cleaner and cheaper [than the one I have]. |

Such forms are common, and ordinarily they are not listed under *no-* in the dictionaries: it is understood that they are to be looked up under the first letter of the comparative itself.

**8.**   "Than" in a comparison may be expressed

(1) by the genitive, if the things compared are nouns or pronouns:[1]

| | |
|---|---|
| Эта кни́га интере́снее то́й. | This book is more interesting than that one. |
| Этот сто́л бо́льше того́. | This table is bigger than that one. |
| Мо́й бра́т ста́рше сёстры́. | My brother is older than my sister. |

(2) by means of the conjunction **чём** (cf. XV 14):

| | |
|---|---|
| Ле́гче писа́ть карандашо́м, чём э́тим ста́рым перо́м. | It's easier to write with a pencil than with this old pen. |
| Ле́гче Ива́ну, чём Пётру́. | It's easier for Ivan than for Peter. |
| Он лу́чше пи́шет, чём говори́т. | He writes better than he talks. |

[1] Or, where idiomatic English translation usually has superlative without "than", if one member of a class is compared with all other members, cf. §§ 2 and 5.1 above.

The genitive may be used *only* with the short comparatives (forms in -e); with compound comparatives **чём** must be used.

Note that **чём** joins two things of the same sort: two adverbs, two verbs, two nouns *in the same case*, etc. The more restricted construction with the genitive may also be replaced by **чём** plus *nominative*: э́та кни́га интере́снее *чем та́*; э́тот сто́л бо́льше *чем то́т*; мо́й бра́т ста́рше *чем сестра́*. Note that **чём** must be used when the genitive would be ambiguous: Мо́й бра́т моло́же *чем ег*о́. 'My brother is younger than *his*.'

**9.**  The adverb **всё** 'always, continually' (cf. XVI 7) is often used with a comparative (which is normally repeated) to show the constant increase of the quality. It is not necessary to translate it specifically into English:

| | |
|---|---|
| Óн всё бóльше и бóльше занима́ется и всё ме́ньше и ме́ньше понима́ет. | He studies more and more and understands less and less. |
| Уро́ки стано́вятся всё ле́гче и ле́гче. | The lessons are getting easier and easier. |

**10.**  To express "as [intense] as possible", **как мо́жно** is used with the *comparative*: e.g.

| | |
|---|---|
| Приди́те как мо́жно ра́ньше. | Come as early as possible. |
| Óн лю́бит реша́ть как мо́жно бо́лее тру́дные зада́чи. | He likes to solve problems that are as hard as possible. |

**11.1**  To show that an increase in one quality is correlated with an increase in another, **чём...тём** is used: e.g.

| | |
|---|---|
| Чём трудне́е зада́чи, тём бо́льше они́ ему́ нра́вятся. | The harder the problems, the better he likes them. |

**11.2**  Occasionally these correlatives are omitted, as in the common proverb

| | |
|---|---|
| Ти́ше е́дешь, да́льше бу́дешь. | The more slowly [quietly] you go, the farther you get. ≅ Slow but sure. |

**11.3**  One of the correlatives is sometimes to be understood from the context:

| | |
|---|---|
| Те́м ху́же для него́! | So much the worse for him! |

**12.1**  **Ещё** + *comparative* intensifies the comparative meaning: e.g.

Óн говори́т ещё быстре́е.          He speaks even more rapidly.

**12.2**  The adverb **гора́здо** (or, colloquially, **куда́**) is used with a comparative to mean "much": e.g.

В Крыму́ гора́здо тёпле́е          In the Crimea it is much warmer
   чём в Москве́.                      than in Moscow.
Э́то куда́ дёше́вле.                This is much cheaper.

**13.**  Beside the adverb **по́зже** 'later' there is an alternate form **поздне́е**.

**14.**  The comparative **скоре́е** or **скоре́й** frequently is used simply to mean "hurry up, quickly", e.g.:

Скоре́й, скоре́й!                   Hurry up!
Я э́то сде́лаю скоре́е.            I'll do it quickly.

But note that when one quality is being compared to another (not one degree to another degree of the same quality), or one noun or verb to another, **скоре́е** is used: e.g.

Э́то скоре́е си́нёё, чём зелё-      This is blue rather than green.
   ноё.

Óн скоре́е умрёт, чём уе́дёт.      He'll $\begin{cases} \text{die rather} \\ \text{sooner die} \end{cases}$ than leave.

Э́то скоре́е расска́з, чём          This is $\begin{cases} \text{more a story} \\ \text{than} \\ \text{a story rather} \\ \text{than} \end{cases}$ a novel.
   рома́н.

**15.**  **Бо́льше не** means 'no longer', and is not significantly different from **уже́ не**; e.g.

Óн бо́льше не обе́даёт у ни́х.      He no longer dines with them.

## УПРАЖНЕНИЯ

**A.**  For oral drill:

1. Ivan's pencil is red, my pencil is redder, and Maria's pencil is reddest.  2. This book is blue, that book is bluer, and my younger brother's book is bluest.  3. This mountain is high, that one is higher, but the one across the river is the highest.  4. Our street is wide, your street is wider, but the main street is the widest.  5. Ivan lives near the school, Peter lives nearer, and we live nearest.  6. This river is clear and deep, the one near the village is clearer and deeper, but the one in the mountains is clearest and deepest.  7. The first war was long, the second was still longer, but the third was the longest of all.  8. This evening his mother is gay, his father gayer, and his little brothers and sisters gayest of all.  9. The ten o'clock train goes fast, the eleven o'clock goes faster, and the one o'clock goes fastest of all.  10. This restaurant is simple but expensive, the one in the station is less simple and more expensive, and the one in the club is least simple and most expensive.  11. Leningrad is far away, Moscow is farther, and Tashkent is farthest.  12. We arrived early (late), the Borodins arrived earlier (later), and Ivan arrived earliest (latest).  13. This book is difficult and boring, our history book (= book of history) is harder and more boring, and the economics book is hardest and most boring.  14. Dinner today was bad, breakfast was worse, supper last night was still (even) worse, and breakfast yesterday was worst of all.  15. Moscow is a big city, London is bigger, and New York is the biggest.  16. This bread is old, the bread we had last night was older, and the bread we had day before yesterday was oldest of all.  17. Anna is pretty, Nadezhda is prettier, and Ljubov' is prettiest of all. She is the prettiest student in the university.  18. His grandfather is strict, his mother stricter, and his uncles strictest of all.  19. This room is cold and unpleasant, that one is colder and unpleasanter, and that other little room is the coldest and most unpleasant.  20. His voice is clear and quiet, his older brother's voice is clearer and quieter, and their aunt's voice is clearest and quietest.  21. The child is happy, his sister is happier, and their mother is happiest.  22. This sentence is short, the last sentence is shorter, and the first sentence is shortest of all.  23. This wine is cheap but pleasant, that is cheaper and less pleasant, and the wine on the table is cheapest and least pleasant.  24. His wife is rich and his father is poor, her mother is richer and his sister is poorer, and her grandmother is richest and his grandfather is poorest.  25. This river is narrow, that one is narrower, and that third river is narrowest.

**B.** Read and translate:

1. Этот высóкий молодóй человéк, котóрый тáк грóмно смеётся, — брáт моегó адвокáта. 2. Вóт ширóкая, зелёная долúна, и тáм — ýзкая, бы́страя, óчень чúстая рекá. 3. Бéдный Ивáн! У негó тáк мáло дéнег, что óн дóлжен покупáть тóлько сáмые дешёвые вéщи. 4. Я рáно встаю́, тáк что мнé легкó приходúть в лаборатóрию рáньше всéх. 5. Нóвая учúтельница оказáлась молодóй, нó стрóгой. 6. У нúх всю́ду мя́гкие дивáны и крéсла. 7. Рекá в э́том мéсте широкá и óчень глубокá. 8. Онá пúшет простúе корóткие фрáзы, котóрые óчень легкó читáются. 9. Почемý вы́ не говорúте тúхо? Ребёнок спúт. 10. Эти бéлые платкú óчень дорогúе, нó хóчется úх купúть! 11. Эти сúние гóры кáжутся блúзкими, нó на сáмом дéле онú далекó. 12. Емý трýдно говорúть по-рýсски и ещё труднéе писáть. 13. Мóй стáрший брáт вы́ше и тóньше меня́, и говорúт óн всегдá грóмче. 14. Рéки в горáх обыкновéнно быстрéе и чúще, чéм рéки в долúнах. 15. Óн беднéе всéх в гóроде, и поэ́тому всегдá покупáет вéщи кáк мóжно дешéвле.

16. Чéм рáньше ты́ встáнешь, тéм лéгче тебé бýдет прийтú вóвремя на рабóту. 17. Хотя́ у нáс учúтель молóже вáшего, óн, кáжется, горáздо стрóже егó. 18. Садúтесь в э́то крéсло, онó мя́гче тогó. 19. Эта кнúга Достоéвского станóвится всё бóлее и бóлее рéдкой. 20. Мáленький мáльчик стоя́л перед нóвыми автомобúлями и дýмал, какóй из нúх красúвее. 21. Чéм быстрéе рекá, тéм глýбже онá станóвится. 22. Я люблю́ фрáзы попрóще и покорóче, онú лéгче длúнных. 23. Говорúте, пожáлуйста, потúше, в дóме спя́т. 24. Дáмы лю́бят вéщи не полýчше, а подорóже. 25. Я óчень люблю́ зúму и веснý, но бóльше всегó я люблю́ óсень. 26. Онá занимáется бóльше всéх в клáссе. 27. Говорúте погрóмче пожáлуйста, я плóхо слы́шу. 28. Идúте поскорéе, а тó мы́ опя́ть опоздáем на урóк. 29. Óн вы́ше нáс всéх, хотя́ я не дýмаю, что óн тáкже умнéе нáс всéх. 30. В лаборатóрии нáм бы́ло óчень жáрко, но здéсь кудá прия́тнее.

**C.** Write in Russian:

1. Is this coffee cheaper or more expensive than that which you bought yesterday? 2. The more you study, the more you learn [use 2nd sg. verb, without pronoun]. 3. The automobiles go faster and faster in our street. 4. Near the little old theater there is now a much larger and newer building in which there is a small theater and a restaurant which is much better than any in town. 5. There it is hotter in January than in June. 6. It rains more frequently in the summer and more rarely in the spring. 7. She talks more than anyone else. 8. Come

a little earlier so that we will be able to talk together without the others.   9. More quietly, children! Sister is talking on the telephone. 10. Maria's voice is louder than Anna's, but not so pleasant. Maria has a less loud and more unpleasant voice.   11. The wife is more intelligent than her husband, and the little child is most intelligent of all.

12. This is bad wine. It's much worse than the wine we drank in this restaurant last time.   13. This atlas is cheaper than that one, and it has more maps in it. It's a better atlas.   14. Ivan translates well, but Vera translates much better.   15. If you had learned all those words at the very beginning, it would be much easier for you to read these long sentences now.   16. This is rather a good book [a rather good b.]; it is shorter and more interesting than the one you showed me.   17. Speak as loudly as possible so that everyone may hear.   18. He arrived at the school before [earlier than] the other teachers.   19. Does it seem to you that Russian [XIV 5.3] is harder than English?   20. Anna dresses more quickly than Vera.   21. Who translates best? 22. His younger sons are students in Leningrad, and the eldest son has become a senior lieutenant somewhere abroad.   23. He writes longer and longer letters because he is getting more and more bored in the little village.   24. Since he saw that I was carrying a Russian book, the old man asked me whether I spoke Russian.   25. The Volga is longer than the Dnepr, and the Dnepr is longer than the Don.   26. It snows a lot here, but the snow is always deeper there in the higher mountains.   27. It is too cold in the mountains, no one lives there. But in the warmer valleys there are many houses.   28. The lower you go, the more houses you see.   29. Please help the younger children. You must remember that it is harder for them.   30. If you study more, the examination will seem easier to you.

## СЛОВАРЬ

| | |
|---|---|
| а то | or else, otherwise |
| вы́сший § 4.2 | superior, upper |
| го́лос (pl. голоса́) | voice |
| гора́здо + comparative | much |
| и так да́лее | and so on |
| и т. д. | etc. |
| Днепр *E* | Dnepr (river) |
| доли́на | valley |
| как мо́жно § 10 | as … as possible |
| куда́ + comparative | much |
| лейтена́нт | lieutenant |
| мла́дший § 4.2 | junior, younger |
| ни́зший § 4.2 | inferior, lower |
| по- | see § 7 |
| скоре́е | rather; see § 14 |
| ста́рший § 4.2 | senior, elder |
| тем | see § 11.1, 11.3 |
| тем бо́лее | the more so, all the more reason that |
| прочесть прочту́т P = прочита́ть past прочёл прочла́ прочли́ | |

*Adjectives* (classed according to short-form accents: see pp. 150–151).
NB: comparatives are not given here:  learn the forms listed on pp.
276–277.

| [A] бли́зкий | бли́зок бли́зко -зки; | близка́ | close, near |
|---|---|---|---|
| дёшёвый | дёшёв дёшёво -вы; | дёшёва́ | cheap |
| дли́нный | дли́нён дли́нно -нны; | длинна́ | long |
| дорого́й | до́рог до́рого -ги; | дорога́ | dear, expensive |
| зелёный | зе́лён зе́лёно зе́лёны; | зелёна́ | green |
| мя́гкий | мя́гок мя́гко -гки; | мягка́ | soft (see App.I, § 17.7) |
| ни́зкий | ни́зок ни́зко ни́зки; | низка́ | low |
| стро́гий | стро́г стро́го -ги; | строга́ | stern |
| ти́хий | ти́х ти́хо ти́хи; | тиха́ | quiet |
| то́нкий | то́нок то́нко -нки; | тонка́ | fine |
| у́зкий | у́зок у́зко у́зки; | узка́ | narrow (short-form often = *too* narrow) |
| ча́стый | ча́ст ча́сто ча́сты; | часта́ | frequent |
| чи́стый | чи́ст чи́сто чи́сты; | чиста́ | clean, pure |

| [C] высо́кий | высо́к высо́ко́ высо́ки́ высока́ | high, tall |
|---|---|---|
| глубо́кий | глубо́к глубо́ко́ глубо́ки́ глубока́ | deep |
| далёкий | далёк далёко́ далёки́ далёка́ | far, distant |
| коро́ткий | ко́ро́ток ко́ро́тко́ ко́ро́тки́ коротка́ | short |
| просто́й | про́ст про́сто́ про́сты́ проста́ | simple |
| широ́кий | широ́к широ́ко́ широ́ки́ широка́ | broad, wide |

## For review

**A.**   Прочтите и переведите:

| 1. Мы вошли в сад. | Мы вышли в сад. |
|---|---|
| 2. Птица влетела в окно. | Птица вылетела в окно. |
| 3. Он подошел к окну. | Он отошел к окну. |
| 4. Самолет прилетел в Москву. | Самолет улетел в Москву. |
| 5. Брат пришел к товарищу. | Брат ушел к товарищу. |
| 6. Когда я пришел домой, все уже пообедали. | Когда я пришел домой, все уже обедали. |
| 7. Уроки начнут в семь. | Уроки начнутся в семь. |
| 8. Все едут куда-то. | Все едут куда-нибудь. |

9. Он долго говорил с Петровым.

Он давно говорил с Петровым.

10. Он пришел работать.

Ему пришлось работать.

**B.** 1. In a small town on the quiet Don lived a very old man. 2. His name was Vasilij Jur'evich Mal'cev. 3. Nobody knew how old he was. 4. Some said that he must be 100 years old. 5. Others said that he was 75 or 80. 6. The old man [use noun старик *E*] himself only remembered that he was born in the reign of [see XX 6] Alexander II.

7. He had no wife, no children, no friends. 8. He lived alone in a very small house in which there were only two rooms. 9. Around the house there was a small garden, and he worked there when the weather was nice, in spring and summer and in the first weeks of September. 10. Sometimes he simply sat in the garden in the sunshine and watched the little birds which were flying about over his house.

11. He did not like to talk with people and the neighbors did not speak to him when they walked by his house. 12. Only one little boy came to see him from time to time.

13. His name was Vanja and he was 10 years old. 14. His family was very poor and often they had no money to buy bread. 15. Vanja used to come to see the old man on Saturdays and Sundays when he did not have to go to school. 16. The old man usually gave him some bread and milk and read him stories from an old book. 17. They liked each other and soon became good friends.

18. One Saturday toward the end of August, Vanja dropped in to see his friend. 19. He came into the house, stood at the door, and waited. 20. The old man was not in the first room. 21. Vanja went into the second room. 22. There he saw the old man sitting [= as he sat] in his chair.

23. He went up to him and said, "Hello", but Vasilij Jur'evich did not answer. 24. Vanja took his hand. 25. It was cold. 26. Suddenly Vanja understood that the old man had died.

27. The old man had seemed to be very poor but it turned out that he was rich. 28. When a judge went to Vasilij Jur'evich's house, he found several thousand rubles [рубль *E*] in a corner under some old German books. 29. There was also a letter which the old man had written in which he asked that all the money and also the house be given to Vanja, his little friend.

# ДВА́ДЦАТЬ ТРЕ́ТИЙ УРО́К

Это был труднейший уро́к! — This was a very hard lesson!

По-мо́ему, э́то са́мый тру́дный уро́к в кни́ге. — In my opinion, it's the hardest lesson in the book.

Я согла́сён с ва́ми. Э́тот уро́к трудне́е все́х други́х. — I agree with you. This lesson is harder than all the rest.

А́нна лу́чше все́х студе́ноток в университе́те. — Anna is the best of all the students in the university.

Я вчера́ чита́л кра́йне интере́сную статью́ о Пётре́ Вели́ком. — Yesterday I read an extremely interesting article about Peter the Great.

Жёна́ о́чень интересу́ётся нове́йшей францу́зской литерату́рой. — My wife is very much interested in contemporary French literature.

Э́тот рома́н ме́нее интере́сён чём то́т, кото́рый о́н написа́л в про́шлом году́. — This novel is less interesting than the one he wrote last year.

Э́ти часы́ сли́шком до́роги. Покажи́те мне́ други́е, пожа́луйста. — This watch is too expensive. Please show me another one.

Ива́н ча́сто хо́дит на конце́рты, ещё ча́ще хо́дит в теа́тр, но́ ча́ще всёго́ хо́дит в кино́. — Ivan often goes to concerts, more often to the theater, and most often to the movies.

Ве́ра пи́шёт ме́дленнее все́х. — Vera writes slowest of all.

Её бра́т та́к же умён, ка́к и она́. — Her brother is just as bright as she is.

Его́ сёстра́ така́я же у́мная, ка́к и о́н. — His sister is just as bright as he is.

Да́йте на́м тако́ё же вино́, како́ё мы́ пи́ли в про́шлый ра́з. — Give us the same kind of wine that we drank last time.

Моя́ ста́ршая сёстра́ бу́дёт ра́да ва́с ви́деть. — My older sister will be glad to see you.

Мы́ о́чень ра́ды э́тому. — We're very glad of that.

Я уве́рен, что о́н придёт во́время.  I'm sure that he'll come on time.

Ему́ понра́вилась та́ но́вая сту-  He liked the new student with
де́нтка с тёмными волоса́ми и  dark hair and blue eyes.
голубы́ми глаза́ми.

---

### 1. The Simple Superlative Adjective

**1.1** The suffix **-ейший** (and all declensional forms), added to the stem of the positive, makes an adjective which can serve in any gender, number or case, but *not* as a predicate *short*-form or adverb. This may be called the *simple superlative* (but cf. 1.4 below). The accent rules are like those for the simple comparative in **-ee** (XXII 1.12).

| | | |
|---|---|---|
| new | но́вый | нове́йший, нове́йшее, нове́йшая, -ейшие |
| fast | бы́стрый | быстре́йший |
| warm | тёплый | тёпле́йший |
| interesting | интере́сный | интере́снейший |
| cold | холо́дный | холодне́йший |
| ordinary | обыкнове́нный | обыкнове́ннейший |

The accent is exceptional in богате́йший, from бога́тый 'rich'.

**1.2** If the positive ends in **-к, -г, -х**, these consonants become **-ч, -ж, -ш**, and the suffix is **-айший**:

| | | | | | |
|---|---|---|---|---|---|
| great | вели́кий | велича́йший | deep | глубо́кий | глубоча́йший |
| high | высо́кий | высоча́йший | fine | то́нкий | тонча́йший |
| light | лёгкий | легча́йший | wide | широ́кий | широча́йший |
| soft | мя́гкий | мягча́йший | stern | стро́гий | строжа́йший |
| rare | ре́дкий | редча́йший | quiet | ти́хий | тиша́йший |

*Note:*

| | | | | | |
|---|---|---|---|---|---|
| low | ни́зкий | нижа́йший | close | бли́зкий | ближа́йший |

**1.3** The declined forms in **-ейший (-айший)** show an intense or extreme degree. If the context indicates that comparison is intended, then the English translation must be superlative. Otherwise the translation may be "extremely, very", or "a most" rather than "the most".

| | |
|---|---|
| Это интере́снейшёё письмо́. | This is a most interesting letter, an extremely interesting letter. |
| Это ёго́ интере́снейшёё письмо́. | This is his most interesting letter. |
| Я э́то сде́лаю в ближа́йшём бу́дущём. | I'll do that in the very near future. |
| Он живё́т в ближа́йшём до́ме. | He lives in the next (closest) house. |
| Во́лга длинне́йшая река́. | The Volga is a very long river. |
| Во́лга длинне́йшая река́ в Евро́пе. | The Volga is the longest river in Europe. |

**1.4**    The forms in **-ейший** are essentially bookish and are thus not frequent in conversation. As a general rule, it is best to avoid this form when translating an English superlative.

**2.1**    The adjective **са́мый**, used together with the positive, in any gender-case form, expresses the superlative (cf. XII 8). This is the *compound superlative*. It is the only form that *specifically* denotes superlative. For example:

| | |
|---|---|
| са́мый жа́ркий де́нь | the hottest day |
| са́мая широ́кая у́лица | the widest street |
| са́моё высо́коё зда́ниё | the tallest building |
| са́мые холо́дные зи́мы | the coldest winters |
| в са́мых мя́гких кре́слах | on the softest armchairs |
| к са́мому лу́чшёму студе́нту | toward the best student |

**2.2**    The adjectives **лу́чший** and **ху́дший** may also express the superlative, but to *specify* superlative they are used with **са́мый**:

| | |
|---|---|
| Она́ здесь лу́чшая студе́нтка. | She is the best student here. |
| Она́ са́мая лу́чшая студе́нтка. | She is the best student. |

**2.21** Note that there is no essential difference between:

| | | |
|---|---|---|
| са́мый большо́й | and са́мый бо́льший | the biggest |
| са́мый ма́ленький | са́мый ме́ньший | the smallest |
| са́мый хоро́ший | са́мый лу́чший | the best |
| са́мый плохо́й | са́мый ху́дший | the worst |

**3.**   You have already learned that the simple comparative used as a predicate adjective with **всех** has the meaning of the superlative (XXII 2.21).

| | |
|---|---|
| Она́ краси́вее всех студе́нток. | She is the prettiest of all the students. |

**4.**   To summarize the comparison of adjectives from the point of view of English:

*Russian expresses the COMPARATIVE by*

  (1) **бо́лее** + positive (all genders and cases), or
  (2) the indeclinable forms in **-e /-ee** and the four adjectives **бо́льший, ме́ньший, лу́чший, ху́дший**.

*Russian expresses the SUPERLATIVE*

  (1) *specifically*, by juxtaposing the appropriate form of the adjective **са́мый** to the adjective being compared, and
  (2) *non*-specifically, in the proper context,
    (a) by the suffix **-ейший (-айший)** in the appropriate declensional form; or
    (b) by the forms in **-e/-ee** + **всех** (only in predicate).

**5.**   The superlative of adverbs is rare. It can be made by the positive with **наибо́лее**: *наибо́лее интере́сно* 'the most interestingly'. But it is more often expressed by means of the *comparative* + **всего́** or **всех**, as explained in XXII 5.1.

| | |
|---|---|
| Он говори́т хорошо́ по-ру́сски, пи́шет *лу́чше* и чита́ет *лу́чше всего́*. | He speaks Russian well, writes better, and reads best of all. |
| Он говори́т по-русски *лу́чше всех*. | He speaks Russian best of all (i. e. better than anyone else). |

**6.**   The intensive prefix **наи-** may also be used with **бо́льший, бо́лее, вы́сший, ме́ньший, лу́чший, ху́дший, ме́нее,** and occasionally other adjectives and adverbs, to express a superlative. These are bookish forms.

**7.**   The prefix **пре-** has the meaning 'very, extremely': e. g. **предли́нный** 'very long, too long', **пренеприя́тный** 'extremely unpleasant'. It is bookish: you need to recognize it, but it is best not to use it.

**8.** A number of adverbs express degrees of intensity. For example: **вóвсе не** 'not at all', **наимéнее** 'least' (often called "negative superlative"), **мéнее** 'less' ("negative comparative"), **немнóго** 'somewhat', **довóльно** 'rather, sufficiently', **óчень** 'very', **совсéм** 'entirely, completely', **крáйне** 'extremely', **слишком** 'too [much]'. For example:

| | |
|---|---|
| вóвсе не интерéсная книга | a quite uninteresting book |
| наимéнее интерéсная книга | the least interesting book |
| мéнее интерéсная книга | a less interesting book |
| немнóго скучная книга | a somewhat boring book |
| совсéм скучная книга | quite a boring book |
| крáйне интерéсная книга | an extremely interesting book |
| слишком тёплая кóмната | a too warm room, too warm a room |

**9.** The comparison of equals is expressed by **тáк же...**, **кáк (и)** or **такóй же...**, **кáк (и)**. **Тáк** is used before short-form adjectives or adverbs, while **такóй** is used (in the appropriate declensional form) before long-form adjectives. For example:

$$\text{Мóй брáт} \begin{cases} \text{тáк же высóк,} \\ \text{такóй же высóкий,} \end{cases} \text{кáк и вы.}$$

My brother is (just) as tall as you.

Ивáн пишет тáк же хорошó, кáк (и) Пётр.

Ivan writes (just) as well as Peter.

**Такóй же...**, **какóй** means 'of the same kind...as'. For example:

| | |
|---|---|
| Это такáя же задáча, какáя у нáс былá вчерá. | This is the same sort of problem as the one we had yesterday. |

**10.** The adjective **рáд**, **рáда**, **рáды** 'glad' has only short forms. Notice that 'glad *of/at*' is **рáд** plus dative.

## УПРАЖНЕНИЯ

**A.** Read and translate:

1. Надéжда мóй ближáйший дрýг. 2. Вы пóмните, кáк во врéмя войны онá пóзже всéх ложилась и рáньше всéх вставáлась? 3. Онá всё ещё такáя же тихая, какóй былá всегдá. 4. Кáк и рáньше, онá бóльше всегó любит игрáть с сáмыми мáленькими детьми. 5. По-móему онá тáк же хорошó говорит по-рýсски, кáк и Михаил Петрóвич,

вы́ не согла́сны? 6. Мы́ уве́рены, что вы́ полу́чите письмо́ от неё в
са́мое ближа́йшее вре́мя. 7. Её ста́ршая сестра́ така́я же краси́вая,
ка́к и она́. 8. Она́ то́лько что прочла́ рома́н, кото́рый на́ш профе́ссор
перевёл с ру́сского языка́. О́н е́й не понра́вился. 9. Я́ согла́сен с
не́й. По-мо́ему, э́то наиме́нее интере́сный рома́н из все́х, кото́рые я́
неда́вно чита́л. 10. Заходи́те к на́м поча́ще. Мы́ всегда́ ра́ды ва́с
ви́деть. 11. Всё у на́с у́мные, но́ са́мый у́мный то́т, кто́ говори́т
ме́ньше все́х. 12. Э́тот уве́ренный в себе́ студе́нт, кото́рый обыкно-
ве́нно сиди́т за ва́ми, хо́чет бы́ть адвока́том. 13. О́н та́к же лю́бит
теа́тр, ка́к и я́.

14. О́н богате́йший челове́к! О́н живёт в са́мом большо́м до́ме в
го́роде. 15. У него́ до́ма всегда́ о́чень ве́село, веселе́е че́м у на́с, хотя́
у ва́с быва́ет не ме́нее ве́село. 16. У него́ све́тлые во́лосы и голубы́е
глаза́, а у его́ бра́та тёмные во́лосы и чёрные глаза́. 17. О́н та́к же
лю́бит теа́тр, ка́к и кино́. 18. Я́ уве́рена, что я́ вчера́ уви́дела в то́м
ма́леньком магази́не в то́й у́зкой у́лице за библиоте́кой таку́ю же
шля́пу, каку́ю ва́ша сосе́дка купи́ла во Фра́нции. И она́ совсе́м
недорога́! 19. Како́е из э́тих кре́сел са́мое дешёвое? Кра́сное кре́сло
та́к же дёшево, ка́к и зелёное, но́ бе́лое кре́сло немно́го деше́вле.
20. Де́душка прочёл на́м сего́дня то́т са́мый предли́нный расска́з,
кото́рый о́н уже́ чита́л на про́шлой неде́ле. 21. На конце́рте бы́ло
мно́го люде́й, кото́рые лю́бят нове́йшую му́зыку. 22. Че́м да́льше
о́н е́хал, те́м веселе́е ему́ станови́лось. 23. Са́д мое́й тёти ме́ньше
все́х в го́роде, но́ о́н са́мый краси́вый. 24. В са́мые жа́ркие дни́ я́
люблю́ ду́мать о са́мых холо́дных дня́х про́шлой зимы́. 25. По-
мо́ему на́ши уро́ки куда́ интере́снее в э́том году́, че́м в про́шлом.

**B.** Write in Russian:

1. They drink only the best wines. 2. The cheapest books are not
always the best books. 3. Do you see the pretty woman at the nearest
table? She's the very one I was telling you about yesterday. 4. Who
translates best? 5. That was an extremely difficult examination! But
it was easier than the examination in October. I never saw a harder
exam than that one. 6. The bank on Third Street used to be the tallest
building in the city, but now there are several taller ones. 7. The
oftener you repeat these words, the easier it will be for you to remember
them. 8. The Ivanovs promised to drop in on us in the very near
future. 9. I told them to come as soon as possible because we would
be going abroad in two weeks. 10. When you have read "Evgenij
Onegin", I am sure you will agree with me that Pushkin is the greatest

Russian poet. 11. This room is too small for us and too dark. Please show us another (which is) a bit larger and brighter. 12. Who was that extremely beautiful lady we saw Lieutenant Markov with at the concert last night? 13. Ol'ga may not be as pretty as Tanja, but she is much more intelligent. 14. All their children have light hair and blue eyes. 15. This exercise is just as short and simple as the last one. 16. This film is just as long and boring as the one we saw last week. 17. Please call us when you come to Moscow next month. You know that we are always glad to see you. 18. That self-assured young lady who is sitting at the next table is a Soviet aviatrix who just flew across the ocean by herself. 19. My wife is very unhappy because our neighbors bought the same kind of sofa we have. 20. I recently read an extremely interesting story about life in Berlin before the last war.

## СЛОВАРЬ

| | |
|---|---|
| вóвсе не | not at all |
| вóлос (see § 2, p. 211) | hair |
| глáз | eye |
| [*Epl* глазá, G. глáз] | |
| голубóй | light blue |
| (see § 3, p. 211) | |
| крáйне | extremely |
| наимéнее | (the) least |
| немнóго | somewhat |
| пре- | see § 7 |
| рáд -а -ы (§ 10) | glad |
| свéтлый | light |
| [свéтёл свéтло -ы: светлá] | |
| слúшком | too, too much |
| соглáсный | in agreement (with) |
| (с + Instr.) | |
| [соглáсён соглáсна] | |
| тáк же..., кáк (и) | as...as |
| такóй же..., какóй | of the same kind as |
| тёмный | dark |
| [тёмён, тёмнó -ы: тёмнá] | |
| увéренный | confident, assured |
| (short) увéрён увéрёна | |
| увéрёны | |
| (adverb) увéрённо | |
| увéрённый в себé | self-confident |
| чёрный | black |
| [чёрён, чёрнó -ы́ -á] | |

# ДВА́ДЦАТЬ ЧЕТВЁРТЫЙ УРО́К

| | |
|---|---|
| Дверь была́ закры́та. | The door was closed. |
| Он услы́шал че́й-то го́лос за закры́той две́рью. | He heard someone's voice behind the closed door. |
| Я сплю с откры́тым окно́м. | I sleep with the window open. |
| Письмо́ наконе́ц напи́сано. | The letter is finally written. |
| Я спроси́л, кто взял напи́санное бра́том письмо́. | I asked who had taken the letter written by my brother. |
| Ска́зано — сде́лано. | No sooner said than done. |
| Из ска́занного мы ви́дим, что э́тот вопро́с труде́н. | From what has been said we see that this question is difficult. |
| Оте́ц принёс обе́щанную кни́гу. | Father brought the promised book. |
| Ве́щи мои́ бы́ли оста́влены на ста́нции. | My things were left at the station. |
| Де́ти съе́ли оста́вленный на столе́ обе́д. | The children ate the dinner which had been left on the table. |
| К ним пришла́ хорошо́ оде́тая де́вушка. | A well dressed girl came to their place. |
| Уже́ решено́ — Петро́вы назову́т ребёнка Па́влом. | It's already decided — the Petrovs will name the child Paul. |
| Решённые Ива́ном зада́чи бы́ли напи́саны на доске́. | The problems solved by Ivan were written on the board. |
| За́нято ли э́то ме́сто? | Is this place occupied? |
| Зада́ча, реша́емая студе́нткой, о́чень трудна́. | The problem being solved by the student is very difficult. |
| Кни́га, чита́емая студе́нтом, была́ о́чень интере́сна. | The book being read by the student was very interesting. |
| Студе́нтка, реша́ющая зада́чу, стои́т у доски́. | The student solving the problem is standing at the board. |

| | |
|---|---|
| Студе́нты, чита́ющие ста́рые газе́ты, должны́ сиде́ть за э́тим столо́м. | Students reading old newspapers ought to sit at this table. |
| Он э́то обеща́л умира́ющему де́душке. | He promised this to his dying grandfather. |
| Студе́нтка, реша́вшая зада́чу, стоя́ла у доски́ и писа́ла. | The student who was solving the problem stood at the board and wrote. |
| Студе́нты, чита́вшие ста́рые газе́ты, сиде́ли за э́тим столо́м. | The students who were reading old newspapers were sitting at this table. |
| Студе́нтка, реши́вшая зада́чу, се́ла и ста́ла писа́ть. | The student who had solved the problem sat down and began to write. |
| Студе́нты, прочита́вшие газе́ты, оста́вили и́х на столе́. | The students who had read the newspapers left them on the table. |
| Де́ти, боя́вшиеся по́езда, запла́кали. | The children, who were afraid of the train, began to weep. |
| Стару́ха вела́ за́ руку пла́чущую де́вочку. | The old woman was leading a weeping little girl by the hand. |

---

## PARTICIPLES

**0.** The Russian verb system includes four sets of forms which combine the verbal meaning with the form and function of an adjective: the *participles*. They express aspect and tense and may take objects in the accusative or other cases and may be modified by adverbs, but they have the gender- and declensional-forms of adjectives.

There is a present and a past active participle and a present and a past passive participle. Of these only the past passive participle is common in conversation, although the others occur in the speech of the educated. All participles are of fundamental importance for journalistic, administrative, and scholarly writings.

**0.1** The passive participles, like most adjectives, have both long and short forms. Only transitive verbs (verbs which take an accusative object) normally have passive participles. Active participles have no short forms. Present participles (active and passive) can be formed only from im**p**erfective verbs.

**1.**   *The forms of the participles.*

**1.1**   The *present passive participle* is not found with all types of verb, and is formed regularly only from verbs with 3 pl. in **-ают** and **-уют** (**-яют/-ююют**). It is found with most verbs in **-авать** and a few (mostly the prefixed imperfectives of "going-verbs") in **-ить.**

The (long masculine) suffix is **-мый**. In verbs in **-авать**, this participle is in **-ава́емый**:

| | | |
|---|---|---|
| дава́ть дают | **дава́емый** | being given |
| *продава́ть продают [1] | **продава́емый** | being sold |

Otherwise the **-мый** replaces the **-т** of the 3rd *singular* (the accent being that of *1st* singular, cf. V 4.2):

| | | | |
|---|---|---|---|
| реша́ть реша́ют | **реша́е-т** | **реша́емый** | being solved |
| объясня́ть объясня́ют | **объясня́е-т** | **объясня́емый** | being explained |
| диктова́ть дикту́ют | **дикту́е-т** | **дикту́емый** | being dictated |
| вводи́ть вво́дят | **вво́ди-т** | **вводи́мый** | being brought in |
| люби́ть лю́бят | **лю́би-т** | **люби́мый** | being loved |

**1.11**   These participles have all the regular adjectival declensional forms. The short forms (e.g. реша́ем, реша́емо, реша́ема, реша́емы) are theoretically possible, but in fact occur only rarely.

**1.2**   The *past passive participle* has three possible (short masculine) suffixes: **-т, -н, -ён.**

NB: Relatively few verbs have the **т**-suffix, and most of those verbs are somewhat irregular in various ways — for the most part these forms must be learned simply as lists. *You should concentrate on* learning thoroughly *the rules under* (b) *and* (c) *on the next page,* for they concern the overwhelming majority of Russian verbs.

**(a)** the **-т** suffix is added to the *past-tense stems* of verbs in **-ереть**:

| | | | |
|---|---|---|---|
| *стере́ть | **стёр, стёр**ла | **стёрт** | wiped off |

and to the *infinitive stem* of

(1) verbs with infinitives in **-ыть, -оть, -уть**:

| | | |
|---|---|---|
| закры́ть закро́ют | **закры́т** | closed |
| забы́ть забу́дут | **забы́т** | forgotten |
| *заколо́ть заколю́т | **заколо́т** | stabbed |
| *обману́ть обма́нут | **обма́нут** | deceived |

---

[1] NB: In this and the next lesson, we give, for the sake of completeness of exposition, some forms which will not be used in the exercises; they will be marked with an asterisk.

(2) verbs with infinitives in **-ать/-ять** *and* present stem in **-н-** or
**-м-**:

| | | |
|---|---|---|
| нача́ть начн-у́т | **на́чат** | begun |
| заня́ть займ-у́т | **за́нят** | occupied |
| взя́ть возьм-у́т | **взят** | taken |

(3) the verbs **де́ть** 'put', **\*гре́ть** 'warm', **\*пе́ть** 'sing', **\*би́ть** 'strike',
**\*бри́ть** 'shave', **\*ви́ть** 'wind', **жи́ть** 'live', **\*ли́ть** 'pour', **пи́ть** 'drink',
**\*ши́ть** 'sew' and their compounds.

| | | |
|---|---|---|
| оде́ть оде́нут | **оде́т** | dressed |
| прожи́ть проживу́т | **про́жит** | lived through |
| вы́пить вы́пьют | **вы́пит** | drunk up |
| **\*уби́ть** убью́т | **уби́т** | murdered |

The accent is normally as in the past tense:

на́чал, на́чало, на́чали : начала́
на́чат, на́чато, на́чаты : начата́

(**b**) the **-н** suffix is added to the *infinitive stem* of verbs with infinitives
in **-ать (-ять)** or **-еть** excepting those mentioned (in **a** 2 and 3) above:

| | | |
|---|---|---|
| (про)чита́-ть | (про)чи́тан | read |
| (на)писа́-ть | (на)пи́сан | written |
| **\*(вз)волнова́-ть** | (вз)волно́ван | disturbed |
| **\*(со)бра́-ть** | (со́)бран | gathered |
| (у)ви́де-ть | (у)ви́ден | seen |
| (про)смотре́-ть | (про)смо́трен | looked through |

The accent is on the second vowel before the **-н**.

    **\*Прода́ть** 'sell' (and other prefixed forms of да́ть) have mobile stress as in the
past: про́дан, про́дано, про́даны: продана́.
    Unprefixed, **да́ть** has suffix stress: да́н, дано́, даны́, дана́.
    But negated: не́ дан -о -ы: не дана́.

(**c**) the **-ён** suffix is added

(1) to the stem of the *first person singular* (look at  V 4.1,  page 58!)
of verbs with infinitive in **-ить** (except those in [**a** 3] above). Accent is
normally that of 3rd *plural* present.

| | | | |
|---|---|---|---|
| реши́ть реша́т | **реш-у́** | **решён** | decided |
| объясни́ть объясня́т | **объясн-ю́** | **объяснён** | explained |
| положи́ть поло́жат | **полож-у́** | **поло́жен** | placed |

| | | | |
|---|---|---|---|
| купи́ть ку́пят | купл-ю́ | ку́плён | bought |
| пригото́вить пригото́вят | пригото́вл-ю | пригото́влён | prepared |
| встре́тить встре́тят | встре́ч-у | встре́чён | met |
| спроси́ть спро́сят | спрош-у́ | спро́шён | questioned |

NB: In the table of consonantal alternations given on p. 58, it was not noted that т alternates with both ч and щ, and д with ж, жд. The alternations т-ч and д-ж are normal in 1st sg., but far less frequent in the past pass. part. Sometimes a verb will have one alternation in 1st sg. and another in the participle. For this reason, for 3rd plurals in -тят and -дят, the 1st sg. and the participle will be given in vocabularies *if* they have щ, жд; otherwise the more typically Russian ч, ж will be derived by the rules:

| | | | |
|---|---|---|---|
| возврати́ть возвратя́т | возвращ-у́ | возвращён | returned |
| [роди́ться родя́тся | рож-у́сь] | рождён[1] | born |

(2) to the *present* stem (look at II 6) of verbs with infinitives in -ти or -сть, -зть. The participial suffix here is normally stressed -ён:

| | | |
|---|---|---|
| нёсти́ нёс-у́т | нёсён | carried |
| (по)вёзти́ (по)вёз-у́т | (по)вёзён | conveyed |
| (пере)вёсти́ (пере)вёд-у́т | (пере)вёдён | translated |
| *приобрёсти́ приобрёт-у́т | приобрётён | discovered |

Note that compounds of идти́ stress the syllable before the suffix:

| | | |
|---|---|---|
| пройти́ пройду́т | про́йдён | gone through |
| найти́ найду́т | на́йдён | found |
| [Exception: перейти́ | перейдён | crossed] |

(3) the -ён suffix replaces the -ёт of the 3rd singular of verbs in -чь (X 8, p. 124):

| | | | |
|---|---|---|---|
| *(ис)пе́чь (ис)пёку́т | (ис)пёч-ёт | (ис)пёчён | baked |
| *(с)же́чь (со)жгу́т | (со)жож-ёт | (со)жожён | burned |

**1.21** All of these are regular short-form adjectives. Those in -ён normally have end-stress: решён, решёно́, решёна́, решёны́.

**1.22** To make the long adjectival forms, add the regular adjectival suffixes -ый, -оё, -ая, -ые, and the other declensional endings to the

---

[1] The historical explanation is that the щ and жд in these forms are borrowed from Church Slavonic, while the ч and ж represent the native Russian ones. It is rare that Russian took over the 1st singular from CS, but since Russian owes almost its entire participal system to CS, it is more frequent that these forms display the "foreign" alternation. In a very few cases, both forms are found.

bases in -т, and -ный, -ноё, etc. to those in -н and -ён. (NB: this makes double -нн- in the long form!)

E.g. закры́тый, на́чатый, оде́тый; прочи́танный, решённый, ку́плённый, возвращённый, переведённый, на́йдённый, испёчённый.

The accent remains on the same syllable throughout the declension.

**1.3**   The *present active participle* is formed by replacing the -т of the 3rd plural present by -щий, -щёё, -щая, etc.

| | | |
|---|---|---|
| чита́ть, **чита́ю**-т | **чита́ющий, чита́ющёё, чита́ющая** | reading |
| писа́ть **пи́шу**-т | **пи́шущий, пи́шущая; пи́шущими** | writing |
| говори́ть **говоря́**-т | **говоря́щий; говоря́щих** | speaking |
| бра́ть **беру́**-т | **беру́щий** | taking |
| идти́ **иду́**-т | **иду́щий** | going |
| пи́ть **пью**-т | **пью́щий** | drinking |
| диктова́ть **дикту́ю**-т | **дикту́ющий** | dictating |

The stress of participles in -ущий/-ющий corresponds to that of the 3rd plural; that of participles in -ящий/-ащий is like the stress of infinitive or first singular.

| | | |
|---|---|---|
| люби́ть **лю́бя**-т люблю́ | **любя́щий** | |
| привози́ть **приво́зя**-т привожу́ | **привозя́щий** | |

**1.4**   The *past active participle* is made by replacing the -л of the past tense with -вший, -вшёё, -вшая, -вшие, etc.

| | | | |
|---|---|---|---|
| чита́ть **чита́**-л | **чита́вший** | прочита́ть | **прочита́вший** |
| писа́ть **писа́**-л | **писа́вший** | написа́ть | **написа́вший** |
| говори́ть **говори́**-л | **говори́вший** | сказа́ть **сказа́**-л | **сказа́вший** |
| бра́ть **бра́**-л | **бра́вший** | взять **взя́**-л | **взя́вший** |
| диктова́ть | **диктова́вший** | продиктова́ть | **продикто** |
| **диктова́**-л | | | **ва́вший** |

**1.41**   If the masculine past form has no -л (per VII 5), then the participial suffix is -ший (without -в-):

| | | | | | |
|---|---|---|---|---|---|
| нёсти́ | **нёс** | **нёсший** | вёзти́ | **вёз** | **вёзший** |
| умёре́ть | **у́мёр** | **умёрший** | лечь | **лёг** | **лёгший** |

**1.42**   For a small group of verbs with present stems in -д- or -т- (specifically, the verbs *брёсти́ 'wander', вёсти́ 'lead', *мёсти́ 'sweep', *плёсти́ [-плёсть] 'braid', *цвёсти́ 'bloom', *-чёсть 'count' and compounds), the suffix is -ший (-шёё, etc.), added to the stem with -д-/-т-:

| перевести перевёд-у́т | перевёл | **переве́дший**[1] |
|---|---|---|
| *плести́ **плету́т** | плёл | **плётший** |
| *счесть сочту́т | счёл | **счётший**[1] |

With **идти́** and compounds, the stem **шед-** is used:

| идти́ ид-у́т | шёл | **ше́дший**[1] |
|---|---|---|
| войти́ войду́т | вошёл | **воше́дший**[1] |

**1.5** The active participles may be accompanied by the particle **-ся** (never **-сь**):

| бояться | **боя́щийся, боя́щееся, боя́щаяся, боя́щиеся** |
|---|---|
| ложи́ться | **ложи́вшийся, ложи́вшаяся; ложи́вшимися** |
| интересова́ться | **интересу́ющийся; (за)интересова́вшийся** |

**2.** *The use of the participles.*

**2.1** The present passive participle means 'being done' at the same time as the action of the clause in which the form is used. E.g.,

| Зада́ча, реша́емая студе́нтами, о́чень трудна́. | The problem *which is being solved* by the students is very hard. |
|---|---|
| Зада́ча, реша́емая студе́нтами, *была́* о́чень трудна́. | The problem *which was being solved* by the students was very hard. |

**2.2** The past passive participle means 'having been done', and like the English participle may be used as an adjective describing the state after the action has been completed.

| Зада́ча, решённая Па́влом, была́ о́чень трудна́. | The problem *which was solved* by Paul was very hard. |
|---|---|
| Оста́вьте до́ма привезённые ва́ми кни́ги. | Leave the books *which were brought* by you (≅ which you brought) at home. |
| Оте́ц принёс обе́щанную кни́гу. | Father brought the *promised* book. |
| Две́рь откры́та. | The door is open (i.e. is in a state of *having been opened*). |

Only the constructions with the short-form past passive participles, as in the last example, are really common in conversation.

---

[1] The **é** for **ě** in these forms shows them to be borrowings from Church Slavonic.

**2.3**  The active participles mean 'doing' or 'having done'. Their time is usually relative to the moment of the action of the main verb. The perfective past active participle means 'having completed'. The imperfective past active participle means simply an action which *started* in the past: it may or may not still be in progress.

Студе́нт, реша́ющий зада́чу, пи́шет на доске́.

The student (who is) solving the problem is writing on the board.

Студе́нт, реша́вший зада́чу, писа́л на доске́.

The student (who was) solving the problem was writing on the board.

Студе́нт, реши́вший зада́чу, сёл.

The student who had solved the problem sat down.

In the second example, **реша́вший** (past *im*perfective active) specifically ties the action to the past time. If it were replaced by the present **реша́ющий**, the meaning would not be seriously changed; however the fact that the action is past would then be expressed only by the context, i.e. the past tense of the main verb, **писа́л**.

**2.4**  The participles used in the written language are extremely close in meaning to the relative clauses which are more normal in speech. For example:

Зада́ча, *реша́емая* студе́нтами, о́чень трудна́.

Зада́ча, *кото́рую* студе́нты *реша́ют*, о́чень трудна́.

Зада́ча, *решённая* Ива́ном...

Зада́ча, *кото́рую* Ива́н *реши́л*...

Студе́нт, *реша́ющий* зада́чу...

Студе́нт, *кото́рый реша́ет* зада́чу...

Студе́нт, *реша́вший* зада́чу...

Студе́нт, *кото́рый реша́л*...

Студе́нт, *реши́вший* зада́чу...

Студе́нт, *кото́рый реши́л*...

**3.**  The form **бы́вший** is the regular past active participle of **быть** 'to be', but it is also found as an adjective meaning 'former, ex-':

В Москве́ о́н встре́тил Петро́ва, бы́вшего у его́ ма́тери.

In Moscow he met Petrov, *who was* [part.] at his mother's place.

Бы́вший судья́ бу́дет та́м.

The ex-judge will be there.

Она́ его́ бы́вшая жена́.

She is his former wife.

Они́ бы́вшие лю́ди.

They are has-beens.

**4.1**  The verb **называ́ть** I / **назва́ть назову́т** P 'name' takes the accusative of thing (or person) named and the instrumental of the name (or epithet).

| | |
|---|---|
| Они назвали девочку Анной. | They named the little girl Anna. |
| Никто не мог бы её пре- | No one could call her beautiful. |
| красною назвать. | |
| Вася назвал все страны Евро- | Vasja named (i.e. recited names |
| пы. | of) all the countries of Europe. |
| Он вошёл и назвал себя. | He came in and gave his name. |

**4.11**  Note the use of the present passive participle in the meaning 'so-called'; так называемый (frequently abbreviated т.н.):

| | |
|---|---|
| После смерти Годунова началось т.н. | After Godunov's death began the so- |
| [так называемое] Смутное Время. | called Time of Trouble. |

**4.2**  Называться is the normal expression for 'to be named':

| | |
|---|---|
| Героиня называется Анной Карениной. | The heroine is called Anna Karenin. |
| Как называется его новый роман? | What's the name of his new novel? |

This verb is usually avoided in speaking of persons, cf. the next paragraph.

**4.3**  For stating names, the verb **звать зовут** 'call' is often used impersonally, in the 3rd plural form (without the pronoun **они**):

| | |
|---|---|
| Как вас зовут? | What's your name? |
| Его звали Иваном. | { He was called Ivan. |
| | { His name was Ivan. |

Sometimes the nominative is used here, instead of the instrumental:

| | |
|---|---|
| Её зовут Анна Петрова. | Her name is Anna Petrov. |

**4.31**  Otherwise, the verb **звать** I / **позвать** P means 'call, invite':

| | |
|---|---|
| Позови Ваню домой! | Call Vanja home. |
| Ивановы нас часто звали к себе. | The Ivanovs often invited us to their place. |

**4.4**  With institutions, "named after" is **имени** plus the genitive of the personal name:

| | |
|---|---|
| фабрика имени Ленина | the Lenin factory |
| библиотека имени | the Saltykóv-Ščedrín library |
| Салтыкова-Щедрина | |

## УПРАЖНЕНИЯ

**A.** Read and translate:

1. Царь Алексей Михайлович оставил ещё одного сына, родившегося в тысяча шестьсот шестьдесят втором году. 2. У них телефон всегда занят. 3. Они решили спросить проезжавшего мимо их дома старика. 4. Книга — это совет умирающего старика молодому человеку, начинающему жить. 5. Оставьте здесь привезённые ими книги, а завтра я их к вам перенесу. 6. Я только что прочитал книгу, переведённую с русского нашим профессором. 7. Госпожа Никулина, написавшая книгу о советах, возвратилась из Советского Союза несколько дней тому назад. Она долго жила за границей. 8. На следующий день она принесла Ване интереснейшую книгу, называемую «Как автомобиль научился ходить». 9. Студентка, готовящаяся к экзамену по французской истории, очень много читает по-французски. 10. На каком языке эти фразы на доске написаны? 11. Я больше всего люблю старую песню «Я забуду тебя очень скоро, как прочитанный, старый роман». 12. Только сегодня мне дали журналы, обещанные мне две недели тому назад. 13. Кто написал книгу, называемую «Герой нашего времени»? Лермонтов, конечно. 14. Вот интересные письма, полученные из-за границы от нашего сына. 15. На книге, найденной моим братом в саду, написана фамилия Петров. 16. Пусть он нам объяснит, где и когда он нашёл эти вещи. 17. Время идёт очень медленно для людей, ждущих доктора. 18. Во Франции почти все завтракающие обыкновенно пьют вино. 19. Гению, показывавшему женщинам в клубе свои фотографии, стало скучно. 20. Она оставила всё у ничего не понимающего дяди и ушла куда-то. 21. Старуха часто пьёт чай у бывшей жены старого судьи. 22. Мы ели привезённое из деревни соседями мясо. 23. Бабушка не знала, где находятся занимаемые нами в театре места. 24. Квартира занята русскими студентами. 25. Это хорошо написанная книга; она гораздо приятнее других романов того же поэта. 26. Все наши вещи уже перевезены в Москву. 27. Их дом находится на широкой улице, ведущей прямо в центр города. 28. Мальчик назвал главные города СССР. Знаете ли вы, где находятся все названные мальчиком русские города? 29. Названные студенты должны явиться на экзамен завтра в половине девятого. 30. Кажется, это было написано для «Нового русского слова».

**B.** Write in Russian the following sentences. Translate all relative clauses (those beginning with "who" or "which") both as relative clauses and by means of a participle. For instance, "The book ·*which we are reading*· is interesting" — ... **кото́рую мы́ чита́ем**... : ...**чита́емая на́ми**...

1. The women ·who were occupying those places· have gone away. 2. The girl ·who is answering the teacher· is Ivan's sister.  3. The answers which Peter gave ($\cong$ given by Peter) were very good.  4. The building ·which is [situated] on the river· is the doctors' club.  5. The girl ·who was living with them for three months· has become a student. 6. They were talking with the man ·who wrote that examination. 7. They are the men ·who were born in the same year· when the war started.  8. An automobile ran over the American woman ·who was returning home after the theater.  9. It is difficult for students ·who are reading a Russian book for the first time.  10. He started to read the book ·which had been placed on the table.  11. One cannot believe a person ·who talks like that. 12. I gave that book to Mrs. Petrov, ·who met me at the concert last night.  13. These problems ·which are solved every year by many students· are very difficult.  14. Do you see the man ·who is sitting there by the window?  15. All the Russians ·who were there yesterday· will be here tonight.  16. Don't forget to tell the old woman about the things ·which I left in the big room. 17. The little boy, ·who is called Vasja·, goes to a German school in the city.  18. The young aviators ·who used to occupy the apartment above ours· fly across the ocean to Europe three times a month.  19. The judge returned to me the money ·which his daughter found in their automobile.  20. Everyone [= all] ·who was [were] late to the examination yesterday· must appear in the professor's office [= to the professor] tomorrow morning at ten sharp.


**C.**  Supplementary sentences:

1. Мы́ говори́ли о расска́зе Макси́ма Го́рького, называ́ющемся «Бы́вшие лю́ди».  2. Все́ лю́ди в метро́, возвраща́ющиеся с рабо́ты, чита́ют газе́ту «Вече́рняя Москва́».  3. Музе́й и́мени Пу́шкина, находя́щийся на углу́ э́той у́лицы, мо́жет бы́ть легко́ найдён все́ми. 4. Но́вая студе́нтка, ча́сто прося́щая учи́теля повтори́ть вопро́сы, хорошо́ отвеча́ла на уро́ке сего́дня у́тром.  5. Ка́ждое у́тро я смотре́л из окна́ на ма́льчика, переводя́щего стару́ху-ба́бушку через у́лицу. 6. Вчера́ я встре́тил И́горя, несу́щего кни́ги в библиоте́ку.  7. Одна́ из кни́г, возвращённая йм, была́ мне́ о́чень нужна́.  8. Ма́льчик, нося́щий на́м газе́ты, учени́к шесто́го кла́сса сре́дней шко́лы. 9. Ученики́, не переше́дшие в сле́дующий кла́сс, реши́ли оста́ться

лётом в го́роде, что́бы занима́ться матема́тикой в ле́тней шко́ле.
10. В конце́ коридо́ра е́сть ма́ленькая две́рь, веду́щая пря́мо на
у́лицу. 11. Обло́мов и Што́льц, учи́вшиеся в одно́й шко́ле, оста́лись
друзья́ми на всю́ жи́знь. 12. Моро́зовы, позва́вшие на́с к себе́ в
дере́вню на всё ле́то, бы́ли за́няты ве́сь де́нь и мы́ и́х ре́дко ви́дели.
13. Лю́ди, живу́щие в э́той стране́, говоря́т и по-неме́цки и по-
францу́зски. 14. Мы́ слу́шали ве́сь ве́чер молодо́го поэ́та, чита́ющего
на́м сво́й но́вый рома́н. 15. Обыкнове́нно мы́ е́здим в го́род у́тренним
по́ездом, но сего́дня мы́ опозда́ли на него́ и на́м пришло́сь дово́льно
до́лго жда́ть авто́буса. 16. Я́ давно́ не слы́шал э́тих ста́рых ру́сских
пе́сен. 17. Де́вочка, не отве́тившая на вопро́сы учи́тельница,
запла́кала и сказа́ла: «Если бы то́лько я́ бо́льше занима́лась!»
18. В Евро́пе опа́здывающие не вхо́дят во вре́мя конце́рта. 19. Вы́
зна́ете кни́гу Замя́тина «Мы́»? Это интере́снейший рома́н о тридца́том
ве́ке, напи́сан уже́ в ты́сяча девятьсо́т двадца́том году́. 20. Че́м
ме́ньше ты́ занима́ешься тепе́рь, те́м трудне́е бу́дет гото́виться к
экза́мену в ию́не.

## СЛОВА́РЬ

бы́вший — former, ex-, § 3

за́нятый (or занято́й) — busy
(за́нят -о -ы; занята́)

ле́тний (aj.) — summer

пе́сня (G pl. пе́сён) — song

стари́к (*E*) — old man

стару́ха — old woman

страна́ (*Spl* стра́ны) — country

вёрну́ть(ся) = возврати́ть(ся)

возвраща́ть I
возврати́ть Р } return, give back
[возвращу́, возвращён]

возвраща́ться I
возврати́ться Р } return, come back

зва́ть зову́т I
позва́ть Р } call, invite (§ 4.3)
позва́л -и; позвала́
по́зван -ы; позвана́

называ́ть I
назва́ть назову́т Р } name (§ 4.2)
назва́л -и; назвала́
на́зван -ы; названа́

называ́ться I
назва́ться Р } be named (§ 4.2)
назва́лся, -ала́сь, -али́сь

оставля́ть I
оста́вить Р } leave (behind)

пла́кать пла́чут I — cry, weep
запла́кать Р — burst into tears

прожи́ть
проживу́т Р
про́жил -о -и;
прожила́ } live (through a period of time)

# ДВА́ДЦАТЬ ПЯ́ТЫЙ УРО́К

Óн сиде́л в саду́, чита́я газе́ту.

He sat in the garden, reading the paper.

Си́дя с на́ми, óн пи́л ча́й.

Sitting with us, he drank tea.

Она́ до́лго смотре́ла на меня́, не отвеча́я.

She looked at me for a long time, not answering.

Вы́пив ча́й, óн посиде́л ещё не́сколько мину́т.

Having finished his tea, he sat there for a few minutes longer.

Прочита́в газе́ту, óн пошёл гуля́ть.

Having read the paper, he went walking.

Возвраща́ясь из теа́тра, мы́ встре́тили мою́ подру́гу.

Returning from the theater, we met my friend.

Верну́вшись домо́й, мы́ нашли́ старика́, лёжа́вшего на дива́не.

On returning home we found an old man lying on the sofa.

Пожела́в все́м споко́йной но́чи, óн попроси́л на́с поду́мать об э́том.

Having wished everyone good night, he asked us to think about it.

Смотря́ в окно́, я ви́дел ка́к óн позвони́л у две́ри и, постоя́в с мину́ту, вошёл.

Looking out the window, I saw him ring the doorbell and, after standing for (about) a minute, enter.

Пойдёмте погуля́ть.

Let's go for a walk.

Мне́ ну́жно с ва́ми поговори́ть по одному́ о́чень ва́жному де́лу.

I must have a talk with you about a very important matter.

---

## GERUNDS

**0.** The Russian verb system includes two types of uninflected forms which combine the verb meaning with a function essentially that of an adverb: the *gerunds*. Gerunds express aspect, may take the particle **-сь**, and govern direct or indirect objects as do other forms of the given verbs. They are common in the spoken as well as in the written language.

Note that the term "gerund" refers to verbal nouns in English and Latin. The Russian gerund is an *adverb*; it is sometimes called a *verbal adverb*.

**1.** *The Forms of the Gerund.*

**1.1** The gerund in -я (often called "present gerund") is formed primarily from *im*perfective verbs. It cannot be formed from all stems.

**1.11** The suffix -я is added directly to the present stem except where the spelling rules forbid this letter (and -a is used; see App. I, § 5.1):

| | | |
|---|---|---|
| читáть **читá**-ют | **читáя** | reading |
| интересовáть **интересу́**-ют | **интересу́я** | interesting |
| говори́ть **говор**-я́т | **говоря́** | speaking |
| пóмнить **пóмн**-ят | **пóмня** | remembering |
| слы́шать **слы́ш**-ат | **слы́ша** | hearing |

**1.111** The accent is normally that of the *first* person singular (V 4.2). Exceptions: **си́дя, стóя, лёжа, мóлча** 'sitting, standing, lying, not speaking'.

**1.12** For verbs in **-авать** -ают this gerund is in **-авая** (cf. imperative, XIII 4.2):

| | | |
|---|---|---|
| давáть дают | **давáя** | giving |
| вставáть встают | **вставáя** | getting up |

**1.13** Certain perfective verbs, principally with infinitives in **-ти, -сть, -зть**, have this type of gerund, notably compounds of **идти́** and **вести́**:

| | | |
|---|---|---|
| прийти́ **прид**-у́т | **придя́** | arriving, having arrived |
| войти́ **войд**-у́т | **войдя́** | entering, having entered |
| привести́ **привёд**-у́т | **привёдя** | leading, having brought |
| прочéсть **прочт**-у́т | **прочтя́** | having read through |

**1.14** This gerund is NOT normally formed from:

(a) verbs with a present stem in **ш** or **ж** which alternates with **с** or **з** in the infinitive: писáть пи́шут (мáзать мáжут);

(b) verbs with infinitive in **-чь**: мóчь, берéчь, пéчь;

(c) most verbs whose present stem has no vowel: пи́ть **пь**-ю́т, ждáть **жд**-у́т;

(d) the verb **éхать** and a few others.

**1.15** NB: there are a number of exceptions to these rules, particularly in the case of forms which are historically this type of gerund but which in the modern language are purely adverbial, or part of fixed idiomatic phrases. Contemporary authors have widely variant usage.

**1.2** The suffixes **-в (-вши)** or **-ши** (often called the "past gerund") are added to the *past* stem (almost exclusively of perfective verbs), according to the rules given in XXIV 1.4, p. 300, so that the gerund in **-в** or **-вши** corresponds to the past active participle in **-вший** and the gerund in **-ши** to the participle in **-ший**:

| прочитáть | прочитá-л | прочитáв, прочитáвши | having read |
|---|---|---|---|
| написáть | написá-л | написáв, написáвши | having written |
| взять | взя́-л | взяв, взя́вши | having taken |
| нестú | нёс | нёсши | having carried |
| везтú | вёз | вёзши | having conveyed |
| умерéть | у́мер | умéрши | having died |
| идтú | шёл | шéдши | having gone |
| войтú | вошёл | вошéдши | having entered |
| *приобрестú | приобрёл | приобрéтши | having gained |

**1.21** Note: the forms *войдя́* and *вошéдши*; *принéся* and *принéсши* are not differentiated in meaning. The tendency here appears to be to favor the **-я** forms where such doublets exist, but the situation varies from verb to verb.

**1.3** Gerunds in **-я** or **-(в)ши** [not those in **-в**!] may have the particle **-сь** [never *-ся*!]:

| смея́ться | смея́сь | засмея́вшись |
|---|---|---|
| готóвиться | готóвясь | приготóвившись |

Thus the gerunds follow the normal rule requiring the shortened form **-сь** after vowel (X 1); it is the participles that violate the rule by having **-ся** after vowel as well as after consonant.

**2.** *The Meaning and Use of the Gerunds.*

**2.1** Gerunds indicate an action secondary to the action of the main verb, *performed by the same subject.*

If the gerund is imperfective, its action is contemporaneous with the main action.

If the verb is perfective, the gerund's action is normally envisioned as completed before the main action, but it may mean simply a completed accessory act.

| Решáя задáчу, он сидéл у окнá. | Working on the problem, he was sitting by the window. |
|---|---|
| Решáя задáчу, он сидúт у окнá. | Working on the problem, he is sitting by the window. |
| Решáя задáчу, он бýдет сидéть у окнá. | Working on the problem, he will be sitting by the window. |
| Решúв задáчу, он сéл. | Having solved the problem, he sat down. |

| | |
|---|---|
| Реши́в зада́чу, о́н обе́даёт. | Having solved the problem, he is dining. |
| Реши́в зада́чу, о́н мне́ позво́нит. | Having solved the problem (= when he has solved the problem), he will call me up. |

**2.2**  While participles, which characterize a person or thing, are more or less equivalent to a relative clause (with "who, which"), the gerunds characterize the main verb, describing manner, time, cause, or other circumstance. They are often approximately equivalent to a clause introduced by some sort of conjunction: e.g.

| | |
|---|---|
| Ка́к? Каки́м о́бразом? | How? In what manner? |
| Си́дя у окна́, о́н реша́л зада́чи. | Sitting at the window... |
| Ходя́ по ко́мнате, о́н слу́шал меня́. | Walking about the room... |
| Когда́? | When? |
| Верну́вшись домо́й, о́н сейча́с же лёг спа́ть. | ⎰ Когда́ о́н верну́лся...<br>⎱ О́н верну́лся домо́й и пото́м лёг... |
| Реша́я зада́чи, о́н всегда́ сиди́т у окна́. | Когда́ о́н реша́ет... |
| Почёму́? | Why? |
| Не поня́вши вопро́са, о́н не отве́тил. | Та́к как о́н не по́нял вопро́са... |

**2.3**  The gerunds in **-вши**, as opposed to those in **-в** alone, have a more specific sense of causality. As a practical rule, use the forms in **-в** except when the particle **-сь** is to be added: then only **-вши** is possible.

**2.4**  Note that a negated gerund may be translated "without ...ing". For example:

| | |
|---|---|
| Она́ вы́шла , не отве́тив. | She went out without answering. |

**3.**  From **быть** 'to be' there is the irregular gerund **бу́дучи**. It is rarely used, and nearly always has a causal sense: e.g., Бу́дучи до́ктором, о́н мо́г и́м помо́чь. 'Being a doctor, he could help them.'

**4.**  **Хоте́ть** 'to want' normally forms no gerund. Instead one finds **жела́я**, from **жела́ть жела́ют** 'wish':

| | |
|---|---|
| Жела́я уви́деть бра́та, я пое́хал к ни́м. | Wishing to see my brother, I went to their place. |

**5.** **Желáть** always takes the genitive:

Чегó вы желáете?                        What do you wish?

This verb is omitted in a number of conventional phrases, but the nouns concerned remain in the genitive:

[Я вам желáю] всегó лýчшего.      (I wish you) all the best.
                     спокóйной нóчи.           good night.
                     счастлѝвого путѝ.       a happy journey.

**6.** The masculine noun **путь** 'path, way, trip' has all the endings of the *third* declension except instrumental singular:

N-A **путь** G-P-D **путѝ** Inst. sg. **путём** N-A pl **путѝ** G **путéй** Pr. **путя́х**

Note the idioms:

Это мнé по путѝ.                        That's on the way for me, on my way.

Емý по путѝ с вáми.                     He's going your way.
Он идёт свойм путём.                   He does things his own way.
Он стойт на моём путѝ.                He's in my way.

**7.** The prefix **по-**, added to a number of imperfectives which denote a state or an action that is essentially continuous, gives the meaning "do for a short while". It also makes the verbs perfective, and thus signifies that this short period of action is viewed as completed. For example:

Онѝ погуля́ли в лесý.                   They had a short walk in the woods.

Посидéв немнóжко, он встáл       Having sat for a short while, he
   и вы́шел из кóмнаты.             got up and left the room.
Он постоя́л у окнá минýты        He stood at the window for a
   двé и опя́ть сéл.                   couple of minutes and then sat down again.

Я хочý с вáми поговорѝть.         I want to have a chat with you.
Мы тáм пóжили нéсколько         We lived there for a few days.
   днéй.
Подýмав немнóго, он отвéтил.    Having thought for a little, he answered.

Я бы хотéл полётáть на           I'd like to fly a bit in an air-
   самолёте.                          plane.

**7.1** NB: The prefix **по-** has this meaning *only with a restricted number of verbs.* With the going-verbs it has the meaning of "beginning" (cf. VII 3.2) and with many other verbs it merely serves to express perfectiveness: e.g., *позáвтракать, пообéдать, позвонúть, полюбúть.*

**7.2 Побывáть** (P) means 'visit' or 'be [somewhere] once':

Óн побывáл в СССР.       He has visited [been in] the USSR.

**8.** The preposition **с** + *Accusative* is used with nouns expressing size, weight, or a period of time to mean 'about, approximately':

с недéлю               about a week

## УПРАЖНЕНИЯ

**А.** Прочтите и переведите:

1. По этому вопросу мне хочется поговорить еще с кем-нибудь.

   По этому вопросу мне хочется поговорить еще с кем-то.

2. Теперь он является на работу поздно.

   Теперь он является профессором.

3. Он казался занятым.

   Он оказался занятым.

4. Будущий доктор может вам помочь.

   Будучи доктором, он может вам помочь.

5. Он купил хлеб.

   Он купил хлеба.

6. Он сказал, что Ирина ушла.

   Он сказал, чтобы Ирина ушла.

7. На столе не было одного документа.

   На столе не было ни одного документа.

8. Я долго читал вашу статью.

   Я давно читал вашу статью.

**В.** 1. Вставáя рáно, молодóй механик всегдá уходил на рабóту до шести часóв. 2. Вернýвшись пóздно с собрáния, я нашёл на столé письмó. 3. Подýмав немнóго, онá началá спокóйно и мéдленно отвечáть. 4. Занимáясь глáвным óбразом языкáми и литератýрой, эта студéнтка, францýженка, интересýется и естéственными наýками. 5. Желáя погулять с дéвушкой на рекé, Сáша не хотéл остáться с товáрищами пóсле урóков. 6. Встáв и одéвшись, мы вышли из дому и слышали, кáк остающиеся нáм пожелáли счастливого путú. 7. Закрыв двéрь и открыв óкна, óн лёг спáть. 8. Вáм нýжно пожить здéсь нéкоторое врéмя, а тó вáм здéсь никогдá не понрáвится.

9. За́втра, возвраща́ясь с рабо́ты, я́ зайду́ к ва́м. 10. Е́сли ва́м нехорошо́, полежи́те зде́сь немно́го. 11. Повторя́я дли́нные фра́зы, Васи́лий Дми́трьевич говори́л всё ме́дленнее и ясне́е. 12. Прожи́в всю свою́ жи́знь гла́вным о́бразом в Нью Ио́рке, мо́й това́рищ та́к и не побыва́л в Калифо́рнии. 13. На́м придётся посиде́ть зде́сь, та́к как ещё о́чень ра́но и до́ктор ещё не пришёл. 14. Поговори́в с сосе́дкой с мину́ту, о́н вдру́г вы́бежал на у́лицу. 15. У и́х дру́га прекра́сный я́сный го́лос, но ему́ необходи́мо научи́ться говори́ть ме́дленно. 16. Не мно́гим, бы́вшим на конце́рте, понра́вилась но́вая симфо́ния. 17. Е́сли о́н не вернётся во́время, я́ до́лжен бу́ду оста́ться, та́к как нельзя́ оста́вить дете́й одни́х. 18. Мне́ на́до бы́ло пое́хать в го́род по дела́м, но поду́мав, я́ реши́ла подожда́ть дня́ два́. 19. Хотя́ я́ уже́ гуля́л сего́дня, я́ с ва́ми ещё погуля́ю, е́сли вы́ хоти́те. 20. Мне́ показа́лось стра́нным, что ему́ не нра́вится америка́нский о́браз жи́зни. 21. Чита́я по́льские газе́ты, на́ша Ири́на у́чится по́льскому языку́. 22. Боя́сь уви́деться с сосе́дями, бра́тья с неде́лю не выходи́ли и́з дому. 23. Снача́ла они́ мне́ показа́лись ру́сскими, но пото́м оказа́лось, что они́ не́мцы, и научи́лись та́к хорошо́ говори́ть по-ру́сски, живя́ в Росси́и. 24. Узна́в, что друзья́ перее́хали за́ реку, ба́бушка захоте́ла уви́деть и́х но́вый до́м. 25. Её сосе́ди прожи́ли в Крыму́ с го́д. 26. Уви́дев меня́, они́ оста́вили рабо́ту и пришли́ пожела́ть мне́ счастли́вого пути́. 27. Не зна́я ру́сского языка́, моя́ ма́ть ничего́ не понима́ла в на́шем кла́ссе. 28. Посмотре́в на часы́, о́н уви́дел, что пора́ е́хать. 29. Они́ оказа́лись ру́сскими, кото́рые научи́лись хорошо́ говори́ть по-неме́цки, живя́ в Герма́нии. 30. Перед кита́йским рестора́ном мы́ встре́тили возвраща́ющуюся из теа́тра подру́гу мое́й сестры́. 31. Она́ мно́го пла́чет. Е́сли бы то́лько о́н звони́л ча́ще! 32. Опозда́в на самолёт, отлета́вший в де́сять мину́т шесто́го, я́ должна́ была́ оста́ться на аэродро́ме до девяти́ часо́в. 33. Прочита́в ва́шу кни́гу, я́ её ва́м сейча́с же возвращу́. 34. Вста́в ра́ньше все́х, де́душка ти́хо вы́шел погуля́ть по го́роду. 35. Услы́шав го́лос ста́ршего бра́та, смею́щиеся де́вушки убежа́ли к себе́ в ко́мнату, что́бы не встре́титься с ни́м. 36. Э́та ве́щь оказа́лась нену́жной, та́к что я́ её возврати́л твоему́ това́рищу. 37. Влете́в в окно́, кра́сная пти́ца полета́ла по фа́брике с мину́ту и опя́ть вы́летела. 38. Верну́вшись из-за грани́цы, о́н ста́л мла́дшим лейтена́нтом. 39. Э́тот высо́кий англича́нин ре́же быва́ет у себя́ до́ма, чем у на́с. 40. Рабо́тая за больши́м столо́м, они́ слу́шали «Пе́сни без сло́в» Мендельсо́на по ра́дио. 41. О́н написа́л оди́н коро́ткий рома́н и не́сколько дли́нных, но хоро́ших пе́сен. 42. Сли́шком мно́го самолётов лета́ет над на́шим до́мом;

придётся переéхать на другóе мéсто. 43. Нрáвясь мнé, éта стрáнная испáнка всё же казáлась мнé неприятной. 44. Я óчень люблю летáть, но éто слишком дóрого для меня. Поэтому я обыкновéнно éзжу домóй пóездом. 45. Взяв старýху пóд руку, мáльчик перевёл её через ýлицу. 46. Прожив три гóда в СССР, с тысяча девятьсóт тридцáтого гóда по тысяча девятьсóт тридцать вторóй гóд, они переéхали в Пóльшу, а потóм в Амéрику. 47. Начáв éтот нóвый ромáн, я не мóг егó остáвить. 48. Чáй был впервые привезён в Еврóпу в тысяча шестьсóт десятом годý. 49. Увидевши, что я нёс пóльскую книгу, старик подошёл и спросил меня, не говорю ли я по-пóльски. 50. Сдéлав всё упражнéния, Миша решил, что тепéрь мóжно и погулять.

**C.** Write in Russian, using gerunds wherever possible:

1. Sitting at home, they were listening to the radio. 2. Hearing (= having heard) the voice of her little son, she went into the house to see what he wanted. 3. Wanting to dine with friends, they went to the city. 4. Having dined well, they went to the theater. 5. Drinking up his tea, the citizen stood up, wished us good night, and went to bed. 6. Carrying the little girl in his arms, the mechanic was walking in the garden. 7. We met Dmitrij by the theater, carrying the little girl in his arms. 8. He stood at the blackboard, repeating every word which the teacher said. 9. Repeat the sentence without looking (= not looking) at the book! 10. Leaving the old lady alone at home, Marija took the little girl to the doctor's. 11. Arriving by fast train, he went at once to the bank and then straight to the meeting at the club. 12. Opening the window, she spoke to her neighbor (f) who was working in the garden. 13. Not being able (= knowing how) to read the letter, she asked the professor to help her. 14. Laughing at him, the girl closed the window. 15. Not believing her mother, she asked her father. 16. Promising her to return soon, he drove away in his beautiful new automobile. 17. Laughing and talking all at once (= together), the students came out of the meeting. 18. Having found my book in the theater, Ivan returned it to me yesterday. 19. Having gone through some broad fields and past a little wood, we came to a clean little village. 20. Having been born in Russia, Il'ja came to the United States in 1920, when he was only two years old. 21. The day has turned out to be (XXI 7.2) clear and beautiful, but colder than yesterday. 21 a. It turned out that the weather was good, much better than before. 22. It seems strange that he didn't come

last night.   23. If it rains (X 5.1) this evening, I must stay home.
24. Since it was snowing, the children couldn't go out of the house.
25. Since it has stopped snowing (XVIII 7.3), you can go buy the evening
paper.   26. It's so cold tonight that I don't want to go to town.   27. He
arrived earlier than usual, so that he could have a chat with the judge
and Mrs. Petrov before supper.   28. She explains the problems so
clearly that a child could understand her.   29. Although the professor
explained this sentence to Ivan many times, he still couldn't understand.
30. Bring your brother when you come to see me, or else I won't be able
to help you.   31. Please call Anna before the meeting; otherwise she
will forget to bring the necessary books.   32. I have to write these
sentences this evening, so that I can't go to the movies with you.   33. I
promised to call her up before dinner.   34. Having promised, I ought
to call her now.   35. Excuse me, I must return home now.

## СЛОВА́РЬ

| | | | |
|---|---|---|---|
| впервы́е | for the first time | снача́ла | at first |
| всё же | all the same | споко́йный | peaceful, quiet |
| [не́которое вре́мя] | (for some time) | (споко́ён, споко́йно, -о́йна) | |
| о́браз | shape, form, mode, image | стра́нный | strange |
| гла́вным о́бразом | for the most part, chiefly | (стра́нён, -нна) | |
| прекра́сный | beautiful | жела́ть I | desire |
| (прекра́сён, -сна) | | пожела́ть P } (+ Gen.) | (§ 4, 5) |
| пу́ть (masc., § 6) | path, way | | |
| с [со] + Acc. (§ 8) | about | побыва́ть P | visit (§ 7.2) |

поговори́ть, погуля́ть, поду́мать, пожи́ть, } see § 7
полежа́ть, порабо́тать, посиде́ть, постоя́ть

## For review

**A.**   1. Кни́ги, принесённые Никола́ем, оказа́лись о́чень интере́сными.
2. Позвони́в домо́й, я узна́л, что бра́т хо́чет уе́хать в Кита́й.   3. Вчера́
пришло́ письмо́ от сестры́, зову́щей меня́ в дере́вню.   4. Мы́ встре́тили
студе́нта, оказа́вшегося дру́гом моего́ бра́та.   5. Зае́хав домо́й за
письмо́м, я встре́тил у двере́й жда́вшего меня́ Ле́вина.   6. Во́т
пришёл Седо́в, опозда́вший на два́ часа́.   7. Зелёный до́м, зани-
ма́емый ра́ньше Гре́миными, тепе́рь ку́плен Ники́той Алексе́евичем.

8. Ко́ротко говоря́, я ва́м скажу́ не́т! 9. Студе́нты, мно́го рабо́тающие по вечера́м, хорошо́ у́чатся. 10. На́до рабо́тать побо́льше и гуля́ть поме́ньше. Вы́ повторя́етесь: об э́том уже́ бы́ло ска́зано ра́ньше. 11. Поу́жинав, мы́ реши́ли пойти́ в кино́. 12. Мы́ уе́хали, увезя́ с собо́й все́ на́ши кни́ги. 13. Мо́й сосе́д, хорошо́ зна́ющий ру́сский язы́к, перево́дит рома́н — и́ли скоре́е дли́нный расска́з — Достое́в-ского «Бе́дные лю́ди». 14. Любя́ му́зыку, о́н ча́сто ходи́л на конце́рты. 15. Это зда́ние уже́ ку́плено сосе́дями. 16. Ста́рший лейтена́нт сиде́л за столо́м и что́-то писа́л, пото́м взя́л напи́санное и вы́шел. Переда́в письмо́ мла́дшему лейтена́нту, стоя́вшему в коридо́ре, о́н сказа́л ему́ не́сколько сло́в и ушёл. 17. Францу́зская кни́га была́ прочи́тана все́ми на́ми. 18. Вы́ехав и́з дому мно́го ле́т наза́д, я тепе́рь опя́ть возвраща́юсь туда́. 19. Си́доров, рабо́тавший на фа́брике, тепе́рь у́чится в университе́те. 20. У меня́ до́ма лежи́т тетра́дка, забы́тая ва́ми. 21. Если они́ не бу́дут е́хать бы́стро, то́ не смо́гут прие́хать во́время. 22. Прия́тно смотре́ть на игра́ющих и ве́село смею́щихся де́вочек. 23. И́м всегда́ прихо́дится жда́ть до́ктора о́коло ча́са. 24. Рубико́н перейдён! Всё решено́! Бу́дет война́! 25. Нача́ло э́того расска́за мне́ показа́лось бо́лее инте-ре́сным, че́м его́ коне́ц. Чем да́льше, те́м ху́же! 26. Всё проси́мые ва́ми кни́ги уже́ поло́жены на ва́ш сто́л. 27. Хотя́ его́ но́вый рома́н дово́льно хорошо́ напи́сан, о́н тако́й же дли́нный и ску́чный ка́к и после́дний. 28. Вели́кий ру́сский писа́тель Макси́м Го́рький ро-ди́лся на Во́лге (реке́), в го́роде, нося́щем тепе́рь его́ и́мя. 29. Все́ кни́ги, взя́тые в библиоте́ке, студе́нтка прочита́ла в оди́н ве́чер. 30. Объясни́те, пожа́луйста, что́ зде́сь напи́сано. Это, ка́жется, кита́йские и́ли, мо́жет быть, япо́нские слова́. 31. Говоря́т, что за́втра бу́дет жа́рче, чем сего́дня. 32. В полу́ченных на́ми вчера́ журна́лах бы́ло мно́го интере́сных и весёлых расска́зов. 33. Студе́нты печа́льно говори́ли с това́рищами, прише́дшими на собра́ние. 34. Хорошо́ вы́ученное не забыва́ется. 35. Всё хорошо́, что́ хорошо́ конча́ется.

**B.** 1a. Could you ask Natal'ja Andreevna if she would send me some of her books on Russian history? b. I'm getting ready for an exam, and I need them very much.

c. I'll speak to her about it, but I can promise you nothing. d. She is an intelligent woman, but not at all interested [use participle] in history — she doesn't understand much more about it than I do.

e. Yes, but she has a great number of books that she got [use parti-ciple] from her father, the great professor of Russian history.

f. His book about Borís Godunóv, which appeared [use participle] just before his death, is one of the best books of the fifties and is translated into several languages.   g. Having left Russia in 1919, he lived for a short time in Poland, and came to the United States in 1920.

2a. Ivan Borisovich, let's repeat the whole matter again.   b. I want you to know everything well, so that there will be no mistakes.   c. Remember, we must all obey the Council in everything.   d. No comrade who made a mistake is still alive (living).   e. At 3:45 on Wednesday, July 27th, Sergej Ivanovich and Anna Pavlovna, carrying briefcases, will be walking toward the bank along 100th street near the corner where the little church is.   f. Having set off by car from the park earlier, you and I will appear in front of the bank at the same time as they enter the bank.   g. As soon as (XXIa) they emerge from the bank with the money, you must open the door of the car for them.   h. The sooner we can get away from there the better.   i. If everything goes well, we will meet under the big clock at the main library at exactly 5:31.

3. Somebody tell old Vanja that no one will ever believe such a story.

4a. The judge's grandfather' who will be ninety years old next month, gets up every day at six-thirty in the morning, dresses, eats breakfast, and leaves the house before eight.   b. He has not once been late for work in sixty-five years.

# УРОК ДВАДЦАТЬ ПЯТЫЙ а

*Читайте и переведите:*

**А.**

1. Он написал без ошибок, но мало.

Он писал без ошибок, зато мало.

2. Он рассказал мне об этом, когда мы возвращались домой.

Он рассказал мне об этом, когда мы вернулись домой.

3. Пригласят кого-то на обед.

Пригласят кого-нибудь на обед.

4. Мы долго играли в шахматы.

Мы давно играли в шахматы.

5. Ошибка должна быть найдена.

Ошибка, должно быть, найдена.

**В.** 1. Телеграмма, посланная ими третьего дня, была получена только через день. 2. Довольны ли вы сделанной мною работой? 3. Сегодня будут передавать по радио хороший концерт новейшей музыки. 4. Я хочу, чтобы вы поправили это упражнение ещё раз. Остаётся много незамеченных ошибок. 5. Встретив Машу, он рассказал ей все свои новости. 6. В шкафах, находящихся в её комнате, стоит много русских книг. 7. Познакомившись с Петровыми, Андрей стал часто приходить к ним в дом. 8. Он ходит каждый день в музей, чтобы читать там интереснейшие письма адмирала Ямамото, умершего во время русско-японской войны. 9. В упражнениях, написанных мальчиками, нет ни одной ошибки. 10. История [= рассказ], рассказанная учительницей, всем нам очень понравилась. 11. Не найдя себе работы дома, я пошёл погулять по городу. 12. В Большом театре, являющемся одним из лучших театров Европы, играют прекрасные актёры и актрисы. 13. К нам пришёл студент, хорошо объяснивший все трудные упражнения. 14. Этот год, не принёсший никаких успехов, хочется забыть. 15. Студент, спрашивающий профессора о французской революции, учится у нас уже третий семестр. 16. Студент, спрашиваемый профессором, не знал ответа. 17. Павел Петров, приехавший из-за границы, рассказал нам много интересных историй. Он рождён быть артистом. 18. Учитель нам вернул поправленные диктовки. 19. Власов, женившийся на Тане Джонс, познакомился с нею через меня. Раньше о́н её ча́сто ви́дел, встреча́ясь с не́й по воскресе́ньям в це́ркви. 20. Между гуля́ющими в па́рке людьми́ я́ вдру́г уви́дел моего́ ста́рого знако́мого Лукина́. 21. Офице́р, захоте́вший учи́ться, бы́л по́слан в университе́т.

22. Вы́ не хоти́те пойти́ с на́ми на ле́кции профе́ссора Попо́ва, неда́вно верну́вшегося из Кита́я? Е́сли смо́жете, пожа́луйста, постара́йтесь прийти́ пора́ньше. 23. Вы́йдя за́муж за Смирно́ва, она́ перее́хала в Росто́в. 24. Не найдя́ его́ в конто́ре, она́ зае́хала к нему́ на кварти́ру. 25. Полу́ченные у́тром пи́сьма лежа́т на э́той по́лке, куда́ я́ и́х всегда́ кладу́. 26. Си́дя у стола́, я люблю́ смотре́ть через откры́тое окно́ на самолёты, летя́щие над реко́й, ка́к больши́е пти́цы. 27. Смотри́те на пти́ц, лета́ющих высоко́ над це́рковью. 28. Петро́в послу́шал отца́, посове́товавшего ему́ побыва́ть в Евро́пе. 29. В прочи́танном на́ми расска́зе бы́ло мно́го незнако́мых сло́в. 30. Переда́йте приве́т друзья́м, гото́вящимся к после́днему экза́мену. 31. Не забыва́йте на́с! Вы́ по́мните ста́рую посло́вицу: «дру́г де́нег доро́же»? 32. Ва́ня, закро́й о́кна, пожа́луйста, хо́лодно на дворе́. —Хорошо́, ма́ма; зна́чит, когда́ о́кна бу́дут закры́ты, на дворе́ ста́нет тепле́е. 33. Она́ ни о чём друго́м не могла́ говори́ть и не могла́ не рассказа́ть Соловьёву своё несча́стье. 34. То́лько когда́ я повтори́л всё, говоря́ о́чень я́сно и ме́дленно, о́н, наконе́ц, по́нял меня́. 35. Она́ продолжа́ла диктова́ть споко́йно и уве́ренно. 36. Генера́л неда́вно жени́лся на тала́нтливой по́льской худо́жнице, не́сколько карти́н кото́рой вися́т в не́которых ва́жных музе́ях и в Евро́пе и зде́сь. 37. Кста́ти, Петро́вы и Бе́лые собира́ются пое́хать вме́сте в Кры́м, в дере́вню недалеко́ от Я́лты, на ме́сяц а́вгуст. И на́с пригласи́ли, но́, к сожале́нию, я бу́ду за́нят ве́сь ме́сяц. 38. На́ши го́сти вы́шли из кино́ как ра́з когда́ пошёл до́ждь. 39. Ко́мната была́ небольша́я, а зато́ с высо́ким потолко́м и больши́м окно́м. 40. Сыгра́йте э́ту пе́сню ещё раз, пожа́луйста, но ти́хо, та́к как э́то мо́жет помеша́ть сосе́дке. Э́ти сте́ны, к сожале́нию, о́чень тонки́, и уже́ дово́льно по́здно.

41. Почему́ вы́ опозда́ли сего́дня на заня́тия? —Рабо́тая в библио́те́ке, я не смотре́л на часы́ и не зна́л, что по́здно. 42. Как то́лько ему́ принесли́ ме́л, о́н уве́ренно на́чал писа́ть о́чень бы́стро на како́м-то всём незнако́мом языке́. 43. Е́сли всё това́рищи бу́дут помога́ть ему́, о́н не мо́жет не де́лать успе́хов. 44. С мину́ту они́ хо́лодно смотре́ли дру́г на дру́га мо́лча. 45. За обе́дом бы́ло по́слано не́сколько телегра́мм лю́дям, интересова́вшимся бу́дущей рабо́той на́шей лаборато́рии. 46. Вошла́ краси́вая ста́рая да́ма, вся́ в

чёрном. 47. Стара́ясь не запла́кать, Ми́шка нам расска́зывал о своём несча́стье. 48. Éсли вы ду́маете, что её ма́ленький брат вам не помеша́ет, то́ вы глубоко́ ошиба́етесь! 49. Запла́кав, она́ ду́мала: «Кéм бы я́ без него́ была́? Кто́ научи́л меня́ рабо́тать?» 50. Я́ стара́лся уйти́ незаме́ченным, но к моему́ несча́стью Ивано́в вдру́г появи́лся как ра́з передо мно́й в дверя́х. Вы мо́жете себе́ предста́вить, как э́то мне бы́ло неприя́тно. 51. Я́ бы хоте́л посла́т её знако́мому худо́жнику откры́тку, но́, к сожале́нию, у меня́ нет его́ а́дреса. 52. Я́ уве́рена, что его́ не́ было до́ма в э́тот ве́чер: он и́ли оста́лся по́здно на аэродро́ме и́ли уе́хал куда́-то в го́сти. 53. Нельзя́ бы́ло не смея́ться над анекдо́тами старика́. 54. —Я́ не собира́юсь бы́ть ничье́й жено́й, крича́ла она́. 55. Мой ста́ршие бра́тья лю́бят игра́ть в футбо́л, хотя́ они́ бо́льше не мо́лоды. 56. В суббо́ту Ири́на Серге́ева-Це́нская наконе́ц посла́ла э́ти прекра́сные то́нкие кита́йские платки́ её подру́ге. —Чье́й подру́ге? 57. Стара́йтесь отвеча́ть погро́мче, пожа́луйста, а то́ мне тру́дно понима́ть ва́ши отве́ты. 58. Éсли бы то́лько у меня́ был ключ к э́тим упражне́ниям! Бы́ло бы гора́здо ле́гче переводи́ть. 59. Да́, да́, тебе́ тру́дно, —сказа́л де́душка. Не подума́вши, ничего́ не начина́й. Но ты́ забы́л: сейча́с лета́ешь хорошо́, а се́сть не уме́ешь. 60. Хоро́шее нача́ло обыкнове́нно, хоро́ший коне́ц ре́док.

**C.** 1. We are all very sorry for Aunt Sonja. 2. I cannot tell you how sad her long life has been! 3. She was born in Japan, as I'm sure I told you once last year, on the 23rd of April, 1889, and she travelled with her parents, Russian musicians whom everybody loved, around Asia (А́зия) and Europe. 4. During the war between Russia and Japan — that was in 1905 — they stayed with their old friends General Sergej (son of Sergej) Popóv-Pokróvskij and his wife in China, far from the frontier where the soldiers were.

5. Aunt Sonja used to tell us children how pleasant it was to live at the Popov-Pokrovskij house, where her father played chess in the mornings with the old general, drank cold Chinese coffee, and talked about the life of a musician in the Russia which they both knew so well. 6. Later, having drunk too much vodka after a concert in the general's garden — I believe it happened in 1906, late in the autumn of that year — he peacefully died, although he was still quite a young man. 7. Of course his wife Marija (daughter of Vasilij) was very sad and lay in bed for six weeks after his death, reading Tolstoj.

8. "I'm bored, so bored, I want to return to my dear old Russia,"

she told the general's wife, Aleksandra (daughter of Semën). 9. "I feel like meeting new people and seeing old acquaintances whom I knew when I went to school with them in the Crimea. 10. Tolstoj's heroines are walking the streets of Moscow; his ideas, which seem so natural to me, are beginning to interest the Poles and the Spaniards too. 11. I want to see those heroines walking in the parks; I want to study those ideas; I'd like to meet Tolstoj himself. What joy!"

12. The general's wife told Aunt Sonja's mother that Tolstoj was too busy with his own work and would not want to make the acquaintance of a woman who ate as much as she did. 13. "I shall eat less, I promise you!" she replied at once, and the following week she left for Moscow by train, taking her little daughter with her.

14. None of the Russians on the train could understand poor Aunt Sonja. 15. Unfortunately she didn't know a word of Russian. 16. Just think how hard it was for her, speaking Chinese with her neighbor, a lady journalist and former school-teacher from Rostóv, who didn't understand a word she said! 17. Her mother didn't help her either, imagine! 18. She just continued to read books on economics and translated nothing for her daughter.

19. They arrived in Moscow late at night on the 12th of November, 1911. 20. It's unclear where Aunt Sonja's mother got the money, but she bought a large house in town — larger than the general's house, I must say — and began to live a merry life. 21. At first only a few old friends dropped in to see them, but later an army of new acquaintances came to them, bringing all the latest books and speaking ever more deeply of the problems which man must solve. 22. For the most part these were students living at home in the city. 23. One of them, a strange boy — from Minsk, I think — said he wanted to become an aviator for the Tsar. 24. The others laughed at him and said he was an idiot.

25. "Why do you want to become a hero? Science, literature, and the revolution are more important than the life of an aviator," they told him. 26. "Just wait a little and you'll soon see what we'll do with your Tsar!"

27. "I don't agree," he would shout at the other guests, "I'm not afraid of your revolutions!"

28. But Aunt Sonja liked the boy, whom she had once caught sight of when he was walking to class with his sister, and at once invited to dinner. 29. She married him — although her mother had told her "It is forbidden!", and he flew for his Tsar during the Revolution.

30. What happened? I'll tell you.

31. Aunt Sonja's first husband never returned after the Revolution. 32. She went off to France, where an Englishmen married her, thinking she must have a lot of money. 33. He left her in a cheap apartment when he found out that she was only a poor musician's daughter, and she cried there a whole month all alone. 34. "Where have you gone, John? Come back! Give me your hand! Don't say you don't need me any longer! We understand each other better than others understand us!"

35. And that's why everyone is sorry for the old lady. 36. But in actual fact that was all a very long time ago. 37. In January, 1923, luckily for her, she married a very rich Italian writer whom she had encountered one afternoon in the park in the summer, and he took her off to Italy. 38. Now she just sits in the sun and plays cards with her neighbors' children. 39. From time to time she invites old Russian friends, with whom she loves to talk about the cold winters and deep snow in Moscow and her sad life and her handsome first husband, the hero-aviator who died for the Tsar. 40. Once a month she goes by bus with her daughter to the city to see a movie and buy several new hats — she loves expensive hats — and she's really, in the final analysis, quite happy.

**D.** 1. When presidents decide to visit one another, this is what usually happens. 2. As soon as he has been invited, he sends several important generals to prepare everything. 3. When he arrives in the country for about two weeks, the great man is met at the airport by many of the most important generals, writers and so forth. 4. At first he says that the two countries have always been and always will remain closest friends and that there never will be a war between them. 5. This simple idea is usually translated as correctly as possible, and then one of the senior officers steps up to the president and answers him with the same kind of pleasant words. 6. A general takes the president by the arm, leads him away and seats him in a waiting black automobile. 7. On the way to town they often cross narrow bridges and drive via the broadest streets past universities and the main schools. 8. Of course, he notices only the most beautiful buildings, and when asked whether he is satisfied with them, he answers that they are taller and more interesting than the ones in the country where he was born. 9. His answer pleases everyone.

10. Arriving in the city, the president of the republic together with

his wife, sons, daughters, aunts and uncles occupy ten or fifteen of the most expensive rooms.   11. First they sit down at their desks to send telegrams and postcards home to their parents and acquaintances. 12. Then in the afternoon, the president and others sleep for half an hour and after this they dress beautifully for dinner.   13. They sit at a long narrow, table; some eat a little cheese, meat, and bread, and drink a lot of French wine, while others, those interested in more serious matters or simply not wanting to eat, explain their future tasks to their neighbors.   14. Everyone is merry at first, but then the later it gets, the more bored they become.   15. Everyone is glad when it's time to go to bed.

# APPENDIX I

## PRONUNCIATION

**1.** The general rules of pronunciation, with the transcription and the meaning of the symbols used, were given in the Introduction, pages 2–6. In the discussion here, an additional compound symbol is used, $\check{z}\check{z}^b$: it represents a long (doubled) $\check{z}$, see § 15 below.

A full description and analysis of the Russian phonemic system may be found in *The Sounds of Russian*, by Prof. Morris Halle of the Massachusetts Institute of Technology and Prof. L. G. Jones of Boston College (Mouton and Co., The Hague, 1959). The total inventory includes five stressed (í é á ó ú) and three unstressed vowels (i a u), a glide (j), four liquids (r r$^b$ l l$^b$), four nasals (m m$^b$ n n$^b$), eleven spirants (f f$^b$ v v$^b$ s s$^b$ z z$^b$ š z x), and thirteen stops (p p$^b$ b b$^b$ t t$^b$ d d$^b$ c č k k$^b$ g).

For pedagogical reasons, it has been found useful to employ extra symbols in the transcriptions in this textbook. Beside the three vowel-letters *é i ə* explicitly noted on page 2, the symbols $g^b$, $x^b$, and $\check{z}\check{z}^b$ are tacitly included for consonantal sounds which are not, strictly speaking, phonemes.

**2.** The distinction of palatalized ∼ non-palatalized is fundamental for the Russian linguistic system and hence for the spelling. The majority of the consonants are paired:

| non-palatalized | p | b | f | v | t | d | s | z | m | n | l | r | k | g | x |
|---|---|---|---|---|---|---|---|---|---|---|---|---|---|---|---|
| palatalized | p$^b$ | b$^b$ | f$^b$ | v$^b$ | t$^b$ | d$^b$ | s$^b$ | z$^b$ | m$^b$ | n$^b$ | l$^b$ | r$^b$ | k$^b$ | (g$^b$) | (x$^b$) |

Palatalized consonants are commonly called "soft", and Russian has no special letters to spell them. Also grouped as soft (but without "hard" equivalents) are *j, č, šč,* and *žž$^b$.* Hard (but without soft equivalents) are *c, š,* and *ž.*

**3.0** Russian has five vowel phonemes – *i e a o u*. They are spelled by means of two sets of symbols, one called "hard vowel-letters", the other "soft vowel-letters". It must be emphasized that "hard" and "soft" here are conventional (and not altogether felicitous) terms for the LETTERS: they have *nothing* to do with the sounds. These letters are:

|  | *i* | *e* | *a* | *o* | *u* |
|---|---|---|---|---|---|
| "hard" | ы | э | а | о | у |
| "soft" | и | е | я | ё | ю |

**3.1** The "hard vowel-letters" represent the vowels and nothing else.

**3.2** The "soft vowel-letters" have two separate functions:

**3.21** Written immediately after a consonant-letter, they signify that the latter stands for a soft consonant followed by the given vowel (but see § 5, below).

**3.22** Written in any other position (i.e. initially, or after a vowel-letter or the signs ъ, ь), they represent the consonant *j* plus the given vowel.

**4.** A consonant letter represents a hard consonant normally. It stands for a soft consonant if followed by any "soft vowel-letter" or the ь ("soft-sign"):

e.g.:  т  *t*      ты  *ti*    тэ  *te*    та  *ta*    то  *to*    ту  *tu*
       ть  *tᵇ*    ти  *tᵇi*   те  *tᵇe*   тя  *tᵇa*   тё  *tᵇo*   тю  *tᵇu*

**5.** Since the consonants *š, ž,* and *c* are always hard and *č* and *šč* are always soft, either "hard vowel-letters" or "soft vowel-letters" would have the same meaning after letters representing these consonants, and thus the distribution is arbitrary. It has little to do with the actual pronunciation.

**5.1** After *š, ž, č, šč* and *c*, the phonemes *u* and *a* are spelled by the "*hard* vowel-letters" **y** and **а**: ша, жа, ча, ща, ца; шу, жу, чу, щу, цу.

**5.2** After *š, ž, č* and *šč*, the phoneme *i* is spelled by the "*soft* vowel-letter" **и**. After *c*, the "hard letter" **ы** is always used in suffixes, but **и** sometimes appears in stems: ши, жи, чи, щи : цы [ци].

**5.3** After *š, ž, č, šč*, the phoneme *o* is usually spelled by the "soft vowel-letter" **ё**. This letter follows **ц** only if *un*stressed.

**6.** The pronunciations *ki, gi, xi* never occur, but only *kᵇi, gᵇi, xᵇi*. Therefore the "hard letter" **ы** never follows **к, г, х**.

**7.** Thus we have these indispensable spelling rules:

| | |
|---|---|
| *After* **к, г, х, ш, ж, ч, щ** : *only* **и**. | [NEVER ы!] |
| *After the same letters and also* **ц** : *only* **а, у**. | [NEVER я, ю!] |

**7.1** Another important spelling rule operates chiefly in declensional endings: if the ending is *stressed*, **o** is written after ш, ж, ч, щ, and ц; but when *un*stressed, the ending is written with **ё** (but see § 11.1322 below).

Specifically, this rules concerns

1. two noun-suffixes of instrumental singular, *-om* and *-oj(u)*:

| | | | | | |
|---|---|---|---|---|---|
| a. отéц | 'father' | отцóм | нéмец | 'German' | нéмцём |
|   кольцó | 'ring' | кольцóм | сéрдце | 'heart' | сéрдцём |
| b. душá | 'soul' | душóй | Мáша | 'Masha' | Мáшёй |
|  |  | душóю |  |  | Мáшёю |

2. the genitive plural noun-suffix -*ov*:

отéц   'father'   отцóв      нéмец   'German'   нéмцев

3. the adjectival endings -*ojə*, -*ovə*, -*om*, -*omu*, -*oj*, -*oju*:

e.g. in the declension of большóй 'big' versus that of бóльший 'bigger' ·

| | | |
|---|---|---|
| neut. sg. Nom.-Acc. | большóё | бóльшёё |
| masc.-neut. sg. Gen. | большóго | бóльшёго |
| Prep. | большóм | бóльшём |
| Dat. | большóму | бóльшёму |
| fem. sg. Gen.-Dat.-Prep. | большóй | бóльшёй |
| Instr. | большóю | бóльшёю |

**8.1**  The symbol **ь** (the so-called "soft-sign", *mʲáxkəj znák*) is written after a consonant-letter to signify a soft consonant *not* immediately followed by a vowel (i.e. final, or followed by a consonant): pʲisʲmó письмó, brátʲ брáть, brátʲjə брáтья.

**8.2**  **ь** is often written after **ш**, **ж**, **ч**, and **щ**. Here it has of course no phonetic value (cf. §2, above).

It may function as an indication that the following "soft vowel-letter" represents the *consonant* j + *vowel*: i. e. **šjót** шьёт, but **šol** шёл; **ružjó** ружьё, but **žóni** жёны; cf. 9.1 below.

**8.3**  Otherwise **ь** may signal that a noun ending in *š*, *ž*, *č*, *šč* is a third-declension feminine and not a first-decl. masc. or some other form:

| | | | | | | |
|---|---|---|---|---|---|---|
| míš | (f) | 'mouse' | мышь | but | kóš (m) | 'basket' | кóш |
| róš | (f) | 'rye' | рожь | but | nóš (m) | 'knife' | нóж |
| nóč | (f) | 'night' | ночь | but | zadáč (Gen. pl.) | 'of problems' | задáч |
| vʲéšč | (f) | 'thing' | вéщь | but | tavárʲišč (m) | 'comrade' | товáрищ |

**8.31**  **ь** is written in the 2nd-sg. verbal ending -**шь**: gəvarʲíš говорúшь.

**8.32**  **ь** is also written in the imperative of stems ending in *š*, *ž*, *č*: e.g.

| | | | | | |
|---|---|---|---|---|---|
| rʲéžut | 'they cut' | rʲéš, rʲéštʲi | рéжут; | рéжь, | рéжьте |
| pláčut | 'they weep' | pláč, pláčtʲi | плáчут; | плáчь, | плáчьте |
| | 'eat' (irreg.) | jéš, jéštʲi | | éшь, | éшьте |

**9.**  The consonant phoneme **j** (pronounced like *y* in *y*es) is spelled in a number of different ways:

1. when *not* before a vowel, by means of **й**:
čitáj, čitájtʲi – читáй, читáйте.
2. when before a vowel, by the "soft vowel-letters" (§3.2): e.g.
maji мой,  majéj моéй,  majá моя́,  majó моё,  majú мою́.

**9.1**  To represent the combination "*consonant* + *j*", the "soft vowel-letters" which contain the *j* must be separated from the consonant-letter by the symbols ь or ъ. ъ (the "hard-sign", *tvʲórdɨj znák*) has no other function; in the orthography in use 1917–56 it could be replaced by the apostrophe (e.g. с'езд, от'езд). For example:

| | | | | | | | |
|---|---|---|---|---|---|---|---|
| sjést | съезд | atjést | отъезд: but cf. sʲéstʲ | сесть | atʲéc | отец |
| padjóm | подъем | pʲján | пьян | | padʲónkə | подёнка | pʲátʲ | пять |
| pʲjóš | пьёшь | pʲjésə | пьеса | | pʲóstr | пёстр | pʲétʲ | петь |
| palʲjót | польёт | sʲimʲjí | семьи | | palʲót | полёт | sʲimʲí | семи |
| šjót | шьёт | šjút | шьют | | šól | шёл | šút | шут |

**10.** It is a principle of Russian spelling to maintain the visual form of a meaningful word-element (a morpheme) in spite of the changes it undergoes in pronunciation. Compare, for example, various forms of the word for 'city' — **górət, górədə, górədʲi, gəratskój, gəradá, zá gərət, zá gərədəm** — and the related word 'orchard' (both contain the idea of "fenced-in place") — **agarót, agaródə, agaródʲi**. In transcription and pronunciation the underlying form, the common denominator of all these ten variants, never really appears, but the Russian is perfectly aware that it is *gorod*, with two *o*'s and a *d*, and he spells accordingly: **город, города, городе, городской, города, зá город, зá городом; огород, огорода, огороде**. The foreigner who knows the rules and the place of the accent on each form can easily pronounce them all correctly. The most complicated problem is that of the vowels.

**11.0** A shift of stress and/or a change of phonetic surroundings may cause the quality of vowels within a morpheme to vary: stól stalá, žɨná žónɨ, dvʲέrʲ dvʲirʲéj; tój, étəj, nášɨj.

**11.01** Phonemically it may be stated thus:

A. under stress there are 5 vowels          :  *i   e   a   o   u*

B. unstressed after *hard* consonants except š, ž, only 3:   *i      a      u*

C. unstressed after *soft* consonants and š and ž, only 2:       *i*      *u*
(for ə instead of unstressed *a*, see below, 12.2)

Thus *e* if not stressed always becomes *i*; unstressed *o* becomes *a* or *i*, according to the quality of the preceding consonant.

The phoneme *i* automatically is pronounced *ɨ* after š, ž, or *c*.

In native words, in specific grammatical suffixes, the unstressed ə (standing for *o* or *a*, cf. 12.2) does exceptionally occur in position C: nominative sing. neuter aknó (A), dʲélə (B), pólʲə (C); dative plural daskám (A), kómnətəm (B), zʲémlʲəm (C).

In words considered as foreign, unstressed *o* and *e* may appear: poét 'poet'.

**11.011** Note that *after* the stress the only vowel that is clearly formed is *u*. The *i* of the transcription is practically never like the English vowel in *beet*, but more like that in *bit*, and sometimes even more obscure, approximately like one of the unstressed vowels in *inhibited*. Nevertheless, after a hard consonant (except the non-paired *š ž c*) there is a distinction maintained between a reduced *i* and an *ə* that stands for a reduced *a* or *o*: dᵇivánə will not be identical with dᵇiváni.

In verbs, the 3rd plural present maintains *ət* as distinct from the singular it/ɨt: vᵇídᵇət/slɨ́šət — vᵇídᵇit/slɨ́šɨt (cf. § 11.151, 11.161 below).

After soft consonants, the unstressed ending of the second-declension Nom. sg. *-a* is usually kept distinct from endings that reduce to *i*: nᵇidᵇélᵇə — nᵇidᵇélᵇi; but in other endings (Prep. and Dat. pl.) the expected *ə* often cannot be distinguished from a weak *i*: nᵇidᵇélᵇəx/nᵇidᵇélᵇix In the neuter Nom.-Acc. sg., many Russians do not retain the *ə* that represents a reduction of *o* in position C, but use a weak *i*: pólᵇi, zdánᵇiji.

After *š ž c*, the potential distinction between *i* and *ə* in declensional endings is retained only in the most careful speech.

**11.1** From the spelling point of view, the picture is totally different. All ten vowel-letters may stand for stressed or unstressed vowels. For that reason it is necessary to discuss the pronunciation of the vowel-letters at some length.

**11.11** The letters for *u* (**y**, **ю**) do not change their pronunciation significantly.

**11.12** The two letters for the phoneme *i* (**и**, **ы**) do not correspond exactly to the distribution of the phonetic variants *i* and *ɨ*: the variant *ɨ* is always pronounced *after a hard consonant*; *i* appears in all other positions (i.e. after a soft consonant, or initial). Note that since *š* and *ž* are hard, the spellings **ши**, **жи** represent *šɨ žɨ*.

An initial **и** is pronounced *ji* only in the pronouns jíx, jím, jímᵇi **úx**, **úм**, **úми**, and the *j* may be very weak or even disappear. After the final consonant of a preposition (cf. § 13.4, 14.1) the spelled **и** is regularly pronounced *ɨ*: vɨtálᵇiji **в Италии** 'in Italy', sɨvánəm **с Ива́ном** 'with Ivan'.

Otherwise initial **и** represents *i*. In contact with the final hard consonant of a preceding word it can become *ɨ*: ón igrál or ónɨgrál **он игра́л** 'he played'.

After a vowel-letter, **и** stands for *ji*, but except in the most emphatic or careful speech, the *j* tends to disappear: vɨtálᵇiji/vɨtálᵇii **в Ита́лии**.

**11.131**   The letter **e** represents *é* or *jé* if stressed (fsᵇé всé, jéš éшь) with the automatic variants *ę́* or *ję́* before a soft consonant (čę́j чéй, dvᵇę́rᵇ двéрь); otherwise *i* or *ji* (jivrapᵇéjkᵇi eвропéйкe), which automatically means *i* after **ж, ш, ц**: žilátᵇ, múži, nᵇémci желáть, мýже, нéмцe.

**11.132**   The letter **ë** represents *ó* or *jó* if stressed (fsᵇó всё, majó моё). Unstressed, it represents (like **e**) *i* or *ji* (sᵇistrá znájit сёстрá знáeт), with the automatic variant *i* after *š*, *ž*, and *c*: žiná pᵇíšit жёнá пишёт.

**11.1321**   An important exception is the use of **ë** for *ə/jə* in the neuter singular Nom.-Acc. grammatical suffixes where the unstressed *ə* corresponds to stressed *ó*: aknó but pólᵇə, zdánᵇijə, окнó ~ пóлё, здáниё; majó but nášə, moë ~ нáшё, also plaxójə, paslᵇédnᵇəjə плохóё, послéднёё. However, many Russians pronounce only *i* here too: pólᵇi, zdánᵇiji; plaxóji, paslᵇédnᵇiji. In the masc.-neut. instrumental singular suffix and the genitive plural, *ə* may be heard, but *i/i* is more usual: aknóm but pólᵇim/pólᵇəm, zdánᵇijim/zdánᵇijəm окнóм ~ пóлём, здáниём; atcóf, čijóf but nᵇémcif/nᵇémcəf, brátᵇjif/brátᵇjəf отцóв, чаёв ~ нéмцёв, брáтьёв, cf. § 11.011 above.

**11.1322**   The distinction between stressed **ë** and unstressed **ë** is not ordinarily made even in textbooks for foreigners. When accent-marks are written, chiefly in dictionaries or in school-books for people whose native language is not Russian, the stressed **ë** is indicated by ordinary **ë** without the additional accent-mark.

In most Russian publications, the two dots (like the accents on other vowels) are written only in rare instances where there might be ambiguity. For example, признает can be read *prᵇiznajót* 'recognizes' or *prᵇiznájit* 'will recognize'; this book writes признаёт versus признаёт. In an ordinary Soviet book, признаёт means only *prᵇiznajót*.

In making alphabetical lists, **e** and **ë** are treated alike, so that after ёлка come елóвый, ёлочка, енóт, ёрш, éсли, etc.

**11.14**   The letter **э** occurs in the native pronoun этот 'this', representing *é* before *t* and *ę́* before *tᵇ* (e.g. *étə*, *ę́tᵇi* это эти). All other words in which **э** occurs are of foreign origin, and unaccented **э** is sometimes pronounced *i*, sometimes *e*: e.g. экономика 'economics' ikanómikə/ekanómikə.

**11.15**   The "soft vowel-letter" **я** represents *a* (*ja*) when accented: vzᵇátᵇ взять, majá моя́. If unstressed and in a declensional suffix where it is not followed by a soft consonant, **я** stands for *ə* (*jə*): dᵇirᵇévnᵇə дерéвня;

brátʰjə бра́тья; sasʰ&#803;édʰəm, sasʰ&#803;édʰəx сосе́дям, сосе́дях. Otherwise it represents *i* (*ji*): jizík язы́к, prʰimój прямо́й, pʰiták пята́к. (Note that unstressed *i* may also be represented by the letters е, и: (cf. pʰitúx [1] питу́х 'drunkard', [2] пету́х 'rooster'.)

**11.151** The letter я in the 3rd plural of verbs is pronounced either *ə* or *u* if *un*stressed; ви́дят vʰídʰət/vʰídʰut, отве́тят atvʰ&#803;étʰət/atvʰ&#803;étʰut (but the stressed suffix is only *á*; говоря́т gəvarʰát).

**11.16** The letter **a** unstressed and directly following the letters ч and щ (which represent consonants which are always *soft*) stands for *i*: часы́ čisí ('hours', but ча́с čás 'hour').

**11.161** The letter **a** after ш, ж, ч, щ, in 3rd plural of verbs, if *un*stressed, is pronounced either *ə* or *u*: слы́шат slíšət/slíšut.

**11.17** The letter **о** represents *a* (*ə*) everywhere except under stress.

**12.0** Here let us examine the pronunciation of the phonemes *o* and *a*. Kept separate only under stress, they fall together in all other positions. Two phonetic variants may be observed, *a* and *ə*.

**12.1** In the syllable *directly* before the accented vowel, or at the *absolute· beginning* of a word, *a* (whether representing stressless *a* or *o*) scarcely differs from stressed *á*, sounding approximately like the vowel of 'f*a*ther':

| | |
|---|---|
| rabótətʰ | рабо́тать |
| tavárʰišč | това́рищ |
| atʰéc | оте́ц |
| abɨknavʰénnə | обыкнове́нно |

**12.2** In any other position (i.e. in any syllable *after* the stress, or more than one syllable before the stress except for absolute initial) it has a reduced sound approximately like that in '*a*bout, sof*a*'. This sound is not significant in itself (is not phonemic), being an automatic variant of the phoneme *a*, and it could be spelled *a* in the transcription. For clarity, we prefer to use the symbol *ə* for it:

| | | | | | |
|---|---|---|---|---|---|
| xərašó | хорошо́ | pólʰə | по́лё | górət | го́род |
| kərandáš | каранда́ш | knʰígə | кни́га | górədə | го́рода |
| kərəndašá | карандашá | kómnətə | ко́мната | gəradá | города́ |
| agarót | огоро́д | prəčitálə | прочита́ла | gərədavój | городово́й |
| vəgaródʰi | в огоро́де | prəčitálə | прочита́ло | nastól | на сто́л |
| nóvəjə | но́воё, но́вая | zágərədəm | за́ го́родом | nətstalóm | над столо́м |

**13.0**  Russian words are of two types, stressless (§ 13.1 below) and stressed. Stressed words are again of two classes, those with a single stressed syllable (14.2), and those which may have more than one stressed syllable (13.3).

The stress is not marked in ordinary Russian books. When you learn a new word, it is essential to learn the stress on the basic forms and to memorize any changes of stress that take place in declension or conjugation.

The stress may fall on any syllable, and it is frequently the only difference between words which are otherwise identical, e.g. плачу *pláču* 'I weep' and *plačú* 'I pay'; купите *kúpʰitʰi* 'you will buy' and *kupʰitʰi* 'buy!': пахнуть *páxnutʰ* 'to smell' and *paxnútʰ* 'to blow'. Further, as will be explained below, words spelled alike may be pronounced quite differently because of the place of the stress, e.g. дорогой *darógaj* 'on the way' but *daragój* 'dear'; and different spellings may represent a single pronunciation, e.g. *nagá* = нага 'naked' and нога 'foot'.

**13.1**  Independent stressless words are very few in number, the most important being the conjunctions й 'and', а 'and/but', да *da* 'and, why' (which differs from stressed да *dá* 'yes'), что *šta* 'that' (which differs from stressed что *štó* 'what?, that which'), the interrogative ли *lʰi*, the conditional бы *bɨ*, the emphatic же *ži*, the adverb как *kak* (which differs from stressed *kák* как 'how, in what manner'), and the particles хоть *xatʰ*, ведь *vʰitʰ*, уж *uš*. The conjunction чтобы or чтоб is usually stressless *štabɨ* or *štap*, but it may be stressed *štóbɨ/štóp*.

**13.2**  The vast majority of Russian words have one single stressed syllable which is in strong contrast to the unstressed syllables, however many there may be. The syllable immediately before the stress is slightly stronger than the other unstressed syllables. It is possible to symbolize the stresses numerically (ignoring further very slight differences which a trained observer might notice), with 4 for maximum stress and 1 for minimum: e.g. *parazgavárʰivalʰi* поразговáривали 1–1–2–4–1–1–1; *vɨkrʰistalʰizavatca* вы́кристаллизоваться 4–1–1–1–1–1–1; *pʰirʰirʰigʰistrʰirujuščimʰisa* перерегистри́рующимися 1–1–1–2–4–1–1–1–1–1. The important point for an English-speaking person is to avoid the secondary stresses which are present in long English words like "incómprehènsibílity".

**13.3**  Words compounded of two (or, rarely, more) roots can have a secondary stress on the first root or roots, but the chief stress always falls on the last root (or its declensional suffix). The secondary stress may be completely suppressed. E.g. *vósʰimsót* or *vasʰimsót* восемьсот '800', *stálʰingrát* or *stalʰingrát* Сталинград 'Stalingrad'. Abbreviations used as independent words are treated as compounds: *ésésésér* CCCP 'USSR', *éššáá* США 'USA', *ágʰitpróp* агитпроп 'department of agitation and propaganda'.

**13.4**  Some syllables which are written as separate units are not in fact independent words. Most prepositions are an integral part of the stressed word (simple or compound) which follows; in relatively rare cases the stress falls on the preposition (e.g. zágərədəm in § 12.2 above; other examples in 14.1 below). The negative particles не and ни likewise are not independent words; both are normally unstressed $n^b i$, becoming distinct $n^b \acute{e}$ and $n^b \acute{i}$ only in the rare cases when they take the stress from the following word. Через may be stressless or stressed: $\check{c}ir^b izj\acute{a}ltu$ or $\check{c}\acute{e}r^b is \; j\acute{a}ltu$ 'via Jalta' через Ялту.

**13.5**  While every word (excepting the small group in 13.1) is, from the phonemic point of view, stressed, not every stress in a sentence is equal in force to every other stress. In general the "structure words" like conjunctions (e.g. $n\acute{o}$ но 'but', $il^b i$ или 'or', $j\acute{e}sl^b i$ если 'if', $t\acute{o}$ то 'then') and personal pronouns have a weaker stress than the "content words" like nouns and verbs, which carry most of the semantic load of the given message. In this book only the phonemic word-stresses will be marked. Accents are placed on stressed monosyllables to distinguish between the stressed independent words on the one hand and the stressless independent words and separately written but dependent stressless units like prepositions on the other. Thus the sentence $n\acute{o} \; \acute{o}n \; j\acute{e}j \; d\acute{a}l \; d\acute{o}m$ (Но он ей дал дом.) 'but he gave her a house' contains five stressed words, while $t\acute{i} \; \check{z}i \; zn\acute{a}l \; \check{s}t\partial \; \acute{o}n \; u\check{s} \; b\acute{i}l \; p^b ir^b idamn\acute{o}j$ (Ты же знал, что он уж был передо мной.) 'but you knew that he was already in front of me' consists of five stressed words (one of which includes the separately written but non-independent three-syllable preposition) and three stressless words.

**14.0**  The voiceless/voiced pairs of consonants ($p/b \; p^b/b^b \; f/v \; f^b/v^b \; t/d \; t^b/d^b \; s/z \; s^b/z^b \; \check{s}/\check{z} \; k/g$) are spelled sometimes by the "voiceless letters" (п ф т с ш к) and sometimes by the "voiced letters" (б в д з ж г).

**14.01**  Voiceless $\check{s}\check{c}$ (щ) corresponds to voiced $\check{z}\check{z}^b$ (which is spelled in various ways), but the only alternations between them occur in a single root, see § 15, below.

**14.02**  The voiceless consonants $\check{c}$, $c$, and $x$ (ч ц х) do not have voiced counterparts that are independent or in any way indicated in the spelling system, although in some cases they may be pronounced with voicing according to rule IIa, below, § 14.2.

**14.1**  In order to know whether to pronounce a given consonant-letter as voiced or voiceless, it is necessary to consider the following —
Two groups of phonemes must be distinguished:

Ai.    Sonants ($m \; m^b \; n \; n^b \; l \; l^b \; r \; r^b \; j$) and vowels, i.e. the letters

м н л р й я е ё ю и ы а о у э.

Aii.   $v$ or $v^b$ followed by $v$, $v^b$ or any of group Ai; i.e. the letter в followed by в or the above.

*Rule I.*   Consonant-letters standing directly before letters representing any phoneme of group A (i.e. either Ai or Aii) in the same word are pronounced voiced or voiceless as spelled.

*Rule IIa.*   Consonant-letters representing voiceless consonants are pronounced voiced if they stand directly before letters representing a voiced consonant or *v* plus voiced consonant.

*Rule IIb.*   In all other positions (i.e. before voiceless consonant-letter or at the end of a word) only voiceless consonants are pronounced.

Examples: (Remember that the letters ь and ъ, being merely signs, do not have any effect on voicing or voicelessness.)

|  | *I* |  |  | *IIa* |  |
|---|---|---|---|---|---|
| slᵇitátᵇ | слётáть | 'fly down' | zbᵇégət | сбéгать | 'run down' |
| prósᵇut | прóсят | 'they request' | prózᵇbə | прóсьба | 'request' |
| atjéxətᵇ | отъéхать | 'ride away' | addátᵇ | отдáть | 'give away' |
|  |  |  |  | *IIb* |  |
| gəradá | городá | 'cities' | górət | гóрод | 'city' |
| gərədavój | городовóй | 'policeman' | gəratskój | городскóй | 'urban' |
| pəjizdá | поездá | 'trains' | pójist | пóезд | 'train' |
| pajézdək | поéздок | 'of trips' | pajéstkə | поéздка | 'trip' |
| búdᵇiš | бýдешь | 'will be' | bútᵇ | бýдь | 'be!' |
| búdᵇitᵇi | бýдете | 'will be' | bútᵇtᵇi | бýдьте | 'be!' |
| rᵇéžiš | рéжешь | 'cut' | rᵇéš | рéжь | 'cut!' |
| rᵇéžitᵇi | рéжете | 'cut' | rᵇéštᵇi | рéжьте | 'cut!' |
| slóvə | слóво | 'word' | slóf | слóв | 'of words' |
| vnasᵇítᵇ | вносúть | 'carry in' | fxadᵇítᵇ | входúть | 'go in' |

Prepositions are part of the word that follows (cf. § 13.4 above):

|  | *I* |  |  | *IIa* |  |
|---|---|---|---|---|---|
| atnᵇijó | от неё | 'from her' | adžiní | от жёны | 'from wife' |
| satcóm | с отцóм | 'with father' | zbrátəm | с брátом | 'with brother' |
| kvám | к вáм | 'to you' | gvdavᵇé | к вдовé | 'to widow' |
|  |  |  |  | *IIb* |  |
| vnᵇéj | в нéй | 'in her' | fknᵇígᵇi | в кнúге | 'in book' |
| padnás | под нáс | 'under us' | patstól | под стóл | 'under table' |
| nadvámᵇi | над вáми | 'over you' | natpólᵇəm | над пóлем | 'over field' |
| pᵇirᵇidjášəj | перед Яшей | 'before Jasha' | pᵇirᵇitsášəj | перед Сáшей | 'before Sasha' |
| bᵇizvnúkə | без внýка | 'without grandson' | bᵇispᵇirá | без перá | 'without pen' |
| izétəvə | из э́того | 'from this' | istavó | из тогó | 'from that' |

**14.2** Rule IIa may, in normally rapid speech, be operative over a word-boundary, so that a final consonant or consonant group which is voiceless by application of rule IIb can become voiced if followed immediately by a word beginning in a voiced consonant or *v* plus voiced consonant.

| | | | |
|---|---|---|---|
| náš dóm | or náždóm | на́ш до́м | 'our house' |
| górət bíl | or górədbíl | го́род бы́л... | 'the city was...' |
| atᵇéc bíl | or atᵇédzbíl | оте́ц бы́л | 'father was...' |
| dóč bɨlá | or dódžbɨlá | дочь была́ | 'daughter was...' |

[Many Russian-speakers carry these rules over into their English, saying "fix" instead of "figs" (i.e. rule IIb), but "hoddok" and "ledz go" for "hotdog" and "let's go" (i.e. IIa, within a word and across a word-boundary)].

**15.** The combination žžᵇ (= long soft ž in standard pronunciation, although a long hard ž is often heard) serves as the voiced mate to šč, but has no separate symbol. It is usually spelled by the combination зж, as in jéžžᵇu éзжу, ujižžᵇátᵇ уезжа́ть. A special case is the root meaning 'rain', where жд + "soft vowel-letter" = žžᵇ: Nom. sg. dóšč (Rule IIb, § 14.1) до́ждь, Gen. sg. dažžᵇá дождя́, Gen. pl. dažžᵇéj дожде́й. In some other words the combination жж represents žžᵇ, e. g. vóžžᵇi 'reins' во́жжи.

**16.** In many cases, a consonant standing before a palatalized consonant is automatically pronounced as palatalized. This change is not indicated either in the Russian spelling or in the transcription. Thus jéstᵇ = jésᵇtᵇ есть, jézdᵇitᵇ = jézᵇdᵇitᵇ е́здить, zdᵇélətᵇ = zᵇdᵇélətᵇ сде́лать, zbᵇégətᵇ = zᵇbᵇégətᵇ сбе́гать, dvᵇérᵇ = dᵇvᵇérᵇ дверь.

The consonants most consistently affected are *t*, *d*, *s*, and *z*, but there is no clear rule, and in many instances the pronunciation of a given consonant-cluster varies from word to word.

**17.** There remain some special cases where the pronunciation is not covered by the rules already given or the tabular summary in § 19, on the following pages.

**17.1** The verbal endings -ться, -тся are always pronounced -*tca*, as if spelled -тца or -цца: bajátcə = both боя́ться 'to fear' and боя́тся 'they fear'; bajítcə бои́тся '(he) fears'.

**17.11** Elsewhere the particle -ся/-сь is pronounced with a *hard s*, but the spelling-pronunciation with soft *s*ᵇ is acceptable: bajálsə or bajálsᵇə боя́лся '(he) feared'; bajáləs or bajáləsᵇ боя́лась '(she) feared'.

**17.2** In the Nom sg masculine of adjectives, final -кий, -гий, -хий may be pronounced -*kəj*, -*gəj*, -*xəj* (M), or else as spelled, -*kᵇij*, -*gᵇij*, -*xᵇij*: e.g. rúskəj or rúskᵇij ру́сский 'Russian'; dólgəj or dólgᵇij до́лгий 'long'; tᵇíxəj or tᵇíxᵇij ти́хий 'quiet'.

**17.3**  The **-г-** in the **-ого/-ёго** suffix of Gen. sg. adjectives and pronouns is pronounced *v*: e.g.

| | | | | | |
|---|---|---|---|---|---|
| tavó | того́ | 'that' | məladóvə | молодо́го | 'young' |
| étəvə | э́того | 'this' | ná\$ivə | на́шего | 'our' |
| nóvəvə | но́вого | 'new' | ból\ᵇ\$ivə | бо́льшего | 'bigger' |
| jivó | ёго́ | 'of him, his' | paslᵇédnᵇivə | после́днего | 'last' |
| majivó | моёго́ | 'my' | trᵇétᵇjivə | тре́тьего | 'third' |

Here also the word *sᵇivódnᵇə* сего́дня 'today'.

**17.4**  The combination **сч** is pronounced as though spelled **щ**: **сч**а́стьё 'happiness' \$částᵇjə.

**17.5**  The consonant clusters **-стл-, -стн-, -здн-** are pronounced without the middle consonants, i.e. *-sl-, -sn-, -zn-*; e.g. \$čislᵇívə счастливо 'happily': rádəsnə радостно 'joyously': póznə поздно 'late'.

**17.6**  In a few common words, **-чн-** is pronounced *-šn-*; kanᵇéšnə коне́чно 'of course'.

**17.7**  **г** before **к, ч** is pronounced **x**: lᵇixkó лёгко́ 'light', lᵇéxči лёгче 'lighter': mᵇáxkəj/mᵇáxkᵇij (cf. 17.2) мя́гкий 'soft'.

**17.8**  Isolated cases:

| | | | | | |
|---|---|---|---|---|---|
| štó | что́ | 'what?' | pažálstə or pažáləstə | пожа́луйста | 'please' |
| štəbɨ | чтобы | 'in order to' | zdrásttᵇi or zdrástvujtᵇi | здра́вствуйте | 'hello' |

The widespread pronunciation **čtó** for что́ is not considered "correct" by Soviet authorities.

**17.9**  Patronymics are ordinarily shortened by one syllable when they are spoken together with the first or Christian name (VI 7.1).

With masculine patronymics the rule for shortening is simple and virtually without exception: the written suffix **-ович/-ёвич** is pronounced **-ыч/-ич** (unless, of course, the **o** is stressed). Thus Ива́ныч, И́горич, Серге́ич, Ю́рьич or Ю́рич.

With feminine patronymics, the situation is less clear, and good usage varies more widely. The **-ов-** is omitted after **в, н,** or **м**: Вя́чеславна, Ива́нна, Степа́нна, Макси́мна. It is retained after **п, б, к**: Ка́рповна, О́сиповна, Гле́бовна, Иса́ковна, Ма́рковна. The unstressed **ё** of forms in **-ёёвна** is usually omitted, and the **-ов-** or **-ёв-** *may* be omitted in most other cases: Андре́вна or Андре́ёвна; Влади́мирна or Влади́мировна; Ю́рьна or Ю́рьёвна.

Here is a list of some of the more common masculine personal names, followed by the *spoken* form of the patronymics. Bracketed letters may be pronounced or omitted: Васи́ль[ёв]на = Васи́льёвна, Васи́льна.

| | | | |
|---|---|---|---|
| Алекса́ндр | Алекса́н[др]ыч | О́сип | О́сипыч [О́спич] |
| | Алекса́нна | | О́сиповна |
| Михаи́л | Миха́лыч | Па́вел | Па́[в]лыч |
| | Миха́лна | | Па́лна |
| Никола́й | Никола́ич | Я́ков | Я́келич |
| | Никола́вна | | Я́кельна |
| | | | |
| Аки́м | Аки́мыч | Макси́м | Макси́мыч |
| | Аки́мна | | Макси́мна |
| Анто́н | Анто́ныч | Плато́н | Плато́ныч |
| | Анто́нна | | Плато́нна |
| Богда́н | Богда́ныч | Святосла́в | Святосла́выч |
| | Богда́нна | | Святосла́вна |
| Владисла́в | Владисла́выч | | |
| | Владисла́вна | Семён | Семёныч |
| Вячесла́в | Вячесла́выч | | Семённа |
| | Вячесла́вна | Стёпа́н | Стёпа́ныч |
| Ефи́м | Ефи́мыч | | Стёпа́нна |
| | Ефи́мна | | |
| Ива́н | Ива́ныч | Яросла́в | Яросла́выч |
| | Ива́нна | | Яросла́вна |
| | | | |
| Алексе́й | Алексе́ич | Бори́с | Бори́сыч |
| | Алексе́[ё]вна | | Бори́с[ов]на |
| Андре́й | Андре́ич | Влади́мир | Влади́мирыч |
| | Андре́[ё]вна | | Влади́мир[ов]на |
| Матве́й | Матве́ич | Прохо́р | Прохо́рыч |
| | Матве́[ё]вна | | Прохо́р[ов]на |
| Серге́й | Серге́ич | Фёдор | Фёдорыч |
| | Серге́[ё]вна | | Фёдор[ов]на |
| Тимофе́й | Тимофе́ич | Федо́т | Федо́тыч |
| | Тимофе́[ё]вна | | Федо́т[ов]на |
| | | | |
| Глеб | Гле́быч | Ка́рп | Ка́рпыч |
| | Гле́бовна | | Ка́рповна |
| Иса́к | Иса́кич | Ма́рк | Ма́ркич |
| | Иса́ковна | | Ма́рковна |

| | | | |
|---|---|---|---|
| Викéнтий | Викéнтич | Демéнтий | Демéнтич |
| | Викéнтёвна | | Демéнтёвна |
| Геóргий | Геóргич | Дми́трий | Дми́трич |
| | Геóргёвна | | Дми́трёвна |
| | | | |
| Арсéний | Арсéн[ь]ич | Юрий | Юр[ь]ич |
| | Арсéнь[ёв]на | | Ю́рь[ёв]на |
| Васи́лий | Васи́л[ь]ич | Порфи́рий | Порфи́р[ь]ич |
| | Васи́ль[ёв]на | | Порфи́р[ь]ёвна |
| Григóрий | Григóр[ь]ич | Прокóфий | Прокóф[ь]ич |
| | Григóрь[ёв]на | | Прокóф[ь]ёвна |
| Евгéний | Евгéн[ь]ич | Савéлий | Савéл[ь]ич |
| | Евгéнь[ёв]на | | Савéл[ь]ёвна |

**18.** Intonation. In American English, the close of a statement is marked by a rather abrupt drop in musical pitch within the last stressed syllable or between the last stressed and following unstressed syllables. (Cf. He's a priest. He's a doctor.) A question is marked by a rising pitch. (Is he a doctor? John?) Other variations in intonation denote the end of a partial statement (i.e. the break between parts of a compound sentence), enumeration (cf. There were books, pamphlets, magazines, and letters on the table.), parenthetical asides, or commands. Still other variations introduce certain emotional connotations, e.g. doubt or surprise.

Russian intonation, in spite of some general resemblances to American English, differs sharply in detail. To describe it meaningfully, a complex notation is necessary, but even a good notation is no substitute for actual Russian utterances, whether live or recorded. In this book no description will be attempted. The student should listen very carefully to his teacher and to recordings and should pay close attention to such matters as, for example, the difference in melodic intervals between the Russian and the American statement-final drop or neutral-question rise. A recognition of the varieties of intonation-patterns and the ability to reproduce them are as fundamental as the knowledge of individual words and grammatical forms.

**19.** The next six pages summarize the use of the Russian letters. The vowels are given first, and then the consonants in alphabetical order. For the "hard-sign" ъ, refer back to § 9.1 (pp. 326–327). For the "soft-sign" ь, see §§ 8 and 9.1 (pp. 326–327).

| letter | pro-nounced | when | example | |
|---|---|---|---|---|
| **а** | a | 1. under stress | tá | тá |
| | | 2. in syllable just before stress, NOT after č, šč | spasʲibə | спасйбо |
| | | | skažitʲi | скажйте |
| | i | 3. in absolute initial position | amʲirʲikánʲic | американец |
| | | unstressed after č, šč (except in inflectional suffix) | čisʲ | часй |
| | u (ə) | unstressed in 3 pl. verbal ending after š, ž, č, šč (§ 11.151) | ščidʲitʲ | щадйть |
| | | | slišut, znáčut | слышат, знáчат |
| | | | palúčut | полýчат |
| | ə | anyplace else | kómnətə, róšče | кóмната, рóща |
| | | | kərəndaší | карандашй |
| **я** | a | under stress after consonant | palʲá, zʲimlʲá | поля́, земля́ |
| | ja | under stress NOT after consonant | majá, jásnə | моя́, я́сно |
| | ə/jə | unstressed in inflectional suffix not followed by soft consonant | rasʲijə, gʲirójə | Россия, герóя |
| | | | dʲirʲévnʲə, lʲúdʲəm | дерéвня, лю́дям |
| | u (ə) | unstressed in 3 pl. verbal ending (§ 11.151) | vʲídʲut, vʲérʲut | ви́дят, вéрят |
| | i/ji | elsewhere | jizík, pójis | язы́к, пóяс |
| | | | pónʲil, pənʲilá | пóнял, понялá |
| **э** | ę | before soft consonant | étʲi | э́ти |
| | e | normally | étə | э́то |
| | i | sometimes when unstressed: in all cases the words are foreign and may have unstressed e | ikanómʲikə/ekanómʲikə | эконóмика |

| Letter | Sound | Rule | Transcription | Cyrillic |
|---|---|---|---|---|
| **е** | ẹ | stressed, after consonant-letter, before soft consonant | čẹj, dvʲẹrʲ, vʲẹščі | чей, дверь, вещи |
| | e | stressed, after consonant-letter | gdʲé, dʲélə, mʲéstə | где, дело, место |
| | je· | stressed, NOT after consonant-letter, before soft consonant | jéstʲ, majéj, jélʲ | есть, моей, ель |
| | je | stressed, NOT after consonant-letter | jél, pajéš | ёл, поёшь |
| | ɨ | unstressed after š, ž, c | žilátʲ, úlʲicі | желать, улице |
| | i/ji | unstressed otherwise | dʲélajitʲi, vmʲéstʲi | делаете, вместе |
| **ы** | ɨ | always (occurs only after consonants) | ví žóni | вы жёны |
| **и** | ɨ | after š, ž, c | žílʲi, círk | жили, цирк |
| | ji | initially in three pronominal forms | jix, jimʲbi, jim | их, ими, им |
| | (j)i | after vowels (the j is very weak) | rasʲiji | России |
| | i | elsewhere | izvʲinʲítʲi | извините |
| **о** | o | stressed ONLY (except foreignisms) | ón, nó (rádʲio) | он, но (радио) |
| | a | 1. in syllable just before stress | gəradá mají | города мой |
| | | 2. absolute initial | agarót, abіknavʲénnə | огород, обыкновенно |
| | ə | elsewhere | kóləkəla, kaləkalá vəgaródʲi, zágərədəm | колокола, колокола в огороде, за городом |
| **ё** | o/jo | stressed ONLY | žóni, majó, jiščó jóš, pʲitʲjó nʲós, žívʲbom, žívʲjóm | жёны, моё, ещё ёж, питьё нёс, живём, живьём |
| | ə/jə | unstressed in certain declensional suffixes | pólʲə, nášə, zdánʲije pólʲəm, zdánʲijem | поле, наше, здание полем, зданием |
| | ɨ | unstressed after š, ž, c | žiná, pʲišit | жена, пишет |
| | i/ji | otherwise | sʲistrá, znájit | сестра, знает |

| letter | pro-nounced | when | example | example |
|---|---|---|---|---|
| у | u | always | živú, pʲíšut ulučšátʲ | живу́, пи́шут улучша́ть |
| ю | u/ju | always | uznajú, uznáju pólʲu, arúžju dʲirʲévnʲu | узна́ю, узна́ю по́лю, ору́жью дере́вню |
| б | b | normally | búdu brátʲ, spasʲíbə | бу́ду брать, спаси́бо |
| | bʲ | before ь or soft vowel-letter | bʲjú sʲibʲé, sʲibʲá | бью себе́, себя́ |
| | p | final or before voiceless consonant | zúp, lóp | зуб, лоб |
| | pʲ | before final ь or ь plus voiceless consonant | zupčátij, ópščij gólupʲ, grápʲ grápʲtʲi | зубча́тый, о́бщий го́лубь, грабь грабьте |
| в | v | normally | vám, vý, svój | вам, вы, свой |
| | vʲ | before ь or soft vowel-letter | vʲjúgə, žívʲjóm vʲéčir, króvʲi | вьюга, живьём ве́чер, кро́ви |
| | f | final or before voiceless consonant | slóf, pʲitróf galófka, afcá | слоф, Пётро́в голо́вка, овца́ |
| | fʲ | before final ь or ь plus voiceless consonant | lʲubófʲ, práfʲ práfʲtʲi | любо́вь, правь пра́вьте |

| | | Rule | Transcription | Cyrillic |
|---|---|---|---|---|
| **г** | g | normally | gəvarᵇú, lᵇágu | говорю́, ля́гу |
| | gᵇ | before *e* or *i* | gdᵇé knᵇíge | где кни́га |
| | | | knᵇígᵇi, fknᵇígᵇi | кни́ги, в кни́ге |
| | | | gᵇénᵇij | ге́ний |
| | k | final or before voiceless consonant | knᵇík, lᵇák | кни́г, ляг |
| | | | lᵇákt̪ᵇi | ля́гте |
| | x | before *k* or *č* | lᵇóxkəj, lᵇéxči | лёгкий, ле́гче |
| | v | in genitive singular masc.-neut. pron.-adj. suffix | tavó, nóvəvə | того́, но́вого |
| | | | majivó balᵇšóvə | моего́ большо́го |
| **д** | d | normally | sᵇádu, gəradók | ся́ду, городо́к |
| | dᵇ | before ь or soft vowel-letter | usádᵇba, dᵇjável | уса́дьба, дья́вол |
| | | | górədᵇi, sasᵇédᵇi | го́роде, сосе́ди |
| | t | final or before voiceless consonant | górət, gəratká | го́род, городка́ |
| | | | pót, pótkup | под, по́дкуп |
| | tᵇ | before final ь or ь plus voiceless consonant | sᵇátᵇ, grúst̪ᵇ | сядь, гру́здь |
| | | | sᵇátᵇtᵇi | ся́дьте |
| **Ж** | ž | normally | užé, úži, ružjó | уже́, у́же, ружьё |
| | š | final or before voiceless consonant | žít̪ᵇ, žmút, arúžje | жить, жмут, ору́жье |
| | | | nóš, rᵇéš | нож, режь |
| | | | nóškə, rᵇéšt̪ᵇi | но́жка, ре́жьте |
| **з** | z | normally | zúp, zvón, glazá | зуб, звон, глаза́ |
| | | | druzᵇjá | друзья́ |
| | zᵇ | before ь or soft vowel-letter | zᵇimá, vzᵇát̪ᵇ | зима́, взять |
| | s | final or before voiceless consonant | glás, rás | глаз, раз |
| | | | gláskᵇi | гла́зки |
| | sᵇ | before final ь or ь plus voiceless consonant | lᵇésᵇ, grᵇásᵇ | лезь, грязь |
| | | | lᵇésᵇt̪ᵇi | ле́зьте |

| letter | pro-nounced | when | example | |
|---|---|---|---|---|
| й | j | always | mój, tájnij<br>rúskaj majór | мóй, тáйный<br>рýсский майóр |
| к | k | normally | kák, skók | кáк, скóк |
| | kʲ | before soft vowel-letter | rúskʲiji, kʲáxtə | рýсские, Кя́хта |
| | g | before voiced consonant | igzámʲin | экзáмен |
| л | l | normally | lúk, stúl, bɨl | лýк, стýл, бы́л |
| | lʲ | before ь or<br>soft vowel-letter | bʲilʲ, stúlʲjə<br>lʲúlʲkə, lʲétə | бы́ль, стýлья<br>лю́лька, лéто |
| м | m | normally | tám, mój, mgnavʲénʲijə | тáм, мóй, мгновéниё |
| | mʲ | before ь or soft<br>vowel-letter | sʲémʲ, sʲimʲjá<br>mʲásə, vazʲmʲóš | сéмь, семья́<br>мя́со, возьмёшь |
| н | n | normally | ón, nó, nánkə | óн, нó, нáнка |
| | nʲ | before ь or<br>soft vowel-letter | kónʲ, lgúnʲjə<br>nʲét, nʲánʲkə | кóнь, лгýнья<br>нéт, ня́нька |
| п | p | normally | spasʲíbə, pústʲ<br>sʲpʲ, pʲjú | спаси́бо, пýсть<br>сы́пь, пью́ |
| | pʲ | before ь or<br>soft vowel-letter | pʲótr, pʲétʲ, pʲítʲ | Пётр, пéть, пи́ть |
| р | r | normally | rás, útrə, dvór | рáз, ýтро, двóр |
| | rʲ | before ь or<br>soft vowel-letter | cárʲ, vʲérʲtʲi<br>carʲá, vʲérʲu | цáрь, вéрьте<br>царя́, вéрю |

| | | | | |
|---|---|---|---|---|
| с { | s | normally | sám, sjést, lʲísɨ | сáм, съéст, лѝсы |
| | sʲ | before ь or soft vowel-letter | vʲésʲ, pʲisʲmó | вéсь, письмó |
| | z | before voiced consonant | sʲádu, sʲudá, lʲísʲji | сяду, сюдá, лисьи |
| | zʲ | before ь + voiced consonant | zdátʲ, zgubʲítʲ | сдáть, сгубѝть |
| | | | prózʲbə | прóсьба |
| т { | t | normally | tót, stól, brát | тóт, стóл, брáт |
| | tʲ | before ь or soft vowel-letter | tʲmá, brátʲjə | тьмá, брáтья |
| | d | before voiced consonant | tʲótʲə, stʲópə, brátʲ | тётя, Стёпа, брáть |
| | dʲ | before ь + voiced consonant | addátʲ, ódzɨf | отдáть, óтзыв |
| | | | məladʲbá | молотьбá |
| ф { | f | normally | fákt, fálʲš | фáкт, фáльшь |
| | fʲ | before ь or soft vowel-letter | fʲivrálʲ, prafʲésər | феврáль, профéссор |
| х { | x | normally | áx, xərašó | áх, хорошó |
| | xʲ | before *i, e* | plóxʲɨ, xʲérʲitʲ | плóхи, хéрить |
| ц | c | always | atʲéc, atcé | отéц, отцé |
| | | | cépʲ, cɨkl | цéпь, цѝкл |
| ч | č | always | čášə, nóč, čjá | чáша, нóчь, чья |
| ш | š | always | šáškə, šút | шáшка, шýт |
| | | | šjút, mɨš | шьют, мышь |
| щ | šč | always | ščí, jiščó, vʲéščʲ | щѝ, ещё, вéщь |

# APPENDIX II

## TRANSLITERATION

The phonemic trans*cription* is to be kept sharply distinct from trans-*literation*. The latter is, as the name implies, simply a substitution of Roman letters for the Russian letters. Since there are 33 Russian letters and only 26 Roman ones, some combinations and modifications are necessary in order to achieve a one-to-one, unambiguous transliteration. Transcription (the one in this book or any of many others) tries to represent somehow the *pronunciation*: nʰičivó, nyeechiVOH, neet-scheevo, etc. Transliteration reproduces the Russian *spelling*, regardless of the pronunciation: ničego or nichego = ничего.

The aim of transliteration is to have a single letter or combination of letters in Roman to represent unambiguously a single letter in Cyrillic, i.e. to reproduce the Russian spelling. There are three instances in which Roman combinations are used: (1) *šč* always stands for **щ**, since **шч** does not occur in Russian; (2–3) *ja* and *ju* represent the Cyrillic "soft vowel-letters" **я** and **ю**, respectively; otherwise *j* always stands for **й** (e.g. mo**ja** mo**ju** mo**j** = моя мою мой). Further, in four cases two letters can, alternatively, be used instead of one; for *č, š* (also *šč*), *ž* and *x* no ambiguity can arise if *ch, sh* (*shch*), *zh*, and *kh* are written, since *h* by itself has no meaning. Thus, *čašax, ščažu* or *chashakh, shchazhu* = чашах, щажу. The two dots are written on **ё** only for the stressed vowel.

| | | | | | | | |
|---|---|---|---|---|---|---|---|
| **а** | a | **и** | i | **р** | r | **ш** | š, sh |
| **б** | b | **й** | j | **с** | s | **щ** | šč, shch |
| **в** | v | **к** | k | **т** | t | **ъ** | " |
| **г** | g | **л** | l | **у** | u | **ы** | y |
| **д** | d | **м** | m | **ф** | f | **ь** | ' |
| **е** | e | **н** | n | **х** | x, kh | **э** | è |
| **ё** | ë | **о** | o | **ц** | c | **ю** | ju |
| **з** | z | **п** | p | **ч** | č, ch | **я** | ja |
| **ж** | ž, zh | | | | | | |

Transliteration is used throughout this book for all proper names, even though in çertain cases some other spelling may be widespread in English. The following list gives typical names: the first column indicates the *pronunciation* in **transcription,** the second column the normal Russian spelling, followed by its equivalent in Roman **transliteration.**

| | | |
|---|---|---|
| *jáltə* Ялта | Jalta (Yalta) | |
| *júrʰij* Юрий | Jurij (George) | |
| *júrʰjiʃ* Юрьёв | Jur'ev (a town) | |
| *pɨ́pʰin* Пы́пин | Pypin | |

| | | |
|---|---|---|
| *ilʰf* Ильф | Il'f | |
| *ólʰgə* Ольга | Ol'ga | |
| *gógəlʰ* Го́голь | Gogol' | |
| *sónʰə* Со́ня | Sonja | |

| | | |
|---|---|---|
| *məjakófskəj (-skʰij)* | Маяко́вский | Majakovskij |
| *čirnɨšéfskəj (-skʰij)* | Чёрнышёвский | Černyševskij or Chernyshevskij |
| *ilʰjá ilʰjič* | Илья́ Ильи́ч | Il'ja Il'ič or Il'ich |
| *trójickəj (-ckʰij)* | Тро́ицкий | Troickij |
| *tróckəjə* | Тро́цкая | Trockaja ⌈Zhemchuzhnikov |
| *žɨmčúžnʰikəf* | Жемчу́жников | Žemčužnikov or |
| *čajkófskəj (-skʰij)* | Чайко́вский | Čajkovskij or Chajkovskij |
| *jizɨ́kəf* | Язы́ков | Jazykov |
| *xəmʰikóf* | Хомяко́в | Xomjakov or Khomjakov |
| *čéxəf* | Че́хов | Čexov or Chekhov |
| *xruščóf* | Хрущёв | Xruščëv or Khrushchëv |
| *muravʰjóf* | Муравьёв | Murav'ëv |
| *tʰútčif* | Тю́тчёв | Tjutčev or Tjutchev |
| *cigánəf* | Цыга́нов | Cyganov ⌈Shchedrin |
| *səltɨkóf ščidrʰin* | Салтыко́в-Щедри́н | Saltykov-Ščedrin or |
| *bəlʰšɨvʰík* | Большеви́к | Bol'ševik or Bol'shevik |
| *vaprósɨ ikanómʰikʰi* | Вопро́сы эконо́мики | Voprosy èkonomiki |
| *pʰiškóf górʰkəj (-kʰij)* | Пешко́в-Го́рький | Peškov-Gor'kij or Peshkov |
| *ʃtarój sjést* | Второ́й съезд | Vtoroj s"ezd |

# APPENDIX III

## I. NOUN DECLENSION

The paradigms illustrate the fundamental declensional types and a few important variants. Remember that the accusative form of animate nouns is like the genitive form for masculine singular (1st decl. only) and for all genders in the plural. Remember that the distribution of the letters ы/и, а/я, у/ю in the suffixes is determined purely by the spelling rules given in §§ 5–7 of Appendix I, as are ó/ë after ш, ж, ч, щ, ц (p. 325).

Do not forget that some masculine nouns have a special partitive genitive in -у/-ю (Lesson XIX) and some a special locative in stressed -ý/-ю́ (Lesson II): none of these forms are illustrated in the paradigms here. It may be noted that a few 3rd declension feminines have a special locative in -и, e.g. *стéпь* 'steppe' — о стéпи, but в степи́.

The rules for the distribution of the plural nominative and genitive endings are given in Lesson VIII; information on accent-patterns below, pp. 350 ff.

Some common irregular paradigms not occurring in the Lessons are given. The noun *телёнок* 'calf' is illustrative of nouns with singular in -ёнок and plural in -я́та; all signify the young of living beings. Ýхо 'ear' has an irregular plural; *плечó* 'shoulder', and *я́блоко* 'apple' have irregular N-A pl., as do certain other neuters in -ко. Like *врéмя* 'time' are declined also *и́мя* 'name', *брéмя* 'burden', *знáмя* 'flag', *плáмя* (no pl.) 'flame', and *плéмя* 'tribe'.

## FIRST DECLENSION: Masculines

|      | club     | table    | tiger     | Peter    | bank      | sin      |
|------|----------|----------|-----------|----------|-----------|----------|
|      | club     | table    | tiger     | Peter    | bank      | sin      |
| N.   | клу́б    | стóл     | ти́гр     | Пётр     | бáнк      | грéх     |
| A.   | клу́б    | стóл     | ти́гра    | Пётрá    | бáнк      | грéх     |
| G.   | клу́ба   | столá    | ти́гра    | Пётрá    | бáнка     | грехá    |
| Pr.  | клу́бе   | столé    | ти́гре    | Пётрé    | бáнке     | грехé    |
| D.   | клу́бу   | столý    | ти́гру    | Пётрý    | бáнку     | грехý    |
| I.   | клу́бом  | столóм   | ти́гром   | Пётрóм   | бáнком    | грехóм   |
| N.   | клу́бы   | столы́   | ти́гры    | Пётры́   | бáнки     | грехи́   |
| A.   | клу́бы   | столы́   | ти́гров   | Пётрóв   | бáнки     | грехи́   |
| G.   | клу́бов  | столóв   | ти́гров   | Пётрóв   | бáнков    | грехóв   |
| P.   | клу́бах  | столáх   | ти́грах   | Пётрáх   | бáнках    | грехáх   |
| D.   | клу́бам  | столáм   | ти́грам   | Пётрáм   | бáнкам    | грехáм   |
| I.   | клу́бами | столáми  | ти́грами  | Пётрáми  | бáнками   | грехáми  |

| | chemist | enemy | German | father | beach | knife |
|---|---|---|---|---|---|---|
| N. | хи́мик | вра́г | не́мец | оте́ц | пля́ж | но́ж |
| A. | хи́мика | врага́ | не́мца | отца́ | пля́ж | но́ж |
| G. | хи́мика | врага́ | не́мца | отца́ | пля́жа | ножа́ |
| Pr. | хи́мике | враге́ | не́мце | отце́ | пля́же | ноже́ |
| D. | хи́мику | врагу́ | не́мцу | отцу́ | пля́жу | ножу́ |
| I. | хи́миком | враго́м | не́мцём | отцо́м | пля́жём | ножо́м |
| N. | хи́мики | враги́ | не́мцы | отцы́ | пля́жи | ножи́ |
| A. | хи́миков | враго́в | не́мцёв | отцо́в | пля́жи | ножи́ |
| G. | хи́миков | враго́в | не́мцёв | отцо́в | пля́жей | ноже́й |
| Pr. | хи́миках | врага́х | не́мцах | отца́х | пля́жах | ножа́х |
| D. | хи́микам | врага́м | не́мцам | отца́м | пля́жам | ножа́м |
| I. | хи́миками | врага́ми | не́мцами | отца́ми | пля́жами | ножа́ми |

| | comrade | hedgehog | style | rain | writer | tsar |
|---|---|---|---|---|---|---|
| N. | това́рищ | ёж | сти́ль | до́ждь | писа́тель | ца́рь |
| A. | това́рища | ёжа́ | сти́ль | до́ждь | писа́теля | царя́ |
| G. | това́рища | ёжа́ | сти́ля | дождя́ | писа́теля | царя́ |
| Pr. | това́рище | ёже́ | сти́ле | дожде́ | писа́теле | царе́ |
| D. | това́рищу | ёжу́ | сти́лю | дождю́ | писа́телю | царю́ |
| I. | това́рищём | ёжо́м | сти́лём | дождём | писа́телём | царём |
| N. | това́рищи | ёжи́ | сти́ли | дожди́ | писа́тели | цари́ |
| A. | това́рищей | ёже́й | сти́ли | дожди́ | писа́телей | царе́й |
| G. | това́рищей | ёже́й | сти́лей | дожде́й | писа́телей | царе́й |
| Pr. | това́рищах | ёжа́х | сти́лях | дождя́х | писа́телях | царя́х |
| D. | това́рищам | ёжа́м | сти́лям | дождя́м | писа́телям | царя́м |
| I. | това́рищами | ёжа́ми | сти́лями | дождя́ми | писа́телями | царя́ми |

| | museum | hero | sanatorium | genius |
|---|---|---|---|---|
| Nom. | музе́й | геро́й | санато́рий | ге́ний |
| Acc. | музе́й | геро́я | санато́рий | ге́ния |
| Gen. | музе́я | геро́я | санато́рия | ге́ния |
| Prep. | музе́е | геро́е | санато́рии | ге́нии |
| Dat. | музе́ю | герою́ | санато́рию | ге́нию |
| Inst. | музе́ём | геро́ём | санато́риём | ге́ниём |
| Nom. | музе́и | геро́и | санато́рии | ге́нии |
| Acc. | музе́и | геро́ёв | санато́рии | ге́ниёв |
| Gen. | музе́ёв | геро́ёв | санато́риёв | ге́ниёв |
| Prep. | музе́ях | геро́ях | санато́риях | ге́ниях |
| Dat. | музе́ям | геро́ям | санато́риям | ге́ниям |
| Inst. | музе́ями | геро́ями | санато́риями | ге́ниями |

|  | house | teacher | brother | son | Englishman | calf | Petrov | Pushkin |
|---|---|---|---|---|---|---|---|---|
| Nom. | дóм | учи́тель | брáт | сы́н | англичáнин | телёнок | Петрóв | Пýшкин |
| Acc. | дóм | учи́теля | брáта | сы́на | англичáнина | телёнка | Петрóва | Пýшкина |
| Gen. | дóма | учи́теля | брáта | сы́на | англичáнина | телёнка | Петрóва | Пýшкина |
| Prep. | дóме | учи́теле | брáте | сы́не | англичáнине | телёнке | Петрóве | Пýшкине |
| Dat. | дóму | учи́телю | брáту | сы́ну | англичáнину | телёнку | Петрóву | Пýшкину |
| Inst. | дóмом | учи́телем | брáтом | сы́ном | англичáнином | телёнком | Петрóвым | Пýшкиным |
| Nom. | домá | учителя́ | брáтья | сыновья́ | англичáне | теля́та | Петрóвы | Пýшкины |
| Acc. | домá | учителéй | брáтьёв | сыновéй | англичáн | теля́т | Петрóвых | Пýшкиных |
| Gen. | домóв | учителéй | брáтьёв | сыновéй | англичáн | теля́т | Петрóвых | Пýшкиных |
| Prep. | домáх | учителя́х | брáтьях | сыновья́х | англичáнах | теля́тах | Петрóвых | Пýшкиных |
| Dat. | домáм | учителя́м | брáтьям | сыновья́м | англичáнам | теля́там | Петрóвым | Пýшкиным |
| Inst. | домáми | учителя́ми | брáтьями | сыновья́ми | англичáнами | теля́тами | Петрóвыми | Пýшкиными |

| **Neuters** | affair | field | building | heart | letter | drink | pen | ear | shoulder | apple |
|---|---|---|---|---|---|---|---|---|---|---|
| N.-A. | дéло | пóлё | здáниё | сéрдцё | письмó | питьё | перó | ýхо | плечó | я́блоко |
| Gen. | дéла | пóля | здáния | сéрдца | письмá | питья́ | перá | ýха | плечá | я́блока |
| Prep. | дéле | пóле | здáнии | сéрдце | письмé | питьé | перé | ýхе | плечé | я́блоке |
| Dat. | дéлу | пóлю | здáнию | сéрдцу | письмý | питью́ | перý | ýху | плечý | я́блоку |
| Inst. | дéлом | пóлём | здáнием | сéрдцем | письмóм | питьéм | перóм | ýхом | плечóм | я́блоком |
| N.-A. | делá | поля́ | здáния | сердцá | пи́сьма | питья́ | пéрья | ýши | плéчи | я́блоки |
| Gen. | дéл | полéй | здáний | сердéц | пи́сем | питéй | пéрьёв | ушéй | плéч | я́блок |
| Prep. | делáх | поля́х | здáниях | сердцáх | пи́сьмах | питья́х | пéрьях | ушáх | плечáх | я́блоках |
| Dat. | делáм | поля́м | здáниям | сердцáм | пи́сьмам | питья́м | пéрьям | ушáм | плечáм | я́блокам |
| Inst. | делáми | поля́ми | здáниями | сердцáми | пи́сьмами | питья́ми | пéрьями | ушáми | плечáми | я́блоками |

# SECOND DECLENSION

|  | school | lady | street | book | student | problem | song |
|---|---|---|---|---|---|---|---|
| Nom. | шко́ла | да́ма | у́лица | кни́га | студе́нтка | зада́ча | пе́сня |
| Acc. | шко́лу | да́му | у́лицу | кни́гу | студе́нтку | зада́чу | пе́сню |
| Gen. | шко́лы | да́мы | у́лицы | кни́ги | студе́нтки | зада́чи | пе́сни |
| Pr.-D. | шко́ле | да́ме | у́лице | кни́ге | студе́нтке | зада́че | пе́сне |
| Inst. | шко́лой / шко́лою | да́мой / да́мою | у́лицей / у́лицею | кни́гой / кни́гою | студе́нткой / студе́нткою | зада́чей / зада́чею | пе́сней / пе́снею |
| Nom. | шко́лы | да́мы | у́лицы | кни́ги | студе́нтки | зада́чи | пе́сни |
| Acc. | шко́лы | дам | у́лицы | кни́ги | студе́нток | зада́чи | пе́сни |
| Gen. | школ | дам | улиц | книг | студе́нток | задач | песён |
| Prep. | шко́лах | да́мах | у́лицах | кни́гах | студе́нтках | зада́чах | пе́снях |
| Dat. | шко́лам | да́мам | у́лицам | кни́гам | студе́нткам | зада́чам | пе́сням |
| Inst. | шко́лами | да́мами | у́лицами | кни́гами | студе́нтками | зада́чами | пе́снями |

|  | line | mistress | article | sister | board | Ivanov[a] | Pushkin[a] |
|---|---|---|---|---|---|---|---|
| Nom. | ли́ния | госпожа́ | статья́ | сестра́ | доска́ | Ива́нова | Пу́шкина |
| Acc. | ли́нию | госпожу́ | статью́ | сестру́ | до́ску | Ива́нову | Пу́шкину |
| Gen. | ли́нии | госпожи́ | статьи́ | сестры́ | доски́ | Ива́новой | Пу́шкиной |
| Pr.-D. | ли́нии | госпоже́ | статье́ | сестре́ | доске́ | Ива́новой | Пу́шкиной |
| Inst. | ли́нией / ли́ниею | госпожо́й / госпожо́ю | статьёй / статьёю | сестро́й / сестро́ю | доско́й / доско́ю | Ива́новой / Ива́новою | Пу́шкиной / Пу́шкиною |
| Nom. | ли́нии | госпожи́ | статьи́ | сёстры | до́ски | Ива́новы | Пу́шкины |
| Acc. | ли́нии | госпож | статьи́ | сестёр | до́ски | Ива́новых | Пу́шкиных |
| Gen. | ли́ний | госпож | стате́й | сестёр | досо́к | Ива́новых | Пу́шкиных |
| Prep. | ли́ниях | госпожа́х | статья́х | сёстрах | доска́х | Ива́новых | Пу́шкиных |
| Dat. | ли́ниям | госпожа́м | статья́м | сёстрам | доска́м | Ива́новым | Пу́шкиным |
| Inst. | ли́ниями | госпожа́ми | статья́ми | сёстрами | доска́ми | Ива́новыми | Пу́шкиными |

## THIRD DECLENSION

|          | joy        | thing    | mother    | daughter  | time       |
|----------|------------|----------|-----------|-----------|------------|
| N.-A.    | ра́дость   | ве́щь    | ма́ть     | до́чь     | вре́мя     |
| G.-Pr.-D.| ра́дости   | ве́щи    | ма́тери   | до́чери   | вре́мёни   |
| Inst.    | ра́достью  | ве́щью   | ма́терью  | до́черью  | вре́мёнем  |
| Nom.     | ра́дости   | ве́щи    | ма́тери   | до́чери   | времёна́   |
| Acc.     | ра́дости   | ве́щи    | матере́й  | дочере́й  | времёна́   |
| Gen.     | ра́достей  | веще́й   | матере́й  | дочере́й  | времён     |
| Prep.    | ра́достях  | веща́х   | матеря́х  | дочеря́х  | времёна́х  |
| Dat.     | ра́достям  | веща́м   | матеря́м  | дочеря́м  | времёна́м  |
| Inst.    | ра́достями | веща́ми  | матеря́ми | дочерьми́ | времёна́ми |

NOUN STRESS.   Three patterns of stress in declension are productive; that is, newly coined or borrowed words may be fitted into them. Mostly there is a fixed stress throughout all forms, either on the stem (group 1 below), or on the first syllable of the ending (group 4); or else the stem may be stressed in the singular and the ending in the plural (group 2). Many common and important nouns belong to various non-productive stress-types, and in some the accent varies according to region and generation, even in the speech of the educated.

For simple reference in the vocabularies, the following abbreviations will be used: $S$ = stem, normally the first syllable of the word; $s$ = the last syllable of the stem, in the few instances where this distinction is necessary; $E$ = first syllable of ending; $pl$ = all plural cases; $Npl$ = nominative plural (+ non-animate Acc.); $pl\ obl$ = only the oblique plural cases (i.e. all but Nom. + non-anim. Acc.). In the vocabularies, you can assume that the stress remains where it is in the nominative singular unless one of the group-symbols defined below is given.

**1.**  Stress is always on stem. This is the largest and most productive group, and no special symbol is needed.

**2.**  Stress on stem in singular and ending in plural (productive for masculines with pl. in -á; non-productive for neuters, ca. 15): symbol *Epl.*

| garden | са́д    | са́да    | о са́де  | — | сады́    | садо́в    |
|--------|--------|----------|----------|---|----------|-----------|
|        |        |          |          |   |          | сада́х    |
| city   | го́род | го́рода  | го́роде  | — | города́  | городо́в  |
|        |        |          |          |   |          | города́х  |
| doctor | до́ктор| до́ктора | до́кторе | — | доктора́ | докторо́в |
|        |        |          |          |   |          | доктора́х |

| teacher | учи́тель | учи́теля | учи́теле | — | учителя́ | учителе́й учителя́х |
| place | ме́сто | ме́ста | ме́сте | — | места́ | ме́ст места́х |

**3.** Stress on stem in singular and Nom. (Acc.) pl., but on ending in plural oblique cases (non-productive; includes some 30 masc., 70 3rd-decl. fem.): *E pl obl.*

| year | год | го́да | го́дом | — | го́ды | — | годо́в | года́х |
| guest | го́сть | го́стя | го́стём | | го́сти | | гостей | гостя́х |
| door | дверь | две́ри | две́рью | | две́ри | | дверей | дверя́х |

**4.** Stress throughout on ending (productive): *E.*

(NB that when there is a zero-ending the stress has to fall on the last vowel present, be it stem-vowel or inserted vowel.)

| table | сто́л | стола́ | столе́ | столы́ | столо́в | стола́х |
| language | язы́к | языка́ | языке́ | языки́ | языко́в | языка́х |
| tsar | ца́рь | царя́ | царе́ | цари́ | царе́й | царя́х |
| father | оте́ц | отца́ | отце́ | отцы́ | отцо́в | отца́х |
| bench | скамья́ | скамьи́ | скамье́ | скамьи́ | скаме́й | скамья́х |

**5.** Stress on ending in singular, stem in plural (non-productive, some 35 neuters, 60 2nd-decl.): *Spl.*

| wine | вино́ | вина́ | вине́ | — | ви́на | ви́н | ви́нах |
| pen | перо́ | пера́ | пере́ | | пе́рья | пе́рьев | пе́рьях |
| war | война́ | войны́ | войне́ | | во́йны | во́йн | во́йнах |

**6.** Stress on ending except in Acc. sing. and in plural (non-prod., rare) *Spl Asg.*

| water | вода́ | воды́ | воде́ | — | во́ду | — | во́ды | во́д | во́дах |
| soul | душа́ | души́ | душе́ | | ду́шу | | ду́ши | ду́ш | ду́шах |
| winter | зима́ | зимы́ | зиме́ | | зи́му | | зи́мы | зи́м | зи́мах |
| price | цена́ | цены́ | цене́ | | це́ну | | це́ны | це́н | це́нах |

**7.** Stress on ending except in Nom. (Acc.) pl. (non-prod., some 20): *S Npl.*

| lip | губа́ | губы́ | | — | гу́бы | — | гу́б | губа́х |
| frying pan | сковорода́ | сковороды́ | | | ско́вороды | | сковоро́д | сковорода́х |

**8.** Stress on ending except Acc. sg. and Nom. (Acc.) pl. (non-prod., 15): *S Npl Asg.*

| board | доска́ | доски́ | — | до́ску | — | до́ски | досо́к | доска́х |
| head | голова́ | головы́ | | го́лову | — | го́ловы | голо́в | голова́х |

**9.** Stress constant either on ending or on first stem-syllable in singular, but on last stem-syllable in plural (non-prod., ca. 15): *s.*

| orphan | сирота́ | сироты́ | сироте́ | — | сиро́ты | сиро́т | сиро́тах |
| wheel | колесо́ | колеса́ | колесе́ | | колёса | колёс | колёсах |
| lake | о́зеро | о́зёра | о́зёре | | озёра | озёр | озёрах |

In the group of about 100 2nd-declension nouns in *-á*, there is a tendency for types 7—8 to adapt to type 5 (i.e. for the plural as a whole to be opposed to the whole singular, cf. type 2). Some of the words at present in 5 occur in poetry and in fixed phrases with stressed oblique pl. -suffixes. The most important of the words remaining in 7—8 are:

7. (*S Npl*) *межá* 'border', *полосá* 'strip', *свечá* 'candle', *строкá* 'line', *строфá* 'strophe', *тропá* 'path'; *волнá* 'wave' may also be *Spl*.

8. (*S Npl Asg*) *горá* 'mountain', *средá* 'Wednesday', *порá* 'time', *рекá* 'river', *рукá* 'hand', *спинá* 'back', *стенá* 'wall', *щекá* 'cheek' [*щёки*], *бородá* 'beard', *сторонá* 'side'.

A few words of the *Spl* group stress the inserted vowel of Gen. pl.:

|          | G sg.   | N pl.   |     | G pl.   | Pr. pl.  |
|----------|---------|---------|-----|---------|----------|
| land     | земля́  | земли́  | — зе́мли | земе́ль | зе́млях |
| sheep    | овца́   | овцы́   | о́вцы    | ове́ц   | о́вцах  |
| pig      | свинья́ | свиньи́ | сви́ньи  | свине́й | сви́ньях |
| family   | семья́  | семьи́  | се́мьи   | семе́й  | се́мьях |
| sister   | сестра́ | сёстры́ | сёстры   | сёстёр  | сёстрах |
| judge (m.)| судья́ | судьи́  | су́дьи   | суде́й  | су́дьях |

## II. ADJECTIVE DECLENSION

### "Soft declension"

|        | masculine     | neuter        | feminine      | plural        |
|--------|---------------|---------------|---------------|---------------|
| Nom.   | после́дний    | после́днее    | после́дняя    | после́дние    |
| Acc.   | (= N or G.)   | после́днее    | после́днюю    | (N. or G.)    |
| Gen.   | после́днего   |               | после́дней    | после́дних    |
| Prep.  | после́днем    |               | после́дней    | после́дних    |
| Dat.   | после́днему   |               | после́дней    | после́дним    |
| Instr. | после́дним    |               | { после́дней / после́днею } | после́дними |

### Normal declension (see tables on next page).

Note: the only spelling difference between types 1A and 1B and between 2A and 2B are in the N sg. masc.: stressed **-óй** ~ unstressed **-ый** or **-ий**. 3B differs from 3A both in this and in the fact that the stressed **o**-endings are replaced by unstressed **e**-endings. 2A and 3A are identical and are presented separately because of the 2B ~ 3B contrast.

### Variant types.

Possessive adjectives in **-ий** are declined like *тре́тий* 'third', see page 357 below, under Numerals; e.g. ли́сий, ли́сье, ли́сья, ли́сьи 'fox's', бо́жий, бо́жье, бо́жья, бо́жьи 'God's, divine' — ли́сьего, ли́сьей, ли́сьих, ли́сьими etc.

Surnames in **-ов** and **-ин** serve as examples of the declension of possessive adjectives with the same suffixes, see above on pages 348 and 349 in the paradigms of masculine and feminine nouns. The neuter form has **-o** in N-A sg and otherwise is like the masculine. Only the prepositional singular differs from the surnames: Петро́ве, but отцо́вом. For example, *отцо́в, отцо́во, отцо́ва, отцо́вы* 'father's'; *се́стрин, се́стрино, се́стрина, се́стрины* 'sister's'.

## A (stressed ending)

### 1

| | m. | n. | f. | pl. |
|---|---|---|---|---|
| Nom. | молодой | молодое | молодая | молодые |
| Acc. | (N. or G.) | молодое | молодую | (N. or G.) |
| Gen. | молодого | | молодой | молодых |
| Prep. | молодом | | молодой | молодых |
| Dat. | молодому | | молодой | молодым |
| Inst. | молодым | | молодой (молодою) | молодыми |

### 2 (in к, г, х)

| | m. | n. | f. | pl. |
|---|---|---|---|---|
| Nom. | плохой | плохое | плохая | плохие |
| Acc. | (N., G.) | плохое | плохую | (N, G.) |
| Gen. | плохого | | плохой | плохих |
| Prep. | плохом | | плохой | плохих |
| Dat. | плохому | | плохой | плохим |
| Inst. | плохим | | плохой (плохою) | плохими |

### 3 (in ш, ж, ч, щ)

| | m. | n. | f. | pl. |
|---|---|---|---|---|
| Nom. | большой | большое | большая | большие |
| Acc. | (N. or G.) | большое | большую | (N., G.) |
| Gen. | большого | | большой | больших |
| Prep. | большом | | большой | больших |
| Dat. | большому | | большой | большим |
| Inst. | большим | | большой (большою) | большими |

## B (unstressed ending)

### 1

| | m. | n. | f. | pl. |
|---|---|---|---|---|
| Nom. | новый | новое | новая | новые |
| Acc. | (N. or G.) | новое | новую | (N., G.) |
| Gen. | нового | | новой | новых |
| Prep. | новом | | новой | новых |
| Dat. | новому | | новой | новым |
| Inst. | новым | | новой (новою) | новыми |

### 2

| | m. | n. | f. | pl. |
|---|---|---|---|---|
| Nom. | русский | русское | русская | русские |
| Acc. | (N. or G.) | русское | русскую | (N., G.) |
| Gen. | русского | | русской | русских |
| Prep. | русском | | русской | русских |
| Dat. | русскому | | русской | русским |
| Inst. | русским | | русской (русскою) | русскими |

### 3

| | m. | n. | f. | pl. |
|---|---|---|---|---|
| Nom. | хороший | хорошее | хорошая | хорошие |
| Acc. | (N., G.) | хорошее | хорошую | (N., G.) |
| Gen. | хорошего | | хорошей | хороших |
| Prep. | хорошем | | хорошей | хороших |
| Dat. | хорошему | | хорошей | хорошим |
| Inst. | хорошим | | хорошей (хорошею) | хорошими |

**A note on diminutives.** Russian has a number of special noun suffixes which, while denoting size (diminutives and augmentatives), reveal the attitude of the speaker (approval, affection; disapproval, scorn). Most important are the affectionate diminutives, e.g. *до́мик* 'little house, nice little house, nice house', *кни́жка* 'booklet, nice booklet, nice book'. For the most part, the emotional content prevails over the notion of physical size: it is possible to call a mansion a *до́мик* or *War and Peace* a *кни́жка*. Compare *винцо́* 'nice little wine', where there can be no question of size. Often two diminutive suffixes may occur together, intensifying the meaning: e.g. *до́мичёк, кни́жёчка*. Here are a few examples of the most common means of formation: *city* го́род, городо́к (-дка́ E), городо́чёк (-чка); *chair* сту́л, сту́лик, сту́льчик: *affair* де́ло, де́льцё; *building* зда́ние, зда́ньицё; *room* ко́мната, ко́мнатка, комнату́шка, комнату́шёчка; *wife* жена́, жёнка, жёнушка; *night* но́чь, но́чка, но́ченька; *thing* ве́щь, вещи́ца, вещи́чка.

In adjectives, the suffix -ёньк- (-оньк- after к г х) conveys the same type of affectionate attitude: **бедне́нький, красне́нький, старе́нький, сине́нький, плохо́нький.**

## III. PRONOUN DECLENSION

**The personal and interrogative pronouns.**

|      | *1 sg.*          | *2 sg.*          | *1 pl.* | *2 pl.* | *m.*  | *n.*  | *f.*  | *pl.*  |       |       |
|------|------------------|------------------|---------|---------|-------|-------|-------|--------|-------|-------|
| N.   | я                | ты               | мы      | вы      | о́н    | оно́   | она́   | они́    | кто́   | что́   |
| A.   | меня́             | тебя́             | на́с     | ва́с     | ёго́   | её́    | и́х    | кого́   | что́   |       |
| G.   | меня́             | тебя́             | на́с     | ва́с     | ёго́   | её́    | и́х    | кого́   | чёго́  |       |
| P.   | мне́              | тебе́             | на́с     | ва́с     | не́м   | не́й   | ни́х   | ко́м    | че́м   |       |
| D.   | мне́              | тебе́             | на́м     | ва́м     | ёму́   | е́й    | и́м    | кому́   | чему́  |       |
| I.   | { мно́й / мно́ю } | { тобо́й / тобо́ю } | на́ми    | ва́ми    | и́м    | { ёю́ / е́й } | и́ми   | ке́м    | че́м   |       |

When used with any preposition, all forms of the third personal pronoun prefix **н**: него́, нему́, ни́м, неё, не́й, не́ю, ни́х, ни́м, ни́ми.

The reflexive pronoun *себя́* ( XV 6) has no Nom., otherwise follows *ты́*. For the emphatic personal pronoun *сам*, see p. 191.

**The possessive and possessive-interrogative pronouns and "all".**

|      | *m.*         | *n.*             | *f.*   | *pl.*      | *m.*         | *n.*      | *f.*             | *pl.*      |
|------|--------------|------------------|--------|------------|--------------|-----------|------------------|------------|
| N.   | мо́й          | моё́              | моя́    | мои́        | на́ш          | на́шё      | на́ша             | на́ши       |
| A.   | (N., G.)     | моё́              | мою́    | (N, G)     | (N., G.) на́шё |          | на́шу             | (N., G.)   |
| G.   | моёго́        |                  | моёй    | мои́х       | на́шёго       |           | на́шей            | на́ших      |
| P.   | моё́м         |                  | моёй    | мои́х       | на́шём        |           | на́шей            | на́ших      |
| D.   | моёму́        |                  | моёй    | мои́м       | на́шёму       |           | на́шей            | на́шим      |
| I.   | мои́м         | { моёй / моёю }   | мои́ми  |            | на́шим        |           | { на́шей / на́шею } | на́шими     |

|    | *m.* | *n.* | *f.* | *pl.* |
|----|------|------|------|------|
| N. | чéй | чьё | чья́ | чьи́ |
| A. | (N., G.) | чьё | чью | (N., G.) |
| G. | чьего́ | | чьей | чьи́х |
| P. | чьём | | чьей | чьи́х |
| D. | чьему́ | | чьей | чьи́м |
| I. | чьи́м | | {чьéй / чьéю} | чьи́ми |

*Твой* and *свой* follow the model of *мой*; *ваш* is like *наш*.

## The demonstrative pronouns.

|    | *m.* | *n.* | *f.* | *pl.* | *m.* | *n.* | *f.* | *pl.* |
|----|------|------|------|------|------|------|------|------|
| N. | тóт | тó | тá | тé | э́тот | э́то | э́та | э́ти |
| A. | (N., G.) | тó | тý | (N., G.) | (N., G.) | э́то | э́ту | (N., G.) |
| G. | того́ | | тóй | тéх | э́того | | э́той | э́тих |
| P. | тóм | | тóй | тéх | э́том | | э́той | э́тих |
| D. | тому́ | | тóй | тéм | э́тому | | э́той | э́тим |
| I. | тéм | | {тóй / тóю} тéми | | э́тим | | {э́той / э́тою} э́тими | |

|    | *m.* | *n.* | *f.* | *pl.* |
|----|------|------|------|------|
| N. | вéсь | всё | вся́ | всé |
| A. | (N., G.) | всё | всю | (N., G) |
| G. | всего́ | | всéй | всéх |
| P. | всéм | | всéй | всéх |
| D. | всему́ | | всéй | всéм |
| I. | всéм | | {всéй / всéю} всéми | |

## IV. NUMERALS

### 1. Cardinal Numerals:

| 1 оди́н | 11 оди́ннадцать | | 100 стó |
|---------|------------------|--|---------|
| 2 двá, двé | 12 двена́дцать | 20 два́дцать | 200 двéсти |
| 3 три́ | 13 трина́дцать | 30 три́дцать | 300 три́ста |
| 4 четы́ре | 14 четы́рнадцать | 40 сóрок | 400 четы́реста |
| 5 пя́ть | 15 пятна́дцать | 50 пятьдеся́т | 500 пятьсóт |
| 6 шéсть | 16 шестна́дцать | 60 шестьдеся́т | 600 шестьсóт |
| 7 сéмь | 17 семна́дцать | 70 сéмьдесят | 700 семьсóт |
| 8 вóсемь | 18 восемна́дцать | 80 вóсемьдесят | 800 восемьсóт |
| 9 дéвять | 19 девятна́дцать | 90 девянóсто | 900 девятьсóт |
| 10 дéсять | 20 два́дцать | 100 стó | 1000 ты́сяча |

**1.01**  *Spelling rule*: up to *40*, ь at the end — after *40*, ь in the middle of word! пятна́дцать — пятьдеся́т, пятьсо́т: семна́дцать — се́мьдесят, семьсо́т

**1.1**  *21, 32, 43* etc. are formed by simply adding the unit to the ten: *два́дцать оди́н (одна́, одно́), три́дцать два́ (две́), со́рок три́,* etc.

**1.2** *1000* is a regular feminine noun (but see 3, below), and further thousands are regular:

*две́ ты́сячи, три́ ты́сячи, четы́ре ты́сячи, пя́ть ты́сяч, со́рок ты́сяч.*

**1.3**  *Миллио́н* 'million' and *миллиа́рд* (or *биллио́н*) 'thousand million' are regular masculine nouns and treated accordingly: *два́ миллио́на, пя́ть миллио́нов; три́ миллиа́рда, девяно́сто миллиа́рдов.*

**1.4**  NOTE: In writing numerals, the Russians use the comma where we use a decimal point: 32,5 means 'thirty-two and a half'. For marking off thousands, they use a period or else a space: 5.321,38 or 5 321,38 (= our 5,321.38).

## 2. Ordinal numerals.

| | | | |
|---|---|---|---|
| 1 пе́рвый | 11 оди́ннадцатый | | 100 со́тый |
| 2 второ́й | 12 двена́дцатый | 20 двадца́тый | 200 двухсо́тый |
| 3 тре́тий | 13 трина́дцатый | 30 тридца́тый | 300 трёхсо́тый |
| 4 четвёртый | 14 четы́рнадцатый | 40 сороково́й | 400 четырёхсо́тый |
| 5 пя́тый | 15 пятна́дцатый | 50 пятидеся́тый | 500 пятисо́тый |
| 6 шесто́й | 16 шестна́дцатый | 60 шестидеся́тый | 600 шестисо́тый |
| 7 седьмо́й | 17 семна́дцатый | 70 семидеся́тый | 700 семисо́тый |
| 8 восьмо́й | 18 восемна́дцатый | 80 восьмидеся́тый | 800 восьмисо́тый |
| 9 девя́тый | 19 девятна́дцатый | 90 девяно́стый | 900 девятисо́тый |
| 10 деся́тый | 20 двадца́тый | 100 со́тый | 1000 ты́сячный |

**2.1**  The ordinals *21st, 32nd, 43rd*, etc. are composed of the *cardinal* of the ten and the *ordinal* of the unit: *два́дцать пе́рвый (-во́е, -вая, -вые), три́дцать второ́й, со́рок тре́тий; се́мь ты́сяч семьсо́т седьмо́й,* etc.

**2.2**  *2000 th, 3000 th*, etc. are formed on the pattern of the hundreds: *двухты́сячный, трёхты́сячный, пятиты́сячный, шеститы́сячный,* etc.

**3.**  The declension of the numeral *1* has already been given in Lesson XIV 7.

*2, 3* and *4* have declensions which are similar: these (*1–4*) are the only numerals with special forms for the animate accusative. For "both" see § 6, below.

The numerals *5–20*, and *30*, are regular nouns of the 3rd declension.

*40, 90*, and *100* have a simple declension which has only two forms, a Nominative-Accusative and a Gen.-Prep.-Dat.-Inst.

The numeral *полтора́* 'one-and-a-half' has in addition a feminine Nom.-Acc.

*50, 60, 70, 80* and the hundreds are treated as compound words, each part having its own declension, although they are written and pronounced as single words.

*1000* is a normal 2nd declension noun except that beside the normal Inst. ты́сячей (ты́сячею) is found the specifically numeral form ты́сячью.

|        | *m./n.*         | *f.*      |          |          |
|--------|-----------------|-----------|----------|----------|
| Nom.   | два́            | две́      | три́     | четы́ре  |
| Acc.   | (Nom. or Gen.)  |           | (N, G)   | (N or G) |
| Gen.-Prep. | двух́        |           | трёх     | четырёх  |
| Dat.   | двум́           |           | трём     | четырём  |
| Inst.  | двумя́          |           | тремя́   | четырьмя́ |

|       | *m./n.*  | *fem.*   |
|-------|----------|----------|
| N-A   | полтора́ | полторы́ |
| G-P-D-I | полу́тора |        |

|       |          |          |              |           |
|-------|----------|----------|--------------|-----------|
| N-A   | пя́ть    | во́семь  | пятна́дцать  | три́дцать |
| G-P-D | пяти́    | восьми́  | пятна́дцати  | тридцати́ |
| I     | пятью́   | восемью́ | пятна́дцатью | тридцатью́ |

|       |        |          |       |
|-------|--------|----------|-------|
| со́рок | девяно́сто | сто́ |
| сорока́ | девяно́ста | ста́ |

Note that in the numerals *50, 60, 70, 80,* and the hundreds, there is potentially a secondary stress. One stress remains primary, however, and that is the one marked. In the forms containing трёх and четырёх the two dots over the ё indicate this secondary stress, and the fact that the vowel may be pronounced *o*: *trᵇoxsót* ~ *trᵇixsót*.

|     |              |            |           |           |              |
|-----|--------------|------------|-----------|-----------|--------------|
| N-A | пятьдеся́т   | пятьсо́т   | две́сти   | три́ста   | четы́реста   |
| G   | пяти́десяти  | пятисо́т   | двухсо́т  | трёхсо́т  | четырёхсо́т  |
| P   | пяти́десяти  | пятиста́х  | двухста́х | трёхста́х | четырёхста́х |
| D   | пяти́десяти  | пятиста́м  | двумста́м | трёмста́м | четырёмста́м |
| I   | пятью́десятью | пятьюста́ми | двумяста́ми | тремяста́ми | четырьмяста́ми |

**3.1** Numerals compounded of the elements given above decline each element: e.g.

|     |                                                    |
|-----|----------------------------------------------------|
| N-A | пя́ть ты́сяч две́сти шестьдеся́т четы́ре [рубля́]  |
| G   | пяти́ ты́сяч двухсо́т шести́десяти четырёх [рубле́й] |
| P   | пяти́ ты́сячах двухста́х шести́десяти четырёх [рубля́х] |
| D   | пяти́ ты́сячам двумста́м шести́десяти четырём [рубля́м] |
| I   | пятью́ ты́сячами двумяста́ми шестью́десятью четырьмя́ [рубля́ми] |

**4.** Ordinal numerals are declined like ordinary adjectives, except for 'third', which has the following forms:

|       | m          | n          | f          | pl.        |
|-------|------------|------------|------------|------------|
| Nom.  | тре́тий    | тре́тье    | тре́тья    | тре́тьи    |
| Acc.  | (N, G)     | тре́тье    | тре́тью    | (N or G)   |
| Gen.  | тре́тьего  |            | тре́тьей   | тре́тьих   |
| Prep. | тре́тьем   |            | тре́тьей   | тре́тьих   |
| Dat.  | тре́тьему  |            | тре́тьей   | тре́тьим   |
| Inst. | тре́тьим   |            | { тре́тьей / тре́тьею } | тре́тьими |

**4.1** In a compound ordinal only the final, adjectival, element is declined: в две́ ты́сячи две́сти девяно́сто тре́тьем году́ 'in 2293'.

**5.** The syntax of the cardinal numerals.

**5.1** If the final element of a numeral is any form of оди́н, the numeral dictates that the noun and any modifiers be singular, but the form of "one" agrees in gender and case with the noun: два́дцать одна́ ру́сская кни́га, ты́сяча три́ста одна́ ста́рая газе́та, се́мьдесят одно́ большо́е окно́. Он принёс два́дцать одну́ ру́сскую кни́гу. Я ви́дел три́дцать одну́ ру́сскую студе́нтку.

For anything but nominative or (non-animate) accusative, a numeral preceding "one" has the proper case-form: о двухста́х семи́десяти одно́й ру́сской кни́ге; пяти́десяти одному́ ру́сскому студе́нту: с восемью́десятью одно́й ру́сской студе́нткой.

**5.2**  If the final element of the numeral is (Nom. or inanimate Acc.) два́ (две́), три́, or четы́ре, the noun is in the GENITIVE SINGULAR, and modifiers may be either *genitive plural* or (less commonly) nominative plural: два́дцать две́ ру́сских [ру́сские] кни́ги: сто́ пятьдеся́т три́ больши́х [больши́е] сту́ла.

**5.3**  If the final element of the numeral is anything else, the noun (and modifiers) must be in the GENITIVE PLURAL: оди́ннадцать ру́сских кни́г, две́сти больши́х сту́льев, две́ ты́сячи четы́реста трина́дцать но́вых домо́в.

**5.4**  When the numeral changes its form to express case, the following noun and modifiers go into the same case as the numeral, but *plural* (that is, the adjective behaves like a normal modifier: it no longer dictates the case, but takes the case from the word it modifies or refers to): из пяти́ ру́сских городо́в; о двухста́х учителя́х; с двумя́ ты́сячами тремяста́ми семью́десятью восемью́ америка́нскими дол-ла́рами: я ви́дел два́дцать двух [трёх, четырёх] ру́сских студе́нтов.

**6.**  The word о́ба 'both' is the only numeral with a complete set of forms which distinguish feminine from masculine-neuter. Like *два́/две́* it takes a noun in the genitive singular with modifiers in genitive or nominative plural: о́ба больши́х [больши́е] стола́, о́бе сёстры.

The declension:

|        | m/n              | fem     |
|--------|------------------|---------|
| Nom.   | о́ба             | о́бе    |
| Acc.   | (like Nom. or Gen.) | |
| G-P    | обо́их           | обе́их  |
| Dat.   | обо́им           | обе́им  |
| Inst.  | обо́ими          | обе́ими |

**7.**  There is a group of so-called collective numerals which are restricted in number and use: those above 5 are not usual, and those over 10 extremely rare. They are: дво́е (2), тро́е (3), че́тверо (4), пя́теро (5), ше́стеро (6), се́меро (7), во́сьмеро (8), де́вятеро (9), де́сятеро (10). They always take the genitive plural. They may be used: (1) with nouns denoting male persons, including the plurals *де́ти* and *лю́ди*, (2) with personal pronouns; and they must be used with nouns which have no singular forms: e.g.

| | | | |
|---|---|---|---|
| дво́е бра́тьёв | two brothers | дво́е часо́в | two watches |
| тро́е дете́й | three children | че́тверо но́жниц | four pairs of scissors |
| пя́теро люде́й | five men | На́с бы́ло че́тверо. | There were four of us. |

The declensions (*пя́теро* is a model for all others):

|          | дво́е | тро́е | пя́теро |
|----------|-------|-------|---------|
| Nom.     | дво́е | тро́е | пя́теро |
| Acc.     | like Nominative or Genitive | | |
| Gen.-Pr. | двои́х | трои́х | пятеры́х |
| Dat.     | двои́м | трои́м | пятеры́м |
| Inst.    | двои́ми | трои́ми | пятеры́ми |

# RUSSIAN-ENGLISH VOCABULARY

After each word is given the number of the lesson in which it first occurs, plus any special paragraph references which are pertinent to the special form or use of the word (supplementary lessons are designated by Arabic numerals, e.g. 5a). For the verb listings, refer to XXI 11 (pp. 258–259). Verb definitions are given under the imperfectives; perfectives are defined specially only if they have special meanings. The abbreviation *см.* = смотри = 'see'.

Personal and place names are for the most part omitted. See VI 7; App. I, 7.1.

## А  а

**а** II 10: and, but
**а то́** XXII: otherwise, or else
**а́вгуст** XVII: August
**авто́бус** XI: bus
**автомоби́ль** (m) VII: automobile
  **на автомоби́ле**: by car
**адвока́т** IV: lawyer
**а́дрес** [*Epl* **адреса́**] 14a: address
**актёр** 11a: actor
**актри́са** 11a: actress
**Алёша**: *см.* XV 10
**Аме́рика** XIV: America
**америка́нец** [**-нца**] X: American
**америка́нка** [G pl. **-нок**] X: American woman
**америка́нский** XIV 5: American
**англи́йский** XIV: English
**англича́нин** [pl. **англича́не**] X: Englishman
**англича́нка** [G pl. **-нок**] X: Englishwoman
**А́нглия** XIV: England
**анегдо́т** 5a: joke, funny story, anecdote
**апре́ль** (m) XVII: April
**а́рмия** 16a: army

**арти́ст** 21a ⎫
**арти́стка** ⎭ performing artist
**а́тлас** IV: atlas
**а́х** III: oh!
**аэродро́м** XXI: airdrome

## Б  б

**б = бы**
**ба́бушка** [G pl. **-шёк**] XV: grandmother
**Баку́** (indecl.) X 11: Baku
**ба́нк** VI: bank
**баскетбо́л** 10a: basketball
**бе́гать (ND)** XXI 1: run
**бе́дный** XII 2.3: poor
**бежа́ть бегу́т (D)** XXI 1.01: run
**без** + Gen. XVII 4.222: without
**бейсбо́л** 10a: baseball
**бе́лый** XII 2.31: white
**[бере́чь берёгу́т (I) XXV 1.14]**
**Берли́н** IV: Berlin
**беру́т**: *см.* **бра́ть**
**библиоте́ка** VI: library
**ближа́йший** XXIII 1.2: nearest
**бли́же** XXII 1.22: nearer
**бли́зкий (от)** XXII: near (to)

богáтый XII: rich
богáче XXII 1.21: richer
бóлее XII 8; XV 12; XXII 1.24, 6:
  more
бóльше XV 12; XXII 1.24: bigger,
  more
  бóльше не XXII 15: no longer
бóльший XXII 3.11–12; XXII
  2.21: bigger
большóй XIV; XXII 2.21: big,
  large
боя́ться (I) + Gen. X 9: be afraid
  of
брáт III [pl. брáтья IX 1] brother
брáть берýт (I) V 6.1: take
бýдут: см. бы́ть
бýдучи XXV 3: being
бýдущёё (neut. aj. used as noun)
  XVII 14.11: the future
бýдущий (aj.) XVII: future
бумáга 5a: paper
бы X 5.2: [conditional particle]
бывáть XX 2, 5 (11a6): be
бы́вший XXIV 3: having been;
  former
бы́стро I; XII 4; XVI 6: quickly
бы́стрый XII 2.3: quick, fast
бы́ть бýдут V 8: be


# В в

в [во] prep. + Prep.: in, at
      prep. + Acc.: into, to
  (II 3; VI 3.1; VI 8, 9; VIII 6;
  XVI 3; XVII 14.11–12, 14.3;
  XVIII 1.2; XX 1.32)
  в гóру XXI 9: uphill
  в окнó V 11.22: out the window
в- (prefix) XVI 1.01, 1.4
вáжный XII 2.3: important
вáм: см. вы́

вáми: см. вы́
вáс: см. вы́
вáш вáшё вáша I: your
  по-вáшёму XIII 3.2: in your
  opinion
вбегáть (I) XXI 1.1 }
вбежáть вбегýт (P) } run into
ввёзти́ ввёзýт (P) XXI 1.1: см.
  ввози́ть
ввёсти́ ввёдýт (P) XXI 1.1 }
вводи́ть -óдят (I) XXI 1.1 } lead in
ввози́ть -óзят (I) XXI 1.1: convey in, import
вдрýг XX (10a): suddenly
вёзти́ вёзýт (D) XXI 1.02, 1.2:
  convey
вёк [Epl векá] XIX: age, century
вёл, вёлá: см. вёсти́
вели́к XIV 1.141: big, large
вели́кий XX: great
величáйший XXIII 1.22: greatest
вéрить (I) + Dat. XIII 2.21: believe
вёрнýть(ся) = возврати́ть(ся)
весёлый XII 2.3: gay, jolly, merry
  [вéсёл -o -ы; весёлá]
вёснá (Spl) XVII 12: spring
  вёснóй XVII 14.15: in the spring
вёсти́ вёдýт (D) XXI 1: lead
вéсь всё вся VIII 5 (p. 355): all
вéчер [Epl вечерá] XVII: evening
вечéрний (aj) XVII 1: evening
вéчером X 12: in the evening
вéшать (I) IX 10: hang
вéщь (f) X: thing
взя́ть возьмýт (P): см. брáть
ви́деть ви́дят (I) II: see
винó [Spl ви́на] XIX: wine
висéть вися́т (I) IV: be hanging
включи́тельно XIX 6.3: inclu-
  sive(ly)

влета́ть (I) XXI 1 ⎫
влете́ть -тя́т (P) ⎬ fly in(to)

вме́сте I: together

внёсти внёсу́т (P) XVI ⎫
1.3, 4 ⎬ carry
вноси́ть -о́сят (I) ⎭ in(to)

во = в

во́время XX: on time

во́все не XXIII: not at all

вода́ (S Npl Asg) XIX: water

води́ть во́дят (ND) XXI 1: lead

во́дка XIX: vodka

возврати́ть (P) XXIV: return, give back

[возвращу́; возвращён: p. 299]

возврати́ться XXIV: return, come back

возвраща́ть (I) XXIV: return, give back

возвраща́ться XXIV: return, come back

вози́ть во́зят (ND) XXI 1: convey

возьму́т: см. взять

война́ [Spl во́йны] XIX: war

войти́ войду́т (P) XVI: enter, walk in

воллейбо́л 10a: volleyball

во́лос [E pl obl, G воло́с] XXIII (16a2): hair

вопро́с VII (5a): question

отвеча́ть на в. VII: answer a question

восемна́дцатый XX: eighteenth

восемна́дцать XVIII: eighteen

во́семь XVII 3 (cf. p. 357): eight

во́семьдесят XVIII: eighty

восемьсо́т XX: eight hundred

воскресе́нье XVII (9a): Sunday

восьмидеся́тый XX: eightieth

восьмисо́тый XX: eight hundredth

восьмо́й XVII: eighth

во́т I: there, look there (voilà)

вошёл вошла́: см. войти́ XVI

впервы́е XXV: at first

вре́мя (n) XX 7: time

во́время XX: on time

не́которое вре́мя XXV: for some time

вс-: см. весь

всё XVI 7 ⎫
всё ещё ⎬ always, continually

всё + comp.: see XXII 9

всё же XXV: all the same, still

всё равно́ + Dat. XIII: it's all the same to

всегда́ IV: always

всего́, всей: см. весь

встава́ть встаю́т (I) XV 5; XXV 1.12 ⎫
вста́ть вста́нут (P) ⎬ get up
[вста́л встала] ⎭

встре́тить -тят (P) V ⎫
встреча́ть (I) ⎬ meet

встре́титься встреча́ться XV 1.2

всю́ду XIII: everywhere

вто́рник XVII (9a): Tuesday

второ́й XVII: second

входи́ть -о́дят (I) XVI: go in, enter

вчера́ IV: yesterday

в. ве́чером X: last night

в. у́тром X: yesterday morning

въезжа́ть (I) XVI ⎫
въе́хать въе́дут (P) ⎬ ride, go into

вы́ II (cf. p. 354): you

вы- (prefix) XVI 1.6

выбега́ть (I) XXI 1 ⎫
вы́бежать вы́бегут ⎬ run out (of), exit running
(P) ⎭

вы́вёзти вы́вёзут (P) XXI 1: см. вывози́ть

вы́вести вы́ведут (P) XXI 1⎱ lead
выводи́ть -о́дят (I) ⎰ out

вывози́ть -о́зят (I) XXI 1: convey out, export

выезжа́ть (I) XVI ⎱ leave, exit
вы́ехать вы́едут (P) ⎰ riding

вы́йти вы́йдут (P) XVI 1.3: *см.* выходи́ть

вылета́ть (I) XXI 1⎱ fly out, exit
вы́лететь -тят (P) ⎰ flying

вы́нести вы́несут (P) XVI ⎱ carry
выноси́ть -о́сят (I) ⎰ out

вы́пить вы́пьют (P) XIX 4: *см.* пи́ть

высо́кий XXII, p. 286 [C]: high, tall

высоча́йший XXIII 1.22: highest

вы́сший XXII 4.2: higher, highest

вы́учить (P) XIV 9.1: learn completely

выходи́ть -о́дят (I) XVI 1: exit, go out

вы́ше XXII 1.22: higher

вы́шел вы́шла: *см.* вы́йти XVI

# Г г

газе́та V: newspaper

Га́млет XVIII: Hamlet

где́ II: where

где́-нибудь III 11.1: somewhere

где́-то II 5.4; VII 8.1: somewhere

генера́л 11a: general

ге́ний II 1.11: genius

Герма́ния XIV 5: Germany

герои́ня VIII: heroine

геро́й VIII: hero

гла́вный XX: chief, main

гла́з [Epl глаза́, G гла́з] XXIII (16a): eye

глу́бже XXII 1.22: deeper

глубо́кий XXII, p. 286 [C]: deep

глубоча́йший XXIII 1.2: deepest

говори́ть II; XIII 8: speak, talk, say

го́д [в году́; E pl obl (годо́в: *см.* XVI 5)] XVII 14.11: year

голова́ (S Npl Asg) XXI 9: head

го́лос [Epl голоса́] XXII: voice

голубо́й XXIII (16a3): (light) blue

го́льф 10a: golf

гора́ (S Npl Asg) XXI 9: hill, mountain

в го́ру: uphill

под гору: downhill

гора́здо XXII 12.2: much

го́род [Epl города́] II: city

за́ городом XI 8: in the country

за́ город: to the country

господи́н VI [pl. господа́ IX 3.2]: Mr., sir, gentleman

госпожа́ VI: Miss, Mrs., mistress

го́сть (m; E pl obl) 21a: guest

(идти́) в го́сти (go) visiting

(бы́ть) в гостя́х (be) visiting

го́стья [G pl. го́стий] 21a: guest

гото́вить (I) XV: prepare, ready

гото́виться к (I) XV: get (self) ready for

граждани́н VI 8 [pl. гра́ждане IX 3.1]: citizen

гражда́нка VI: citizeness

грани́ца XXI: border, frontier

за грани́цей: abroad

за грани́цу: (to) abroad

из-за грани́цы: from abroad

гро́мкий XXI: loud

гро́мче I (XXII 1.11): louder

гуля́ть XIX: walk, stroll

## Д д

да́ I: yes

да (*unstressed*) 10a: why, and

дава́й, дава́йте VII 6: let's

дава́ть даю́т (I) XIII 4.2; XXIV 1.1; XXV 1.12: give

давно́ XVI 10: long ago; for a long time

да́же XVII: even

да́лее XXII 1.22: further

и т. д. = и та́к да́лее: etc. = and so forth

далёкий XXII: distant

[далёк далеко́ далёка́]

да́льше XXII 1.22 (5a): next, further, more distant

да́ма IV; XII 9: lady

да́ть даду́т (Р) XIII 4.1: give

два́ две́ XVII (p. 357): two

двадца́тый XIX: twentieth

два́дцать XVIII: twenty

двена́дцатый XVII: twelfth

двена́дцать XVII: twelve

две́рь (f) I; (*E pl obl*) IX 8.4: door

две́сти XX (p. 357): two hundred

дво́р (*E*) XXI: court, yard

на дворе́: outside, outdoors

при дворе́: at court

двухсо́тый XX: two hundredth

де́вочка [G pl. -чёк] VIII: little girl

де́вушка [G pl. -шёк] XVII 16: girl, maid, virgin, waitress

девяно́сто XVIII (p. 357): ninety

девяно́стый XIX: ninetieth

девятисо́тый XX: nine hundredth

девятна́дцатый XIX: nineteenth

девятна́дцать XVIII: nineteen

девя́тый XVIII: ninth

де́вять XVII: nine

девятьсо́т XX: nine hundred

де́душка (m) XV: grandfather

дека́брь (m *E*) XVII: December

де́лать (I) V: do

де́ло [*Epl* дела́] XII: affair, matter

на са́мом де́ле XII 7: in fact

де́нь [G sg. дня́] XVII; XVIII 6 (9a): day

до́брый де́нь: good afternoon

де́ньги (pl. only) IX 9.1: money

дере́вня [G pl. дереве́нь]: village

в дере́вне: in the village, country

в дере́вню: to the village, country

деся́тый XVIII: tenth

де́сять XVII: ten

де́ти XI 1.22, 10: children

дешёвле XXII 1.22: cheaper

дешёвый XXII: cheap, inexpensive

[дёшев -о -ы; дёшева́]

дива́н IV: sofa

диктова́ть (I) V 4.21: dictate

дикто́вка V: dictation

дли́нный XXII: long

[дли́нён, дли́нно; длинна́]

для + Gen. XVI 3.4: for

для того́ чтобы XVIII 9.1: in order to

днём XVIII 6: in the afternoon

Днепр (*E*) XXII: Dnepr (river)

до + Gen. (XVI 3.1; XVII 11; XIX 6.3–4; XX 8): up to, to, before [*of time*], prior to

до́брое у́тро (p. 8): good morning

до́брый ве́чер (p. 8): good evening

до́брый де́нь (p. 8): good afternoon

дово́льно XII: rather; sufficient

дово́льный + Inst. 14a: satisfied, pleased (with)

до́ждь (*E*) XVIII 7.3; *see* App. I, § 15: rain

до́ктор [*Epl* доктора́] VI: doctor

докуме́нт IV: document

до́лгий XVI: long [*in time*] [до́лог, до́лги; долга́]

до́лго IV; XVI 10: for a long time

до́лжён [-жно́ -жны́ -жна́] XIII 6: ought

должно́ быть XIII 6: *see* p. 163

доли́на XXII: valley

до́льше XXII 1.2: longer [*of time*]

до́м [*Epl* дома́] II: house

до́ма II: at home

домо́й VII: homewards, (to) home

До́н [на Дону́] II 3: (the river) Don

доро́га XXI: road

дорого́й XIV 1.11: dear, expensive [до́рог -о -и; дорога́]

доро́же XXII 1.1: dearer, more expensive

доска́ (*S Npl Asg*) I; IX 8.3: (black)board

достава́ть достаю́т (I) ⎱ V: get,
доста́ть доста́нут (P) ⎰ obtain

до́чь [f; G до́чери] VI 9; IX 7; XI 1.22: daughter

дру́г [*Epl* друзья́ друзе́й] XI 9: friend

дру́г дру́га XV 8: each other

друго́й XVI: other

ду́мать (I) VII [XXV 7] (5a): think

дя́дя [m; G pl. дя́дей] XV: uncle

### Е е

Евро́па IV: Europe

европе́ец [-е́йца] XIV: European

европе́йка XIV 5.2: European woman

европе́йский (aj.) XIV: European

его́ I 2.1 [III 12]: his (possessive)

её I 2.1: her (possessive)

е́здить (**ND**) VII: go, ride, travel

е́м: *см.* XIX 3

е́сли V; X 5: if

е́сли б(ы) X 5.2: if

е́ст: *см.* XIX 3

есте́ственный XIV: natural

есте́ственные нау́ки XIV: natural sciences

е́сть VI 1: there is [XX 5: is]

е́сть едя́т (**I**) XIX 3: eat

е́хать е́дут (**D**) VII 1–4: go, ride

ещё IV; VII 10; XVI 7; XVII 8; XXII 12.1: still; more

ещё не IV; VII 10: not yet

ещё ра́з I; XVII 8: again, once more

### Ж ж

ж = же

жа́ль + Dat. (+ Acc.) XIII: be sorry (for)

жа́ль, что . . .: it's a pity that . . .

жа́ркий XVIII: hot [жа́рок, жа́рко -и; жарка́]

жа́рче XXII 1.1: hotter

жда́ть жду́т (I) XV 9: wait (for)

же XI 11 (9a4): [*see* p. 138]

жела́ть (I) + Gen. XXV 4, 5 (21a): wish

жёна́ (*Spl*) III; IX 8.3: wife

жена́тый 16a1: married

жени́ться же́нятся (**IP**) 16a1: marry

жени́х (*E*) 16a: bridegroom, fiancé

же́нщина XIII 9: woman
живу́т: *см.* жи́ть
жи́знь (f) XX: life
жи́ть живу́т (I) II; IV 5: live
журна́л V: magazine
журнали́ст VIII: journalist
журнали́стка VIII: journalist

## З з

за + Instr.: behind, beyond
+ Acc.: [to] behind, beyond
XI 5.4, 7, 8; XVI 3, 3.5
за мно́й (p. 8): after me
за- (*prefix*) XVIII 8.2
забыва́ть (I) V ⎫
забы́ть забу́дут (P) ⎬ forget
за́втра V: tomorrow
за́втра ве́чером X: tomorrow
evening
за́втра у́тром X: tomorrow
morning
за́втрак XIX: breakfast
за́втракать (I) XIX: to breakfast,
lunch
зада́ча V: task, assignment, problem
заезжа́ть (I) ⎫ XVIII 8.2:
заéхать -éдут (P) ⎬ drop in on, visit
заинтересова́ть (P) XIV ⎫ *см.* интересова́ть(ся)
заинтересова́ться XV ⎭
за́йм-: *см.* заня́ть
зайти́ зайду́т (P) XVIII 8.2: *см.* заходи́ть
закрича́ть -ча́т (P) 21a: (start to) shout
закро́ют: *см.* закры́ть

закрыва́ть (I)·V ⎫ close, shut
закры́ть закро́ют (P) ⎭
заме́тить (P) ⎫ IX: notice
замеча́ть (I) ⎭
замолча́ть: *см.* молча́ть
за́муж выходи́ть 16a1: marry
за́мужём бы́ть 16a1: be married
занести́ -нёсут (P): *см.* заноси́ть
занима́ть (I) XXI: occupy, take up
занима́ться + Instr.: be engaged in
заноси́ть -о́сят (I) XVIII 8.2: drop in on, carrying; bring
заня́тие 21a6: occupation, work, pastime, studies, class
за́нятый (заня́той) XXIV: busy [за́нят -о -ы; занята́]
заня́ть займу́т (P) XXI: *см.* занима́ть
заня́ться: *см.* занима́ться
запла́кать -пла́чут (P): *см.* пла́кать
засмея́ться -смею́тся (P): *см.* смея́ться
зато́ XXI: to make up for it; on the other hand
заходи́ть -о́дят (I) XVIII 8.2: drop in on
захоте́ть захотя́т (P): *см.* X 6
зашёл зашла́: *см.* зайти́
зва́ть зову́т (I) XXIV 4.3, 4.31: call [зва́л -о -и; звала́]
звони́ть (I) XIII 7: ring, call
звоно́к [-нка́] 5a: bell
зда́ние II: building
зде́сь II; VI 6: here
здра́вствуйте (cf. p. 335): hello

зелёный XXII: green
[зе́лен, -о, -ы: зелёна́]
зима́ (*Spl Asg*) XVII 12: winter
зимо́й XIII: in winter
знако́м 11a1: acquainted, known
знако́мить (I) 16a: make acquainted
знако́миться (I) 11a: become
acquainted
знако́мый 14a: acquainted, familiar; acquaintance
зна́ть зна́ют (I) II: know
зна́чить 16a: mean
зову́т: *см.* зва́ть

# И и

и I; II 9 (9a4): and; also, even, too
и . . . и IV: both . . . and
игра́ть (I) XI (10a): play
иде́я VIII: idea
идио́т XIV: idiot
идти́ иду́т [*past* шёл, шло́, шли́,
шла́] (D) VII 1; XVIII: go
из + Gen. XVI: from, out of
извини́те I: excuse (me)
из-за + Gen. XVI: from behind
из-под + Gen. XVI: from beneath
и́ли I: or
и́ли . . . и́ли VI: either . . . or
и́мёни XXIV 4.4: named after
импера́тор XX: emperor
императри́ца XX: empress
и́мя (n.) VI 10; XX 7: name
иногда́ XVII (9a): sometimes
интере́сный XII: interesting
интересова́ть (I) XIV: interest
интере́сова́ться + Inst. XV: be
interested (in)
испа́нец [-нца] XIV 5: Spaniard
Испа́ния XIV: Spain

испа́нка [G pl. -нок] XIV 5.2:
Spanish woman
испа́нский XIV: Spanish
исто́рия XIV: history; story
Ита́лия XIV: Italy
италья́нец [-нца] XIV: Italian
италья́нка XIV 5: Italian woman
италья́нский XIV: Italian
итти́: *alternate spelling for* идти́
и́х I: (possessive) their
ию́ль (m) XVII: July
ию́нь (m) XVII: June

# К к

к (ко) + Dat. XIII 3.1; XVI 3:
to, toward
ка́ждый XVII: every, each
каза́ться ка́жутся (I) XXI 7:
seem
ка́к I: how; as
та́к как XXI: since
как мо́жно + comp. XXII 10:
as . . . as possible
ка́к-нибудь: somehow (or other)
как ра́з 21a: just, exactly, precisely
ка́к-то: somehow, in a certain way
как то́лько 21a: as soon as
како́й XIV: how, of what kind
како́й-нибудь: of any sort at all
како́й-то: of some sort
календа́рь (m E) VI: calendar
кани́кулы [pl. only, G кани́кул]
9a3: vacation
капита́н 11a: captain
каранда́ш (E) I: pencil
карма́н VI: pocket
ка́рта IV: map; playing-card
карти́на IV: picture
кварти́ра XI: apartment, flat

ке́м: *см.* кто́ [cinema

кино́ (neut. indecl.) X: movie,

кита́ец [-а́йца] XIV: Chinese (man)

Кита́й XIV 5: China

кита́йский (aj) XIV: Chinese

китая́нка [G pl. -нок] XIV Chinese woman

кла́сс III: class, classroom

кла́сть клад́ут [кла́л, кла́ла] (I) VII: put, place

клу́б VII: club

ключ (*E*) VI: key

кни́га I: book

когда́ II: when

когда́-нибудь: sometime, at some time (or other)

когда́-то III 11.2: once, at one (certain) time

коммерса́нт 11a: businessman

ко́мната I: room

коне́ц [-нца́] XX: end

коне́чно [pron. -шн-] III: of course

конто́ра 10a: office

конце́рт VII: concert

на конце́рте: at the concert

конча́ть (I) XV (5a): finish (*trans.*)

конча́ться (I) XV: end (*intrans.*)

ко́нчить (P): *см.* конча́ть

ко́нчиться (P): *см.* конча́ться

коридо́р XXI hall, corridor

коро́ткий XXII: short

[ко́рото́к, ко́рото́ко́, ко́ро́тки коротка́]

коро́че XXII 1.22: shorter

кото́рый XII 6: who, which, what, that

тот . . . кото́рый: the (one) . . . who/which

ко́фе (masc. indecl.) XIX: coffee

кошелёк [*E* -лька́] IV: purse

кра́йне XXIII 8: extremely

краси́вый XII: pretty

кра́сный XVII: red

[кра́сён, кра́сно -ы; красна́]

кре́сло [pl. кре́сла] IV armchair

кри́кнуть (P) 21a: (give a) shout

крича́ть крича́т (I) 21a: shout

крова́ть (f) VIII: bed

Крым [в Крыму́] II: The Crimea

кста́ти 16a: by the way

кто́ II: who

кто́-нибудь III 11.1: anyone, someone

кто́-то II 5.4: someone

куда́ VII: (to) where, whither

куда́-то -нибудь: (to) someplace

куда́ + comp. XXII 12.2: more

купе́ц [*E* -пца́] 11a: merchant

купи́ть ку́пят (P): *см.* покупа́ть

## Л л

лаборато́рия IV: laboratory

ла́мпа IV: lamp

лёгкий XIV (p. 335, § 17.7): light, easy

[лёгок лёгко́ -й лёгка́]

легча́йший XXIII 1.22: lightest

ле́гче [pron. -хч-] XXII: lighter, easier

лёжа́ть лёжа́т (I) IV; XXV 1.111: lie, be lying

лейтена́нт XXII (11a): lieutenant

ле́кция 10a: lecture

чита́ть ле́кцию: deliver a lecture

Ленингра́д IV: Leningrad

лес [в лесу́; *E* pl леса́] II: forest, woods

лет (G pl.): *see* XVI 5

лёта́ть (ND) XXI: fly

лёте́ть лётя́т (D) XXI: fly

ле́тний (aj) XXIV: summer

ле́то [*Epl* лета́] XVII: summer
  ле́том X: in the summer
лётчик XXI: flyer, aviator
лётчица XXI: flyer, aviatrix
ле́чь ля́гут (**P**) XV 5.2: *см.*
  ложи́ться
ли II 8; X 5.3: *question particle*,
  whether
литерату́ра XIV: literature
ложи́ться (**I**) XV 5: lie down
лу́чше I (XXII): better
лу́чший (aj) XXII 3.13: better
  всего́ лу́чшего (p. 8), *see also*
  XXV 5: all the best, good luck
люби́ть лю́бят (**I**) XVIII 11: love,
  like
лю́ди (pl. only) IX 5: people, men
ля́гут: *см.* ле́чь

# М м

магази́н VII: store
ма́й XVII: May
майо́р 11a: major
ма́л, -о; мала́: *see* XIV 1.142
ма́ленький XIV: little, small
ма́ло VIII 4: a little
ма́льчик VIII: little boy
ма́ма 9a: mamma
ма́рт XVII: March
ма́сло XIX: butter; oil
матема́тика XIV: mathematics
материа́л 21a: material
ма́ть (f. irreg.) VI 9 (p. 350):
  mother
медици́на XIV: medicine
ме́дленно I: slowly
ме́дленный XII 4: slow
ме́жду + Instr. XI 6: between,
  among
ме́л XI: chalk

ме́нее XII; XXIII 8: less
ме́ньше XV 12: less
ме́ньший XXII 3.11; XXIII 2.21:
  lesser
ме́сто [*Epl* места́] XXI: place,
  room
ме́сяц XVI: month
метро́ (neut. indecl.) X: subway
меха́ник VI: mechanic
меша́ть (**I**) + Dat. 14a: hinder,
  bother, prevent
миллио́н XX: million
ми́мо + Gen. XVI: past, by
мину́та XVIII: minute
мла́дший XXII 4.2: junior
мне́, мно́й: *см.* я
мно́гие XVII 6.1: many
мно́го VIII 4; XVII 6: many, a lot
може́-: *см.* мо́чь
мо́жет быть IV: perhaps
мо́жно + Dat. XIV 8.1: one may,
  is permitted
  как мо́жно + comp. XXII 10:
  as . . . as possible
мо́й мое́ моя́ I: my, mine
молодо́й XII: young
  [мо́лод -о -ы; молода́: моло́же
  XXII 1.21]
молоко́ XIX: milk
молча́ть молча́т (**I**) V; XXV 1.111:
  be silent, not speak
Москва́ IV: Moscow
мо́ст [на мосту́; *Epl* мосты́] XVI:
  bridge
мо́чь мо́гут (**I**) X 7: be able, can
  [мо́г могло́ могли́ могла́]
му́ж II [pl. мужья́ муже́й IX 1.1]:
  husband
мужчи́на (m) XV: man, male
музе́й II: museum
му́зыка XIV: music

музыка́нт 11а: musician (m)

музыка́нтша 11а: musician (f)

мя́гкий [pron. -xк-] XXII: soft [мя́гок мя́гко -гки; мягка́]

  мя́гче XXII 1.1 [pron. -xч-]: softer

мя́со XIX: meat

## Н н

на + Prep.: in, at

  + Acc.: into, to; for II; VII 8, 9; XIV 3, 3.6; XVII 14.13, 14.4

над + Inst. XI 5.4: over, above [надо XI 6]

наде́яться -е́ются (I) X: hope

на́до + Dat. XXI 5.21: one must

наза́д: тому́ наза́д XVII: ago

назва́ть назову́т (P): см. XXIV 4.1 [назва́л -и; назвала́] [на́зван -ы; названа́]

назва́ться назову́тся: см. XXIV 4.2 [назва́лся назвала́сь]

называ́емый: см. та́к [XXIV 4.11]

называ́ть (I) XXIV: call, name

называ́ться XXIV 4.2: be called

наи-: см. XXIII 6

наибо́лее XXIII 5: most

наиме́нее XXIII 6, 8: least

найти́ найду́т (P): см. находи́ть

найти́сь найду́тся (P): см. находи́ться

наконе́ц XII: finally, at last

написа́ть напи́шут (P) V: см. писа́ть

нау́ка XIV: science

научи́ть -у́чат (P) XIV 9: teach

научи́ться -у́чатся (P) XV 3.2: learn

находи́ть -о́дят (I) IX: find

находи́ться (I) XX 5: be found, located

нача́ло XX (9a): beginning

нача́ть начну́т (P): см. начина́ть [на́чал -о -и; начала́]

нача́ться начну́тся (P) XV: см. начина́ться [начался́ -ло́сь -ли́сь -ла́сь]

начина́ть (I) VII (5a): begin (trans.)

начина́ться (I) XV: begin (intrans.)

на́ш на́ше на́ша I: our, ours

нашёл нашла́: см. найти́

не I (see also 21a): not

  ещё не: not yet

  уже́ не, бо́льше не: no longer

не ра́з XVI (9a2): more than once

не то́т XI 12: the wrong

небольшо́й XIV: not large, small

неве́ста 16а: fiancée, bride

неда́вно XVI: recently, not long ago

неде́ля XVI (9a2): week

недово́льный + Inst. 14а: displeased, dissatisfied (with)

недорого́й XIV: inexpensive

незнако́мый 14а: unknown, unfamiliar, unacquainted

нельзя́ + Dat. XIV 8.2: be forbidden, impossible

не́мец [не́мца] XIV 5: German (man)

неме́цкий (aj) XIV: German

не́мка [G pl. не́мок] XIV: German woman

немно́гие XVII 6.1: some, few

немно́го VIII 4; XXIII 8: some, a bit

немно́жко = немно́го

нену́жный XXI: unnecessary, useless

необходи́мый XXI: necessary

непого́да XVIII: bad weather

непра́вильно 5a: incorrect(ly)

неприя́тный XVIII: unpleasant

не́скольки-: *see* XVII 6.2

не́сколько VIII 4.1: several

нёсти́ нёсу́т (D) VII 2: carry
[нёс нёсло́ нёсли́ нёсла́]

несча́стный 21a: unhappy, unfortunate, miserable; (aj. as noun) wretch

несчастли́вый XXI: unhappy

несча́стьё 21a: unhappiness, misfortune, ill luck, calamity

не́т I (21a1.22): no

не́т + Gen. VII 1.1 (21a1.21): there is no(t)

не́ту: *see* VI 11

неуже́ли: *см.* 11a5.1

нехоро́ший: poor

нехорошо́: poorly, not well

ни: not even

ни . . . ни IV: neither . . . nor

ни оди́н: *см.* XVI 8.1

ни ра́зу XVI: not once

-нибудь III 11.1: (*indefinitizing particle*)

нигде́ II 5.3: nowhere

ни́зкий XXII: low
[ни́зок ни́зко -зки; низка́: ни́же]

нижа́йший XXIII 1.2: very low, lowest

ни́зший XXII 4.2: lower, subordinate

ника́к 21a: in no way

никако́й XIV 10: of no kind, no

никогда́ IV 7: never

никто́ II 5.1: no one

никуда́ VII 8.1: to nowhere

ниотку́да XVI: from nowhere

ничего́ = Gen. of ничто́

ниче́й ничьё ничья́ 21a: no one's

ничто́ II 5.1: nothing

но́ II 10: but

но́вость (f) 16a: news

но́вый [но́в -о -ы; нова́] XII: new

носи́ть но́сят (ND) VII 2: carry

но́чь (f) XVII: night

на́ ночь XVII 13; XVIII 6: for the night

но́чью XVIII 6: at night

ноя́брь (m *E*) XVII: November

нра́виться (I) + Dat. XV 3.1; XVII 11: be pleasing to ≅ like

ну́ VII: well, now

ну́жно + Dat. XXI 5.2: one must

ну́жный XXI 5 (14a): necessary
[ну́жён ну́жно ну́жны́ нужна́]

## О о

о prep. + Prep. II: about, concerning
[об *before vowels*; обо мне́]

о́ба о́бе (p. 358): both, the two

обе́д XIX: dinner

за обе́дом: at dinner

на обе́д: for dinner

обе́дать (I) XIX: dine

обеща́ть (IP) + Dat. XIII 2.21: promise

обо = о

о́браз XXV: shape, form, manner

гла́вным о́бразом: chiefly

каки́м о́бразом XXI: how?

таки́м о́бразом XXI: thus

объясни́ть (P) XIII ⎫ (+ Dat.):
объясня́ть (I) ⎭ explain (to)

обыкнове́нно VII: usually
обыкнове́нный XII: ordinary
одева́ть (I) XV: dress (*trans.*)
одева́ться (I) XV: get dressed
оде́ть оде́нут (P): *см.* одева́ть
оде́ться: *см.* одева́ться
оди́н одно́ одна́ XVI 8: one, alone
  ни оди́н: *см.* XVI 8.1
оди́ннадцатый XVIII eleventh
оди́ннадцать XVII: eleven
оказа́ться ока́жутся (P)⎱
ока́зываться (I) XXI 7⎰ turn out
океа́н XXI: ocean
окно́ I; IX 8.5: window
  смотре́ть в окно́ V 11.22: look
  out (the) window
о́коло + Gen. XVI 3.2: around,
  about
октя́брь (m *E*) XVII: October
о́н оно́ она́ они́ I: he, it, she, they
опа́здывать (I) [на] XXI: be late
о́пера 9a: opera
опозда́ть (P): *см.* опа́здывать
опя́ть XX: again
о́сень (f) XVII: autumn
  о́сенью XVII: in autumn
остава́ться остаю́тся (I) XVII:
  remain, be left over
оста́вить (P)⎱ XXIV: leave,
оставля́ть (I)⎰ abandon, give up
оста́ться оста́нутся (P): *см.* остава́ться (I)
от + Gen. XVI; XIX 6.4 (14a):
  from, away from
отбега́ть (I) XXI 1.1⎱
отбежа́ть -бегу́т (P)⎰ run away
отвезти́ -вёзу́т (P) XXI 1.1: *см.* отвози́ть
отвести́ -ёду́т (P): *см.* отводи́ть
отве́т VII (5a): answer

отве́тить -е́тят (P)⎱
отвеча́ть (I) V⎰ answer
  ∼ на вопро́с VII: answer
  question
отводи́ть -о́дят (I) XXI 1.1: lead
  from
отвози́ть -о́зят (I) XXI: take
  away
оте́ц [*E* отца́] II 2: father
открыва́ть (I) V⎱ open,
открыть откро́ют (P)⎰ uncover, discover
откры́тка [G pl. -ток] 14a: postcard
отку́да XVI 2: from where
отку́да-то XVI: from somewhere
отлета́ть (I) XXI⎱ fly away
отлете́ть -тя́т (P)⎰ (from)
отнести́ -несу́т (P)⎱ XVIII 8:
относи́ть -о́сят (I)⎰ carry away (from)
отойду́т отойти́: *см.* XVIII 8 отходи́ть
  [отошёл отошла́]
отсю́да XVI 2: from here
отту́да XVI 2: from there
отходи́ть -о́дят (I) XVIII: move
  away (from)
о́тчество VI: patronymic
отъезжа́ть (I)⎱ XVIII 8:
отъе́хать -е́дут (P)⎰ go, ride away (from)
офице́р 11a: officer
о́чень I (XIII 10): very, very
  much
ошиба́ться (I) 11a⎱
ошиби́ться ⎰ be mistaken
ошибу́тся (P) 11a4⎰
оши́бка [G pl. -бок] 5a: mistake,
  error

## П п

**Пари́ж** IV: Paris

**па́рк** VIII: park

**пе́рвый** XVII: first

**перебега́ть** (I) XXI ⎫
**перебежа́ть -бегу́т (Р)** ⎬ run across

**перевёзти́ -вёзу́т (Р):** *см.* **перевози́ть**

**перевёсти́ переведу́т (Р)** ⎫ 1. trans-
[**перевёл, -вёла́**] XIV ⎮ late
(5a1) ⎮ 2. lead
**переводи́ть -о́дят (I)** ⎭ across

**перевози́ть -о́зят (I)** XXI: transport through, across

**перед** + Inst. XI 5.4; XX 8: before, in front of; prior to
[**передо** XI 6]

**передава́ть -даю́т** ⎫
(I) 14a ⎮ hand over,
**переда́ть -да́м (Р)** ⎬ pass on,
14a2 ⎮ communicate

**переезжа́ть** (I) XXI ⎫ go, ride
**перее́хать -е́дут (Р)** ⎬ across, over

**перелёта́ть** (I) XXI ⎫ fly across,
**перелёте́ть -тя́т (Р)** ⎬ over

**перейти́ перейду́т (Р)** ⎫ XXI 2:
**переходи́ть -о́дят (I)** ⎬ cross, go
⎭ over, across

**перешёл перешла́:** *см.* **перейти́**

**пери́од:** period

**перо́** I [*Spl* **пе́рья** IX 1]: pen

**пе́сня** [G pl. **пе́сён**] XXIV: song

**Пётр** [*E* **Пётра́**]: Peter

**печа́льный** XII: sad
[**печа́лён, печа́льна**]

**пешко́м** VII 1.21: afoot

**пи́во** XIX: beer

**писа́тель** IV: writer (m)

**писа́тельница** IV: writer (f)

**писа́ть пи́шут (I)** V: write

**письмо́** I [*Spl* **пи́сьма**]: letter

**пить пью́т (I)** XIX 4: drink
[**питьё** p. 348: drink]

**пла́кать пла́чут (I)** XXIV: weep

**плато́к** [*E* **-тка́**] VI: kerchief, handkerchief

**плохо́й** XIV 1.11: bad
[**пло́х, пло́хо пло́хи; плоха́**]

**по** + Dat. XIII 3.2: around, about
+ Dat. pl. XX 1.4 (9a1.2): on (regularly) ⌈including)
+ Acc. XIX 6.3: up to (and

**по-** + comp. XXII 7: somewhat
+ verb: *см.* XXV 7

**по-. . . ски:** *см.* XIV 5.3

**по-англи́йски** I: in English

**побежа́ть -бегу́т (Р)** XXI: *см.* **бе́гать**

**побыва́ть (Р)** XXV 7.1: visit

**по-ва́шёму** XIII 3.2: in your opinion

**повёзти́ повёзу́т (Р):** *см.* **вози́ть**

**пове́рить (Р)** + Dat. XIII: *см.* **ве́рить**

**пове́сить (Р)** IX: *см.* **ве́шать**

**повёсти́ повёду́т (Р):** *см.* **води́ть**

**повтори́ть (Р)** ⎫ V: repeat
**повторя́ть (I)** ⎭

**поговори́ть** XXV 7: have a chat

**пого́да** XVIII: weather

**погуля́ть (Р):** *см.* XXV 7; **гуля́ть**

**под** [**подо**] XI 5.7; XVI 3
+ Inst.: under, below
+ Acc.: (to a place) under

**подбега́ть** (I) XXI ⎫ approach
**подбежа́ть** ⎮ running,
**-бегу́т (Р)** ⎭ run up to

**подлёта́ть** (I) XXI ⎫ approach
**подлёте́ть** ⎮ flying,
**-тя́т (Р)** ⎭ fly up to

поднести -несут (P) ⎱ XVI 1.8:
подносить -осят (I) ⎰ carry up to
подождать подождут (P): *см.*
ждать
подойти подойдут (P): *см.* подходить XVI 1
[подошёл подошла]
подруга XV 11: (girl-)friend
подумать (P) VII (5a); XXV 7:
*см.* думать
подходить -одят (I) XVI 1.8:
approach, come up to
подъезжать (I)
XVI 1.8 ⎱ approach,
подъехать -едут (P) ⎰ ride up to
поезд [Epl поезда] XI: train
поехать поедут (P) VII 1: *см.*
ехать
[*imperative* поезжай(те)]
пожалуйста I: please
пожелать (P): *см.* желать XXV
пожениться поженятся (P): *см.*
16a1
пожить поживут: *см.* XXV 7
позавтракать (P): *см.* завтракать
позвать позовут (P) XXIV: *см.*
звать
[позвал, -и; позвала]
позвонить (P) XIII: *см.* звонить
позднее XXII 13: later
поздно XV: late
позже XV 13 [XXII 13]: later (on)
познакомить (P) 16a: *см.* знакомить
познакомиться (P) 11a: *см.*
знакомиться
поиграть (P) XXII 7: play (a little)
поймут: *см.* понять [7.3]
пойти пойдут (P): *see* VII 1 (XVII
[пошёл пошло пошла]

показать покажут (P): *см.* показывать
показаться (P): *см.* казаться
показывать (I) XIII: show
покупать (I) X (9a2): buy
пол [на полу Epl] (IV): floor
поле [Epl поля, G полей] IV: field
полежать -ёжат (P): *см.* XXV 7
полететь -тят (P) XXI: *см.* лётать
полка [G pl. полок] IV: shelf
половина XVII: half
положить положат (P) VII: *см.* класть
получать (I) V ⎱ receive,
получить получат (P) ⎰ get
полчаса (not declined) XVIII: half-hour
полька [G pl. полёк] XIV: Polish woman
польский XIV Polish
Польша XIV 5: Poland
полюбить -юбят (P) XVII 11: *см.* любить
поляк XIV: Pole
помешать (P) 14a: *см.* мешать
помнить (I) IV: remember
помогать (I) + Dat. XIII: help
по-моёму XIII 3.2: in my opinion
помочь помогут (P) XIII 5: *см.* помогать
понедельник XVII (9a): Monday
понести понесут (P) ⎱ *см.*
VII 2 ⎰ носить
[понёс, понесли]
понимать (I) II, V: understand
понравиться (P) XV 3.1: *см.* нравиться
понять поймут (P): *см.* понимать
[понял -ло -ли; поняла]
пообедать (P): *см.* обедать XIX

поправить (P) 5a ⎫
поправлять (I) ⎬ correct
поправить -осят (P): *см.* просить
пора + Dat. XIII 2.3 (5a): it's time (for)
поработать (*см.* XXV 7): work a little
портрет 16a: portrait
портфель (m) VIII: briefcase
по-русски I (XIV 5.3): in Russian
посадить -адят (P): *см.* сажать
по-своёму (cf. XIII 3.2c): in one's own way
посидеть (P): *см.* XXV 7
послать пошлют (P): *см.* посылать
после + Gen. XVIII (10a): after
последний XVII 1, 17: last
послезавтра XVIII: day after tomorrow
пословица 25a: proverb
послушать (P) IX (5a): *см.* слушать
послушаться: *см.* слушаться
посмотреть -отрят (P): *см.* смотреть
посоветовать (P): *см.* советовать
поспать поспят (P): *см.* XXII 7
поставить (P): *см.* ставить
постоять (P): *см.* XXV 7
посылать (I) 14a: send
по-твоёму XIII 3.2: in your opinion
потерять (P): *см.* терять IX
потолок [*E* -лка] IV: ceiling
потом VII (5a): then, afterwards
потому что VIII: because
поужинать (P): *см.* ужинать
почёму II: why?
почёму-то IV: for some reason
почти VIII: almost

пошёл пошла: *см.* пойти VII 1.1
пошлё-: *см.* послать
поэт XX (11a3): poet
поэтому XXI 7.1: therefore
правда 10a: truth
  не правда ли: isn't it so?
правильно 5a: correctly
пре- XXIII 7: (*intensive prefix*)
представить (P) ⎫ 16a: present,
представлять (I) ⎬ introduce
представлять -вить себе 21a: imagine
президент XX: president
прекрасный XXV: beautiful
[прекрасён, прекрасна]
при + Prep. XX 6: at, next to
прибегать (I) XXI ⎫ come
прибежать ⎬
  -бегут (P) XXI 1 ⎭ running
привезти -вёзут (P): *см.* привозить
привёл -вёла: *см.* привёсти
привёсти -вёдут (P) ⎫ lead,
приводить -одят (I) XXI ⎬ arrive
привёт 14a: greeting
привозить -озят (I) XXI 1: bring
пригласить (P) ⎫ 21a: invite
приглашать (I) ⎬
приготовить(ся) (P) XV: *см.* готовить(ся)
придётся (P): *см.* приходится XXI
приезжать (I) XVI ⎫ arrive riding,
приехать -едут (P) ⎬ come
[*imperative* приезжай(те)]
прийти придут (P): *см.* приходить
прилетать (I) XXI ⎫ come flying,
прилететь -тят (P) ⎬ arrive
принести -несут (P) XVI ⎫ bring, come
приносить -осят (I) ⎬ carrying

приходи́лось: *см.* XXI 6

прихо́дится (I) + Dat. XXI 6: must

приходи́ть -о́дят (I) XVI: arrive

пришёл пришла́: *см.* прийти́ XVI 1

пришло́сь: *см.* прихо́дится XXI 6

[прия́тно: *see* 11a]

прия́тный XVII: pleasant [прия́тён прия́тна]

пробега́ть (I) XXI ⎱ run through,
пробежа́ть -бегу́т (P) ⎰ past

провёзти́ -вёзу́т (P): *см.* провози́ть

провёсти́ -вёду́т (P) ⎫ XXI: lead
проводи́ть -о́дят (I) ⎬ through, past

провози́ть -о́зят (P) XXI: convey through

продава́ть продаю́т (I) ⎱
прода́ть продаду́т (P) ⎰ 21a: sell

продиктова́ть (P) V 4.21: *см.* диктова́ть

продолжа́ть (I) ⎱ 21a: continue
продо́лжить (P) ⎰ (*trans.*)

продолжа́ться ⎱ go on, continue
продо́лжиться ⎰ (*intrans.*)

проезжа́ть (I) XVI ⎫ go, ride
проéхать -éдут (P) ⎬ through, past

[*imperative* проезжа́й(те)]

прожи́ть проживу́т (P) XXIV: live through (period)
[про́жил -о -и; прожила́]

пройти́ пройду́т (P): *см.* проходи́ть

пролета́ть (I) XXI ⎱ fly through,
пролете́ть -тя́т (P) ⎰ past

пронёсти́ -нёсу́т (P) ⎱ XVI: carry
проноси́ть -о́сят (I) ⎰ through, past

проси́ть (I) [по- (P)] XI 13: request

простóй XXII: simple [прост про́сто про́сты проста́]

про́ще XXII 1.11: simpler, more simply

профéссор I [*Epl* профессора́]: professor

проходи́ть -о́дят (I) XVI 1.7: go, walk through or past

прочéсть прочту́т (P) XXII = прочита́ть [прочёл прочли́ прочла́]

прочита́ть (P) V: *см.* чита́ть

прошёл прошла́: *см.* пройти́

про́шлоё (aj. as noun) XVII: the past

про́шлый (aj.) XVII 17: past

про́ще: *см.* просто́й

пря́мо XVII: straight, directly

пти́ца XXI: bird

пуска́й VII ⎱ let (*introduces 3rd*
пу́сть VII 7 ⎰ *person imperative*)

пу́ть (masc. 3rd decl.) *see* XXV 6: road, way

пью́т: *см.* пи́ть

пятидеся́тый XIX: fiftieth

пятисо́тый XIX: five hundredth

пятна́дцатый XIX: fifteenth

пятна́дцать XVIII: fifteen

пя́тница XVII (9a): Friday

пя́тый XVIII: fifth

пя́ть XVII 3.4; XVIII 5.2 (p. 357): five

пятьдеся́т XVIII: fifty

пятьсо́т XX: five hundred

## Р р

рабо́та XX: work на рабо́те: at work

рабо́тать (I) II: work

[равно́:] всё равно́ + Dat. XIII: it's all the same (to)

ра́д + Dat. XXIII 10: glad for/of

ра́дио (neut. indecl.) XV: radio

ра́дость (f) VIII: joy

ра́з [G pl. ра́з] XVI: time, occasion

ра́з (adverbially used Acc.): once
  ещё ра́з: once more, again
  не ра́з XVI (9a2): more than once
  ни ра́зу XVI (9a2): not (even) once

ра́зве: *см.* 11a2

ра́но XV: early

ра́ньше XV 13: earlier, before

расска́з IV: story

рассказа́ть расска́жут (P) } recount, narrate, tell
расска́зывать (I) 9a }

ребёнок XI 10: child
  [G sg. ребёнка; pl. де́ти]

револю́ция XIX: revolution

ре́дкий XIV: rare
  [ре́док ре́дко -дки; редка́]

ре́дко VII: seldom, rarely

ре́же XXII 1.22: rarer, more rarely

река́ (*S Npl ASg*) XXI 9: river
  [ре́ку, за́ реку; ре́ки река́х]

респу́блика XX: republic

рестора́н VII: restaurant

реша́ть (I) V 9 } solve, decide
реши́ть (P) }

реша́ться реши́ться XV 1.1: be solved; make decision

ро́вно XVIII (with time): sharp, exactly

роди́тели [pl. only, G -лей] 14a: parents

роди́ться (IP) XIX: be born
  [роди́лся роди́ли́сь роди́ла́сь]

ро́ль (f; *E pl obl*) 21a: part, role

рома́н V: novel

Росси́я II: Russia

[ружьё; *Spl* ру́жья ру́жей gun]

рука́ (*S Npl Asg*) VI: hand, arm
  [ру́ку, за́ руку; ру́ки рука́х]
  за́ руку: by the hand
  под руку: by the arm

ру́сский (aj.) XIV: Russian

ру́сский (aj. as noun) XIV 4: Russian

ру́сская (aj. as noun) XIV 4: Russian woman

## С с

с [со] + Instr. XI 5.4, 6: with, accompanying
  + Gen. XIV; XVI 3; XVIII; XIX 6.4: from
  + Acc. XXV 8: about

са́д [в саду́; *Epl* сады́] II: garden

сади́ться (I) XV 5: sit down; land, come to rest, perch

сажа́ть (I) IX 10: seat, sit

са́м XV 7: self

самолёт XXI: airplane

са́мый: *see* XII 7; XXIII 2.1
  то́т са́мый: the (very)

са́хар [2nd Gen. са́хару; *Epl* сахара́] XIX: sugar

све́тлый XXIII (16a): light, bright

[свида́ние: rendezvous]
  до свида́ния (p. 8): goodbye

сво́й своё своя́ III 12; VI 5.1: own (*see* p. 43)

сде́лать (P) V: *см.* де́лать

себе́ себя́ XV 6: self

сего́дня V: today
  сего́дня ве́чером X: tonight
  сего́дня днём: this afternoon
  сего́дня у́тром X: this morning

седьмо́й XVIII: seventh

сейча́с же V: right away, at once
секрета́рша 11a: secretary
секрета́рь (m *E*) 11a: secretary
семе́стр 21a: semester
семидеся́тый XIX: seventieth
семисо́тый XX: 700th
семна́дцатый XIX: seventeenth
семна́дцать XVII 5: seventeen
се́мь XVII; XVIII 5 (p. 356): seven
се́мьдесят XVIII 5: seventh
семьсо́т XX (p. 357): 700
сентя́брь (m *E*) XVII: September
сестра́ III: sister
[pl. сёстры сёстёр сёстрах]
се́сть ся́дут (P) XV 5; XXI: *см.* сади́ться
сиде́ть сидя́т (I) V [XV 5; XXV 1.111, 7]: sit, be sitting
симфо́ния XVI: symphony
си́ний -нёё -няя XVII: (dark) blue
сказа́ть ска́жут (P) V; XIII 8: say, tell
ско́лько XV; XVII 6: how many
скоре́е [скоре́й] XXII 14: sooner, hurry, rather
ско́ро XVI 6: quickly
ско́рый XVI: quick, fast
ску́чный [-*šn*- App. I, § 17.6] XI: dull, boring
[ску́чён ску́чно -чны, скучна́]
сле́дующий XVII 17: next, following
сли́шком XXIII: too (much)
слова́рь (m *E*) VI: dictionary
сло́во [*Epl* слова́] IX 8.5: word
случа́ться (I) } 16a4: happen
случи́ться (P) }
слу́шать (I) IX (5a): listen
слу́шаться (I) + Gen. XV 1.2: obey

слы́шать -шат (I) XXI: hear [*imperative* слу́шай(те)]
сме́рть (f; *E pl obl*) XX: death
смея́ться -ею́тся (I) X 1: laugh
~ над + Instr.: *см.* XI 8.1
смотре́ть смо́трят (I) [на] V 11: look
~ в окно́: look out the window
смотри́(те): *см.* ви́деть *и* V 7.1
смо́чь смо́гут (P) X 7: be able, manage to
смо́г, смо́жёт: *см.* X 7
снача́ла XXV: at first
снег [в, на снегу́, *Epl* снега́]; снег идёт XVIII 7.3: snow
собира́ться (I) 11a: be about to
собо́й: *см.* XV 6
собра́нѣ VII: meeting
на собра́нии VII 9: at the m.
собра́ться соберу́тся: *см.* собира́ться
сове́т XX: advice, counsel; council; soviet
сове́товать (I) 14a: advise
сове́тский (aj.) XX: soviet
совсе́м XXI: entirely, quite
согла́сный (с + Instr.) XXIII: in agreement (with)
соедине́нный XX: united
к сожале́нию 21a: unfortunately
солда́т [G pl. солда́т] 11a: soldier
со́лнцё [*sónцə*: no *l*!] XVIII: sun; sunshine
на со́лнце: in the sun
со́рок XVIII 5.1 (p. 357): forty
сороково́й XIX: fortieth
сосе́д [pl. сосе́ди IX 4] VI: neighbor
сосе́дка [G pl. -док] VI: female neighbor
со́тый XIX: hundredth

социалисти́ческий XX: socialist(ic)

сочине́ниё V: written work, composition, paper

сою́з XX: union; alliance; league

спаси́бо (за + A) I: thanks (for)

спа́ть спя́т (I) XV: sleep
спи́тся XV 4: be sleepy

специали́ст XIII: specialist

споко́йной но́чи (p. 8), *see also* XXV 5: good night

споко́йный [-ко́ён -о́йно] XXV: peaceful

спра́шивать (I) III; VI 3.1 ⎱ ask, question
спроси́ть спро́сят (P) ⎰

среда́ (*S Npl Asg*) XVII 12 (9a): Wednesday

СССР XX: USSR

ста́вить (I) IX 10: stand, put (standing)

станови́ться -о́вятся (I) + Instr. XX 4 (11a2): become

ста́нция VII: station
на ста́нции: at the station

старе́е XXII 4.1: older

стари́к (*E*) XXIV: old man

стару́ха XXIV: old woman

ста́рый XII 2.31: old
ста́рше XXII 4.1: senior
ста́рший XXII 4.2: senior

ста́ть ста́нут (P) XX (11a2): become; start

статья́ IV: article

стена́ (*S Npl Asg*) IX 8.3: wall

сто́ XVII 5.1 (p. 357): hundred

сто́л (*E*) I: table
за столо́м XI 8: at table

стоя́ть стоя́т (I) IV; XV 5; XXV 1.111, 7: stand, be standing

страна́ [*Spl* стра́ны] XXIV: country

стра́нный XXV: strange [стра́нён -нна]

стро́гий XXII: stern, strict [стро́г -о -и; строга́: стро́же]

строжа́йший XXII 1.2: strictest

студе́нт III: student

студе́нтка [f; G pl. -ток] III: student

сту́л I [pl. сту́лья IX 1]: chair

суббо́та XVII (9a): Saturday

судья́ (m) XV: judge [су́дьи судей су́дьях]

суме́ть (P) XIV 7: *см.* уме́ть

су́мка [G pl. су́мок] IV: handbag, pocketbook

су́п [2nd Gen. су́пу; *Epl* супы́] XIX: soup

счастли́вый XXI: happy

сча́стьё 21a: happiness, luck, fortune
к сча́стью: luckily, fortunately
на (моё) сча́стьё: luckily for (me)

США XX: USA

съе́сть съедя́т (P) XIX 5: *см.* е́сть [съе́л съе́ли съе́ла]

сыгра́ть (I) XI: *см.* игра́ть

сы́н VI: son [pl. сыновья́ сынове́й IX 2]

сы́р [2nd Gen. сы́ру; *Epl* сыры́] XIX: cheese

сюда́ VII 8.1; XVI: (to) here

ся́дут: *см.* се́сть [сади́ться]


**Т т**

та́к I; XXI 8.1: thus, so; right

та́к же . . . ка́к (и) XXIII 9: just as

та́кже (и) IV: likewise, also

та́к как XXI 8.2: since

та́к называ́емый XXIV 4: so-called

[т. н. = та́к называ́емый]

та́к что XXI 8: so that

та́к . . . что: so . . . that

тако́й XIV: such, of this kind

тако́й же (. . . како́й): *see* XXIII 9

тала́нт 11a: talent

тала́нтливый 21a: talented

та́м II; VII 8.1; XVI 2: there

та́м же XI 11: in the same place

твой твоё твоя́ II: your

по-твоёму: *см.* XIII 3.2

теа́тр VII: theater

телегра́мма 14a: telegram

телеграфи́ровать (IP) 14a: telegraph

телефо́н XIII: telephone

по телефо́ну XIII 3.2e: by phone

те́м: *see* XXII 11.1, 11.3

те́м бо́лее: *см.* XXII

те́м ху́же XXII 11.3: the worse

тёмный XXIII (16a): dark

[тёмен темно́ тёмна́]

те́ннис 10a: tennis

тепе́рь III: now

тёплый XVIII: hot

[тёпел тепло́ тёплы́, тёпла́]

теря́ть (I) IX: lose

тетра́дка [G pl. -док] I: notebook

тётя [G pl. тётей] XV: aunt

ти́хий XXII: quiet

[тих ти́хо ти́хи; тиха́]

ти́ше XXII 1.11: quieter

то́ (*particle*): *см.* X 5.1

-то (*indefinitizer*): *см.* II 5.4; III 11.2

това́рищ VI 8: comrade

тогда́ VIII: then

то́-есть [т.-е.] XX: that is, i.e.

то́же IV; XI 11: also

то́лько XII (9a): only

то́лько что XVI 9: just

тому́ наза́д XVII: ago

то́нкий XXII: slim, fine

[то́нок то́нко -нки; тонка́: то́ньше]

то́т то́ та́ I 2.3 (p. 357): that, the

то́т же XI 11: the same

не то́т XI 12: the wrong one

то́т . . . кото́рый XII 6.1: the one who/that

для того́ чтобы XVIII 9.1: in order to

чём . . . те́м XXII 11.1: the . . . the

трамва́й XI: streetcar

тре́тий тре́тьё тре́тья XVII 2 (p. 357): third

тре́тьего дня́ XVII: day before yesterday

трёхсо́тый XX: 300th

три́ XVII (p. 357): three

тридца́тый XX: thirtieth

три́дцать XVIII 5: thirty

трина́дцатый XIX: thirteenth

трина́дцать XVIII 5.2: thirteen

три́ста XX (p. 357): 300

тру́дный XII: difficult

[тру́ден тру́дно -дны; трудна́]

туда́ VII 8.1; XVI 2: (to) there

ту́т VI 6: here

ты́ II 7: you

ты́сяча XX (p. 356 § 2.2): thousand

ты́сячный XX: thousandth

# У у

у prep. + Gen. VI 3, 5; XVI 3: at, near

у- (*prefix*) XVI 1.5: *see* p. 200

убега́ть (**I**) XXI 1 ⎤ run away
убежа́ть убегу́т (**P**) ⎦ (from)

увезти́ увезу́т (**P**): *см.* увози́ть

уве́ренный XXIII (21a): sure, confident, assured
[уве́рен, уве́ренно -а -ы]

уве́ренный в себе́ XXXII: self-confident

увести́ уведу́т (**P**) [увёл увела́] XXI: *см.* уводи́ть

уви́деть уви́дят (**P**) V 9: see, catch sight of

уводи́ть -о́дят (**I**) XXI 1: lead off

увози́ть -о́зят (**P**) XXI: cart off

у́гол [*E* угла́; в углу́] IV: corner

уезжа́ть (**I**) XVI ⎤ go, ride off,
уе́хать уе́дут (**P**) ⎦ away
[*imperative* уезжа́й(те)]

уже́ IV; VI 10: already

уже́ не IV; VI 10: no longer

у́же XXII 1.22: narrower

у́жин XV: supper

за у́жином XV: at supper

у́жинать (**I**) XVII: sup, have supper

у́зкий XXII: narrow
[у́зок, у́зко у́зки; узка́: у́же]

узна́ть (**P**) V: know, find out

уйти́ уйду́т (**P**) XVI: *см.* уходи́ть

улета́ть (**I**) XXI ⎤
улете́ть -тя́т (**P**) ⎦ fly off, away

у́лица XIII: street

умере́ть умру́т (**P**) XIX: *см.* умира́ть
[у́мёр, умерла́; уме́рший]

уме́ть (**I**) XIV 7: know how to

умира́ть (**I**) XIX: die

у́мный XII 2.31: intelligent, bright
[умён у́мно́ умны́ умна́]

унести́ унесу́т (**P**): *см.* уноси́ть

универма́г 9a: department store

университе́т VI: university

уноси́ть -о́сят (**I**) XVI: carry off, away

упражне́ние V: exercise

уро́к III (21a6): lesson

на уро́ке: at the lesson

услы́шать (**P**): *см.* слы́шать XXI

успе́х 10a: success

де́лать успе́хи: make progress

у́тренний -нёё -няя XVII: morning

у́тро [*см.* p. 217]: morning

у́тром X: in the morning

вчера́ у́.: yesterday morning

сего́дня у́.: this morning

за́втра у́.: tomorrow morning

уходи́ть -о́дят (**I**) XVI: go away

уче́бник V: textbook

учи́тель [m; *Epl* учителя́] III: teacher

учи́тельница III: teacher (f)

учи́ть у́чат (**I**) XIV 9: 1. teach; 2. learn

учи́ться у́чатся (**I**) XV 3.2: learn

ушёл ушла́: *см.* уйти́

# Ф ф

фа́брика II: factory

на фа́брике VIII 9: at the factory

фа́кт XII: fact

фами́лия VI: surname

февра́ль (m *E*) XVII: February

фи́льм XIII: film

фотогра́фия VIII: photograph

фра́за V: sentence

Фра́нция XIV 5: France

францу́женка [G pl. -нок] XIV: Frenchwoman

францу́з XIV: Frenchman

францу́зский XIV: French

футбо́л 10a: soccer, European football

## X x

хи́мия XIV: chemistry

хлеб XIX: bread

ходи́ть хо́дят (ND) VII 1: go, walk

хокке́й 10a: hockey

холо́дный XVIII: cold
 [хо́лоден хо́лодно -дны; холодна́]

хоро́ший XIV 1.31: good
 [хоро́ш, хорошо́, -ший -ша́]

хорошо́ I: well; good

хоте́ть хотя́т (I) IV 6; X 6: want

хоте́ться + Dat.: см. XV 4

хотя́ (и) XX: although

хо́чешь, хо́чет: см. хоте́ть

худо́жник 11a: artist (m)

худо́жница 11a: artist (f)

ху́дший XXII 3; XXIII 2.2, 4: worse, worst

ху́же XXII 1.23: worse

## Ц ц

цари́ца XX: empress, tsaritsa

царь (E) XIX: tsar, emperor

це́рковь [f. irreg.; G-D-Pr. це́ркви, I це́рковью; pl. N-A це́ркви, G церкве́й; -ква́х, -ква́м, -ква́ми] 9a: church

## Ч ч

чай [2nd Gen. ча́ю; Epl чай] XIX: tea

час XVI; (see XVII 10 for stress): hour
 [в часу́; Epl часы́]

ча́сто IV: often

ча́стый XXII: frequent
 [част ча́сто -ы; часта́: ча́ще]

часы́ (pl. only) IX 9.2: watch, clock

ча́шка [G pl. ча́шёк] XIX: cup

ча́ще XXII 1.1: more often

чей чьё чья I (p. 355): whose

челове́к VI; IX 5; XVII 7: man, human being

чем XV 14; XXII 8, 11.1: than

че́рез + Acc. (see App. I, § 13.4) XVI 3.3; XXI 2.1: through, across; in

чёрный XXIII (16a): black
 [чёрен чёрно́ чёрны́ чёрна́]

четве́рг (E) XVII (9a): Thursday

четвёртый XVIII: fourth

че́тверть (f) XVIII: quarter

четы́ре XVII 3.31; XVII 5.1 (p. 357): four

четы́реста XX (p. 357): 400

четырёхсо́тый XX: 400th

четы́рнадцатый XIX: fourteenth

четы́рнадцать XVIII: fourteen

число́ XIX 6.1: number; date

чи́стый XXII: clean, pure
 [чист чи́сто -ы; чиста́: чи́ще]

чита́ть (I) III: read

чи́ще XXII 1.11: cleaner

что I (p. 354): what; that which

что V, см. X 3, p. 121: that

что́ за + Nom. IV: what sort of

чтобы, чтоб X 4, 6; XVIII 9: to, in order to, that

 для того, чтобы XVIII 9: in order to

что-нибудь III 11.1, 3: something

что-то II 5.4; III 11.2–3: something

## Ш ш

ша́пка [G pl. -пок] IV: cap

ша́хматы [pl. only, G -т] 10a: chess

шёл шло́ шла́ шли́: см. идти́

шестидеся́тый XIX: sixtieth

шестисо́тый XX: six hundredth

шестна́дцатый XIX: sixteenth

шестна́дцать XVIII 5.2: sixteen

шесто́й XVIII: sixth

ше́сть XVII; XVIII 5.2 (p. 356): 6

шестьдеся́т XVIII 5.3: sixty

шестьсо́т XX (p. 357): 600

ши́ре XXII 1.22: wider

широ́кий XXII: wide, broad

 [широ́к широко́ широ́кй широка́]

шка́ф [в, на шкафу́; Epl] VI: wardrobe, cupboard

шко́ла VII: school

шля́па IV: hat

шта́т XX: state (of U.S., Australia)

## Э э

экза́мен (по + Dat.) XV: examination (on)

эконо́мика XIV: economics

э́тот э́то э́та I; p. 355: this, that

## Я я

я I; p. 354: I

яви́ться (P) XX 3: report, appear

явля́ться (I) XX 3, 5: be, appear

язы́к (E) XIV 5.3: language, tongue

Я́лта II: Jalta (Yalta)

янва́рь (m E) XVII: January

япо́нец [-нца] XIV: Japanese man

Япо́ния XIV 5: Japan

япо́нка [G pl. -нок] XIV: Japanese woman

япо́нский (aj.) XIV: Japanese

я́сный XXI: clear

 [я́сён я́сно я́сны; ясна́]

# ENGLISH-RUSSIAN VOCABULARY

These listings are intended only as reminders: they do not give accents or grammatical information, except in special cases.

## A

about о(б); около; по; XVII 4
 to be ~ to: собираться
above над
abroad за границу, за границей
 from ~ из-за границы
acquaint (по)знакомить
acquaintance знакомый
acquainted знаком(ый); become
 ~ with (по)знакомиться
across через, за; *verbs with prefix*
 про-
actor актёр
actress актриса
actual: in ~ fact на самом деле
address адрес
advice совет
advise (по)советовать
affair дело
afoot пешком
afraid: be ~ of бояться + Gen.
after за, после, по
afternoon: in the ~ днём
again еще раз, опять
age век
ago тому назад
airdrome аэродром
airplane аэроплан, самолёт
all весь
 all at once (suddenly) вдруг
almost почти
already ужé

also тоже, и
although хотя
always всегда; всё
A.M. *see* XVIII 6
America Америка
American (aj.) американский;
 (man) американец; (woman)
 американка
among между
analysis: in the final ~ в конце
 концов
and и; а
answer ответ
any (*usually omitted in R.*)
 (not) ~ = none III 11.3
anybody кто-нибудь
 (not) ~ никто
apartment квартира
apparently *see* XXI 7.1
appear XX 3 являться явиться
 (по)казаться
approach *verbs with prefix* под-
 XVI 1.3
approximately около; с + Acc.;
 *numeral after noun*
April апрель
arm рука
armchair кресло
army армия
around около
arrive *verbs with prefix* при-
artist художник; художница; артист, артистка

as как; так как
  as...as так же... как (и)
  as...as possible как можно +
    *comparative*
ask (question) спрашивать спро-
    сить
ask (request) просить попросить
assignment задача
at в, на, у
August август
aunt тётя
automobile автомобиль; by ~
    на автомобиле; автомобилем
autumn осень; in ~ осенью
aviator = flier
away *verbs with prefixes* у-, от-

### B

back: come back *see* return
bad плохой
badly плохо
bank банк
baseball бейсбол
be быть; бывать; XX 5
beautiful красивый, прекрасный
because потому что
become становиться стать
bed кровать
beer пиво
before перед, до, раньше
begin начинать(ся) начать(ся)
  ~ to стать становиться 5а4
beginning начало
behind за
  from ~ из-за
believe (по)верить + Dat.
bell звонок
below под
  from ~ из-под
beneath под

best (самый) лучший; (= greeting)
    привет
better лучше; лучший
between между
big большой
bigger больший
bird птица
black черный
blackboard доска
blue (dark) синий; (light) голубой
board доска
book книга
boring скучный
born: be ~ родиться
both оба
  both...and и...и
bother (по)мешать
bread хлеб
breakfast завтрак; (по)завтракать
bride невеста
bridegroom жених
bridge мост
briefcase портфель
bright светлый; (intelligent)
    умный
bring *verbs with prefix* при XXI 1.2
  bring in вносить вводить ввозить
broad широкий
brother брат
building здание
burst into tears заплакать
bus автобус
business дело, дела
businessman коммерсант
busy занятый
but но; а
butter масло
buy покупать купить
by *instrumental case*; у, при,
    около; мимо

## C

calendar **календарь**

call (by name) **звать позвать**
  be called **называться** *see* XXIV 4

call (up) **(по)звонить (по телефону)**

calm **спокойный**

can **мочь, уметь**

cap **шапка**

captain **капитан**

car *see* automobile

card **карта**

carry **носить (по)нести; возить**
  ~ out **вы-носить**
  ~ away **у-носить, от-носить**

catch sight of **увидеть**

ceiling **потолок**

century **век**

chair **стул**

cheap **дешёвый**

cheese **сыр**

chemistry **химия**

chess **шахматы**

chief **главный**

chiefly **главным образом**

child **ребёнок**; children **дети**

China **Китай**

Chinese (aj.) **китайский**; (man)
  **китаец**; (woman) **китаянка**

church **церковь**

cinema **кино**

citizen **гражданин; гражданка**

city **город**

class **класс, урок, занятия**

classroom **класс**

clean **чистый**

clear **ясный**

clock **часы**

close (shut) **закрывать закрыть**

close (near) **близкий**

club **клуб**

coffee **кофе**

cold **холодный**

comrade **товарищ**

concerning **о(б)**

concert **концерт**

confident **уверенный**

continue **продолжать(ся)**

convey **возить везти повезти**

corner **угол**

correct **поправлять -ить**

correct(ly) **правильно**

council **совет**

counsel **совет; (по)советовать**

country **страна**

country (not city) **деревня**
  in the ~ **в деревне; за городом**

course: of course **конечно**

court **двор**
  at ~ **при дворе**

Crimea **Крым**

cross **пере-ходить -езжать -летать**

cry (weep) **плакать заплакать**

cup **чашка**

cupboard **шкаф**


## D

dark **темный**

daughter **дочь**

day **день**; ~ after tomorrow **послезавтра**; ~ before yesterday
  **третьего дня**

deal: a great ~ **(очень) много**

dear **дорогой**

death **смерть**

December **декабрь**

decide **решать решить**

deep **глубокий**

department store **универмаг**

desire **желать**

desk **стол**
dictate **(про)диктовать**
dictation **диктовка**
dictionary **словарь**
die **умирать умереть**
difficult **трудный**
dine **(по)обедать**
dinner **обед**
directly **прямо**
displeased **недовольный**
dissatisfied **недовольный**
distant **далекий**
do **(с)делать**
  how do you do **как вы поживаете**
doctor **доктор**
door **дверь**
downhill **под гору**
dozen ≅ about twelve
dress **одевать(ся) одеть(ся)**
drink **пить выпить**
  ~ up **выпить**
drive **возить везти повезти**
drop in (to see) **заходить, заезжать**
  XVIII 8.2
dull **скучный**
during **во время**

### E

each **каждый**
  ~ other **друг друга**
earlier **раньше**
early **рано**
easy **лёгкий**
eat **есть съесть**
economics **экономика**
eight **восемь**
eighth **восьмой**
eight hundred **восемьсот**
eight hundredth **восьмисотый**
eighteen **восемнадцать**
eighteenth **восемнадцатый**
eighty **восемьдесят**
eightieth **восьмидесятый**

either...or **или...или**
elder **старше; старший**
eleven **одиннадцать**
eleventh **одиннадцатый**
else: or ~ **а то**
emperor **царь, император**
empress **царица, императрица**
encounter **встречать встретить**
end **конец; кончать(ся)** 5а4
be engaged in **заниматься за-**
  **няться** + Inst.
England **Англия**
English (aj) **английский**
  (language) **английский язык**
  in ~ **по-английски**
Englishman **англичанин**
Englishwoman **англичанка**
enter **входить войти; въезжать**
  **въехать**
entirely **совсем**
etcetera **и так далее**
Europe **Европа**
European (aj.) **европейский;**
  (man) **европеец**; (woman) **евро-**
  **пейка**
even **ровный; даже, и**
evening **вечер**
  in the ~ **вечером**
  this ~ **сегодня вечером**
evening (aj.) **вечерний**
every **каждый**
everyone **всé** (*plural*!)
everywhere **всюду**
ex- **бывший**
exactly (of time) **ровно**
examination (in) **экзамен (по)**
excuse (me) **извините**
exercise **упражнение**
expensive **дорогой**
explain **объяснять -нить**
extremely **крайне**
eye **глаз**

## F

fact **факт**
  in (actual) ~ **на самом деле**
factory **фабрика**
fairly = rather **довольно**
fall **осень**
  in the ~ **осенью**
far **далекий, далеко**
father **отец**
fear **бояться** + Gen.
February **февраль**
feel like (do)ing: *see* XV 4
few **немного, немногие**
fiancé **жених**
fiancée **невеста**
field **поле**
fifteen **пятнадцать**
fifteenth **пятнадцатый**
fifth **пятый**
fifty **пятьдесят**
  fiftieth **пятидесятый**
film **фильм**
final **последний**
finally **наконец**
find **находить найти**
fine (not coarse) **мелкий**; (excellent) **хороший**
finish **кончать кончить** 5a4
first **первый**
  at ~ **сначала**
  for the first time **впервые**
five **пять**
  500 **пятьсот**; 500th **пятисотый**
flier **лётчик, лётчица**
floor **пол**
fly **летать лететь полететь**;
~ across **перелетать**; away **у-,
  от-летать**; out **вылетать**; thru,
  past **пролетать**
for: *dative case*: **для**; **за**
forest **лес**
forget **забывать забыть**

former **бывший**
forty **сорок**
  fortieth **сороковой**
four **четыре**; fourth **четвёртый**
$^1/_4$ (одна) **четверть**
400 **четыреста**; 400th **четырехсо-
  тый**
fourteen **четырнадцать**; ~th
  **четырнадцатый**
France **Франция**
French **французский**
Frenchman **француз**
Frenchwoman **француженка**
Friday **пятница**
friend **друг**; **подруга**
from **из, от, с**; *verbs prefixed with*
  **вы-**: (= because of) **из-за**
~ behind **из-за**
~ here **отсюда**
~ there **оттуда**
~ under **из-под**
~ where **откуда**
front: in ~ of **перед**
frontier **граница**
fun, be ≅ **весело**
further **дальше**
future (noun) **будущее**; (aj.) **будущий**

## G

garden **сад**
gay **весёлый**
general **генерал**
genius **гений**
gentleman **господин**
  ladies and gentlemen **господа**
German (aj.) **немецкий**; (man)
  **немец**; (woman) **немка**
Germany **Германия**
get **получать -чить**
get dressed **одеваться одеться**
get ready **(при)готовиться (к)**

get up вставать встать

girl девочка; девушка XVII 16

give давать дать; передавать передать

glad рад

glad (to meet you): *see* p. 143

go: *see* VII, *particularly* § 1.2; XIV

go in входить въезжать XVI

go on продолжать(ся)

go out выходить выезжать XVI

go to see: XIII 3.1

good хороший ;∼ evening добрый вечер; ∼ morning доброе утро; ∼ afternoon добрый день

grandfather дедушка

grandmother бабушка

great великий

green зеленый

greeting привет

guest гость, гостья

## H

hair волос

half половина

half-hour полчаса

hand рука

handbag сумка

handkerchief платок

hang: (trans.) вешать повесить; be ∼ing висеть

happen случаться случиться

happiness счастье

happy счастливый

hard трудный

hat шляпа

have *see* VI: быть у; have not нет у

have to должен, нужно, надо, приходится

head голова

hear (у)слышать

help помогать помочь

her (possessive) её

here здесь; тут (VI 6)

here is (pointing) вот

(to) here = hither сюда

from here отсюда

hero герой

heroine героиня

high высокий

hill гора

hinder (по)мешать

his его

history история

hockey хоккей

home: (to) ∼ домой

at ∼ дома

hope надеяться

hot жаркий

it's ∼ жарко

hour час

how как, каким образом

how many сколько

human being человек

hundred сто

hundredth сотый

## I

I я

idea идея

idiot идиот

if если, если бы (X 5.3)

imagine представлять себе

immediately сейчас (же)

important важный

in в, на, через (VII 8, 9; XVII 3.3; XVII 14; XVIII 4; XX 1)

in (a language) по-...ски

inclusive *see* XIX 6.3

incorrect(ly) неправильно

indispensable необходимый

inexpensive недорогой, дешёвый

instead зато

intelligent **умный**
interest **(за)интересовать**
  be ~ed in **(за)интересоваться**
    **+ Inst.**
interesting **интересный**
introduce **представлять**
invite **звать позвать; приглашать**
Italian (aj.) **итальянский;** (man)
  **итальянец;** (woman) **итальянка**
Italy **Италия**


# J

Jalta **Ялта**
January **январь**
Japan **Япония**
Japanese (aj.) **японский;** (man)
  **японец;** (woman) **японка**
jolly **весёлый**
journalist **журналист, журналист-**
  **ка**
joy **радость**
judge **судья**
July **июль**
June **июнь**
junior **младший**
just **только; только что; как раз**


# K

keep (doing) *see* XVI 7
key **ключ**
kind: of what ~ **какой;** of this ~
  **такой**
know **знать**
know how (to do) **(с)уметь**
known **знаком(ый)**


# L

lady **дама**
lamp **лампа**

language **язык**
  in (x) language **на .. языке**
large **большой**
last (XVII 17) **последний; прош-**
  **лый**
  at last **наконец**
last night **вчера вечером**
late **поздно**
  be ~ **опаздывать опоздать**
later **позже, позднее**
lawyer **адвокат**
lead **водить вести повести;** ~ in
  **вводить;** ~ out **выводить;** ~
  through **проводить;** ~ away
  **уводить, отводить**
learn **учить(ся), научиться, выу-**
  **чить**
leave **у-ходить -езжать -летать;**
  **от-, вы-**
leave (behind) **оставлять оставить**
lecture **лекция**
left: be ~ (behind) **оставаться**
  **остаться**
less **менее, меньше**
lesson **урок, задача, занятие**
let **пусть, пускай**
let's: *see* VII 6
letter **письмо**
library **библиотека**
lie **лежать**
  ~ down **ложиться лечь**
lieutenant **лейтенант**
light **светлый;** (not heavy) **лёгкий**
like **(по)нравиться** XV 3.1
like (to do) **(по)любить;** would ~
  X 6.2
likewise **также**
listen **(по)слушать**
literature **литература**
little **маленький**
  a little **немного, немножко, мало**
live **жить**

long **долгий, долго; длинный**
  for a ~ time **долго, давно**
  ~ ago, ~ since **давно**
  not ~ ago **недавно**
longer **дольше**
  no ~ **уже не, больше не**
look (at) **(по)смотреть [на]**
loud **громкий**
louder (av.) **громче**
love **(по)любить**
low **низкий**
lower **ниже; низший**
luck **счастье**
  ill luck **несчастье**
luckily **к счастью**
  ~ for (me) **на (мое) счастье**
lunch **завтрак; (по)завтракать**

### М

magazine **журнал**
main **главный**
major **майор**
man (human) **человек**; (male) **мужчина**
many **много, многие**
map **карта**
March **март**
marry: *see* 16a1
master **господин**
material **материал**
mathematics **математика**
matter **дело**
  what's the ~ with you? **чтó с [вами?**
may **можно, может быть**
May **май**
maybe **может быть**
mean **значить**
meat **мясо**
mechanic **механик**
medicine **медицина**
meet (by chance) **встречать(ся) -тить(ся)** (11a7)

meeting **собрание**
merchant **купец**
merry **весёлый**
milk **молоко**
million **миллион**
minute **минута**
miserable **несчастный**
misfortune **несчастье**
Miss **госпожа**
mistake **ошибка** [биться
mistaken: be ~ **ошибаться оши-**
mister, Mr. **господин**
Monday **понедельник**
money **деньги**
month **месяц**
more **ещё; более** (XII 8; XV 12; XVII 8; XXII 9; XXIII 6)
more than once **не раз**
morning **утро**; good ~ **доброе утро**; in the ~ **утром**; this morning **сегодня утром**
morning (aj.) **утренний**
most **самый** XII 7; XXIII 6
mother **мать**
mountain **гора**
move **переезжать переехать; перевозить перевезти**
movies **кино**
Mrs. **госпожа**
much **много; гораздо, куда**
museum **музей**
music **музыка**
musician **музыкант, музыкантша**
must **должен; надо; должно быть**
  must not **нельзя**
my **мой**

### N

name **имя, фамилия**
name **называть назвать**
  be named **называться назваться**
narrate **рассказывать рассказать**

narrow **узкий**

natural **естественный**

near (to) **близкий (от)**

necessary **нужный; нужно**

need **нужный** (XXI 5)

neighbor **сосед, соседка**

neither...nor **ни...ни**

never **никогда** (+ neg. verb)

new **новый**

news **новость**

newspaper **газета**

next (XVII 17) **следующий, будущий; дальше** (5а)

nice **хороший, красивый**

night **ночь**

  at ~ **ночью**

  last night **вчера вечером**

nine **де́вять**

  ninth **девя́тый**

  nine hundred **девятьсот**

  nine hundredth **девятисотый**

nineteen **девятнадцать**

  nineteenth **девятнадцатый**

ninety **девяносто**

  ninetieth **девяностый**

no **нет; никакой**

no longer **уже не, больше не**

no one **никто**

no one's **ничей ничье ничья**

none **никакой**

not **не**

  not any **никакой**

  not at all **во́все не**

not once **ни разу** (+ neg. verb)

not until *see* XXI 10

notebook **тетрадка**

nothing **ничего; ничто**

notice **замечать заметить**

novel **роман**

November **ноябрь**

now **теперь**

nowhere **нигде, никуда** (+ neg.
  verb); from ~ **ниоткуда**

## O

obey **(по)слушаться**

obtain **доставать достать**

occasion **раз**

occupy **занимать занять**

  be ~d **заниматься заняться**

ocean **океан**

o'clock *see* XVII 9

October **октябрь**

of: *genitive case*; **из, от**

office **контора**

officer **офицер**

often **часто**

oh! **ах**

old **старый**

  ~ man **старик**

  ~ woman **старуха**

on **на** (XVII 14; XX 1.4)

  on time **во́время**

once **(один) раз**

  at once **сейчас же**

one **один**; *see also* XII 5

  not one **ни один, никакой**

  one time **раз, один раз**

one another **друг друга** XV 8

only **только**

open **открывать открыть**

opera **опера**

opinion: in my ~ **по-мо́ему**

  in your ~ **по-ва́шему [-тво́ему]**

order: in ~ to **(для того) чтобы**

ordinarily **обыкновенно**

other **другой**

  each other **друг друга** XV 8

otherwise **а то**

ought **должен**

our, ours **наш**

out **из, от**; *verbs with prefix* **вы-**

outdoors ⎫
outside ⎭ **на дворе, на двор**

over **над**

own, one's own **свой**

## P

paper **бумага**; newspaper **газета**; written composition **сочинение** (5а6)

parents **родители**

park **парк**

part **роль**; for the most ~ **главным образом**

pass: *verbs with prefix* **про-**

pass on **передавать передать**

past **прошлый**; **прошлое**

patronymic **отчество**

peaceful **спокойный**

pen **перо**

pencil **карандаш**

people **люди**

per: *see* XVII 14.3

perhaps **может быть**

photograph **фотография**

picture **картина**

pity: it's a (great) ~ **(очень) жаль**

place **место**

play **играть сыграть**

playing card **карта**

pleasant **приятный**

please **пожалуйста**

please **(по)нравиться** XV 3.1

pleased (with) **довольный**

P.M. *see* XVIII 6

pocket **карман**

pocketbook **сумка**

poet **поэт**

Poland **Польша**

Pole **поляк, полька**

Polish **польский**

poor **бедный**; **нехороший**

portrait **портрет**

possible: as...as ~ **как можно** + *comparative*

postcard **открытка**

prepare (for) **(при)готовить(ся) [к]**

president **президент**

prevent **(по)мешать**

probably **должно быть**

problem **задача**

professor **профессор**

progress: make ~ **делать успехи**

promise **обещать**

prove to be **оказываться оказаться**

pure **чистый**

purse **кошелек**

put **класть положить** (*see* IX 10)

put on (= dress) **одевать одеть**

## Q

quarter **четверть**

question **вопрос**; **спрашивать спросить**

quick **быстрый, скорый**

quickly **быстро, скоро**

quiet **тихий**

quite **довольно**; **совсем**

## R

radio **радио**

rain **дождь**; **дождь идёт**

rare **редкий**

rarely **редко**

rather **довольно**; **скорее**

read **(про)читать**

really **на самом деле**

receive **получать получить**

recently **недавно**

red **красный**

reign: during the ~ of **при**

remain **оставаться остаться**

remember **помнить**

repeat **повторять повторить**

republic **республика**

request **(по)просить**

restaurant **ресторан**

result: with the ∼ that **так что**
return (give back) **возвращать -атить**; (come back) **возвращаться**
review = repeat
revolution **революция**
rich **богатый**
ride **ездить ехать поехать**
right away **сейчас (же)**
ring **(по)звонить**
river **река**
road **дорога**
role **роль**
room **комната**
run **бегать бежать побежать**; ∼ away **убегать, отбегать**; ∼ in **вбегать**; ∼ out **выбегать**; ∼ through, past **пробегать**; ∼ across **перебегать**
run over (something) **переезжать**
Russia **Россия**
Russian (aj.) **русский**; (man) **русский**; (woman) **русская**
in ∼ **по-русски**

## S

sad **печальный**
same **тот же (самый)**
it's all the ∼ to **всё равно** + Dat.
all the same (= even so) **всё же**
(of the) same (kind) **такой же**
in the same place **там же**
satisfied (with) **довольный**
Saturday **суббота**
say **говорить сказать**
school **школа**
science **наука**
seat **сажать посадить**
second **второй**
secretary **секретарь, секретарша**
see **видеть увидеть**
seem **(по)казаться**

seldom **редко**
self **сам; себя** XV 6, 7
self-confident **уверенный в себе**
sell **продавать продать**
semester **семестр**
send **посылать послать**
senior **старший; старше**
sentence **фраза**
September **сентябрь**
set out **пойти, поехать**
seven **семь**; seventh **седьмой**; 700 **семьсот**; 700th **семисотый**
seventeen **семнадцать**; seventeenth **семнадцатый**
seventy **семьдесят**; seventieth **семидесятый**
several **несколько**
severe **строгий**
shallow **мелкий**
sharp (of time) **ровно**
shelf **полка**
short **короткий**
shout **(за)кричать, крикнуть**
show **показывать -зать**
shut **закрывать закрыть**
sight: catch ∼ of **увидеть**
silent, be **молчать**
simple **простой**
since (because) **так как**
sister **сестра**
sit **сидеть**; sit down **садиться сесть**
six **шесть**; sixth **шестой**; 600 **шестьсот**; 600th **шестисотый**
sixteen **шестнадцать**
sixteenth **шестнадцатый**
sixty **шестьдесят**; sixtieth **шестидесятый**
sleep **спать**; be sleepy: *see* XV 4
slow **медленный**
slowly **медленно**
small **маленький**
snow **снег**; it snows **снег идёт**

so так; таким образом
 so that так что; чтобы (XXI 8.11)
 isn't it so? не правда ли
soccer футбол
socialist (aj.) социалистический
sofa диван
soft мягкий; тихий
soldier солдат
solve решать решить
some: *see* XIX 1
some sort of какой-нибудь; какой-
 то
somebody кто-то
someone (specific) кто-то; (general)
 кто-нибудь
sometimes иногда
somewhere (specific) где-то, куда-
 то; (general) где-нибудь, куда-
 нибудь
son сын
song песня
soon скоро
 as soon as как только
sorry: be ~ (for) жаль + Dat.
 (+ Acc.)
soup суп
soviet совет; советский
Spain Испания
Spaniard испанец
Spanish испанский
speak говорить сказать
specialist специалист
spend проводить провести
spring весна
 in ~ весной
stand стоять; (по)ставить IX 10
stand up вставать встать
start начинать(ся) начать(ся)
state (of U.S.) штат
station станция
stern строгий
still (av.) ещё, всё ещё; (aj.)
 тихий

store магазин
 department store универмаг
story рассказ
straight прямо
strange странный
street улица
streetcar трамвай
stroll (по)гулять
student студент, студентка
study учиться, заниматься
subway метро
success успех
such (of this kind) такой
suddenly вдруг
sugar сахар
summer лето
 in ~ летом
sun, sunshine солнце
Sunday воскресенье
supper ужин
 have ~ (по)ужинать
 at ~ за ужином
sure уверенный
surname фамилия
symphony симфония

## T

table стол
 at ~ за столом
take брать взять (*also* XIX 1.2)
take up занимать занять
talent талант
talented талантливый
talk говорить
tall высокий
task задача
tea чай
teach (на)учить
teacher учитель, учительница
telegram телеграмма
telegraph телеграфировать

telephone **телефон**; **(по)звонить по телефону**

tell **говорить скáзать**; **расскáз[ыв]ать**

ten **дéсять**; tenth **десятый**

textbook **учебник**

than **чем** (XV 14; XXII 8)

thanks, thank you **спасибо**

that: *see* I 2.3; X 3 (5a5)

theater **теáтр**

their, theirs **их**

then **тогда, потóм**

there **там, туда**

   there is (= exists) **есть** (*see* VI)

   there is no[t] **нет** (*see* VI)

   there is (pointing) **вот**

therefore **поэтому**

thin **тóнкий**

thing **вещь**

think **(по)думать**

third **трéтий**

thirteen **тринáдцать**

thirteenth **тринáдцатый**

thirty **трúдцать**; thirtieth **тридцáтый**

this **этот это эта** (I 2.3)

thousand **тысяча**

thousandth **тысячный**

three **три**; 300 **трúста**; 300th **трехсóтый**

through **чéрез**; *verbs with prefix* **про-**

Thursday **четвéрг**

thus **так, такúм óбразом**

time **врéмя**; what ~ is it **? котóрый час?** in the time of **при**; it's time (to) **порá**; on time **вóвремя**; for the first time **впервые**; have a good time **вéсело** + D

to **до, в, на, к**; *dative case*

today **сегóдня**

together **вмéсте**

tomorrow **зáвтра**

   ~ morning **зáвтра утром**

   ~ night **зáвтра вéчером**

   day after ~ **послезáвтра**

too *see* XIV 1.4

too (much) **слúшком**

town **гóрод**

train **пóезд**

transfer **переводúть переносúть перевозúть**

translate **переводúть перевестú**

truth **прáвда**

tsar **царь**; tsaritsa **царúца**

Tuesday **вторник**

turn out **окáзываться оказáться**

twelve **двенáдцать**; twelfth **двенáдцатый**

twenty **двáдцать**; twentieth **двадцáтый**

twice **два рáза**

two **два две**; 200 **двéсти**; 200th **двухсóтый**

## U

uncle **дядя**

under **под**; from ~ **из-под**

understand **понимáть понять**

unfortunate **несчáстный**

unfortunately **к сожалéнию**

unhappiness **несчáстье**

unhappy **несчáстливый**

union **союз**

united **соединéнный**; USA **США**

university **университéт**

unknown **незнакóмый**

unless *see* 21a3

unnecessary **ненýжный**

unpleasant **неприятный**

until **до**; not ~ XXI 10

uphill **в гóру**

used to: *past tense, imperfective verb*

USSR **СССР**
usual **обыкновенный**
usually **обыкновенно**

## V

vacation **каникулы**
valley **долина**
very **очень**; the ~ **самый** XII 7
village **деревня**
visit *see* XIII 3.1 and Less. 21a
vodka **водка**
voice **голос**

## W

wait **ждать подождать**
walk **ходить**; **гулять**
wall **стена**
want **хотеть захотеть** (X 6.1)
war **война**
wardrobe **шкаф**
warm **тёплый**
watch **часы**; **смотреть**
water **вода**
way **путь**; **дорога**
  by ~ of **через**; **путём**
  by the ~ **кстати**
weather **погода**; bad ~ **непогода**
Wednesday **среда**
week **неделя**
weep **(за)плакать**
well **хорошо**
what **чтó**
  what a (what sort of) **какой**
wheat **хлеб**
when **когда**
where **где**; **куда**
  from ~ **откуда**
whether **ли**

which **который, какой**
  which one **который, какой**
who? **кто**
who (relative) **который**
whose **чей чьё чья**; *see* XII 6.3
why **почему**
wide **широкий**
wife **жена**
wine **вино**
winter **зима**
  in ~ **зимой**
wish **желать**
with **с**; *instrumental case*
without **без**
woman **женщина**
woods **лес**; **лесá**
word **слово**
work **работа**; **работать**; **занятие**
  work on (problem) **решать решить**
wretch **несчастный**
write **(на)писать**
write down **написать**
wrong **не тот, не та**

## Y

yard **двор**
year **год**
yes **да**
yesterday **вчера**
  ~ evening **вчера вечером**
  ~ morning **вчера утром**
  day before ~ **третьего дня**
yet **уже**; **ещё**
  not yet **ещё не**
you **вы, ты**
young **молодой**
younger **моложе**
your, yours **ваш, твой**

# INDEX

Consult also the Russian and English vocabularies.
Abbreviations: VI 2 = Lesson VI, section 2; Intro. 5.3 = Introduction,
section 5.3; A 1 4 = Appendix I, section 4